Developmental Reading in Middle and Secondary Schools: Foundations, Strategies, and Skills for Teaching

Lawrence E. Hafner

Florida State University

Macmillan Publishing Co., Inc.
New York
Collier Macmillan Publishers
London

To My Parents, Erhardt and Minna Hafner

Macmillan Publishing Co., Inc.
855 Third Avenue, New York, New York 10022

Collier Macmillan Canada, Ltd.

Library of Congress Cataloging in Publication Data

Hafner, Lawrence E
  Developmental reading in middle and secondary schools.

  Includes bibliographies and index.
  1. Reading (Secondary education) 2. Developmental reading. I. Title.
LB1632.H28   428'.4'3   76-20811
ISBN 0-02-348820-4

Printing: 2 3 4 5 6 7 8   Year: 8 9 0 1 2 3 4

Preface

The main thrust of this book is to help classroom teachers and reading specialists improve reading skills among average and superior readers; however, chapters such as those on teaching reading acquisition skills and applying learning principles to the teaching of reading bear directly on teaching the nonreader and the below-average reader.

In the first section—"Reading Foundations"—I explain the importance of reading, what reading is, and how learning principles are applied to the teaching of reading.

Section Two is devoted to strategies for developing concept-vocabulary skills, comprehension skills, and study-reference skills.

The third section explains how to teach general and specific reading skills in the content areas of science, mathematics, English, social studies, business education, vocational-technical courses, foreign languages, art, music, and physical education.

The final section is devoted to a chapter on basic procedures for teaching (a) additional systematic, comprehensive reading lessons which are applicable to teaching in the content areas and (b) independent word identification skills and a chapter on teaching reading acquisition skills to the nonreader and the reader who has attained minimal reading skills.

Because this is a comprehensive textbook it can be used in a number of ways. Let me suggest several possible tracks:

Chapters (Titles Abbreviated)	Undergraduate		Graduate		
	First Course: Developmental Reading Course	Second Course: Content Areas Reading Course	Developmental Course for Classroom Teacher: Content Emphasis	Developmental Course for Reading Specialist. (A foundations course assumed.)	Comprehensive Content Reading Course for Reading Specialists: All content areas. (Developmental courses assumed)
1. Uses and Nature of Reading	√	†	√	†	†
2. Theories of Learning		√		√	†
3. Teaching for Retention	(√)	(√)	√	√	†
4. Measurement in Reading	√	†	√	†	†
5. Developing Vocabulary	√	†	√	†	†
6. Developing Comprehension	√	†	√	(√)	†
7. Research-Study Skills	(√)	√	√	(√)	†
8. Social Studies Foundation		√			√
9. Social Studies: Skills Strategies	√*		√*	√	√
10. Mathematics Foundations					√
11. Mathematics Skills Strategies					√
12. Science Foundations		√*			√
13. Science Skills Strategies		√			√
14. English Poetry		√		√	†
15. English Fiction, Drama, Essays		√		√	†
16. Business Education					√
17. Vocational-Technical	√	†	√		†
18. Foreign Languages					√
19. Art, Music, and Physical Education	√	†		√	√
20. Basic Procedures	√		√	(√)	†
21. Reading Acquisition	√	†	√	√	†

*Plus a content area the student is majoring in.

†Assumed this was taught in the first course or some reading foundations course.

Acknowledgments

I want to thank my wife, Mary, who was so understanding in the several years that this manuscript was in preparation. She gave me encouragement and support in many ways, not the least of which was her typing of the manuscript. She also gave me some valuable suggestions for reading in art.

I wish to thank our daughter Becky, who read the rough draft of the foreign language chapter and gave me suggestions for improving it. The endeavors of Linda, Katie, and Charlie—our middle school and secondary school children on whom I tried out various ideas—are also appreciated.

Next I would like to thank my colleagues and friends who encouraged me and who loaned me materials that would otherwise have been hard to obtain.

A special note of appreciation goes to Eva Berg, a graduate student of mine who prepared the appendix on curriculum materials in reading.

Finally, I want to thank my parents, who have always believed in me and who instilled in me a love for learning.

L. E. H.

Contents

Section One: Reading Foundations

    1. Uses of Reading and the Nature of Reading Acts   3

    2. Psychological Foundations for Reading Instruction. I.   17
       Theories of Learning, Concept Development, and Discovery
       Learning Versus Expository Teaching

    3. Psychological Foundations for Reading Instruction. II.   39
       Teaching for Retention

    4. Measurement and Evaluation of Mental Aptitude, Capacity   57
       for Reading, and Reading Achievement

Section Two: Developing and Organizing Meanings

    5. Developing Concepts and Vocabulary Representing Concepts   95

    6. Comprehending Explicitly and Implicitly Stated Meanings   127
       and Reading Critically

    7. Reading and Organizing in Research-Study Situations   161

**Section Three: Teaching Strategies for Improving Reading Skills
in the Content Areas**

    8. Teaching the Reading of Social Studies. I. Foundations   189

    9. Teaching the Reading of Social Studies. II. Strategies for   207
       Improving Reading Skills

10. Reading Mathematics. I. Developmental, Psychological,   239
    and Pedagogical Foundations

11. Reading Mathematics. II. Strategies for Improving the   257
    Reading of Mathematics

12. Reading in Science and Technology. I. Foundations   279

13. Reading in Science and Technology. II. Strategies for   293
    Improving Reading Skills

14. Teaching the Reading of English. I. Foundations and   327
    Strategies for Improving the Reading of Biography, Folk
    Literature, and Poetry

15. Teaching the Reading of English. II. Strategies for Improving 363
    the Reading of Fiction, Drama, and Essays

16. Reading in Business Education   387

17. Reading in Vocational-Technical Education: Construction   401
    Trades, Automotive Science, Electronics, Home Economics

18. Teaching the Reading of Foreign Languages   429

19. Teaching Reading in Art, Music, Health, and Physical   451
    Education

Section Four: Basic Procedures—Teaching Comprehensive Content Area Reading Lessons and Teaching Reading Acquisition Skills

20. Some More Basic Procedures for Teaching Reading Lessons   485
    in the Content areas

21. Teaching Reading Acquisition Skills to the Nonreader and   503
    the Reader Who Has Attained Minimal Reading Skills

Appendixes   523

Index   571

Section One

Reading Foundations

CHAPTER 1
Uses of Reading and the Nature of Reading Acts

USES OF READING

Problems of Illiterates

How many millions of adolescents and adults would like to read a letter or a newspaper but cannot? They are also unable to communicate in writing with friends and family. They enjoy the comic section of a newspaper but miss many of the subtleties conveyed through the dialogue. The world of print is closed to them. Illiteracy brings other problems. When they are out of work and looking for jobs, illiterates cannot read the "Help Wanted" signs or advertisements in the newspaper or participate in training that requires reading skills. These unfortunate people cannot read bedtime stories to their children or check the program schedule in *TV Guide*. These common uses of reading are valuable.

Basic Uses of Reading

In Promoting Family Welfare and Harmony. The householder-citizen needs to read in order to accomplish numerous tasks that, if performed properly, should promote family welfare and harmony. Planning a budget, reading advertisements and shopping intelligently; reading job descriptions, job application forms, and so forth, are some of these tasks.

Hundreds of thousands of people in this country get an extremely poor start in life because their parents are not adequately informed about nutrition. Hafner and Guice (1974) have discussed the deprivation associated with lack of adequate nutrition, love, and language stimulation. One means of learning about nutrition is to read material on the subject. Individuals have to be able to read about these things because they cannot always depend on their physicians for advice. Furthermore, people need to read about other healthful practices, such as the kinds and amounts of exercise to strengthen the pulmonary

3

and cardiovascular systems of the body, adequate rest and recreation, and the development and pursuit of reasonable vocational goals.

In Learning a Trade or Profession. In recent years the Agency for International Development discovered that much of the money spent to aid the economy of foreign countries was being wasted. Millions of dollars were spent on farm and industrial equipment that stood idle because the workers and farmers could not read the technical manuals that explained how to operate and repair the equipment. Similarly, many individuals cannot learn to be plumbers, carpenters, mechanics, electricians, teachers, lawyers, or physicians because they do not have adequate reading proficiency. Instructional manuals for repairing automobiles effectively and efficiently, for example, are quite technical and are written on a high school or college level. Instructional materials, technical reports, and journals used by professionals are written on the college and graduate level.

The Examined Life

Reading to Become More Intelligent and to Broaden One's Perspective. People can become more intelligent and broaden their perspective in a number of ways, one of which is certainly reading. The reader can select from a plethora of writers and topics in order to promote the examined life that is worth living. One such topic could be progress and happiness, since these seem to be goals of many people throughout the ages.

World opinion differs about the definition of such terms as *progress* and *happiness*, whether these are worthy goals, how such goals might be attained, and when and where they might be attained. Utilitarian doctrine states that one ought to seek the greatest happiness of the greatest number of people. Furthermore, the rightness of a given action is determined by the consequence of the action. In like manner, pragmatists such as C. S. Peirce, William James, and John Dewey claim that one judges the truth of a proposition by its results. This idea has a utilitarian tone and reflects the American idea of valuing things on the basis of the good one can expect from these things.

To be useful to people, to help them, however, might not mean that one should pander to the masses. Goethe, for example, wrote, "I have never asked, what does the great mass want and how can I be useful to the totality? But I have always endeavored only to make myself more intelligent and better, to increase the content of my own personality and then to utter only what I have recognized as being good and true." What is good and true, it has been suggested, is what is spiritual, what is of the "next world" rather than what is in "this world." Numerous individuals, among the more prominent being Friedrich Nietzsche, have deplored the idea of a "next world." But today many people practice the "this world - next world" dichotomy, claiming one world to be of value while denigrating the other. Yet nearly two hundred years ago, Goethe attempted to clarify the issue: "I pity the people who make a big fuss about the transitoriness of things and lose themselves in the contemplation of earthly vanity. For are we not here for the very purpose of making the transitory everlasting? And this can, of course, happen only when we are able to value both."

Many individuals have written on happiness and the moral ethics related to who should attain it, when, and in what degree. Immanuel Kant, J. S. Mill, Russell Kirk, and James Baldwin provide some diverse ethical points of view.

Although Kant did not travel far from home, his reading, observation, and contemplation yielded profound results in the area of ethics. Kant "reinstated" the soul, God, and immortality because he felt that people need them in order to be happy. Kant's categorical imperative, "Do your ethical duty," illustrates an important view of motivation, even though many people have challenged this view. He explains further, "Act in such a way that the maxim of your will may at all times have validity as the principle of a Universal law . . ." In this view, the essence of morality can be found in the motive underlying an act.

Other arguments may be as compelling as any Kantian categorical imperative. For example, if one would agree with J. S. Mill that moral good is definable from society's vantage point as "the greatest happiness of the greatest number," then the power of moral imperatives such as Kant's might be increased. Also, by espousing the happiness of many people and the judgment of good in terms of effects of action rather than the motive of the action, one obviates such horrible results as Hitler's genocide, which supposedly was justified on the basis of well-intentioned motives. Herein lies the danger of justifying an action by its intent.

But some people distrust the majority and would not want the masses to set the tone of society, and, at first blush, this attitude might seem reasonable. Such leaders are said to respect tradition and authority and should be emulated by the proletarian masses. Russell Kirk espouses this view in his book, *Prospects for Conservatives*. Kirk defines the proletarian as "a rootless man, a social atom, without traditions, without enduring convictions, without true home, without true family, without community, ignorant of the past and careless of future generations." He states further that "although most members of the proletariat belong to the poorer classes, economic status is not the distinguishing feature of a proletarian." The proletarian is not the same as the laboring man; the proletarian is not directed from within. "Since he does not have any traditions or private convictions of his own, he rushes to embrace the follies and schemes of the charlatans and demagogues of the moment."

Just how much experience Kirk has had with the exigencies of life that faced (1) the poor blacks who were working in slavery before, during, and after the Civil War or (2) the poor whites in the sweat shops of the industrial North so that generations of nonproletarian Southerners and Northerners could maintain roots, traditions, enduring convictions, and true home and family is not known. (Many poor Caucasians and American Indians were also in difficult plights.)

One need only search the objective *Chronicles of Black Protest* edited by Bradford Chambers and the *Negro Pilgrimage in America* by C. Eric Lincoln to understand not only the problems of blacks, but also the roots of these problems. James Baldwin has captured the essence of many problems faced by blacks in their long years of struggle. In his novel, *Go Tell It on the Mountain*, Baldwin tells of a Harlem ghetto family haunted by lust as it searched for saint-hood. He tells of a young adolescent's (John) hatred of his father, Gabriel, a lecherous man who hid under a cloak of pretended piety, and of John's struggle with sin, his fighting the attempts of family and friends to convert him, and his vain attempts to be accepted and loved by his father. Confusion, harrassment, and despair mark the lives of the blacks in this story from the time of John's slave grandmother to his own time. In a flashback, Baldwin summarizes an aspect of the days of formal slavery as John's father Gabriel, his aunt Florence, and his grandmother, lived it:

> Thus had her mother lived and died; and she has often been brought low, but she had never been forsaken. She had always seemed to Florence the oldest woman in the world, for she often spoke of Florence and Gabriel as the children of her old age, and she had been born, innumerable years ago, during slavery, on a plantation in another state. On this plantation she had grown up as one of the field workers, for she was very tall and strong; and by and by she had married and raised children, all of whom had been taken from her, one by sickness and two by auction; and one whom she had not been allowed to call her own, had been raised in the master's house. When she was a woman grown, well past thirty as she reckoned it, with one husband buried—but the master had given her another—armies, plundering and burning, had come from the North to set them free. This was in answer to the prayers of the faithful, who had never ceased both day and night, to cry out for deliverance.

It appears that roots, traditions, home, and family would be difficult to develop and maintain under the conditions just described. Yet throughout the generations in this story ran a thread of hope in the lives of blacks, surety of forgiveness, and the hope of a better life—if in this world only in dim adumbration, in the next world in effulgent consummation.

But Kirk has also claimed that the proletarian is ignorant of the past. Perhaps some blacks cannot read about the past, but they *feel* it every minute, every day. Why can these blacks not read about the past? They cannot because of the conditions described in the works of such black writers as Baldwin, in the objective histories by Lincoln and Chambers, as well as in the writings of nutritionists and psychologists. These conditions render many of these un-fortunate people physically, socially, and psychologically incapable of profiting from the meager education proferred in the past or the better education now be-ing offered. But the effects of the psychological and physical wounds of hatred, deprivation, and exploitation do not vanish in decades much less in a few years.

NATURE OF READING ACTS

Common Misconceptions

A person must pass through developmental phases in order to become a mature reader. For various reasons alluded to not all high school students become mature readers. Another reason is that the abilities of these students are not capitalized on by either the teachers or the students as the students proceed (not progress) through the schools. The abilities of some students may be minimal, but their teachers fail to teach in terms of these minimal abilities. Other students have maximal abilities, but their teachers' view of reading maturity is so undeveloped that they neither set the proper goals for these students nor aid them in reaching such reading maturity goals.

What, then, are the goals of reading? What is reading? It is more than looking at print and saying words. It is more than understanding details, although one wishes that more students could reach that goal. Yet H. K. Smith (1961) found that twelfth-grade students classified as poor readers read for details regardless of the purpose set for reading.

Most teachers probably think reading is getting meaning. However, the reader brings meanings to the printed page. The more meanings the reader brings to the page, the more he or she will be able to use the cues on the page to develop further meaning. Still others feel that all reading material should be easy to understand; that is not a realistic view. But saying that all reading material will not be easy to understand should not be used by teachers as an excuse for not providing less-capable readers with appropriate reading materials for a given topic. Finally, one hears secondary teachers say that, after all, it is the job of elementary teachers to teach reading skills so that the secondary teacher can proceed with teaching the content of a discipline. What a quaint view! If only the proponents of the liberal arts were more acquainted with the liberal arts! Not only do the findings of present-day research in psychology and the keen observations and deductions of educators inform us that all the reading skills that an individual will need in secondary school cannot be developed in the elementary schools,[1] but no less a person than Goethe said, "The dear people do not know how long it takes to learn to read."

The Reading Process

The Gist of Reading. While reading, a person reconstructs the facts that lie behind the symbols. This fact implies that symbols reflect experience and that reading is an active process for ascertaining the experiences encoded in language and, in turn, encoded in print. Korzybski, the semanticist, points this out in *Science and Sanity*. Similarly, Ortega y Gassett, in *Origins of Philosophy*, claims that in reading a person is engaged in reconstructing formed experiences.

The Language Base for Reading. Language is related to symbolic thinking, but it is not synonymous with symbolic thinking. Language is substitutive behavior that stands for or represents primary behavior processes. In other words, language has a referential function, because it links external or internal events with speech behavior. People can communicate because language uses

---

[1] For a further explanation, see *Improving Reading in Middle and Secondary Schools,* Second Edition, by Lawrence E. Hafner, pp. vii, viii.

conventional speech symbols for meanings; certain signs of language have been used by many people to refer to particular events.

In order to preserve speech symbols in visual form, people have developed systems of writing. The Egyptians and Chinese, for example, have developed forms of picture writing. The Japanese basically use the Chinese written symbols. Thus, a Japanese person may read Chinese symbols although he or she may not understand spoken Chinese. The Chinese symbols are not alphabetic but are based on pictures that represent things and ideas. Thus, the word *nihon*, which means "origin of the sun," is developed from the pictograph ▭, which means "sun" and the pictograph 本 , which means "origin." The following sketches show how the transformations were made over the years from a regular picture to a more abstract rendition of the picture.

(sun)   (pronounced *nichi*)

(tree)   ← note the root   (pronounced *hon*)
                                                     (meaning root or
                                                     origin or source)

Therefore, 日 本, (nichihon), means "origin of the sun." *Nihon* (short for *nichihon*) denotes "Japan" or "the land of the rising sun."

In contrast with some other languages English uses an alphabetic code. Letters and letter combinations (graphemes) represent sounds. A given grapheme may represent one sound (phoneme) in one word, *sun*, and another sound in a different word, *sugar*. Certain graphemes, then, have phonemic options. For example, the grapheme ⟨ough⟩ has four phonemic options: /ō/, dough; /ü/, through; /aù/, bough; and /ò/, thought. Note also the different sounds represented by *ch* as you pronounce *champion, chamois, orchestra,* and *Bach.* In the English language a letter combination and a sound are seldom in one-to-one correspondence. The sound that a letter combination represents—as just illustrated—is contingent on the other letters that appear in the word and, sometimes, the context in which the word appears.

The Basic Tasks of Reading

Visual Perception of Printed Symbols. First, the individual learning to read needs to understand the idea of printed symbols. One indication of readiness to read is a child's knowledge that print is "talk written down." The secondary school student who is not seriously mentally retarded should understand this concept.

Second, the learner should be able to differentiate one printed symbol from another. The learner may have to learn to make this differentiation but he or she should be able to do it, for it is propaedeutic to further learning. When presented with *A A*, the learner should say, "They are alike" or, "They are the same." The response to *A X* should be "They are different" or, "They aren't the same."

Third, the learner should know the name of the symbol. Actually associating *a* phoneme with the grapheme transfers to reading better than knowing the name does.[2] Knowing the name of the symbol, the learner can use the symbol names (letter names) to refer to component parts of a word. Furthermore, in being able to differentiate the letters and learn the spoken counterparts (letter names), the learner has learned tasks that should transfer to learning the names of words and differentiating the configurations of words.

Fourth, the learner, before learning to read words or sometime in the beginning stages of learning to read, should know some of the more common sounds attached to letter combinations; that is, the learner should learn phoneme options.

Fifth, the learner makes associations between speech symbols and the printed symbols that represent them, that is, the student learns to read words.[3] In differentiating one word from another word, that is, in noting the clues that guide the pronunciation of a word, the student should look through the word from left to right for appropriate letter and letter combination clues.

Sixth, the learner engages in a variety of word identification and word recognition exercises that help one to learn the word so well that on seeing it in print the learner can say it without hesitation. It is in failing to develop such step-by-step mastery in the beginning reading stages that failure in reading is precipitated.

Comprehension of Words, Phrases, and Sentences. While reading, a person could encounter the printed word *dog*. What does the word *dog* mean? It means a lot of things depending on the context in which you encounter it. *Dog* means a four-footed animal, the kind of house a husband may be in if he does not shape up, a type of leg at golf courses, and so forth. In the phrase "a big German shepherd dog," the meaning of dog becomes more proscribed and, consequently, explicit. Similarly, in reading sentences, the reader needs to perceive the words accurately, decode them correctly, and understand their meanings in the particular array of the sentence.

In addition to the context aids just mentioned, there are formal or recurring explicit and implicit context aids to understanding the meaning of certain words and phrases. The contrasting element is one type of explicit context aid or clue. Note the use of the word *however* in this sentence: "Mr. Smith's topic, was thought provoking and interesting; however, Mr. Jones' topic was *jejune*." The word *however* informs the reader that the two parts of the sentence are contrasting elements; therefore, *jejune* must mean the opposite of thought provoking and interesting. It does; a synonym for *jejune* is *insipid*.

---

[2] The name for ⟨t⟩ is /tē/; the phoneme or sound is /t/—one sound rather than the two you get with /tē/.

[3] The student may have at his or her disposal several methods for yielding the speech symbol needed to make the association. These methods are discussed thoroughly in chapter 21.

To the extent that the writer uses meanings familiar to the reader and couches the words in familiar sentence patterns, communication will result. If the context is strong enough, the writer may occasionally use words that are not very familiar.

Decoding and Comprehending: A Unified Process. Decoding or converting print to "speech" is a necessary (but not a sufficient) first step in reading. To decode words independently, a person brings to the page a knowledge of grapheme-phoneme associations, also termed phonic elements. Obviously a person cannot use phonic elements alone to decode words if he or she knows only a few phonic elements. The student will pronounce the known part of the word and use the *context* of the sentence as a further aid in decoding. For example, let us assume a student knows the following phonic elements ⟨ch⟩ → /ch/, ⟨e⟩ → /e/. Furthermore, the student can read all of the sentence except ⟨cherry⟩.

Mother baked a cherry pie.

By reading what he or she can, the student knows that Mother baked a pie. Knowledge of the English language and experience with pastries tells the student that the word preceding ⟨pie⟩ identifies the kind of pie. Through partial pronunciation the student gets /ch/ . . . /e/. Combining the meaning from the sentence and the partial pronunciation yields /ché-rē/, that is "cherry." A stronger context is provided by

Mother baked a red cherry pie.

or

On Washington's Birthday, mother baked a red cherry pie.

This kind of decoding requires that the individual be a fairly fluent reader so that the contexts are generally strong. Therefore, sequential, systematic instruction in which the student masters the concepts as he or she goes along will enable the student to read fluently and develop the meanings. Through questions, discussion, and at times asking the student to illustrate meanings, one can keep a check on meaning.

Developing Literal and Inferential Comprehension. The instructional reading materials encountered at the first reading level provide few meaning problems. Students will understand the meanings of words, phrases, and sentences that they decode—provided they can decode them fluently enough for the sentence to hang together.

Meanings are developed in sentence contexts and the reader has a double job in understanding the author. The reader must "read the lines," that is, understand the basic, directly stated ideas of the author. These are called the *literal* meanings.

Examples: The person reads, "Canberra is the capital of Australia" and is able to answer questions such as, "What is the capital of Australia?" (direct reference) or "Which city is the seat of government for Australia?" (indirect reference).

You can always keep the person honest by first asking, "Which is the most populous city in Australia?"

But the reader must also "read between the lines" in order to garner the implied or indirectly stated meanings. This process is also called interpretation. Familiar settings for inferential reading are love letters, letters to editors, and editorials. When one infers, one develops meanings by bringing together pieces of information in the selection, by bringing in (1) additional information from experience and (2) one's reasoning processes to develop the relationships among these bits of information.

Examples. The temperature at 7:00 A.M. is 70° and rising steadily; whereas the humidity is 30 per cent.

> Exercise A. What kinds of inferences can you make about existing weather conditions? About the weather in succeeding minutes or hours?
>
> Exercise B. On the basis of the statement about temperature and humidity, check the numbered conclusions that can safely be drawn. (You may want to state degrees of probability or qualify your answer.)
>
> 1. The temperature at 8:00 A.M. will be 75°. _____
> 2. It will rain during the day. _____
> 3. The temperature at 7:10 A.M. will probably not be 65°. _____
> 4. It is not raining. _____
> 5. All the people in town are up. _____

IMPORTANT DEVELOPMENTAL READING SKILLS

The attempt to analyze and state a definitive list of reading skills is like trying "to nail Jello to the wall." Theoretically and practically a person will come up with an overlapping of skills and will not give the emphasis that will satisfy everyone. Someone who has done this piece of research or that bit of theorizing may take umbrage at some part of my delineation; others will experience a warm glow as they see something that agrees with their predilections.

It is my opinion that one uses a number of processes to get the products often termed skills. These processes are mainly deductive, inductive, and analogical reasoning processes. For example, a main idea is, in a sense, a product, and it can be obtained by one or more processes. At any rate, someone who thinks that I have mixed apples and oranges can still enjoy the fruit of my labors. Organizational reference skills will be discussed in another chapter and the developmental reading skills listed here will be elaborated on throughout the book.

Developing and Using Vocabulary Meanings

1. Understanding one or more meanings of a word.
2. Learning to use context clues.

3. Understanding figures of speech.
4. Analyzing word structure—root, affixes—for meaning clues.
5. Knowing what a word or expression denotes or connotes in a given context.

Developing and Applying Independent Word Identification Skills

1. Analyzing words for grapheme-phoneme associations and for phonemic options.
2. Looking for familiar syllables, roots, affixes, and inflectional endings.
3. Checking pronunciation of a word against the context.
4. Using context and partial pronunciation to identify a word.

Using Verbal Reasoning to Comprehend

1. Recalling word meanings.
2. Following the structure of a passage.
3. Finding answers to questions answered explicitly or in paraphrase.
4. Noting explicitly stated relationships such as cause-effect.
5. Noting explicitly stated main ideas and relevant clarifying and supporting information.

Using Verbal Reasoning to Infer

1. Drawing conclusions from content.
2. Recognizing and appreciating [noting influence of] of a writer's purpose, tone, attitude, and mood.
3. Inferring implicit and/or complex relationships such as cause-effect.
4. Inferring implicitly stated main ideas and relevant supporting information.

Coping With Difficult Writing

1. Adjusting speed and approach to one's purpose and to the difficulty of the writing.
2. Comprehending compact writing.
3. Analyzing a sentence for the key elements.
4. Clarifying devious, circuitous language.
5. Reading other materials on the same subject.

Noting and Interpreting Feeling and Tone

1. Noting indications of feeling or emotion in a situation.
2. Noting one's own feeling reactions to a situation.
3. Being aware of literary devices used to obtain a certain tone or mood.

Understanding Various Patterns of Explanation

1. Definition
2. Analysis
3. Cause and effect
4. Comparison and contrast

5. Analogy
6. Chronology
7. Dialogue

SUMMARY

Some common uses of reading that we take for granted would be sweet attainments for nonreaders and poor readers. Through reading, aspects of family welfare and harmony might be promoted, a trade or profession might be learned, and a person might lead the examined life on a different plane.

In the past, certain groups of people have been deprived of the opportunity to improve economically and socially. Today some individuals denigrate the apparent lack of roots and traditions in these groups, but the latter indices of prized conservatism are hard to acquire and maintain when one's life and culture are rooted in slavery instituted by the forefathers of certain kinds of "conservatives," who do not know the meaning of classical conservatism.

Misconceptions of reading acts contribute to the miseducation of countless individuals. In reality, teachers and parents should conceive of reading as a process whose development requires nurturing over a period of many years. The best teachers in the middle and secondary schools will conceive of reading development as a long-term process and will accept responsibility for doing their part in stimulating and guiding the reading development of their students.

While reading, a person reconstructs the facts that lie behind the symbols. Decoding or converting print to "speech" is a necessary (but not a sufficient) first step in reading. Reading and reading instruction involve decoding *and* comprehending—a unified process. Reading instruction focuses on teaching both inferential and literal comprehension.

There are a number of important developmental reading skills. One uses deductive, inductive, and analogical reasoning processes in developing and exercising these skills which, in a very real sense, are products. In discussing the nature of the reading process I have sketched the broad lineaments of some of the key skills. Further development will be found in the following chapters.

ACTIVITES AND QUESTIONS
TO PROMOTE LEARNING AND APPLICATION[4]

1. Construct a questionnaire or checklist about reading materials and activities in the home and have each student complete it. Tabulate your data, state the important findings, and draw appropriate conclusions.

---

[4] These activities may apply to pre-service and/or to in-service situations. In either case students should be involved as much as possible.

2. Form committees to investigate the basic teachings of several philosophers, educators, and theologians. State their views about the purposes and values of education and, where possible, the role of reading in obtaining an education. Some possibilities: Christ, Aquinas, Luther, Comenius, Goethe, Horace Mann, C. S. Peirce, Booker T. Washington, William James, Alfred North Whitehead, Jacques Maritain, and Adolph Haentzschel. (Also, what do your reactions to this assignment and your ability to tackle it say about your liberal education to this point?)

3. Examine several recent issues of such magazines as *Time, Newsweek, Atlantic Monthly, Harper's,* and *Psychology Today.* What are people saying about who can and should be educated and how it should be done? State how you agree with the authors' contentions; disagree. How will these matters affect the way you feel you can carry on your work as a teacher?

4. Why do you suppose Goethe said it takes a long time to learn to read?

5. People make statements orally and in writing about what they think reading is and how it should be taught. Collect these statements and list them in ascending order of sophistication. How have these views affected educational practice? How can you promulgate the better views to the advantage of the schools? How can you mitigate the effect of the poorer views?

6. What might be the advantages or disadvantages of considering decoding and comprehending a unified process?

7. List the courses you have had in the last year or two that you have considered (a) educationally valuable and (b) educationally worthless. List the courses in which you have had to make (a) many inferences and (b) few inferences. What is the relation between your perception of the value of a course and the number of inferences you had to make in the course?

SUGGESTED ADDITIONAL READINGS

DOUGLASS, MALCOLM (Ed.). *Reading in Education: A Broader View.* Columbus, Ohio: Charles E. Merrill, 1973, Unit one.

GOODMAN, KENNETH. *The Psycholinguistic Nature of the Reading Process.* Detroit: State University Press, 1973.

HAFNER, LAWRENCE E. (Ed.). *Improving Reading in Middle and Secondary Schools.* New York: Macmillan, 1974. Sections 1 and 2.

MELNIK, AMELIA, and JOHN MERRITT. *Reading: Today and Tomorrow.* Morristown, N.J.: General Learning Press, 1972. Unit one.

SINGER, HARRY. "Theoretical Models of Reading." In Ekwall, Eldon E. (Ed.). *Psychological Factors in the Teaching of Reading.* Columbus, Ohio: Charles E. Merrill, 1973. Pp. 402–422.

——, and ROBERT B. RUDDELL. (Eds.). *Theoretical Models and Processes in Reading.* Newark, Del.: International Reading Association, 1976.

SMITH, FRANK. *Understanding Reading: A Psycholinguistic Analysis of Reading and Learning to Read.* New York: Holt, Rinehart and Winston, 1971.

——,(Ed.). *Psycholinguistics and Reading.* New York: Holt, Rinehart and Winston, 1973.

STICHT, THOMAS G. (Ed.). *Reading for Working.* Alexandria, Va.: Human Resources Research Organization, 1975.

ZINTZ, MILES V. *The Reading Process.* Second Edition. Dubuque: Wm. C. Brown, 1975, Chapter 1.

BIBLIOGRAPHY

BALDWIN, JAMES. *Go Tell It on the Mountain.* New York: Dial, 1963.

CHAMBERS, BRADFORD (Ed.). *Chronicles of Black Protest.* New York: Mentor, 1969.

HAENTZSCHEL, ADOLPH. *The Great Quest.* St. Louis: Concordia, 1953.

HAFNER, LAWRENCE, and BILLY M. GUICE. "Nutrition, Love, and Language: Keys to Reading." In Lawrence E. Hafner (Ed.). *Improving Reading in Middle and Secondary Schools. Second Edition.* New York: Macmillan, 1974.

KIRK, RUSSELL. *Prospectives for Conservatives.* Chicago: Henry Regnery, 1956.

KORZYBSKI, ALFRED. *Science and Sanity.* Lancaster, Pa.: The Science Press Printing Co., 1941.

LINCOLN, CHARLES ERIC. *Negro Pilgrimage in America.* New York: Praeger, 1969.

ORTEGA Y GASSETT, JOSÉ. *The Origins of Philosophy.* New York: W. W. Norton, 1941.

SMITH, HELEN K. "Research in Reading for Different Purposes." In J. Allen Figurel (Ed.). *Changing Concepts of Reading Instruction.* Newark, Del.: International Reading Association, 1961.

CHAPTER 2

Psychological Foundations for Reading Instruction. I. Theories of Learning, Concept Development, and Discovery Learning Versus Expository Teaching

A person who learns acquires the behavior or ability to perform as a result of experience. The person who learns well remembers how to perform the behavior at a later time. The abilities to work a mathematics problem, to play a musical selection, and to read and perform a physics experiment are learned behaviors.

Methods of retaining learning, techniques for measuring retention, and methods of transferring training to other situations will be discussed in the next chapter. I will first discuss several important theories of learning, principles that follow from them, and applications of the principles to the teaching of reading.

THEORIES OF LEARNING

Pavlov's Classical Conditioning

Pavlov discovered that he could get a dog to salivate on hearing a bell. Big deal, you say? Dogs do not salivate when they hear bells. How did he achieve this monumental feat and what does it mean for the teaching of reading?

He preceded the presentation of meat powder to the dog with the ringing of a bell. After a number of such paired presentations the sound of the bell elicited the salivation before the appearance of the meat powder. What Pavlov succeeded in doing was to get the animal to respond to a stimulus with a given response that it previously would not make. What is an application of this phenomenon to reading instruction?

Let us assume we want a child to look at the printed word ⟨peach⟩ and say /pēch/. How do we get the child to do it? We can say /pēch/, but the student may not learn it on one or two trials, and we do not have time to do that sort of thing for many students.

What we do is provide the student with a picture that will elicit the word. (The picture is called an unconditioned stimulus; the printed word, the conditioned stimulus.) Next, place the printed word to the *left* of the picture because reading is done from left to right in English and the unconditioned stimulus (remember the bell?) should come first in the sequence. After a number of paired presentations of ⟨peach⟩ and 🍑 , the printed word alone elicits /pēch/.

According to Pavlov's paradigm this would be represented as follows:

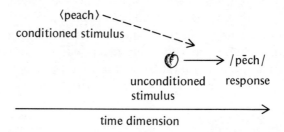

We have students learn "several words at a time" so that they have to differentiate a given word from other words. This technique will help students learn many words (and phrases) on their own.

Thorndike's Connectionism

Edward L. Thorndike developed a learning theory that became known as connectionism. From his observations of learning situations, he developed three major laws of learning: (1) the law of *exercise*, (2) the law of *effect*, and (3) the law of *readiness*.

Law of Exercise. This law states that other things being equal, learning occurs to the extent that the particular acts involved in the learning are practiced. The more a person practices an act in a situation the more likely he will respond that way the next time he is in the situation. Thorndike felt that the S-R connection was strengthened by the vigor and duration of the practice periods. Therefore, in reading situations many practice periods and active responses to stimuli during these periods should be arranged for so that associations will be made and remembered when learning such phenomena as:

1. At-sight words
2. Phonic elements
3. Vocabulary terms
4. An outline one has developed
5. Formulas, equations, and the like
6. The steps in a reading-study technique

Law of Effect.   We have noted, now, that repetition is an important(although not sufficient) factor in the acquisition of responses. For efficient learning, motivation should be present at least to the extent that rewards will be satisfying to the individual.

The law of effect, then, states that the strength of an association (connection) is increased when the response is followed by a satisfying state of affairs. Learning situations need to be monitored so that (1) incorrect responses are corrected and (2) only correct responses are rewarded (satisfying state of affairs).

Another way of stating the law of effect is that one tends to do that which is pleasant and to avoid doing that which is unpleasant. Now let us look at the middle or secondary school student who cannot read a word. For what has this student been rewarded? He or she has been rewarded for many things but *not* for making correct responses in reading—because this student has made none.

Law of Readiness.   Readiness means a preparation for action. If you get a student ready—set up an action tendency—by developing a set or attitude, it will be satisfying for him or her to act. When we "set the student up" we should be sure that the response for the situation is available. It is doubly important to develop activity sets in which the student can be successful because one's successes are a guide to future activities. Therefore, the teacher is responsible for providing a learning environment that develops positive sets for student responses so that associations can be learned and the law of effect can thereby be capitalized on.

A subordinate law of *set* or *attitude* operates here. It states that set or attitude determines not only what a person will do but what will satisfy or annoy him. This law helps to explain a youngster's satisfaction in learning to identify ten words one week when accustomed to learning two words per week.

Theory of Transfer and Intelligence.   Since transfer of training and intelligence are highly related in Thorndike's theory, they will be treated as one topic. Thorndike espoused a theory of identical elements transfer. If one has as an original task—the spelling of the word *shall*—there will be greater transfer from this task to spelling the word *shell* than to *shut* because the former has more elements identical to *shall* than the latter does. Similarly, the study of Latin should transfer to elements of English study that are closely related to Latin elements. In considering these two lists, we are assuming that the meaning of the Latin word was learned first.

Latin		English
avunculus	(uncle)	avuncular
geminus	(twin)	geminate
opus	(work)	opera
sacer	(sacred)	sacerdotal
timeo	(fear)	timorous

Thorndike believed that intelligence consists of a large number of specific abilities. An ability is a bundle of independent reactions. Ability A might be comprised of reactions a, b, c, and h, and ability B of a, b, f, g, and h. (Note the identical elements.) Because of partial identity of abilities A and B, a relationship between the two should be evinced. For example, Ability A might be skill in playing the clarinet and Ability B might be skill in typing. Can you see overlapping abilities?

Let me make an application in mathematics reading. Let $X = abc$ be a mathematics pattern. If $a = 2$, $b = 3$, and $c = 4$, then $X = (2) (3) (4)$ or 24. Note the identical elements in the formula (required to solve the following physics problem) and the mathematics pattern:

> Problem: A baseball dropped from the top of a building took three seconds to hit the ground. Using the physics formula $\underline{D} = \frac{1}{2} g t^2$, where $\underline{D}$ is distance or height, $\underline{g}$ is a constant of 32, and $\underline{t} =$ time in seconds, we compute
>
> $$\underline{D} = (\tfrac{1}{2}) \ (32) \ (3^2)$$
> $$= (16) \ (9)$$
> $$= 144 \qquad \text{The building is 144 feet high.}$$

Also, because there are more identical elements between Latin and French than between Latin and German, knowledge of Latin transfers to the study of French more readily than it does to German. Since to Thorndike intelligence is a matter of having bonds or connections (what we would today call S-R connections, facts, concepts, and the like), the person who has more bonds will likely have more elements to transfer. By such reasoning, knowing Latin gives a person more bonds, making him or her more intelligent with more elements that can be transfered to learning French and to learning new cognate words in English. Thus, we see the relationship between intelligence and transfer in Thorndike's theory.

I have selected five Latin words at random and shown their German and French counterparts below:

German	Latin	French
kalt	frigus	froid
(die) Milch	lac	lait
(die) Gelegenheit	occasio	occasion
(der) Stern	stella	étoile
(die) Schulter	umerus	l'épaule

Because learning results from the acquisition of connections or bonds in the brain, and the right experiences will lead to acquiring more, or at least different, connections than the lack of such experiences, one function of home and school is to provide the type of environment and training conducive to the acquisition of connections.[1] Thorndike also claimed that the brightest people have the most connections. Therefore, the more one learns, the more connections one has and the more connections (of the right and useful kind) that one has, the more educated and intelligent one is.

[1] One should teach for transfer, not assume that it will occur.

It is known that vocabulary is an important factor in intelligence. Furthermore, how many words one knows depends on how often the learner is rewarded for using appropriate terminology, (Snelbecker,1974). Bugelski (1971), commenting on Thorndike's theory, states that one should be rewarded for using a precise vocabulary, and the teacher should not allow a vague approximation. I would add that perhaps a student could learn a technical definition *and* be able to say it in his or her own words *if* the paraphrase is conceptually correct.

Commins and Fagin (1954) criticized Thorndike's multifactor theory of ability on the grounds that it (1) overemphasizes environmental contributions to growth of ability by overemphasizing stimuli, specific reactions, and identical elements in subject matter. Constitutional factors contributing to differences in ability appear to be neglected. (2) The factor of maturation appears to be slighted; actually it is difficult to understand as a practical concept in this theory. (3) His theory seems to hold that no abilities are fundamental and that there is no general mental ability. Yet evidence points to a general mental ability.

Skinner's Connectionism

Operant Conditioning and the Reinforcement Situation. B. F. Skinner has for many years studied the control of behavior. He conditions organisms to behave in a certain manner. In early studies, Skinner devised a situation in which an animal can perform an operation that it is likely to do (anyway); for example, press a bar with a foot or peck at it. When the desired response is made, it is rewarded with, say, a food pellet. The pellet is called a reinforcer. Such reinforcement is followed by the organism making the response with greater frequency. This operant conditioning increases the frequency of a given response. Most human behavior is thought to be of the operant type: We operate on our environment in order to change it in some way and bring reinforcers.

Reinforcement. Food, drink, touch, and the like that are necessary for survival are primary positive reinforcers. But a stimulus associated with primary reinforcement is able to reinforce behavior and is known as a *secondary reinforcer*. Praise, money, gestures, words, tokens, smiles, grades, titles, and gold stars are examples of secondary reinforcers with which we are familiar. These secondary reinforcers are very useful conditioners of behavior. However, if money could not buy food and good grades did not lead to acceptable jobs and thence (eventually) to food, they would most likely cease to be secondary reinforcers, they would lose their symbolic value.

Actually, secondary reinforcers have wide applications. Response after response can be kept going by the reinforcement at the goal, because these milestones—social approval, money and the like—serve as signs, as secondary reinforcers, that assure the person of satisfaction on approaching the goal. Secondary reinforcers, then, can serve very effectively as motivators of behavior.

An Application to Reading Instruction.   The operant conditioning phenomenon can be used in reading instruction. Let us imagine that Charlie, a ninth-grade student reads only 150 words a day outside of school, the equivalent of a brief news item in a newspaper. The frequency of response (or, in effect, the total number of words read) can be increased by giving him a suitable reward for making such a response. The reinforcement might mean permission to engage in a higher frequency behavior, that is, something he really likes to do (Premack principle). Or the reward may be a token that could at another time be traded for money; or it could be money itself. To be effective the reinforcement should (theoretically) be given within five seconds after the response. The paradigm follows:

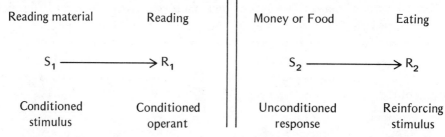

Reading material	Reading		Money or Food	Eating
$S_1 \longrightarrow R_1$			$S_2 \longrightarrow R_2$	
Conditioned stimulus	Conditioned operant		Unconditioned response	Reinforcing stimulus

Knowledge of Results as Feedback.   Knowing that a response one makes is correct is positive feedback and a good reinforcer. A nod of the head at a correct verbal response is a common method of reinforcement. The trouble in teacher-student exchanges is that when one person is responding 29 other students are not responding. Provision should be made for many individuals to make many responses during the day and get positive reinforcement. Programmed learning is one means of providing this opportunity.

Programmed Learning.   Programmed texts are comprised of highly organized material that is presented in short sequences ranging from a word and a picture, for example, through sentences to a brief paragraph. Following the presentation of material, a problem is posed, the student constructs a response, and then moves a marker to reveal the correct answer. In this way the student can move at his or her own rate and receive immediate feedback on the correctness of the responses. These programs are usually organized so carefully and with such gradual increments that a student who can read the material with good comprehension gets 90 per cent or more correct responses.

Ausubel's Meaningful Verbal Learning Theory

Millions of hours are wasted daily in American schools on useless rote learning. A prime example is the recitation of the "Pledge of Allegiance," which, data show, is largely meaningless as a *cognitive* exercise. More concrete, meaningful expressions of what is entailed in being loyal, in being a good citizen, can certainly be formulated for pupils in the elementary, middle, and secondary schools.

Reception Learning.   Ausubel (1968, 1969) believes that reception learning is superior to, and certainly more efficient than, discovery learning. Reception learning results from the learner relating to his or her cognitive structures material that has been carefully selected, organized, and presented by such means as textbooks, lectures, and technological devices such as computer-assisted instruction, programmed learning, and the like.

Subsuming Material into Cognitive Structures. As stated, individuals have cognitive structures or meaning hierarchies. Any verbal material presented to a person must be able to fit into these structures if it is to be considered meaningful. By fitting, Ausubel means it can be subsumed into a structure. Let me give an example:

Existing Structure	(New) Information Presented	Relationship	Conclusion
Flowers have stems, leaves, petals, etc.	The rhododendron is a flower	Flower (superordinate) rose lily (rhododendron)	A rhododendron also has stems, leaves, petals, and the like.

If the new material can be subsumed into an existing cognitive structure, it is meaningful. After all, the human brain does not do a good job of grasping and remembering material that cannot easily be related to a cognitive structure. (It is the repetition of the "Pledge" rather than the meaningfulness that allows children to remember it. Much less repetition would be required of a more concrete pledge and it would also be meaningful.)

Unrelated words and other arbitrary materials are very hard to remember. But if the learner can somehow impose one or more structures on the material, he or she might be better able to retain the material as well as see relationships among the concepts involved. Let us say a person is given the names of several cities and towns and asked to remember them: San Francisco, Gary, Frankenmuth (Mich.), Sydney, Birmingham, Altenburg, (Mo.), Ft. Wayne, New York, and Pittsburgh.

What kind of cognitive structures could be imposed on these cities or under what kinds of meaning hierarchies could these cities be subsumed in order to remember them? How about these?

Excellent Harbors	Major Centers of Steel Production	Early Lutheran Settlements in Mid-America
San Francisco	Gary	Frankenmuth
New York	Birmingham	Altenburg
Sydney	Pittsburgh	Ft. Wayne

You see, the learner can bring to the learning process organized knowledge that can be used to retain much new material. New information fitting the above categories can neatly be slipped into the structures. A key role of education is to develop new categories or "hooks." For example, you probably knew about major ports and steel production, but may not have known about early Lutheran settlements in mid-America. Mouly (1974) points out that material may be logical, but it is the psychological (idiosyncratic, personalized) meaning of the material that gets slotted into the learner's cognitive structures. One must want to relate the material into one's cognitive structure. The key to effective learning, retention, and transfer of information is to make sure that adequate subsumers (or categories) are available.

Advance Organizers. Appropriately general and inclusive frameworks can be introduced in advance of the material to be read so that ideational scaffolding is provided for the stable incorporation and retention of the more detailed and differentiated material that follows. Ausubel calls these frameworks advance organizers. With the passage of time, details in the structure, and also their import, tend to be reduced to the broad, general meaning of the few inclusive concepts and propositions (Mouly, 1974 on Ausubel). I feel that these concepts and propositions are easier to retain, but some of the power of explanatory illustrations and detail will be lost, too.

Types of Subsumption. Two types of subsumptions relate new ideas to superordinate categories, that is more abstract and inclusive categories: derivative subsumption and correlative subsumption. These and other kinds of subsumption are discussed below:

Derivative subsumption: In derivative subsumption the new information merely illustrates (or is an example of) a known superordinate or can be deduced from it. For example, the person who knows what an explosive is (either inductively or deductively) can understand the meaning of a new term, *nitroglycerine*, when it is related to the superordinate *explosive* by a sentence such as, "Nitroglycerine is an explosive." In this case the subordinate nitroglycerine *derived* its meaning from a more general proposition.

Correlative Subsumption: In correlative subsumption the new information or proposition is an elaboration or qualification of a previously learned one. For example, in relating *nitroglycerine* to the previously learned superordinate *explosive* we *must* elaborate on or qualify the meaning. If a person thinks of explosives in terms of those that do not necessarily explode when dropped and handles nitroglycerine in a "careful" manner, it could result in his or her death. Why? Because nitroglycerine is very unstable and explodes easily when jarred!

Combinatorial Subsumption: Some ideas cannot (1) be related specifically to either a superordinate or subordinate category or (2) be transformed. However, they are congruent to, or consistent with, a broad background of relevant ideas. These ideas carry a *combinatorial* relationship to existing cognitive structures (Ausubel and Robinson, 1969). I would think that comparing cognitive structures to the model of the basic structure of a house would be an example of a combinatorial relationship.

Obliterative Subsumption. A general reductionist trend in cognitive organization produces cognitive economy. It is easier to remember the more general, stable, established concepts and propositions that we use as anchors than all the new ideas "tied" to them. An abstract concept is easier to manipulate than the many diverse examples of the concept. The assimilating of examples, details, and illustrations in the general structure results eventually in *obliterative subsumption;* details sort of "get lost in the shuffle." Trying to remember all the supporting data for a general meaning is much more difficult than remembering the "more general and inclusive meaning of the established subsumer." Correlative, derivative, and combinatorial subsumption are all subject to the phenomenon of obliteration.

On the negative side, when propositions lose their identifiability and can no longer be distinguished from their subsumers, a real loss of knowledge occurs. If you wanted to talk about a particular correlative proposition and had in your memory only the subsumer, the abstract category, then you could not reconstruct the substance of the forgotten material. For example, have you already obliterated the concept of correlative subsumption? That is, can you talk only about subsumption in a general way or can you specifically discuss correlative subsumption? "The acquisition of knowledge, therefore, is largely a matter of counteracting the trend toward obliterative assimilation and retaining correlative, superordinate, and combinatorial learnings" (Ausubel and Robinson, 1969).

In sum, Ausubel's meaningful learning theory states that the use of existing meaning hierarchies for subsuming new information is a key to learning and retaining information. When new material is introduced, a writer or teacher can develop and/or reactivate meaningful cognitive structures to which the learner can relate new material. New materials that can be subsumed into existing cognitive structures are meaningful. Teachers and students should work toward (1) using existing meaning hierarchies, (2) expanding those hierarchies, and (3) rearranging old ones as well as (4) developing new ones. Such strategies are the key to effective learning, retention, and transfer of information and ideas.

PIAGET'S PRINCIPLES OF DEVELOPMENT RELATED TO LEARNING

What Is Thinking?

Instrumentalists such as John Dewey would say that thinking is something that precedes action, that thinking is a prelude to action. But for Jean Piaget operational thinking is an interiorized action in which things in the environment are transformed into objects of knowing. One form of transformation is that of classifying an object. Another is transforming the operation 6 X 3 into the operation (6 X 2) + (6 X 1) (Furth, 1969). In growing from childhood to adulthood a person develops a series of concrete and then formal thought structures with which he or she operates on the concrete level and then on the abstract hypothetical level.

What Are the Developmental Stages?

In developing from an infant into an adult a person goes through a series of stages:

Sensorimotor Stage (C.A. 0–2). The child in this stage learns to represent the world with (1) visual images, which serve as internal symbols and (2) motor symbols, such as imitation, which serve as signs. Toward the end of this period verbal symbols are also used to represent thought. In other words, during this stage, visual images, motor symbols, and verbal symbols are used to represent thought. For Piaget, thought precedes language, and only later does the process become somewhat reciprocal.

Preoperational Stage (C.A. 2–7). During the first substage (2–4) the child begins to use mental symbols, especially words, to represent absent things or events. And the child runs these events off in a serial order. During the second substage (4–7) the child's reasoning is (1) *egocentric*—cognitive operations and language are determined by present action and from the *child's* viewpoint; (2) *perceptually oriented*—words are defined by describing them (an *orange* is round and orange) or showing how they are used (you eat it); and (3) *marked by irreversibility*, shown by the child's difficulty in classifying; for example, the child loses sight of the original criterion and becomes confused when trying to move from an example or instance to a class and then back from the class to the instance. Understanding the number system is predicated on understanding the operations of classes and seriation; this understanding is a product of the synthesis of the two operations according to Furth (1969, p. 64).

During the latter part of this stage, the child is able to decenter so that he or she (1) will look at events from more than his or her own viewpoint and (2) will focus upon several aspects of a configuration such as a printed letter or word in order to differentiate it from similar-appearing letters or words. The child who is centering might have trouble in differentiating *l* and *h* because he or she is centering only on the vertical line; such a child fails to differentiate *tree* and *tent* because of centering on the *t*. This child needs to decenter and note the second letter, which makes it possible to differentiate the two words:

centering	decentering
👁	👁
↓	↓↓
l	l↓
h	h
👁	👁
↓	↓↓
tree	tree
tent	tent

Concrete-Operational Stage (C.A. 7–11 or 12). During this stage the child acquires the ability to *classify*, to *order*, and to *reverse thinking action*. Reversibility means, for example, that the child can go back and forth in the vertical classification hierarchy (flower ⟷ rose) and also note that $3 + 5 = 8$, so does $5 + 3$. This "power" is attained at about age seven.

At this level the child also acquires the ability to *conserve* (principle of invariance):

1. *Conservation of quantity.* An amount of substance—clay, for example—is the same amount whether it is in the form of a ball, a sausage, or in small pieces. This ability is acquired at about age seven.

2. *Conservation of weight.* The same principle is in operation here, and the ability is acquired at the age of nine.

3. *Conservation of volume.* This ability is acquired at age eleven.

Formal-Operational Stage (C.A. 11 or 12–14 or 15). Operations developed during this stage are in their incipient form at eleven or twelve years of age and in their stable or more mature form at age fourteen or fifteen. At this stage the child develops formal, abstract thinking operations and can state hypothetical propositions and deduce possible consequences from them. If-then propositions are probably quite familiar to the reader. This level of thought, then, expresses itself in linguistic formulations containing propositions and logical constructions (implication, disjunction, etc.) (Furth, 1969).

A problem solvable by the formal-operational child, but not by that child in the concrete-operational stage, is the following question dealing with *abstract relations:*

> Gene is shorter than Larry; Gene is taller than Charlie. Who is the tallest of the three?

Another example of formal thinking involves *combinatorial logic:*

> Five bottles of colorless liquid are placed before the child. Bottles one, three, and five when combined will yield a brownish color. The second bottle is neutral, and the fourth bottle contains a color-reducing solution. The task for the child is to discover how to produce a colored solution. In this formal stage the child learns how to construct a table of all the possible combinations and thereby determines which combinations will yield the colored solution.

Further applications of Piaget will be made in later chapters.

CONCEPTS

Development of Concepts

What Is a Concept? The word *cat* is the name of a concept; so are the words *intelligence, love,* and *justice.* A concept is a class of things or ideas with common elements or characteristics. The common physical elements and characteristics of *cat* are animal, claws, whiskers, good night vision, carnivorous, and so forth. There are differing characteristics among the cat or feline species—differences in size, coloring, form, and so forth—but the things that have the common characteristics listed above are called cats or *feline.*

Johnson (1972) tells us that any word or phrase that points to or designates a referent is called a term. A *singular* term such as Socrates and Statue of Liberty refers to one object. *General* terms refer to a class of objects such as dog or small red triangles.

Concept Attributes and Values.   An attribute is a distinctive characteristic of a concept. Thus, a distinctive attribute that distinguishes the house cat from a dog is vocal sound (what we call "Meow"). Johnson (1972) differentiates the extensional significance of terms from intensional significance. By *extensional* significance he means the entire set of objects denoted by a term; by the term *dog*, then, is meant all members of the class living or yet to be born. By *intensional* significance (and this is what we are most interested in) he means all the properties that define the class and characterize its members. These properties are also called *attributes, qualities,* and *dimensions.*

We can list the attributes for a given concept and then use this list, called a criterial features list, to judge whether a given thing belongs to this class of concepts. Following is the criterial features list for insects; row A is a check-off list for the spider; row B is the check-off list for the ant; and row C is for the cat. Which is an insect, the spider, the ant, or the cat?

Insects ——→	Three body segments	Six legs	Spiracles for breathing	No backbone	Complete metamorphasis	Cold blooded
A. spider	0	0	0	+	0	
B. ant	+	+	+	+	+	+
C. cat	0	0	0	0	0	0

DeCecco and Crawford (1974) note that the number of attributes varies among the concepts. There are two attributes in the concept *blue squares*—color and form. But there are three in *small blue squares*—size, color, and form. How many attributes are listed above for insects? Do you think that exhausts the attributes of insects? Try listing the number of attributes for the concepts *republic, agape* (love), and *justice.* Much reading, study, and discussion would be involved in such an endeavor. We may not be able to attend to all the attributes of a concept. We may need to emphasize certain attributes and neglect others; possibly some attributes can be combined. There is always a danger—particularly when the concepts have to do with basic concepts such as *agape, justice,* and so forth—that we fashion incomplete, detrimental-to-certain groups concepts. For example, we may falsely assume that *agape* (1) is something to be received by certain groups of people only, (2) is meritable, and (3) has only spiritual dimensions. The same kinds of false assumptions have been made about *justice.* The application to reading interpretation seems obvious.

For various reasons teachers and learners may tend to neglect certain attributes of concepts. A teacher must try to note the important attributes that may escape student attention and then take steps to give those attributes visual and oral emphasis. For example, in discussing the concept of *mastery,* one may underline master and show the learner with his or her thumb pressed against some visual depiction of another concept in order to show mastery or depict a person "nailing down" an idea or fact or rule so that it cannot "get away." Also, one's tone of voice and inflection can serve to emphasize the importance of certain aspects or attributes of mastery.

Types of Concepts

Conjunctive Concepts. The attributes and values of conjunctive concepts are simply additive according to De Cecco and Crawford (1974). A person in a sense learns a list of attributes and appropriate values. For example, *dog* has color, shape, texture, behavior, and size attributes. The values of attributes will vary from the Weimaraner to the Chihuahua.

Disjunctive Concepts. Disjunctive concepts can be defined in several ways. For example, they have an *and/or* dimension or an *or* dimension:

> two-point score (basketball): Awarded when ball goes through the hoop or opposing player interferes with ball on downward path to goal (or dimension).
> walk (baseball): Awarded when a batter receives four balls or is hit by a pitched ball (or dimension).
> member of big women club: A woman who is taller than 70 inches and/or who weighs more than 150 pounds (and/or dimension).

As an exercise, define *strike* (baseball) and *extra point* (football) to see if the concepts are conjunctive or disjunctive. Disjunctive concepts seem to be harder to think of and to learn than conjunctive concepts.

Relational Concepts. *Slenderness* is a relational concept because it depends on the relation between height and weight. *Average* is another relational concept, because it refers to a general tendency relationship. Bruner (1959) suggested that since *income tax brackets after deductions* depend on the relationship between the amount of net income and the number of dependents, they can be considered relational concepts. These concepts are more difficult to teach than conjunctive concepts since they are not facets of the attributes; they are, rather, a function of the relationships among the attributes.

Development of Rules

What Is a Rule? Gagné (1970) defines a rule as a relationship between two or more concepts. It might be useful to think of rules as *if-then statements*: (1) *If* you multiply eight by four, *then* the result is thirty two. (2) *If* you want better results from reading instruction, *then* pace to each student's ability to master material before going on to new challenges.

Gagné (1974) points out that knowing rules enables a person to react to a group (class) of things with a class of responses or performances.

Therefore, a class of remediation strategies can be applied to a class of reading difficulties so that one does not have to develop entirely discrete techniques for difficulties that can be grouped as a class because of many shared attributes.

Using Concepts and Rules

If we did not have concepts we would be hard put to use all the detailed language necessary to describe our environment and the myriad interrelationships among people, and between the environment and people, and between things in the environment. If we did not have the concept or class of *things*, we would have to detail perhaps hundreds ___ _____ and then say, "You know what I mean." Think of the detail you would have to produce before somebody would know you are talking about your house. Someone will say, "Oh, I would just refer to my domicile or abode or home." But these, too, are class names, that is, concepts. Therefore, we can be much more parsimonious in denoting things by using concepts and appropriate vocabulary for the concepts.

Another item of importance: Rules are derived from relating two or more concepts. To the extent that we are weak in concepts, we are lacking in the ability to develop or understand rules. "If you work outdoors with electrical equipment, stand on insulated material" is a rule based on the concept that electricity has a strong proclivity to go to the ground. If there is defective wiring or insulation in the equipment, the charge of electricity will tend to go through you to the ground and likely kill you.

Many rules help a person identify words, develop word meanings, and understand connected discourse. A small sampling of these rules follows:

1. ⟨ea⟩ in a word is usually pronounced /ē/ or /e/.

2. The meaning of the context will help you decide the correct phonemic option in a word.

3. ⟨ai⟩ usually represents the /ā/ sound.

4. Read through a word for important graphic cues to the pronunciation of a word.

5. *If* ⟨ch⟩ → /ch/ does not sound right in pronouncing a word, *then* try /k/, and, if necessary, /sh/.

6. In order to determine the meaning of a word, relate it to the surrounding context.

These rules are taught by a number of strategies and techniques over a long period of time—years—and are reviewed and applied in reading—content reading materials as well as general reading materials. Whether the rules are learned inductively or deductively, they must be applied and reviewed periodically, and, if necessary, retaught until they can be used appropriately and facilely.

DISCOVERY LEARNING VERSUS EXPOSITORY TEACHING

Discovery Learning

Discovery learning has been variously characterized as a way of learning and a goal of learning, as a student-centered learning activity, and as a problem-solving process. Wittrock (1963) differentiates *unguided* discovery from *guided* discovery. In the former the teacher may not give the principle (rule) that applies nor the problem solution; in the latter the teacher helps with recall and application of appropriate rules but not with the problem solution.

Bruner (1961) *claimed* four advantages of discovery learning (1) Discovery learning increases intellectual power by acquiring information in a manner that makes it readily available for problem solving. (2) Discovery learning builds intrinsic motivation by using the reward of discovery itself. (3) Discovery learning teaches the individual discovery techniques. (4) Discovery learning results in better retention of material because the student organizes his or her own information and, since he or she has stored it, knows how to retrieve it when needed. These claims have been seriously questioned by eloquent opponents.

Bruner (1959) reported on his discovery approach with a class of fifth graders in a "good" school in the East. He hit upon the idea of presenting the geography of the North Central States as a set of unknowns. The class was presented with blank maps that contained only tracings of the rivers and lakes of the area as well as the natural resources. The students were then asked to locate the principal cities. One child pointed his finger at the foot of Lake Michigan and was very happy that the big city of Chicago is located there, confirming his hypothesis. If this was in truth a discovery lesson then the schools of the East are not as great as many people claim, for children in the fifth grade in a "good" Eastern school should have been able to not only locate the cities but *name them.*

At any rate, one group, according to Bruner, "learned geography as a set of rational acts . . (while the other group learned passively that there were arbitrary cities at arbitrary places by arbitrary bodies of water and arbitrary sources of supply)." As I see it, either Bruner stacked the deck in favor of discovery learning by having the other group try to learn by an inferior method that did not ordinarily characterize the school or this inferior method characterized what Bruner would call a good Eastern school.

Wittrock (1966) scores Bruner on a different basis:

1. Bruner concluded that the children presented with blank maps were thinking. It would have been better to have empirical data that indexed their thoughts.

2. The groups that received blank maps received better treatment. (See my argument above.)

3. "When learning and discovery are measured by one event, discovery cannot be given as a cause for learning."

4. Empirical data on the consequences of "discovery learning" are needed in order to evaluate it.

Proponents of discovery learning, Wittrock says, claim that a person must learn to produce answers and knowledge, not reproduce them. Some people feel that only students who have *already* learned how to discover may learn by discovery. Also, it assumes that all people learn best by one method, discovery learning; however, individual differences may necessitate several different approaches. For example, Grimes and Allinsmith (1961) found that first-grade children who are highly compulsive and also highly anxious overachieve greatly when taught to read by a phonics method, which provides a structured setting of rules, systematic arrangement, and certainty of problem solving. Children who are highly anxious and *low* in compulsivity underachieve when taught by the whole-word method, which operates in a relatively unstructured setting.

Corman (1957) studied the effects of varying degrees of guidance on the learning, application, and verbalization of principle and procedure used to solve Katona's matchstick problems. In one of his problems the task is to make four squares instead of the five given. All sixteen original matches must be used in the solution.

Corman used three degrees of guidance: *no* information, *some* information, and *much* information about the key principle and procedure. In general, he found

1. *Learning.* Successful learning of the principle was a function of the amount of information about the principle.

2. *Verbalization.* Verbalization (in writing) of the method was not affected by the amount of information. Verbalization of the principle was affected by receiving information about the principle. (Some or much information was better than no information.)

3. *Application.* Subjects who were given information applied the principle to new matchstick problems better than those receiving no information. However, ability to make applications also varied as a function of intelligence, problem difficulty, and the amount of information provided about the principle.

What did Corman finally conclude? Guidance helps people to learn and apply principles and methods, whereas lack of guidance might interfere with problem solutions. For this reason I prefer much more directed reading instruction than is being done in the schools.

Gagné and Brown (1961) presented a program in which cues relating to problem solutions, not methods, were given to the subjects. Through use of programmed instruction, subjects learned principles used in solving number-series problems. The students were divided into three groups for differentiated instruction. After this experimental teaching period, post- (experimental teaching) tests, which involved solving four new number-series problems, were administered to all three groups. The *guided discovery* group performed best. In explaining the results, Gagné and Brown state that the guided discovery approach was effective, because it required the learner to reinstate (actually practice) the concepts that will be used later to solve new problems. The practice used in the rule and example (R & E) group *did not require* the use of these necessary concepts. Therefore, R & E led to very poor problem-solving performance.

Rather than agreeing with Gagne's contention that provided the concepts are learned, it should make no difference how they are learned, Wittrock (1966) states that all groups learned to the same criterion and therefore must have differed only with respect to how it was learned.

Finally Ausubel (1964), although not opposed to discovery learning per se, comments on misconceptions about discovery learning:

1. A pupil may spend much time solving a trivial problem, although the teacher could explain the solution in a matter of minutes.

2. Students rote memorize problem types and forms of solutions of these types in response to problem-solving techniques that are ostensibly creative.

3. Discovery procedures are not necessary for intuitive understanding and need not be a routine aspect of teaching technique.

Expository Teaching

If an inductive approach characterizes the discovery method, then a *deductive* approach marks expository teaching. In expository teaching, the instructor presents facts, concepts, and principles, illustrates them, and points up applications and implications. Good expository teaching, of course, will use appropriate technology, discussions, field work, laboratory work, and practicums. And the teaching will be done so that the ideas and their applications and implications can be further clarified and enhanced.

A comprehensive expository unit or lesson also has room for aspects of discovery learning. Good unit teaching in social studies, mathematics, and science has for years used expository teaching as well as relevant aspects of discovery learning.

Mouly (1973) points out that generally speaking rote learning is to be condemned. But one cannot repudiate reception learning as a corollary statement. Ausubel and Robinson (1969) have listed some of the worst abuses of expository teaching, for example:

1. Using only verbal techniques with cognitively immature pupils.
2. Arbitrarily presenting unrelated facts without the support of organizational or explanatory principles.
3. Not integrating new learning demands with previously learned materials.
4. Using evaluation techniques that measure only the ability to recognize facts and recall ideas verbatim or merely in the same context in which they were originally presented.

A caveat: These abuses should not be thought of as inherent characteristics of expository teaching.

Mouly also notes that in the interest of economy and efficiency most of the learning in the schools will be accomplished through expository teaching. Even though the primary-age child relies heavily on concrete experiences in concept development, by junior high school the students can acquire many concepts through a more verbal approach. Ausubel (1963) states that at this age "students acquire most new concepts and learn most new propositions by *directly* grasping higher order relationships between abstractions." Such a level of abstract understanding is "qualitatively superior to the intuitive level in terms of generality, clarity, precision, and explicitness."

Some research has been done on expository teaching. Ausubel has developed the idea of advance organizers to aid students in recalling relevant principles to be used in reading a selection. Advance organizers are definitions, concepts, or principles introduced before the chief reading (or other instructional) material is presented. The organizers provide a kind of conceptual framework for explaining and organizing the ensuing material. Research studies on the value of certain kinds of organizers have yielded equivocal results.

Ausubel (1960) had experimental and control groups read a passage on the metallurgical properties of ordinary carbon steel. Prior to reading the material the experimental group was permitted to read advance organizers—principles on the chief similarities and differences between metals and alloys, their advantages and disadvantages, and why alloys are made and used. The control group read an introductory passage sans advance organizers. The experimental group, which used these special organizing principles, more successfully retained the material on carbon steel than did the control group.

Johnson and Stratton (1966) taught concepts by means of three expository programs, one discovery program, and one mixed program. The mixed program was illustrative of a teacher-textbook approach and was the most successful. An example of mixed method instruction follows:

> To chide someone is to talk to him to get him to correct his mistakes. Chide means to criticize or reproach. Thus a mother might chide her children for fighting with each other. An example might be a group of fellows poking fun at a boy with dirty clothes. Now write in your words what chide means. (Following this was a block of synonyms for matching and a block of events for classification; correct answers were available.)

Ausubel and Youssef (1963) studied the effect of advance organizers on the ability of college seniors to learn doctrines of two eastern religions (Y and Z). The organizers aided the learning and retention of the doctrines of the Y religion but not of the Z religion.

What we have here is the fact that we can understand better and retain more if we relate ideas to a cognitive framework or hierarchy. If such a framework is lacking or in need of reactivation and refurbishing, then the advance organizer should be developed in order to provide it.

SUMMARY

A person who learns acquires a behavior or the ability to perform as a result of experience. The person who really learns remembers how to perform the behavior at a later time.

A number of individuals have proposed theories of learning. Pavlov developed the theory of classical conditioning, which can be used to explain how one can condition a person to identify a printed symbol that was not previously identifiable.

Thorndike advanced three major laws of learning: the law of *exercise*, the law of *effect*, and the law of *readiness*. Briefly, they tell us that we strengthen associations by long, vigorous practice periods (exercise), by correcting incorrect associations and rewarding correct responses (effect), and by introducing learning situations after favorable sets or attitudes toward the situation are developed.

Thorndike espoused a theory of identical elements transfer. One learning or concept or task transfers to another to the extent that they contain identical elements; this theory can be applied, for example, to learning of vocabulary and to word identification tasks. Also, because intelligence is a function of the number of bonds or connections one has, the more intelligent person will have more elements to transfer to the learning of another task. According to his theory, then, the brighter a person is the greater is this person's vocabulary.

Skinner's connectionism features operant conditioning. Most human behavior is thought to be of the operant type: we operate on our environment in order to change it and bring reinforcers. Those things necessary for survival are primary reinforcers; however, stimuli such as praise, money, smiles, and the like become associated with primary reinforcers and are useful conditioners of behavior.

Knowing that a response is correct is positive feedback and a good reinforcer. Programmed learning paces the introduction of material to be learned so that a large percentage of the learner's responses are correct and thus positively reinforced. This procedure allows the student to master material and keep active in the learning environment.

Ausubel's meaningful verbal learning theory espouses meaningful learning that uses an individual's cognitive structures or meaning hierarchies. Verbal material should be introduced to an individual so that it intersects with, and is subsumed into, existing cognitive structures. In that way the material will be meaningful and will be retained more readily.

Consonant with the ideas of cognitive structures is the concept of receptive learning; that is, a person does not have to go out and discover everything. Rather, material can be organized in such a way that it fits into an individual's existing cognitive structures. Advance organizers help to develop or to quicken ideational scaffolding so that detailed information can be more readily incorporated and stably retained by the learner.

Piaget has advanced a cognitive theory of development and learning. In growing from childhood to adulthood a person develops a series of concrete and then formal (and more abstract) thought structures with which he or she operates on the concrete level of experience and thought and then on the abstract hypothetical level.

A concept is a generalization, a class of things or elements with common elements or characteristics. A given concept has certain criterial features that enable one to judge whether a given thing belongs to that concept or class of concepts. Basic abstract concepts such as *agape* and *justice* are important to our survival and must, therefore, be rightly conceived. Throughout life we develop, refine, relate, and apply concepts. It is important that the schools foster conceptual development rather than neglect it.

One can think of a rule as a relationship between two or more concepts. Rules devised as if-then statements are useful guides in reading pedagogy.

ACTIVITIES AND QUESTIONS
TO PROMOTE LEARNING AND APPLICATION

1. What are some of the responses that you have been (classically) conditioned to make?
2. Try to develop further applications of classical conditioning to reading instruction.
3. List some of your activities that require practice. How can you improve the *quality* of response? The *quantity*? Keep records of your efforts over a period of time and then discuss the results in class.
4. In what ways do you agree and/or disagree with Thorndike's identical elements theory of transfer and intelligence?
5. Make an application of the identical elements theory to teaching in your subject-matter area.
6. To what extent do you agree with Bugelski's assertion that one should be rewarded for using a precise vocabulary? Do you experience any difficulty in trying to apply that principle in teaching? In everyday living?
7. What do you think "general mental ability" means? Check your conception of it against the view presented in a psychology text.
8. Which secondary reinforcers have diminished in value in your life? Why?
9. State some specific applications of the Premack principle to motivating people to read and to make more responses.
10. Write an advance organizer (AO) for a section of a content chapter that has presented problems to readers. Also write some neutral material (NM) that might be of interest to your students. List students alphabetically and number them. Give students 1, 3, 5, . . . the AO material and students 2, 4, 6, . . . the NM material and ask them to read the material (without comment and discussion) and then the text. After the students have finished reading, administer an objective test over the material. Determine any differences in mean scores of the two groups. (If you know how to determine the statistical significance of differences, do so, or perhaps your instructor can do it or have it done.) If the AO was effective, discuss reasons for its being effective; if not, scrutinize the AO in terms of the content of the text.
11. Analyze some content in your subject-matter area. What kinds of tasks require the student to use concrete operations? Formal operations?
12. Write criterial features lists for several concepts in your subject matter area.
13. Develop rules that might be of value in teaching some topic.
14. Prepare a plan for teaching a concept. Teach it and report on the results.
15. Compare and contrast discovery learning and expository teaching.

SUGGESTED ADDITIONAL READINGS

AUSUBEL, DAVID P. *The Psychology of Meaningful Verbal Learning.* New York: Grune and Stratton, 1963.

____, and F. G. ROBINSON. *School Learning: An Introduction to Educational Psychology.* New York: Holt, Rinehart and Winston, 1969.

BIGGE, MORRIS L. "Theories of Learning." In Eldon E. Ekwall (Ed.). *Psychological Factors in the Teaching of Reading.* Columbus, Ohio: Charles E. Merrill, 1973.

DI VESTA, FRANCIS J., and GEORGE G. THOMPSON. *Educational Psychology: Instructional and Behavior Change.* New York: Appleton-Century-Crofts, 1970.

FURTH, HANS G. *Piaget and Knowledge.* Englewood Cliffs, N.J.: Prentice-Hall, 1969.

GAGNÉ, ROBERT M. *The Conditions of Learning.* Second Edition. New York: Holt, Rinehart and Winston, 1970.

GINSBURG, HERBERT, and SYLVIA OPPER. *Piaget's Theory of Intellectual Development.* Englewood Cliffs, N.J.: Prentice-Hall, 1969.

KLAUSMEIER, HERBERT J., and WILLIAM GOODWIN. *Learning and Human Abilities Educational Psychology.* Fourth Edition. New York: Harper and Row, 1975.

LOWE, A. J. "Recent Research Sources for Middle and Secondary School Reading Problem Areas." In Lawrence E. Hafner (ed.). *Improving Reading in Middle and Secondary Schools,* Second Edition. New York: Macmillan, 1974, pp. 224–247.

PHILLIPS, JOHN L., JR. *The Origins of Intellect: Piaget's Theory.* San Francisco: W. H. Freeman, 1969.

SNELBECKER, GLENN E. *Learning Theory, Instructional Theory, and Psychoeducational Design.* New York: McGraw-Hill, 1974.

SPRINTHALL, RICHARD C., and NORMAN A. SPRINTHALL. *Educational Psychology: A Developmental Approach.* Reading, Mass.: Addison-Wesley, 1974.

BIBLIOGRAPHY

AUSUBEL, DAVID P. "Use of Advance Organizers in the Learning and Retention of Meaningful Verbal Material." *Journal of Educational Psychology.* 51 (1960), 267–72.

____. "Some Psychological and Educational Limitations of Learning by Discovery." *Arithmetic Teacher.* 11 (May 1964), 290–302.

____. *Educational Psychology: A Cognitive View.* New York: Holt, Rinehart, and Winston, 1968.

____ and F. G. ROBINSON. *School Learning: An Introduction to Educational Psychology.* New York: Holt, Rinehart and Winston, 1969.

____ and MOHAMED YOUSSEF. "The Role of Discriminability in Meaningful Parallel Learning." *Journal of Educational Psychology.* 54 (1963), 332–36.

BRUNER, JEROME S., "Learning and Thinking." *Harvard Educational Review.* 29 (1959) 184–92.

____. "The Art of Discovery." *Harvard Educational Review.* 31 (1961), 21–32.

BUGELSKI, B. R. *The Psychology of Learning Applied to Teaching.* Second Edition. New York: Bobbs-Merrill, 1971.

COMMINS, W. D., and BARRY FAGIN. *Principles of Educational Psychology.* Second Edition. New York: Ronald Press, 1954.

CORMAN, BERNARD R. "The Effect of Varying Amounts and Kinds of Information as Guidance in Problem Solving." *Psychology Monographs* 71 (2) (No. 431).

DE CECCO, JOHN P., and WILLIAM R. CRAWFORD. *The Psychology of Learning and Instruction. Second Edition.* Englewood Cliffs, N.J.: Prentice-Hall, 1974.

DONIMOWSKI, R. L. "Role of Memory in Concept Learning." *Psychological Bulletin.* 63 (1965), 271–80.

FURTH, HANS G. *Piaget and Knowledge.* Englewood Cliffs, N.J.: Prentice-Hall, 1969.

GAGNÉ, ROBERT M. *The Conditions of Learning.* Second Edition. New York: Holt, Rinehart and Winston, 1970.

_____. *Essentials of Learning for Instruction.* Hinsdale, Ill.: Dryden Press, 1974.

_____ and LARRY T. BROWN. "Some Factors in the Programming of Conceptual Learning." *Journal of Experimental Psychology.* 62 (1961), 313–21.

GRIMES, J. W., and W. ALLINSMITH. "Compulsivity, Anxiety and School Achievement." *Merrill-Palmer Quarterly.* 7 (1961), 247–71.

JOHNSON, DONALD M. *The Psychology of Thinking.* New York.: Harper and Row, 1972.

_____ and R. PAUL STRATTON. "Evaluation of Five Methods for Teaching Concepts." *Journal of Educational Psychology.* 57 (1966), 48–53.

KATES, SOLIS L., and LEE YUDIN. "Concept Attainment and Memory." *Journal of Educational Psychology.* 55 (1964), 102–109.

KLAUSMEIER, HERBERT J., and WILLIAM GOODWIN. *Learning and Human Abilities: Educational Psychology.* Fourth Edition.: New York: Harper and Row, 1975.

MOULY, GEORGE J. *Psychology for Effective Teaching.* Third Edition. New York: Holt, Rinehart and Winston, 1973.

PAVLOV, IVAN P. *Conditioned Reflexes.* London: Oxford University Press, 1927.

SKINNER, B. F. *Science and Human Behavior.* New York: Macmillan, 1953.

_____. "Operant Behavior." *American Psychologist.* 18 (1963), 503–15.

SNELBECKER, GLENN E. *Learning Theory, Instructional Theory, and Psychoeducational Design.* New York: McGraw-Hill, 1974.

THORNDIKE, EDWARD L. *Educational Psychology. The Psychology of Learning.* New York: Teacher's College, Columbia University, 1913.

_____. *Human Learning.* New York: Century, 1931.

WITTROCK, MERLIN C. "Verbal Stimuli in Concept Formation: Learning by Discovery." *Journal of Educational Psychology.* 54 (1963), 183–90.

_____. "The Learning by Discovery Hypothesis." In L. S. Shulman and E. R. Keislar (eds.). *Learning by Discovery.* Chicago: Rand McNally and Co., 1966. pp. 33–76.

CHAPTER 3

Psychological Foundations for Reading Instruction.II. Teaching for Retention

MEASURING RETENTION OF LEARNED MATERIAL

With the passage of time one tends to forget what one has learned. Learned behaviors, for example, may become less skilled if they are not practiced. A person may forget a step in a mathematics strategy, a word or phrase in a foreign language, a grapheme-phoneme association used in word identification, and so forth. Remembering or retaining worthwhile information and skills is important.

Kinds of Retention

Recognition. When we recognize we *know again*. If we pass a girl without *knowing* her *again*, that is, without recognizing her, there is a reason. The original learning may have been tenuous or her appearance may have changed; we did not re-cognize her. If a person is presented with a printed word such as ⟨chimerical⟩ that he or she had correctly identified previously, and pronounces it /kimerikəl/, the person recognizes it.

Recall. If one asks a person who has learned to play Brahms' Waltz in A♭ to play it and the person responds by doing so without looking at the music, one can say that the person has recalled it. Or, if I ask a student, say Geri, to write a given reading expectancy formula, and she is able to do so, I say she is able to recall it, that she has retained that ability or behavior.

Relearning. If person A brings a partly retained skill back to perfection faster than person B who learned the same skill to the same degree of mastery at the same time, it can be said that person A has retained the skill better. Let us look at some ways of measuring retention.

Measuring Retention

Recall. A way to measure recall is to calculate the percentage of material that a person can recall. In reading, for example, one can administer a learning rate test: First teach a person to recognize several printed words to mastery criterion. An hour later show the stimulus array of printed words to the person one at a time, and ask the person to respond with the appropriate spoken words. The percentage correct is recorded. The score can be compared with that of other individuals who learned the same words under identical conditions.

I learn a piano piece to mastery criterion; that is, I am able to play it from memory without a mistake. After a given number of days have elapsed, during which I have not played the piece, I play it again. The percentage of notes or percentage of bars played correctly is "noted."

Reading and recalling: Ask a person to read a selection and then recite what was read. Next record the number of correct chunks of information recalled. You, as examiner, will have a list of specified chunks. Those correctly recalled— exactly or in paraphrase—are checked off the list. Number correct or percentage correct is the score.

Recognition. The recognition method of measuring learning has the subject (1) select the correct choice from among an array of foils or (2) mark a statement as true or false. (Actually, the matching format could be used, but I will not go into that.)

Multiple-choice examples:

1. One way of encoding /ī/ is: A. eigh   B. ay   C. oa   D. ia.
2. The highest level of comprehension according to Bloom's cognitive taxonomy is:
   A. synthesis   B. extrapolation   C. translation   D. knowledge.

The foregoing choices require finer discrimination and make a better test item than the following array of choices for the same stem: A. memory   B. extrapolation   C. autonomy   D. perception.

Whether or not a person really knows and retains a piece of information can better be tested by an item that requires *fine* discrimination such as having to differentiate extrapolation from synthesis, translation, and knowledge, which are closely related and all a part of Bloom's taxonomy.

True or false examples:

_____1. /ī/ cannot be encoded ⟨igh⟩.
_____2. Reading has been called the "reduction of uncertainty."

Savings upon Relearning. In this type of measurement a person first learns a task. The number of trials it took to learn it is recorded. (An alternate way is to record the time it took the subject to learn.) After a specified amount of time has elapsed (enough so that one can assume some forgetting will occur), the individual relearns the material. The number of trials (or the time) it takes to relearn the task is recorded.

$$Savings\ Score = 100 \left[\frac{\text{Original trials (or time)} - \text{Relearning trials (or time)}}{\text{Original trials (or time)}} \right]$$

How would one actually compute savings scores and recall scores?

1a. Word identification (savings score): Suppose that it took a person twenty trials to learn to identify *eight* printed words. By that I mean the criterion of mastery is the ability to identify all eight words perfectly three times in succession where the cards are shuffled after each trial. So during the last three of the twenty trials the person correctly identifies all eight words. Therefore, *original trials* = 20. Two days later it takes six trials to relearn to mastery criterion. Therefore, relearning trials = 6.

$$Savings\ Score = 100 \left[\frac{20 - 6}{20} \right] = 70\%$$

1b. Word identification (recall score): In that same example the learner remembered five words on the first relearning trial, which in effect was a test.

$$Recall\ Score = \frac{\text{number correct on first relearning trial}}{\text{number of total words in experiment}}$$

$$= \frac{5}{8} = 62\frac{1}{2}\%$$

2a. Vocabulary (savings score): A person learned the meanings of ten new words in *thirty minutes*. A week later the person was tested. On the *first trial* he or she remembered the meanings of four words. It took the subject fifteen minutes to relearn all ten words to mastery criterion.

$$Savings\ Score = 100 \left[\frac{30 - 15}{30} \right] = 50\%$$

2b. Vocabulary (recall score):

$$Recall\ Score = 4/10 = 40\%$$

Forgetting Curves

Ebbinghaus's Classical Model. The course of forgetting over a period of time when no relearning trials are interpolated shows an initial rapid decline or fall off of remembered items. Ebbinghaus (1885) taught himself nonsense syllables, which were learned to a criterion of tenuous mastery. At specified intervals such as 20 minutes, one hour, nine hours, two days, and six days, he would relearn the materials and compute a savings score percentage. Thus, the more trials it took him to relearn the syllables the lower his savings score would be.

Ebbinghaus's model is called a classical model because he first developed such a model and because general retention (or forgetting) curves approximate closely his curve. Figure 3–1 is his curve.

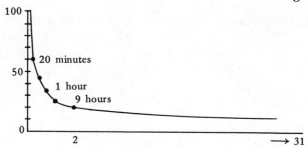

Figure 3-1. Ebbinghaus's Retention Curve for Nonsense Syllables. The Points Plotted Represent Savings Scores for Relearning. (After Ebbinghaus, 1885)

Measures of Retention.   If one measures retention of nonsense syllables after one day and two days by *recognition, relearning,* and *recall* methods, one will find as did Luh (1922) that the following percentages are obtained by the different methods.

	one day	two days
Recognition	80%	72%
Relearning	52%	50%
Recall	20%	10%

You know how to compute relearning and recall scores. Recognition scores are computed according to the following formula:

$$Recognition\ Score = 100 \left[\frac{right - wrong}{total} \right]$$

Thus one can easily conclude that nonsense material dissipates from memory quite rapidly, as it should.

STRATEGIES FOR LEARNING AND REMEMBERING

Remembering Organized Material

The sense or gist of a reading selection can be remembered longer than the major points and the latter can be retained longer than the details. George Miller (1956) found that memory is to a large extent a function of the number of things to remember. If information can be chunked or hooked into some meaningful category, it can be retained longer. Therefore, it pays to organize material so that one can use existing categories. An alternative is to develop new categories.

Reciting material can aid retention because recitation allows a person to associate it with existing known material, or slot it into a category, or develop a mnemonic device or an acronym. Slotting into a category may be more formal. An example is developing an outline in which superordinates and subordinates are used. Category slotting is also done when one paraphrases and in effect uses synonyms, superordinates, and subordinates:

Sentence: My Dad's brother's children sank their teeth into watermelon after the main part of the meal.

Paraphrase 1:   My Dad's nephews (synonym) ate (synonym) fruit (superordinate) for dessert (s.o.).

Paraphrase 2:   The dessert (s.o.), watermelon, was devoured (synonym) by relatives (s.o.), my cousins (synonym of Dad's nephews).

In doing the above the material may be contracted (made more abstract) or expanded (using illustrations).

Recitation (Test for Retention) Without Correction.   Spitzer (1939) studied the ability of five groups of secondary school students to retain a meaningful reading passage of factual material. Five equated groups read the same material. However, each group recited on different days. The first group recited on the same day that it read the material. Recall on recitation was 52 per cent. About eight days later the group recited again and the recall was 43 per cent. After 60 days, 40 per cent was retained.

Group five first had the opportunity to recite after 20 days. These students remembered 8 per cent. Forty days later they recited again; retention was 7 per cent.

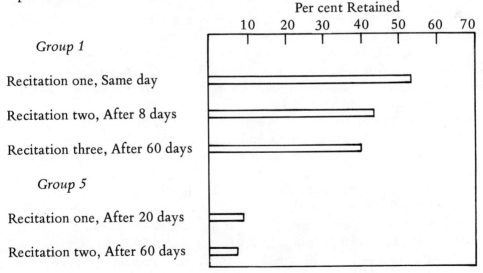

Figure 3-2. Retention of Material Read Under Varying Conditions of Recitation.

In the Spitzer study recitation on the same day seemed to put a damper on forgetting. You will notice that little forgetting took place after that first recitation on the same day. The application to the teaching of reading is obvious: Recite newly learned material the same day.

In order to retain material better, recitation with correction should be used. This means that errors would be corrected. If the material were retaught to mastery at certain points and recitation with correction were interpolated, retention would be even better. This brings us to short-term memory, long-term memory, and overlearning.

Short-term and Long-term Memory

Some information, such as a telephone number or a detail in a conversation, need only be remembered for seconds and then forgotten. Other information needs to be retained for a long time. Hebb (1949) posited two systems of storage for human memory. One is short-term memory, STM; the other is long-term memory, LTM.

How do we transfer things important to us to long-term memory? We do it by rehearsing the information immediately in order to remember it long enough (STM) to work on it and transfer it to long-term memory. If we do not put it into STM, it will disappear in less than one minute. As I stated previously, in order to put the material into LTM it must be revamped or reorganized in such a way that it fits into the cognitive structures we already have. In other words we need to reorganize creatively or restructure the information in some way.

In order to put information into LTM, we can use any of the following schemes:

Coding. If I am given the task of remembering the telephone number (818) 198-1483, I can rehearse it quickly, perhaps already beginning to recode it: I remember (818) 198 and notice that 1483 is the year Martin Luther was born. Then I recode the rest 818 → HAH (number-alphabet sequence correspondence); that leaves me with 198, my weight. I can now transfer the number into LTM by remembering HAH, weight, Luther's birth year. This is easily recovered and translated.

A familiar type of coding is the *mnemonic* device. Most of us are familiar with Roy G. Biv, the device for remembering the color spectrum: red, orange, yellow, and so forth. However, *mnemonic* devices may backfire. Fifth grader Jerry, on being asked why he missed the date of Columbus' first great voyage when, after all, he had been taught, "In 1492 Columbus sailed the ocean blue," replied, "Oh, I thought you said, 'In 1493 Columbus sailed the deep blue sea!' "

Imagery. In teaching persons to identify printed words we often use word-picture and phrase-picture cards (Hafner and Jolly 1972). Pictures are the unconditioned stimuli for eliciting the unconditioned response. By pairing the printed word (conditioned stimulus) with the picture, the response after awhile antedates looking at the picture. In this manner people can be taught to identify printed words and phrases. These images are imposed from the outside.

In a 1960 study Hafner taught fifth graders to use certain kinds of context cues in an attempt to improve their reading achievement. It was assumed that the context could be "strengthened" if students were encouraged to develop images of what they were reading. A stronger context would provide better cues to the meanings of difficult words. A statistically significant greater number of students in the experimental group than in the control group made gains in reading achievement but it could not be ascertained that the gains were due to imagery.

Anderson and Kulhavy (1971) gave high school seniors a written passage to read; some students were instructed to visualize what they were reading, whereas the other students were not. The students reporting that they used imagery extensively recalled more of what they read than the students who reported little or no (use of) imagery.

Levin (1972) studied fourth graders in an attempt to manipulate the extent to which supposed nonimagery producers who were poor readers would generate visual images during reading. As expected, the imagery strategy improved comprehension. The poor readers who had adequate vocabulary skills benefited more than the pupils who lacked adequate vocabulary skills. Imagery production in children who need an organization framework is a reasonable strategy. As to the contribution that imagery makes to retention, it is implied that one needs to know and understand something before one can retain it readily.

Mediating Instructions. We can teach a person to read an English word by first teaching him the written Chinese symbol for the spoken English word. Thus 木 木 木 groups of trees, is the Chinese symbol for forest. In this way, Chinese symbols can be used as mediators that provide the stimulus for the spoken English word, which is then associated with the written English word:

In teaching the association of a foreign language word with an English word, a picture mediator can be used:

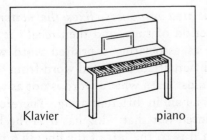 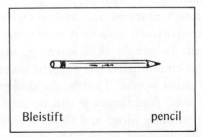

Those who learn foreign languages may profit from developing their own mediators. I have developed the following for myself: (the pronunciations do not always jibe).

	Word	Mediator	Meaning
Japanese	mizu	Missouri (river)	water
	tomodachi	tomo (I take, in Spanish) friend	(Or I think, "I take you for a friend.")
	dachi	(name similar to a friend of mine)	
	warúi	war	bad, awful
	kawaii	Hawaii	
		Kaui	cute (girls)
Chinese	hǎukàn	How can (you be so good looking?)	be good looking
	lèi	He lay down.	tired
	tàitai	tie (bond)	wife
	dzàijyan	'bye, Jan	goodbye
	táng	Tang drink tangy	candy
	chàng	chant	sing
	tsūngming	Zunge / tsúŋə / (tongue in German)	clever (as in clever speaker)

With such mediators, certain foreign language terms can be stored fairly easily in one's long-term memory. Once the material is coded (generic term here for coding, imagery, and mediating instruction) and stored in LTM, it is resistant to being forgotten.

Practice

The Purpose of Practice. I have found that whether practicing piano, Chinese, or shooting baskets it is *what* I do when I practice that counts; it is as much a *quality* as a quantity thing. In all instances I "aim" at correct responses. As I work at making correct responses, I strive to eliminate incorrect responses. So practice is not a matter of making responses, but rather of making correct responses. Also in verbal learning one needs to understand the material before committing it to memory.

Through practice one *makes differentiated responses, fixes the material* in one's repertoire, *retains* it over some period of time, and then *recalls* it when needed. In simple skill learning, such as associating a printed word with a spoken counterpart, the student must differentiate a printed word from one or more other words. That is, the student must learn what a word is not as well as what it is. And language can be used as an aid in differentiating. Therefore, in differentiating ⟨dog⟩ and ⟨boy⟩ it is pointed out that "dog has *d* at the beginning but boy has *b*" or "The tummy in d is to the left of the line; in b it is to the right." "They both have *o* in the middle," and so forth.

Practice in the first stage is devoted to *differentiation*. In the next stage we try by various means to *fix* the material. We *retain* it by making responses, that is, *recalling* it, from time to time; therefore, we are distributing practice or making responses over several periods. The words can be presented (1) in isolation on cards, with the word and picture on the other side of the card to check correctness of response, (2) on Language Master cards, (3) in sentence contexts, (4) in games, and so forth. In this manner, practice will be meaningful, differentiations can be made, and enough correct responses (plus positive feedback) can be made to assure learning.

The Uses of Self-recitation. In reading a text for the purpose of differentiated acquisition and recall practice, self-recitation may be used to advantage. By differentiated acquisition I mean you do not try rote memory of the whole reading selection. You read for a purpose such as answering teacher- or self-generated questions, summarizing the information, or outlining it. In any case, the main ideas of paragraphs and sections must be developed, relevant supporting details marshaled, and appropriate conclusions drawn.

In the first place, self-recitation can be useful in clarifying concepts. You should read a segment—sentence, several sentences, or a paragraph—look away from the material, and see if you are able to recite the gist of it, showing you understand the concepts involved. If you cannot, you possibly do not understand it. When the ideas are understood, they can be used in developing the main idea of the paragraph and in drawing conclusions based on information in it. The ideas are then clearly understood so that questions can be answered, summaries written, and outlines developed.

In the second place, once the questions are answered and the summary or outline made, steps can be taken to retain the information for recall on demand. Self-recitation plays a role here, too. One can look at the question and try to recite the answer to it. The recitation need not be in the exact form written but essential points should be recited in paraphrase. A similar procedure can be used in memorizing an outline. One may not remember all the points the first time one recites during a review of questions and answers or outlines. Distributed practice will help to fix the material in long-term memory.

One should devote about two thirds of study time to active self-recitation. Gates (1917), Seibert (1932), and Forlano (n.d.) have shown that self-recitation is superior to (re)reading in developing recall efficiency of short biographies, French vocabulary, and spelling and arithmetic, respectively.

Distributed Practice Versus Massed Practice. *Distributed practice* means spreading practice time over several days or weeks so that practice periods are interspersed with rest periods. *Massed* practice is grouping practice time into a one-shot practice period. A person who does not read the book until the night before an exam and then spends several hours cramming is engaging in "massed" practice.

If immediate recall, with no thought of how much is remembered after some days, weeks, or months is the consideration, massed practice is best. If material is to be retained for a long time, distributed practice is best (Underwood, 1964). Another consideration of importance is that if material is very difficult, a long massed practice may be needed to untangle concepts, to clarify them. This practice could be followed to advantage by a series of distributed practices. Once the material is understood and brought to a level of mastery, one should distribute practice periods in order to fix the material so that it can easily be recalled. These periods may not have to be as long as time goes by, just long enough to assure the individual that he or she remembers the information or can still perform the skill with a high level of proficiency.

Therefore, many practice periods of short duration are superior to an occasional massed practice if the goal is the ability to perform a skill or recite information "on call!"

Overlearning. A good example of overlearning is the radioman who learns Morse Code and receives it four to eight hours a day for several years. He does not forget it even after 20 to 40 years. Other examples of overlearning are speaking, typing, and the like.

Overlearning can be quantified, and quantification is useful in research as well as in the classroom. We can talk about overlearning a certain percent. For example, if someone wants 100 per cent overlearning of vocabulary items and it takes 30 trials to reach initial mastery, then 60 trials would be required for 100 per cent overlearning of the items. The effect of various percentages of overlearning could be noted in terms of per cent of material retained at given intervals, that is, determination of a recall score (discussed earlier).

Proper Instruction. People generally want to know how they are succeeding in an endeavor. In reading, students can be taught to want to know how they are doing, if the teacher can arrange for students to receive positive feedback when they make correct responses.

Making the correct response is a part of proper instruction. What does proper instruction mean? It means teaching each student at his or her level and pacing instruction so that a student can master material at that level before going on to new levels and more difficult materials. Not many people like to work at things in which they do not feel confident. Mastery is an indication of success, and we know that success in an endeavor breeds confidence and interest in doing further work along those lines (Hafner and Jolly, 1972).

Programmed Instruction. One kind of instruction that makes the foregoing possible is programmed instruction. In programmed material designed to teach reading skills, (1) information is presented, (2) a problem is posed, and (3) the student has an opportunity to respond. The student then uncovers the correct answer (by moving a marker or turning the page) and, if he or she has been correctly placed in the material, sees that he or she has made a correct response. This positive feedback is reinforcing and motivates the student to try another information-problem sequence.

The reason that students can learn so much in programmed instruction is that this method keeps one in the learning situation longer than some other methods and thus enables one to make many more correct responses, thereby making associations, learning concepts, developing principles, and so forth.

Examples of Programmed Instruction:

1. Linear Programming: The following eight frames were designed to give the reader an idea of what programmed learning is about. It is not a sophisticated sequence.

Directions:
1. The answers following the reading material are below the reading material and to the left. The answers should be kept covered until responses are made.
2. Read the material in frame one carefully and write the answer in the blank.
3. Check your answer against the correct answer in the box below the reading material.
4. If an incorrect response is made, insert the correct response and reread the material to see why it is the correct response.
5. Proceed to frame two and repeat the procedure.

1

One of the problems in education is that for many students instruction is paced so rapidly that they generally make incorrect responses to reading materials or to questions. A system should be devised so that they are able to make more _____ responses.

correct

2

Also, in order to learn enough skills and content the students must make a great many correct responses. Systems have been devised that meet the problem and allow students to make a _____ number of _____ responses during a day.

larger (greater)   correct

3

In addition to making many correct responses during the course of a day, a student must get feedback on the correctness of responses. If the student checks each response against the correct answer immediately after making it, he or she will get instant _____ on the correctness of the response.

feedback

4

Being correct has positive value; it enhances one's self-concept. When a person knows that he or she has answered correctly he or she experiences _____ feedback.

positive

5

To ensure a high percentage of correct responses, the programmed learning sequences are presented in small, easy steps. Such carefully prepared material will consist of small, _____ steps that will result in a person making a _____ percentage of correct responses.

easy   high (large)

6

As a rule of thumb, programs are designed so that approximately 95 per cent of the students who are appropriately placed in the material make 90 per cent (or better) correct responses. So if a person is making at least _____ per cent correct responses, one can say the person is _____ placed in the material.

90   appropriately

7

In order to ensure storing meaningful material in Long Term Memory (LTM), review frames must be appropriately interspersed. In this way, a check or understanding and _____ of material is made and necessary ret __ch __ g is done.

retention   ea   in

8

The aim of this kind of programmed instruction is mastery of material. Pacing the material in easy, small steps, providing positive _____ , and providing review frames in the program ensures a high degree of _____—understanding and retention.

feedback   mastery

Encouraging Self-instruction. To make instruction possible, make available materials that have some or all of the following characteristics:

1. Are sequentially and logically organized.
2. Are presented in optimal size steps.
3. Afford many opportunities to respond.
4. Are geared so that approximately 90 (or more) per cent of the pupil's responses will be correct.

5. Are geared so that pupil receives immediate feedback about correctness of responses.
6. Will teach all the basic reading skills, plus concept development in content areas.
7. Could be used without disturbing other pupils in the classroom.
8. Could be used individually and in small groups.
9. Would actually instruct.
10. Would be supportive to the direct instruction of the teacher.
11. Would keep pupils profitably occupied in real instructional activities when not receiving direct instruction from the teacher or not engaging in project and other types of independent or small group activities (Hafner and Jolly, 1972).

Summary of Advantages of Programmed Reading Instruction

1. The best student works at his or her own rate and gets positive feedback.

2. The middle student works at his or her own rate and gets positive feedback.

3. The "low" student works at his or her own rate and gets positive feedback.

4. The "low" student can now be called an *achieving* student.

5. Each student makes more correct responses during the day than formerly.

6. Each student works independently rather than leaning on somebody else.

7. The student develops a sense of responsibility because of the newly-formed ability to develop answers.

8. Students do not develop cumulative deficits as they do when work is not individualized.

9. A student competes with self, not with someone else.

10. The student is in an ongoing instructional program and can pace effort so that learning is continuous.

Transfer of Training or Learning

If we learn a concept or a rule in one situation and can apply it in a somewhat different situation, let us say new contexts, then we are transferring training or learning.

Teaching for Transfer. We sometimes think that any person of reasonable intelligence should be able to transfer the principle of inductive learning of phonics to a different language so that after learning a number of words in that language plus knowing some of the English cognates of the language he or she could transfer the principle and learn "the phonics" of the language.

It is entirely possible that transfer for such a task would not be automatic. You might have to give a student or a teacher of foreign languages some cues on how this is done.

> T: You remember how you learned the phonics of English. Your teacher took words that you had learned to pronounce which contained a common element. She aligned them vertically so the common elements would be adjacent:

cherry

cheap

chill

She then asked you how they looked alike and how they sounded alike. You were then helped to develop the rule which would aid you in pronouncing some of the words containing ⟨ch⟩. After you learned words such as choir and orchestra you were taught a phonemic (sound) option for the grapheme ⟨ch⟩, /k/.

c̲h̲oir

orc̲h̲estra

You know quite a few French words, that is, English words taken from French. What can you do with these words that could be an aid to you in developing the pronunciation of words not previously encountered?

Actually many English words are taken directly from French. So that individuals who do not know French can take part in this exercise, I will use English words that have come from the French language:

Teaching Strategy

T: Here are some English words that are taken from the French. Let us see which phonic elements they have in common and what sounds these elements represent." [Underline the elements after the students note them. The sounds (phonemes) can be noted using slash marks]. The first one is done for you.

bo̲u̲quet	cherie	bon soir	chateau
mo̲u̲sse	Chevrolet	Renoir	beau
ou → / ü /	ch → / ___ /	oir → / ___ /	eau → / ___ /

T: Now that we have indicated what sounds are represented by these elements, can you give more examples of English words that contain these elements and they can be listed in the appropriate categories? [Discuss the relationships and doublecheck their grasp of them.]

T: Now let us see if we can apply our new knowledge about "French phonics" and pronounce these French words.

mouchoir   couteau

T: Who knows what these words mean or what they are? (You may have wanted to ask your students of French to "lay low" in order to let the other students make some of the discoveries. Now is the time to let them star.) Let us use the words in sentences. Please give me a sentence for each word.

What Other Kinds of Things Transfer?

1. Attitudes. If a person develops good attitudes toward reading in school life, there is a better chance that this attitude will transfer to out-of-school and post-school life. The person who developed good attitudes toward reading in school is more likely to subscribe to newspapers, magazines, and books. There may be some specificity involved. If the attitude toward reading mathematics books was negative, the person may find excuses (maybe reasons) for not doing the family bookkeeping and income tax returns. Related to attitude is skills. A poor attitude toward an activity or subject may be rooted in poor skills in that area.

2. Skills. I have already illustrated how to transfer the principle of inductive teaching of phonics to teaching an aspect of French phonics. *Comprehension skills* should also be taught in such a way that individuals learn to understand not only *how* to develop main ideas, relevant supporting details, and conclusions, but also to *understand* the general procedures and processes involved. The reading teacher teaches students to develop the main idea or thrust of a paragraph and the deductive and inductive means by which this is done. (See the chapter on comprehension.) The reading teacher should also make forays into one or two of the subject-matter areas to give cues on the applicability of the skills to those areas. Then the question might be asked, "Are there any other subject-matter areas in which this skill is applicable?" Then try to make the application. Next ask, "Are there any subject-matter areas in which this skill is not applicable?" The stage might be set for altering the approach to fit certain kinds of materials. The subject-matter teacher should not expect that all the skills can be taught by a reading teacher. If that were so, we might not need content-area teachers! Where there is a residue of comprehension skills, one needs to revivify the skills and then help the student make applications to the area. After all, reading is a thinking skill and content-area teachers are paid to help students think well about materials and ideas in a content area. In this book I discuss processes of thinking and teaching. If you study these processes, their application to subject-matter reading—in the few cases where I have not made the application (in order to give you a chance)—will be relatively simple for the alert teacher who has a sense of responsibility for students.

You will find that the *reference-study skills* taught in Chapter 7 are easy to apply to most subject-matter reading materials. Some adaptations may have to be made; that is your chance to be creative.

SUMMARY

The measurement of the retention of learned material can be accomplished through checking a person's ability to recognize or recall the material. The time or trials needed to relearn a partly retained skill to the original degree of mastery is also used as a retention measure and is indexed as a savings score.

Teachers should teach strategies for learning and remembering useful material. An author organizes material, and students should note the organization and use it. In addition, the student will use existing categories (and at times develop new ones) in order to learn better and retain information. Furthermore, recitation with correction is an excellent method for accurate and better retention of material.

In order to put material into short-term memory, one rehearses it immediately. To put material into long-term memory, one codes it through imagery, coding, and mediating instruction.

One practices a skill in order to improve its quality and retain it. A practice period should be marked by making correct, quality responses in smooth sequence; a system for provision of feedback on correctness of responses should be set up; and any errors should be corrected at once. Even where practice is devoted to learning to identify words in isolation, such as differentiating a given word from other words, one will follow it with contextual practice so that these words can be read fluently in meaningful sentence contexts. Meaningful acquisition and retention are thus served.

Self-recitation can be used to advantage when the purpose is differentiated acquisition and ability to recall. Differentiated acquisition means to acquire material meaningfully, in a way that necessitates the learner's reorganizing it in some way. Self-recitation is an excellent learning strategy.

Distributed practice is used when material is to be retained for a long period of time. Massed practice should be used initially when the material to be learned is very difficult.

Proper instruction, the *sine qua non* for learning to read well, can be seen to be lacking where individuals are not reading up to capacity. Proper instruction is marked by teaching a student on his or her level, pacing the introduction of material so that the student makes many correct responses during a day, resulting in mastery of the material before moving on to new challenges, the mastery of which is predicated on those earlier learnings. Programmed instruction is one kind of instruction that makes mastery learning possible.

A major goal of education is the accomplishment of transfer of training in as many situations as possible. If you expect transfer of training, you should teach for transfer. Whether you use an identical elements theory or a generalization theory of transfer it is incumbent upon you to teach concepts, rules, skills, and attitudes for transfer to similar concepts, rules, and the like and for transfer to related life situations.

ACTIVITIES AND QUESTIONS
TO PROMOTE LEARNING AND APPLICATION

1. List some things that you recognize visually. How do you recognize them? What, if any, are the similarities between the recognition of printed words and other things that you recognize?

2. What are some things that people have to relearn?

3. Test several people with a number of difficult words to determine five to ten printed words that they do not recognize. Using word-picture cards teach the words to mastery criterion. After one hour, test the people individually to determine how many words they can recognize or recall. Note the percentage of recall for each individual.

4. Using the same people that you did in the previous problem, test their recall after one day; after one week. Try to account for any differences that may exist.

5. Select several paragraphs of reading material. Determine a specific list of chunks of information. Have a student read the selection and then relate as much as possible of it. Do this for several students.

6. Using the same students that you did in the previous problem, determine what is remembered after a delayed period of time.

7. Devise a "savings upon relearning" experiment. Report your results in class.

8. Devise an experiment in which two equal groups are determined by random assignment. Have group A read a mimeographed selection and recite to themselves after each paragraph read. Have group B read and underline what they consider to be the important points. Each group has only its directions at the top of the reading selection. Control for time by giving each group the same amount of time. Administer to both groups a test on the reading selection. Compute mean scores and range of scores for each group.

9. Set up an experiment similar to the Spitzer experiment and execute it. Note the results and try to account for differences. Discuss the results with the students. What principle of reading and studying can you develop as a result of this experiment?

10. Have a class discussion to see what kinds of mediating devices the students use.

11. Invent mediators for learning foreign language terms. Share them in class.

12. Devise a distributed practice versus massed practice experiment for your content area. Report your results in class.

13. Make a list of tasks that lend themselves to overlearning. Have students overlearn material in an area in which they are weak; they can note the degree of overlearning. Discuss any change in self-concept and/or attitude toward the task and/or the subject matter related to the task.

14. Select a topic that you are interested in teaching to someone. Construct a programmed learning sequence of 25 to 40 frames. Have the first ten frames critiqued in class before continuing. Then finish the sequence and try it out with some people. Refine your program.

15. Observe a content-area class and/or a class in reading. Note the quantity and quality of self-instruction taking place. Devise a set of concrete recommendations for improving self-instruction in the class.

16. Devise teaching techniques that use transfer strategies. Did you use the identical elements theory or the generalization theory? A combination? Neither? Explain.

SUGGESTED ADDITIONAL READINGS

DI VESTA, FRANCIS J., and GEORGE G. THOMPSON. *Educational Psychology: Instruction and Behavior Change.* New York: Appleton-Century-Crofts, 1970.

EKWALL, ELDON E. (Ed.). *Psychological Factors in the Teaching of Reading.* Columbus, Ohio: Charles E. Merrill, 1973. Chapters 3-7.

HAFNER, LAWRENCE E. *Improving Reading in Middle and Secondary Schools.* Second Edition. New York: Macmillan, 1974. Section 8.

KLAUSMEIER, HERBERT J., and WILLIAM GOODWIN. *Learning and Human Abilities: Educational Psychology.* Fourth Edition. New York: Harper and Row, 1975.

MILLER, GEORGE A. "The Magical Number Seven, Plus or Minus Two: Some Limits on Our Capacity for Processing Information." *Psychological Review. 63.* (1956), 81-97.

TRAVERS, ROBERT N. W. *Essentials of Learning.* Third Edition. New York: Macmillan, 1972.

ZINTZ, MILES V. *The Reading Process.* Second Edition. Columbus, Ohio: Charles E. Merrill, 1975. Chapter 2.

BIBLIOGRAPHY

ANDERSON, R. C., and R. W. KULHAVY. "Imagery and Prose Learning." Unpublished Manuscript. University of Illinois, 1971.

EBBINGHAUS, HERMANN. "Über das Gedächtnis." Translated as "Memory." *Educational Reprint No. 3.* New York: Teachers College Press, Columbia University, 1913.

FORLANO, G. "School Learning With Various Methods of Practice and Rewards." *Teachers College Contributions to Education,* No. 688.

GATES, ARTHUR I. "Recitation As a Factor in Memorizing." *Archives of Psychology,* N.Y., No. 40.

HAFNER, LAWRENCE E. "An Experimental Study of the Effect on Reading Achievement Scores of Teaching Selected Aids to a Group of Fifth Grade Pupils," Unpublished Doctoral Dissertation, University of Missouri, 1960.

____ and HAYDEN B. JOLLY. *Patterns of Teaching Reading in the Elementary School.* New York: Macmillan, 1972.

HEBB, DONALD O. *Organization of Behavior.* New York: John Wiley and Sons, 1949.

LEVIN, JOEL R. "Organization, Comprehension and Some Evidence 'How.' " Paper presented at the annual meeting of the American Educational Research Association, Chicago, April 1972.

LUH, C. "The Conditions of Retention." *Psychological Monographs, 31,* No. 142.

SEIBERT, L. C. "A Series of Experiments on the Learning of French Vocabulary." *Johns Hopkins University Studies in Education,* No. 18.

SPITZER, H. F. "Studies in Retention." *Journal of Educational Psychology, 30* (1939), 641-56.

UNDERWOOD, BENTON. "Laboratory Studies of Verbal Learning." In E. R. Hilgard (Ed.) *Part I of the 63rd Yearbook of the NSSE.* Chicago: University of Chicago Press, 1964. Pp 133-52.

CHAPTER 4

Measurement and Evaluation of Mental Aptitude, Capacity for Reading, and Reading Achievement

Any capable teacher is concerned with how well students learn. To make adequate instructional decisions that foster learning a teacher needs to know something about his or her students. For example, the teacher should know their capacity for academic performance as well as the actual performance. How does one determine a student's capacity and performance? The teacher measures reading performance, for example, by administering and scoring tests designed to determine (1) how well a student understands printed material and (2) what strategies the student has for identifying printed words. Measurement, then, is the process of determining how much of a thing or attribute exists.

In placing a value on a score or interpreting it in the light of a standard or objective, a person is evaluating performance. To know that a person is 6'4½" is not very interesting. We can place some value on this height by comparing this measurement with the average height of various groups of people. We would discover that a 6'4½" adult male would be considered a fairly tall American, a very tall Japanese, an extremely tall Hottentot, a slightly above average Watusi, a short TOPS club member, or an improbable center on a professional basketball team.

The teacher who obtains intellectual capacity and reading achievement scores for an individual and then interprets the discrepancy between the scores is evaluating. The effective teacher will have to measure various kinds of academic performance, evaluate these performances in terms of capacity and personality measures, and then plan instructional sequences in light of these evaluations.

Determining the Quality of Measuring Devices

Validity. A test is valid if it measures what it purports to measure. Any given test should have various kinds of validity. A test has *predictive validity*, for example, if it predicts well scores on some criterion such as another test of its kind or school marks. It has *concurrent validity* if it correlates highly with an accepted test of its kind. A correlation on the order of .80 is generally needed to establish concurrent validity. If the test grows out of psychological theory, it has *construct validity*. One such theory states that intelligence is the ability to see relationships and to understand abstract concepts. To have construct validity according to this theory, an intelligence test would need to have a large proportion of items that require the seeing of relationships and understanding abstract concepts. *Content validity* is particularly important when considering the validity of achievement tests. To have high content validity, a test should reflect a large portion of the material presented in a course of instruction. A test has *face validity* when it looks as though it tests what it is supposed to test.

Reliability. A test is considered reliable if it yields consistent results. A test must be reliable if it is to be considered valid. However, a test may be reliable and still not be valid. For example, if a person wanted to measure the range of vocabulary in a typical middle school and all items were taken from Thorndike's first one thousand words, the test would not be valid even if it yielded consistent results. To be valid it would have to contain an adequate sampling of words from other Thorndike levels.

Steps in the Measurement and Evaluation Process

According to Hafner and Jolly (1972), there are basic steps in the measurement and evaluation process. They are presented here and elaborated upon:

1. *Determine what is to be measured and evaluated.* Do you want to measure intelligence? If so, do you want measures of verbal intelligence and performance intelligence? If you want to measure and evaluate reading achievement, do you want to use measures of ability to translate printed verbal information, ability to extrapolate printed verbal information, cognitive knowledge of graphemic options, and so forth? These facets should be determined in light of the next step.

2. *Understand the nature of the thing to be measured and evaluated.* It is less than satisfactory for teachers not to know what is meant by such terms as general information, translating and extrapolating printed verbal information, and graphemic options and such concepts as reading and intelligence if they are going to interpret academic measures and plan instructional sequences.

3. *Set up criteria that the tests should meet.* Of course, the tests should meet the criteria of validity and reliability. A survey reading test designed to test reading comprehension should meet especially the criterion of *construct validity*. The psychological theory underlying reading comprehension would relate to such concepts of meaning derivation as understanding vocabulary in isolation and in context, seeing relationships among ideas, weaving together ideas in context, and understanding abstract ideas.

4. *Check available tests against the criteria.* First of all, it is necessary to understand the criteria thoroughly. Then one must study the test passages and test items. Relate passages and corresponding items to the criteria. The final

decision about the appropriateness of the test should be weighted heavily by the actual comparison of test passages and items with the criteria, especially the construct validity criterion. Additional useful information is found by following the next step.

5. *Study interpretation manuals and technical manuals that accompany the tests and study reviews of the tests written by competent specialists.* The better tests are produced according to test-construction guidelines furnished by the American Psychological Association. Specialized information regarding a test's construction, validity, reliability, and interpretation is found in the interpretation manuals and the technical manuals provided by the publisher. Outside, objective assessments of capacity and reading tests can be found in such volumes as *The Seventh Mental Measurements Yearbook,* edited by O. K. Buros (1972) and *Reading Tests for the Secondary Grades* edited by Blanton, Farr, and Tuinman (1972).

6. *Select the test.*

7. *If existing tests do not satisfy the criteria, choose the test that most nearly satisfied them, or else develop a test.* Certain criteria, already discussed, are more important than others and must be given more weight in the decision making. Developing a test can be difficult, but there is no reason why a suitable test cannot be produced by a group of knowledgeable teachers.

8. *Administer and score the test.* Directions must be followed explicitly if the results are to be valid. Test-scoring services are provided by most publishers. But if the analysis of scores and the test answer sheets are not returned immediately, the value and utility of the testing enterprise may be lost.

9. *Evaluate the results.* One can take the answer sheets and test booklets and ask certain students why they answered particular items as they did. In this way one can get at the dynamics of their reasoning processes. Possibly one could duplicate the answer sheets of the students in question and probe their reasoning processes immediately.

10. *Apply the findings as a guide to teaching, to placement in self-instructional materials and so on.* A person who scores at the 7.5 reading grade level in reading comprehension should not be placed in material that has a reading difficulty rating of 9.0 grade level. For example, if you want Tony and Maria to learn and have a good attitude toward the educational experience, you will place them in reading material that they can handle. In summary, the purpose of meaningful measurement and evaluation in reading is to aid proper instruction. In turn, proper instruction should contribute not only to improved achievement but also to the mental health of student and teacher alike. And it shows what students can do when well taught under good conditions.

BASIC AREAS FOR MEASUREMENT

A teacher will measure and make evaluation in several areas.

1. *Capacity.* What are the pupil's basic abilities? Intelligence, language, and so forth?

2. *Reading skills.* How well do the students read? How well do the students pronounce words? How well do they understand the basic, literal meaning? Do they get the gist of what they read? Do they relate supporting details to the main ideas, and so on? Can they make adequate inferences while reading, that is, can they draw conclusions while they read? Can they read and understand vocabulary?

3. *Word analysis skills.* Do the students have the basic skills underlying the ability to learn and use phonics? That is, how do the students function in auditory discrimination and visual discrimination tasks? Do they know the important phonemic options? Can they apply knowledge of phonemic options and context skills to aid word-identification in reading.

4. *Study-reference skills.* Can a student apply important reading skills such as getting the main idea and relating the important details to the main idea? Can the students shift gears, so to speak, and read for various purposes? Can they locate information? Do they know which resources and skills to use in locating information? Can they select materials pertinent to their reading purposes? Can they evaluate these materials? Finally, can they organize the information that they glean for their particular purposes?

MEASURING ACADEMIC APTITUDE AND CAPACITY FOR READING

What Capacity for Reading Means

If we are going to predict ability to read, obviously we cannot use a test with nonreaders that involves reading.[1] Therefore, we will have to use some form of a test called language auding, because language auding relates to verbal comprehension, which is the basic factor in language understanding. It is listening comprehension, and it underlies reading ability. Actually the basic capacity involved is intelligence, and verbal comprehension and performance ability are two basic factors in intelligence.

Verbal comprehension or language auding can be measured in various ways. Of course, the problems, tasks, and questions will be given in an oral form so that reading is not involved. Some basic factors tested are vocabulary, general information, and arithmetic reasoning. When you measure vocabulary you are to some extent measuring a built-in reasoning factor, too, because reasoning processes are used to acquire, retain, and use vocabulary.

The verbal comprehension factor can also be measured by a listening comprehension test such as the *Durrell Listening Test* (1968–1970) or a teacher-constructed test. For example, one can read a story to the students and then ask questions on the story. This kind of test can even be used in group situations when the answer is indicated by marking the correct picture out of four or

[1] For average and good readers, reading ability may exceed language auding ability. For example, a sixth grade girl who obtained a *Slosson Individual Intelligence Test* I.Q. of 104 earned an I.Q. of 125 on the *Kuhlman-Anderson Intelligence Test.* The latter test involved much reading.

five choices or by marking a category designated by a picture under which a spoken word fits. Listening comprehension tests, being verbal comprehension tests, are good predictors of reading achievement.

Generally speaking, performance factors do not predict reading nearly so well as verbal factors do, because there is less verbal comprehension involved in performance tasks. However, one performance task correlates well with the total intelligence test and reading. That task is Block Design, which measures a visual-spatial factor.

Some people feel that performance or nonlanguage factors show the basic intelligence of a person. They may indicate what might have been had the person had better language stimulation as a child. The fact remains that language factors are the best predictors of reading achievement.

A person with fairly good language ability may still have problems with reading because he or she has not learned to decode words. If there are problems in auditory or visual perception, a person can be handicapped in learning to decode printed symbols. One can try to remedy the perceptual deficits of students who are not reading up to their basic language capacity level. However, research by Cynthia Deutsch (1964) has shown that auditory perception deficits that exist as late as third grade are most difficult to remedy.

The deficits are often in auditory perception, making ordinary phonics approaches to reading acquisition rather inefficacious. One must then use special techniques, some of which are adumbrated in the chapters on learning and discussed more fully in the chapter on reading acquisition.

MEASURING ACADEMIC APTITUDE

Verbal and Nonverbal Group Tests

Some of the subtests of the tests discussed in this section require reading; some do not. These academic aptitude tests are to a large extent indices of previous academic accomplishments and cultural background. For this reason they are fairly good predictors of academic achievement in an individual's immediate future. If some persons could concentrate for longer periods of time and work as assiduously on their studies as they can on a "one-hour" test, the correlations between academic aptitude tests and school marks would be higher.

On the other hand—and this will give you something to think about—Benjamin Bloom some years ago found that academic aptitude tests correlated .70 with algebra achievement among ninth graders. Such results are a joy to elitists. However, he then proceeded to teach like groups of students on a pacing and mastery basis and extended the period of instruction from nine months to something like eleven months; the students then achieved well. The correlation dropped to .00.

Descriptions of Several Intelligence and Aptitude Tests. On the following pages several representative intelligence and aptitude tests are described and discussed.

1. *Title:* *Lorge-Thorndike Intelligence Tests.*
2. *Authors:* Irving Lorge and Robert L. Thorndike.
3. *Publisher:* Houghton Mifflin Company, Boston, 1964.
4. *Grade Levels:* Levels 1–5 (kindergarten through grade 12). Levels 1 and 2 are nonverbal. Levels 3–5 are verbal and nonverbal. Multilevel edition, Levels A–H (grades 3–13).
5. *Areas Tested:* Verbal intelligence and nonverbal intelligence. The types of items used to measure verbal intelligence are sentence completion, verbal classification, arithmetical reasoning, and vocabulary—all accepted measures of verbal ability. The following kinds of items are used to estimate nonverbal intelligence: figure (pictorial) classification, number series, and figure (pictorial) analogies.
6. *Comments:* The verbal tests provide a good index of ability to deal with the kinds of verbal abstractions found in textual materials. The correlations with achievement tests are usually in the .70s. The nonverbal tests measure spatial factors not closely related to the general intelligence factor; therefore, these nonverbal portions would not be useful in predicting ability to read. However, the types of items used in the nonverbal tests can help predict achievement in studies involving spatial thinking, for example, physics, architecture, drafting, and mechanics.

Since the verbal tests require reading, they will predict reading achievement. But they are not the best measures of capacity to improve reading achievement or to acquire reading skills; individual intelligence tests and listening comprehension (auding) tests are. (See the next section of this chapter on individual tests of capacity.)

1. *Title:* *Kuhlmann-Anderson Intelligence Test-Seventh Edition.*
2. *Author:* Rose G. Anderson.
3. *Publisher:* Personnel Press, Inc., Princeton, N.J., 1960.
4. *Grade Levels:* Grade 5, Book E; 6, F; 7–8. G; 9–12, H.
5. *Areas Tested:* Verbal intelligence and quantitative intelligence.
6. *Comments:* These tests are designed to be scholastic aptitude measures. They are based on the research findings of a significant relationship between verbal intelligence and achievement in secondary and college English, social studies, and language studies. Quantitative intelligence is a necessary ability for success in science and mathematics.

As with other capacity tests, the IQs derived should be used in conjunction with knowledge of the student's interests, motivation, and study habits and the family's and the student's goals.

1. *Title:* *Analysis of Learning Potential*
2. *Authors:* Walter N. Durost, Eric F. Gardner, and Richard Madden.
3. *Publishers:* Harcourt Brace Jovanovich, Inc., New York, 1970.
4. *Grade Levels.* Elementary, 4–6; Advanced I, 7–9; Advanced II, 10–12. (Also available at lower levels.)
5. *Areas Tested:* Word-relational concepts, number concepts, and figure concepts.

6. *Comments:* The ALP series was not designed to match a specific theoretical framework regarding the nature of mental ability or intelligence. Rather, the subtests were designed to contribute to the prediction of academic success. National norms for the series are derived from the testing of almost 165,000 students in 44 states.

The *Index or Learning Potential* (ILP) indicates a student's general scholastic ability in terms of chronological age group, regardless of grade placement.

A *Composite Prognostic Score* (CPS), the estimate for a student's ability to learn in a given subject matter area, may be obtained by administering a given cluster of subtests.

An unpublished study by the author showed that a verbal aptitude test correlated .70 with the ability to *retain* organized verbal information over a three-week period when the original learning was on a mastery basis and the re-test was not announced ahead of time and consisted of the same course examination administered three weeks before.

A Final Note. Since aptitude tests are to some extent achievement tests and are useful in short-term prediction, they generally—as in the case of the present tests—require reading. To the extent that a person does not read well, his or her scores will suffer on a number of the subtests. But the purpose of these kinds of tests is to predict achievement in the near future, so reading tasks are used. We now turn to listening tests and intelligence tests, which do not require reading, and are, consequently, fairer measurements of capacity to learn to read.

MEASURING CAPACITY FOR READING

Group Listening Test

The Durrell Listening-Reading Series: Listening is ostensibly a no-reading test. As you read the description you will understand why I say ostensibly.

1. *Title: Durrell Listening-Reading Series: Listening*
2. *Authors:* Donald D. Durrell and Mary T. Hayes.
3. *Publisher:* Harcourt Brace Jovanovich, Inc., New York, 1968–1970.
4. *Grade Levels:* Intermediate (grades 3.5–6) and Advanced (grades 7–9). Also available: Primary.
5. *Areas Tested:* Vocabulary comprehension and paragraph comprehension.
6. *How Tested:* The discussion here is on the advanced test, but it generally applies to the intermediate test as well. These listening tests are administered orally by the teacher. The students' booklets have no words except the option words, which are read by the teacher. Therefore, the students are not required to exhibit reading skill.

The *vocabulary comprehension* test for the advanced level has two parts. Part one asks the student to relate the meaning of a word to one of five categories in a cluster; sometimes the stimulus word is a category synonym at other times it is a subordinate. Sample categories are:

a. ANIMAL   b. TIRED   c. RICH   d. STORE   e. DANGER

Sample spoken stimulus words—the ones to be categorized—are *wealthy, beast, shop, risk,* and *costly.* The second part asks the student to relate a spoken stimulus word to one of five topics or subjects about which he or she might be reading when the word was first seen. For example, the topics or subjects might be

a. PETROLEUM   b. RELIGION   c. NUTRITION,   d. BOTANY,
e. LIGHTING.

The stimulus words might be 1. *protein*   2. *fluorescent*   3. *derrick*   4. *gospel*   5. *stamen.* (I had to devise these samples because none were given in the test manual or test.)

The *paragraph comprehension* test also contains two parts. The first part is comprised of passages followed by five statements the student then judges as true, false, or information not given in the passage. A sixth item following each passage is multiple choice, with four options provided.

Sample Paragraph (read *to* the students)

Unicorn is the name of a plant which is commonly found in the southwestern part of the United States. Its flowers are yellowish white spotted with purple. It is used by the Indian women of the Southwest, who weave the black pods into their baskets for ornamental purposes. The plant itself often serves as a pattern for the design.

Sample Statements (also read by the teacher)

After each sample statement the teacher says,

"What space should be marked for this statement?"

1. Part of the unicorn plant is useful in making baskets.
2. The unicorn plant grows in the United States.
3. Leaves of the unicorn plant can be cooked and eaten.
4. The flowers of the unicorn plant are black.
5. The unicorn plant is small.
6. According to this paragraph, <u>unicorn</u> is the name of a (a) decorative plant (b) fabulous animal (c) fragrant flower (d) useless weed. Which is the right answer for this sample?

Sample Answer Boxes (T = True; F = False; NG = Not Given)

The first three in our illustration are done.

S1	(X)	(F)	(NG)		S4	(T)	(F)	(NG)
S2	(X)	(F)	(NG)		S5	(T)	(F)	(NG)
S3	(T)	(F)	(XG)		S6	(a)	(b)	(d)

The second part of the *paragraph comprehension* test consists of passages comparing and contrasting two people or places that are alike in some respects but different in others. Each passage is followed by statements for the student to classify as true of the one, true of the other, true of both, or as information not given in the passage.

Comments: These appear to be excellent tests and they fit the meaning hierarchy theory espoused in the present text. With respect to the vocabulary comprehension section, however, some students might have difficulty in remembering the categories. Possibly the use of semi-abstract designs to indicate the categories would have been useful.

KINDS OF INTELLIGENCE

In an effort to clarify the nature-nuture controversy some years ago Hebb (1949) posited two kinds of intelligence. Intelligence A is innate and is defined as the potential or capacity for development. Hebb states that Intelligence A is rooted in the "possession of a good brain and a good neural metabolism." I feel that a problem arises when people attribute Intelligence A solely to genetic endowment.

Intelligence B is the functional ability of the brain that has been influenced by experience (that is, this intelligence is developed through interaction with the environment.) Intelligence A and Intelligence B are hard to measure. Vernon (1970) refers to scores on intelligence tests as Intelligence C.

Vernon (1970) and Hafner and Guice (1974), among others, do not agree that the proportion of intelligence not accounted for by experience can be accounted for solely by genes. I agree with Vernon that what the hereditarians would call genetic intelligence is strongly influenced by such pre- and peri-natal factors as (stated negatively) malnutrition, birth injury, and anoxia. Hafner and Guice noted in their review of research that protein malnutrition is especially damaging to brain development from 5 months prior to birth to 25 months after birth. So there are physical development—pre-, peri-, and post-natal—factors not accounted for by genes.

The potential intelligence attributable to genes and the physical development factors up to 25 months I will call pyramidal intelligence. I choose this name because the pyramidal tracts of the brain are completely myelinized at about 25 months of age. This pyramidal intelligence can be called Intelligence D. The total working intelligence I shall call Intelligence E; it is a result of the "interaction" of pyramidal intelligence (D) and functional intelligence (B). We have, then, two formulas:

(1) $$E = D \times B$$

Total working intelligence = Pyramidal intelligence $\times$ Functional intelligence

(2) $$C = f(E)$$

Measured intelligence is a function of total working intelligence

A Caveat Against Pride and Greed.   In the sixties and seventies certain people in the United States, as a result of their hereditarian predilections and the research and theorizing of such people as Coleman, Shockley, Jensen, and Herrnstein, ascribed more influence in the determination of intellectual capacity to genes than the genes actually possess.[2] The latter four men seem to have become the prophets for elitists in and out of government who denigrate those of lower caste and use the hereditarian argument as an excuse to vote down funds (or to withhold appropriated funds—remember Nixon) that would go to (1) supplying adequate nutrition to indigent mothers and to their offspring (as well as to educate these families in nutrition and other developmental, homemaking, and economic matters), (2) setting up more infant cognitive therapy centers such as that of Rick Heber (1970) in Milwaukee, and providing much-needed educational materials, and special teachers for the schools.

The resultant increase in pyramidal and functional intelligence and, in turn, of working and measured intelligence as a result of such nutritional and cognitive therapy bodes well for our country. More people would be able to learn and earn, and there would be less need for the extremely expensive correctional, penal, and educational facilities, the latter for the retarded.

Not only do we have a moral obligation to help people—do not forget that the blacks were held slaves de juris and de facto until the Civil War and de facto in many respects since; and do not bypass the poor whites who were held slaves by industrial, mining, and agricultural tycoons for generations or the Indians who were raped culturally and economically by white intruders. There is no longer any logical excuse for not helping indigent people, and of course, there never was a moral reason for not helping.

Finally, I recommend to the reader a cogent book by Arthur Whimby and Linda Shaw Whimby titled *Intelligence Can Be Taught*. It clarifies the issues, rectifies incorrect solutions proferred by certain individuals, and offers appropriate solutions.

TESTS USEFUL IN MEASURING AND EVALUATING CAPACITY FOR READING

I am almost sure that working intelligence and measured intelligence are flexible rather than fixed entities. Both general education and specific cognitive therapy influence them positively. But we still should try to use appropriate instruments to get estimates of measured intelligence. Nonreaders and poor readers should be given individual intelligence tests that do not require reading.

The *Slosson Intelligence Test* (SIT), the *Stanford-Binet Individual Intelligence Test*, and the Wechsler tests—the *Wechsler Intelligence Scale for Children* (WISC) and the *Wechsler Adult Intelligence Scale* (WAIS)—can be used by

[2] Also, in 1976 much of the work of the hereditarian Cyril Burt on this issue was seriously questioned by scholars.

trained personnel to obtain indices of intelligence. Of the three, the Slosson requires minimal training and could be used by the classroom teacher for individual testing. For a rapid estimate of intelligence certain duos of the Wechsler such as General Information and Block Design subtests or trios, for example, Vocabulary, Arithmetic Reasoning, and Block Design, may be administered. The Slosson Test correlates highly with the Binet because many Binet items are used (with permission) in the Slosson.

Wechsler tests use five verbal subtests and five performance subtests. The *General Information* test asks such questions as, "How far is it from Seattle to Los Angeles?" and "What is the Forum?" The *Comprehension* tests asks such questions as "Why are houses insulated?" and "What should you do with a parachute before you hit the ground?" The *Arithmetic Reasoning* test poses such questions as "How many grains of red sand can you buy for two dollars if each grain costs 1/100 of a cent?" In taking the *Similarities* test one responds to such queries as, "How are a spider and a rhinoceros alike?"

In the *Digit Span* test, a set of numbers is presented and the subject is required to repeat the set. The more numbers a person can repeat accurately the better his or her auditory memory. Finally the *Vocabulary* test (which is actually an optional test) asks for definitions of words ranging from "banana," through "parapet" to "casuistry." (The foregoing are not actual items in the tests.)[3]

The five Performance subtests call for placing in the correct order a series of pictures that tell a story, telling what part of each picture in a series is missing, putting together a picture puzzle, arranging colored blocks to match a given pattern, and writing under a series of symbols the proper number (according to a provided key). These performance tests are timed and bonus points are given for speed. Separate scaled scores can be computed for each subtest; verbal, performance, and total intelligence quotients can be ascertained.

Typical research relating WISC results to reading scores has shown that students who are good readers do well on subtests that can be classified as abstract, for example, Information, Arithmetic Reasoning, Digit Span, and Coding. Conversely, poor readers do poorly on these same kinds of tasks. Hafner (1974, p. 451) used certain Wechsler subtests in developing a formula for ascertaining capacity for reading.

MEASURING AND EVALUATING READING ACHIEVEMENT

Standardized Reading Survey Tests

Survey tests are designed to measure reading achievement in the basic areas of vocabulary and comprehension. These tests are to be used as screening devices

---

[3] It is possible for good readers to rank higher on an intelligence test that requires reading than on one that does not. For example, a mathematics education major—a good reader and honor student—obtained an IQ of 112 on the *Wechsler Adult Intelligence Scale* (WAIS) and an IQ of 140 on the *California Test of Mental Maturity* (CTMM). According to the *WAIS* she ranked at the 79*th* percentile in intelligence. Her percentile rating on the *CTMM* was 99.4

to compare a class group with other groups of students. They also provide a rough estimate of the instructional level of students. Research dictates a rule of thumb for determining a more realistic instructional level from the results of standardized reading survey tests: subtract one grade level from the result. It is best, however, to validate that procedure for particular tests by noting how students perform when placed according to the initial result compared to the adjusted score. Survey tests are also widely used in reading research to show class and individual gains in achievement following instruction.

The intent of the following presentation is to provide an understanding of what to expect from some widely used tests.

1. *Title: Iowa Silent Reading Tests.*
2. *Coordinating Editor:* Roger Farr.
3. *Publisher:* Harcourt Brace Jovanovich, Inc., New York, 1972.
4. *Grade Levels:* Level 1: upper elementary, basic adult. Level 2: high school, community college, other post-high school groups. Level 3: college-bound high school, college, professional groups.
5. *Areas Tested and How Tested:* Vocabulary: reading comprehension; directed reading: part A. Locating information, part B. skimming and scanning; and reading efficiency in Levels 1 and 2; Vocabulary, reading comprehension, and reading efficiency in Level 3.

The *vocabulary* test requires a student to select the synonym for a given word. Four choices are given, so a chance score is one-fourth the number of items in the test.

Most items in the *comprehension* test seem to be related to the area of social studies. In reading comprehension, part A, the student may look back into the selection while answering the questions. In part B, once the student has read the selection and turned the page to the questions, he or she may not look back.

In the *directed reading test*, part A-*locating information*, the student is required to demonstrate skill in the use of the dictionary, knowledge of the best sources for finding certain information, familiarity with the purposes of parts of a book, and knowledge of sources of information.

In the *directed reading test*, part B-*skimming and scanning*, the reader is directed not to read the article carefully but to glance over it in order to answer the questions. For Levels 1 and 2 the questions are listed on the answer sheet.

The *reading efficiency* test uses a modified cloze procedure and is designed to yield an index of speed and accuracy.

6. *Comments:* The revision of this test has been so extensive that it bears little relation to its predecessor. For example, the poetry test has been dropped, the directed reading test uses a different set and format, a general vocabulary test has been substituted for the four content-area vocabulary tests, and the thorough treatment on the use of the index has been replaced. The test user should consult the publisher's technical manual to obtain further information about the rationale for the test, its validity and reliability, and how it should be used.

1. *Title: Davis Reading Test.*
2. *Authors:* Frederick B. Davis and Charlotte Croon Davis.
3. *Publisher:* The Psychological Corporation, New York, 1957, 1961.
4. *Grade Levels:* Series 1, for average and above average students in grades 11–13. Series 2 for students in grades 8–11. Four parallel forms.
5. *Areas Tested:* Level of comprehension and speed of comprehension.
6. *Categories of Skills Tested:* (1) Finding the answers to questions answered explicitly or in paraphrase in a passage; (2) weaving together the ideas in a passage and grasping its central thought; (3) making inferences about the content of a passage and about the purpose or point of view of its author; (4) recognizing the tone and mood of a passage and the literary devices used by its author; (5) following the structure of a passage.
7. *Comments:* An excellent theoretical rationale undergirds this test. The test is not insipid; it is considered hard. Therefore, it provides the student with opportunities to do some real thinking. The test is easy to administer and requires a total testing time of about 50 minutes.

1. *Title: Durrell Listening–Reading Series: Reading.*
2. *Authors:* Donald D. Durrell and Mary T. Hayes.
3. *Publisher:* Harcourt Brace Jovanovich, Inc., New York, 1968–1970.
4. *Grade Levels:* Intermediate (grades 3.5–6) and Advanced (grades 7–9). Also available: Primary.
5. *Areas Tested:* Vocabulary comprehension and paragraph comprehension.
6. *How Tested:* The format for the tests is the same as for the listening test discussed in the section on capacity, except that a printed material stimulus is used. In the vocabulary test the stimulus words are classified into one of five categories. In the paragraph comprehension test, the students read a passage and then mark statements about the passage as True, False, or Not Given.
7. *Comments:* These tests appear to be excellent, and they fit the meaning hierarchy theory espoused in this book.

Standardized Diagnostic Reading Tests

The *Stanford Diagnostic Reading Test* is a comprehensive test that, when used with discretion, provides useful diagnostic information.
1. *Title: Stanford Diagnostic Reading Test II.*
2. *Authors:* Bjorn Karlsen, Richard Madden, Eric F. Gardner.
3. *Publisher:* Harcourt Brace Jovanovich, Inc., New York, 1966.
4. *Grade Levels:* Level 2, grades 4^2 to 8^2. Also available: Level 1, grades 2^2–4^2.
5. *Areas Tested:* (1) Reading comprehension: literal and inferential; (2) vocabulary; (3) word-recognition skills: syllabication.
6. *Comments:* Since this test was devised to assess performance of below-average readers it has a larger percentage of easy material than some tests do.

Each subtest contains instructions for interpreting performance. Suggestions for remedial instruction include specific directives under a number of headings. Schools that avail themselves of the special service—the instructional placement report—receive a special test-score analysis that places pupils in one of eleven groups. Instructional suggestions for each group are listed.

Individual Word-Recognition Test

The *Hafner Quick Reading Test: Expanded Version* is an individual reading test that provides information about a student's ability to pronounce words presented in a visual printed stimulus array.

1. *Title: The Hafner Quick Reading Test: Expanded Version.*
2. *Author:* Lawrence E. Hafner.
3. *Publisher:* Published in this work, Macmillan, New York, 1977.
4. *Grade Levels:* 1–14.
5. *Area Tested:* Word identification. Ten words at each of 14 levels constitute the stimulus array. A copy of the test is in the appendix of the present text.
6. *Comments:* The HQRT:EV correlates well with the Slosson Oral Reading Test, Peabody Individual Achievement Test, and the Gates-McGinitie Reading Test. It agrees with one or the other of these tests in given cases more than the other tests agree with one another.

A Comprehensive Group Reading Inventory

Because classroom teachers can seldom obtain standardized commercial reading tests to use as they see fit, I am including a comprehensive group reading inventory in the appendix. A teacher can select the test segments he or she deems appropriate. Teachers may want to experiment and devise their own test, also.

1. *Title: The Hafner Comprehensive Group Reading Inventory.*
2. *Author:* Lawrence E. Hafner.
3. *Publisher:* Published in this volume, Macmillan, New York, 1977.
4. *Reading Levels:* Prereading through College Level.
5. *Areas Tested:* A. *Readiness:* visual discrimination, letter names, auditory discrimination; B. *Silent Reading:* word recognition, (RL 1–2); comprehension (RL 1–16[+]); C. *The (Independent) Word-Identification Skills Test* (TWIST).
6. *Supplemental Tests:* (in this volume) Individual word-recognition test: *Hafner Quick Reading Test: Expanded Version*; a syllable test. (Directions are given in this section for constructing a simple, *meaningful* syllable test for students on the basis of results on the *Letter Name Test* and the TWIST.)
7. *Comments:* These tests cover a wide range of skills and levels of difficulty. The upper levels of the comprehension test are quite difficult.[4] The comprehension test uses a cloze, multiple-choice format. The tests use a multiple-choice format and have the ordinary advantages and disadvantages of tests of this kind.

[4] The comprehension test is difficult more by dint of the semantic complexity than syntactic complexity.

At this point none of the tests except the TWIST needs much explanation.

LN Letter Names. Being able to read the letters of the alphabet can be useful in discriminating words of similar appearance. The test is easy to administer and interpret.

CB Consonant Blends. Some individuals do not see the value of testing and teaching the consonant blends if the letter names are known; others consider it a moot point. Since blending is not all that easy a task, teaching the blends obviates a step or two in blending the parts of certain words.

CD Consonant Digraphs. What you have here is a digraph (two letters) representing a uniphone (one sound). This concept is discussed further in the next paragraph.

VC Vowel Clusters. In reading, given graphemes have phonemic options. For example, ⟨ea⟩ → (yields) /ē/ and /e/ depending upon the word. In like manner, phonemes have graphemic options; that is, phonemes can be encoded in several ways. For example, /ē/ → ⟨e⟩ me, ⟨ee⟩ free, ⟨ie⟩ chief, ⟨e-e⟩ complete, etc.

For indicating the phoneme stimuli for CD, VC, and OC I have used the pronunciation key of *Webster's Eighth New Collegiate Dictionary*. This key should provide no real problem for any teacher of IQ 110⁺ (who eats nutritionally balanced meals).

Some examples:

> /ȯi/ as in boy /bȯi/ and oil /ȯil/
>
> /au̇/ as in how /hau̇/ and round /rau̇nd/
>
> /iŋ/ as in sing /siŋ/ and sink /siŋk/
>
> /ü/ as in cool /kül/ and blue /blü/
>
> /ō/ as in no /nō/, dough /dō/, and toe /tō/, and the like.
>
> /ə/ as in fun /fən/, about /ə-bau̇t/, and couple /kəp-əl/

There are other ways of encoding the phonemes given above, but the examples provided should give one an idea of the concept.

Syllable Test. Syllable tests as usually constructed provide ammunition for people who look askance at education. They are usually a farrago of items such as *leat, kem,* and *chob*, that do not take into consideration individual needs. That procedure makes absolutely no sense. When a person fails to respond to such items you never really know whether it is because that person does not know one of the elements or more than one.

What one should do (and this procedure is not foolproof) is to make up syllables from elements the student knows. The following procedures may have minor flaws but it is better than other procedures I have seen. You will not be interested in devising and administering such tests to very many students.

Procedure: 1. Select a problem reader and survey the results of the TWIST to locate some of the known elements. 2. List the elements. 3. Construct syllables from known elements. 4. Administer your test. (There still is no guarantee that a given student will respond, but the chance is much greater than if you use the not-too-rational procedures of yesteryear.)

Example:

| | Some Syllables That Can Be Constructed |
Some Known Elements	from the Known Elements
LN (all)	wroon
CB bl, cr, cl	kaich
CD ch /ch/; sh /sh/	vur
VC ea /ē/; ai /ā/; oo /ü/	soo
OC wr /r/; ur /ər/	bleav

Some Tongue-in-Cheek Contextual Applications:

1. If you eat that candy, it will <u>roon</u> your appetite.

2. You pitch, and I will <u>kaich</u>.

3. That old boy was <u>vur</u> smart.

4. It is <u>soo</u> nice to have you back, my dear.

5. I <u>bleav</u> this foolishness should stop.

GROUP DIAGNOSIS → PRESCRIPTION PATTERN

Tests

Reading: 1. *Stanford Diagnostic Reading Test;* 2. *Letter Knowledge Test;* 3. Any appropriate survey or diagnostic test.

Reading Programs: 1. Individualized or small group, programmed, linguistically based: *The Sound Reading Program*, Education Achievement Corporation, Waco, Texas. 2. *SRA Reading Labs,* Science Research Associates, Chicago. 3. *Reading for Meaning,* Lippincott Corporation, Philadelphia. 4. *Reader's Digest Skillbuilders,* Reader's Digest Company, Pleasantville, New York. 5. Teacher-directed: (LEA) Language Experience Approach or program of one's choice.

MEASURING AND EVALUATING STUDY-REFERENCE SKILLS

Group (or Individual) Study-Reference[5] Skills Inventories

Efficient, effective methods of acquiring and organizing information for later use help people to use their brain power fully. Most great composers, artists, scientists, and writers developed special regimens that permitted them to acquire, organize, and produce information and images (visual and auditory) in creative ways. Einstein, for example, worked for years in a patent office. His discoveries are based on systematic analysis and synthesis of organized information.

[5] You are also measuring comprehension skills; that is inherent in the concept.

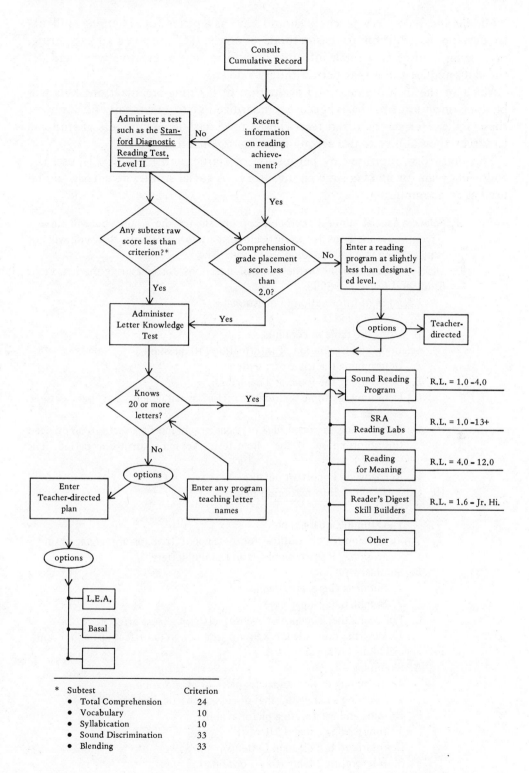

```
                              ┌─────────────────┐
                              │  Consult        │
                              │  Cumulative     │
                              │  Record         │
                              └─────────────────┘
```

*   Subtest   Criterion
  * Total Comprehension   24
  * Vocabulary   10
  * Syllabication   10
  * Sound Discrimination   33
  * Blending   33

Middle and secondary teachers should have as a prime focus helping students to develop in addition to basic funds of ideas: (1) purposes for acquiring, organizing, and setting forth information and images in creative ways and (2) the skills and attitudes that permit them to do so.

Much of the measurement and evaluation of learning-organization skills will be done on an informal basis because standardized instruments tap only a few of these skills. Yet standardized tests can be used with large numbers of students to survey their ability to use certain learning-organization skills.

This inventory, reprinted by permission of Hafner and Jolly (1972), uses the following plan for making such an inventory. A social studies inventory will be used as an example.

1. Select a (social studies) textbook appropriate for the group you will survey. If you know the book is too difficult for certain individuals, then you will not subject them to a test based on that book.

2. Develop items, usually in the form of questions, for measuring the important Study and Reference Skills.
   I. Location of Information (5 questions)
      A. Using the index.
      B. Using the table of contents.
   II. Selection and Evaluation of Information (10 questions)
      A. Determining the topic of a sentence.
      B. Determining the topic of a paragraph.
      C. Determining topic sentences. (Use a paragraph that has a topic sentence.)
      D. Determining the main idea of a paragraph and of a section. (You need this information. If the whole test takes more than one period, it is worth it.)
      E. Recognizing important details.
   III. Organization of Information (5 items)
      A. Outlining
         1. Outlining a paragraph.
         2. Developing an outline for a segment (two or three pages) of a section. Roman numerals and capital letters.
      B. Summarizing
         1. Summarizing a paragraph.
         2. Summarizing a page.
      C. Following the sequence of events [related to cause-effect]
         1. Describe events leading to a phenomenon (an effect or major event).
   IV. Special Skills (7 items)
      A. Skimming
         1. Skimming to find a specific piece of information.
         2. Locating a paragraph that discusses a particular phenomenon.
      B. Reading and interpreting pictorial aids.
         1. Interpreting a map (2 items).
         2. Interpreting a diagram (3 items).
         3. Interpreting a table (this is optional).

Study-Reference Skills Inventory

Social Studies: Your Country and the World, level-7 text, Ginn (1960)

I. Location of Information
  A. Index
    1. On what pages can you find information about the population of Brazil? [pages 363–364]
    2. On what page can you find information about the soil in the Belgian Congo? [page 106]
    3. Read the sentence that describes Holland's most famous dairy product. [Page 148, see Netherlands.]
  B. Table of Contents
    1. In what unit would you find a chapter on U.S. trade with Asia? [Unit 3]
    2. How large is the continent of North America? [See Appendix-8,300,000 square miles.]
    3. How much of the earth's surface is covered by the oceans? [Three-fourths, page 321.]

II. Selection and Evaluation
  A. Topic of a Sentence
    1. What is the topic of sentence 1, paragraph 1, column 2, page 30?
    2. What is the topic of sentence 1, paragraph 2, page 32? [Man's speed in conquering space and distance.]
  B. Topic of a Paragraph
    1. What is the topic of paragraph 2 under "We Become a World Power." page 56? [trade by ships]
    2. What is the topic of the last paragraph, page 67? [Crops that grow well in subtropical climate]
  C. Topic Sentences
    1. What is the topic sentence of paragraph 2, page 155? [First sentence]
    2. What is the topic sentence of paragraph 2, page 395, under "India . . ."? [last sentence]
  D. Main Ideas
    1. What is the main idea of the last paragraph, first column, pages 340 and 341? [stated in the last sentence]
    2. What is the main idea of the section "Our Richest Soils Are in the Middle of the Country," page 103? [last two sentences]
  E. Recognizing Important Details.
    1. [Read second paragraph, page 189] What tropical woods are described in this paragraph? [mahogany, ebony, teak] What are mahogany and teak used for? [mahogany used in furniture and ships? teak in boat keels, furniture]
    2. [Read first two paragraphs, page 339,] What is the most valuable wood product? [paper] What products rank second? [furniture]

III. Organization
  A. Outlining
    1. Outline the first paragraph, page 363.
    2. Indicate the major headings and capital letter headings for an outline of pages 374–375.

       B. Summarizing

          1. Summarize paragraph 2 under "China . . .," page 400.

          2. Summarize "China has many other problems," page 402.

       C. Following the Sequence of Events

          1. [Read paragraph 1, page 412.] Describe the events leading to the establishment of the Communist government in Russia.

    IV. Special Skills

       A. Skimming

          1. "When did Brazilia become the capital of Brazil; [1960, page 363]

          2. Locate the paragraph that describes India's problems.

       B. Reading and Interpreting Pictorial Aids

          1. [Map, page 446]

             a. What color on the map represents the aggressor countries in World War 1? [black]

             b. To what group did the United States belong? [Allies] Persia? [neutrals]

          2. [Diagram, page 329]

             a. What is the fourth step in the assembly line? [chemical treatment]

             b. What happens to a car after colored enamel is applied? [It is oven-dried.]

             c. Name one operation that takes place away from the assembly line. [dashboard assembly or weather stripping]

      3. Administer the inventory (without the answers)

        a. Explain to the students that the purpose of the inventory is to obtain diagnostic information about their comprehension and study skills.

        b. Provide each student with a copy of the text in which the inventory is based.

        c. Allow the students to work during the entire period. Collect the papers at the end of the period. If another period is required to finish the inventory, let the students finish it during the next class period.

        d. Correct the inventory yourself and make transparencies of appropriate pages of the text and explain the answers, pointing to appropriate segments of the text, and how they are obtained. Thus the whole process becomes a learning situation!

NOTE: Regarding the development of inventories for *other subject-matter areas.*

    1. Inventories are provided throughout the book. After studying them, you should be able to *generalize the procedures* and prepare inventories for your subject-matter area even if a specific sample inventory is not provided.

    2. When preparing inventories for science or technical subjects, you will have to take special care that you do not ask students to sample material that is totally unfamiliar to them.

    3. Therefore you will want to prepare your inventory carefully and administer it at the right time so that the above considerations are taken care of.

    4. For scientific, technical, and mathematical courses, add questions about

      a. particular formulas, what they mean, and how they are used.

      b. particular laws, principles, theorems, and how they are applied in the text.

    c. certain directions such as the steps in an experiment, how something is put together, how to make something.

    d. the meanings of symbols used in mathematical formulas, equations, and problems.

    e. the meanings of certain technical vocabulary items.

    f. the basic steps in solving mathematical word problems.

5. You can devise items on the use of *library resources* that are appropriate to the maturity of the students and the resources of your school library: (A special test on the use of library resources is included in one of the appendices.)

Standardized Study-Reference Skills Tests

1. *Title: Survey of Study Habits and Attitudes.* (SSHA) [Spanish edition available]

2. *Authors:* William F. Brown and Wayne H. Holtzman.

3. *Publisher:* The Psychological Corporation, New York, 1952.

4. *Grade Levels:* 7–12.

5. *Areas Tested:* (1) Delay avoidance, (2) work methods, (3) teacher approval, and (4) education acceptance. (Combine the first two subscale scores to get the *study habits* score and the last two to get the *study attitude* score. All four combined yield the *study orientation* score.)

6. *Comments:* (1) The authors suggest that the reading teacher or counselor use the subscale scores rather than individual items to counsel and plan. (2) Research by Brown and Holtzman (1968) with students in grades 7–12 showed that SSHA + SA (scholastic aptitude) correlated .67 with GPA.

The learning-organization skills measured by the *Iowa Tests of Basic Skills - Work Study Skills* are reading maps, reading graphs and tables, and knowing of and using reference materials. Unless teachers have valid data, they tend to overestimate the proficiency of their students in these skills.

1. *Title: Iowa Tests of Basic Skills-Work-Study Skills.*

2. *Authors:* E. F. Lindquist and A. N. Hieronymus.

3. *Publisher:* Houghton Mifflin Company, Boston, 1955.

4. *Grade Levels:* 3–9.

5. *Areas Tested:* (1) Map reading, (2) reading graphs and tables, (3) knowledge and use of reference materials.

6. *Comments:* (1) These scores can be profiled along with other scores; the profile depicts strength and deficit areas in a student's achievement. (2) The mastery of these skills should be a goal of teachers and students for their mastery is basic to quality academic achievement.

The Informal Reading Inventory (IRI)

Purpose. The IRI is designed to yield information about a student's ability to pronounce words, define words, and understand what he or she is reading. Basically it is used to determine (1) the grade level at which reading instruction can be done, (2) the suitability of a given selection, chapter, or book for use as "text" material for a given student, and the level at which students can read independently. For example, the student who answers 75 per cent or more of the questions on a particular reading level selection, say grade eight, and pronounces 95 per cent of the words correctly can be instructed in reading at that level; in our example that would be the eighth reading level.

Description. The informal reading inventory (IRI) consists of a series of graded reading selections from either literary or expository material and a set of questions for each of the selections. There are four basic steps in administering the inventory: (1) The student reads a selection silently. (2) The student answers questions posed by the teacher. (3) The student then reads the same selection orally as the examiner notes pronunciation errors on a duplicated copy of the story. (4) Finally, the student defines a list of ten vocabulary words taken from the selection or from similar material.

Construction. To prepare a set of selections for the inventory, choose reading materials of given readability. A readability formula such as that associated with the Fry Readability Graph can be used to determine the readability level of a given selection. You have to keep at it until you have your set of reading selections. A table showing length of selections by readability levels follows; the lengths are approximate:

Readability	1.1–1.5	1.6–2.0	2.1–3.0	3.1–4.0	4.1–5.0	6.1–7.0	7.1–13.0+
Length (in words)	50	100	100	150	200	200	300

Next you will need to write your literal comprehension and interpretation questions. The interpretation questions require that the reader (1) see relationships such as cause-effect and (2) draw conclusions. Ten vocabulary words of appropriate difficulty in isolation and/or in context could also be included in the inventory.[6] As you know, a "what" question is not necessarily a literal comprehension question, nor does a "why" question necessarily require interpretation. The selection plus questions, vocabulary items, and coded designation of readability level, such as RL 7.3, are typed (double spaced) and duplicated. The student's reading selection is printed on a separate page. (See Appendix for a sample of IRIs.)

Administering the Test. After determining an approximate level for entering IRI by using the results of the *Hafner Quick Reading Test* (HQRT:EV level minus one should give you a good entering level), select the appropriate selection, establish rapport with the student and ask him or her to read the selection silently.

After the student reads the selection *silently*, pose the literal comprehension and interpretation questions. Note the responses and compare them quickly with the correct responses on your copy. Write the number of points in the

[6] Such a vocabulary inventory can help you understand the student's comprehension performance. You may also want to note the difference in ability to define the words in isolation and in context.

margin so that the student's total score can be quickly computed. Partial credits may be given.

Then ask the student to read the selection orally; note errors in pronunciation according to the "Code for Checking Oral Processing Errors."

Scoring the Test. Compute the percentage correct in comprehension by totaling the points. Determine the word-recognition accuracy by dividing the number of errors by the number of words in the reading selection. To facilitate computing an odd-number-of-words selection set up a table; for example, on a 148-word selection, carried down to 90 per cent:

Number of Errors	0	1-2	3	4-5	6	7-8	9	10-11	12	13	14-15
Percentage Correct	100	99	98	97	96	95	94	93	92	91	90

Performance Criteria for Informal Reading Tests. To simplify matters I will discuss only the independent reading level, the instructional level, and the frustation reading level.

Independent level: This is the level on which a person can read on his or her own, pronounce 98 per cent of the words correctly, and score at least 90 per cent correct on comprehension-interpretation questions designed for the selection. What is Sam's independent level when he scores as follows on these grade levels?

	Per Cent Correct	
	Pronunciation	Comprehension-Interpretation
Tenth grade	87	68
Ninth grade	95	79
Eighth grade	98	91

It is eighth grade. Can you explain why?

Instructional level: To determine at what level daily reading instruction should be carried on or what level textbook a person should read in, use the following criteria: at least 75 per cent correct in comprehension-interpretation and from 92 per cent to 95 per cent pronunciation accuracy, depending upon the level of the selection.

Table 4-1. **Pronunciation Criteria for the Various Readability Levels**

Readability Levels	1-2	3-4	5-6	7-12+
Pronunciation Criteria, Percentage Correct	92	93	94	95

What is Katie's instructional level based on this performance?

		Per Cent Correct
	Pronunciation	Comprehension-Interpretation
Seventh	88	70
Sixth	94	80
Fifth	98	84

It is sixth grade. Can you explain why?

The frustration level: Any reading performance that falls much below 75 per cent correct comprehension can be frustrating; so can pronunciation that falls below the frustrational level criterion. Frustrating refers to *blocking* of meaning development and learning and may be associated with such internal feelings as anxiety and hopelessness and such external behaviors as moving lips during silent reading, pointing with one's finger, and restlessness. One does not try to obtain a person's frustration level, but it sometimes shows up in testing.

Following are Yolanda's scores on several inventories. Please indicate her independent, instructional, and frustration reading levels:

		Per Cent Correct
	Pronunciation	Comprehension-Interpretation
Twelfth grade	80	50
Eleventh grade	86	72
Tenth grade	95	80
Ninth grade	98	83
Eighth grade	98	92

Code for Checking Oral Processing Errors. As the student reads the selection, the examiner notes on a duplicated copy of the selection mispronunciations, omissions, substitutions, insertions, repetitions, and word-order inversions. Each error is recorded, but they will be subjected to a misprocess analysis to see how they are to be interpreted.

1. *Supplying a word.* (✓) If the student pauses for three seconds, seemingly unable to pronounce a word or after five seconds of attempting to pronounce it, put a check mark (✓) over it and pronounce it (1 error).

2. *Mispronunciations and substitutions.* (___) Underline the word and write the student's pronunciation over it. If the student reads quite rapidly, you may only have time to underline it.

$$sky \qquad [\text{1 error}]$$
$$\underline{berry}$$

Count a subordinate or a superordinate substitution as ½ error:

bananas [½ error]　　*jewelry* [½ error]
<u>fruit</u>　　　　　　　　　<u>bracelet</u>

Exception: Do not count a synonym as an error:

sofa [0 error]　　　　*a* [0 error]
<u>couch</u>　　　　　　　　　<u>one</u>

however [0 error]
<u>but</u>

Count a closely related substitution as ½ error:

hook [½ error]

He got the fish with a <u>spear</u>.

3. *Partial mispronunciations.* (＿＿) Underline the mispronounced segment and write the student's mispronunciation over it. If the pronunciation is partially correct and the meaning is seriously affected, count the mispronunciation as 1 error; if the meaning is not seriously effected, do not count the mispronunciation as 1 error; if the meaning is not seriously affected, do not count the mispronunciation as an error:

hatful [1 error]

<u>fanciful</u>

4. *Omissions.* (O) Circle omitted elements. Omitting an important word counts as 1 error.

They gave (food) to the hungry man.　　[1 error]

If less than half the word is omitted and the meaning is affected in only a *minor* way, do not count the omission as an error:

follow(ing)　　[0 error]

If an omission affects the meaning seriously and the word is important to the meaning of the sentence, count the omission as 1 error:

The man fell out of the air(plane.)　　[1 error]

She gave a condition(al) promise.　　[0 error]

Omitting the following counts as ½ error each:

<u>prepositions</u>: in, of
<u>conjunction</u>: and
<u>articles</u>: a, an, the

lots (of) fun　　[½ error]

man (of the) hour　　[1 error]

5. *Insertions.* (∧) The insertion of an element into a word or a word into a sentence counts as ½ an error if it does not seriously affect the meaning such as ascribing bad traits to someone good or vice versa. Insertion of *and* between

coordinated sentences or a contrasting word such as *but* or *however* where it would be appropriate does *not* count as an error.

The small *est* animals went in last.   [½ error]

The *cute* little girl came to visit us.   [½ error] (assuming she is cute or there is no indication that she is not cute)

The big *bad* man walked into the store.   [1 error] (when there is no basis for assuming he is bad)

The football team was successful. *and* The baseball team had a good season, too.   [0 error]

Jan is pessimistic. *however* Becky is hopeful.   [0 error]

If one inserts *that* or *which* in places where they fit, it is not considered to be an error:

The ice cream cone was so good *that* Jerry wanted another one.   [0 error]

6. *Repetitions.* (〜〜) Count one error for every three sets of repetitions. Of course, they need not be in consecutive sentences. But do not count one set as 1/3 error. Indicate a repetition with a wavy line.

Mary is an excellent artist.

Socialism is anathema at our house.

I am sure the seeds will germinate.   [1 error]

We love to play the toccatas.

7. *Inversions.* (〜) Count 1 error for every inversion except when the inversion would change the meaning or be quite ungrammatical:

The discussion was enlightening.   [1 error]

Word knowledge is a basic ability in reading.   [0 error]

8. *Dialects.* Teachers may need to familiarize themselves with the dialects of their students. Students for whom English is a second language have to be given special consideration. Teachers in a school district might want to work out their own dialect code. Examples of usage from several different dialects that one might *not* want to count as errors are

/siŋk/ for think	/gif/ for give	/de′di/ for Daddy
/jis/ for just	/gi′mē/ for give me	/hant/ for hadn't
/gi/ for give	/wē wəz/ for we were	/ə-sept/ for accept
/wif/ for with	/rē-spä′/ for respond	/aks/ for ask
/skrēt/ for street	/sim-yü-l ə (r)/ for similar	/di′-tint/ for didn't
/sē′-in/ for seeing	/ən-daut′-ə b-lē/ for undoubtedly	

Here is my point: If you count /wif/ (with) and /aks/ (ask) from one of the black dialects as wrong, then you must count /sim′-yü-lə(r)/ (similar) and /ən-daut′-əb-lē/ from one of the southern white dialects as wrong! The point is not debatable.

Below is a reading selection at the college readability level. Pronunciation errors made by a student are noted, the types of "misprocesses" are indicated in column one, and numerals indicating error scores are given in column two:

A Newton Vignette

Reading text	Type of error or misprocess	Error
During 1665 and 1666 Newton completed		
first his <u>initial</u> investigations on gravity and	Synonym Substitution	0
great motion. For twenty years his∧ideas were	Insertion	½
universe kept from the <u>world</u>. His original theory	Superordinate Substitution	½
was posited on inaccurate measurement(of the)	Omission	1
however earth's radius, <u>but</u> Newton noted differ-	Synonym Substitution	0
ences between the facts and the theory.		
One day several <u>English</u> scientists	Repetition	0
✓ tried to determine what law of force	Supplying a Word	1
could account for the motion of the		
(planets around) the sun. Halley decided	Non-meaningful Inversion	1
aks to go to Cambridge to <u>ask</u> Newton what	Dialect	0
that he thought about it. He discovered ∧	Meaningful Insertion	0
Newton (had already) solved the problem	Meaningful Inversion Repetition	0 0
the and had proof for <u>his</u> solution . . .	Closely-related Substitution	½
the law of gravity.		
	Total	4½

The person who read this 100-word selection scored 95.5 per cent correct. He passed the 95 per cent criterion for this readability level. As far as pronunciation is concerned, the material is at this person's instructional reading level. Under the older codes for checking oral errors, this selection would have been rated at the reader's frustration level. The present approach of taking into consideration semantic, syntactic, and phonological (dialect) factors in ascertaining oral reading performance is a reasonable one.

Using Cloze to Assess Reading Achievement

What the Cloze Is. In the cloze technique students have as a task supplying words that have been systematically deleted from a reading selection. The usual approach is to delete every fifth word. The score is an index of ability to read with comprehension, since the student has to read and make inferences and recognize language patterns in order to supply the deleted words. When every nth word is deleted the reading task is thought to be a general comprehension task. Deleting nouns and verbs rather than every nth word makes it a test of knowledge of the specific content of the selection.

Validating Studies. Bormuth's (1962) study at the elementary level showed cloze scores (one in five deletion) to be highly related ($r = .93$) to scores on inventories carefully constructed to measure a number of reading skills. His test, however, used a multiple-choice format along with the deletions. The correlation for main idea, however, was not as high as the other correlations.

Jenkinson (1957) obtained a correlation of .78 between cloze scores and the comprehension test of the *Cooperative English Test C-2*. Friedman (1964) administered cloze tests and the *Metropolitan Reading Test (MRT)* to students in the elementary grades. Correlations of cloze with *MRT* Vocabulary ranged from .63 to .85, with MRT Total, .71 to .87, showing marked to high correlations.

Byrne, Feldhusen, and Kane (1971) studied the relationships among three divergent thinking abilities and regular and modified cloze performance of seventh-grade students. They found that "cloze performance" is related to the divergent thinking ability of associational fluency. Students high in associational fluency perform better on both standard and adapted cloze procedures than students low in associational fluency.

Use of the Test in Measurement. The cloze test can be used as a measure of reading comprehension of a given piece of material. As such, it could be used to determine how well students read given pieces of material. Research has shown that a completion score of 42 per cent on every fifth-word-deletion cloze test is equivalent to a comprehension score of 75 per cent on an informal reading inventory constructed on the same material. Therefore, if a person reaches the 42 per cent criterion on a cloze selection, the material in the selection is considered to be on the individual's instructional reading level. Fifty per cent completion is the criterion for one's independent reading level. Before students take a cloze test they should be told that they are doing quite well if they get about half the items right (when the material is about on their readability level).

Construction of the Cloze Test. Generally speaking, one should use a selection that has somewhat more than 250 words. In the first sentence no words are deleted, and following that every fifth word is deleted for a total of 50 blanks (each 15 spaces long). The material is typed double spaced and is prefaced by a set of directions.

In order to give you an idea of what a cloze test is like, I shall include a twenty-five blank, 1–5 deletion, sample cloze test:

Cloze Reading Test

Reading Level: High School-College.

Directions: The following selection has had some words deleted. Your ability to replace the deleted words is one indication of your reading ability. If you are able to complete correctly 40 to 50 per cent of the items you are doing quite well. Read carefully in order to determine the words you think have been deleted and write them in the blanks accordingly.

The smoke of the Battle of Waterloo rolled back to the borders of Belgium, and then to the confines of Europe. A field of desolation _____ 1

revealed without a parallel _____ 2 modern history. The wrecks

_____ 3 heaped on every coast. _____ 4 was at

once apparent _____ 5 a bloody transformation had _____ 6

effected among the Western _____ 7 . Nor might the prescience

_____ 8 statesmen or philosopher discover _____ 9

the existing condition the _____ 10 results of the Revolutionary

_____ 11 .

One of the first _____ 12 discoverable in the then _____ 13

of Western Europe was _____ 14 Great Britain had been _____ 15

of all shaken from _____ 16 political moorings. It was _____ 17

as the roar of _____ 18 receded to the horizon, _____ 19

England had, even through _____ 20 epoch of turmoil and _____ 21 ,

held on her tedious _____ 22 labored course, like a _____ 23

ship, toiling with the _____ 24 , battered with the storms,

_____ 25 nevertheless, essentially sound in her structure.

(The answers are found on a later page. Remember, the exact word has to be replaced to be counted correct. Research shows this to be a good procedure; it is more objective and saves the teacher a lot of bother.)

READABILITY

Development of meanings is a cardinal goal of education and meaningful instruction is the primary approach to this goal. For instruction mediated by reading to be meaningful it must use readable materials. However, what is readable for one student may not be readable for another. Factors that contribute to the ease of reading (readability) are simple vocabulary, short sentences, uninvolved sentence structure, human interest, clear explanation, easy concepts, and good organization.

Detailed guidelines for improving the readability of materials can be found in an article by Hafner (1967). A summary of these guidelines follows: (1) write from a well-organized plan, (2) pay attention to your reader, (3) state your ideas clearly by cutting out needless words, making positive statements, and amplifying concepts that are far-removed from the reader's experience, (4) generally prefer the short sentence to the long sentence, (5) be specific, definite, and concrete, (6) ground your generalizations in specific facts, (7) emphasize nouns and verbs because they give to writing its toughness and color, and (8) use special organizational devices such as topic headings, summaries, and enumeration.

To make a precise, objective assessment of the difficulty of reading materials the teacher can employ one or more readability formulas. These formulas are designed to determine readability by looking at two or three measurable areas that involve the above factors: sentences/hundred words; syllables/hundred words; and human interest.

A teacher should not just determine the readability of textbooks. To introduce meaning into the teaching-learning situations for all students the teacher must match difficulty of materials to the reading ability of each student.

Graph for Estimating Readability. Fry (1968, 1969) has developed a means for determining the readability of materials. His method is based on two factors: average number of syllables per 100 words and average number of sentences per 100 words; three randomly selected 100 word samples are used. Fry obtained high correlations of his readability ratings with SRA, Dale-Chall, Flesch, and student comprehension scores. The present author has found this readability graph easy to use.

Answers to the Cloze Test: 1. was   2. in   3. day   4. It   5. that   6. been   7. nations   8. of   9. in   10. true   11. conflict   12. facts   13. condition   14. that   15. least   16. her   17. discerned   18. battle   19. that   20. the   21. violence   22. and   23. heavy   24. breakers   25. but.

GRAPH FOR ESTIMATING READABILITY

by Edward Fry, Rutgers University Reading Center,
New Brunswick, New Jersey

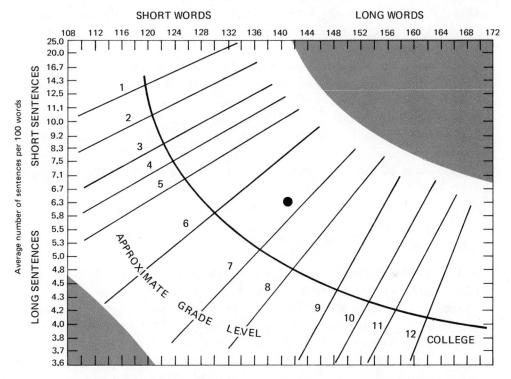

Average number of syllables per 100 words

DIRECTIONS: Randomly select 3 one hundred word passages from a book or an article. Plot average number of syllables and average number of sentences per 100 words on graph to determine the grade level of the material. Choose more passes per book if great variability is observed and conclude that the book has uneven readability. Few books will fall in gray area but when they do grade level scores are invalid. When counting words include proper nouns but do not include numerals.

EXAMPLE:

	SYLLABLES	SENTENCES
1st Hundred Words	124	6.6
2nd Hundred Words	141	5.5
3rd Hundred Words	158	6.8
AVERAGE	141	6.3

READABILITY 7th GRADE (see dot plotted on graph)

For further information and validity data see the April, 1968 Journal of Reading and the March, 1969 Reading Teacher.

The SMOG Grading Plan. McLaughlin (1969) adapted and simplified the Fog Index and called it the SMOG grading plan. If a piece of material is classified as 9.3 grade level, then a person who expects to comprehend the material fully must have a reading achievement level of *at least* 9.3 (reading grade level).

This SMOG formula is not very accurate for material below the fourth grade level.

SMOG Formula: One obtains the readability of a piece of material by applying the following steps of the SMOG formula:

1. Select three samples from the material. Select ten consecutive sentences near the beginning of the material, ten in the middle, and ten towards the end.

2. Using this sample of 30 sentences, count each word of three or more syllables. Count each repetition of a polysyllabic word.

3. Estimate from a table of square roots the square root of the number of polysyllabic words in the samples. If the number of polysyllabic words is 81, the square root is 9.

4. Add three to the square root and you have the SMOG grade. (*Example:* 9 + 3 = 12.)

SUMMARY

Wise instructional plans are based on adequate measurement and evaluation of students' capacity for academic performance as well as on their actual performance. A teacher is especially interested in determining a student's reading instruction level so that he or she can be taught developmental reading at that level and be placed in content reading material of the appropriate level. The quality of measuring devices is determined by ascertaining their validity and reliability. Certain basic steps in the measurement and evaluation process, when followed, result in better diagnosis of capacities and achievements and placement in instructional materials. The basic measurement areas are capacity, reading skills, word-analysis skills, and study-reference skills.

It is important to determine an individual's capacity to profit from reading instruction. One would not ask a poor reader or nonreader to take a capacity test that requires reading. Instead, one would give a test in which the stimuli are administered orally or that utilizes performance tasks which correlate well with academic tasks. Verbal tests such as listening tests and the verbal section of the WISC and WAIS are suitable capacity measures.

A teacher who does not have access to standardized capacity tests will use informal tests such as the ones presented in the present work. Such a teacher may, however, want to develop norms for these tests.

In this work I have delineated five kinds of intelligence. I have also issued a caveat against the pride and greed that have had such deleterious effects on the thinking of individuals in high and low places. We now know that nutritional therapy for pregnant women and infants and cognitive therapy from infancy on result in increases in the various kinds of intelligence.

Reading achievement can be measured by using standardized reading survey tests, diagnostic reading tests, and informal reading inventories. The latter can be constructed by alert teachers and reading specialists. A model group diagnosis-prescription pattern was included as an aid to the teacher who is inexperienced in diagnosis and in the placement of students into appropriate reading programs.

Only a few standard study-reference skills tests are available to the teacher; they are only group survey tests. They do not tap as many skills as one would like, nor do they fit particular texts. To satisfy the latter two requirements, a teacher would want to develop inventories.

The informal reading inventory is designed to yield information about the student's ability to pronounce words, define words, and understand what is being read and to determine a student's instructional reading level. I conceive of oral reading errors as due to misprocessing. Oral reading errors can be subjected to a misprocess analysis that is guided by a set of criteria rooted in semantic, syntactic, and phonological considerations.

Another technique for assessing reading achievement is the cloze procedure. The procedure, which entails supplying words deleted from textual material, has been validated as a reading comprehension measure by a number of researchers.

The importance of determining the readability of materials was explained, and two means of assessing readability, were explained.

ACTIVITIES AND QUESTIONS
TO PROMOTE LEARNING AND APPLICATION

1. Select several informal tests (including exam papers) and standardized tests and try to determine what kind of validity each has. What can be done to improve the validity of the tests?
2. Compare your findings for the standardized tests with the experts' comments in the latest Buros *Mental Measurements Yearbook.*
3. Why is reliability an important factor in testing?
4. Try to figure out why the Block Design subtest of the Wechsler intelligence tests is a fairly good predictor of reading achievement. Consult the *Education Index* or the ERIC system in order to find appropriate theory or research articles.
5. Remember Benjamin Bloom's mastery work in ninth-grade algebra. Teach a unit of material such as algebra, science, or reading on a mastery basis. How did the students like it? How do you feel about it yourself?
6. Administer the *Durrell Listening-Reading Series: Listening Test* to students. What do the results tell you about your students that you did not know?
7. Collect newspaper, magazine, and research articles that comment on what intelligence is, how it is developed, and the like and criticize them in terms of the discussion in the present text. What additional insights did you obtain from these articles?

8. What are the advantages of individual intelligence tests over group intelligence tests?

9. Read recent research articles relating individual intelligence test results to results on reading tests. What information do they add to that found in the test?

10. Examine copies of standardized reading tests. Which tests measure the kinds of skills that you consider important? Note strengths and weaknesses of the tests.

11. Obtain a copy of the *Davis Reading Test* and a tape recorder with a microphone. As you take the test, record your reasoning in answering some of the items. This exercise is qualitative: you are interested in developing insight about your reasoning processes. Check your answers against the correct answers and try to note the reasons for any incorrect answers. Have a student do this and conduct the same kind of analysis.

12. Apply the group-diagnosis → prescription pattern for teaching to a group of students. As you get students appropriately placed in suitable materials, note their reactions. What kinds of gains in reading achievement do the students make as a result of this placement and instruction?

13. Construct a study-reference skills test for a textbook of your choice. Administer the test to an individual or a group of students. What do the results tell you about the students' strengths and weaknesses in these areas?

14. Administer the Brown-Holtzman *Survey of Study Habits and Attitudes* to the same group of students that you used for the study-reference skills test. What patterns do you see among good students? Among poor students?

15. Prepare several levels of an Informal Reading Inventory. Administer them to a group of students, score, and interpret your results. Administer a standardized reading test to these same students. Which test seems more useful, more in keeping with the students' achievement in a given content area?

16. Determine the readability of a segment of reading material from a textbook. Construct a "cloze" test, following directions, and administer it to a group of students who use the text. Determine the average cloze score and the range of scores on the test. What percentage of students obtained satisfactory scores?

SUGGESTED ADDITIONAL READINGS

BURMEISTER, LOU E. *Reading Strategies for Secondary School Teachers*. Reading, Mass.: Addison-Wesley, 1974. Chapter 3.

BURNETT, RICHARD W. "Assessing Reading Progress." In Gerald G. Duffy (Ed.). *Reading in the Middle School*. Newark, Del.: International Reading Association, 1975. Chapter 6.

DULIN, KENNETH L. "The Middle Half: How Alike Are They, Really?" In Lawrence E. Hafner (1974, pp. 198–203).

HAFNER, LAWRENCE E. (Ed.). *Improving Reading in Middle and Secondary Schools*. Second Edition. New York: Macmillan, 1974. Section 7.

HARRIS, ALBERT J., and EDWARD R. SIPAY. *How to Increase Reading Ability.* Sixth Edition. New York: David McKay, 1975. Chapters 8 and 9.

SHEPHERD, DAVID L. *Comprehensive High School Reading Methods.* Columbus, Ohio: Charles E. Merrill, 1973. Chapter 2.

SMITH, EDWIN H., BILLY M. GUICE, and MARTHA C. CHEEK. "Informal Reading Inventories for the Content Areas: Science and Mathematics." In Lawrence E. Hafner (1974, pp. 204–12).

TUINMAN, J. JAAP and B. ELGIT BLANTON. "Problems in the Measurement of Reading Skills." In Lawrence E. Hafner (1974, pp. 212–22).

ZINTZ, MILES V. *The Reading Process. Second Edition. Dubuque: Wm. C. Brown, 1975.* Chapter 4.

BIBLIOGRAPHY

BLANTON, WILLIAM, ROGER FARR, and JAAP TUINMAN (Eds.). *Reading Tests for Secondary Grades.* Newark, Del.: International Reading Association, 1972.

BORMUTH, JOHN R. "Cloze Tests As Measures of Readability." Unpublished Doctoral Dissertation. Indiana University, 1962.

BUROS, OSCAR K. *The Seventh Mental Measurements Yearbook.* Highland Park, N.J.: Gryphon Press, 1972.

BYRNE, MARY A., JOHN FELDHUSEN, and ROBERT B. KANE. "The Relationships Among Two Cloze Measurement Procedures and Divergent Thinking Abilities." *Reading Research Quarterly.* 6 (Spring 1971), 378–93.

DEUTSCH, CYNTHIA P. "Auditory Discrimination and Learning: Social Factors." *Merrill-Palmer Quarterly of Behavior and Development.* 10 (1964), 277–96.

FRIEDMAN, M. "The Use of the Cloze Procedure for Improving the Reading Comprehension of Foreign Students at the University of Florida." Unpublished Doctoral Dissertation, University of Florida, 1964.

FRY, EDWARD. "A Readability Formula That Saves Time." *Journal of Reading.* 11 (April 1968), 513–16.

____. "The Readability Graph Validated at Primary Levels." *Reading Teacher.* 22 (March, 1969).

HAFNER, LAWRENCE E. "Critical Problems in Improving Readability of Materials at the Secondary Level." In J. A. Figurel (Ed.) *Vistas in Reading.* Newark, Del.: International Reading Association, 1967. Pp. 116–19.

HAFNER, LAWRENCE E., and HAYDEN B. JOLLY. *Patterns of Teaching Reading in the Elementary School.* New York: Macmillan, 1972.

____. "Teaching the Nonreader to Read." In L. E. Hafner (Ed.). *Improving Reading in the Middle and Secondary School.* Second Edition. New York: Macmillan, 1974.

HEBB, DONALD. *Organization of Behavior.* New York: John Wiley and Sons, 1949.

HEBER, RICK, and H. GARBER. "An Experiment in the Prevention of Cultural-Familial Mental Retardation," *Proceedings Second Congress of the International Association for the Study of Mental Deficiency,* August 25–September 2, 1970.

JENKINSON, MARIAN E. "Selected Processes and Difficulties in Reading Comprehension." Unpublished Doctoral Dissertation, University of Chicago, 1957.

MC LAUGHLIN, HARRY G. "SMOG Grading—A New Readability Formula." *Journal of Reading.* 12 (1969), 639–46.

VERNON, PHILIP E. "Intelligence." In W. B. Dockrell (Ed.). *On Intelligence.* London: Methuen, 1970. Pp. 99–117.

WHIMBY, ARTHUR, and LINDA SHAW WHIMBY. *Intelligence Can Be Taught.* New York: Dutton, 1975.

Section Two

Developing and Organizing Meanings

Developing Concepts and Vocabulary Representing Concepts

Talk to anyone with an outstanding vocabulary and you will soon notice that he or she is well informed and able to use a variety of words with precision in order to communicate effectively. Words are facilitators of thinking and have power because they are labels for the concepts we use in thinking. We interact with others through the use of words and use words as the "chief vehicle of all learning, in school and out" (Hafner and Jolly, 1972).

Hafner, Weaver, and Powell (1970) at the elementary level and Davis (1968) at the secondary level have shown word knowledge to be the most important factor in reading comprehension. Inherent in a deep and broad vocabulary is a knowledge of relationships among ideas and the reasoning power that enables one to acquire concepts and associated vocabulary.

Of course, difficult concepts can be expressed in "easy" as well as in "difficult" words. Easy concepts can also be formulated in unusual words. I would like to illustrate this point in a contrived sentence and show additionally how a student with a poor vocabulary feels when reading news magazines, essays, and literary texts: "The refractory attitude would militate against a palliation of the opprobrium directed toward the chimerical lugubrious termagant."

I believe it was Piaget who contended that organization and intelligence can be equated. If that is true, it is possible to understand the high correlation between vocabulary knowledge and intelligence. In a real sense we improve aspects of our intelligence by building our vocabulary. Words help in organizing the world of experience, for words are used to refer to the things and ideas in our environment and the interrelations among them. Through words we can zero in on particular aspects of our environment and disregard other aspects. We can look at, analyze, and then synthesize them into new meaning-organization patterns.

Vygotsky (1962) tells us that a word denotes a group of referents. The word *cat* refers (in some contexts) to Persians, Siamese, Calico, Burmese, Manx, and the like. Thus, it is a category label for animals that share a number of distinctive features. Words also refer to or indicate *relations* (between, therefore), *actions* (read, play), *nonphysical entities* (democracy, justice), and *qualities* (beauty, big). Such words are, in effect, generalizations (Brown, 1958). In that sense the word *run* has several meanings depending on context and it can be said to refer to general categories of movement and operation.

The meanings of words, then, are made specific and clear by interverbal relations, by verbal context, and sometimes by graphic illustrations. Anglin (1970) states that the choice of referents for a word is narrowed and made specific by these relations in context. Irving Lorge once studied 576 of the more common English words and found 800 meanings for the word *run*.

CONCEPTS: CRITERIAL FEATURES AND HIERARCHICAL RELATIONSHIPS

An introduction to the study of concepts was given in the chapter on learning theory. In this section, I shall discuss concepts in greater depth.

Criterial Properties

The word *shirt* can be used generically if I avoid to some extent the properties of a particular shirt and refer to the *features* or criterial properties that shirts have in common. Note the features in Table 5-1 for shirts and trousers.

Table 5-1. Construction and Use Features for Shirts and Trousers

	made of fabric	sleeves	collar	front	back	fasteners	legs	cover part of body	decorative	practical	put arms through	put legs through
Shirts	X	X	X	X	X	X		X	X	X	X	
Trousers	X			X	X	X	X	X	X	X		X

Here you see not only the criterial features for shirts and trousers, but also their common features. The category label for the common features of shirts and trousers is clothing. Clothing is the *superordinate* of shirts and trousers in this scheme.

Hierarchical Relationships

My recent unpublished analysis of items on a reading test shows that knowledge of a large number of hierarchical relationships in the text and in the test

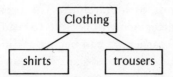

items is called for in order to answer correctly the reading test items. Expansion of the incipient hierarchy both "upward" to higher levels of abstraction and "downward" to less abstract (more concrete) levels might yield

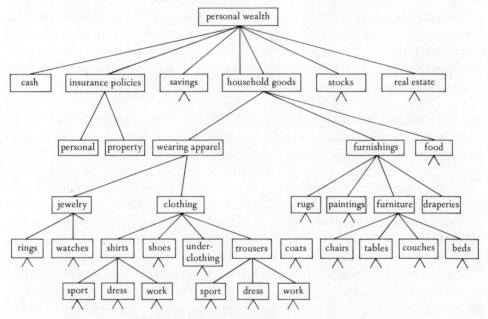

Figure 5-1. Hierarchy of Personal Wealth

Note that a shirt is *clothing,* clothing is *wearing apparel*, wearing apparel is *household goods,* and household goods is an aspect of *personal wealth*. The other categories added do not exhaust the possibilities and could have been approached in somewhat different ways. Going down the ladder from shirts, one could classify them first by color and then by use or by type of fabric, then color and the like.

Anglin (1970) has pointed out that such hierarchically organized features are redundant. In our hierarchy, for example, if personal wealth is clothing, it is of necessity wearing apparel, household goods, and so forth. If two words, such as *shirts* and *trousers,* "share a given feature in a nest they will necessarily share all higher order features within that nest." This means that if a person really understands the concept *personal wealth*, he or she will know how to delineate its subcategories. As concepts and relationships are learned, they can be added to a meaning hierarchy such as that in Figure 5-1. They should be added *as* they are learned. Ability to read and comprehend depends on a functional grasp of many similar kinds of hierarchies. The broader and deeper the hierachies one possesses the better one will be able to read.

We learn to learn and the earlier we can begin building our concept-vocabulary hierarchy the better we can use it to organize, acquire, and retain information. As we listen and read, we rechunk material and process it by relating it to our hierarchical organization. This may be done by some kind of intermediate step such as reducing complex sentences to simpler sentences.

Short- and Long-Term Memory. Bever (1968) points out that short-term memory of semantic information is aided by reducing "sentential material to simple declarative sentences." Clark and Clark (1967) adduce evidence that people process information in such a way that main features of a sentence are remembered by combining the semantic information. A person who needs to reproduce (encode) the information at a later time can then use new syntactic structures. Deese (1970) notes that "meaning or semantic information is not bound to the particular syntactic form in which it may occur on some particular occasion." After all, we can remember *not ugly* as *pretty*. And "In Tokyo riding the subway system is a memorable occasion. The trains are crowded with friendly people who smile a lot and generally seem to be quite happy," can be recalled and mapped as "Riding the subway trains in Tokyo was really something. The trains were crowded but the people were happy and friendly."

When we paraphrase material we can use our hierarchical organization and select superordinates to represent several "detailed" pieces of information. At other times our memory might be aided by selecting more concrete words, subordinates if you will, in order to aid memory; we can then map these onto a surface structure (spoken or written sentences) at various levels of abstraction.

What we retain in long-term memory, then, is the semantic component. When we are forced to recall something, we use the semantic component (verbal information) to some extent to fashion the structure of our sentences (Deese, 1970). Hierarchical organization provides a good model for organizing and remembering information, because it breaks "the informational bottleneck" of an otherwise limited memory by characteristically organizing or grouping information coming to us—the input sequence—into units or chunks (Miller 1956a, 1956b).

We remember information as chunks in hierarchies rather than in sentences that require some kind of syntactic arrangement. When we recall the information and transmit it, we encode it in appropriate syntactic form in order to develop sentences. Chomsky might say that we get the semantic content from deep structure and map it onto a surface structure.

CONCEPT-VOCABULARY GROWTH IS A GENERALIZATION PROCESS

Anglin (1970) has adduced evidence for viewing concept-vocabulary growth as a generalization process in which the child first appreciates the similarity among small groups of words and only later sees the similarity among increasingly broad classes. For example, at first the child sees that roses and tulips are *flowers*, collies and poodles are *dogs*, oaks and elms are *trees*. Later the child might realize that the objects classed as flowers are similar to the objects classed as trees in that both exhibit the criterial features of the concept labeled *plants*. Later still the child might form even more general concepts of *living things*, *objects,* and finally *entities*, which would apply to most nouns. The development of other parts of speech proceeds in a similar fashion.

Of course, generalization and differentiation processes are both involved in lexical growth. To generalize in the sense we have been discussing implies a previous differentiation of features. In order to see that a rose and a tulip are similar (both flowers) one must ignore the fact that they are different in such dimensions as fragrance and leaves.

Growth of Word Meaning

The growth of word meaning can be studied in several ways. One way is to study the similar and different ways that children and adults classify words in a conceptual hierarchy. One method of classifying words is the *sorting* method. The subjects are given a set of cards with a word and a definition of the word on each card. The subjects are then asked to sort the words on the basis of similarity of meaning.

Miller (1969a) had subjects sort 48 common nouns. The adult subjects grouped words by ignoring the features that differentiate the words and by paying attention to the features that the words share. The results seem to be consistent with the hierarchical model of organizing words as well as with the generalization hypothesis.

In order to replicate the basic findings, a different task—the *free recall* task— was used. Bousfield (1953), a pioneer in the use of free recall, presented subjects with a list of 60 random words drawn from four categories. Immediately after the presentation, the subjects were asked to recall as many words as they could. The subjects tended to group words; for example, they might recall *celery, spinach,* and *carrots* as a group. Bousfield thought the lexical items activated superordinates. *Celery* and *spinach*, though not in serial order on the list, activated the superordinate *vegetable,* so in recall these words were grouped.

Bower, et al. (1969) attempted to determine adults' ability to use structural relations among words in recalling words. An experimental group of subjects was presented with a number of words that were neatly slotted into their places in a visually displayed hierarchy of the words involved. The control group also had the words in a visual display but in a scrambled order. After studying the words, the subjects were asked to recall items. The subjects who had the structured material recalled two to three times as many words as the people who had the scrambled material.

From these studies and ones by Miller (1956), Mandler (1968), and Tulving (1968) one can determine that the subjects were *active* participants who have a knowledge of the relations among words and of language as a system and who organize the input in terms of this knowledge.

Another method of studying growth in meaning is the *free association* task. A word is spoken and a person is asked to say the first thing that comes to mind. Children tend to give syntagmatic responses; a child might respond to *girl* with *fall*. As people get older they tend to give hierarchical relationships; that is, an adult might respond to *boy* with an opposite (*girl*) or a superordinate (*child*). These hierarchical relationships are known as paradigmatic relationships.

ANGLIN'S STUDIES OF THE GENERALIZATION HYPOTHESIS[1]

Anglin (1970) conducted several studies to test the generalization hypothesis. He used 20 words: 6 nouns, 4 prepositions, 5 verbs, and 5 adjectives. As an example of how he conceptualized the relations among the words, the nouns and their relations are shown below:

Idea can be classed only as *entity*, but all the words below idea are entities. A given word, such as *horse*, falls into the category *animal*, but also under all the categories above it.

A concrete grouping would be for a person to group *boy* and *girl* A very abstract grouping would be *boy* and *idea*—both entities. An immature grouping would be *girl–grow*. A likely development in the progression from the child's development to the adult's development in classifying words is shown in Table 5–2.

Table 5–2. Concrete-Abstract Gradient

Words Classified Together	Relationships in Various Tasks		
	Recall-Sort	Free Association	Provide Label for the Relationship
1. girl–grow		syntagmatic	predication
2. banana—peach	fruit	paradigmatic	fruit
3. boy–girl	children	paradigmatic	children
4. banana—milk	food	paradigmatic	food
5. banana—milk—water–air	organic	———————	support life, organic

---

[1] The material in this section is somewhat difficult. It may be treated as an Advanced Topic.

Number one is also redolent of the *syntagmatic* relationship in free association in which an immature person might respond to *girl* with the word *grow*. Then as he or she matures the individual might respond to *girl* with *boy*, a *paradigmatic* or hierarchical relationship.

Support for the Generalization Hypothesis

The main findings of the sorting, free recall, and free association experiments support the generalization hypothesis. Although the applications are not always readily apparent, the findings are included for the benefit of the serious student:

The Original Sorting Study   (Anglin)

1. Children's clusters are often thematic: children might group (a) *eat* and *apple* or (b) *needle, suffer, doctor,* and *weep*.

2. Conversely, children tend to ignore form class distinctions; that is, they do not group words by part of speech.

3. Children's clusters are more *syntagmatic* than those of adults.

4. Relatively concrete words such as *apple* and *cheese* were paired paradigmatically almost as much by children as by adults. This also holds true for the relatively specific opposites such as *hard* and *soft* and *quickly* and *slowly*.

5. On such concrete tasks as those in 4 children did almost as well as adults, but on words that were abstractly related adults did better than children.

The First Sorting Experiment

6. The clustering of two words decreases with the level of abstractness that seems to bind them, that is, adults clustered *boy* and *girl* 98 per cent of the time; *boy* and *idea*, 18 per cent of the time.

7. Adults often cluster concrete words, but seldom cluster words in which the relations are thought to be abstract (correlate of 5).

8. The basis for clustering seems to be shared features.

The Second Sorting Experiment

9. The tendency to group words from different parts of speech such as *girl* and *cry* and *white* and *flower* decreases systematically with age. (This tendency supports the generalization hypothesis.)

10. Abstract notions are difficult for children to master. The more abstract the relations are between words—*boy–chair, boy–idea* (abstract) compared to *boy–girl* (concrete)—the less often will children cluster them. (Supports the generalization hypothesis.)

11. There is a tendency for adults to group words by part of speech more often than children do. Children do not seem to understand the concept of parts of speech. (This tendency supports the generalization hypothesis.)

The Free Recall Study

12. Adults' clusters are more paradigmatic than those of children. Probably the organization into paradigmatic clusters in the free recall task is done on the basis of shared features. (cf. 8.)

13. The more general the relation between words the more the curves (representing percentage clustered) of adults diverge from those of children. (This divergence supports the generalization hypothesis.)

The Hierarchically Organized Study Materials Experiment   (Bower)

14. When adults are given material that is organized spatially to conform to hierarchical relations among words, the recall of adults seems to be enhanced, whereas the recall of children in grades 3–4 is hardly benefited at all by such relations.

15. (Expanding on 14) Children from grades 3–4 benefited very little from study material showing the hierarchical relations among words relative to the scrambled material.

The Bruner–Olver Experiment

16. An adult's ability to produce predicates (superordinates) that show the relation binding a pair of words decreases with the generality of the relations among words.

17. A child can generate predicates for words bound by a concrete relation almost as well as an adult can.

18. A child does not do nearly so well as an adult at generating predicates for words which are related in an abstract manner.

FALLACIES IN VOCABULARY DEVELOPMENT

"A Given Word Has One Meaning"

One does not teach the meaning of a word; a meaning of a word is derived from its context: different contexts, different meanings. McDonald (1964) correctly points out that "words serve as stimuli to call up a category of meanings, the appropriate one of which must be selected by the individual in accord with the context."

Note, for example, how the meaning of the word *punch* varies in the following contexts:

1. Dempsey gave Firpo a punch in the mouth.
2. Did you read the article on marriage in the latest issue of Punch?
3. I would like to have the recipe for that punch.

In asking for punch I'd hate to have someone confuse the meaning of punch in sentence three with its meaning in sentence one.

Teachers are not only responsible for teaching students the various meanings of words, but also for teaching them to be alert to the multiple meanings of words.

"The Reader Must Understand Each Word in the Text He Is Reading"

McDonald (1964) claims the above statement is a fallacy about vocabulary development. Although I tend to agree that a person who reads widely could not possibly know every word, I would not like to see this idea become an excuse for inundating students with material that is too difficult for them. Nor would I like to see students neglect the habit of using the context of a word in conjunction with the dictionary in developing the meanings of words in reading. Improper use of a dictionary and overdependence on it are not acceptable practices. If a person is reading such difficult material that the flow of thought is broken by the number of unfamiliar words, or by having to look them up, then that person should probably be reading easier material.

"Roots and Affixes Are Efficient Aids in Vocabulary Learning"

In one method of teaching vocabulary the student is taught the meanings for the most common Latin and Greek affixes and roots that occur in English. The student is then supposed to analyze the various affixes and the roots in words and synthesize the meaning of any given word.

Verbs in Greek and Latin had many variant meanings acquired during the long developmental history of those languages. Therefore, a root may have as many as twenty possible meanings. Also, the force of the prefix may have been lost someplace along the way (McDonald, 1964).

Research in vocabulary teaching at the seventh-grade level by Jenkins (1957) shows that the study of roots and affixes was not nearly so good an approach as was the use of word cards in which the meanings were studied in context followed by class discussions of the meanings of the words. A lively discussion is generally a good way to clarify meanings and enhance the retention of the meanings.

"Wide Reading Is a Guaranteed Means of Building Vocabulary"

Some individuals who I am sure have read widely do *not* have top-notch vocabularies; others do. The difference in level of vocabulary acquisition is probably related to the individual's having or not having: (1) high intelligence, (2) vocabulary conscience, (3) vocabulary consciousness, (4) the habit of using the new words he encounters, (5) the opportunity to discuss the new words, and so forth.

Sachs (1943) studied 416 college freshmen in order to determine the extent of their meaning vocabularies. He concluded that the reading method of improving vocabulary has some real limitations. McCracken (1971) discussed a program of *Sustained Silent Reading* (SSR) directed by Floyd Davis in the Seattle Schools. Based initially on six special rules and 25 minutes per day of sustained reading, the program adheres rigidly to the six rules for a month and then variations can be introduced. There were no hard data about improving vocabulary or comprehension, but reports from hundreds of classrooms produced thousands of positive testimonials. Levine (1972) has provided a convincing *apologia* for quantity reading.

"Quickie Vocabulary Courses Erase Long-standing Vocabulary Deficiencies"

Many years of teaching reading improvement courses at various educational levels have convinced me that *small* gains can be made on standardized vocabulary tests during a ten-week period. Since each word on a vocabulary test represents many hundreds of words, raising the grade-level equivalent appreciably in an "honest" course is most difficult. What I am trying to say is that long-standing vocabulary deficiencies—serious deficiencies of thousands of words—cannot be erased in a quarter or a semester. This is especially true if you are thinking about these words becoming a part of an individual's working vocabulary.

THE RESPONSIBILITY FOR TEACHING VOCABULARY

Middle school teachers must make a concerted effort, in cooperation with the home wherever possible, to study the capacities, achievements, and weaknesses of their students as well as their own commitments in preparation for embarking on a full-scale, long-term effort to improve the vocabularies of their students. Nor can secondary teachers be blasé about the matter. They, too, have a responsibility for the vocabulary development of their students. This development should be a result of an ongoing schoolwide effort. Lack of an all-out effort by the school does not excuse the individual teacher from doing his or her best to help students acquire a good vocabulary.

PRINCIPLES OF TEACHING VOCABULARY

Vocabulary development involves more than setting up an association between a known word and an unknown word. Meanings develop over a period of time and must be rooted in a number of contexts. Furthermore, a good teacher will constantly work with students to help them develop proper *diction*, that is choose the correct words to convey ideas.

The following guidelines, assiduously and intelligently applied, should help the teacher develop a first-rate, perhaps in some instances nonpareil, vocabulary program.

Create a Good Climate for Learning Words

Show Your Love of Words. The teacher who is alive to the world of words and ideas will strive to use the appropriate word, the fresh, alive phrase. Such a teacher will not be afraid to interject unusual words into speech and writing. Many of these words will be enountered by the young reader in the future, and if the student does not have the opportunity to use them, they will serve as a barrier to understanding and may result in the student's turning away from reading more challenging works. The teacher should also show a love for word play and figurative language. Above all, the teacher will be seen reading a variety of paperbacks and will stand ready to share and discuss ideas with students and colleagues.

Use a Variety of Methods.   One or two methods do not constitute a variety. As good as some methods are, they can become tiresome if overdone. Once a person has learned a number of methods he or she can select the ones that facilitate learning.

Use Positive Reinforcement.   When a student uses a word that you have introduced or that he or she has come across in reading, show your appreciation by nodding, smiling, or using the word in your conversations with him or her and your discussions with the class. A really tangible way to indicate you appreciate nascent vocabulary is to let ability to use new words in discussions and written work contribute positively to students' grades.

Let Students Study Words That Interest Them.   Soon after I started a vocabulary program with her, my fifth grade daughter came up with the word, *tabard*. I have not found it to be as useful as she has; neither do I find that I can use it as facilely as she can. Let students just look up unusual words to start with and then guide them into interesting reading material that contains some of the unusual words as well as general vocabulary items in a variety of materials that interest them. Finding the word in context will enable them to use the words with precision.

Create a Vocabulary Consciousness and Conscience.   One method I have used to create a vocabulary *consciousness* in secondary school students is to bring to class copies of the morning newspaper and either premark the front page by circling unusual words or let the students mark the front page. The next step is to talk about the words. Did they know that there were so many words they did not know? What are they going to do about them? Let us figure out what some of the words mean.

My self-concept regarding words is this: I feel that I am the sort of person who should know just about all the general vocabulary words in the English language. I am realistic enough to know that I probably will not succeed, but new and unusual words are a challenge to me and I must come to grips with them. I have a highly developed *conscience* about learning words.

What about Johnny, who does not feel that he should know so many words? Also, he may really know a lot of words and not be aware of the discrepancy between his store of words and that of someone with a truly outstanding vocabulary. Then his conscience would not bother him because he is convinced that he has reached the zenith of vocabulary knowledge. June, being aware of having a mediocre vocabulary, may feel she is not bright enough to learn more words when in fact she is. A third person may scoff at the person with an excellent vocabulary, point out personality idiosyncrasies and be glad that he or she has a good working vocabulary as well as a host of good personality traits.

The point is that we learn what we intend to learn and that many people who do not intend to learn vocabulary will not do a very good job of it. This is not to say that there is no such thing as incidental learning, but those individuals who do not like vocabulary may also be the ones who are not reading enough to come across words incidentally.

Root Vocabulary Development in Concept Development

A person who uses words without knowing their meaning engages in verbalism. Verbalism has humorous facets but also serious aspects. A political candidate who uses empty phrases may fail to be elected if the voters are intellectually sophisticated. However, if they are not, they may elect someone who is stupid or cunning or some combination of those two and possibly more traits.

I suppose there is always the danger of any given person engaging in verbalism if he or she gets too far afield in an area outside his or her competence. In fact, one only need pick up the daily newspaper to read about someone who excels in a particular field and who essays to pontificate in some other fields: actors who are instant experts in the fields of government or finance, bankers who are curriculum experts for the public schools, and accountants who develop new principles of hermeneutics for theologians. Let these self-proclaimed experts study these second fields thoroughly before spouting eternal truths. After all, the only real pansophists are the reading specialists, right?

Develop Vocabulary in Oral and Written Language Contexts

Illustrate Meanings. If you wanted to illustrate what is meant by the word *petulance* you could say, "The legislature exhibited *petulance* when the group of teachers asked for both cost of living and merit pay increases." Or, "She did not need to exhibit such *petulance*. This is only the third year in a row that I got the blue ribbon and she got the red ribbon for rhubarb pies." Since various people have different attitudes about legislatures and pay increases, it can be seen that a given context can evoke different meanings. One probably needs to use a number of illustrations, give the synonyms of the word in question, and discuss the meanings.

Make Words Interesting. Some people will think the illustrations for *petulance* were interesting (maybe even fantastic). If there is a choice of making them interesting or dull, which would you choose? What does *milquetoast* mean? These illustrations might be classified as interesting (to teachers). "The teachers union leadership was anything but a group of *milquetoasts*; these leaders fought vigorously for the improvement of working conditions and for better pay." "Had Samuel Adams been a *milquetoast* we might still be flying the Union Jack."

Increase Chances Words Will Be Remembered and Used. The person who wants to make a word his or her own will use it often in appropriate language contexts. Vocabulary work that is not done in language contexts is likely to be *nugatory*. Consider the social studies teacher and the class who wants to learn the meaning of this word and be able to use it. You might say, "Well, the word itself is *nugatory*; I would not give you a dime for it." But the word *nugatory* can be used in reference to the value of a continental dollar, a confederate dollar in 1866, or a dollar today for that matter. Or, "After the 1929 stock market crash, many stocks were *nugatory*." You might give some kind of credit for using the word correctly in oral recitation or in written work. Positive reinforcement or reward might bring *nugatory* out of the *nugatory* class into the class of worth or merit.

A Key Strategy: Jenkins' Study. Jenkins (1957) experimented with five seventh-grade classes to discover the better methods of developing vocabulary. Which were the two better methods? Individual word study—using dictionary and index cards (containing word, pronunciations, meanings, and the words in sentence contexts)—plus discussion ranked first, and study of synonyms, antonyms, and word lists ranked second.

Discussion of Experiences Is a Basic Strategy for Vocabulary Development

Real Experiences. One should make a list of the kinds of real experiences that one's students are likely to have during the year. Also, keep in touch with upcoming events of interest through newspapers, radio and television, and brochures and handbills. Try to visit as many of these events as you can. Be careful to guide and stimulate the discussion and not take off in a soliloquy or monologue. If you do so, you may find yourself the focus for obloquy. Some of the real experiences that students may have in common are

1. Rose Bowl, Cotton Bowl, Sugar Bowl, Orange Bowl, etc. Parades.
2. Calgary Stampede.
3. Darlington 500.
4. Milwaukee Circus Parade.
5. Science fairs.
6. Springtime Tallahassee.
7. Rebuilding or repairing an automobile.
8. Centennial and bicentennial celebrations.
9. Billy Graham Crusade.
10. County Fair, State Fair, World's Fair.
11. Tour of naval ship: U. S. S. Alabama in Mobile, U. S. S. North Carolina in Wilmington, or active ships docked in ports such as Bremerton, Norfolk, Brooklyn, Philadelphia, Jacksonville, Honolulu, San Diego, and so forth.
12. Music Festival.
13. Tutoring Experience.
14. Boy Scout and Girl Scout Projects.
15. Future Farmers of America Projects.

Vicarious experiences relate to reading or watching or listening to a record of experiences. Not only can people engage in experiences such as the above, they can also partake of those experiences vicariously. Some good sources of vicarious experiences are

1. *Print:* newspapers, *National Geographic, Reader's Digest, Boy's Life, Seventeen,* brochures, *Southern Living, Popular Mechanix, Mechanix Illustrated, Christianity Today,* mail-order catalogues, encyclopedias, books and so forth.
2. *Film, T-V:* Movies, filmstrips, slides, television, video cassettes . . .
   a. Locally produced documentaries, displays, lessons . . .

   b. Commercially produced documentaries, displays, lessons, travelogues
      . . . (see catalogues of publishers) and various guides to free and in-
      expensive AV materials.
 3. *Audio:* Radio, records, audio (tapes) cassettes

STRATEGIES FOR TEACHING VOCABULARY

If vocabulary learning is left to chance, that chance will not be very successful
in developing an exquisite vocabulary. (You cannot fool Mother Nature, and
Father Chance can trick you.) You can teach quite directly by setting up
exercises, games, and techniques. You can also teach in a somewhat more
oblique, but not laissez faire, manner by using certain ongoing strategies we
have discussed. In this section I provide some tactics—patterns, exercises, and
games—that I find useful in working with middle and secondary school students.

Vocabulary Cards, Dictionaries, and Booklets

Vocabulary Cards. In using vocabulary cards to study word meanings one has
a flexible, personal, meaningful tool. A vocabulary card should contain the
word, its *phonic respelling*, one or more *meanings*, a *synonym* where possible,
the *source sentence* or sentences in which the word was found, and (on the
back side of the card) the sentences the learner makes up, *original sentences,*
to show that he or she understands the meaning(s) of the word. Note the
example:

(Front side of the card)

synonym for meaning 1	phonic respelling in parentheses
	bagatelle (bag′ ə tel)
definitions	1. a trifle: something that is not very important, not much value 2. a short musical composition
source sentence	1. The Americans paid off the Indians with one bagatelle after another.
source sentence	2. Although bagatelles are short pieces of music, they are nevertheless often quite pretty.

(Back side of the card)

1. I thought the gift was precious, but she just considered
   it a bagatelle.

2. It did not take her too long to perform the two Beethoven piano bagatelles.

It is most important for the student to devise original sentences for the word. If the student does something meaningful with the word, he or she will have a two-way investment in the word: the student will invest it with meaning and will invest time in it. One does not forget that kind of investment! And that kind of investment pays off.

Although the first word had several meanings, the following kind of word card might be a more common one: one word, one basic meaning:

(Front)

---

babbitt   (bab' it)

    A self-satisfied conventional person who is interested mainly in business and social success and who cares very little for cultural values, *philistine*.

1. It is the babbits of this world who are so eager to strike the musical and graphical arts from the school curriculum.
2. He was playing Babbitt to perfection as he paraphrased Pinckney: "Millions for defense but not one cent for the symphony orchestra."

(Back)

---

1. He was such a babbitt that he thought that the three B's were . . . . rather than Bach, Beethoven, and Brahms.
2. His Babbittry was never so evident as when he thought it was a compliment to be called the Goliath of the country club set.*

---

*Cue: Remember Goliath's nationality and size.

Dictionaries. Through the efforts of a number of students one can build an illustrated, multicontext dictionary. Whenever a student comes across a word to enter in the dictionary, he or she writes it in the upper left-hand corner of a 3 X 5 index card, the sentence in which the word was found and a synonym for the word. The words are filed alphabetically in a card file. One can do a dictionary page whenever there are enough illustrative sentences on the cards. If a word has more than one meaning, additional pages for the word can be made up. The dictionary will differ from a word card in that pictures and/or drawings can be made for pictorial illustrations.

Synonym Booklet. In this fun technique one selects a word or phrase and then lists synonyms: The synonyms should always be in context in order to develop the meaning and to bring out the color. A few illustrations:

1. Sports
   a. make a basket: Williams made a basket.
      (1) Jones stuffed it in the hoop.
      (2) He made a quick bucket on a turn-around shot.

      (3) The ball was <u>canned</u> from twenty feet out.

      (4) It was good for a <u>two pointer</u>.

   b. <u>home run</u>: He hit a <u>home run.</u>

      (1) Aaron hammered more <u>round trippers</u> than any baseball player.

      (2) Allen's shot against the screen wound up being a <u>four bagger</u>.

      (3) Ruth hit 714 <u>circuit clouts</u> in his career.

2. <u>General</u>

   a. <u>express</u>: I would like to <u>express</u> my thoughts on the subject.

      (1) She is not diffident about <u>voicing</u> her opinion on any matter that may come up.

      (2) He was so overwhelmed by the unexpected compliment that he could not <u>utter</u> a single word.

      (3) You can be sure that they will <u>air</u> their differences.

   b. <u>vituperated</u>: He <u>vituperated</u> from his rocking chair the vices of youth.

      (1) They <u>reviled</u> the man who had attacked the two girls.

      (2) Old Jones got a <u>tongue-lashing</u> from his wife when he came in at two o'clock in the morning.

      (3) The poor fellow gets <u>jawed</u> by his boss everytime he runs out of gas.

Special Contexts: Newspapers, Books, and Catalogues

Newspapers. One technique that is hard to beat for interest, currentness, and meaningfulness is that of bringing a morning newspaper to class and studying selected words in context. It is best for each person in the class or group to have a copy of the paper.

Distribute the newspapers and ask the students to mark a given page of the paper by drawing a line with a pen under each word that they do not understand. (Modify according to the ability of the class.) Then discuss the meanings in light of the headlines and the context of the story or article. An interesting follow-up is to select (or have the students select) certain words for further study, possibly to find their places on vocabulary cards or in a group dictionary.

Books. A technique that I first devised when tutoring some middle school students whose teachers insisted they read social studies texts that were too difficult for them is the following:

1. Skim the text, preferably with the student, and select words that he or she cannot pronounce and/or does not know the meaning of.

2. Place in sequence the unknown words in column one.

3. For each word develop a sentence similar to the one in the text or use the text sentence.

4. Go over each word and sentence, note problems, and rectify them through helping the student use whatever phonic, structural, and context cues that are applicable.

5. Allow the student to take the study sheet home in order to study it further.

This activity should be done before the text section is assigned or in conjunction with an assignment. Since students should be working on texts that are on their readability level one would hope that not too many words have to be developed for each assignment. Also, this activity is particularly valuable for those students who, for whatever reason, are not adept in word identification skills.

Catalogues. A nonpareil source of interesting information and vicarious experience and vocabulary is the mail-order catalogue. If the depression years had any advantage over the affluence of today with respect to reading materials it must lie in the sedulous manner that rural and small-town youth read mail-order catalogues. It was a source for the development of concepts, vocabulary, and reading skills. We first read pictures, then made associations between words and pictures that were obviously associated, and finally made associations between the printed descriptions and the pictorial descriptions.

Reading catalogues also affords one an opportunity to compute the total cost of a fantasy order or a real order. One can try to determine which trombone, which mackinaw, which basketball, or which blouse, is the best value. Finally, one can learn to use the index in order to locate items in a catalogue.

It is interesting to note that we could seldom afford to buy the fun things from the catalogues—although our parents bought necessary things such as clothing and some bagatelle now and then. Yet the avidity with which we attacked the reading material in the catalogue was not notably diminished.

One activity that might help students to read catalogues is to have students mark with a red pencil those items that they would like to read about. They could then underline in red the words that caused them difficulty. These words could be printed and recorded on *Language Master* cards, first the word and then the phrase containing the word. (Some *Language Master* cards can hold an entire sentence.) A series of entries can be recorded on tape cassette. One also writes the page number of the catalogue on each card. The cards can be filed by page number.

Word Relationships: Superordinates, Coordinates, Subordinates, Contrasts, etc.

Meaning is a relationship between *referent* (thing or idea) and a *reference* (language referring to the referent) and between a *reference* and a *symbol* (sets of phonemes or sets of graphemes)(Ogden and Richards, 1923). In developing vocabulary in the schools one should use a particular context or semantic network and develop the relationships among the words in the context or network. Increasing the links among the words allows one to say more with them. Ten words from one context or semantic network allow more possibilities for meaningful associations or relationships that one word from each of ten different contexts. Furthermore, associated words are easier to remember. For any given word in our language the richness of associations will vary from person to person (Mackey, 1965).

I will show some of the kinds of relationships as they relate to one semantic network:

- *superordination* (industry—citrus) industry is the superordinate
- *coordination* (orange—apple) both are fruits
- *subordination* (citrus fruit—lemon) lemon is the subordinate
- *similarity* (writing advertisements—printing advertisements)
- *contrast* (sweet—sour)
- *part—whole* (seed—orange)
- *whole—part* (grove—tree)
- *predication* (tree—grows)
- *completion* (productive—season)
- *assonance* (cold—fold)

Note how these relationships, as well as the hierarchies of things and ideas discussed earlier in the chapter cut across the factors of word knowledge, reasoning, and seeing relationships—the three most important factors in reading. I posit this as an important insight into the nature of the reading process.

Paradigmatic and Syntagmatic Relationships. Note, also, the predication, completion, and assonance (above) are syntagmatic relationships, whereas the others are paradigmatic relationships. The latter relationships, paradigmatic, are more mature. Association studies in which stimulus words are given to a subject who responds with a word have shown that as a person gets older (grows up) his or her responses become more paradigmatic (Entwisle, 1966).

Bickley, Dinnan, and Bickley (1970) studied high IQ and low IQ adults using the P/S Language List and the *Otis Quick-Scoring Mental Maturity Test*. The high IQ subjects made significantly more paradigmatic responses than the low IQ group. One can predict, then, that among adults those who produce fewer than 50 per cent paradigmatic responses will do poorly on the Otis test.

On the P/S Language List, each subject is tested individually with the list. The directions are, "Give me the first word you think of when I say this word." Each subject is then given the 30 words, one at a time, and the examiner writes the response next to the stimulus word.

P/S Language List

in	life	keep	pay	mine
she	call	open	laugh	South
me	father	law	front	common
up	money	kind	short	pretty
over	city	run	poor	please
old	war	morning	happy	foreign

Furthermore, my own analysis of standardized reading tests shows that a person must know a large variety of paradigmatic relationships—hierarchical conceptual networks in depth and breadth—in order to score high on these reading tests as well as on mental aptitude tests such as the *Miller Analogies Test, Lorge-Thorndike Tests,* and the *Ohio State Psychological Test*.

It becomes apparent that teachers (and parents) must continually work at helping young people develop concepts, semantic networks, and language relationships if they are going to excel in reading comprehension. The next few sections deal with paradigmatic relationships: Opposites; Synonyms; Superordinates and Subordinates.

Opposites (Contrast Relationship). If one stops to think that all relationships have a spatial-quantitative dimension, it might become easier to teach opposite relationships. Opposites are actually a relative matter: Two opposites are at two different points along a spatial-quantitative continuum. Sometimes they are polar, but many times they are not:

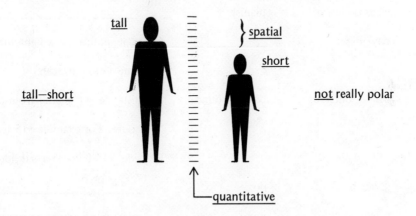

Tall-short is a relative matter, depending on one's frame of reference, or reference, or reference of frame! A height of 6′4¾″ is tall if the comparison group is 1,000 randomly selected American adult males. In that case, if one were to diagram the relationship, he or she could come up with polar opposites, 6′4¾″ versus about 5′2¼″. One could then speak of opposite, meaning the two ends of the distribution:

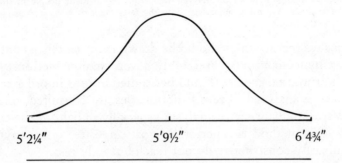

Tall and short in this continuum could be thought of as polar opposites. Some readers, however, are going to be 4′9″ and some 6′9″. The 4′9″ person may think the 5′2¼″ person is relatively tall. The 6′9″ person will not think of the 6′4¾″ person as tall. The kinds of drawings and comments above may serve as starters to bring out the idea of opposites involving spatial-quantitative relationships.

As an exercise develop the spatial-quantitative relationships for the following (it can be done). Complete the following:

Dimension	Specific Example	Spatial-Quantitative Scale
good—bad	pie	_____
poor—rich	in money	number of dollars
rich—poor	in spirit	_____
virtuoso—tyro	pianist	_____
day—night	_____	scale points on a light meter plus time (24-hour scale)
inside—outside	house (round)	distance (on plane) from center of house. For example +15 feet is outside, +14'8" or less is inside.
good—bad	dog	_____
bright—dull	mind	number of points on a general information test
kind—mean	teacher	_____
destitute—affluent*	_____	_____

* Not only do I use different words here than poor—rich but there is also a connotation—even denotation—that destitute not only means fewer, if any (quantitative) dollars, clothes, etc. but spatially the people may be further removed from the affluent people in the suburbs. This kind of analysis may bring objectivity into the assessment of areas such as competency, morality, and the like.

These opposites relationships should be drawn from sentence contexts and/or placed into sentence contexts. Preferably, given chapter sections, news stories and magazine or journal articles should be studied *in toto* in order to find opposites that may be analyzed. Even if dictionaries are consulted, one should do some of this spatial-quantitative analysis, especially in light of the conditions in the context. This method is superior to most opposites or antonym exercises, which, as ordinarily constructed, do not teach but only test.

Synonyms. As with antonyms or opposites, there are three basic sources of synonyms in the classroom—printed materials, people, and audio materials.

One activity that can be used to arouse sensitivity to synonyms and to varying connotations of synonyms is the following:

Search—Insert—Verify:

1. Select textual material—paragraph or more. Retype (doublespaced), duplicate, and distribute copies.

2. Students underline words that could have synonyms.

3. Students write a synonym (or two) for each designated word. If necessary, they may consult a dictionary, synonym dictionary, or thesaurus to see if the word has different connotations.

4. Have a brief group discussion of synonyms and their connotations. Decide which sentences retain their original meaning when a given synonym is substituted and which sentences would have meanings changed so as to change the original intended meaning.

5. Students may rewrite selections to give them divergent meanings.

Synonym Jamboree: Each of two teams is given a word. The team that comes up with the longest list of synonyms in a given time period is declared the winner. Discuss particular words.

Building Meaning Hierarchies. The present work contains much information about concept development and meaning hierarchies. Teachers and students in the content areas should devote much time to classifying phenomena and building hierarchies for bold graphic display in the classroom. Start with what people know and add to the hierarchies as concepts and their relationships are learned.

Below is a portion of a food hierarchy. Fruits, grains, and vegetables did not provide many problems in classifying. "Animal" food provided many problems as far as parallelism is concerned. Only the fruit part is included here. Fruits can be classified in many ways. Here they are classified by *design* and by *climate* (in which they are generally produced). The listings of fruit are representative rather than exhaustive.

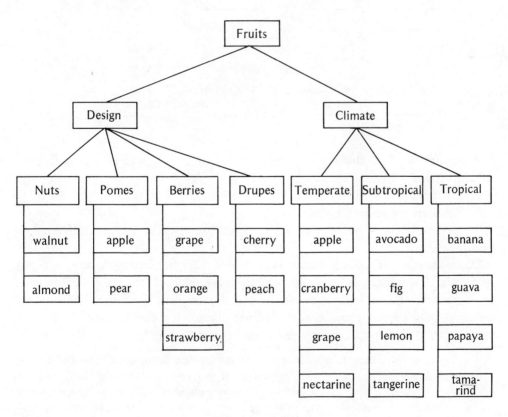

Classification: Add a Word

1. List several coordinates in a column; for example, chair, table, credenza.

2. List a different set of coordinates, followed by as many sets as you want to work with.

3. Have students provide further coordinates for each list.

4. Have students provide superordinates for each list; for example, the word *furniture* is the *superordinate* for chair, table, etc. The latter, you will remember, are coordinates of one another and subordinates of *furniture*.

5. The meanings of unknown words should be discussed and illustrated. The design of a fugue may be illustrated and the teacher, student, or outside consultant may play a fugue on the piano or organ. If the class has several musicians, they may, with the help of the music teacher or possibly on their own, present a fugue arranged for the instruments they play. This activity may be preceded by or followed by listening to records of fugues. (Failing all that, try for a sonatina.)

Furniture	_____	_____	_____
chair	chandelier	condenser	Tokyo
table	drapery rods	resistor	London
credenza	_____	transformer	Taipei
_____	_____		_____
_____		Cloth Material	_____
Boyle's	fugue	organdy	Tyndale
Charles'	sonata	gingham	Luther
Avogadro's	passacaglia	broadcloth	Scofield
_____	_____	_____	_____

A Variation: The above exercise can be made into a game requiring fluency of production:

1. List headings.

2. Students list subordinates.

3. A time limit may be set and competition may be on an individual or group basis.

Classification: of Coordinates. Provide, or have students provide, a group of words. The task is (1) to find words that are related, that are coordinates of one another, and arrange each set of coordinates into a column—six sets, six columns—and (2) to provide superordinate labels for the categories. For example, sort these words into six sets of categories.

> gnu, violin, chemist, kind, clarinet, mason, sympathetic, creek, sparrow, giraffe, president, tuba, sea, electrician, viola, river, platypus, glockenspiel, finch, senator, emu, trumpet, governor, suspicious, physician, plumber, wallaby, saxophone, superintendent of education, scarlet tanager, ocean, cheerful, oboe, koala bear, maracas.

You will notice that the categories may be labeled:

		Musical	Bodies of	Government	Personality
Occupations	Animals	Instruments	Water	Officials	Traits

The words within each category are *coordinates* of one another. They are *subordinates* of the categories of Animals, Personality Traits, and so forth.

Further inspection will reveal that each category can be divided into two or more categories. (Also, a given word may fit in more than one category.) Some of the subcategories are provided. Others will result as you apply your intelligence and divergent thinking abilities. (There are one or two problem cases.)

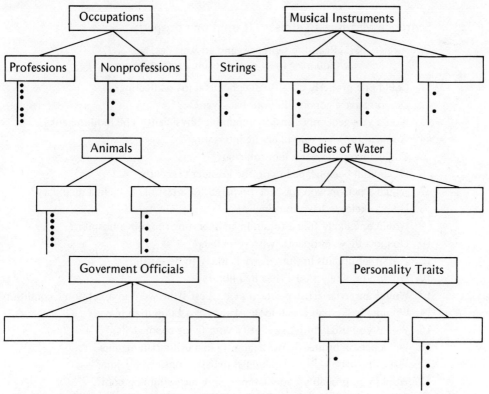

Sentence Meaning Exercise. This kind of study can be approached in a number of ways:

1. Read, Answer

    a. Distribute copies of the sentences.
    b. Students read each question and answer Yes, No, or ?.
    c. The sentences are discussed.

2. Read, Discuss, Answer, and Discuss

    a. Distribute copies of the sentences.
    b. Students work alone or in groups in answering the questions.
    c. They may consult reference works such as dictionaries and encyclopedias for facts and word meanings.
    d. The class discusses their findings as a group.

Sentence-Meaning Exercises, Follow-up Exercises, and Check Tests. One great problem with much vocabulary work is the lack of follow-up exercises, or enough application so that the words can be recalled and used with precision and facility and become part of one's working vocabulary. Follow-up exercises, activities, games, discussions, and the use of words by teachers and students in and out of class are great aids to solid vocabulary growth.

Following are examples of *sentence-meaning* exercises, follow-up exercises, and check tests. A basic set of directions that can be altered to fit the situation is provided for each exercise. The exercises are made difficult so that you the reader, can still be challenged by some of the sentences and thereby find them interesting. You may want to do these as exercises in your college reading methods class.

Sentence-Meaning Exercise: "Could one properly . . .?"

<u>Directions</u>:   1. Read the sentences and answer Yes, No, or ?.
                 2. You may (may not) consult a reference work.

1. Could one properly classify an <u>ephemeral</u> joy as fleeting?
2. Do you have a <u>gondola</u> in your back yard?
3. Would you generally consider reputable physicians to be <u>mountebanks</u>?
4. Would a <u>motley</u> group likely be interesting?
5. Could a woman wear a <u>mouton</u> coat?
6. Has <u>odium</u> been heaped upon the President recently?
7. Would a person who was well prepared for a test likely be in a <u>quandary</u>?
8. Does a skeleton have any <u>sinews</u>?
9. Would one likely find a <u>tocsin</u> in an operating room in a hospital?
10. Do most bicycles operate with <u>sprockets</u>?
11. Are street <u>urchins</u> in slum districts likely to be squalid?
12. Would you likely find a <u>rhea</u> in a library?
13. Would an aerial artist perform at his best if he were in a <u>catatonic</u> condition?
14. Would a basketball coach look askance at a <u>Lilliputian</u> player?
15. Would you use <u>lignite</u> to beautify your living room walls?
16. Will a person ordinarily use a <u>jalousie</u> in a utilitarian manner?
17. Were the historic Lincoln-Douglas debates considered <u>jejune</u>?
18. Would you probably enjoy <u>lamprey</u> in your swimming pool?
19. Would you expect <u>laminated</u> wood to be a single piece of wood?
20. Are executives likely to find themselves in a <u>maelstorm</u> on occasion?
21. Is Cher Bono a <u>fastidious</u> dresser?
22. Would an excuse be an <u>egress</u>?
23. Is a <u>palatial</u> abode commodious?
24. Would a person with <u>contraband</u> fear the port authorities?
25. Was Marie Antoinette <u>decapitated</u>?

Follow-up Exercise to Sentence-Meaning Exercise:
"Could one properly . . ?"

<u>Directions</u>: Write the correct word in each blank. Use a word from the original exercise, "Could one properly . . . ?"

1. He was caught with _____ flown in from Mexico.

2. The beautiful intaglio ring was the work of a _____ jeweler.

3 The muscles were attached to the frame by _____ .

4. Few people make favorable impressions by making _____ remarks.

5. A _____ condition is associated with a psychosis.

6. Paul Revere sounded the _____ on his famous ride.

7. The power of many people in high places is often _____ .

8. People who cannot back their boastful words with action are considered

   _____ .

9. Most palaces can be considered _____ , quite roomy.

10. _____ people are not gigantic in size.

11. She thought it was a seal fur, but it was _____ , from sheep.

12. It may be hard to determine whether _____ is peat or bituminous coal.

13. Being _____ makes it pretty hard to swallow.

14. He did not heap _____ upon the uniformed, only upon the lazy and unwilling.

15. One could be shocked by the improper use of a _____ knife.

16. She made her _____ gracefully, but she never returned.

17. (A) _____ will get you nowhere if you do not slant it correctly.

18. A _____ resembles an ostrich; however, it is not as large.

19. _____ are malapert youngsters.

20. Watergate was a _____ that ruined some careers.

21. He thought he was a big wheel, but his _____ was not engaged.

22. I like your pizza; I love your singing; but your _____ is far out— in the canal.

23. The _____ is one of a _____ group of pests in Lake Michigan. Does that leave you in a _____ ?

Vocabulary Check: Based on Sentence-Meaning Exercise: "Could one properly . . . ?"

Directions: Read each pair of words and determine whether the words are the same (synonym or superordinate-subordinate relationship), opposite, or neither of these. Indicate your answer with S, O, or N. Also explain what the word in the N pair is; note the examples:

Examples:

Word Pairs	Relationship	
A. house:building	S	
B. frigid:hot	O	
C. caparison:instrument	N	A caparison is an outfit. The queen was elegantly caparisoned on the day of her coronation.

1. hatred:odium ____

2. maelstrom:peace ____

3. lasting:ephemeral ____

4. urchin:capital ____

5. palatial:commodious ____

6. jejune:interesting ____

7. lamprey:animal ____

8. mountebank:charlatan ____

9. mechanism:sprocket ____

10. tocsin:evergreen ____

11. decapitated:joined ____

12. rhea:bird ____

13. sinews:ligaments ____

14. loot:contraband ____

15. catatonic:rigid ____

16. lignite:coal ____

17. fastidious:sloppy ____

18. boat:gondola ____

19. mouton:color ____

20. exit:egress ____

21. small:Lilliputian ____

22. quandary:sure ____

23. laminated:single ____

24. jalousie:decoration ____

25. motley:regular ____

Sentence-Meaning Exercise: "Was Sennacherib's . . . ?"

If you found the other exercises too insipid, this one might be a bit more challenging.

Directions: 1. Read the sentences and answer <u>Yes, No</u>, or <u>?</u>.

                2. You may consult reference works after the first time through.

1. Was Sennechacerib's army <u>decimated</u>?
2. Will we have a <u>crenulated</u> football team this year?
3. Has anyone ever called you <u>mavourneen</u>?
4. Do you like people who <u>pontificate</u>?
5. Do you have a <u>stentorian</u> voice?
6. Would you like for someone to <u>objurgate</u> you?
7. Were you a <u>wunderkind</u>?
8. Are you a <u>dreadnaught</u> on the playing fields?
9. Do you like for people to use <u>obscurantist</u> arguments against you?
10. Do you operate under anybody's <u>aegis</u>?
11. Are you generally <u>gauche</u> in social situations?
12. Are your feelings <u>infrangible</u>?
13. Do you have <u>regalia</u> in your closet?
14. Do you have a <u>refulgent</u> mind?
15. If you were in trouble, would you like to be <u>exonerated</u>?
16. Are women generally <u>espousers</u> of equal rights?
17. Would you be inclined to pull somebody's <u>legume</u>?
18. Have you ever seen a vulture engage in <u>necrophagia</u>?
19. Would you enjoy having <u>porcine</u> features?
20. Would you like to be known for <u>sciolism</u>?
21. Have people ever pronounced <u>maledictions</u> over you?
22. Do you have a <u>propensity</u> for taking vacations?
23. Do you sometimes feel like a <u>chrysalis</u>?
24. Are you a <u>habitue</u> of nocturnal festivals?
25. Have you brought you endeavors to a high degree of <u>fruition</u> this term?

SUMMARY

Words are facilitators of thinking and have power because they are labels for the concepts we use in thinking. Word knowledge should be the most important factor in reading comprehension; research shows this contention to be true. A word denotes a group of referents. In a real sense some words have different meanings depending on the context in which they are found.

Concepts are defined and pinpointed by criterial properties or features. A given concept such as *clothing* can be set into a meaning hierarchy. An aim of academic instruction should be to develop a large number of germane, meaningful hierarchies. The broader and deeper the hierarchies one possess the better one will be able to read since these meaning hierarchies are used to acquire, organize, and retain information.

Concept-vocabulary growth was explicated as a generalization process. The results of a number of studies were adduced as proof for the hypothesis.

The fallacies in vocabulary development were quickly dispatched. A really basic point is that vocabulary development is a long-term process, should be begun early, and carried out sedulously.

Principles for teaching vocabulary should be intelligently and assiduously applied. A particularly important point is that vocabulary development should be rooted in concept development. Another basic principle is that vocabulary should be developed in oral and written language contexts.

The strategies for teaching vocabulary are grounded in the above principles and feature meaningful instruction, much practice and discussion, and the development of individual vocabulary card packs, dictionaries, and booklets.

At various points in the book meaning hierarchies are discussed. A special discussion of word relationships is included in the chapter. Relative to these ideas is the idea of paradigmatic and syntagmatic relationships. The more mature individuals make more paradigmatic responses when presented the P/S Language List. They think and operate more in terms of meaning hierarchies and consequently obtain higher scores on intelligence and reading tests than individuals of the same age who are more syntagmatically oriented.

Examples of techniques for building meaning hierarchies are given in the chapter as are special techniques for developing vocabularies through sentence-meaning exercises. The latter can be planned and executed so that the much needed element of humor and fun can be included and capitalized on.

ACTIVITIES AND QUESTIONS
TO PROMOTE LEARNING AND APPLICATION

1. In what sense does one improve one's intelligence by improving one's vocabulary? What, in your estimation, is the best way to improve intelligence by improving vocabulary?
2. What does *democracy* mean to you? *Justice*? What problems do you encounter in trying to explain what such concepts mean? Discuss the explanations in class.
3. Did your "definition" of *justice* lean toward a law-and-order legalistic definition?
4. Develop criterial attributes for concepts in your content area. Of what value do you think such feature lists might be in concept teaching? Explain.
5. Develop a meaning hierarchy for an aspect of a content area of interest to you. Discuss portions of the hierarchy that appear to be difficult to teach. Why is this so?
6. Prepare a lesson or strategy that would help a person put information into long-term memory.
7. How can you apply the discussion on word meaning growth as a generalization process to vocabulary improvement?
8. Add examples that further illustrate the fallacies in vocabulary development.

9. Make a list of *incorrect* uses of words, for example, *diction* to mean enunciation; *tuition* to mean tuition fee, etc.
10. Explain why so many people do not use words with precision. Is a teacher doing students a favor by not having a first-class vocabulary development program?
11. Outline your plans for a self-improvement vocabulary program.
12. Outline your plans for vocabulary improvement program for your students.
13. Why should vocabulary development be rooted in concept development?
14. Develop vocabulary tests for a series of content chapters. For chapters A, B, and C give the tests when you complete work on the chapters. For chapters D, E, and F have the students use prestudy vocabulary worksheets following the procedure outlined in the text. What differences do you note on the vocabulary tests for chapters A, B, and C compared with those for D, E, and F?
15. Administer the P/S Language List to several good readers and several poor readers. What performance differences do you note. Explain differences in reading achievement in terms of differences in *P/S Language List* performance.
16. Write a *search—insert—verify* exercise for material of your choice and use it according to the directions in the text. Report on your experience.
17. Develop classification (meaning) hierarchies exercises and try them out on people who are majoring in the same content area that you are. Use them in game-like atmospheres.
18. Develop sentence-meaning exercises, appropriate follow-up exercises, and check tests for given sets of words. Use them in class.

SUGGESTED ADDITIONAL READINGS

BURMEISTER, LOU E. *Reading Strategies for Secondary School Teachers.* Reading, Mass.: Addison-Wesley, 1974, Chapter 6.

CRAWFORD, EARLE E. "Teaching Essential Reading Skills—Vocabulary." In Lawrence E. Hafner (1974, pp. 140–52).

DALE, EDGAR, and JOSEPH O'ROURKE. *Techniques of Teaching Vocabulary.* Palo Alto, California: Field Educational, 1971.

FREDERICK, NANCY and BARBARA C. PALMER. "Word Processing: Explaining and Implementing the Skills." In Lawrence E. Hafner (1974, pp. 152–59).

HAFNER, LAWRENCE E. (Ed.). *Improving Reading in Middle and Secondary Schools.* Second Edition. New York: Macmillan, 1974. Section 5.

HARRIS, ALBERT J., and EDWARD R. SIPAY. *How to Increase Reading Ability.* Sixth Edition. New York: David McKay, 1975. Chapter 16.

KAHLE, DAVID J. "Student-Centered Vocabulary." In Lawrence E. Hafner (1974, pp. 136–139.)

PETTY, WALTER, CURTIS P. HEROLD, and EARLINE STOLL. *The State of Knowledge About the Teaching of Vocabulary.* Champaign, Ill.: National Council of Teachers of English, 1968.

ROBINSON, H. ALAN. *Teaching Reading and Study Strategies.* Boston: Allyn and Bacon, 1975. Chapter 4.

SHEPHERD, DAVID L. *Comprehensive High School Reading Methods.* Columbus, Ohio: Charles E. Merrill, 1973. Chapter 3.

ZINTZ, MILES V. *The Reading Process.* Second Edition. Dubuque: Wm C. Brown, 1975. Chapter 11.

BIBLIOGRAPHY

ANGLIN, JEREMY M. *The Growth of Word Meaning.* Cambridge, Mass.: The M.I.T. Press, 1970.

BEVER, T. G. "Associations to Stimulus-Response Theories of Language." In T. R. Dixon And D. L. Horton (Eds.). *Verbal Behavior and General Behavior Theory.* Englewood Cliffs, N.J.: Prentice-Hall, 1968.

BICKLEY, A. C., JAMES A. DINNAN, and RACHEL BICKLEY. "Language Responses As a Predictor of Performance on Intelligence Tests." *Journal of Verbal Learning and Verbal Behavior. 8* (1969), 323–43.

BOUSFIELD, W. A. "The Occurrence of Clustering in the Recall of Randomly Arranged Associates." *Journal of General Psychology. 49* (1953), 229–40.

BROWN, ROGER. *Words and Things.* Glencoe, Ill.: Free Press, 1958.

CLARK, H. H., and E. V. CLARK. "Semantic Distinctions and Memory for Complex Sentences." *Quarterly Journal of Experimental Psychology. 20* (1968), 129–38.

DAVIS, FREDERICK B. "Research in Comprehension in Reading." *Reading Research Quarterly. 3* (4) (Summer 1968), 499–545.

DEESE, JAMES. *Psycholinguistics.* Boston: Allyn and Bacon, 1970.

ENTWISLE, D. "Form Class and Children's Word Associations." *Journal of Verbal Learning and Verbal Behavior. 5* (1966). 558–65.

HAFNER, LAWRENCE E., and HAYDEN B. JOLLY. *Patterns of Teaching Reading in the Elementary School.* New York: Macmillan, 1972.

_____ , WENDELL WEAVER, and KATHRYN POWELL. "Psychological and Perceptual Correlates of Reading Achievement Among Fourth Graders." *Journal of Reading Behavior. 2* (4) (Winter 1970), 281–90.

JENKINS, MARGUERITE. "Vocabulary Development: A Reading Experiment in Seventh Grade English." *Peabody Journal of Education. 19* (May 1942), 347–51.

LEVINE, ISIDORE. "Quantity Reading: An Introduction." *Journal of Reading. 15* (8) (May 1972), 576–83.

MACKEY, WILLIAM F. *Language Teaching Analysis.* Bloomington: Indiana University Press, 1965.

MANDLER, G. "Association and Organization: Facts, Fancies, and Theories." In T. R. Dixon and D. L. Horton (Eds.). *Verbal Behavior and General Behavior Theory.* Englewood Cliffs, N.J.: Prentice-Hall, 1968.

MCCRACKEN, ROBERT A. "Initiating Sustained Silent Reading." *Journal of Reading. 14* (8) (May 1971), 521–24, 582–83.

MCDONALD, ARTHUR S. "Vocabulary Development: Facts, Fallacies and Programs." In E. L. Thurston and L. E. Hafner (Eds.). *New Concepts in College-Adult Reading.* Milwaukee: National Reading Conference, 1964.

MILLER, GEORGE A. (a) "The Magical Number Seven Plus or Minus Two: Some Limits on Our Capacity for Processing Information." *Psychological Review. 63* (1956), 81–96. (b) "Human Memory and the Storage of Information." *IRE Transactions on Information Theory. 2* (1956), 129–37.

_____ . "A Psychological Method to Investigate Verbal Concepts." *Journal of Mathematical Psychology. 6* (1969), 169–191.

OGDEN, C. K., and I. A. RICHARDS. *The Meaning of Meaning.* London: Routledge and Kegan Paul, 1923.

SACHS, H. J. "The Reading Method of Acquiring Vocabulary." *Journal of Educational Research. 36* (1943), 457–64.

TULVING, E. "Theoretical Issues in Free Recall." In T. R. Dixon and D. L. Horton (Eds.). *Verbal Behavior and General Behavior Theory.* Englewood Cliffs, N.J.: Prentice-Hall, 1968.

VYGOTSKY, LEV S. *Thought and Language.* Cambridge, Mass.: The M.I.T. Press, 1962.

CHAPTER 6

Comprehending Explicitly and Implicitly Stated Meanings and Reading Critically

Language can be encoded in graphic forms such as pictograph and alphabet codes and decoded by the process called reading. Compared to radio and television, reading does have at least ten unique values or uses (Hafner, 1974). For example, in reading (1) time is allowed for reflection, (2) information is easily rechecked, and (3) sources can be compared readily. Such values can aid the comprehension of ideas.

Defining Comprehension

Comprehension is a familiar term and relates to a reader's ability to follow the pattern of thinking intended and structured in the author's writing. In this sense, comprehension is rooted in and synonymous with intelligence: the ability to make a thorough logical analysis of conceptual or cognitive relationships. Comprehension means to *grasp with*; the proficient reader grasps with, that is, understands, the meaning intended by the author. To the extent that one comprehends one reduces any cognitive uncertainty that one may have had prior to reading.

PROBLEMS IN COMPREHENDING THE TEXT

Comparing Good and Poor Readers

Helen K. Smith (1961) provided an invaluable service in comparing good and poor readers in grade twelve. Table 6-1 shows that good readers can read for stated purposes, whereas the poor readers do not. Good readers try to relate information to what I would call a cognitive structure—restructuring material, cataloguing details, and connecting details with something else—whereas the poor readers try to remember points in isolation.

Table 6-1. Comparisons of Good and Poor Readers in Grade 12

Factor	Good Readers	Poor Readers
Stating Purpose	stated it correctly	1/2 stated correctly
Reading for Stated Purpose	did	did not
Establishing Own Purposes	did	did not
Reasons for Rereading	• to find definite information • to place information in mind	because did not understand something

Proportion reading every word:
  reading for details
  reading for general impressions
	1/2
	1/3
		all
		all

Approach to organization of material when reading for details	• restructured material • catalogued details • connected detail with something else • fixed information in mind	tried to remember points in isolation
Review While Reading	frequently	seldom
When Reading for General Impressions	read for ideas	tried to remember details in isolation

Understanding Paragraph Structure

Williams and Stevens (1972) studied the ability of middle school and secondary school students to summarize the *main idea* and determine the *topic sentence* of paragraphs. Paragraphs for middle grade students were written at the fourth-grade level. The selections for the secondary students were written at the sixth-grade level. Each student was asked to (1) identify the main idea when it occurred at the beginning, middle, and end of the paragraph (they were not told the position) and (2) write a title for each paragraph in order to identify the main idea.

The middle grade students were able to determine about 40 per cent of the topic sentences and 50 per cent of the titles. However, when the topic sentence was not at the beginning of the paragraph, they could identify it only 30 per cent of the time. The secondary school students identified 57 per cent of the topic sentences and 65 per cent of the titles. Placement of the topic sentence in the middle of the paragraph apparently caused the secondary students the most difficulty.

COMPREHENSIBILITY OF MATERIALS

Factors Affecting Comprehensibility

Semantic and Syntactic Factors. Semantic factors relate to meaning. Difficult concepts stated in short words, brief sentences, and unfamiliar idiomatic expressions—not difficult according to formula but difficult conceptually—can render a selection harder to understand than one would imagine if relying on the results of readability formulas.

On the other hand, simple ideas can be made difficult to understand when they are couched in unusual syntactic patterns or lengthy, run-on sentences. In such cases a burden is placed upon the long-term memory and consequently the *reasoning* ability of the reader, making it hard for the reader to *follow the structure of the content* and to *make inferences about the content*. *Word-meaning* problems, as noted already in Chapter 5 also increase the difficulty of making inferences.

COMPREHENSION SKILLS IN MATURE READING

It is precisely these three factors—word meanings, making inferences about the content, and following the structure of the content—that Davis (1968) found to be the most important comprehension skills in mature reading among secondary school students (Table 6–2). He found that comprehension is not a unitary mental skill or operation.

In the next segment I shall analyze passages drawn from the *Cooperative Reading Comprehension Tests* (Davis, et al., 1941-49) and the *Davis Reading Tests* (Fred Davis and Charlotte Davis, 1958; 1961) in order to show the kinds of thinking involved in reading the passages and answering the questions about them. The skill passages will be grouped into the three areas listed in Table 6-2: comprehension of explicitly stated meanings (CE), comprehension of implicitly stated meanings (CI), and appreciation (A). A more general factor for subsuming these three areas is verbal comprehension.

Comprehension of Explicitly Stated Meanings

Table 6-2 shows that the following skills are grouped under comprehension of explicitly stated meanings: remembering word meanings, following the structure of the content, understanding the content stated explicitly or in paraphrase, and weaving ideas in the content.

Table 6–2. Comprehension Skills in Mature Reading Among Secondary School
Students and the Order of Importance of the Five Chief Skills

Comprehension of Explicitly Stated Meanings	Order of Importance Among All Skills
Remembering word meanings* (recognition vocabulary test)	1
Following the structure of the content	3
Understanding the content stated explicitly or in paraphrase	5
Weaving ideas in the content†	
Comprehension of Implicitly Stated Meanings	
Inferring word meanings from context	
Making inferences about the content	2
Appreciation	
Identifying the author's literary techniques	
Recognizing author's attitude, tone, mood and purpose	4

*Thirty-two per cent of the nonerror variance of this skill is not involved in any of the other seven comprehension skills used in the Davis study.
†Twenty-two per cent of the nonerror variance is unique.
According to Davis (1968), weaving ideas together and getting the central thought of a passage are probably subsidiary steps to drawing inferences.

Illustrations of Test Items and the Dynamics of Thinking Involved in Their Solution

CE–1 Remembering Word Meaning

Guffaw
A. make fun of
B. sneeze
C. cough
D. laugh

It should be obvious that remembering word meanings is basic to comprehending meaning. This skill ranked first in importance among the reading comprehension skills. The task is to find a synonym for the item. There are no great dynamics involved in this particular item but they may be involved where part-whole or whole-part relationships are involved in reading passages.

CE–2 Following the Structure of the Content

Only the adult male cricket chirps. On a summer night, they sing by the thousand in unison, so that the forest seems to pulsate and the tiny unseen orchestra becomes its very voice. "Its" (last line) refers to

A. "adult male cricket"
B. "summer night"
C. "forest"
D. "tiny unseen orchestra"

One could not very well substitute *adult male cricket* for *it* since *tiny unseen orchestra* means the many singing male crickets, for then the passage would read "the many singing male crickets become the male cricket's voice." If we choose D, *tiny unseen orchestra*, the passage section would read, "the tiny unseen orchestra becomes the tiny unseen orchestra's very voice." The answer cannot be A, *on a summer night*, because it is merely an adverbial phrase modifying the word *sing*. In a broad sense forest includes trees, bushes, vines, and living creatures (remember the meaning hierarchies!); it is the *forest* that seems to pulsate. The *tiny unseen orchestra* is the voice of the forest; therefore, "its" refers to *forest*, choice C. One can understand from the complexity of the task and the reasoning processes involved in the correct solution how this skill ranked third in importance among the comprehension skills.

CE-3 Understanding Content Stated Explicitly*

All program changes must be recorded on blanks furnished by the Registrar and filed with him after they have been approved by the student's advisor, or, in the case of applicants for advanced degree, by the Director of the School of Education or the Dean of the College of Liberal Arts.

Program changes are to be filed with the

A. Registrar
B. Student's advisor
C. Director of the School of Education
D. Dean of the College of Liberal Arts

Understanding content stated explicitly (or in paraphrase) is not a high-level skill; it seems to be related to reading for details, although, strictly speaking, a person might infer details at times. The test passage states rather explicitly that program changes are to be filed with the registrar. To some extent skill CE-2, following the structure of the content, is involved in that in order to answer this item (CE-2) one must know the antecedent of the pronoun *him*. This should serve as a warning that there are no truly pure single reading skills.

CE-4 Weaving Ideas in the Content

One early April I visited a man who had an outdoor swimming pool. The first night my host asked, "Are you a morning plunger?"

Thinking he referred to a tub plunge in a warm bathroom, I glowed and said, "You bet!"

*Research by Gray and Rogers (1956) showed that few high school graduates in the study could be considered mature readers. More recent studies such as the National Reading Assessment and the SAT analysis indicate a decline in reading ability over the past few years.

"I'll call for you at seven, then, and we'll go out to the pool."

It was evidently his morning custom, and I wasn't going to have it said that a middle-aged man could outdo me. My visit lasted five days, and I later learned from one to whom my host confided that they were the worst five days he had ever gone through. "But I couldn't be outdone by a mere stripling," he said, "and the boy surely enjoyed it."

The writer and his host both

A. like to swim
B. disliked swimming
C. were amused by the other's behavior
D. misunderstood the other's real feelings

In the test the stem states, "The writer and his host both . . . " Choice A, like to swim, can be eliminated by inference based on the statement by the host that the days were the worst five days he had ever gone through. There is not enough information to say they disliked swimming or that they were amused by the other's behavior. Choice D must be correct because if they had understood the other's real feelings, they would not have had to engage in the "morning plunging," which, evidently, neither enjoyed.

Comprehension of Implicitly Stated Meanings

CI-1 Inferring Word Meanings from Context

Into the muddy pool of my heart some healing drops had fallen—from the music of the passing birds, from the crimson disc that had now dropped below the horizon, the darkening hills, the rose and blue of infinite heaven; and I felt purified and had a strange apprehension of a secret innocence and spirituality in nature—a fore-knowledge of some bourn, incalculably distant perhaps, to which we are all moving.

"Apprehension" (line 5) most nearly means

A. fear
B. perception
C. recollection
D. seizure

This passage can be used to illustrate the point that a reading passage might have so many difficult words that there is not enough meaning in the context to enable a person to infer the meanings. Actually, I am illustrating the importance of skill CE-1, remembering word meanings. Being able to infer the meaning of the word *apprehension* is predicated on the idea that the reader knows a number of words that would be rather difficult for average readers in secondary school: *crimson, disc* (not to mention the concept of *crimson disc*), *infinite, purified, spirituality, foreknowledge, bourn,* and *incalculably.* To select the correct synonym—perception—for the word *apprehension* as used in this context requires the reader to understand the difficult words just listed and to understand the gist of the selection.

CI-2 Making Inferences About the Content

The delight Tad had felt during his long hours in the glen faded as he drew near the cabin. The sun was nearly gone and Tad's father was at the woodpile. He was wearing the broadcloth suit that he wore to church and to town sometimes. Tad saw his father's hands close around a bundle of wood. He was doing Tad's work— and in his good clothes. Tad ran to him. "I'll git it, Pa."

When Tad saw his father, he felt

- A. disappointed
- B. impatient
- C. angry
- D. guilty

The root *fer* means to bear or bring; *in* means in or into. When we infer we bring in meanings and reasoning processes in order to determine the "hidden" meanings of a passage. To the explicit meaning that Tad was engaged in enjoyable pursuits for many hours, we add our knowledge of what a glen is (from real or vicarious experience); poetic references describe glens as places of real natural beauty. We combine the explicit meanings with the inferred meanings we develop and say that Tad was having a good time. From the information that Tad stayed a long time, that it was nearly dark, and from the experience and/or reasoning ability that chopping wood in the dark would be a foolhardy and nonproductive type of experience, we conclude that there was little time left in this day for finishing the wood-chopping and bringing-in chores; it had to be done. The task evidently was Tad's; Father was doing Tad's work. And his father was doing it in his good suit. Even if the test were not a multiple-choice type, we would have to produce the response that Tad felt guilty. Choice D, guilty, has to be the correct answer, at least for people who have both reasoning skills and a conscience. One can see why this skill ranked second in importance among reading-comprehension skills.

Appreciation

A-1 Identifying the Author's Literary Techniques

Thomas Girard once remarked of George V: "King George does not reign; he merely sprinkles."

Girard was making use of

- A. exaggeration
- B. understatement
- C. a play on the word "reign"
- D. a play on the word "sprinkles"

Girard's remark was probably spoken. The words used to denote *rule* and *precipitate* use the homophone /rān/; Girard was making a play on the word *reign*. One would infer, also, by the use of the word *sprinkle* in conjunction with *reign* (rain) that Girard did not think much of George V's ability to rule.

A-2 Recognizing the Author's Tone, Mood, and Purpose

The golf links lie so near the mill
   That almost every day
The laboring children can look out
   And see the men at play.

This verse was written about 1915 and refers to a social problem of the period—child labor. The tone of the verse is

A. resigned
B. belligerent
C. bitterly ironic
D. mournful

In addition to being able to develop the meanings in the passage, the reader must have rather broad experience with the terms used in the answer choices. This fact is certainly a prime example of the fact that author and reader have to be on the same "wave length" if communication is to take place. Choice C, bitterly ironic, appears to be the correct choice.

As a result of studying the preceding analyses one should have better grasp of the following aspects of reading comprehension in the secondary schools: (1) what is meant by the various comprehension skills, (2) the relative importance of those skills, (3) the structure of reading test items, (4) some of the dynamics of thinking involved in attempting to ascertain correct responses, and (5) the problems that can be encountered in trying to read certain kinds of materials for particular kinds of purposes.

What have I been doing? I have been making thorough logical analyses of the cognitive relationships in the reading passages; in essence, it has been intelligence in action. As you will see, this comprehension ability—this intelligence—can be trained.

TEACHING STRATEGIES THAT IMPROVE READING COMPREHENSION

Promoting Careful Reading

Transformational Strategy: Manzo's Re-Quest Procedure. Many learners have not been taught to attack the printed page actively and mine it for all it is worth. This Re-Quest procedure will help teach the student to do that.

The goal: to improve the student's reading comprehension by promoting careful reading.

Basic technique: provide an active learning situation for developing questioning behaviors:

Teacher is the model of questioning behavior. The student is encouraged to ask questions, using the teacher as a model, about textual material and to set the purpose for reading.

The teacher guides the student's reading through a series of sentences through giving the rules and playing the game.

The rules: Teacher says, "This lesson is designed to improve your comprehension of what you read. We will both read the first sentence silently. Then we will take turns asking questions about the meaning of the sentence. You can ask questions first, then I'll ask some. See if you can ask the kind of questions a teacher might ask.

When you ask me questions I will shut the book. Then when I ask the questions you will please close the book."

Questions should be answered as completely and honestly as possible. An unclear question should be rephrased or clarified. The responder should be prepared to verify his answer by referring back to the text.

Playing the Game:

1. S and T read the first sentence silently.
   T closes the book and S proceeds with the questioning.
2. T answers the questions. If the questions are not clear, T requires S to rephrase them.
3. T asks as many questions as might prove useful in adding to the student's understanding of the material. (Both literal and interpretation questions should be used.)
4. Beginning with the second sentence, T and S can ask questions which require integration and evaluation of previous questions.
5. To improve student questioning, give positive feedback, explaining, "in order to answer that question I have to do such and such (or think about this and that.)"
6. Reading is continued until T feels sure that S has a good enough grasp of the paragraph to provide a reasonable answer to the question, "What do you think is going to happen in the rest of the selection? Why?" In other words, what have you read that permits you to make that prediction?
7. If conditions—short first paragraph or insufficient information in it—do not permit a reasonable prediction, T may continue into the second paragraph. Very rarely would one go into the third paragraph.
8. Follow-up activities may be used.

It appears that this Re-Quest procedure of Manzo's (1969) should help us to reach the goal for reading encapsulated in Mortimer Adler's statement: "In the case of good books, the point is not to see how many of them you can get through, but rather how many can get through to you."

Developing the Main Idea

One great mistake in considering comprehension is to think of "getting" the main idea as a skill; it is a product. One uses deductive, inductive, and analogical reasoning processes to develop the main idea(s) of a paragraph. One cannot really determine if the first sentence is a topic sentence until one reads the whole paragraph and then determines that the import of the details and the argument are encapsulated in that first sentence. If they are not, one must take the conclusion reached about the import of the material and consider it the main idea. It may be necessary for the reader to write a note in the margin regarding the main idea of the paragraph as he or she has determined it.

A person uses the details to develop the main idea. If one understands the relevant details and sees how they support the main idea, one will have a firmer grasp of the main idea. Also, there will be less chance that one will talk about the main ideas in meaningless ways, that is, that one will be guilty of verbalism. You see, we often talk in generalities, and if we cannot support the generalities, the main ideas, with relevant information, we not only will appear ludicrous in the eyes of others but we may also mislead them.

Hypothesis-Testing Strategy. D. E. P. Smith's Pattern. Donald E. P. Smith and his staff (1960) developed a model for teaching paragraph comprehension that in "preliminary tryouts with dull-normal children resulted in substantial increases in comprehension."

The steps: The steps in Smith's hypothesis testing pattern for teaching paragraph comprehension are

1. Read the first sentence; assume that it is the main idea.
2. Read the second sentence; then,
   a. if the meaning of the first sentence encompasses the second, continue to assume that the first sentence is the main idea; or,
   b. if the first sentence is too narrow, broaden it to include the second sentence idea.
3. Continue with each succeeding sentence as in the second step.

Application: Apply the procedure to the following paragraph:

> All milk has some fat in it. Butter is made from this fat. Butter as we buy it is mostly fat. But some water from the milk is still left in it, and usually a little salt has been added as seasoning. More important, butter has in it some of the vitamins we need to keep us well.

(The pupil is CA 10–11 and IQ (Slosson) of 118.)

> T: "Read the first sentence, and then tell me the meaning in your words."
> P: 1. "There is some fat in all milk." (This is the paraphrase form).
> T: "Read the second sentence and tell me the meaning in your own words."
> P: 2. "This fat is used to make butter."
> T: "Which idea seems most important?"
> P: "This fat is used to make butter."
> T: "Can you put the ideas together and make a main idea?"
> P: "Butter and milk have fat in them."
> T: —
> P: "Butter is made from milk fat."
> T: "Read sentence three and see if it adds anything to your main idea."
> P: "Now I would say, Butter is made from milk fat and it is then more fat than milk."
> T: "Can you combine your ideas?"
> P: —

T: "Butter is made from milk fat and it is ... "
P: "mostly fat?"
T: "Yes."
T: "Let us look at the next sentence and see if ... "
P: (Reads it.)
T: "Does it add anything important in it?"
P: "Yes, that salt is added for seasoning."
T: "Can you ... ?"
P: "Butter is made from milk fat and salt is added for seasoning."
T: "We do not want all the details, do we? You dropped out the fact that butter is mostly fat; that is O.K."
T: "Now read the last sentence."
P: (Reads)
T: "Do you think that is important?"
P: "Yes."
T: "Do you think that the milk fat is most important—or the vitamins?"
P: "Milk fat."
T: "Can you state the big idea with main ideas of the paragraph?"
P: "Butter, made from milk fat and salt added for seasoning, has some vitamins which help keep us well."

Related follow-up exercises. The related exercises below are of varying levels of difficulty. Apply the hypothesis-testing strategy to the following selection. Compare your results with those of a colleague.

1. *Hypothesis-testing exercise:*

The Language of the Street

The language of the street is always strong. What can describe the folly and emptiness of scolding like the word jawing? I feel too the force of the double negative, though clean contrary to our grammar rules. And I confess to some pleasure from the stinging rhetoric of a rattling oath in the mouths of truckmen and teamsters. How laconic and brisk it is by the side of a page of the North American Review. Cut these words and they would bleed; they are vascular and alive; they walk and run. Moreover they who speak them have this elegancy, that they do not trip in their speech. It is a shower of bullets, whilst Cambridge men and Yale men correct themselves and begin again at every half sentence. (Ralph Waldo Emerson)

Main Idea: _____

_____

NOTE: If you as a teacher (or when you become a teacher) do not take the time to discuss with your students what they are doing and why they answer the way they do, if you do not get at the dynamics of their thinking and discover the logical fallacies in their thinking, you are not teaching; you are merely testing.

2. *The 1, 2, 3, 4 exercise:* (1) Read through and clarify words and explicitly stated ideas. (2) Read through, assuming the first sentence is the main idea, etc., as in the first kind of exercise. (3) Write down the main idea. (4) Write down the relevant supporting details. Try this 1, 2, 3, 4 method on the following paragraph; do not be afraid to have a dictionary at hand:

Example

> Consider the savage: he has bodily strength, he has courage, enterprise, and is often not without intelligence. What makes all savage communities poor and feeble? The same cause which prevented the lions and tigers from long ago extirpating the race of men—incapacity of cooperation. It is only civilized beings who can combine. All combination is compromise: it is the sacrifice of some portion of individual will for a common purpose. The savage cannot bear to sacrifice, for any purpose, the satisfaction of his individual will. His social cannot even temporarily prevail over his selfish feelings, nor his impulses bend to his calculations. (John Stuart Mill, Civilization: Signs of the Times)

Main idea: _____

_____

Relevant supporting details: _____

_____

_____

Developing Inferences (Drawing Conclusions)

In order to make inferences or draw conclusions one uses such subprocesses as weaving ideas together, making deductions, and making inductions. The process yields a product—information. The information might be the meaning of a word or a fact. The fact may be a detail or a more inclusive idea such as a main idea. Details and ideas can be explicitly stated or they may be implied, requiring one to use the context—weaving ideas together, making deductions, making inductions—in order to draw the conclusions. And at other times, one might also need to develop the gist of the selection, the main idea, in order to make inferences.

Dynamic Process-Product Strategies.   The following questions were developed after I worked out a way of showing the dynamics of thinking involved in making inferences. First are the questions, then the selection, and finally an analysis explicating this aspect of comprehension as process yielding product. (The questions do not exhaust all possibilities):

1. What is the import of the word flagship?
2. Who discovered America?
3. What is the name of Columbus' flagship?
4. What generalizations can you make about the captains?

The expedition set out for the New World in 1492. (A German geographer was later to call this world America.) The commander of the flotilla was Christopher Columbus. Rizzuto commanded the Pinta and Durante, the Niña. Columbus boarded his flagship, which flew his, the flotilla commander's, flag. After sailing for three months the flotilla landed on a small island, a part of the New World. Columbus debarked from the Santa Maria and soon was on dry land.

Process	Product

Question 1. What is the <u>import</u> of the word flagship?

· Inferring meaning from context ⟶ Information: meaning of <u>flagship</u>.

· Note that Columbus was commander of the group of ships. (Need to know— by recall or inference—meaning of flotilla.)

· Note that the Commander has his own flag which is flown from the mast.

∴ (deduce) that ⟶ the flagship is the most important ship, and it flies the commander's flag and is a symbol of authority.

Question 2. Who discovered America?

· inference arrived at through two subprocesses of weaving ideas together and making a deduction

Information:
  · fact that Columbus discovered America

· Inferring meaning from context

a. Note that America is the New World.
b. Columbus was the commander of the expedition because he commanded the flagship.
c. Flotilla is a small group of ships so Columbus' group is referred to by word flotilla.
d. Commander of flotilla would get credit for discovery of New World (America)
e. Columbus was the commander.

Weaving ideas together {
Deductive reasoning {

P
R
E
M
I
S
E
S

∴ ⟶ Columbus discovered America.

(The two subprocesses of weaving ideas together and deductive reasoning comprise the process of inferring meaning from context. The process yielded the information [the product] at the right.)

Question 3. What is the name of
                Columbus' flagship?

· Another deduction

Deductive
reasoning

{
· Columbus was on board his ship—
  the flagship—that he commanded.
· He would stay with his ship until
  he landed.
· He disembarked from the <u>Santa Maria</u>.

∴ _____ → The name of Columbus' flagship
                                        was the <u>Santa Maria</u>.

Question 4. What generalizations can
                you make about the captains?

<u>An induction</u>

a. Note that the captain of the
   Niña was an Italian.
b. Note that the captain of the
   Pinta was an Italian.
c. Note that the captain of the
   Santa Maria was an Italian.

P
A
R
T
I
C
U
L
A
R
S
↓

The generalization process   Generalization →   All the captains in the flotilla
involves noting the common   were Italian. [This can be con-
element in the three particulars.   sidered a detail.]

(This exercise should also help to explode the myth that <u>what</u> questions
always involve literal comprehension alone.)

A Six-Step Strategy for Drawing Conclusions.   The following strategy for
drawing conclusions is a model *teaching* paradigm:

Procedure:

1. Clarify the ideas of the selection through discussion.
2. List some of the key ideas of the selection in paraphrase. (Some of these will
   be main ideas and others will turn out to be supporting details.)
3. Develop the main ideas and supporting details from the key ideas listed.
4. The teacher lists conclusions that can be drawn from the information in the
   paragraph. (Sprinkle in some statements that cannot be drawn; these will provide the foils.)
5. Ask the students to check which listed statements are valid conclusions that
   can be drawn on the basis of the ideas in the selection.
6. During the verification—discussion period the students will be called on to explain or verify their choices.

The Selection: There are two basic kinds of sleeping habits which Sir William Osler
once labeled as "owls" and "larks." Some people, like owls, prefer to work late
and get up late; others, the larks, get up early in the morning and retire early.
Whichever you are, it makes no difference, provided that you get the right amount
of sleep.

There is no substitute for the total number of hours of sleep required. While it is best to sleep soundly, the important point is to sleep at least the minimum number of hours, seven or eight.

It is perfectly satisfactory to break up your periods of sleep. Many people, Edison being the most famous, sleep a few hours at night and take frequent naps during the day. This is particularly true in the entertainment world. Yet most who do this suffer no ill effects. However, one interesting point: resting in bed is much more satisfactory than sleeping in a chair.

The Procedures:

A. Clarify the ideas of the selection through discussion.

B. List the key ideas of the class as they are developed by the class as a result of the discussion.

   1.

   2.

   3.

     etc.

C. Develop the main ideas and supporting details from the key ideas listed.

   Main idea 1: _____

   Supporting detail _____

   Supporting detail _____

   Main idea 2: _____

   Supporting detail _____

   Supporting detail _____

D. The students read the conclusions (and foils) the teacher has prepared and check the statements that are valid conclusions that can be drawn on the basis of the ideas in the selection.

E. The teacher then calls upon various students to explain or verify their choices. They will need to resort to the text and to the ideas listed as key ideas and possibly to the outline developed.

After several of these exercises are completed, committees or individuals may be allowed to select reading materials, develop the conclusions (and foils), and lead the other students through the steps of the exercise. This experience should be a valuable motivation for drawing conclusions. After a while it should generalize as a procedure applicable to the various content areas. Encourage students who have learned the procedure in another class to apply it to the content-area materials of your class, that is, of your subject-matter area. If they have not—you may be the only person in your school who knows the procedure —teach them the approach using the procedures we have just been through. NOTE: I suggest that the reading methods instructors who are using this text guide their students through the above story and accompanying procedures.

Chaining Strategy. Some reading instruction programs use a chaining strategy designed to promote the student's ability to make inferences while reading.

What Chaining Is: Chaining is an aspect of programmed learning. Information is given, a word or words are deleted from the context, and the student supplies the deleted word. If the material is matched to ability, the student should not find it difficult to infer the missing word. Through syntax, paraphrasing, analogy, and other such cues, the answer becomes rather obvious. The word constituting the answer will always appear in an adjacent context so that the individual has cues for spelling the word.[1]

Rationale: Although this kind of chaining is not classical, it jibes with the programmed format in that it requires a person to think and to make a response in connected discourse, and it provides immediate and generally positive feedback.

Materials: Very few materials designed to *teach* reading comprehension correctly use this type of chaining pattern. A common problem is the failure to use adequate connected discourse; another is the lack of appropriate cues.

A reading program that does use chaining is the *Sound Reading Program* by Edwin Smith, C. Glennon Rowell, and Lawrence E. Hafner. Since this program begins with initial reading acquisition—decoding and comprehension—and proceeds through second and third reading levels to the fourth level, the authors provide one further clue: the initial letter of each deleted word is provided. Following are examples from the *Sound Reading Program*, Book Six, a comprehension book:

> Great grandfather's name was Bill. They called him Rider Bill in those days. In th____ days there were no cars. Men looked up to those who were good with horses. Rider Bill, your gr____ grandfather, was a g____ rider. He was the best in the West.
>
> Rider Bill liked to go to church. On Sunday he would come to church. There was a red-haired girl who went to the same ch____ . . .

Further stimulation of comprehension development is provided by a small group of questions at the end of each selection. The correct answers on an ensuing page provide feedback. Research by Briggs, *Journal of Reading Behavior*, 5(1):35–46, with second-grade disadvantaged pupils showed that the experimental (SRP) group made a statistically significantly greater achievement in reading over the control group. In the experimental groups the average gain for black and white students was about the same!

A Hierarchy of Patterns: Hafner's and Jolly's Explication of Bloom's Taxonomy

In this series of exercises I will try to explicate aspects of the Comprehension segment of Bloom's (1956) Cognitive Taxonomy. By comprehension Bloom means translating, interpreting, and extrapolating; the latter refers to what most of us call interpretation (drawing conclusions).

---

[1]   Edwin H. Smith, personal communication.

This discussion is based heavily on a section of *Patterns of Teaching Reading in the Elementary School* by Hafner and Jolly.

1.0 Translation Patterns. Basically a translation is a paraphrase. Generally a paraphrase is an attempt to make material clearer. Various kinds of relationships can be involved in translation; usually whole-part, part-whole, and coordinate relationships are involved. To the extent that directions which point to the relationships involved and/or a discussion are used, instruction is taking place. To the extent that these are not involved testing is being done.

1.1 Parts-Whole Translation Pattern

Directions: In the following paragraph you will read some related points (parts). These points refer to a more general term or heading (whole). What heading (adjective) can we use to describe this scene?

> Besides the vineyard, you would see the hayfields, pastures, and fields of grain. In smaller patches you would also see vegetable gardens, potato fields, and orchards.

This scene can best be described as _____ .

or

This scene can best be described as

A. irrigated
B. agricultural
C. industrial
D. mechanized

1.2 Whole-Parts Translation Pattern. (Translate an abstraction, such as a generalization, by giving an illustration or an example.)

Directions: Read the following sentence and be prepared to respond to an item relating to *contrasts*.

> Bombay is a city of contrasts.

Basing your thinking on the main idea in the sentence, you might expect to see in Bombay:

A. Many legal agreements to be made
B. Crowded tenement sections and areas of fine residences
C. Many Indian people living there
D. Extreme poverty and many starving people

NOTE: The above exercise could be one of several comprehension exercises done in conjunction with a Directed Reading Lesson on a segment of social studies material. It is not a substitute for direct teaching—concept development, word-recognition work, discussion of the material, and the like—but a related activity to use in conjunction with these activities.

1.3 Predication Relationship & Contrast Relationship. In the following problem two important kinds of relationships are involved—a predication relationship, vagabond travels, and a contrast (paradigmatic) relationship. Vagabond does not cling or settle; this means it *moves*.

The scallop is a vagabond. It does not cling to rocks or settle in beds on the bottom of the ocean, but is constantly

A. eating   B. idle   C. traveling   D. learning

(This item, paragraph and multiple choices, is from SRA's *Reading for Understanding Jr.* by Thelma G. Thurstone.)

NOTE: Can you not see how students would make much more progress in these kinds of materials if teachers would provide some guidance on occasion?

2.0 Interpretation Patterns

In interpretation a person is required to understand the basic ideas in a communication and go a step further to understanding the relationships of those ideas; he must grasp the significance, the point, of the selection he is reading. There are various ways of showing understanding of relationships and so on; one way, according to Bloom is by reordering material by writing a summary (Hafner and Jolly, Patterns, 1972).

The task: Below is a paragraph on soybeans. Write a one-sentence summary of that paragraph, please.

Directions: (You will need to find the common elements or "threads" running through the paragraph.)

Step 1: Note the first sentence, especially the noun and the verb.

The subjects are _____, _____ .
                         (1)

What is said about the subject(s)? _____ ,
                                                    (2)

_____ .

Step 2: Do the subject and verb occur in other sentences—pronouns standing for the subject and synonyms (or related verbs) for the verb?

Subject: _____ Verb: _____
                (3)   (4)

Step 3: Note the direct objects; generalize where possible _____

_____ (omit as many details as possible)
                  (5)

_____

Possible answers for the blanks:
  (1) soybeans, they
  (2) they have uses, furnish
  (3) they, soybeans, soybeans
  (4) supply, used (make)
  (5) food, fertilizer

Soybeans

Soybeans . . . are used as food for man, and they furnish him with vegetable oil, flour, breakfast foods, and so on. They supply animals with hay and pasture, and they enrich the soils in which they grow by adding needed nitrogen. . . Soybeans are used in making such products as soap, paints, and varnishes. Plastics and water-proof coatings for cloth are also made from soybeans.

After studying these relationships (noun—verb—objects) you should be ready to write a one-sentence summary of the paragraph: _____

_____

(The students might produce such sentences as the following. (Discussion and mediation can be fruitful.):

Example 1: Soybeans are used for food, fertilizer, plastics, paints, varnish, and waterproof coatings.

Example 2: Soybean products and by-products include such things as food, fertilizer, plastics and protective coatings such as paint and waterproofing material.
NOTE: A superordinate, protective substances, was provided for paints, varnishes, and waterproof coatings.)

Example 3: Some foods, fertilizers, plastics, and protective substances are soybean products or byproducts.

NOTE: If the students are not sophisticated enough to follow the directions entirely, the teacher and the students should discuss the process as they do it. It may be necessary for the students to do a number of these exercises under teacher guidance before they catch on to the procedure. Do not force the instruction if they are not catching on. They may not be ready for it.

3.0 Extrapolation Pattern

A person extrapolates when he makes inferences, draws conclusions, or predicts outcomes on the basis of some data. Pupils need much practice in this skill if they are to acquire the ability and propensity to use it. Discussions should accompany this work in order that the teacher can get some insight into the reasoning processes of his students.

Directions: Read the following segment of material, picture the conditions, and note the effect of the sun's rays. Enter the number of the correct answer in the blank.

. . . the south-facing slopes receive much winter sunshine. The slanting rays of the winter sun strike these south-facing slopes rather directly and bring warmth to this part of the Alps.

Therefore, we probably find that _____.

1. Farms of this region have a shorter growing season than some of the surrounding areas.
2. The area is famous as a winter resort.
3. Nothing is planted on these slopes.
4. The summer sun strikes the north-facing slopes rather directly. (From Hafner and Jolly, Patterns, 1972.)

NOTE: For other exercises and activities see chapter 7 of *Patterns*.

CRITICAL READING

A Working Definition of Critical Reading

Critical reading uses a set of complex processes for the purpose of determining the truth of written material; it is undergirded by interpretation abilities, the noetic impulse, and the proclivity for rectifying cognitive dissonance and social injustice.

Reasons for Reading Critically

Generally one reads critically to determine truth in a matter so that one can act on accurate information. The person who does not want to deceive or be deceived will want both to dispense and receive valid information. In many instances in everyday life a person needs to read critically. A person will read critically to note, for example, misinformation circulated about welfare recipients; to know more exactly the role of a country in getting into, prosecuting, and trying to get out of a war; and to determine why numbers of millionaires pay no income taxes while the rest of us pay and pay.

Basic Guidelines for Critical Reading

To improve critical reading performance the reader should *first* be well informed generally and try to develop background on the specific topic that he or she is reading about. If one is just beginning to read on a certain topic, one should proceed with caution. *Second,* one should check the assumptions of the writer. Some writers may make blithe assumptions in their opening statements, throwing the reader off balance with a cute remark, a half truth, or with the mucker pose. *Third,* note the specific competencies of the author. What is his or her standing in the profession, what research has he or she done and of what quality is it, and what are the author's qualifications according to the better national and international biographical publications? *Fourth,* check the purported facts in standard reference works and in articles and books by recognized authorities in the field. *Fifth,* look for propaganda devices and logical fallacies of thinking. Chase (1956) has written a book on the latter. There is a tendency to associate events that are contiguous in space and/or time, but this phenomenon can lead to incorrect judgments about cause and effect (*post hoc ergo propter hoc* fallacy).

In the *ad hominem* fallacy, the writer or speaker, failing to make a point in legitimate ways, attacks an adversary with innuendo, belittling, and so forth. The *ad hominem* attack is a means of focusing attention on the worth or implied worth of one's opponent rather than on the issues under discussion. Abraham Lincoln was once debating another lawyer in a trial case when Lincoln's opponent, in the process of losing the argument, turned to make unfavorable comments about Lincoln's mode of dress, thereby hoping to discredit Lincoln personally and to get the jury to look with favor on himself. *Sixth*, be open-minded and flexible—be willing to look at all the evidence and to change views when the evidence warrants it.

What Are Critical Readers Like?

Critical readers come in all shapes, sizes, colors, and political and religious persuasions, but they are already to some extent well informed.[2] They cannot tolerate cognitive dissonance; they are keyed to note discrepancies in written material; and when they do, they attempt to rectify the discrepancies. They are—or should be—reflective thinkers, in that they try to determine the facts of a situation before making judgments. Critical readers may or may not do something positive about their findings. But there is some sense of urgency about the true critical reader. Ortega y Gassett (1967) writes: "Only the individual who is in a position to question things with precision and urgency—whether they definitely exist or not—is able to experience genuine belief or disbelief."

Critical Readers of Times Past

At his trial in 399 B.C., Socrates claimed that he philosophized because "the unexamined life was not worth living." He maintained that his contemporaries devoted their lives to the pursuit of fame and riches without stopping to question their importance. If they did not ask how important the things that they were doing were, they could not know if they were living right and pursuing worthwhile goals. Socrates developed and used a method of inquiry that featured the habit of asking a series of questions in order to elicit a clear and reliable declaration of something that all rational beings supposedly know implicitly.

Another famous iconoclast was Martin Luther. Reared in the dominant Christian denomination of the time, he received his doctorate in theology at Wittenberg University and became professor of Biblical exegesis at that school. In preparing his lectures on Galatians and Romans, he found that these scriptures contradicted the basic doctrines of his church. He challenged the scholarly community to debate 95 theses regarding his view of incorrect practices in the church. These 95 statements questioned the accuracy and worth of a number of religious doctrines promulgated by the church. Many of his writings received wide circulation in Europe and later, in translation, throughout the world.

Martin Luther King, Jr., a black American leader, called into question many prevalent social practices. He was a critical reader in the broad sense of reading both the environment and history for the purpose of determining truth in the form of social justice, that is, civil rights for black people. On August 28, 1963, during the civil rights march on Washington, D.C., King said, "We must not

---

[2] Someone who is critical is not necessarily well informed, and a person might note a logical fallacy in a writing without being well informed on the topic; yet, we would say that critical readers are either well informed and/or trying to become better informed.

allow our creative protests to degenerate into physical violence. Again and again, we must rise to the majestic heights of meeting physical force with soul force." In recent years he was found to be the victim of a malicious watchdog and slander campaign of the F.B.I.

Some Research on Critical Reading

Piekarz (1956) at the elementary level, and H. K. Smith (1961) and Swain (1953) at the secondary and college levels, respectively, have shown how the poorer readers zero in on word perception and literal meanings, eschewing interpretation, whereas the better readers can analyze and restructure meanings in order to grasp implied meanings and make critical reactions.

McKillop (1952) studied eleventh-grade students and found that to some extent the type of question asked determined the relationship between the students' attitude toward a topic and their ability to provide answers to questions on the topic after reading. Smith (1961) found, however, that it was the good reader who could change approach according to the purpose set, whereas the poor reader could not; the latter read for details regardless of the purpose set for reading. Nardelli (1957), on the other hand, has shown how sixth-grade pupils can improve their ability to detect propaganda devices and to draw inferences as a result of specific instruction.

Howards (1965) reported his study of the effect of teaching propaganda techniques in the higher grades in which he had students (1) analyze media advertisements and then write advertisements and (2) analyze, during a presidential campaign, 12 different newspapers from across the country for 30 days. The students determined, by inference, the biases of the papers and then compared the biases with the election returns of the specific areas.

Jensen and Knecht (1968), using male and female college students as subjects, sought to identify personality factors that would predict attitude change resulting from three types of written messages (conforming, emotional, and factual appeals). The messages were designed to show the undesirable effects of yearly chest X rays. Attitude changes following the *factual* presentation were not related to any personality type. Attitude change following the *emotional* appeal was related only to manifest anxiety among females. Attitude change following the *conforming* appeal was related positively among women to self-esteem and among men to intolerance of ambiguity. Attitude change following the *conforming* appeal was related negatively among men and women to manifest anxiety and among men to authority.

Examples of Materials That Must Be Read Critically. The following examples illustrate the need for determining the truth of ideas in reading material:

> 1. A majority of our colleges admit B and C students, and in some it is still possible for a student to accumulate the requisite credits for a bachelor's degree by picking courses in different subjects that are all or nearly all at freshmen level. (H. Rickover, <u>American Education—A National Failure</u>, 1963, p. 159).

2. Elect Jeremiah Smith Mayor of Smithton. Born and reared in Smithton. Attended local school. Fought in Viet Nam conflict. Member of Kiwanis, American Legion, and the Smithton Community Church. Married and the father of three children. Honest.
3. Never before have men gone for a razor like they have for <u>Slicko</u> Razors.

Further examples of the need to read critically will be found in the next two sections. The next section will suggest several strategies for improving critical reading. The last section of the chapter will provide "Checkpoints for Teaching Reading"; these will, in effect, provide further important strategies.

TEACHING STRATEGIES THAT IMPROVE CRITICAL READING

Teaching critical reading skills is not a matter of providing a number of (in effect) insipid testing exercises labeled critical reading exercises. However, a few exercises done in connection with general strategies and discussion can be useful. Following are some exercise starters. (The illustrations will be at various reading levels):

1. **"Change a Word."** Have students find absurdities or errors of fact in sentences and paragraphs. The sentences can be corrected by substituting or inserting or deleting words or by rewriting. Always discuss responses and reasoning behind them.

    a. All airplanes have five wheels.
    b. (On a beautiful, sunny day post this): Be sure to use your umbrella today.
    c. Dogs are great tree climbers.
    d. Colonial loyalists in the Revolutionary War were traitors.
    e. High school graduates are qualified to do college work because they have high school diplomas.

2. **"What's Stupid About That?"** Have students analyze the following assertions. They should place a + by those that are true, a 0 by the ones that are ridiculous, and a question mark by the ones that they are not sure of. Then they should write the reasons for the judgments they made. Discuss.

    a. The cat had four puppies.
    b. Katie is 12 years old. Linda is 14 years old. In two years Katie will be as old as Linda.
    c. She has got 30 sixth graders in her class so she needs 30 sixth-grade social studies books. (Our fifth grader solved this. Too bad so many principals cannot.)
    d. President Lincoln died when he was eight years old.
    e. An apple a day keeps the doctor away.
    f. Sailors have more fun.
    g. You do not have to stop at a stop sign if a car is not coming.
    h. Men are more intelligent than women.
    i. "They are dumb. They say /aks/ (ask) and /wif/ (with). I can't /ə-sept/ (accept) that kind of talkin'. /ən-daút'-əb-lē/ (undoubtedly) those people are dumber'n us."

    j. People who are loyal to their country would not go to another country during wartime to escape being drafted.

    k. There is no God, because I have not seen Him.

    l. What goes up must come down.

    m. If you do not agree with me, you're probably a Communist.

    3. "Let's Try That Again." The following exercises based on Musson's (n.d.) book, *Reading and Reasoning*, are designed to make one aware of how certain words appeal to the emotions and to show that meaningless words and phrases, metaphors, and pseudoscientific terms must be analyzed. Musson's exercises were used with twelve-year-old boys. This experiment resulted in their reading material more thoughtfully.

    1. Using experience to be critical of words used without precision.

        a. The underlined words are not so informative as they might be. Replace them with more precise and informative words or phrases or clauses:

           (1) The movie was great.

           (2) Do justice.

           (3) He is very intelligent.

        b. Translate the following into accurate, honest English, correcting any errors of fact:

           (1) They do not teach the way they used to.

           (2) Loud noise stunts the growth of plants.

           (3) Them pseudointellectuals at the university . . .

    2. Using experience to be critical of figurative language.

        a. The following passages appeal to emotion; rewrite them so they will appeal to reason:

           (1) You will love her, mother; she's an angel in disguise.

           (2) He was as sharp as a mashed potato sandwich.

           (3) As sure as my great-grand daddy fought for Lee, I promise you . . .

    3. Using experience to be critical of fake scientific terms.

        a. Determine the real meaning of the terms used in the following. Start by reading and circling doubtful words and phrases.

           (1) Metaphysical commands can help you. Take fabulous astral journeys outside your bodies into other time dimensions.

           (2) Are you tired, cranky, and feeling as though you are losing your mind? You need to saturate your circulatory system with organic magnesium and nonfattening carbohydrates. Try Supermag today. It provides you with all the organic magnesium you need and can use.

CHECKPOINTS FOR TEACHING CRITICAL READING

Use Materials at Hand   □

If one waits for money enough to purchase the ideal kit or workbook for teaching students to read critically, one may never get around to teaching these skills.

Furthermore, one is not always assured of a transfer from such materials to real-life reading tasks. Use the materials at hand—textbooks, newspapers, magazines, bulletins, editorials, letters to the editor, and the like—for sources to be read critically. They provide opportunities for checking assumptions, detecting logical fallacies, noting propaganda devices, and the like.

Ask students to bring to class reading materials that they have read critically and in which they found problems. These samples can be marked appropriately (critical notes in margins, underlining, question marks, etc.) or left unmarked so that the class can analyze them. These materials can be placed on the bulletin board or duplicated and/or prepared on overhead transparencies. A series of overlays to be superimposed on the text can unfold the analysis step by step. A student may want to lead the discussion, helping the other students to discover the problems he or she has discovered. The teacher may even get to chime in.

The teacher may want to keep the materials filed by topics for use at a later time or with another class. (Some of this material could become outdated, though.)

Investigate the Relevancy and Authenticity of Information □

Assume you are doing a unit of work and individuals are reading text and other materials. The students should be shown how to be on the lookout for extraneous information, arguments, and divagations—material that is not relevant to the topic at hand and may even cause distortion of the truth. Teacher and students should explain how and why the information is irrelevant.

One method of checking the authenticity of information is to investigate the qualifications of the author. A way of doing this is to check biographical reference works. Some biographical sources are more authentic than others.

One should also check given items of information in textual materials against standard reference works and against relevant notable books in the field. If necessary, one may need to check original sources (for example, letters, diaries, official documents and the like for history matters; scientific journals and original data of science experiments, etc., for science topics). Where necessary and feasible, experts may be brought into the classroom and the people mentioned in letters to the editor or in news items may be interviewed or in some other way given a chance to tell their side of an issue and *be subjected to questioning*.

Another related strategy, and it can be used as a part of the above activities, is to discover on which of the following elements the generalizations are based:

(1) general experience	(5) experiments
(2) facts of history	(6) scientific facts
(3) historical trends	(7) accepted laws or principles
(4) specific observations	(8) others (specify)

Another strategy is to compare the approaches of different source materials on a given question or topic:

1. In what ways did the various authors differ in reporting the same event?
2. Why do you suppose they differed?

Some of the reasons for differing are obvious: differences in philosophy of the writers (and publishers), background of authors, sources, purposes in writing, temperament, intelligence, and writing ability.

Try to Determine the Motives of the Writer   □

One way to prevent wrong decisions in various situations is to investigate the motivations of the people who are trying to influence your decisions. First, get at the actual, sometimes veiled, reasons for the writer's statement, argument, or action versus the ostensible seemingly plausible reasons. The field of advertising offers many examples of the need to be wary:

Come on down to Sam's for a good buy. We've marked the price of our merchandise down 25%. Come in and save money.

1. How well do you know Sam; that is, What has his "track record" been?
2. How much might the merchandise have been overpriced before it was marked down?
3. How much is being charged for the item in other stores?
4. What is the quality of the merchandise at that price compared to other brands of the same price or similar price?
5. Another question which does not have anything to do with Sam's honesty is: Am I really saving if the cost of the merchandise plus transportation costs to and from the store exceed those costs in trading at a nearby store?

Writers of editorials, letters to the editor, and press releases for manufacturers, legislators, and people with vested interests in certain corporations or small businesses often stand to profit in some way by your believing something they are saying. There is, of course, nothing wrong with making an *honest* profit. But are these people making an unfair profit? Is the profit they are making related to something detrimental to the people—for example, ten-year-long undeclared wars, conflicts here and there, or cutting off education funds (because so much tax money is going to support a nonsensical military fiasco and because those making the decisions say such expenditures for education are part of a "welfare state?"). The people have to get at facts, investigate assumptions, watch for nonsequiturs, and so forth. But first ask, *Cui bono* (who profits) by my believing these missives?

Question "Custom"   □

Question the "this is the way we have always done it" argument. Claiming that something should be done a particular way because it has always been done that way is a non sequitur; it just does not follow that something should be done that way because it is the custom. Let me list a few things that need to be questioned; for each problem in the list the following questions apply:

1. What makes anyone think the present approach is logical?
2. What have the results been?
3. Would the results have been better had another way been tried?
4. Could the results have been more meaningful?
5. What is logical about the new approach?
6. What research supports the old approach?
7. What research supports the suggested new approach?
8. Might a more efficient way that yields the same or better results be substituted for the customary way?

A few customary practices to be questioned (Please add to the list):

1. How textbooks are adopted.
2. How a person's worth is ascertained.
3. How education is supported.
4. How educational funds are apportioned.
5. How congressional and legislative leaders are selected.
6. How people of genius potential are treated.
7. How educational achievements are publicized.
8. The basis for setting up certain "Christian" schools in the post-integration order era.

Commonly held ideas or sterotyped opinions to be questioned: (Again, be my guest):

1. Fallacy 1: People of genius are spindly and emaciated looking.
   Fact: Studies have shown that on the average highly intelligent people are taller and healthier than people of average intelligence are. (See, for example, Lewis Terman's Genetic Studies of Genius.)
2. Fallacy 2: The people of certain minority groups are not intelligent because they are genetically inferior.
   Fact: Studies have shown that when pregnant women are deprived of adequate amounts of animal protein, especially during the last five months of pregnancy, and their children are deprived of such protein, especially during the first 25 months of life, the brain cells of such children do not develop adequately. Indicators of this phenomenon are reduced brain size and head circumference and lower (on the average) birth weight. There is a correlation between birth weight and later measured intelligence. On the average, bright children weighed significantly more at birth than children of average or low intelligence did. (See the article: "Nutrition, Love, and Language: Keys to Reading" by Hafner and Guice in Hafner (1974). Also work by Heber (1970) in Milwaukee attests to the value of very early (beginning ten days or so after birth) environmental intervention and concept-language enrichment for the intellectual development of black slum infants.)

If you doubt what I am saying about people of genius potential and the relationships of nutrition to birth weight and subsequent intellectual development try this little study. From sources at your disposal randomly select 25 people of IQ 120$^+$ of a given age, sex, and educational opportunity and 25 people of IQ 100$^-$ who are of the same age, sex, and educational opportunity as the first 25. Ascertain birth weight and present height, weight, and general health of the two groups and compare. Send me your data and results, please. I would be very interested in what you find.

Probe for Information   □

What are the facts? How many times is one asked to believe something, to act on it or be the "beneficiary" or "victim" of it when one has not been able to ascertain the factualness of the information. What questions should one ask in these situations?

1. What kind of fact is involved here? (Philosophers tell us there are different kinds of facts, different ways of knowing, for different disciplines.)

2. Given the *kind* of fact involved, what are the facts?

3. Is there some pertinent information missing?

4. To what extent does its omission alter the truthfulness of what is being presented?

During the early 1800s Bible doubters pointed out what they considered to be a hundred or so discrepancies in the Bible accounts of geography and history phenomena. Archeological expeditions during that century uncovered information that proved that the Bible accounts were indeed accurate all along.

Ascertain Causes of Effects   □

One fairly burns at the rhetoric based on false information—and the consequent wrong assignment of cause—used to put people down and to influence voters. In the sixties and seventies it was apparent that misinformation abounded:

1. *Date, 1964:* One candidate for high office put down poor people en masse. He said in effect, "Why don't those people get out and work like I did and they might amount to something." He was implying that his affluence, and it was considerable, was due to his initiative and hard work.

Fact: He happened to inherit one of the better businesses in his home state.

2. *Date, any year:* "We worked hard for what we got. If those people would get out and work the way we do, they could make it, too." Speakers? Midwestern farmers.

Fact: Many of these people inherited hundreds and sometimes thousands of acres of the best farmland in the world, plus machinery, buildings, and many times no small bank account. They have the advantage of the knowhow of state and federal employees and programs—extension agents, bulletins, 4-H, seminars, etc. Granted they worked hard, but look at the affluent base from which they started. Many farmers also use terminology for profit and loss and what they consider profit that differs from that of nonfarmers.

What was the legacy of many of the people upon whom these de facto wealthy people heap calumny? It was what you get when your ancestors were slaves and you were denied *actual* equal education, civil rights, equal opportunity employment, and fair wages and you were kept in such a state of fear that life was miserable. I suggest such affluent people whether they be farmers, business men, professors, bankers, lawyers, doctors, or whatever read the books of Isaiah and Amos in the Bible; Amos gets to the point faster. You might also understand, then, why so many downtrodden blacks thought Amos was a fine name!

3. *Date, any year:* What is the cause for inferior intelligence of numbers of white and black and "red" people? (See my arguments under "Commonly held ideas or stereotyped opinions")

4. *Non sequitur.* I have been talking about non sequiturs here and there; non sequitur means "it does not follow." Here are some more examples:

a. "Those lower class people have grits for breakfast every day because they're crazy about grits."

Fact: They might not be able to afford anything else; that is a basic reason. If you are hungry and grits are all you can afford, the food would likely taste good and you might develop an affection for something that keeps you alive, even though barely so. Even when people can afford something else, they may lack the education that would help them prepare a more nutritious and economical breakfast. [Once again, please see the Hafner and Guice article in Hafner (1974).]

b. "He'll get a good education because he's in the best school in the county."

Fact: It does not follow that he will get a good education; the best school in the county might be a rather mediocre one.

c. "Mr. Smith should be sent to Congress because he is a veteran of the X conflict, he belongs to Y church, and he is married."

What are his specific qualifications for the office? Also, what are the teachings of that church, and does he abide by the teachings?[3]

d. "The American colonists were right in revolting because they felt that they weren't being treated properly."

Fact: Applying that rule today would result in anarchy. Students are taught that the revolutionaries were heroes and then people are surprised that they take steps to fight against injustice, undeclared wars, and the like.[4]

e. "He is a 'hippie' therefore he's not any good."

Fact: Hippies are distributed in morality like bankers, teachers, preachers, bakers, hunters, barmaids, university presidents, and the like. Some are good; some are so-so; and some are not good.

---

[3] Abiding by the teachings that are sanctimonious and law oriented, rather than Gospel oriented could pose problems. (See Strommen, et al. 1972 for a penetrating analysis of this phenomenon.)

[4] There are, of course, cogent reasons for promoting justice. (See the U.S. Constitution—based on English law; Amos, chapter 6; Micah 3 and 6: 6–16; and Luke 4: 14–21).

Check for Evidence of Overgeneralization   □

Overgeneralization is jumping to a conclusion on the basis of too few cases or incorrect sampling procedures. Some types of generalization:

1. *I know a man who* . . . "Why, I know a man who gave a hitchhiker a ride. The hitchhiker drove off with the car when the man stopped at a service station. This proves that you should not help people in need anymore" (After Chase, 1956).

2. *In a nutshell*

a. *Headlines:* Jonesville *Daily Blade*: Jonesville Tigers Slaughter Smithton's Lions. The story goes on to tell how the score was 5–2 in favor of Jonesville. Some kind of standard should be set for the use of terminology. By the way, the Smithton *Herald* had Jonesville winning a squeaker from Smithton.

b. *Popular magazine story titles:* "The Child Loretta Young Didn't Want." She did not want a particular child to be in the cast of a show that she was in.

c. *Improper encapsulating of events into a story and a story into headlines.* Numbers of people who have had an article written about them or have been part of a news report attest to the distortion, overgeneralizing, and omission of facts in the stories. Distortion can be made in headlines. Compare the headlines of newspaper X with those of newspaper Y for identical AP or UP or UPI news reports and also for syndicated columns. Teach students how to note the biases of newspapers by comparing content with headlines and the general tenor of articles and editorials in the newspapers. Show them, then, how these biases affect the writing of headlines and editorials. Of course, headlines will be different because different people write them. But one needs to watch out for distortion.

Editors prefer the neatly packaged story to the story with qualifications. These editors know that qualifications prevent the writers from supplying "easy" answers (after Chase, 1956).

3. *Lovers and wheeler-dealers.* Think of a man who has a date with a woman, then another date. He sees wedding bells. She was just filling time. What happened is that the young man overextrapolated. He established several points on the "chart," drew a line through them and extended it all the way to "wedding bells."

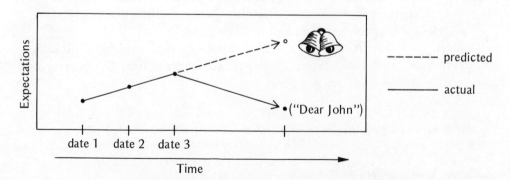

This situation can be heartbreaking, and there are people who are not fair in their treatment of others, but young people must be careful in their assessments of certain situations. What really happened is that the young woman did not like the caramel corn the man's mother bought at the movie!

A similar thing happens to some individuals who play the stock market. The diagram is self-explanatory.

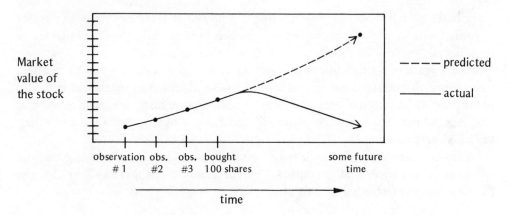

Ce la bear!

SUMMARY

In order to comprehend written material well, the reader must make a thorough logical analysis of conceptual or cognitive relationships. Through comprehension the reader reduces certain areas of cognitive uncertainty that may have existed prior to reading.

Great differences exist between good and poor readers. In grade twelve, for example, good readers read for established purposes and can establish their own purposes, whereas poor readers do not. In keeping with our meaning hierarchy phenomenon, good readers restructure material and slot details into their meaning structures, whereas poor readers do not. Finally, good readers read for ideas, for general impression, whereas poor readers try to remember details in isolation.

According to Davis there are three basic comprehension factors: comprehension of explicitly stated meanings (CE), comprehension of implicitly stated meanings (CI), and appreciation (A). The dynamics of thinking involved in the logical analyses of the cognitive (and affective) relationships in passages used in several kinds of reading test items were presented.

Several important strategies designed to improve comprehension were thoroughly explicated. They feature intensive *interaction* among teacher, student, and reading material—a *much-neglected* principle in teaching reading.

Included among the strategies were the author's *dynamic process-product strategies,* which illustrate the paradigms and dynamics related to processing reading material in order to obtain products.

Finally, a working definition of critical reading was couched in somewhat esoteric terms (in order to help keep the reader from dozing off). Reasons for reading critically relate to determining the truth in order that justice might reign.

Six basic guidelines for critical reading can be posited; for example, the better informed one is and the more knowledgeable one is about logical fallacies of thinking the more accomplished one will be as a critical reader.

Critical readers cannot tolerate cognitive dissonance, and they have a propensity to try to rectify such dissonance. This tendency to criticize in order to obtain social justice has cost the lives of many great historical figures such as Socrates, Christ, Paul, Lincoln, Ghandi, and King; a few others, such as Luther, have had narrow escapes.

Teaching strategies that improve critical reading require intelligent and sedulous preparation and execution. For best results teachers should also use the checkpoints included in this chapter.

ACTIVITIES AND QUESTIONS
TO PROMOTE LEARNING AND APPLICATION

1. Reflect on your development to this point. How would you change the balance of time devoted to reading and TV watching in order to accomplish goals you now see as important?
2. What advice do you have for parents and young people regarding use of time in reading versus TV watching?
3. What are some definitions of reading comprehension? How do you suppose the various definitions affect the way reading is taught?
4. Try to replicate H. K. Smith's study. What results did you get? How do you account for any differences between your results and Smith's results? (The interviewing and testing tasks may be done by various members of your methods class. You will use the same tests and techniques.)
5. Design a study similar to that in item 4 to use with middle school students. Try to execute it in the same school district. Note differences between your results and the secondary school results. Are there developmental differences? Explain similarities and differences in your findings.
6. Rewrite some materials in order to make them easier to read and understand. What did you have to do to accomplish the task successfully? Design a study to prove your rewritten materials are easier to understand.
7. If you did not analyze your reasoning processes as you did test items in the *Davis Reading Test* (an activity suggested for chapter 4), do so now: record on tape the steps in selecting the correct responses. Try to determine where you "went wrong" on the items that you miss.

8. Have a group discussion to try to determine why comprehension skills are not better taught in the schools. Group reasons into categories. What can be done to improve such instruction?

9. In class try out Manzo's *Re-Quest Procedure.* Teach the procedure to a poor or average reader in middle school or in secondary school. Can it be successfully taught in just one session? Explain.

10. Try out D. P. Smith's *Hypothesis-testing Strategy* in class with middle or secondary school students. If possible, tape the procedure. Report the results in class.

11. Write and teach exercises designed to teach the main idea and relevant supporting details.

12. Design exercises and execute them following Hafner's *Dynamic Process-Product Strategies.* What kind of insight did you obtain about comprehension processes?

13. Select appropriate reading material and apply the *Six-step Strategy for Drawing Conclusions.* Does this procedure seem worthwhile? Explain.

14. Obtain copies of the *Sound Reading Program* and use them with problem readers. What kinds of results did you get?

15. Write some exercises using the strategies based on Bloom's taxonomy. What difficulties do you encounter in writing interpretation and extrapolation patterns?

16. Gather from your reading of newspapers and magazines examples of logical fallacies of reasoning. Discuss.

SUGGESTED ADDITIONAL READINGS

BURMEISTER, LOU E. *Reading Strategies for Secondary School Teachers.* Reading, Mass.: Addison-Wesley, 1974. Chapters 7–9.

FISHER, JOSEPH A. "Improving Comprehension–Interpretation Skills." In Hafner, Lawrence E. (Ed.). *Improving Reading in Middle and Secondary Schools.* Second Edition. New York: Macmillan, 1974. Pp. 104–114.

GOODMAN, KENNETH S. "Comprehension-Centered Reading." In Eldon E. Ekwall. *Psychological Factors in the Teaching of Reading.* Columbus, Ohio: Charles E. Merrill, 1973. Pp. 292–302.

HARRIS, ALBERT J., and EDWARD R. SIPAY. *How to Increase Reading Ability.* Sixth Edition. New York: David McKay, 1975. Chapter 17.

HERBER, HAROLD L. *Teaching Reading in the Content Areas.* Englewood Cliffs, N.J.: Prentice-Hall, 1970. Chapters 5 and 6.

LEVIN, HENRY, and E. L. KAPLAN. "Grammatical Structure and Reading." In H. Levin and J. P. Williams. (Eds.). *Basic Studies on Reading.* New York: Basic Books, 1970. 119–33.

MELMED, PAUL JAY. "Black English Phonology: The Question of Reading Interference." In James L. Laffey and Roger Shuy (Eds.). *Language Differences: Do They Interfere?* Newark, Del.: International Reading Association, 1973. Pp. 70–85.

RUSSELL, DAVID H. [Robert Ruddell, (Ed.)]. *The Dynamics of Reading.* Waltham, Mass.: Ginn, 1970. Chapter 7.

SHEPHERD, DAVID L. *Comprehensive High School Reading Methods.* Columbus, Ohio: Charles E. Merrill, 1973. Chapter 4.

ZINTZ, MILES V. *The Reading Process.* Second Edition. Dubuque: Wm. C. Brown, 1975. Chapters 11 and 13.

BIBLIOGRAPHY

CHASE, STUART. *Guides to Straight Thinking.* New York: Harper, 1956.

DAVIS, FREDERICK B., and MARY WILLIS. *Cooperative Reading Test C-2.* Princeton, N. J.: Educational Testing Service, 1943.

—— and CHARLOTTE CROON DAVIS. *Davis Reading Tests.* New York: Psychological Corporation, 1961.

——. "Research in Comprehension in Reading." *Reading Research Quarterly.* 3 (4) (Summer 1968), 499–545.

GRAY, WILLIAM S., and BERNICE ROGERS. *Maturity in Reading: Its Nature and Appraisal.* Chicago: University of Chicago Press, 1956.

HAFNER, LAWRENCE E., and HAYDEN B. JOLLY. *Patterns of Teaching Reading in the Elementary School.* New York: Macmillan, 1972.

—— (Ed.). *Improving Reading in Middle and Secondary Schools.* Second Edition. New York: Macmillan, 1974.

—— and BILLY M. GUICE. "Nutrition, Love, and Language: Keys to Reading." In Lawrence E. Hafner (Ed.). *Improving Reading in Middle and Secondary Schools.* New York: Macmillan, 1974.

HEBER, RICK and H. GARBER. "An Experiment in the Prevention of Cultural-Familial Mental Retardation." Proceedings, Second Congress of the International Association for the Study of Mental Deficiency, August 25–September 2, 1970.

HOWARDS, MELVIN. "Ways and Means of Improving Critical Reading Skills." In J. A. Figurel, (Ed.). *Reading and Inquiry.* Newark, Del.: International Reading Association, 1965.

JENSEN, L. C., and SUSAN KNECHT. "Type of Message, Personality, and Attitude Change." *Psychological Reports.* 23 (1968) 643–48.

MANZO, ANTHONY. V. "The Re-Quest Procedure." *Journal of Reading.* 13 (November 1969), 123–26.

MUSSON, J. WINDSOR. *Reading and Reasoning.* Sussex, England: John Crowther, no date.

NARDELLI, ROBERT R. "Some Aspects of Creative Reading." *Journal of Educational Research.* 50 (1957), 495–508.

ORTEGA Y GASSETT, JOSE. *The Origin of Philosophy.* New York: W. W. Norton, 1967.

PIEKARZ, JOSEPHINE A. "Getting Meaning from Reading." *Elementary School Journal.* 56 (March 1956), 303–309.

SMITH, DONALD E. P. "Reading Comprehension: A Proposed Model." In O. S. Causey and E. P. Bliesmer (Eds.). *Research and Evaluation in College Reading.* Ft. Worth: National Reading Conference, 1960.

SMITH, EDWIN H., GLENNON C. ROWELL, and LAWRENCE E. HAFNER. *The Sound Reading Program.* Waco, Texas. Education Achievement Corporation, 1972.

SMITH, HELEN K. "Research in Reading for Different Purposes." In J. Allen Figurel (Ed.). *Changing Concepts of Reading Instruction.* Newark, Del.: International Reading Association, 1961.

STROMMEN, MERTON P., MILO L. BREKKE, RALPH C. UNDERWAGER, and ARTHUR L. JOHNSON. *A Study of Generations.* Minneapolis: Augsburg, 1972.

SWAIN, EMELIZA. "Conscious Thought Processes Used in the Interpretation of Reading Materials." Unpublished Ph. D. Dissertation, University of Chicago, 1953.

WILLIAMS, MAURICE, and VIRGINIA STEVENS. "Understanding Paragraph Structure." *Journal of Reading.* 15 (1972), 513–16.

CHAPTER 7

Reading and Organizing in Research-Study Situations

The current propaganda about our not needing reading skills in the near future reminds me of the rumors that the clever students in high schools and colleges circulate about never cracking a book and still getting good grades. While you are misled into thinking it is possible, they study sedulously but do not let you know it. Guess who gets the good grades and guess who gets the not-so-good grades? There will be a need to read to organize what we read for some time to come. Most students finish high school without learning how to read comprehensively and organize information effectively. Consequently, they are not skilled in writing papers and examinations.

Intelligence and organization are two sides of a coin; they are, in a sense, reciprocal agents. If we apply intelligence to organization, results are clearly superior; and if we organize our efforts, our products will seem to be done more intelligently. This means according to my definition of intelligence-comprehension that we conduct a thorough logical analysis of cognitive relationships.

Organization can increase our fund of knowledge, its accessibility, its retrievability, and its reproduction or statement for a variety of purposes. In this way intelligence is increased.

We reproduce information orally in the form of everyday speech, in speeches, in formulating plans, in discussions, and in soliloquies. Written reproduction takes the form of term papers, news articles, letters to the editor, magazine articles, journal articles, and books. For students it means such things as term papers, essays, articles for the school newspapers, and tests.

In this chapter we are particularly interested in improving reading-organization skills of the middle and secondary school student, both in terms of general inquiry skills and of the ability to write better themes, term papers, and examinations.

161

WHAT ARE THE READING ORGANIZATION SKILLS?

I. *Ability to Develop a Particular Purpose for Reading and to Determine Method of Organization*
   A. Reading to be informed, but not to organize formally.
   B. Reading and organizing for a written presentation—theme, article, paper.
   C. Reading and organizing for reproduction on quiz or examination.
II. *Ability to Initiate Inquiry*
   A. Developing questions to be answered and/or points about a topic.
   B. Writing preliminary answers or points known about a topic.
   C. Arranging questions and/or points into a preliminary outline.
III. *Ability to Select Appropriate Sources of Information*
   A. Using general sources to get an overview.
      1. encyclopedias.
      2. standard books or texts.
      3. cyclopedias and handbooks.
   B. Consulting a librarian when necessary.
IV. *Ability to Pinpoint Information*
   A. In an encyclopedia.
      1. using the index.
      2. noting cross references and related topics.
      3. using headings and typographical aids.
   B. Through the card catalogue.
      1. knowing the kinds of cards.
      2. knowing what each kind of card tells you.
   C. Through *Readers' Guide to Periodical Literature*.
   D Through vertical file index.
   E. Through subject matter indexes.
   F. In subject-matter cyclopedias and handbooks.
   G. In a book.
      1. using the table of contents.
      2. using the index.
      3. using headings, summaries, and typographical aids.
V. *Skill in Selecting and Evaluating Information*
   A. Judging the validity of one's sources.
   B. Determining relevant information.
   C. Determining the validity of one's information.
   D. Judging when one has enough information.
VI. *Ability to Comprehend Written Material* (treated in a previous chapter)
   A. Determining the big ideas in a paragraph or section.
   B. Noting the relevant details that explicate or support the big ideas.
   C. Making inferences, drawing conclusions, making predictions.

    D. Seeing implications of ideas read and making applications.
    E. Reading directions and following them correctly.
    F. Interpreting pictorial and other graphic aids.
       1. pictures and cartoons.
       2. tables, figures, and graphs.
       3. maps and globes.

VII. *Skill in Recording and Organizing Information for Retention, New Synthesis, and Reproduction*
    A. Abstracting and paraphrasing information and organizing information.
       1. making notes.
       2. keying note cards to the preliminary outline.
       3. revising the preliminary outline.
       4. writing summaries.
       5. comparing and contrasting views, processes, theories, etc.
       6. making outlines.
    B. Special formalized study techniques.
    C. Synthesizing information.

VIII. *Writing the Paper, Article, etc.* (Based on VII)
    A. The first draft.
    B. The cooling period.
    C. Revising the first draft.
    D. Writing the final draft.

IX. *Writing the Examination* (Based on VII)
    A. The essay exam.
    B. The objective exam.
    C. The application exam.

NOTE: The rest of the chapter will be devoted to illustrating skills noted in the preceding outline.

READING TO BE INFORMED BUT NOT TO ORGANIZE FORMALLY

We often read to be informed but we do not make a great effort to remember what we read, and we make little effort to organize it formally. Reading a newspaper and a weekly news magazine, reading nonfiction topics to broaden our horizons or see what is new in a particular field, and even desultory reading that ranges over a variety of topics fall into this class. To be sure, we may clip an article now and then and file it, we may underline in texts and write marginal notes, but this organization is informal.

Reading Newspapers and Weekly News Magazines

Newspapers should be readily available in the middle and secondary school if we are to teach students how to read them! In teaching students to read newspapers I have noticed that some individuals do not read them because they cannot read all they want to because of their slow rate of reading. They seem to have compulsive traits of starting in the upper left-hand corner of the first page and then reading every word. Often these students are mathematics or science majors who are successful in these fields. However, an inflexible approach applied to news reading will result in not being selective, not knowing when and how to shift gears, and generally, then, not enjoying reading the paper because it takes such a long time to get through.

One of the first steps in teaching students to read newspapers is to help them be selective. They should read the sections that interest them and gradually be led into other kinds of materials. Tips in reading some of the main sections of newspapers and news magazines follow.

News

1. Read the index or table of contents to see where certain stories or sections are located.
2. Read headlines to see if one is interested in reading further.
3. Read the opening paragraph or two to find answers to the classical who, what, when, where, why, and how questions. (Newswriters are instructed to pack the first paragraph or two with answers to these questions.)
4. Read the article further if more detail and/or clarification is desired.
5. Raise critical questions if necessary.
6. If critical questions are raised and a bias in the headlines or article is suspected, read the news story in another paper or news magazine of different political persuasion.
7. Provide time in class for discussions and clarification of ideas in selected news articles.

Editorials and Letters to the Editor

1. Note assumptions of the author. (If you grant the author's assumptions, you may be hooked into believing the rest of what he or she writes, whether it is true or not.)
2. Check the facts. (If the letter or editorial is about something where printed facts exist or one can get information in person from an expert or talk to the people involved, do so.)
3. Note the logic or lack thereof. (One should be particularly careful about overgeneralizations and nonsequiturs.)
4. Ask *cui bono*? Who will profit from my believing this?
5. If possible, determine qualifications of editor or letter writer with respect to the topics involved.

Political cartoons

1. Note assumptions of the cartoonist.
2. Note the appropriateness of the symbols used.
3. Beware of overgeneralization.
4. Check the facts involved.

Keeping Up with Serious, Nonfiction Books

Read Reviews of the Books. If one has the time and reviews written by competent reviewers are available, one should read them. Bright secondary school students in particular should be shown the value of reading such reviews and should be taught where to find them. Sources of reviews are in professional journals and in such reference sources as *Book Review Digest* and *The New York Times.*

Reading the Book

1. Read the preface. In the preface the author tells you why he or she wrote the book, how it is organized, its emphases and biases, and why some material was included and other material omitted. Reading the preface helps one to get the gist of the book and may help greatly with the proper understanding and interpretation of the work. There may also be suggestions for studying the book more profitably.

2. Read the table of contents and skim the index.

3. Determine which parts you want to read and how you want to read them. (You may feel that you do not need to read certain sections, that you can skim others, and that still others you may want to read thoroughly. You may decide, too, that you want to underline, make marginal notes, and use other standard or idiosyncratic symbols to help you remember your interpretation and emphasis.)

WRITING A PAPER: READING, ORGANIZING, AND WRITING

The main *steps* are: (1) Initiating the Inquiry and Writing the Preliminary Outline, (2) Getting an Overview . . . , (3) Zeroing in on Specific Sources . . . , (4) Recording and Organizing Information Skillfully . . ., and (5) Writing the Paper.

After the compact discussion of the first subtopic—Initiating the Inquiry—the remaining subtopics will be expanded and detailed.

Step One: Initiating the Inquiry and Writing the Preliminary Outline

Developing Questions to Be Answered. Since a person is not likely to write a paper on a topic about which he or she knows nothing or could not ask a single question, he or she should first, after selecting a topic, write some questions that he or she and/or the reader of the paper would like to have answered. The writer may also list points known about the topic.

Writing Preliminary Answers or Points Known About a Topic. At this stage the answers and points known should be combined into a list of points about the topic. They should not be run together into a paragraph form but listed as separate points.

Arranging Points into a Preliminary Outline. Major points receive a Roman numeral. Points that fit under a major heading should be given a capital letter.

Some points may also be parallel, but have no major heading or superordinate. One will have to be devised at that time. Still other points may be subordinate to the minor headings labeled A., B., C., etc., and can be placed under them.

Now the matter of determining the order of the major headings takes place. Order them in correct sequence and give them the appropriate Roman numerals. Then determine the order of the minor headings under each major heading and note the sequence with A., B., C., and so forth. Finally, sequence the subpoints under these letters and assign the numbers 1., 2., and 3., and so forth. Of course, you may not have enough detailed information to go that far with each heading.

As you are developing the outline, you may think of other points. They may be slotted into the appropriate places in the outline.

Step Two: Getting an Overview. Selecting Appropriate General Sources of Information
Using Encyclopedias. Information in the overview of encyclopedia articles can be used to verify facts and to add relevant points to the outline. Younger middle grade students might find the following encyclopedias useful:

1. *The Golden Book Encyclopedia.* Edited by Bertha M. Parker. Golden Press, New York. Sixteen, accurate, fact-filled volumes illustrated with more than 6,000 color pictures.
2. *The New Book of Knowledge.* Grolier, Inc., New York. For children in grades 3–6. Very carefully written to meet the reading abilities of elementary school children. The accuracy is outstanding.
3. *The World Book Encyclopedia.* Field Enterprises Educational Corporation, Chicago. The emphasis is on serving the needs of students in the upper middle school through high school, but excellent readers in lower middle school grades can use it. Accuracy is outstanding.

Other top-rated encyclopedias, according to *General Encyclopedias in Print*, that may be used by the somewhat older and better middle and secondary students are

Collier's Encyclopedia, Compton's Encyclopedia and Fact Index, and *Encyclopedia International. The Encyclopedia Britannica* is recommended for high school and college students, and the *Merit Students Encyclopedia* is recommended for good students in grades 7 through 12.

Using Single- or Double-Volume Basic General References. Brief, panoramic views on a topic may be gained from reading such works as:

1. *The Columbia Encyclopedia.* Third Edition, Edited by William Bridgwater and Seymour Kurtz. New York and London: Columbia University Press, 1963. Pp. 2388.
2. *Dunlop Illustrated Encyclopedia of Facts.* Norris McWhirtor and Ross McWhirter (compilers). Garden City, N.Y.: Doubleday, 1969. Pp. 864. Information on various nations, the United States, and on all the basic disciplines.
3. *Harper Encyclopedia of the Modern World.* Edited by Richard B. Morris and Graham W. Irwin. New York: Harper and Row, 1970. Pp. 1271. A concise reference history from 1760 to the present.
4. *The Lincoln Library of Essential Information.* Edited by William J. Redding. Two volumes. Columbus, Ohio: The Frontier Press Company, 1971. This work was prepared in order to embody in two volumes the most helpful information ever placed in two volumes and to do it with thoroughness and accuracy. It offers a vast array of practical information on fundamental subjects.

5. *Through the Canadian Index.* This index is a guide to Canadian periodicals and films. Ottawa, Ontario: Canadian Library Association, 1947 to present.
6. *Through Good Reading—a Guide for Serious Readers.* J. Sherwood Wever, New York: Weybright and Talley, 1969. The main contents of this book are (1) a list of 100 significant books, (2) a listing of thousands of good works under the following headings: Historical regional cultures; literary types; humanities, social sciences, and sciences.

Specialized reference works for the various content areas follows:

Selected science reference works:

1. *The Book of Popular Science.* New York: The Grolier Society, Inc., 1969. Ten volumes. Each volume contains encyclopedic articles that treat a number of important scientific topics. Volume ten contains such special features as: selected readings in science (by topics); general outline (by topics with volume and page for each topic); and the alphabetical index of topics.
2. *McGraw-Hill Encyclopedia of Science and Technology.* Revised Edition. New York: McGraw Hill, 1966, 15 volumes.
3. *Science Year—The World Book Science Annual.* Chicago: Field Enterprises, Yearly.
4. *Van Nostrand Scientific Encyclopedia.* Fourth Edition. Princeton: D. Van Nostrand, Inc., 1968.
5. *Young People's Science Encyclopedia.* Edited by the staff of National College of Education. Evanston, Ill.: Children's Press. 20 volumes. Practical aid for school work. Has Parents' and Teacher's Guide. For middle school students.

Selected history reference works

1. BERGMAN, PETER M., and MORT N. BERGMAN (Eds.) *The Chronological History of the Negro in America.* New York: Harper and Row, 1969. Pp. 698.
2. BRINTON, CRANE. *Modern Civilization—A History of the Last Five Centuries.* Second Edition. Englewood Cliffs, N.J.: Prentice-Hall, 1967. Pp. 961.
3. COMMAGER, HENRY STEELE. *Documents of American History.* Sixth Edition. New York: Appleton-Century-Crofts, 1957. Pp. 842.
4. DURANT, WILL and ARIEL. *The Story of Civilization.* N.Y.: Simon and Schuster. Eleven volumes: 1. Oriental Heritage. 2. The Life of Greece. 3. Caesar and Christ. 4. The Age of Faith. 5 The Renaissance. 6. The Reformation. 7. The Age of Reason Begins. 8. The Age of Louis XIV. 9. The Age of Voltaire. 10. Rousseau and Revolution. 11. The Age of Napoleon.
5. EDWARDS, I. E. S., C. J. GADD, N. G. L. HAMMOND and E. SOLLBERGER. *The Cambridge Ancient History.* Two volumes. Cambridge, England: Cambridge University Press, 1973.
6. GARRETT, ROMEO B. *Famous First Facts About Negroes.* New York: Arno Press, 1972. Pp. 212.
7. JOHNSON, THOMAS H. *The Oxford Companion to American History.* New York: Oxford University Press, 1966. Pp. 906.
8. MORRIS, RICHARD B. *Encyclopedia of American History.* New York: Harper and Row, 1970. Pp. 850.
9. TERRELL, JOHN UPTON: *American Indian Almanac.* New York: World, 1971. Pp. 494.

Selected art reference works

1. DANIEL, HOWARD. *Encyclopedia of Themes and Subjects in Painting.* New York: Harry N. Abrams, 1971. 242 black and white and full color illustrations. Pp. 252.

2. HAGGAR, REGINALD G. *A Dictionary of Art Terms.* New York: Hawthorn Books, 1962. Pp. 416.
3. JANSON, H. W. *History of Art.* New York: Harry N. Abrams, 1969. A survey of the major visual arts from the dawn of history to the present day. 1970 color illustrations, including 88 color pages. Text. Pp. 616.
4. MAILLARD, ROBERT (Ed.). *New Dictionary of Modern Sculpture.* New York: Tudor Publishing Company, 1970. Illustrated text. Pp. 328.
5. OSBORNE, HAROLD. *The Oxford Companion to Art.* Oxford, England: Oxford University Press, 1970. Designed as a nonspecialist introduction to the fine arts. Illustrated. Pp. 1277.

Selected literature reference works

1. COURTNEY, WINIFRED F. (Ed.). *The Readers' Adviser: A Guide to the Best in Literature.* Eleventh Edition. New York: R. R. Bowker, 1968. Two volumes. In each volume the background or reference books necessary to the general reader precedes the main divisions of literature: Chapter 1, Books About Books; Chapter 2, Bibliography; Chapter 3, Reference Books—Literature; Chapter 4, Broad Studies and General Anthologies. The divisions of literature are poetry, essays and criticism, fiction, drama. American, British, Roman and Greek Classics, French, German, and Russian Literature are treated. There are also special chapters on Other Foreign Literature in Translation, on Shakespeare, and on Literary Biography and Autobiography.
2. BENÉT, WILLIAM ROSE. *The Reader's Encyclopedia.* Second Edition. New York: Crowell, 1965. This work explains allusions from art, music, history, and geography as well as all facets of literature. The illustrations are charming. For secondary school students.
3. FIDELL, ESTELLE A. *Play Index* 1961–67 (Updated from time to time). New York: Wilson, 1968. This volume indexes 4,793 plays: collections of one-act and longer, radio, T.V., and amateur plays.

Selected music reference works

1. LLOYD, NORMAN. *The Golden Encyclopedia of Music.* New York: Golden Press, 1968. This very comprehensive work covers nearly every phase of music. Included are symphony analyses, biographies, technical glossary, and stories of operas. 800+ illus.
2. SCHOBES, PERCY A. *The Oxford Junior Companion to Music.* Fairlawn, N.J.: Oxford University Press, 1963. For students 8 to 16 years of age.

Miscellaneous references

1. *Book Review Digest.* New York: Wilson, 1906– -. Monthly except February and July, with annual cumulation. Indexes reviews in many American and English periodicals. Digests and excerpts included.
2. BRANDT, SUE R. *How to Write a Report.* New York: Watts, 1968. For middle grades.
3. HALSEY, WILLIAM D. (Ed.). *The School Dictionary.* New York: Macmillan, 1974. Sources of the 65,000 entries are children's literature and basal readers. Each entry is syllabicated, and pronunciation, part of speech, and spellings of related words are included. Of special interest are the geographical entries. For middle grades.
4. MORRIS, CHRISTOPHER G. (Ed.). *Beginning Dictionary.* New York: Macmillan, 1975. Popular basal readers and children's literature were subjected to a computerized study to produce the 30,000 words in this dictionary. Each definition is followed by syllabication, pronunciation, part of speech, and spelling of plurals or various forms of the word. Guide words are appropriately placed, and each spread contains a pronunciation key.

5. *Vertical File Index.* New York: Wilson, 1935- -. Monthly except August. Pamphlets references are arranged by subject, with title, publisher, date, paging, and price. A descriptive note for each of these selected and current pamphlets is usually included.

Step Three: Zeroing in On Specific Sources: Books and Pamphlets

Finding the Right Books

Through the Card Catalogue. Books in a library will be grouped into broad, general types. For example, sections might be devoted to biography, reference books, fiction, education, and so forth. These broad groups are usually subdivided into smaller groups.

Libraries generally arrange books according to the Dewey Decimal System or the Library of Congress System. Using the Dewey Decimal System, the librarians divide all books into 10 subject areas. Each area will have a set of numbers. For example, education books are numbered from 300 to 399; science books are numbered from 500 through 599. Astronomy books are numbered in the 520s, physics books are numbered in the 530s, and so forth.

Large libraries that contain many scholarly works classify books by the Library of Congress System. In this system the major headings are indicated by capital letters of the alphabet, rather than by numbers.

How does one know whether to use a subject card, title card, or an author card? If one does not know any titles related to a topic or authors in the field, one will need to use the subject cards. If one has located a title in a general reference or specialized reference or through a bibliography, one will locate the book through the title card or the subject catalogue. Students need specific instruction in order to develop this skill. Following are examples of an author card, a title card, and a subject card.

      Adams, Edwin Plimpton, 1878–   tr.

530.11   Einstein, Albert, 1879–1955.
E35mYa   The meaning of relativity; four lectures delivered at
        Princeton university, May, 1921. [Tr. by Edwin Plimpton
        Adams] Princeton, N.J., Princeton University Press, 1923
        [^{c}1922]
          123 p.   illus.

      1. Relativity (Physics) 1. Adams, Edwin Plimpton, 1878–
  tr. II. Title.

Author Card

The meaning of relativity.

530.11   Einstein, Albert, 1879–1955.
E35mYa   The meaning of relativity; four lectures delivered at
           Princeton University, May, 1921. [Tr. by Edwin Plimpton
           Adams] Princeton, N.J., Princeton University Press, 1923
           [^{c}1922]
              123 p.   illus.

              1. Relativity (Physics) 1. Adams, Edwin Plimpton, 1878–
           tr. II. Title.

Title Card

Relativity (Physics)

530.11   Einstein, Albert, 1879–1955.
E35mYa   The meaning of relativity; four lectures delivered at
           Princeton University, May, 1921. [Tr. by Edwin Plimpton
           Adams] Princeton, N.J., Princeton University Press, 1923
           [^{c}1922]
              123 p.   illus.

              1. Relativity (Physics) 1. Adams, Edwin Plimpton, 1878–
           tr. II. Title.

Subject Card

Activities for Learning to Use the Card Catalog

1. The teacher, an advanced student, or a student library helper may make a mock-up of a library card on poster board or reproduce it on a transparency for overhead projection Explain the function of the various parts of the cards. Provide a paper and pencil check, "open book" style.

2. Allow each student to select a book from the library shelves, then let him or her find the author card and title card and verify the information on the card by referring to the actual characteristics of the book.

3. Allow the students to make three or four author cards for that number of books and then verify the completeness of their work by checking against the information from the appropriate cards in the card catalogue.

4. Provide a bibliography or set of references and let the students look up the Dewey numbers or the Library of Congress numbers and put them in the margin by the corresponding books.

5. As a part of unit work, have secondary students annotate their references as well as provide the call numbers of each reference.

6. If there is a classroom library, the students can organize and prepare a card catalogue for the collection of books.

Ability to Pinpoint Information in a Book. Reading the *preface* of a book can be a valuable experience. The *table of contents* will help you zero in on particular chapters that treat the topics in which you are most interested. If you are looking for a particular point, consult the *index*. The table of contents, of course, gives a general idea of a book's contents. Of greater value is the index, but many people do *not* know how to use an index intelligently.

Using the index:

A. *Finding the key word.* For the following questions, which is the important or key word?

    1. What is the population of California? (A little trick will help here. If the book is on California the key word in the index would be *population*. If the book is on population, the key word in the index would be *California*. This is a basic point.)

    2. Who invented the vacuum tube? (Again, if the book is on inventors, look under *vacuum tube* or *tube, vacuum*. If it is on vacuum tubes, look under *inventor*.)

B. *Choosing a subtopic in the index.* Choose a subtopic to help you answer these questions:

    1. Which European country first owned Cuba?

    2. Does it generally snow in Cuba?

    3. Are radios manufactured in Cuba?

> Cuba, climate in, 87; history of, 24; industries of, 127; migration from, 202; products of, 150.

This exercise demonstrates the value of knowing hierarchies of ideas, for the successful completion of this activity is related to knowing the superordinates of certain words, that is, perceiving relationships among ideas. This activity serves to remind us that reading ability will not transcend general intelligence and its related hierarchy of concepts. Ownership would be a subordinate of history, snow is a subordinate of climate, and radios would be a subordinate of either industries or products. This concept is basic.

C. *Choosing alternate key words.* Which words might you need as key words to locate information in a book? Select a main key word and an alternate key word. (How would you proceed if words in the sentences did not yield the information?) Think of words that are superordinates or subordinates or even coordinates of the important words in the questions:

    1. How is carbon used in manufacturing a microphone?

    2. Is solar energy used in space satellite flights?

    3. What kinds of fuels are used in rocket sled experiments?

Finding Pamphlets, Pictures, and Newspaper Clippings Through Use of the Vertical File Index. Vertical files are filing cabinets in which pamphlets and the like are stored. Such items are difficult to store on shelves because they would be hard to find and easily damaged. Separate folders are used to store these materials alphabetically by subject. The material is classified in a Vertical File Index. Otherwise a person can go directly to the file(s) and look up the subject alphabetically. One has to use classifying skills similar to those with an index.

Through the Reader's Guide to Periodical Literature. This guide gives the titles of individual articles appearing in such periodicals as *Newsweek, Atlantic Monthly, Popular Mechanics,* and about 125 periodicals in all. Articles are listed alphabetically by subject and author. The H. W. Wilson Company also publishes special guides or indexes in other subject areas. Below is an entry from the *Reader's Guide* plus an explanation of its notational system.

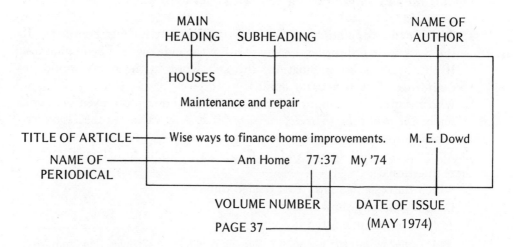

The front matter of each *Reader's Guide* contains an explanation of how to use it. Abbreviations are also explained.

Activities for Learning to Use the Reader's Guide

1. Reproduce several entries from the *Reader's Guide* on transparencies. Project on screen and ask individuals to come and identify title, author, journal, date, heading, subheading, and so forth.

2. Reproduce an entry on a piece of poster board. Mark title, author, and so forth and discuss the function of each segment of the entry.

3. Select several topics from a number of *Reader's Guides* for which there are no headings using the same words or not as much information as you think might be available. Have students suggest alternate headings. For example, there is not much information on *giants* (people) in *Reader's Guide.* You will find such information under *Stature.* (These exercises are important because the person who cannot come up with alternate headings will miss much information.)

4. Have students develop a small bibliography on a topic in which they are interested, listing the various headings they used.

Selecting and Evaluating Information

In selecting and evaluating information that one has located one must answer these basic questions:

1. *Is the information pertinent to the topic?*
   a. Does it answer questions I have asked?
   b. Does it fit the basic outline?
   c. Can it be used as a logical extension of the outline?
2. *Is the information accurate?*
   a. Is the author an expert in the field?
   b. Does the information jibe with authoritative sources?
   c. Has the information been validated by experience or by research?
   d. Is the material up-to-date?
   e. Does the writing contain logical fallacies of reasoning?
3. *Would the information be understandable for my readers or would I have to translate it* (paraphrase, expand, illustrate it, and so forth)?
4. *Do I have enough information to explain what I am trying to explain?*
   a. In answering this question am I thinking of the sophistication of my reader or of other experts in the field?
   b. Is it better to err on the side of redundancy or brevity? [redundancy]
   c. Do I feel there are things the reader needs to know that he or she is not aware of?

Step Four: Recording and Organizing Information Skillfully for Retention, New Synthesis, and Reproduction.

Making Notes on Material Read

1. *Make a preliminary notation of location of pertinent material.* This material could have been discussed in an earlier section, but I think it is a good idea to group these subtopics in a way that shows the process of noting the material and making the notes. What one does then is to (1) make a bibliography card for each reference, (2) read through pages (to which you were guided by the index), and (3) note pages and lines relevant to the topics and subtopics in your outline, always being aware that new information may cause you to develop new subtopics.
2. *Read the information carefully and make paraphrased notes.* In order to be able to move notes flexibly and to slot them correctly into your outline, write one basic bit of information on each card. If you put too much information on one card, you will likely find that part of the information belongs in one part of your outline and part of it belongs in another; that renders the placement of note cards in proper sequence rather difficult.

<u>Original statement</u>   ["Therefore, it behooves us to 'exercise our inalienable right
<u>in Adamson:</u>   to petition the government for a redress of grievances.' "]

a. *Write the note in paraphrase.*
b. *Write one basic bit of information on each card.*[1]
c. *Write the reference on each
   card.*

> II_A_1
>
> • It is our responsibility to exercise our
> right to present lawful complaints to the
> courts and thereby see that justice is done.
>
> Adamson, T. Constitutional Rights, p. 271.

3. *Keying the notes to the outline.* This piece of information is sub-subtopic 1 under subtopic A under topic II. The information is from page 271 of the T. Adamson reference titled, *Constitutional Rights.*
4. *Revise the outline if necessary.* Revision might entail moving subtopics around and/or adding subtopics. Outline notations on cards must be changed accordingly.
5. *Arrange all the note cards in proper order according to the notations on the cards.* With one bit of information per card it is easy to key the notes to the outline and then to arrange them in proper outline order prior to writing.

Step Five: Writing the Paper

Several drafts may need to be written before an acceptable one is completed.

Write a First Draft. With note cards (including synthesized notes) in place it is relatively easy to write the first draft. Write or type the draft in triple space so that there will be room for later revisions. Make sure you use the proper headings.

Let the Draft Cool. If you do not let a draft cool, you will be in danger of not taking an objective look at your work. It is not too bad an idea to allow some qualified person to read your draft critically.

Revise Your First Draft. Make emendations in the space between lines and in the margin. Check for accuracy, clarity, coherence, and interest appeal. Check both text and references.

Write Your Final Draft. Always have your drafts read for content, style, and accuracy (typographical accuracy as well as accuracy of ideas).

Activities for Making Notes, Keying Notes to Outline, Synthesizing Notes, and Writing the Draft

If students have started writing a paper—chosen a theme or topic, jotted points, and arranged them into a preliminary outline, and located, selected, and evaluated information—they may continue by making notes for their paper.

1. Have students zero in on a paragraph in which the information fits part of the outline. They should lift out the essential information (a) by paraphrasing it, (b) by paraphrasing and abstracting it, and (c) by paraphrasing it and explaining it. If the expansion or explanations get into subpoints of the outline, the subpoints should be placed on the appropriate keyed card. Remember only one basic piece of information per card.

---

[1] Although one basic bit of information is written on each card, a writer will at times want to synthesize pieces of information into integrated, more complete sentences when such synthesis makes a needed contribution.

2. Submit examples of a student's work—paragraph plus transformations—to other students for constructive criticism. The critics should point out (a) how the information does or does not fit the outline, (b) whether it is paraphrased well, (c) whether it needs to be explained further.

3. Have students synthesize two or more pieces of related information into a smooth sentence or two. Check their work and offer constructive suggestions for needed improvement.

PREPARING FOR AND WRITING EXAMINATIONS

One can use a number of procedures in preparing for an examination. The *first* procedure is to have a thorough systematic grasp of the content—the various concepts and interrelationships among the concepts. The *second* is to anticipate the form of the examination as well as some of the questions on it. The *third* is to write practice examinations. *Fourth*, one should know the meanings of the various terms used in essay examinations. *Finally*, one should know several basic strategies to use in writing examinations, especially essay examinations.

Reading a Chapter and Organizing It for Retention and Reproduction

Writing Summaries. Of course, the key skill in writing summaries is to develop the main idea of a paragraph. One begins the writing of summaries by practice in *developing the main idea of a sentence.* It might be helpful to have a student read the sentence and paraphrase it or, better yet, give the gist of it. First locate the subject of the sentence, then the predicate, and then what is said about the subject and the predicate or what the subject and predicate do.

How does one write a one-sentence *summary of a paragraph? One* approach is to read quickly through the paragraph and then go back to the first sentence to see if that sentence summarizes the thought of the paragraph. *Another* approach is to note the key words and phrases as you read through the paragraph. Then synthesize the thoughts to capture the gist of the paragraph. *Still another* method is to read through the paragraph and note the important details and then see what these details point to. What is the import of the details? What are they about? Write a summary sentence.

Finally, one can try the hypothesis-testing approach discussed in the comprehension chapter. Read the first sentence. Assume it is the main idea; paraphrase it. Read the second sentence to see if it supports the first sentence. Continue through the paragraph to see if each succeeding sentence might be the main idea or to see if it contributes to the main idea or contradicts what was considered the main idea. Of course, it may work out that one sentence was a major premise, another served as a minor premise, and to get the main idea one must draw a conclusion that then serves as the main idea. This skill is not one that you take care of through a few lessons; it requires careful attention in all content areas for many months and years. *It is a key reading task.*

One continues through the paragraphs of a section and then *combines the summary sentences into a summary paragraph.* It may well be that you should read this summary paragraph to determine the thrust of the sentences so that you can write a topic sentence for the paragraph. Proceed with the other sections in like manner, and you will have developed a summary (comprised of several summary paragraphs, each of which has a good topic sentence!)

Making Notes (A Creative Process). If you ask a person to take notes, he or she might well say, "Show me where they are; I will take them." We should not take notes; we should *make* notes. Making notes implies a creative process in which we invest our thinking and purposes in order to develop a meaningful product that we understand.

Making notes is not so formal a process as outlining nor so straightforward a procedure as writing summaries. The nature of the material, one's familiarity with it, and the purpose for reading the material dictate the approach to making notes at any particular time.

When making notes for the purpose of mastering subject matter, one does the following kinds of things in a spiral omnibus manner; that is, one does these things as they come along in the reading material:

1. Lists the main points with necessary clarifying statements.

2. Lists illustrations (graphic and/or verbal) and experiments useful for clarifying points.

3. Lists important terms and their definitions.

4. Lists terms or concepts that need further clarification.

As implied in the term *spiral omnibus,* this would *not* be four separate listings, but the notes would be made in the material as one comes to the particular things.

NOTE: To cut down on the amount that would need to be written suggest that the student read a paragraph and try to recall the main idea. Some paragraphs and their main ideas might be so well known that the student would need to write only an expanded phrase or a sentence.

The idea of reciting and "boiling down" the information is helpful in keeping the notes from getting too bulky and unmanageable. Remember, too, that paraphrasing is an essential activity because it is a safeguard against recording verbatim notes that may not be understood—a cardinal "sin"!

Outlining. Outlining forces a person to develop the main ideas and supporting details; it makes one look at material and organize it in a logical manner. In outlining one takes a giant step toward being able to reproduce it accurately in test situations, being able to go either the objective test route—true-false, multiple choice, and so forth—or the essay route. Numbers of excellent students that I have had over the years outlined material assiduously and well.

Basically two types of notations are used in outlining:

One: I. MAIN TOPIC
       A. Subtopic
          1. Supporting detail
          2. Supporting detail
            a. Supporting or explanatory detail
              1) Further support
              2) Further support
       B. Subtopic

   II.
       A.
          1.
          2.
              (and so forth)

If the material being outlined contains excellent headings, the outline headings *may* correspond to headings in the chapter, for example:

   I. Center Heading.
       A. Free-standing heading
          1. Indented boldface heading
          2. Indented boldface heading
            a. paragraph main idea
              1) supporting detail
              2) supporting detail

  II. Center Heading
           (and so forth)

Two: Another method uses numbers only:
    1.0   Center Heading
    1.1   Free-standing heading
    1.1.1   Indented boldface heading
    1.1.1.1   paragraph main idea
    1.1.1.1.1   supporting detail
    2.0   Center Heading
            (and so forth)

People will probably use the method with which they are most familiar. There seems to be some kind of advantage to using the number system, because one can note the outline headings on note cards better using the numbers. However, the standard outline system has the advantage of yielding a neater, less cluttered-looking outline.

A Sophisticated Study Approach: Modified SQ3R

Many people say they have heard of the SQ3R study approach by Robinson (1970) but surprisingly few people use it well or diligently. They do not use it effectively because (1) they do not understand it well, (2) they are not willing to devote the time to perfecting it, and (3) after an assignment is made, they wait so long before starting the approach that they do not have enough time to do the last step adequately; that is, they do not have enough time to *Review* properly.

The five steps of the SQ3R (modified) approach are

S   = Survey
Q   = Question
R^1 = Read
R^2 = Recite and 'Rite
R^3 = Review

Survey. In order to get the big picture of what the chapter is about one conducts an overview of the chapter. One reads the chapter title, the introduction, the summary (to see how the basic ideas tie together), the headings and subheadings (to see the structure and the main topics or ideas), and then examines the pictures, charts, maps, tables, and figures.

The survey is the first step in making it possible to have a purpose for reading so that one will not get to the end of the chapter and make the common remark, "I read the whole chapter and cannot remember a thing I read," or "I cannot concentrate when I read." It is the first step in developing pegs upon which ideas can be hung, or categories into which related ideas can be slotted.

Question. As the reader surveys he or she should develop questions over the chapter. An aid to developing questions is to take the headings and convert them into questions. The questions should be written down. This act develops structure and provides a focal point for reading and organizing a series of ideas. If the headings and subheadings do not seem adequate for developing questions, one may have to read a portion of the first paragraph following a heading in order to get enough information for a suitable question. However, one should not write all the questions first, but should at first write only the question for the first heading or section and then read to find the answer before proceeding to the other sections.

Read. Now take the first section and read it through with the purpose of finding the answer to your question. Search actively for the answer.

Recite and 'Rite. After you have read the first section, you should look away from the book and try to *recite* the answer to the question. Put the answer into your own words and try to give a meaningful example. (If you cannot give a meaningful example, there is a high probability that you do not really understand the material.)

When you can recite the answer satisfactorily and give a meaningful example, then *write* the answer under the question. An alternative way of writing the answer is to write key words, phrases, and drawings needed to recall the whole idea.

Now take the next heading and turn it into a question and repeat the process of reading, reciting, and writing the answer until you have completed the chapter.

Review. After you complete the entire reading-reciting-writing assignment, you need to pull together loose ends. Look over your notes in order to get a bird's eye view of the chapter. Proceed by covering up the notes and trying to recall the main points. Then show each point one by one and as you do try to recite the subpoints, or try to recite the answers to the questions. Check your recitation against your written notes.

REAP—A Reading-Writing-Study Skills Strategy

Eanet and Manzo (1976) have devised REAP—a strategy for improving reading/writing/study skills. It is predicated upon a theme which is espoused in this book, that one needs to process information and organize it in a way that is useful to oneself and to others. The four steps in the REAP Strategy are, in brief:

R — <u>Read</u> to discover the writer's message.

E — <u>Encode</u> the message by putting it into one's own language.

A — <u>Annotate</u> by cogently writing the message in notes for oneself or in a thought book to share with others.

P — <u>Ponder</u>—in other words, process the message, now in annotation form, through internal dialectic thinking or through discussion with others.

In writing annotations the reader must differentiate the author's ideas, translate them into his own language, and encapsulate the results in writing. Eanet and Manzo delineate seven kinds of annotation, three of which are discussed here.

1. *Summary*—condenses the selection in a brief, clear, and to-the-point manner. In nonfiction the significant ideas are stated so that relationships are clear but explanatory detail is omitted.

2. *Thesis*—cuts to the heart of the matter, producing a telegram-like, clear statement.

3. *Questions*—directs attention to the answers to the significant questions which the reader feels the author is trying to answer.

Eanet and Manzo select the *summary annotation* to demonstrate how each of the annotations may be effectively taught. In order to teach REAP, the students must have several short selections written at their independent reading level. Following are the steps for teaching students to write annotations.

Step 1—<u>Recognizing and defining.</u> As students read the first selection the teacher writes a summary annotation on the board. Then the teacher gently probes and guides them to state how the summary statement is related to what they have just read. In this manner the concept of summary annotation is developed.

Step 2—<u>Discriminating.</u> Students read another selection. This time one good and three poor summary annotations are presented. Through class discussion students select the best annotation, defend their choice, and explain what makes the others unsatisfactory.

Step 3—<u>Modeling the process.</u> After the students read another selection, the teacher shows the students how to write a summary annotation by "thinking aloud" and noting the <u>thought processes</u> used in arriving at the major ideas and their relationships as well as the writing and <u>rewriting</u> needed to compose a thorough yet concise summary.

<u>Step 4—Practicing</u>. Students read another selection and each student writes a summary annotation. Next they work cooperatively in twos or threes to develop the best summary annotation possible. They may refer back to the selection. The group productions may be placed on the board or duplicated and then compared and evaluated by the class under the teacher's direction. The next summary annotation, using another selection, should be analyzed diagnostically by the teacher and needed help given.

The authors give several examples of how these student annotations can be used; for instance:

> Scene. A secondary English class. Students read a selection from a classroom library of short story or essay anthologies. After reading a selection, a student writes and signs an annotation in a "thought book," a looseleaf notebook kept in the library. The thought book can be used by subsequent readers to aid in choosing a story or essay and as a "cognitive organizer" for reading it.

NSL: A Notetaking System for Learning

Palmatier (1973) describes a notetaking procedure that provides a means for (1) making reading or lecture notes that can easily be synthesized with related notes taken from another source, and then (2) systematically reviewing and mastering the synthesized notes. This procedure is known as the Notetaking System for Learning (NSL). Palmatier (1971) found NSL to be superior to three other methods in an experiment involving high school juniors.

Notes are written on one side of 8½ inch by 11 inch loose-leaf sheets. A margin *three* inches from the left side of the paper may be added to lined paper that has no margin.

Notes from lectures or reading are written to the right of the margin. A method which uses subordination and space should be used. After making notes, numbers and letters can be used to identify the various segments of material. In the left-hand margin the student writes labels that correspond to the segments of information recorded in the original notes. The labeling process also allows the student to fill gaps in notes while the lecture or reading material is still fresh.

Next, the student can insert reading notes into appropriate positions in the original notes. This synthesis is important.

When studying the material, the pages are spread out—second page on first, third on second, etc.—so that only left-hand margins show. The labels in the left-hand margin can be converted to questions. The student attempts to answer a question and then checks his notes to see if he has correctly recalled the material. When a page has been mastered, it can be placed in an "I already know" stack.

If a person is studying for an objective test, he may take the labels in any order. If he is preparing for an essay exam, he will probably take a block of related material that would logically constitute the answer to a particular question. The student should have no trouble in predicting essay questions because the areas on which the most notes are written will likely be the areas on which the essay questions will be based. NSL appears to be a flexible, logical system that "covers the bases" quite well.

Study Strategies Involving Underlining.

Underlining. Adams (1971) studied college students' use of underlining in textbooks used in courses in teaching reading, science, and social studies. She found that the extent of underlining was related to grade point averages.

Underlining and Making Study Sheets. A study at the university level which should have application for average and superior readers in senior high school was conducted by Ritter (1971). Emphasized in Ritter's study skills course were lessons on (1) listening and making notes, (2) underlining, (3) skimming, (4) making study sheets in outline form, and (5) taking examinations, including the writing of essays and term papers. Students considered underlining and making study sheets to be the two most beneficial activities.

Students were taught to differentiate (through an underlining scheme) various parts of paragraphs and chapters in their textbooks and in lecture notes. They underlined enough of the subject, verb, and object to get the full sentence meaning.

The following color system was used:

Yellow — main ideas and topics
Red — important names, dates, chemical formulas, and words to be defined
Blue — details, examples, definitions of words, numbered items, and reasons why something was underlined in red.

[Detailed items were numbered, if not already so, and the numbers were circled to insure catching the reader's attention during review.]

This system was taught the students, they were given a chance to practice in a homework assignment, and they applied the system to the textbooks they were using. The students were encouraged throughout the term to keep up with their reading and underlining.

Study sheets were made by using the students' homework assignments. They "reread their underlinings, constructing a mental outline of the main topics and details at the same time." Next they outlined their underlinings, condensing and reorganizing as they worked through the given chapter. Each chapter was condensed into an outline on one side of a sheet of paper. Furthermore, four to six weeks of class notes could be summarized on *one* sheet of paper. At the end of a year a student would have only about twenty pages in outlines and summarized study sheets to study.

Several months following the study skills program the students showed a mean gain on grade point average of .30, a significant gain.

Writing the Examination

The difficulty in writing objective examinations is that a person must not only know what something is, but what it is not. If one does not have such knowledge, one may experience difficulty in answering multiple-choice questions because they are often cleverly devised to make the student err when he or she (1) fails to note a half truth, (2) answers on the basis of a clang association, (3) does not carefully and logically eliminate incorrect alternatives, and so forth.

Essay examinations may cause difficulty if, for example, the examinee (1) does not understand the meaning of key directional terms such as define, compare, explain, criticize, and discuss, (2) fails to anticipate examination questions, and (3) does not outline answers before beginning to write them. In the following sections, you will find suggestions that you may practice in taking examinations and, in turn, teach your students.

Taking Objective Examinations. *First*, one notes the time limits of the test and checks to see if there is a penalty (a "correction") for incorrect answers. *Second*, one proceeds to read the items carefully, doing the easier items first and not spending too much time on the difficult ones. *Third*, one comes back to the harder items and does them. If in doubt about an answer, one can flag it with a question mark and then come back and read the item more carefully. If one is strongly convinced that one should change a response, one should by all means do so. If there is a penalty for guessing, one should be chary about wild guessing.

If the student has prepared for the examination by thorough preparation such as outlining, doing the SQ3R or NSL, he or she likely will find objective examinations easier than if preparation was cursory. Also, preparation that involves comparing two points of view, or mechanisms, or theories will make it easier to obtain a good score on multiple-choice and matching items, because the examinee has already done valuable differentiation that will stand him or her in good stead when differentiating among choices on the multiple-choice items.

New Types of Examinations. Most of the objective types of examinations in the past have dealt with the recall and recognition of facts. Newer kinds of examinations give data to the students and ask them to draw conclusions on the basis of the data. For example, data couched in a sentence or paragraph are given on the exam and a set of statements or conclusions is listed under the information. The examinee is asked to note if the statement is *true, false,* or (that) *not enough information is given.* One variation on this theme is to insert degrees of probability of truth or falsity. Such tests should be discussed when returned to the students for it will help them understand the process by engaging in related kinds of thinking.

In a similar type of test the student not only answers the question but checks appropriate reasons for the answers from a list. Each item has a separate list. Discussion of returned tests can be of value if it familiarizes students with some of the logical fallacies of thinking such as overgeneralization, reasoning by false analogy, half truths, assuming something as true, irrelevant reasons, and *post hoc ergo propter hoc.* The discussion should be related to the tests and not be a discussion of these fallacies in the abstract or of situations that are not applicable to the test.

Writing the Essay Examination.   The key to writing successful essay examinations is two-fold: preparation and organization. Successful exam writing is predicated on the examinee's being thoroughly prepared; in fact, it is useful not only to study but also to anticipate exam questions and practice writing answers to them.

When you[2] sit down to answer essay examination questions, you should follow these steps:

1. *Estimate the time.* Look at the exam questions and estimate how much time will be required on each; you should write the time in minutes by each question.

2. *Recall and jot key phrases.* In the upper right-hand corner of your page jot the key phrases that you recall for each test question. Allot ¼ to ½ of the time you have for each question to this and the following step.

3. *Organize the jotted key phrases.* Toward the end of the time allotted for jotting and organizing organize the phrases by numbering them in a logical order; you may find also that some of the phrases are subordinate to others. In actuality, then, you will have outlined your answer.

4. *Write the answer.* Once you have organized your responses, you will find little or no trouble in writing your answer.

The *rationale* for this approach is logical. Many people panic on essay questions; panic results in concretizing, that is, a person cannot think flexibly and fluently about abstract ideas. If one is prepared, one will have no trouble in recalling ideas. One will not panic because he or she does not mix the three basic procedures: the *recalling,* the *organizing,* and the *writing.* My students and I verify the value of this approach. Once again, this system assumes (1) thoughtful, active preparation for the examination, (2) anticipation of examination questions, and (3) practice runs of jotting phrases and writing on the basis of an organization of the phrases.

SUMMARY

Positive results accrue academically to the individual who intelligently organizes information that comes within his or her purview. Organization is useful not only in obtaining and comprehending information but also in retaining and reproducing it, that is, in writing better themes, term papers, and examinations.

A first step in reading and organizing information is to develop a particular purpose for reading and to determine a method of organization. Since poor readers, as you will remember, have such difficulty in developing and executing worthwhile purposes for reading as well as in organizing information, special attention would need to be given such readers.

There are special techniques to use in initiating inquiry, and they revolve around the idea of developing a theme, writing preliminary points, and

---

[2] I have used the word "you" because you need to practice these steps if you are going to teach the method well and convincingly.

arranging the points into a preliminary outline. In addition to points that come to mind, answers to specific questions are also used in developing the preliminary outline.

Students must be taught how to select appropriate sources of information to be used in writing a paper. First one uses general sources such as encyclopedias, standard texts, and handbooks to get an overview, and then, when necessary, one consults a librarian for expert help.

One must learn to pinpoint information through use of such aids as the card catalogue, the *Readers' Guide, Vertical File Index,* subject matter cyclopedias, and the index of books. Intensive instruction by the various content-area teachers should be given to students to make sure they learn the many skills needed to pinpoint information.

One of the more difficult skills is that of carefully selecting and evaluating information. The reader has to judge the validity of the information and select that of suitable validity or quality and also judge when he or she has enough information. In other words, a person must read critically, carefully, and selectively.

The ability to comprehend written material was treated in a different chapter, but one will remember that in reading and writing information must be processed in order to make it understandable. This means that information may have to be paraphrased, expanded, contracted, illustrated, and so forth. In addition, specialized instruction in interpreting pictorial and other graphic aids will need to be given.

As just noted, information must be processed; that is, it will have to be abstracted, paraphrased, and organized in terms of one's preliminary outline. Revisions of one's outline are sometimes necessary After suitable drafts are written and appropriate emendations made, the final draft is typed.

Special formalized study and organization techniques, such as REAP, NSL, SQ3R and outlining, were discussed as was the relation of these skills to writing examinations. Finally, the reader was shown how to write more successfully certain kinds of examinations.

ACTIVITIES AND QUESTIONS
TO PROMOTE LEARNING AND APPLICATION

1. Why could it be true that intelligence and organization are two sides of a coin?
2. Find a "slow" reader who does not read the newspapers because he or she is frustrated at not being able to read all of it. Help this reader apply the text suggestions on reading selectively. What resistance did you encounter? How did you handle it? (Is the reader still your friend?)
3. Read book reviews from *Book Review Digest* and the *The New York Times.* Select a target group of young people and write reviews that would be appealing to them.

4. Allow your students to write book reviews in an interesting way. Perhaps they could develop multimedia presentations. Does this seem to result in an increase in the reading of books?
5. Why should people read the preface of a book?
6. Select a topic of great interest to you. Following the procedures suggested in the text write a nonfiction paper of about 11 double-spaced typewritten pages including references. After you finish the paper, allow other people to read it. Be sure you follow the steps, especially that of careful revising. Do you feel more confident about your ability to write as a result of doing the paper?
7. Teach your students (or a peer) how to write a paper by this method.
8. Write a summary of a chapter in a text you are using this term. Use the procedure suggested in the text. Compare it with the summary of a friend in the course who agrees to do the same.
9. Make notes of a segment of a chapter in a technical book, using the procedures outlined in the text. Teach a student to make notes in this manner.
10. Why is it a cardinal "sin" to record notes verbatim?
11. Outline a section in a chapter in this text. What features of the text make outlining easy? Difficult? Compare the organization of this book with a book that is less well organized. What are the advantages of a well-organized book?
12. What is the theory underlying SQ3R? NSL?
13. Apply SQ3R or NSL to the reading of a chapter in a course you are taking and on which you will be tested. Allow enough time for several review periods. Did it help your examination grade?
14. Prepare for an essay examination by diligently applying SQ3R or NSL. Develop a number of possible essay questions and practice writing them according to the technique outlined in the text. Use the technique in writing your exam. Did it pay off?

SUGGESTED ADDITIONAL READINGS

AUKERMAN, ROBERT C. *Reading in the Secondary Classroom.* New York: McGraw-Hill, 1972. Chapter 4.

BURMEISTER, LOU E. *Reading Strategies for Secondary School Teachers.* Reading, Mass.: Addison-Wesley, 1974. Chapter 11.

CARMAN, ROBERT A., and W. ROYCE ADAMS, JR. *Study Skills: A Student's Guide for Survival.* New York: John Wiley and Sons, 1972.

HAFNER, LAWRENCE E. (Ed.). *Improving Reading in Middle and Secondary Schools.* Second Edition. New York: Macmillan, 1974. Section 6.

JOLLY, HAYDEN B. "Determining Main Ideas: A Basic Study Skill." In Lawrence E. Hafner (1974, pp. 162–72).

KARLIN, ROBERT. *Teaching Reading in High School.* Second Edition. Indianapolis, Ind.: Bobbs-Merrill, 1972. Chapter 7.

MOE, IVER L. and FRANK NANIA. "Reading Deficiencies Among Able Pupils." In Lawrence E. Hafner (1974, pp. 172–85).

PAUK, WALTER. *How to Study in College.* Boston: Houghton Mifflin, 1962.

ROBINSON, FRANCIS P. "Study Skills for Superior Students in Secondary School." In Lawrence E. Hafner (1974, pp. 185–91).

SHEPHERD, DAVID L. *Comprehensive High School Reading Methods.* Columbus, Ohio: Charles E. Merrill, 1973. Chapter 5.

ZINTZ, MILES V. *The Reading Process.* Second Edition. Dubuque: Wm. C. Brown, 1975. Chapter 12.

BIBLIOGRAPHY

ADAMS, EFFIE K. "Underlining: The Graphical Aid to College Reading." In George B. Schick and Merrill M. May (Eds.). *Reading Process and Pedagogy.* Milwaukee: National Reading Conference, Inc., 1971.

EANET, MARILYN and ANTHONY V. MANZO. "REAP—A Strategy for Improving Reading/Writing/Study Skills." *Journal of Reading.* *19* (8) (May 1976), 647–652.

PALMATIER, ROBERT A. "A Notetaking System for Learning." *Journal of Reading.* *17* (1) (October 1973), 36–39.

RITTER, JOYCE H. "University Study Skills Program." *Journal of Reading.* *14* (6) (March 1971), 377–380.

ROBINSON, FRANCIS P. *Effective Study.* Fourth Edition. New York: Harper and Row, 1970.

Section Three

*Teaching Strategies for Improving
Reading Skills in the
Content Areas*

CHAPTER 8

Teaching the Reading of
Social Studies. I. Foundations

This foundation chapter is perhaps written more for the general reader, teachers in other content areas, and reading specialists than it is for some social studies teachers. Not everyone who has completed the liberal arts requirements in college has a liberal education, but such instruction is a good start towards the life-long effort to become liberally educated.

Sydney J. Harris, the columnist, recounts an interview that Phil Donahue conducted with a 70-year-old man released after 20 years of imprisonment in Germany. The man's remarks are an excellent testimonial for liberal education. The man is Albert Speer, the architect and Nazi who was Hitler's master logistics expert in the fields of armaments, munitions, and slave labor control.

Speer lamented his receiving only a technical education, learning little of humanities and the liberal arts and nothing whatsoever of philosophy. He stated that he and others were technical barbarians who never probed the reasons for and end results of the things they did for Hitler.

Not having a liberal education, which would have helped them ask questions and probe for information and evaluate it, and not being educated to the probable moral and social consequences of Nazism had deleterious effects. Speer stated that if they had been educated and informed they might have taken steps to abort the revolutionary Nazi movement. But like the Watergate people, he said, the German leaders thought they were being loyal and had never learned what real loyalty ought to mean.

So many people think that subjects such as religion, history, and philosophy are not practical. But are they not the only subjects that ask the perennial existential questions, "Who am I?" "Where did I come from?" "What am I doing here?" "Where am I going?" These questions are not academic and the answers to them mean life or death. If you do not answer them now and try to rectify wrong answers and intelligently and compassionately fill vital lacunae, your children may have to do it on some future battlefield or in some other kind of holocaust that ensues. The problem is that these latter "solutions" require blood and lives and are seldom effective anyway. *So a liberal education that educates cognitively and affectively is a very practical education!*

What Do We Mean by the Term "Social Studies?"

Trying to find a definition of social studies is unbelievably difficult. I have had to infer that the social scientists in their studies of human and social behavior in such fields as history, psychology, geography, politics, and economics provide the content. The authors of social studies materials use their own assumptions and biases of what is important for the social and psychological education of humans and select and interpret content accordingly.

Educators involved in social studies education have had as a central goal the development of the knowledgeable, good citizen. Any failures that result are traceable to the quality of their assumptions and biases, the tenacity with which they hold them, and the fervor with which they propagate them.

As with almost any concept, the meaning with which a term is invested depends on the people defining the term Social studies as noted seems to be a farrago of concepts, principles, and values from a number of fields. In the past, social studies educators have tried mainly to integrate history and geography, with some attention given to related fields. Ideas were represented in terms of the philosophies of the writers of the texts and how far they would allow their principles to be compromised and their materials to be emasculated in order to appease pressure groups. The fact that these materials have been unreadable by the majority of the students in the grades in which they were used may have proved to be a boon to society rather than a bane.

A more modern and intelligent concept has been to shun single text adoptions and go to a variety of paperback texts that have more or less escaped the obscurantist emasculators of truth. One way to test the veracity of my claims is to list the facts and interpretations of social studies from primary sources in one column and the facts and interpretations from emasculated texts in another column. Then see what conclusions can be drawn Even where facts in the texts are accurate, discussions may be slanted such that incorrect implications result.

Furthermore, the assumptions of the writers of "patriotic" texts need to be examined very carefully. May I point to the treatment of the Revolutionary War in most texts? In the average text of the past (and in some today) Samuel Adams and others are treated as heroes rather than the revolutionaries they were. On the other hand, may I point to the shoddy treatment given by "patriotic" groups to some people today who espouse nonviolent dissension in the spirit of "Your country—love it and improve it" rather than the ludicrous alternative, "Your country—love it or leave it." The young people who try to improve the country are treated like criminals even though their actions in many instances are more rational than those of many of the radical heroes of history and the present "Your country—love it or leave it" supporters. If you love your country, you stay and try to improve it.

The "patriots" in backing Samuel Adams have taught that violent dissension is democratic and desirable. It is, however, demeaning and destructive. How can they be surprised that the recipients of such instruction should employ dissent? The miracle is that the majority of modern dissenters have been as peaceful as they have been—much more peaceful than Adams and Washington.[1]

Spector's (1971) brilliant article questions the necessity of the Revolutionary War: (1) "Was there any grievance or set of grievances so vital and impelling that it could not have been settled in the courts by constitutional processes?" (2) Were any of the grievances so immediate that they were worth breaking up the British Empire–Union? These questions must be considered in light of those times and in the context of world civilization since that time. I will try to list a few of the major ideas of the article, but you should read the original:

1. These two wars were fought only for self-determination, because a minority group—colonial leaders—and slave holders wanted to lead a different life from the majority.

2. The problems could have been solved where 1,200 years of English history demand they be solved, in the courts. Oddly enough, Americans try to justify a period of history that in its resort to violence negates constitutional processes —the bedrock of our democracy.

3. Only a small, vociferous minority wanted the separation from Britain.

4. There was *nothing* mentioned in the Declaration "that could not have been settled by reasonable litigants in courts of law." (Spector makes a brillant rational analysis of all this.)

5. Did the colonial leaders want taxation with representation or did they merely desire to be free of taxation per se?

6. The Welsh and Scots had been granted representation already and the Irish were to receive it in 1801. The colonials would have gotten representation also.

7. We boast about the radicals illegally ruining someone else's tea, but did we hold Martin Luther King's philosophy of nonviolence in esteem?

8. In the American–British situation machinery was present for fruitful change. Several times early in the war the British made conciliatory offers that the colonials would have accepted if they truly wanted representation in the Parliament and status in the Union.

9. "We must accept the bitter truth that the War was a departure from constitutional processes."

Fortunately, some excellent texts that have not been subjected to the crude scalpels of ignorant people are now being published and people are thus beginning to have a chance at free inquiry into truth.

A LOOK AT GEOGRAPHY

What is Geography?

Leinwand and Feins (1968) define geography as the "study of Man's relationship to the earth on which he lives." They note that geography is unique in the

---

[1] I accept the establishment of the United States as a *fait accompli* and uphold the Constitution and the Bill of Rights. It is a nonsequitur to say that I must condone the manner in which the colonists flouted British law and revolted against the mother country.

in the social studies because it uses the physical and natural sciences in addition to the behavioral and social sciences. Mathematics is used in making and interpreting map projections. Physics is used in dealing with problems in climate. Geology and chemistry are basic to obtaining detailed insight into the earth's soils and minerals.

The two main branches of geography study are physical geography and human or cultural geography. The physical geographer will emphasize studies of the world's surface—its "flora, fauna, climate, the distribution of its land and water areas, the location, size, and shape of the land masses, and the soil upon which men depend for a livelihood." The physical geographer usually divides the world into natural regions based on climate, vegetation, or land forms. Some of the common regional arrangements based largely on climate are rainy tropics, tropical deserts, dry continentals, and subarctics. Geography study, however, involves more than just giving a physical description of an area. The focus of study must be the human *relationship* to the region and its environment (James, 1959).

Human geography uses physical geography as a starting point and tries to (1) determine how geographic factors have curtailed or expanded human activities and (2) study the methods and means used by humans to transform their natural environment successfully. Some cultural regions studied are *Soviet:* the Soviet Union and Eastern Europe; *Anglo-American:* Canada and the United States; and *South Asian:* India, Pakistan, Ceylon, and border countries (James, 1959).

Increasing Cruciality of Geographic Knowledge

Hanna and others (1966) point out that we need to pay more attention in the formal curriculum to preparing the young to grasp the structure of relationships existing between the natural conditions of one's environment and the human activities taking place there. Also, we must develop the skills so that we can deal rationally with matters that have geographic aspects.

Several examples of our growing awareness of natural phenomena might clarify the point. For instance, the Western Hemisphere nations, Hanna, et al. note, are working hard to "create social technology that will help foster peace, order, prosperity, and the dignity of humans throughout the Americas." Knowledge about our "natural environment—diversities in such natural characteristics as soil, flora and fauna, minerals, climate, and terrain" throughout the spacious Americas—would enable us to anticipate or understand the responses of peoples who inhabit environments strange to us in the United States. In the past, lack of such knowledge has been responsible for our making mistakes that have helped frustrate the progress universally desired.

Geography begins at home, and the geographical method is done justice where the data are fully available and the ground quite accessible for study. A taste for geography is firmly rooted in the experience of roaming, map in hand, in one's native countryside. (Wooldridge and East, 1958) This method is a favorite of British social studies teachers and has much to commend it. Take groups out into the community, but take groups that are prepared and have been supplied with the proper tools and instruments and have a good idea of what they are about.

A LOOK AT HISTORY

What Is History?

History is a kind of inquiry or research—a science of asking questions and trying to answer them. As part of this inquiry history explores the "actions of human beings that have been done in the past" (Collingwood, 1946). The philosopher Ortega y Gassett (1960) states that because man is each living being who thinks with meaning and whose thinking we can understand, history assumes it can understand man.

Of course there are purposes for delving into the past. One purpose is to take the *second look* in order to find the reason for what appears to be unreason. This statement implies that when we are looking the second time—intelligently, creatively, and with a critical eye at the first "reporter," I would say—we somehow find the reason that the first time around appeared to be unreason. The second purpose, as generally stated, is to *apply history* to the present in order to improve social living.

The historian is guided in questioning and in the search for answers by interests and by the outlook and assumptions of the era—of his or her time and place as he or she interprets them. (Danzer, 1973) Just as theologians tell us that each generation reinterprets theology so that it can be understood by that generation, Frederick Jackson Turner has stated that each age attempts to reconceptualize the past for itself with reference to the salient conditions in its own time, that is, the time being investigated. I concur in the necessity for such reconceptualization.

The actions of humans in ages past are explored, then, in order to develop a meaningful explanation of the facts and an application to the present. In fact, history is not really history and does not fulfill its inner mission unless it develops an understanding of humans in whatever period the historian is investigating (Ortega y Gassett, p. 27).

Facts by themselves often turn out to be quite meaningless. A point of view has to be taken toward them, and an interpretation relating them to one another and to the present must be made. Kotarbinski (1966) discusses historical explanation. The genetic problem type pertains to the *origin* of something and is identified by questions such as, "Why has something happened?"

The Three Processes of History. According to Commager (1965), the *first* process of history is collecting facts relevant to the questions being asked. The *second* is organizing the facts into some coherent pattern. The *third* process is interpreting the facts and the pattern. By now the reader has said that the first point is really asking questions. Yet it is quite possible that we do not even ask some of the better questions until we have collected facts.

Collecting Facts: Historians have broad interests and a proclivity for digging up countless details. But it is just these phenomena that create the danger that the historian will be inundated in a vast sea of data. But the things that guide the search and are of central importance are questions, for they help the historian find the facts and the relationships that can be selected and arranged to yield an explanatory device. The facts ultimately selected are only those of significance to the historian, those that can be strung as beads along the thread of the explanation. But the string of beads must carry conviction if it is to appeal to the reader. (Danzer, 1973) The important test of credulity and whether the arguments command agreement does not depend so much on the logic that conveys them as it does on the climate of opinion in which they are upheld (Becker, 1959).

One assumes, of course, that the historian will use only genuine data. Yet historical data and sources must be subjected to external criticism. External criticism seeks to determine the genuineness of the document itself, whether it is valid (Is it what it purports to be?) and true to the original. Internal criticism is concerned with the meaning and trustworthiness of statements remaining after invalid material has been deleted from the text. External criticism relates to form and appearance of content, whereas internal criticism works on the meaning, weighing the document's testimony in relation to the truth, or what really happened.

Organizing and Interpreting Data. The second and third processes of history are organizing and interpreting data into some new, coherent schema or pattern so that a clearer understanding may be developed (Commager, 1965). The key point seems to be that the historical method is in essence a matter of interpreting evidence. Yet, as Commager states, these three processes of collecting, organizing, and interpreting facts flow into each other. One cannot collect the facts in the first place unless one is guided by a theory of relationships among them. One cannot organize them into a pattern without a theory to dictate that pattern. The interpretation, then, on the basis of the material selected and the pattern developed.

There is a presumed fourfold advantage of the historian's arrangement over the natural matrix:

1. It is simpler, less unwieldy, and easier to grasp.

2. It reveals a relationship among an inner meaning of events that seemingly have no rationale or significance. In other words, the historian is developing a new pattern that handles the totality of the situation.

3. There is power to the explanation that goes beyond the individual events used. Other data can be fit into the structure.

4. The schema or pattern can be moved across time and space and used to analyze other situations, and, with minor alterations, to invest another area with meaning (Danzer, 1973).

Factors that influence the historian's organization and interpretation are one's *general philosophy* of history and also one's *specific school* of historical interpretation. Students will be affected by the philosophies and schools to which authors and teachers subscribe. It is important for history teachers and reading teachers to be aware of this phenomenon so that they know what can happen if the assumptions of a particular philosophy of history or school of historical interpretation are granted.

Christian Philosophy of History. Among the broad philosophies of history is the Christian philosophy, which places Christ at the center of history. Historians espousing a Christian philosophy of history see God "as dominant in human affairs, controlling and moving all things for His purposes." On the material level, God is concerned with such things as the preservation and protection of the human race by such human institutions as government and commerce. On the spiritual level, God uses history to show people their need for God. And He uses misfortunes and disasters as chastisements useful for turning people to God. In the beneficent events and trends in history and in the disasters, the Christian sees God's hand seeking out humanity so that God might glorify people by humbling them. In the Christian philosophy of history the greatest event is the one in which God most directly intervened to manifest His love to humans. That event is the incarnation of Jesus Christ and the subsequent redemption of humanity by Christ. All the other events of history have the sole function of turning people to find Christ before He returns in Judgment to end history and begin the new heaven and the new earth (Caemmerer, 1975).

Marxian Philosophy Applied to History Versus Capitalist Philosophy. Marx borrowed Hegel's idea of thesis, antithesis, and synthesis to show why the future is to bring, according to Marx, a classless or socialist society. Capitalism's *thesis* is that one must work in order to show a profit. A corollary is that a class of privileged few own the means of production and the others, the workers, are controlled by the few. Another thesis, *antithesis,* works against the original thesis of control by the privileged few. The antithesis, then, results in conflict between the mass of poor workers and the few capitalists. Following an open conflict or revolution, the capitalist system goes under and the resulting synthesis is a new socialist or classless society.

The Marxists illustrate the process by claiming that the historical King state societies divided into opposite forces—the King rulers versus the have-nots and slaves. The struggle between these forces resulted in the synthesis of feudalistic society. Feudalism, in turn, yielded the factions of lords and serfs; the synthesis resulting from this conflict was capitalism. Marxists aver that they do not develop class struggles but only highlight their existence in a way that favors communistic growth. There evidently was an assumption prevalent among many classes of people prior to the World War I that this kind of social evolution was yielding Utopia.

Popkin and Stroll (1956) state that the defenders of capitalism attack Marxism's contention that the capitalist system will inevitably produce depressions, accumulation of wealth by the owners of business, and the increasing distress and misery of the workers. The capitalist's response is this: First, the workers in capitalist societies rather than being miserable are doing well. The worker makes more money and has a higher standard of living, even though he or she works fewer hours and has better working conditions. Second, capitalism has been quite creative in solving difficulties within the system: growth of labor unions, antitrust laws, and social security provisions, for example. (It might be, may I add, that labor unions in generally providing rational and effective solutions to management-labor have helped to stall off the radical solutions of communism, thereby helping capitalism survive!)

But the Marxists contend that these provisions were socialist measures, not capitalist ones. What this means for the study of history is that it is necessary to inquire into the various sides of issues, that more original sources be consulted, and that the political and philosophical leanings of local and national pressure groups not be allowed to stifle the right to spirited active pursuit of knowledge in these spheres.

Platonic Political Philosophy. It may seem as though I am not approaching these philosophies in the correct order. Yet it may prove to be of value to note the deep roots of modern political philosophies. An important, yet perplexing, problem in political philosophy is, "Who should rule?" Those people favoring democracy say, "The people should rule themselves." (John Locke) Monarchists such as Thomas Hobbes feel that one person should rule. Hobbes, therefore, favored a very powerful centralized state.

Plato, who lived almost two thousand years before Hobbes, espoused rule by a specially groomed cadre of elite *intellectuals* guided by pure reason. The other two social groups in his immutable system of social classes were the strong, courageous *soldiers* who were to defend the state, and the *workers,* a sort of motley, sensual, barbaric group who were fit only to support themselves and the other two groups. The workers were kept on an even keel by having to obey the laws imposed on them. Plato also felt that his views (which were really antidemocratic) were just, because they were in keeping with the "nature of things." Thus, Plato held that by nature some people are born to rule and others to be ruled. The social divisions had an analogue in the makeup of the human soul—the rational element, the spirited element, and the appetitive element (Wiener, 1964).

It is quite easy to see how Plato's philosophy leads to an antidemocratic, authoritarian philosophy. If you peruse American history you can pick out the ardent followers of Plato who used his arguments and suppositions to bolster their master–slave morality, with the soldier class used to safeguard the master-slave relationship.

What Are the Purposes and Values of History?

In stating what history is we have already suggested two basic *purposes* of history One is to understand humanity in the periods that we investigate and the other is to make applications of what we learn about human interactions to present day living. What follows will be variations on these fundamental themes.

History Provides Answers to Basic Questions. Most of us are by now familiar with the basic existential questions. Of course, not enough people seem to confront these questions seriously. Some individuals who deem their answers adequate have not conducted a thorough investigation of history in order to be able to claim that they have adequate answers.

Saunders (1956) points out that if these questions are not answered, society will not have cohesion, organization, or purpose. If history does not provide society with a sense of unity and being, we shall die. And may I add, parenthetically, that we have died in countless personal and social rifts and in many wars because we have not found that sense of unity. Christian philosophers of history tell us that saving unity comes only through Jesus Christ. It may just be that this is one of the neglected areas of history, and because of the neglect inadequate answers to the existential questions are held by so many people.

Connecting the Past with the Present. History should look at the past as a whole and connect the past with the present. Barraclough (n.d.) feels that the only adequate history is one that looks to humanity in all lands and all ages. The whole system of reality must be dealt with. Therefore, history will gain meaning and relevance for our lives and help us know where we stand in a changing world, if we think of the whole world as one and realize that the fortune of each person in the world is linked with the fortune of every other person in the world.

A notable example of obscurantism and its resulting inability to see the interdependence of peoples was shown in the complaints of numerous people during the United States sea-and-air lift of hundreds of thousands of Vietnamese who were subsequently brought to this country. Some people were so compassionless that all they could say was, "Why did they bring them over here? There are not enough jobs to go around the way it is." That one of the great rescue operations of all times elicited such prosaic and heartless responses is dumbfounding!

In order for the historical approach to succeed in helping us make a wellinformed, critical judgment of modern society's problems (with a view, no doubt, to solving some of those problems), we must (1) look at the past as a whole and shun fragmentation of knowledge, (2) look outside the historical process for an end or goal of history, (3) test the relevance (of historical data), and (4) strive to redevelop the connection between history and life, between then and now.

Social Purpose of History. John Donne said "No man is an island unto himself." Yet we have seen people who do not realize that we stand or fall together; that is, we are social beings who need one another.

Plumb (1964) believes that the most important feature of human history is humanity's increasing control over its environment. (Some people today will certainly question that contention.) However, we must look to such phenomena as Egypt's development of mensuration and irrigation, Jenner's and Salk's vaccines, Edison's electric light, and hydro-electric power and admit that great strides in environmental control have been made over the centuries. (And how would I have known that had I not studied history!) The historian's investigation of the past should lead to the application of insights in order that humans may exert an intelligent and compassionate control over their future. (If it is not compassionate, it will not be intelligent!)

Plumb continues by saying that teachers of history should emphasize broad movements of great impact such as the effects of geographical discoveries and of the scientific revolution. (See above.) The social purpose of history should help mold the teachers' and students' studies and help them to understand better the past so that their attitudes toward the past will be more informed.

Furthermore, the history teacher and the students *will* engage in pentrating discussions and make broad generalization in order to draw sound conclusions or lessons from history. History must fulfill its social function in government and in administration as well as in all the many affairs of people.

History Is Necessary for Social Education. Today some people want to abolish history in favor of more "relevant" contemporary studies. It is true that these latter studies have a place in educating young people in their struggle with current problems. However, adequate social education cannot be achieved without substantial attention being paid to history (Cartwright, 1966).

Through history, Cartwright avers, the student should see people at work on matters of universal, never-ending importance in different times and settings. In this way, the student should come to understand different peoples and to see that humankind is one.

Also, it is incumbent upon the historian and the history teacher to select from historical data elements of enduring value. It is for this capacity to select such enduring elements that history has singular importance in the social studies. What Cartwright is saying is that historical study should guide social action. Wise decisions about any matter of social significance can be made only by considering similar decisions made by people in the past.

The Writing of History With Clues to the Reading of History

Certainly, knowing how history is written by the better writers will provide the alert teacher and student with cues. Vaughn (1969) states that the historian has a duty to disseminate the facts and their meanings as widely as possible in order that society's memory of its past may be enriched and preserved. Yet the important aspect of an event is its description in terms of thought, as we shall see.

Bodies and Thoughts: Aspects of Historical Description. In investigations an historian differentiates between the outside of an event and the inside of the event. The former refers to all things belonging to the event that can be depicted in terms of bodies and their movement, Caesar's passage across the Rubicon on one date or the shedding of his blood on the senate house floor on another. The *inside* of the event refers to its description in terms of thought. The historian, then, is interested in the crossing of the Rubicon in its relation to the Republican law only, and in the shedding of Caesar's blood only as it relates to a constitutional conflict. Thus, the historian's job is to think himself or herself into the action, that is, to discern the thought of the agent of the action. The processes of history, then, are the processes of thought. The historian then searches for these processes of thought. Therefore, all history is the history of thought (Collingwood, 1946).

Such is the case with the most famous person of history. The central figure in history, the man who is so dominant in history that we figure time around him (in terms of Before Christ and Anno Domini). His blood was shed, too. That is the outer part of the event. But the significance of it (the inside of the event) is not that certain Jews killed Christ; they were only the precipitating cause.

Christian philosophy of history interprets the event as being caused by all humankind, and the real purpose of the death is in atonement for humanity's sins. Those who do not understand this might use the Jews as scapegoats, as has often been done in history. Hitler even used it as one of several pretenses for slaughtering millions of Jews.

So, it is *not* true that we should not talk about religion in the schools or in textbooks such as this. It *is* true that we must study Judeo-Christian history and correctly interpret it so that lives will be spared, both now and in the future. Our timorousness in coming to grips with this kind of history has left people ill-informed and heartless and prone to side with totalitarian minds (in this country and abroad) in persecuting Jews and other peoples.

As you can see, the historian's values and beliefs shape the account, and it should be so. We hope the historian will have such values and beliefs that he or she will dig into *all* facets of history, not just those that are marketable in the public or private schools, not just those that will receive the nihil obstat and the imprimatur of a publisher or this pressure group or that pressure group.

Truth as an Important Goal of the Historian. The author's hortatory remarks should not be construed as the voice of one crying in the wilderness; he is not alone. Danzer (1973), for example, states that the nature of reality and of existence obscures truth from both the historian and the audience. Yet truth is an important goal and the historian must be able to communicate with readers in order to develop a dialogue between past and present. Such dialogue requires that the historian not only break existence into pieces and divide it into artificial segments but also that he or she clearly outline the message and then convey the rich texture of the past through metaphor.

Common Elements in the Writing of the Masters of History. A teacher of the social studies in the middle school and in the secondary school should write. The teacher who writes history should be able to do a better job of teaching history, including helping students to read better and to write history also. Good and Scates (1954) have some suggestions about the writing of history.

First, one should saturate one's mind with the subject before beginning to write. Second, use a preliminary outline to guide the selection of notes. Third, use a thesis or principle of synthesis in order to delineate cause-effect relationships. Fourth, in each major segment of the historical work, develop several more-detailed generalizations or conclusions related to the basic guiding thesis or principle of synthesis. Fifth, discard enough data so that the resulting condensation and precision will prevent unwanted detail from crowding the main actors and narrative events from the scene. Sixth, write simply and clearly and shun improper appeal to emotions.

Trevelyan maintained that historians should present history in a variety of forms readable by various sections (or kinds) of people. Also, the general reader should study history unless his or her education both as a citizen and as an intellectual and imaginative being is to be lacking. However, few readers study history for patriotic reasons or to improve their minds. They read because they like reading, and they choose those books that interest or delight them. If history materials fascinate them, they will read them. Therefore, it is incumbent upon historians to make history as fascinating and readable as possible. This brings us to factors that impede the readability of textbooks in the middle and secondary schools.

THE CONCEPT-VOCABULARY BURDENS OF INSTRUCTIONAL MATERIALS

Because of the tendency of authors and publishers to give their readers their money's worth there has arisen in the educational field a phenomenon I have termed *competitive concept stuffing* (Hafner, 1965). What does it mean? Publisher B's sales representatives tell prospective users of a world history text that it contains more concepts in its 490 pages than publisher S's world history text. That may be true; B's text broaches more topics, but it sacrifices the explanatory text necessary to explain and clarify those concepts.

Competitive concept stuffing, then, has been one of the great trapdoors of middle and secondary school students. It has rendered some texts almost impossible to read.

Readability Problems in the Social Studies. Some years ago Ritter (1941) found 2,195 technical, difficult, or unusual terms introduced in a fourth-grade text. At the time authors of reading texts thought that pupils would do well to acquire 1,000 *general* vocabulary terms in a year.

In 1974 I found two state-adopted social studies texts, a regular text and a history of Florida text, designed for use in the fourth grade to have readability grade placements of 9.5 and 8.7, respectively. The regular text contained a list of about 40 consultants from various fields, but, to my knowledge, not a single consultant from the field of reading. Of course, that is belaboring the obvious.[2] A representative study by Campbell (1972) showed that about one-fifth of the middle grades students he studied could not adequately understand the social studies textbooks assigned to them.

Increasing Comprehension

Authors and readers must share the responsibility in developing meaning and thereby increasing comprehension. An author can increase comprehension by

[2] L. E. Hafner, Unpublished study, Florida State University, 1974.

attending to such factors as concept density, language structure, and diction (choice of words.) Wilson (1944) studied middle school students and found that reading comprehension increased when general statements found in textbooks were amplified. Conversely, reading comprehension increased to the degree that concept density was decreased. The fewer the concepts per page the greater the comprehension achieved. Serra (1954) summarized her review of the studies on the effect on comprehension of amplifying and simplifying instructional materials by stating that "Vocabulary simplification has less effect on understanding than does simplification of language structure and the relative difficulty of the concept involved. Since concept burden is a factor in readability, a valid evaluation of reading materials can be made only by considering the number and difficulty of concepts." She also warned that concepts acquired vicariously through language often lead to verbalism. The implication is that words and concepts should, wherever possible, be grounded in real experiences.

SUMMARY

There is much evidence that a good liberal education can help a person to ask the perennial existential questions and find answers that contribute to an intelligent, compassionate life. Thus, a liberal education is a practical education.

Consonant with that idea is the social studies educator who has as a key goal the development of the knowledgeable, good citizen. There are other goals, of course, but their attainment should contribute to a better life for more people.

Truth can be rather hard to come by in social studies texts, which have been so consistently and viciously emasculated by so many people who propagate myths detrimental to truth and freedom.

Geography has been defined as the study of humanity's relationship to the earth on which it lives. Teachers must help prepare the young to understand the structure of relationships existing between their physical environment and human activities.

History is a kind of inquiry that explores and reconceptualizes the past actions of humans with reference to the salient conditions of the time so that a more reasoned and clear interpretation can be made of what is found and applications can be made to the present in order to improve social living.

The processes in history have to do with collecting facts relevant to the questions being asked and organizing and interpreting the facts into a new coherent pattern so that a clearer understanding may be developed. The collection and the organization of facts are guided, possibly even dictated, by a theory.

The historian's arrangement of facts has a number of advantages over the original matrix of facts: it is easier to grasp, it reveals a new pattern that interprets the totality of the situation, it develops greater explanatory power, and it can be moved across time and space to analyze other situations and invest other areas with meaning.

Marxian philosophy was compared with capitalist philosophy, with the former trying to show why a classless society is inevitable and the capitalist philosophy trying to prove that since capitalism is so successful the classless society will never come into being.

Plato's political philosophy was explored and found to be an antidemocratic, authoritarian philosophy, which has been used even into this century to bolster a master-slave morality.

The Christian philosophy of history places Christ at the center of history, seeing God as dominant in human affairs and being concerned with humans on material and spiritual levels. He preserves and protects humans through institutions such as government and uses misfortunes as chastisements to turn humans to God. The incarnation of Jesus Christ and His subsequent redemption of humanity are viewed as the greatest events in history. The other events of history have the sole function of turning humans toward Christ before He returns in judgment.

Purposes and values of history have been touched upon. Further purposes and values follow: history provides answers to basic questions, connects the past with the present, teaches us that we are social beings who need one another, and helps humans make wise decisions about matters of social significance by considering similar decisions made by people in times past.

The historian differentiates the outside of an event from the inside of the event. The former refers to aspects of an event that can be depicted in terms of bodies and their movement, whereas the latter refers to describing an event in terms of thought. In this chapter was shown the necessity of applying a truly Christian philosophy of history to interpreting events that in the past have been badly misinterpreted, resulting in the loss of millions of lives.

An understanding of how the masters of history write history should contribute to an understanding of how to teach students to read and properly interpret history. The reader should try especially to uncover the historian's guiding thesis, for that will be an aid in discovering the other generalizations that guide the historian's interpretations and, in turn, the reader's.

There is a never-ending quest for readable social studies materials. Competitive concept stuffing results in social studies texts being more difficult to read. Various studies have shown typical social studies material to be too difficult for the intended readers.

ACTIVITIES AND QUESTIONS
TO PROMOTE LEARNING AND APPLICATION

1. Select a topic in history. Locate primary sources or good secondary sources on the topic. Select a middle school or secondary school history text. Note areas of agreement and disagreement between the sources and the textbook.
2. Select a topic in history. Note the slant or bias in the text. Question the suppositions of the author, especially in the light of Biblical and philosophical maxims.

3. Note examples of compartmentalized thinking extant today. For example, some people think armed revolt was all right as a reaction against taxation without representation, whereas they object to peaceful (though at times somewhat noisy) demonstrations by people who object to fighting in an undeclared war that cost hundreds of thousands of lives.

4. What does it mean to be patriotic? That is, how does a real patriot think and act? Does it have to do with externals—waving flags, marching in parades, pledging allegiance, using abstractions that are not understood—or does it relate to trying to improve concretely laws, the obeying of laws, and the way the country is run? Does it relate to the letter of the law (legalism) or the spirit of the law?

5. Make an investigation of your own. Was the Revolutionary War (a) necessary? (b) Just?

6. What, in your opinion, is the relationship of geographic knowledge to ecology?

7. Select a small segment of history and reconceptualize it for today with reference to the salient conditions of that time. Also develop a meaningful explanation of the facts and make an application to today.

8. What are the advantages and disadvantages of using a single state-adopted history text? Do the disadvantages outweigh the advantages? Discuss this in class. What evidence of legalism do you see in the arguments?

9. Have students make reports on internal criticism as it has been applied to certain documents by historians, by theologians, etc.

10. Have selected students write critiques of social studies texts used in the schools today.

11. Have someone who is interested write a report on several Christian philosophies of history. Where there are areas of disagreement in the philosophies, relate them to hermeneutical differences of the philosophers. (These hermeneutical differences may need to be inferred or there may be rather direct indications of differences.)

12. Compare and contrast historical materialism (Marxism) and capitalism.

13. The author assumes that aspects of Platonic philosophy have had a deleterious influence in this country. Do you agree or disagree? Explain.

14. Write your answers to the basic existential questions. Now check your comments on question 13.

15. John Donne has stated, "No man is an island unto himself." What did he mean? To what extent do you agree? Disagree?

16. Select several important events in history and discuss them in terms of the *inside* of the events. Is this interpretation or slant what most people think of?

17. Do you agree with the author's contention that it is important to interpret history in the light of a Christian philosophy of history as well as in the light of secular philosophies? Why or why not?

18. Determine the readability of a social studies text used in a given classroom. Determine the reading ability of the class. Does the text seem to be suitable for use in the classroom?

SUGGESTED ADDITIONAL READINGS

DANKER, FREDERICK W. *Jesus and the New Age.* St. Louis: Clayton Publishing House, 1972.

ESTES, THOMAS. "Reading in the Social Studies: A Review of Research Since 1950." In James L. Laffey. (Ed.). *Reading in the Content Areas.* Newark, Del.: International Reading Association, 1972. Pp. 177–190.

HAENTZSCHEL, ADOLPH. *The Great Paradox.* St. Louis, Mo.: Concordia, 1959.

HAFNER, LAWRENCE E. (Ed.). *Improving Reading in Middle and Secondary Schools.* Second Edition. New York: Macmillan, 1974. Section 10.

SHEPHERD, DAVID L. *Comprehensive High School Reading Methods.* Columbus, Ohio: Charles E. Merrill, 1973. Chapter 9.

TILLICH, PAUL. *The Eternal Now.* New York: Scribners, 1963.

BIBLIOGRAPHY

BARRACLOUGH, GEOFFREY. "The Historian in a Changing World." In *History in a Changing World.* Oxford, England: Basil Blackwell, Publisher. (n.d.)

BECKER, CARL. "What Are Historical Facts?" In H. Meyerhoff (Ed.). *The Philosophy of History in Our Times.* New York: Anchor Paperback, 1959.

CAEMMERER, RICHARD. "Christian Philosophy of History." In Erwin Lueker (Ed.). *Lutheran Cyclopedia.* Second Edition. St. Louis: Concordia, 1975.

CAMPBELL, BILLY. "A Study of the Relationships of Reading Ability of Students in Grades, 4, 5, and 6 and Comprehension of Social Studies and Science Textbook Selections." Unpublished Doctoral Dissertation, Florida State University, 1972.

CARTWRIGHT, W. H. "The Enduring Relevance of History." *View.* 1 (1) (Winter 1970), 1–2.

COLLINGWOOD, ROBIN G. *The Idea of History.* New York: Oxford University Press, Inc., 1946.

COMMAGER, HENRY STEELE. *The Nature and the Study of History.* Columbus, Ohio: Charles E. Merrill, 1965.

DANIELS, ROBERT V. *Studying History: How and Why.* Englewood Cliffs, N. J.: Prentice-Hall, 1966.

DANZER, GERALD A. "History and the Concept of Structure." *The Social Studies.* 64 (3) (March 1973), 99–106.

GOOD, CARTER V., and DOUGLAS E. SCATES. *Methods of Research.* New York: Appleton-Century-Crofts, 1954.

HAFNER, LAWRENCE E. "Implications of the Cloze." In E. L. Thurston and L. E. Hafner (Eds.). *Fourteenth Yearbook of the National Reading Conference.* Milwaukee: National Reading Conference, 1965.

—— "Critical Problems in Improving Readability of Materials—Secondary Level." In J. A. Figurel (Ed.). *Vistas in Reading.* Newark, Del.: International Reading Association, 1966.

HANNA, PAUL, ROSE E. SABAROFF, GORDON F. DAVIES, and CHARLES R. FARRAR. *Geography in the Teaching of Social Studies.* Boston: Houghton-Mifflin, 1966.

JAMES, PRESTON. "The Use of Culture Areas As a Frame of Organization for the Social Studies." In Preston James, (Ed.), *New Viewpoints in Geography,* The National Council for the Social Studies, Twenty-Ninth Yearbook, 1959.

KOTARBINSKI, TADEUZ. *Gnosiology: The Scientific Approach to the Theory of Knowledge.* New York: Pergamon Press, 1966.

LEINWAND, G., and D. M. FEINS. *Teaching History and Social Studies in Secondary Schools.* New York: Pitman Publishing Corporation, 1968.

MORRILL, RICHARD L. *The Spatial Organization of Society.* Second Edition. North Scituate, Mass. Duxbury Press, 1974.

ORTEGA Y GASSETT, JOSÉ. *What Is Philosophy?* New York: W. W. Norton, 1960.

PLUMB, J. H. "The Historian's Dilemma." In *Crisis in the Humanities.* London: Penguin Books, 1964.

POPKIN, RICHARD H., and AVRUM STROLL. *Philosophy Made Simple.* New York: Made Simple Books, 1956.

SAUNDERS, R. M. "Some Thoughts on the Study of History." *Canadian Historical Review 37* (2), (June 1956) 109–110, 117–18.

SERRA, MARY C. "Amplifying and Simplifying Instructional Materials: Effect on Comprehension." *Elementary School Journal.* (October 1954), 77–81.

RITTER, OLIVE P. "Repetition, Spread, and Meanings of Unusual, Difficult, and Technical Terms in Fourth Grade Geography Texts." Unpublished Doctor's Dissertation, University of Iowa, 1941.

SPECTOR, ROBERT M. "The American Revolution: Something Beyond the Causes." *The Social Studies. 42* (March 1971), 99–106.

TURNER, FREDERICK JACKSON. "The Significance of History." In Ray Allen Billington (Ed.). *Frontier and Section: Selected Essays of Frederick Jackson Turner.* Englewood Cliffs, N. J. Prentice-Hall, 1961. (Turner's essay was originally published in 1891.)

VAUGHN, ALDEN. "Early New Englander Reintroduced." *Saturday Review. 52* (February 15, 1969), p. 42.

WIENER, PHILIP. "Philosophy of Political History." In Daniel J. Bronstein and Yervant R. Krikorian. *Basic Problems of Philosophy.* Third Edition. Englewood Cliffs, N. J.: Prentice-Hall, 1964.

WILSON, MARY C. "The Effect of Amplifying Material Upon Comprehension." *Journal of Experimental Education. 13* (September 1944), 5–8.

WOOLDRIDGE, S. W., and W. GORDON EAST. *The Spirit and Purpose of Geography.* London: Hutchinson Publishing Group, Ltd., 1958.

CHAPTER 9

Teaching the Reading of Social Studies. II. Strategies for Improving Reading Skills

CONCEPT-VOCABULARY PROBLEMS

To the extent that knowledge of social studies concepts and the vocabulary representing those concepts is indicative of knowledge of and good attitudes toward the study of history, geography, economics, and political science, attempts to dissuade people from serious study are most regrettable.

The responsibility for mediocre vocabulary ability can be laid at many doors, including those of parents, but the phenomena that characterize the active and passive denigrators of serious study are underdeveloped vocabulary consciousness and vocabulary conscience.

Difference Between Concept and Vocabulary

A concept is a generalized idea. One saves a lot of time in communicating by using generalized ideas. Describing the detailed elements of dwelling places each time one referred to the latter would not be efficient. Instead, one uses the vocabulary term *house* to refer in English-speaking countries to what most of us live in. So a concept is a generalized idea about a set of features that several given things may have in common. Vocabulary is the label we give the concept. In the following discussion when I use the term *vocabulary* I will be especially concerned about *students'* inability to assign meanings to words and their failure to connect vocabulary with referents.

Examples of Vocabulary Difficulties

Following is just a *sampling* of difficult terms from a fifth-grade history text:

heritage	national feudal monarchies	man the measure of all things	men of every degree
traditions	religion	classical past	primitive
medieval culture	paid dearly	optics	

Middle Graders Try Some Words.   An example of social studies terms used to test middle school students comes from a study by Springman (1941). Sam, Ed, and Joe—fictitious names—were subjects of the original study, done when more people rode trains. Jane, Lee, Al, and Sally are four children of today who have never ridden on a train and do not live in a port city. Table 9–1 gives the results.

Table 9-1

Grade	Person	Word and Definition	Educational Age	Reading Age	Intelligence Quotient
4	Jane	tributary: combination of chemicals express train: something that goes under the ground like a train wharf: Do not know	12-1	12-2	123
5	Al	tributary: Do not know express train: carries passengers wharf: Do not know	12-9	12-6	120
6	Sam	tributary: Do not know express train: where the trains meet main line (or railroads): where the railroads are	9-7	9-7	82
6	Ed	tributary: a city express train: Do not know wharf: big wheel used to unload boats	11-0	11-5	101
6	Lee	tributary: kind of tribute express train: a train that does not stop at every town wharf: Do not know	13-0	14-0	118
6	Joe	tributary: Do not know express train: trains that do not stop at small cities wharf: Do not know main lines: the ones that go to Paris where they all connect and go out to smaller cities	12-5	16-0	123
7	Sally	tributary: Do not know express train: means of transportation wharf: Do not know	12-5	12-5	115

Pledge of Allegiance. A practice of questionable merit on *cognitive* grounds is the recitation of the pledge of allegiance. For years I doubted that adults, much less children, understood it. Some evidence collected by Hafner and Buck (1973) should be considered. We studied the ability of 25 sixth-grade students to give the meaning of the main terms in the pledge of allegiance and compared their performance with their reading ability and intelligence. Table 9–2 gives a random sample of performances.

Table 9–2. The Ability of a Small Sample of Sixth Graders to Explain Concepts That Are Part of the "Pledge of Allegiance"

Subject 1 Reading grade placement 6.8; Slosson IQ 126; CA 11–10

Words	Definitions	Correctness
pledge allegiance	D. K. (Do not Know)	—
flag	stands for our country	+
republic	a group that evolved from a group	—
nation	group of people—same land, government, and language	+
indivisible	D.K.	
liberty	freedom	+
justice	the right thing to do	½+

Subject 2 Reading grade placement 7.0; Slosson IQ 94; CA 12–4

Words	Definitions	Correctness
pledge allegiance	obey, salute	½+
flag	represents a country	+
republic	like a Democrat	—
nation	country, home	+
indivisible	yourself	—
liberty	D.K.	—
justice	D.K.	—

Subject 3 Reading grade placement 3.8; Slosson IQ 73; CA 12–5

Words	Definitions	Correctness
pledge allegiance	say it to them	—
flag	D.K.	—
republic	D.K.	—
nation	D.K.	—
indivisible	can't see it	—
liberty	D.K.	—
justice	D.K.	—

The results of this study showed a positive correlation (.55) between reading ability and knowledge of the concepts in the "Pledge of Allegiance." Many young people, after 5½ years of reciting the "Pledge" know next to nothing about its meaning. I assume a more concrete approach over a five-year period gradually leading up to using the "Pledge" or some more suitable substitute would be more profitable. It would also jibe with the developmental theory of Piaget.

Some Problem Terms in Secondary School Texts. Geography texts in the secondary schools pose many problems. Several such terms selected from a human geography text are *decentralization of industrial plants, dark continent, international date line,* and *isobars.*

A Sample of Other Problem Terms Found in Secondary Geography Texts

meridians	relative humidity	conterminous
physiographic	latitude	inanimate energy consumption
rivulets	chernozems	molybdenum
erosion cycle	habitat	petrochemicals
cirque	cultural scene	cretaceous
monadnocks	agglomeration	mid-latitude
troposphere	subsidization	marine

A Sample of Difficult Terms from a United States History Text

agrarian	abolitionist	diplomacy
piedmont	catalyst	injunction
tyranny	reconnaisance	electorate
confederation	neolithic	isolationism
amphibious	immigrant	ratification
artisans	tariff	ecocide
transcendentalists	blockade	

WAYS OF DEALING WITH VOCABULARY AND WORD-RECOGNITION CHALLENGES

I have already discussed the consummate intelligence of using social studies materials that more closely match the reading achievement level of the particular student. Even material at the proper instructional level will contain an occasional unfamiliar word; that is to be expected. The question is, "How do I teach new vocabulary in social studies materials?" Since so many words present both meaning and pronunciation problems, some of the exercises will deal with both facets. (See Chapter 6 for more strategies.)

Take-Home Study Sheets

A simple approach that yields great benefit is to preview material with a student (or students), select hard vocabulary, place each item into a written sentence context related to the content in question and go over the sentences with the students. Then allow the students to take the sentences home for further study. If possible, put the sentences on a tape cassette.

If you carry out this procedure several days before the topic is taken up in class, it will make a more willing and capable reader out of a reluctant, poor reader. This relatively simple procedure (and others in the chapter) can be used in other content areas, of course, and it pays handsome dividends in terms of student learning and teacher satisfaction. Below is a sample exercise. These words are from a fourth-grade text, but some of your students can only read fourth-grade texts.

Christopher Columbus	"Young Christopher Columbus lived in Italy. . . ."
Mediterranean Sea	Columbus lived in an old city beside the blue Mediterranean Sea. (Med it er ra ne an)
jewels	The sailors talked of the beautiful jewels in China and India.
dangerous	The trip to China and India was long and dangerous.
captains	Some sea captains tried to sail south around Africa.
compass	The needle of a compass points to the north.
currents	The wide bands of water that move through oceans are called currents.
supplies	Columbus needed money to buy ships and supplies and to hire sailors.
discover	"If I discover new lands, I will claim them for you," Columbus said.
Isabella	The queen of Spain was named Isabella.
Niña	Niña is pronounced Neen'ya. / nēn'-y∂ /
rudder	The rudder on the Pinta broke.
Indies	The islands that Columbus found were later named the West Indies.
natural	Natural rubber comes from the sap of the rubber tree.

Categorizing Words

Category Game. This game allows students to produce exemplars for given categories and seeks to emphasize the importance of meaning hierarchies.

Directions: 1. Teacher and/or students provide categories related to the topic being studied. These are listed vertically. Across the top of the page some word is written; it may or may not be thematic. 2. Competition is carried out on an individual or a group basis. 3. Teams write in as many examplars as possible. 4. A time limit is announced. 5. Scoring procedures allow a team more points for an exemplar that other teams do not have.

	V	A	P	O	R	S
Topographical Features						
Rivers in America (or France)						
Cities in America (or France)						
Metals						
Canals						

Twenty Questions.   This popular game uses interesting cognitive strategies.

Purpose: To guess in 20 questions or less a word that represents something or somebody concrete.

Materials: None.

Players: Two or more.

Procedure: One person X selects the name of a person or thing. The other players ask questions trying to zero in on it. X answers *yes* or *no*. In order to narrow the possibilities, people begin with such questions as, "Is it *animal*?" or "Is it *mineral*?" or "Is it *vegetable*?" If it is neither of the first two, the person knows it is *vegetable* and will not waste a question. The players then continue to quiz in an attempt to eliminate certain possibilities and focus on others.

Simple Categorizing Game

Purpose: To categorize words under headings. This may be done in conjunction with a particular unit or chapter or it may be a general information game.

Materials: Chalkboard and chalk.

Players: Students or students and teacher.

Procedure: Headings are placed on the chalkboard. Team one provides a term for team two to classify and it is written under the proper heading. Then team two reciprocates. The team with the highest score after a certain time wins.

Example 1: Great Lakes Region of Minnesota, Wisconsin, Illinois, Michigan, and Ohio

(Middle School Level)

Headings:

Mining	Football	Largest City in its State	State Capitals	Baseball
.	.	.	.	.
.	.	.	.	.
.	.	.	.	.

People and Things in Duluth-Superior	Basketball	Rivers	Geographical Features
.	.	.	.
.	.	.	.
.	.	.	.

Cities on Lake Erie	Cities on Lake Huron	Cities on Lake Michigan	Cities on Lake Superior
.	.	.	.
.	.	.	.
.	.	.	.

People and Things in Greater Chicago	People and Things in Greater Milwaukee	People and Things in the Twin Cities
.	.	.
.	.	.
.	.	.

People and Things in Greater Detroit	People and Things in Greater Cleveland
.	.
.	.
.	.

Words to be classified: Reliance Electric; Washington Park Zoo; General Mills; Mesabi Range; Madison; Green Bay Packers; Minneapolis; St. Croix; Chicago; Minnesota Twins; Milwaukee; St. Paul; Richard Daley; Superior Uplands; O'Hare Airport; Wayne State University; Martin Marty; Great Lakes Steel Corporation; Kettle Moraine; Chicago Bulls; Illinois; Lansing; Fox; Menominee; Milwaukee Bucks; Detroit Lions; Duluth; Wrigley Building; Detroit Tigers; Marquette University; Swift Meat Packing; St. Louis; DePaul University; Bucyrus Erie; White Sox; Allen Bradley Corporation; Skyline Parkway; Springfield; Argonne National Laboratory; General Motors Corporation; Sears Tower;

Heil Corporation; Straight of Mackinac; Chicago; Peabody; Marshall Field & Co.; Cuyuna Range; Dardanelles of America; Columbus; S. Skrowaczewski; Cleveland; Brookfield Zoo; A. B. Dick Corporation; Northwestern University; Milwaukee Brewers; Standard Oil; Mather; Cuyahoga; Ishpeming; Columbus; Merchandise Mart; Ford Motor Corporation; Mitchell Park (geodesic dome) Botanical Gardens; Macalester College; Museum of Natural Science and Industry; Greek Orthodox Church (Frank Lloyd Wright); Saginaw River; Concordia Teachers College; Cobo Hall; Hamline College; Starved Rock; Marquette Range; Case Western Reserve University; Wisconsin Dells; Newberry Library; Paul Manz.

Example 2:   World History: Renaissance and Reformation (College Prep: Highly Gifted)

Headings:

Luther	Erasmus	Michaelangelo	DaVinci
.	.	.	.
.	.	.	.
.	.	.	.

Loyola	Alberti	Copernicus
.	.	.
.	.	.
.	.	.

Cosimo de'Medici	Melcanchthon	Calvin
.	.	.
.	.	.
.	.	.

Words to be classified: *Spiritual Exercises; On the Revolutions of Celestial Bodies; Praise of Folly;* Laurenziana; *Preceptor Germaniae; The Babylonian Capitivity of the Church*; pansophist; Vittoria Colonna; the Pieta; Colet and More; designed fortifications for Milano; *Christian Soldiers Manual;* "all revolt is wrong"; *Mona Lisa;* Council of Trent; *Treatise on Painting*; audited chrysoloras; *Theological Common Places;* "great art is thought wrought in stone;" *Re de Aedificatoria*; Institute of the Christian Religion; Dutch; Ninety-Five Theses; Geneva; Eisleben; robbed astrology of its traditional foundations; hymnist; patron par excellence of new Renaissance culture; remodeled the papal palace; Augsburg Confession; Sistine Chapel; Small Catechism; Greek New Testament; Finish St. Peter's; Holy Roman Emperor; *Description of the City of Rome*; Renaissance prince; heliocentric theory of the universe; the Will; translated entire Bible; "Here I stand . . ."; *David* (sculpture); Jesuits; Pope; India; Huguenots; *The Last Supper; Day and Night;* presbyterian; architect; frescoes on *Bondage of Laurenziana.*

Example 3: History, Government, and Economics (Secondary Level)

Some of it may be classified under more than one category.

Headings:

Writ or Document	Official	Belief or Philosophy or One Who Holds Such
.	.	.
.	.	.
.	.	.

Governing Group	Act or Action of Official	Act or Action of People
.	.	.
.	.	.
.	.	.

Economic Condition or Action	Pertaining to Legislative	Pertaining to Executive	Pertaining to Judicial
.	.	.	.
.	.	.	.
.	.	.	.

Words to be classified: edict; Industrial Revolution; indict; Diet; parliament; bigotry; monopoly; carte blanche; deism; incumbent; gubernatorial; jurisprudence; liberal; concordat; parley; emissary; negotiate; consul; abrogation; pantheism; lobby; habeas corpus; plebiscite; ex post facto; arbitrate; injunction; initiative and referendum; post mortem; corpus delecti; truce; speculation; filibuster; precedent; concurrent; pro tem; coalition; collateral; deficit; secede; patronage; aristocrat; propaganda; electoral college; plutocrat; provocation; bureaucrat; demagogue; plurality; gerrymandering; quorum; rebate; unicameral; promissory note; chattel; mortgage; pro rata; accrued; inflation; franchise; subpoena; determinism; proletarian; bourgeois; coup d'etat; laissez faire; alliance; boycott; capitalist; tariff; embargo; doctrine; suffrage; reciprocity; insurrection; allegiance; constitution; insolvency; plaintiff; impeach; contraband; amnesty; nullify; envoy; reconstruction; mandamus; manumission.

Applying Pronunciation Skills to Social Studies Reading

Many students above the primary grades have a working knowledge of structural analysis and phonetic-analysis skills. Although analysis of words for meaning and pronunciation cues is fraught with difficulties, certain skills may be applied in order to yield at least an approximation of the correct pronunciation. If concept vocabulary work is an ongoing procedure in the classroom, the student will encounter more words that he or she can reconstruct through use of syllabication, approximate pronunciation, and context cues. Let us look at some helpful syllabication rules:

The Open Syllable and Closed Syllable Rule. The following are *open* syllables: hi–, be–, ma–, ve–, la–. Why do you think they are "open?" Right, because the vowel is "open" to its right. In *accented* syllables (the catch is: "How can you tell it is accented?"), the vowel often sounds the way it does in the alphabet:

me	/mē/	la -dy	/lā-dē/
hi	/hī/	he -ro	/hē-rō/ (one type of "Southern" dialect)

These are *closed* syllables: met, hit, un–, Can you see why? In closed, *accented* syllables, the vowel has the sound it has in these words:

/a/	/e/	/i/	/ä/	/ə/
cat	met	hit	cot	run
fat	set	sit	lot	bun

Breaking down Multisyllabic Words and Pronouncing Syllables Sometimes it helps to cut words down to size before trying to pronounce them. The following rules and examples may refresh the memories of you and your students. Note the open and closed syllables. The approximately correct pronunciations that sometimes result can be rectified by (1) reflection, (2) checking against context, or (3) using the dictionary.[1]

1. <u>Divide between double constants.</u> Vc-cv

	<u>Words similar to the syllables</u>
At-lan-tic	At <u>land</u> <u>tic</u> or <u>tick</u>
Den-ver	Den <u>verna</u>
Dec-can	Deck <u>can</u>

I have no argument with people who want to keep *geminate* consonants together rather than separate them, since you pronounce *one* consonant, not two: Decc-an, Nass-au, Suff-olk. (Vcc-v)

[1] Strategies for developing grapheme-phoneme associations and applying them in identifying the pronunciation of words are found in Chapter 20.

2. In a vowel-consonant-vowel setup, divide before the consonant.

v-cv

	Word similar to the syllables
ve-to	ve Venus
	toe
Mo-zam-bique	Mo Shazam pique, antique

3. In words ending with consonant le (Cle), divide before the consonant.

	Words similar to the syllables
Se-at-tle (or Se-att-le)	See at battle
ma-ple	may

4. Consonants clusters (blends and digraphs) are not usually divided.

	Words similar to the syllables
Con-stance	Con stance
Mon-tre-al (Mont-re-al)	Money tree all

Common Prefixes That Should Be Learned. The prefix provides the first syllable of the word and does not provide much of a pronunciation problem. The headings can be placed on a large sheet of chart paper. Students and teacher or a committee of students can add to it as they dig out the information. Illustrative sentences can be placed on an adjoining chart.

Prefix	Meaning	Examples	Meaning	Root	Meaning
un	not	unorthodox	not regular	ortho	straight
ex	out	expatriate	somebody sent out of his fatherland	patri	father
		export	send or carry out	port	carry
pre	before	prescience	knowing before hand	science	knowledge
		pre-existing	being beforehand	exist ex+ sistere	be (out-stand)
ab	from; away	aborigine	existing from the beginning (native)	origin	source; beginning
		abolition	do away with		

Prefix	Meaning	Examples	Meaning	Root	Meaning
ad	to; toward	adequate	equal to the task	aequare	equal
		admit	allow in	mit	send
com	with	combine	put together	bi(ne)	two
en	in; into	endemic*	regularly found in a locality (among the people)	demos	the people
in	in; into	indented	make a "tooth" in	dent	tooth
re	back; again	reconstruct	build again	con- structus (struere)	build
de	from; down from	depopulate	take people from	populus	people
sub	under	subterranean	underground	terra	ground
		submarine	being, acting, or growing underwater	mare	sea (water)
be	1. thoroughly	bespatter	thoroughly spatter	spatter	splash
	2. make	belittle	make little (put someone "down")	little	small
dis	apart; not	disarmament	not arming (more exactly reducing arms or guns)	arma- menta	arms (guns)
		discover	reveal or find (uncover or reveal)	cover	close; conceal
pro	for; in front of	pro- democracy	for the democratic form of government (i.e., for the people)	demos	people

*Since cholera is regulary found among the people in India we say cholera is endemic in India.

Learning Meanings of Prefixes and Roots Inductively and Deductively

For a given prefix or root, you might want to start inductively, develop the meaning of the segment in question, and then have the students provide more examples. At other times you may want to develop rules and examples based on the above chart. Since we should study words and their parts in meaningful contexts, I provide two sentences below for each word in the above chart. These sentences should be discussed with the students to see the derivation of a word and its meaning in the particular sentence. (You may also expand the context and then see what interpretation might be placed on it by different kinds of people.)

1a. He has an <u>unorthodox</u> view on the role of the legislator in education.

  b. Luther considered Tetzel's teachings on the role of indulgences to be <u>unorthodox</u>.

2a. Solzhenitsyn is an <u>expatriate</u> of Russia.

  b. Mobsters are sometimes <u>expatriated</u> from countries where they hold citizenship to the land where they were born.

3a. In recent years the United States has <u>exported</u> much grain to the U.S.S.R.

  b. Japan <u>exports</u> beer to the United States.

4a. Some successful investors in the stock market seem to have a certain <u>prescience</u> about future developments.

  b. Prophets receive nice <u>prescience</u> on their birthdays.

5a. The president must abide by the <u>pre-existing</u> rules.

  b. The Arctic explorers discovered <u>pre-existing</u> cairns.

6a. When the English settled Australia they found the <u>aborigines</u>.

  b. Cave-dwelling <u>aborigines</u> were discovered in the Philippines in the early 1970s; they were living in a Stone Age culture.

7a. The <u>abolitionists</u> wanted to do away with slavery.

  b. I favor the <u>abolition</u> of schools founded on prejudice.

8a. Military leadership on the Union side was not <u>adequate</u> during the early years of the Civil War.

  b. The sherpas were the only <u>adequate</u> worker guides that would be scalers of Mt. Everest could find.

9a. Missouri was <u>admitted</u> to the Union as part of a compromise situation.

  b. The man's testimony was <u>admitted</u> as evidence.

10a. Several countries <u>combined</u> forces to form the ANZAC in World War II.

  b. She was a <u>combination</u> of her father's good looks and her mother's intelligence.

11a. At one time hookworm was <u>endemic</u> in South Georgia.

  b. Obscurantism is <u>endemic</u> among school boards in certain areas.

12a. He had "marginal" ability in <u>indenting</u> paragraphs correctly.

  b. Cleopatra made several <u>indentations</u> in the grapes that Marc Antony gave her.

13a. The immediate years following the destructive Civil War were known as the <u>Reconstruction</u> Period.

  b. Economics utilizes a number of intellectual constructs as it <u>reconstructs</u> the causes of recessions.

14a. The H-bombs practically <u>depopulated</u> Nagasaki and Hiroshima.

  b. A <u>depopulated</u> town is called a "ghost town."

15a. Caves are made up of <u>subterranean</u> passageways and rooms.

  b. Troglodytes inhabit <u>subterranean</u> dwellings.

16a. A fish is a <u>submarine</u> animal.

  b. <u>Submarines</u> are useful in warfare because they are relatively difficult to detect but have adequate firepower.

17a. The conservative curators of the art museum would probably look askance at the suggestion that <u>bespattered</u> canvases be considered works of art.

  b. The advancing troops at Gettysburg were <u>bespattered</u> with grape shot.

18a. McClellan's military leadership was <u>belittled</u>.

  b. The poor were <u>belittled</u> by most of the rich, but not by the Psalmist.

19a. It would be interesting to compare the psychological profiles of people favoring armament with those of people favoring <u>disarmament</u>.

  b. In 1922 Charles Evans Hughes outlined a bold plan for naval <u>disarmament</u>.

20a. He <u>discovered</u> oil on his third try.
   b. Balboa is usually credited with <u>discovering</u> the Pacific Ocean for the Europeans.

21a. Lincoln's <u>pro-democracy</u> views eventually led to his death at the hands of an anti-democracy assassin.
   b. Greed and <u>pro-democracy</u> are mutually exclusive because the greedy are actually fascists.

PROBLEMS IN COMPREHENDING AND READING CRITICALLY

Comprehension

Comparision of Good and Poor Readers in Grade Twelve. Helen K. Smith's remarkable study in 1961 was analyzed in a previous chapter. You may remember that

1. Good readers read for stated purposes, whereas poor readers did not.
2. Good readers restructured material and tried to relate the detail with something else, whereas poor readers tried to remember points in isolation.
3. Good readers reviewed frequently while reading and tried to read for ideas and general impression, whereas poor readers seldom reviewed and tried to remember details in isolation.

Dewey's Landmark Study of Eighth Graders.   J. C. Dewey (1935) made a thorough study of the comprehension difficulties that a group of eighth graders had with several social studies topics. The test selections were on colonial lighting, the invention and development of the reaper, a description of the Dred Scott decision, and the articles of Confederation. Both objective tests and a free-expression inference test were given.

These words caused great difficulty:

   selection A: tender; primitive; projecting
   selection C: recourse; territory
   selection D: requisitioned; by-word; not worth a continental

This sentence was particulary difficult:

   Aside from the fireplace, the candle was the chief source of light.

Many students omitted "aside from the fireplace." Others thought the phrase meant *away from* or *beside* the fireplace.

Typical reading comprehension difficulties:

1. Ignorance of word meaning.
2. Disregarding certain parts of the sentence. (I am reminded of Thorndike's (1917) classical study in which he found pupils have trouble in giving proper emphasis to segments of a passage.)
3. Tendency to consider the reading process a matter of memorizing words that are given back to the teacher regardless of meanings:

   <u>Example:</u> A student repeated the phrase "sue for liberty" but had no idea what it meant. Do you know?

Some Conclusions:

1. Children may know certain meanings for words, but lack the particular meaning needed to properly understand a given sentence.

2. Do not place too much confidence in verbal responses as evidence that students understand or in verbal presentation as an adequate teaching method.

3. Use concrete materials such as maps, models, pictures, and charts when possible to make more certain a genuine grasp of the meanings.

4. The fact that few correct answers were made on the inference test is open to two interpretations:

     a. Part of the inability to infer well is due to inadequate understanding of facts.

     b. Inferences may be difficult for eighth graders to make even though the facts necessary for a thorough understanding are adequate. NOTE: We must remember that some people even by this age have not fully entered into the formal-operational period. Also, at the time of Dewey's study, and even today, we see too little excellent teaching of inferential reading in the content areas.)

5. Children in the eighth grade did not seem to possess sufficient backgrounds in the fields of history, civics, economics, and geography, and general experience to understand and interpret such technical material as (1) judicial decisions and (2) problems of federal finance.

6. More than a casual explanation of difficult ideas in words is needed in order to teach children to comprehend what they read. The children need to receive an adequate experience regarding each idea presented in words in the reading material.

Critical Reading Problems. Critical reading is context processing done to sift facts from fallacies and correct conclusions from incorrect conclusions. A more complete discussion was given in Chapter 6. Some phenomena that interfere with the process of reading critically in order to determine truth in social studies writing are the following.

1. Failure to note qualifications of the writer: Newspapers are included among social studies materials and there are fewer areas than newspapers where writers have to deal with so many disciplines. Writers—including reporters, general columnists and editorial writers—have to deal with subject matter that lies outside their area of competence It is true that many newspeople are quite bright, but we must warn students of the problems of would-be pansophists so that they will be on guard when reading newspapers. Where possible, try to find the area(s) of competence of particular newswriters.

In addition to teaching students to check the credentials of writers by consulting various *Who's Who* type publications, one might address a letter to a person asking about his or her training, experience, and so forth or invite the person to class where these questions can be asked.

2. Misinterpreting motives of the writer: It is terrible to impugn a writer's motives incorrectly but it is worse to assign altruistic motives to a person who is trying to enlist you in the cause of social injustice, demagoguery, totalitarianism, obscurantism, and the like.

3. Failure to note and question the writer's assumptions: If an author succeeds in getting you to grant his or her assumptions, you are practically hooked into believing the rest of what he or she writes. Joseph Goebbels, Hitler's minister of propaganda, appealed to the needs and fears of the German people and fashioned his assumptions to allay those fears and meet those needs. Many Germans granted the assumptions and believed his arguments rooted in those assumptions. Millions died as a result of their diabolical output.

Richard Nixon had certain assumptions about the value of the common man, the interdependence of people, interrelationships between business and government, and anthropology. He was only too willing to grant the assumptions in the writings of Jensen, Shockley, and Coleman about the educability of lower class children. That Shockley's and Jensen's assumptions left much to be desired and Coleman's research was found to have flaws was small comfort to the thousands of educators and millions of children whose teaching and learning suffered due in part to (1) lack of materials and facilities; (2) lack of stipends for advanced training of teachers; and (3) poor pupil–teacher ratio caused by Nixon's withholding federal education funds voted by Congress.

The pitiful part is that adequate evidence had been available for years of Nixon's antipathy toward the disenfranchised and his proclivity for allying himself with powerful, greedy people. He apparently preferred mendacity to the mendicant and the powerful to the poverty stricken. Voters have ample opportunity to see these devastating faults in candidates before they go to the polls, but "Having eyes they see not and having ears they hear not." People perceive in terms of what is nearest and dearest to them, and this is often self.

Bias of Textbooks. For years well-meaning but rather uninformed pressure groups such as certain veterans organizations and daughters of this and sons of that, as well as segments of some religious bodies, have exerted undue influence to withhold truth, or at least divergent points of view, from American social studies texts. *Facts* and interpretations based on facts have been excised from textbooks. Teachers, should have a strong voice in selecting books. If school boards find certain texts objectionable, then let teachers and school boards go to *primary* historical sources and settle differences. Let these portions of primary documents be published in the press in columns parallel to the text material in question.

Some results of not including an unbiased presentation of the loyalist side in the history of the Revolutionary War and not interpreting the acts of revolutionary leaders in terms of the Judeo-Christian writings are the following:

1. Children are brought up to think that revolution is all right.

2. Revolutionaries, such as Samuel Adams and Benjamin Franklin, become heroes.

3. The value of court proceedings, bargaining, and appeal is denigrated.

4. Children learn that whatever emanates from our inclinations and disclinations is acceptable if we get enough people to band together to enforce it, that is, might makes right.

5. The value of loyalty is deprecated.

I think you can probably add to the list. Certainly you should discuss the above ideas in your college reading class as well as in your communities and in the classrooms where you teach. You might entertain this question, "Do espousers of revolution (1776) have a right to decry young dissenters because they wear beards rather than powdered wigs?"

For a scholarly discussion of this issue I recommend Spector's article (1971) "The American Revolution: Something Beyond the Causes", which I analyzed in the previous chapter. One of many popular articles giving the loyalist side in the Revolutionary War appeared in the April 1975 issue of *National Geographic*.

Overgeneralizing. When one makes a remark about a group of people and states that all these people do or believe a certain thing, one is in danger of overgeneralizing. General, as well as racial, prejudice is rooted, in part, in overgeneralizing. If you will pardon a pun, it is so much easier to think in "blacks and whites" than to differentiate. We find some unfavorable characteristics about a group of people and, then, in order to save ourselves the problem of differentiating among people so that we might accept at least some of the people rather than others, we reject the whole group.

In a democracy this approach can pose problems. On the one hand we vote on issues, and 51 per cent of the people can "control" the 49 per cent when the plurality criterion is used. Then the latitude of opinion and willingness to differentiate do not hold. The minority group then complains it has no choice. On the other hand, when people are given an opportunity to differentiate—to choose to accept some people on the basis of a number of criteria rather than just one (say, color)—they do not exercise this wholesome, positive freedom, but enslave themselves and delimit their options by using only one criterion.

Churches, families, friendships, and political parties are often split on the basis of poorly selected, irrelevant, or minor criteria. Interestingly enough a common thread—selfishness and inability to rethink values—seems to run through many of the institutions and situations. How many people choose religious denominations, spouses, friends, and political parties only on the basis of what these institutions and people can do for them, for self!

1. *Excoriating the whole bunch:* There is a dangerous propensity among some teachers to overgeneralize the personality traits, voting record, and general worth of school boards, administrators, regents, and legislators. We may, for example, lump all legislators together. For its effect on us, even if 49 per cent are "good guys", it does not do us much good, if the plurality voting rule is in effect. We still do not get the raise or the materials or the better teaching conditions so that children (including those of the legislators) may be helped if there are 2 per cent more "bad guys" than "good guys." But, it is not logical or fair to overgeneralize and excoriate the whole bunch.

2. *I know a man who . . . :* Sometimes we take one instance of a phenomenon and generalize with a great degree of certitude. For example, "I know a person who gave a ride to a young man and the young man flailed the side view mirror of the car with three wet noodles. This proves that you must not help

people in trouble." If we followed that line of thought, a lot of people who really need help would not receive it.

3. *How old are you?:* Two teachers were discussing a subject once and the one who evidently was losing the point involved suddenly said to the person who was winning, "Jim, how old are you?" (Jim was the youngest of several people at the table.) Jim said, "Oh, no. That will not work. That is an ad hominem attack. Try again. Come up with some facts and a better developed argument. Do not try ad hominem on me!" (What does ad hominem mean?)

Nonsequitur. A nonsequitur is a logical fallacy in which a statement thought by the writer to follow from another statement does *not* follow. As I stated in the chapter on comprehension, it does not follow that a school is a good school just because it is the best one in a town or country; that is a nonsequitur.

A hundred years ago tomatoes were poison: A newspaper ad by Tobacco Associates, Inc. started with this statement and tried to establish an assumption that if the tomato, over the years, was found not to be poisonous, then tobacco is not poison. There is absolutely no link between the finding that tomatoes are not poison and what tobacco is or is not. This argument is a classical example of a *non sequitur* (does not follow). The "argument" concludes: "There is good reason (never stated) to think that within a few years we will look back and laugh about 'the great tobacco scare of the 1960s.' In the meantime, there is a vicious, unfair attempt to destroy a great American agricultural industry, affecting the livelihood of millions of people. Think about it!"

Post hoc ergo propter hoc.: *Post hoc* . . . means "after this, therefore because of this;" it is a logical fallacy. Stuart Chase (1956) has provided us with some illustrations of *post hoc.*

1. Night air ———➤ malaria.

   (Research showed the blame must be pinned on the pesky little mosquito.)

2. Wet feet ———➤ colds.

   (Lumbermen state that a person who keeps his blood circulating well through exercise can have wet feet for days and still not develop a cold.

PROCESSES FOR DEVELOPING COMPREHENSION

Remember that comprehension involves a thorough logical analysis of cognitive relationships. In the comprehension chapter I analyzed a number of items prepared by Fred and Charlotte Davis and showed you the thinking dynamics involved. That was followed by analyses of dynamic strategies and concomitant processes involved in developing main ideas, relevant supporting details, drawing conclusions, and the like. Applications of these strategies to social studies content follow.

Developing Main Ideas Through Literal and Inferential Reading

D. E. P. Smith's Hypothesis-Testing Pattern. You will recall from Chapter 6 that Smith's model for teaching paragraph comprehension used with *dull-normal*

children resulted in substantial increases in comprehension. You will also remember the application of the procedure with a relatively bright (IQ = 118)
fifth-grade pupil. Let it not be thought that successfully teaching pupils to
develop the main idea of a paragraph is easy to do. I must at this point disabuse you of the idea, also, that topic sentences do a very good job of encapsulating the real thrust of a paragraph. It is necessary, therefore, to teach
students how to use a hypothesis-testing pattern for developing the main idea
of a paragraph.

The steps for teaching the H-T pattern are

1. Read the first sentence; assume that it is the main idea.
2. Read the second sentence; then
   a. if the meaning of the first sentence encompasses the second, continue
      to assume that the first sentence is the main idea; or,
   b. If the first sentence is too narrow, broaden it to include the second
      sentence idea.
3. Continue with each succeeding sentence as in the second step.

Apply the procedure yourself, please, to the following paragraph by reading it
and developing step-by-step the main ideas of this statement by Teddy Roosevelt related to the ability of a corporation to make more profit by demanding
longer hours from employees while at the same time cutting their wages:

> The great coal-mining and coal-carrying companies, which employed their tens of
> thousands, could easily dispense with the service of any particular miner. The
> miner, on the other hand, could not dispense with the companies. He needed a
> job; his wife and children would starve if he did not get one.

TMI = Tentative Main Ideas

TMI 1 _____

TMI 2 _____

TMI _____

TMI _____

Now help someone else, through skillful questioning, develop the main idea:
(See questioning procedure in the comprehension chapter.)

Compare the main idea that you developed with the main idea developed by
the person you taught. How do you account for any difference between that
which you obtained alone and that which your student obtained with your
help? Were the differences explainable in terms of education, intelligence,
philosophy, religion, compassion, social class, and wealth of one's parents . . . ?

Paraphrase and Infer. One problem in trying to develop an inclusive main
idea is that of expecting students to develop the central thrust of a paragraph
(or longer selection) when you have not checked to see if they understand the
basic ideas of the paragraph. You *check* it by having the students give you the
important ideas in paraphrase. Any point that they cannot develop, you, the
teacher, through questioning and illustration *help* them to clarify. Once they

understand the basic ideas of the paragraph they have a fighting chance of seeing the relationships among the ideas and what the big thrust of the paragraph is. If, after a number of attempts at paraphrasing material in a text, it is still difficult to paraphrase the segments, you might well conclude that you have the students in material that they cannot process.[2] You should very seriously consider using material that your students *can* process.

I. *Directions:* Read this paragraph to discover some facts about the significance of lakes.

> Considering the great size of the seas and oceans, the smaller water bodies seem insignificant. However, significance cannot be measured by size alone. A lake, or group of lakes, may have a local or even an extralocal importance far out of proportion to the area or depth of water involved. Lakes may furnish domestic and industrial water, transportation, fish, and recreational opportunities. In such manner, they may be more truly and directly entwined with the lives of many people than are seas and oceans.

II. *Important Ideas:* We will list the important ideas on the chalkboard.

1. _____

2. _____

3. _____

4. _____

III. *Main (Thrust) Idea:* Let us analyze the ideas, looking for relationships among the ideas, and develop two (or possibly one) summary statements.

1. _____

2. _____

Now combine the two summary statements to give the real thrust of the paragraph.

1. _____

You might say that you thought one of the sentences in the paragraph was a pretty good summary statement. I think it is too vague and does not encapsulate information that may reduce uncertainty. After all, if information reduces uncertainty—that is, tells you something you did not know before—that is what you want to process and remember. Hence the quest for an information-giving central thrust statement.

---

[2] However, one must differentiate between inability to work and unwillingness to work.

Extending the Process to Drawing Conclusions

Important Ideas ⟶ *Main Idea* ⟶ *Conclusions:*   Continuing with the paragraph on the significance of lakes we can work with conclusions in at least two ways: (1) students draw conclusions; (2) teacher or small group of students lists valid and invalid conclusions and students check the valid ones. Rather than draw conclusions, I will leave both methods for a class exercise in your methods class.

IV. A. *Drawing Conclusions:*   Considering the facts that you have developed and the main idea based on these facts, list the conclusions you can safely draw.

1. _____

2. _____

3. _____ , etc.

   B. *Checking valid conclusions:* Which of these conclusions can we draw according to the information that the paragraph contains. Check them ( ). Be prepared to support your choices.

_____   _____

_____   _____

_____   _____

Actually the conclusions drawn in Method A should be subjected to the scrutiny of the class and the teacher. Permutations and combinations of this method can be developed.

NOTE: The above method can and should be used with segments larger than paragraphs.

Drawing Conclusions: Internal and External Interpretation

By now you should see that the ideal method of developing comprehension skills is *not* to have separate books on facets of comprehension but to take a selection and reduce uncertainty by "mining" the important ideas, the central thrusts, and the conclusions. In commercials materials, the *Reading for Meaning Series* published by Lippincott comes much closer to my idea of developing concepts, vocabulary, and comprehension all in one selection than, for example, Richard Boning's materials, which, in my estimation, are merely testing materials—used largely as busy work.

At this point let me show you an instructional framework that can be used to develop comprehension of larger segments of material. This framework is useful in various content areas.

Using an Instructional Framework. Reading teachers and elementary teachers are familiar with the directed reading format as an aid in teaching students to read with comprehension. The components are usually (1) preparation for reading, (2) guided reading, and (3) teaching skills. Whether the way this format is ordinarily taught prepares the students to transfer many structures to reading on their own is not known. The basic idea is good and perhaps aspects of it transfer, but other useful kinds of instructional framework are needed. The various organizational skills provide good instructional frameworks, as do several of the strategies discussed in the chapter on comprehension.

Let us now discuss an instructional framework that uses two of those steps—preparation and guidance—and adds a third, independence.

1. Preparation: When we have some idea of what we are looking for in reading and know we are reading for a worthwhile purpose we have a more impelling purpose (motivation) for reading and are more attentive. Fourteen-year-old Charlie's interest in reading increases as he realizes he needs to improve his reading skills in order to read the driver training handbook. But a given chapter of social studies material that needs to be read may not be that interesting to him because he sees no purpose in reading it. In developing instructional frameworks we should make sure to devise clear-cut purposes for reading such material.

When reading somewhat unfamiliar material a student needs what Herber (1970) calls a *frame of reference*, an aid in acquiring the new ideas so that his or her idea intake will be organized. The teacher will develop background information by identifying the concepts that are prerequisite to and undergird the concepts to be studied. The teacher will draw on the student's experience to obtain information that will clarify particular points and will draw on his or her own expertise in the topic to develop interest and make the problem clear.

The teacher, Herber points out, has the purpose of providing a framework or context into which new information can be placed. The student with little experience with or knowledge of a topic can gain through the teacher and fellow students enough vicarious and actual experience to sustain interest.

The teacher uses a review in order to develop intellectual categories into which information can be slotted. In doing this the teacher draws on knowledge of students' backgrounds to elicit a common experience that can be related to the new unit in order to strengthen and clarify the framework for the unit topics. One type of review, I would think, would be going over or developing a related meaning hierarchy.

Anticipation and purpose are also part of preparation. If the preparation has been successful to this point, anticipation should certainly be developing. However, anticipation can be heightened by developing purpose for reading. For this facet to work, the instructor has to determine (1) the important ideas, those of great enough import for the student to make his or her own (integrate into cognitive and/or affective structures) and (2) how the students must read the text in order to fashion those ideas.

Direction, then, is needed so that the important ideas are ferreted out by appropriate skills. If obtaining the idea requires drawing conclusions, then guidance must be directed toward that skill.

Language development, including the important aspect of technical vocabulary, is fostered through discussion prior to reading. We have discussed a number of ways of doing this.

2. Guidance: Herber suggests that students be guided in executing the reading plan. The guidance will be structured enough to give purpose and direction but flexible enough to allow discoveries. Use of induction and concomitant discovery pays off in student enthusiasm; it also increases the likelihood that students will become independent in reading-reasoning analysis.

The use of reading guides that show students how to apply pertinent skills while they read enhances skill development. This can be accomplished by asking questions: for example, those on drawing conclusions where that is the purpose. Other kinds of structures derived from Herber's work will follow.

Two important goals of learning are concept and principle development. You will remember a thorough discussion of concept and principle development in the two chapters on psychology of learning. When concepts and rules are well developed, they form important aspects of meaning hierarchies, which we discuss throughout this text. These hierarchies are useful in allowing a person to process and assimilate ideas while reading. They are likewise useful in further analysis of material read.

Herber differentiates reading skills and reasoning skills. The latter refer to what I call, at least according to the Gray Model of Reading, reaction to ideas read and application of ideas read. It is not enough for a student to have a vague idea of the analytic processes in reading. The student must be so familiar with these processes that he or she is able to apply them in various kinds of reading matter over a period of time after direct instruction is no longer available. As the student becomes adept at applying these skills, he or she will become a much more independent thinker. Herber feels that reading and reasoning guides foster thinking development and independence in applying needed structures. But the student has to generalize this process in order to make it his or her own.

As I have stated throughout this book, students need more than a motley array of facts. They need to know how to develop and organize and apply concepts and rules and generalizations. Certainly, guide material for such development should be developed by the teacher, using the various strategies presented in the present text. Further strategies developed by Herber (1970) in the form of reading-reasoning guides will now be discussed. Credit must be given Herber for providing useful principles for construction of such guides as well as examples of them.

Reading-Reasoning Guides

Three levels of comprehension skills are used in Herber's reading-reasoning guides: the literal level, the interpretive level, and the application level.

Literal comprehension is an understanding of directly stated processes of information. This is in keeping with the way it is usually defined. There is a danger if students are not required to translate information, for example, by paraphrasing, that they will get by with verbalism.

In adapting Herber's work, I shall refer to the interpretive level as comprised of internal interpretation and external interpretation. In internal interpretation one uses pieces of information from various parts of a page or several pages and notes the relationships between the parts; that is, relationships among ideas. That is why this is called internal interpretation.

External interpretation involves development of information by seeing relationships between the author's meanings and meanings brought in from the outside—what the reader remembers or can find in other material or both.

In addition to reading guides for the literal level, we shall have reading-reasoning guides for the internal and the external interpretation levels. Furthermore, I shall also give examples of cause-effect reading guides based on Herber's structures and a format for differentiating ideas through comparison-contrast analyses. I do recommend Herber's (1970) work to the reader.

Examples of Reading-Reasoning Guides

The reading selection below is followed by three kinds of comprehension exercises—literal comprehension, internal interpretation, and external interpretation. In the first exercise the statements following the selection on comets are read *first* and then the "comets" selection is read.

Comets

1. If you look into the sky and see a heavenly body with shining "hair" streaming from it you likely are looking at a comet
2. (unless it is accompanied by loud trumpet music).
3. In fact, the word comet is derived from a Latin word meaning "hair."
4. Although there are hundreds of comets in our solar system
5. most people have not seen one because most comets do not come close enough to earth to be visible without a telescope.
6. Whenever the appearance of a large comet such as Halley's Comet (last appearance, 1910) or Kohoutek is predicted, many people become frightened because they believe such a comet portends evil.
7. In 1456, Halley's comet instilled so much fear in Europeans that Christians there prayed to be saved from "the Devil, the Turk and the comet."
8. Today most people have given up that idea.

LITERAL LEVEL

Directions: Please follow these steps: (1) read the statements below, (2) read the above selection on comets, (3) as you read the selection, look at the statements in the guide and indicate by circling the number which statements the author made. Substantiation may be indicated by placing in the blanks numbers corresponding to the text. (Some of the statements below may be false.)

_____ 1. You might see an angel in the sky.

_____ 2. The sky contains heavenly bodies.

_____ 3. A hobo with clean hair might be called a comet.

_____ 4. There are hundreds of comets in the solar system.

_____ 5. Christians generally pray for deliverance from Turks and comets.

_____ 6. Christians today probably still pray for deliverance from the Devil.

_____ 7. Many people fear large comets.

_____ 8. A telescope is usually needed in order to see most comets.

_____ 9. Halley's comet was large.

INTERNAL INTERPRETATIONAL LEVEL

Directions: Having read the selection, you are now ready to check each statement that you feel the author was trying to get across. Several pieces of information may coalesce to form the relationship indicated by the statement. To show which pieces of information back your contention (or are elements in the coalescence) write the numbers referring to the information on the lines by the statements. You have to ask, "Do code 'numbers' J and T combine to imply what statement Y infers?"

_____ 1. There is some chance that a person could see a comet if he looked into the sky.

_____ 2. If more people had telescopes, there would be more fear.

_____ 3. There will probably be a flurry of excitement the next time Halley's comet becomes visible.

_____ 4. There is an element of truth in the statements made about Hollywood starlets, " 'Hair' today; gone tomorrow."

_____ 5. Some people today fear comets.

EXTERNAL INTERPRETATION LEVEL

Directions: Since you are familiar with the selection you may proceed to the exercise below. If you think a statement can be supported when the author's ideas and related ideas on the subject from other sources are taken into consideration, check the statement. Keep in mind especially the internal relationships developed at the internal interpretational level.

_____ 1. Today people fear large comets less because they have a naturalistic attitude about them.

_____ 2. The author probably knows about Gabriel's big impending role.

_____ 3. Mr. Kohoutek and Mr. Halley discovered comets.

_____ 4. More familiarity with comets might lessen fear of them.

_____ 5. Most living astronomers saw Kohoutek's comet.

_____ 6. There may still be places where people pray for deliverance from the "Devil, the Turk and the comet."

Differentiating literal comprehension, internal interpretation, and external interpretion. Personal, social, and political development and maturity would be fostered, it seems, by the ability to differentiate among actual statements, conclusions drawn on the basis of statements, and conclusions drawn on the basis of statements and information we decide to kind of "mix in" with the author's statements.

Directions: A list of statements is placed after the selection. Some of the statements are literal, some internal interpretive, and some external interpretive. Identify in the blank preceding each statement the nature of the statement.

L = Literal; II = Internal Interpretive and EI = External Interpretive.

William the Conqueror

William the Conqueror was born in France but he became the King of England. At age eight when his father, Duke Robert of Normandy, died, William became the ruler. By the time he became a man he had quelled a number of disorders. At the age of twenty, he, with the help of King Henry of France, put down a great rebellion. After this he ruled Normandy with an iron hand. His enemies even admired him.

In 1051 when William visited England, King Edward the Confessor (a relative of William's) named William to be his successor to the English throne. Upon Edward's death in 1066, Harold, a brother-in-law of Edward, obtained the throne on the basis of a deathbed grant and election by the nobles and ranking clergy of England.

William proceeded at once to invade England with an army that numbered 5,000; that seems small by today's standards. Harold had just gone north to try to stave off the invading Norwegians; he succeeded. William landed before Harold could get back. William was fortunate that he had powerful archers and horsemen and that Harold's men were exhausted. In the decisive Battle of Hastings, Harold was killed and William became king.

There were a number of attempts to overthrow him but they failed. Noblemen and peasants had to swear allegiance to William. From those who would not support him he took lands and gave them to those who were loyal. He soon developed a strong nation.

William brought with him the French language and many French customs. He also instituted the building of great castles and cathedrals.

During William's reign Danegeld, a national tax on landed property, was imposed. William kept a record of all the lands in England, the principal landholders, the farm population and the resources of his kingdom. These records were the basis for assessing taxes. To insure fairness and keep the records accurate he appointed in each district a group of twelve men to check these records. The system of juries evolved from similar groups two hundred years later.

_____ 1. Robert was just out of his teens when he quelled a great uprising.

_____ 2. Strong rulers are known for their ability to command respect and obedience.

_____ 3. During Edward the Confessor's reign England lagged behind France in church architecture.

_____ 4. It is always a good idea to ensure equitable tax assessment and collection for rich and poor alike.

_____ 5. Duke Robert owed allegiance to a French king.

_____ 6. Andrew Jackson didn't invent the "spoils system."

_____ 7. State university regimes are not above a form of "spoils system."

_____ 8. In a sense we owe William the Conqueror a debt of gratitude.

Cause and Effect

In the real world people continually work in the realm of cause and effect. A person, for example, exhibits a certain behavior pattern and rather than try to attribute the cause to the person a parent makes statements about the personality of and conduct of the other parent and adduces such statements as causes . . .

We have the advantage in history and literature—if not in current events—of "coolly" reading documents, determining effects and possible precipitating and underlying causes in a situation (Civil War), and then matching effects with their likely causes. Being able to read and engage in such matching of causes and effects is actually a luxury, which we may not appreciate as we should until we get older.

> *Directions:*   Identify cause and effect relationships and (2) place effects in one list and causes in another. (3) Students read the text to note relationships of details in the text and (4) relate causes and effects on the basis of the relationships; place letters in appropriate blanks.

Reading Selection

("Israel: 25 Years Under Arab Siege")
by Jan Bushinsky
1974 World Book Yearbook, p. 403

Effects

a. Israel devoting more effort and gross national product (GNP) to defense than any other nation.
b. Deficit in the balance of payments
c. Sixfold increase by Israel In GNP between 1952-1970
d. Lack of constitution
e. Complicated social problems

Causes

_____ 1. Inability of Orthodox Jews to accept basic laws not derived from the Torah.

_____ 2. Diverse cultural and ethnic backgrounds of post-independence immigrants.

_____ 3. Israeli-Arab wars in 1956 and 1957; two-year war of attrition against Israel 1968-1970.

_____ 4. Massive imports of warplanes and armor, mainly from the United States.

_____ 5. Modern production methods introduced.

NOTE: It is important to discuss the cause-effect pattern with students. Guide the students' reading in a way that will make them consciously aware of the process. Students need to develop an understanding and feeling for the process so that they will be able to do such reading without the aid of a structure prepared by the teacher.

Compare and Contrast

Most of us have experienced some difficulty in differentiating related ideas. A comparison-contrast paradigm can be used to show how two phemonema are similar and how they are different. Features characterizing X are placed in one column and related features characterizing Y are placed opposite in an adjoining column. Below is a comparision-contrast of Luther and Erasmus, two great Renaissance theologians.

Table 9-3.

Luther	Erasmus
. German	. Dutch
. Biblical humanist	. Biblical humanist
. Earthy firebrand	. Esthete
. Saw in the classical languages the media for the rebirth of Christianity	. Saw in the classical languages the media for the rebirth of Christianity
. Believed in justification by faith	. Believed that man struggled to make himself worthy of God's salvation
. Wrote "Bondage of the Will"	. Wrote "Freedom of the Will"

A direct application of the compare and contrast paradigm to reading behavior follows:

Table 9-4. A Comparison-Contrast of Reading Behaviors of an Average Student and a Gifted Student*

	Average Student	Gifted Student
	CA 14.3; IQ 101; Reading Grade Placement 8.0	CA 13.9; IQ 130; Reading Grade Placement 12.4
Task	Performance	Performance
Use phonic rules, word analysis.	Not able to apply principles in multi-syllable words.	Able to apply principles, even to unfamiliar words. Had trouble with words that deviated from the normal patterns.
Derive hint of meaning or singular meaning from word in context (contexts selected from texts and manuals designed for grades 6 through 14).	Could perform as long as the words and context were within the interest range and vocabulary knowledge level	Able to perform task with both concrete and abstract words within experience level. Made serious efforts to determine meanings of words outside experience level. Shows curiosity over unknown contexts and words.

Task	Performance	Performance
Derive main idea from a paragraph.	Able to do this task only when main idea was expressed in outstanding way such as the topic sentence.	Could perform this task with positive degree of success in both concrete and abstract material, regardless of position.
	Not successful when main idea was expressed in various positions in the paragraph, that is, not explicitly expressed.	Did show some difficulty in dealing with abstract ideas in which the main idea was not expressed.
Select supporting details.	Able to perform if the paragraph was conventionally organized.	Able to perform task and also reorganize details into order of sequence or importance.
	If presented with a group of reworded ideas, was not able to derive idea from supporting details.	
Outline material.	Showed only a general knowledge of outlining and was able to do a simple, basic outline.	Was able to outline and refine outline.
	Showed difficulty in separating main ideas from supporting details.	Was able to separate main idea from supporting details as long as the material was within interest range and experience level. Had difficulty with material outside experience range.
Answer inference question on a selection.	Has not refined behavior enough to be successful. Still relies on concrete concepts.	Succeeded on concrete and abstract material through eleventh grade material. Succeeded on higher level with more concrete material.
	Difficulty in answering inference questions on selections above the seventh-eighth grade level.	

*This table is based on an unpublished study done at the University of Georgia, 1970, by Sarah Harper, under the direction of the author.

COMMENTS: We will let you draw your own conclusions. Also, the gifted child would not have done as well if he or she had not been exposed to appropriate reading instruction. The child of average ability might have made more quality responses if he or she had (1) received specialized instruction in reading and (2) been the recipient of teachers' efforts to emphasize reading skills in the content areas. He also stated that he did not like to read about anything except cars.

SUMMARY

Few adults are really knowledgeable about social studies concepts and associated vocabulary. Part of the reason might be the failure to teach the meanings of the difficult vocabulary items in social studies texts. Another problem is the way so many difficult concepts and words are stuffed into textbooks. Furthermore, verbalism is encouraged by meaningless rote recitation of textual materials and certain abstract passages such as the "Pledge of Allegiance."

A number of methods of dealing with vocabulary and word-recognition problems are explained in the chapters. Vocabulary exercises use the ideas of sentence contexts, meaning hierarchies (classification), and inductive teaching of prefixes and roots. Aids to pronunciation featured syllabication and open and closed syllable rules for pronunciation.

Remember that by the last year of secondary school good readers read for stated purposes, whereas poor readers do not; good readers take advantage of their meaning hierarchies, whereas poor readers do not; and good readers develop the general impressions and review frequently, whereas poor readers do neither of these.

Social studies teachers should realize that at various grade levels students do not have sufficient experiential backgrounds to handle certain technical materials, that teachers and students too often memorize material meaninglessly rather than process it and relate it to existing meaning categories or develop new meaningful categories, that teaching of inferences must be grounded in knowledge of facts [and that these facts must be related to real experiences and carefully developed vicarious experiences through the use of models, maps, pictures, movies, charts, illustrated articles (*National Geographic*, for example), and the like.]

Several critical reading problems were discussed. A key problem in critical reading is the failure to note and critically scrutinize a writer's assumptions. Another is the failure to check content against primary sources; the latter is at least one way truth can be disseminated in our classrooms. Some of the tacts used by people in overgeneralizing were also mentioned. Two especially important logical fallacies are the nonsequitur and the post hoc ergo propter hoc.

Strategies or patterns for teaching main ideas were reviewed. Then a three-step strategy for teaching students how to draw conclusions was given. Finally you were shown how to construct reading guides for processing larger sections of reading material: literal comprehension, internal interpretation, and external interpretation guides. Finally, formats for teaching students to make cause-effect analyses and compare-contrast analyses were shown.

ACTIVITIES AND QUESTIONS
TO PROMOTE LEARNING AND APPLICATION

1. What is the difference between *concept* and *vocabulary?*

2. In order to improve readability, rewrite segments of social studies texts designed for middle school students. How does your rewritten segment appeal to below-average readers compared to the original text?
3. Replicate the "Pledge of Allegiance" study described in this chapter.
4. Write several concrete pledges of allegiance and try them out in middle school classes.
5. Develop take-home study sheets for students in a social studies class. Try them out and notice the results.
6. Develop a number of category games that use important concepts in social studies and play them in class.
7. Develop a Simple Categorizing Game such as the one developed for the "Great Lakes" topic and the "Renaissance and Reformation" topic and play it in class.
8. Select social studies terms and develop a minimum of two sentences for each term. (Use terms different from the examples already given.)
9. What does J. C. Dewey's study mean to you?
10. Design a study like Dewey's study, using current texts. Execute the study, detail your findings, and draw conclusions. (This may be done as a small group project.)
11. What critical reading problems do you observe in the schools? Among adults?
12. Investigate textbook controversies of the past and critique them. Do the same for a current controversy.
13. What evidence of overgeneralizing do you observe in popular reading materials; academic materials?
14. Make a list of nonsequiturs that you have observed. Why do you think people make nonsequiturs?
15. How have you been affected by the post hoc ergo propter hoc fallacy? That is, have you been the victim of such a fallacy? Explain.
16. Select a section of a social studies chapter and write appropriate reading guides at the following "levels:" literal internal interpretation, external interpretation, cause and effect.
17. Do a comparison-contrast analysis of two (a) philosophies of history, (b) explanations of the cause of a war, and (c) presidential candidates' platforms.

SUGGESTED ADDITIONAL READINGS

AUKERMAN, ROBERT C. *Reading in the Secondary School Classroom.* New York: McGraw-Hill, 1972. Chapter 7.

FAIR, JEAN. "Materials for the Unit Plan in Social Studies." In Lawrence E. Hafner (Ed.). *Improving Reading in Middle and Secondary Schools.* Second Edition. New York: Macmillan, 1974. Pp. 385–90.

HERBER, HAROLD L. "Reading in the Social Studies: Implications for Teaching and Research." In James L. Laffey, (Ed.). *Reading in the Content Areas.* Newark, Del.: International Reading Association, 1972. Pp. 191–210.

HUUS, HELEN. "Antidote for Apathy." In Lawrence E. Hafner (Ed.). *Improving Reading in Middle and Secondary Schools.* Second Edition. New York: Macmillan, 1974. Pp. 374–85.

PIERCEY, DOROTHY. *Reading Activities in Content Areas.* Boston: Allyn & Bacon, 1976. Chapter 14.

SANDERS, PETER L. "Teaching Map Reading Skills in Grade 9." In Lawrence E. Hafner (Ed.) *Improving Reading in Middle and Secondary Schools.* New York: Macmillan, 1974. Pp. 191–95.

ROEHLER, LAURA R. "Techniques for Improving Comprehension in Social Studies." In Gerald G. Duffy (Ed.). *Reading in the Middle School.* Newark, Del.: International Reading Association, 1974. Pp. 140–52.

BIBLIOGRAPHY

CHASE, STUART. *Guides to Straight Thinking.* New York: Harper, 1956.

DEWEY, JOSEPH C. "A Case Study of Reading Comprehension Difficulties in History." *University of Iowa Studies in Education.* *10* (1935), 26–54.

HAFNER, LAWRENCE E., and JUDY BUCK. "The Ability of Sixth Graders to Explain the Basic Concepts in the Pledge of Allegiance." Unpublished Study, Florida State University, 1973.

HARPER, SARAH. "A Comparison-Contrast Study of Reading Behaviors of an Average Student and a Gifted Student." Unpublished Study, University of Georgia, 1970.

HERBER, HAROLD. *Teaching Reading in Content Areas.* Englewood Cliffs, N.J.: Prentice-Hall, 1970.

SMITH, HELEN K. "Research in Reading for Different Purposes." In J. Allen Figurel (Ed.). *Changing Concepts of Reading Instruction.* Newark, Del.: International Reading Association, 1961.

SPECTOR, ROBERT M. "The American Revolution: Something Beyond the Causes." *The Social Studies.* *42* (March 1971), 99–106.

SPRINGMAN, JOHN H. "A Study of Sixth Grade Pupils' Understanding of Statements in Social Studies Textbooks." Unpublished Doctoral Dissertation. Colorado State College, 1941.

THORNDIKE, E. L. "Reading as Reasoning: A Study of Mistakes in Paragraph Reading." *Journal of Educational Psychology.* *8* (June 1917), 323–32.

CHAPTER 10

Reading Mathematics.
I. Developmental, Psychological,
and Pedagogical Foundations

The Language of Mathematics

"The confidence of an individual to pursue the study of a subject is increased if he develops facility in using the language of the subject. This facility, in turn, is developed by meaningful, correctly paced exposure to this language" (Hafner, 1974). Lerch (1974) explains how to teach students the distinct vocabulary for the language of mathematics and its unique form of symbolization.

He points out that in reading English, in reading mathematics, or in reading any kind of language one uses the same basic process. However, the language of mathematics is written in verbal and mathematical symbols. These symbols or signs represent words and also concepts or phrases with complex meanings. In studying mathematics one goes from the use of a simple sign representing a quite simple concept to the use of more complex symbolization, which often represents concepts that are more complex or hard to understand.

Lerch further explains that a qualitative symbol may be comprised of one sign or several signs. He asks us to consider such symbols as 3, -4, y^2, and $\sum\limits_{x=2}^{n}$ and explains that in order to interpret the meaning of these symbols one must comprehend the meaning of each sign in relationship to the total symbol and combine these meanings into a mathematical concept. Furthermore, one has to deal with "symbols representing comparative ideas, operational ideas, descriptive or definitive ideas, and other mathematical abbreviations."

GOALS AND OBJECTIVES OF MATHEMATICS

Objectives and Basic Mathematical Needs

In keeping with the research of Davis (1968) and Hafner, et al. (1971) it is safe to say that the *objectives* of any educational endeavor relate to the utilization-development of word knowledge (concepts and their labels in the forms of words, phrases, etc.), reasoning, to determine relationships among ideas and some concrete form of carrying out the implied mental operations. In the case of mathematics the mental operation would be computation.

However, *basic mathematical needs* serve as goals toward which teachers and students strive. Johnson and Rising (1972) summarize these needs as follows:

1. The student needs to know how mathematics contributes to his understanding of natural phenomena.
2. He needs to understand how he can use mathematical methods to investigate, interpret, and make decisions in human affairs.
3. He needs to understand how mathematics, as a science and as an art, contributes to our cultural heritage.
4. He needs to prepare for vocations in which he utilizes mathematics as a producer and consumer of products, services, and art.
5. He needs to learn to communicate mathematical ideas correctly and clearly to others.

These needs imply that students not only learn how to do mathematics in the narrow sense but that they learn (1) the various applications of mathematics, (2) the interrelationships of the various disciplines, and (3) the language means for learning mathematics ideas and relating them to other ideas as a means of improving the lot of humankind.

Behavioral Objectives

My own bias is that behavioral objectives may be useful in developing certain aspects of mathematics curriculum and teaching methods and materials, but that there is a danger in fragmenting objectives to the point that meaningfulness is curtailed and higher order cognitive and affective learnings are impeded, if not totally stymied.

Johnson and Rising (1972) point out that behavioral objectives do provide a framework useful in developing accountability in instruction, but that there is some difficulty in stating behavioral objectives for higher cognitive levels and in measuring these achievements with simple pencil and paper tests. Consequently, these higher cognitive processes do not get measured and "the more important goals of teaching—independence, critical thinking, creativity, skill in attacking truly original problems and solving them—are lost in the shuffle."

Instructional objectives are developed in terms of what we know about logical and psychological sequence of learnings, including child development theory and research findings generated by such theory.

PIAGET'S PSYCHOLOGY IN EARLY MIDDLE SCHOOL: CONCRETE OPERATIONS

(If you have not read the basic Piagetan theory in Chapter 2, you may want to do so before proceeding.)

In grade 5 practically all students are in the concrete-operational stage. The transition to the early stages of the formal-operational stage begins during the latter part of grade 5 and, for some, grade 6. If mathematical ideas refer to concrete objects, the concrete-operational child can operate logically on ideas in order to develop conclusions.

Concrete Logic in Conservation

The hallmark of the concrete-operational stage is the students' use of the conservation principle in solving various kinds of problems. The "concrete" child will conserve or maintain the fact that two equal sets of numbers are equivalent regardless of the configurations of the two sets. This feat is a triumph of operation over perception (Fremont, 1969, on Piaget, 1952). Conservation of number, then, means that a set of numbers remains the same so long as nothing is added to or taken away from the set.

Mental Differentiation

Mental Reversibility. A key to the logic of cognitive activity in the concrete-operational stage is mental reversibility, which means that a person can start at a certain point in an operation and return to the point. Lefrancois (1975) offers this definition of reversibility:

> A logical property manifested in the ability to reverse or undo activity in either an empirical or a conceptual sense. An idea is said to be reversible when a child can unthink it and when he realizes that certain logical consequences follow from so doing.

Examples of reversibility:

(1) $5 + 3 = 3 + 5$
(2) Ability to move from an instance of a class, or from a subclass and then reverse the movement:

a. A pear is a fruit.　　　　　　　　One kind of fruit is the pear.
b. A car is a type of vehicle.　　　　One kind of vehicle is the car.

Grouping ability is a first fundamental structure of operational intelligence.

Seriation. The concrete-operational child can put things, such as sticks of various sizes, into serial order. This task requires a grasp of the double principle of seriation, which requires that each stick or element be compared with its neighbors on both sides. When this is mastered and the seriation operation is reversible and firmly developed, the principle of transitivity is comprehensible: If T is larger than U and U is bigger than V, it is understood internally (through thinking alone), without recourse to a model, that T is bigger than V (Furth, 1969). Writers of intelligence tests include this kind of intellectual task in logical thinking subtests.

Comprehending the System of Numbers. Comprehension of the number system is predicated on the operations of classes and of seriation and is a synthesis of these very operations. In other words, it is reasonable that the set of natural numbers 1, 2, 3, 4 . . . , infinity manifests the properties of seriation where each element is related to both its prior element and its following element, $(n - 1)$ and $(n + 1)$, respectively. The characteristic of classification is shown in the number system because each lower number is included in the higher number (Furth, 1969).

Mental Inversion. A concept that leads to the attainment of conservation is that of mental inversion. It is the *mental* operation whereby an operation already performed can be canceled:

Applied more directly to numbers this concept means that for every element there is another element that cancels or negates it; the negating element is called an *inverse.* When the first element and the inverse are combined, the identity element is the result:

$$A \times A' = I \quad \text{(Identity)}$$

In addition: $A + (-A) = I$ (In addition, the Identity element $= 0$.)
                   $1 + (-1) = 0$

In multiplication: $A \times 1/A = A/1$ (In multiplication, the Identity
                        $1/1 \times 1/1 = 1$ element $= 1$.)

(Phillips, 1969), p. 70)

Mental Reciprocity. In bouncing a ball off a wall the angle of incidence (approach to wall) equals the angle of reflection (exit from wall). By throwing the ball back at the path of the original angle of reflection, it will bounce off on the path of the original angle of incidence. This is termed reciprocity. An application is this: In order to hit an object by bouncing a ball off a wall, one makes the angles of incidence and reflection equal angles, that is, equivalent or reciprocal:

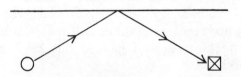

Principles That Characterize Operational Thought

Several principles basic to operational thought have been discussed either explicitly or implicitly; the principles follow:

> *1. Closure:* Any two operations can be combined to form a third operation; for example, all boys and all girls = all children; $3 + 4 = 7$.
>
> *2. Reversibility:* For any operation there is an opposite operation that cancels it; for example all boys plus all girls equals all children, but all children except all boys equals all girls: $3 + 4 = 7$ and $7 - 4 = 3$.
>
> *3. Associativity:* When three operations are combined it does not matter which two are combined first; or the same goal can be reached by different routes. For example, all adults plus all boys and girls equals all boys plus all girls and adults: $(1 + 4) + 2 = 1 + (4 + 2)$.
>
> *4. Identity:* This is a "null operation" performed when any operation is combined with its opposite. For example, all human beings except all those who are human beings equals nobody: $5 - 5 = 0$ (Lovell, 1966).

Applying Piaget's Theory in the Concrete-Operational Stage

Attitudes and Expectations Affecting Scholastic Educability. Lovell (1972) has long been a student of Piaget's work. He contends, as a result of his review of research, that it is the general ways of knowing that determine the way in which taught material is understood. Lovell has two suggestions that aid our understanding of the scholastic educability of students in the early years:

1. The value judgments of parents, language function within the home, and the attitudes of parents toward education affect scholastic educability. It is a most difficult job to change parental attitudes.

2. Teacher expectation affects pupil performance (Pidgeon, 1970). Therefore, the mathematics teacher should think well of pupils in a way that they know. Yet the teacher should set appropriate standards of work, expectations that are high for a given individual or group. (I do not interpret this to mean the expectations should be mind breaking, only mind stretching.)

Applications Relating to Classroom Organization and General Teaching Techniques. Home attitudes and teacher expectation greatly affect students' willingness to act on and transform reality and thereby develop new knowledge. Transformations should be aided by these suggestions of Lovell (1972) for classroom organization and general teaching approaches. (They are paraphrased.)

1. Play down much teacher talk directed to the whole class and emphasize pupils working in small groups, or individually, at tasks set by the teacher.

2. Provide opportunity for pupils to act upon physical materials and to use games as suggested by Dienes. It is not the objects themselves but the abstractions from actions performed on objects that advance knowledge of mathematical ideas. Only when students reach the flexible formal-operational stage of thought can mathematics be learned using words and symbols only; and it is *only* at that time that intuitive data can be dispensed with.

3. A child is forced to organize thoughts into a coherent structure and to bring forth available thinking strategies by engaging in social intercourse using verbal language. Through discussions and oppositions the child is faced with different viewpoints that must be reconciled in some manner with his or her own. Therefore, mathematics teaching must emphasize much teacher-child interaction. Actually, dialogue and action should be used together because language helps the child to organize experience and express thinking.

4. The teacher has the responsibility of initiating and directing student work so that the structured and interlocked system of relations of mathematics governed by firm rules and expressed in symbols may be learned. This is not to imply that students never have a choice of activities but the tasks should have the right amount of structure and be viewed by students as having relevance to life.

5. Concomitant with the abstracting of mathematical ideas from the physical contexts is the introduction of appropriate symbolization and the working of examples in drill, practice, and the working of problems on paper.

PIAGET'S PSYCHOLOGY IN MIDDLE AND SECONDARY SCHOOL: FORMAL OPERATIONS

Thinking About Thinking

In formal thinking one thinks about thought and reverses the relations between what is real and what is possible. (Inhelder and Piaget, 1958). In this kind of thinking one can examine the thinking process itself, reflecting on thinking's own operations. One can reason on the basis of the operational relations themselves no matter what the content, or, better yet, disregarding the content; examples follow.

The Classical Syllogism. The order of the syllogism is (1) major premise, (2) minor premise, and (3) conclusion.

Major premise:	All X's do Y.
Minor premise:	B is an X.
Conclusion:	Therefore, B does Y.

Upon that contentless form all kinds of content can be impressed:

M.O.:	All floobies park against yellow curbs.
m.p.:	Klod is a floobie.
∴	Klod parks against yellow curbs.

Being able to think in terms of the classical syllogism means that the person can follow the form of the argument but disregard its specific content. Regardless of the content that may be inserted in the place of the abstract S, Y, J, and so on, the child in the formal-operational stage can (ostensibly) draw the correct conclusions from a proposition such as the one following:

Some green X's deserve Y. Since one of the most green X's was J, the R, therefore:

1. J, the R, deserved Y.
2. J may have deserved Y.
3. J did not deserve Y.
4. None of these conclusions logically follows.

Difference Between C.O.P. Child and F.O.P. Child. Children in the concrete-operational period, when presented with the following sentence: "I am very glad I do not (like) onions, for if I liked them, I would always be eating them, and I hate eating unpleasant things." will respond to the *content* of the sentence by saying, for example, "Onions are unpleasant; it is wrong not to like them; and so on." The child in the formal operational period will respond to the *form* of the argument, noting the contradicitons between "if I like them" and "onions are unpleasant." (Ballard in Hunt's *Intelligence and Experience*).

Operating in the Area of Possibilities

Basis for Hypothetico-Deductive Thinking. The hypothetico-deductive thinking that characterizes formal thinking is based on hypotheses that lead to certain logical deductions. This kind of thinking opens up areas of possibilities closed to the concrete-operational child. Now the child can develop hypotheses so that the larger set of possibilities that are envisionable contains reality as only a subset. The child can even try out hypotheses in his or her mind and discard those that seem inappropriate (Phillips, 1969).

Types of Hypotheses. Several forms or types of hypotheses are

1. *What if hypotheses:* What would happen if the average height of women were 6'4" and that of men, 5'10"?

What would happen if only women could be gainfully employed?

What would happen if twins had to fill the position of president and vice-president of the United States? (This can get into the area of probabilities.)

2. *If-then hypotheses: If* children had to be six years of age by July 1 of the year they want to enter grade 1, *then*, a larger proportion of the children will attain the concrete-operational stage in grade 1.

If I finish this book, *then* my editor will be happy.

Floating Bodies Problem: C.O. Solution vs. F.O. Solution. The child in the formal-operational stage can be differentiated from the child in the concrete-operational stage in a number of ways; one is in the way the child derives Archimedes' law of floating bodies.

1. *Apparatus:* The subject is given a pail of water and a number of different objects that will fit into the pail plus three cubes of different densities and an empty plastic cube to help make accurate comparisons with the density of water.

2. *Procedure:* The subject has the task of (1) classifying objects into floatable and nonfloatbale, (2) explaining why he or she classified each object as he or she did, (3) experimenting with the materials, (4) summarizing what was observed, and (5) looking for a law that will account for the findings.

3. Concrete-operational solution: The concrete-operational child thinks of each object as having an absolute weight. At one time the child says the water will push an object up, and then it will push one down. The child seems to classify objects somewhere on the scale between small, light to large, heavy; size and weight are considered one. Some objects sink because they are iron or stone, according to our C.O. child. What the child needs to do is place each object (1) on a continuum of volume *and* (2) on a continuum of weight. Then object A might be considered small and light; B, small and heavy; C, medium and heavy, and so forth. The C.O. child cannot do this and consequently fails to develop the law.

4. Formal-operational solution: The formal-operational child does deal with weight and volume as separate interacting dimensions, conceiving an object as small and light or small and heavy, and so forth. When weight and volume become operational, the child places them into a logical relationship called *proportion* and determines that an object that has a specific gravity less than that of water will float (Phillips, 1969). The next segment discusses proportion along with the details of the solution.

Proportion, an Operation on Operations

Before continuing with the solution of the floating bodies problem, I should like to explain proportion. Two objects that are proportional will have the same general figure or contour even though one is larger than the other. A standard football field is 60 yards wide and 100 yards long. If we wanted to develop a smaller field proportionate to the standard field we could first determine how long we wanted the field to be, let us say 50 yards. Since 50 is ½ of 100 our proportion is ½. Therefore, the width will have to be in the same proportion, that is ½. One half of 60 yards is 30 yards. For this reason a 50 × 30 football field is proportional to a 100 × 60 field.

In the floating bodies problem we proceed to determine the proportion of the weight of the object W_o to the volume of the object V_o; that ratio $W_o/V_o = d$, the density of the object. If the density of the object is less than the density of the water, $W_o/V_o < W_w/V_w$, then the object will float. Since the specific gravity (density) of water is 1.00, an object must have a specific gravity of less than 1.00 if it is to float in water. (After Inhelder and Piaget, 1958, and J. L. Phillips, 1969.)

Combinatorial Logic

In the earlier overview of the stages, combinatorial logic was shown to be involved in determining which combination of five colorless liquids would produce a colored solution. The formal-operational child can do this because he or she learns how to construct a table of all possible combinations and so determines which combinations will yield the colored solution.

The Lattice as a Mathematical Model. One kind of table is the lattice, a mathematical model that uses the concept of the number of possible combinations in X number of binary propositions. If one wanted to consider the possible arrangements for any given committee of professors, by color and by sex (assuming only two colors and two sexes), one would have four binary propositions to work with: black women, white women, black men, and white men. We see the following lattice of possible arrangements of a committee.

no professors	black women only	black men and white women	white men and women, and black women
white men only	white men and white women	women only, white and black	black men and women, and white men
white women only	black men and black women	men only, white and black	black men and women, and white women
black men only	white men and black women	white men and women, and black men	white men and women, and black men and women

These solutions may not be practical, but they present the committee formulator with 16 possible solutions. This kind of thinking is pure thinking, eschewing the exigencies of the practical situation.

Basis for Scientific-Reasoning Tasks. Piaget often states that the adolescent's understanding of combinations and proportions undergirds the ability to solve successfully many of the scientific-reasoning problems that he and his associates set for these young people. He means such tasks as those involving discovery of the measurement regularities involved in shadow projections, determining the chemical properties of a set of identical-appearing liquids, and solving probability problems. (After Flavell's discussion in Mussen (1970); Inhelder and Piaget, 1958; Piaget and Inhelder, 1951.)

Probability

Probabilistic thinking is based on cognitive processes that are developed enough to organize by means of rational operations that which is inherently certain, lawful, and predictable, for only then can things that are inherently uncertain, unlawful, and unpredictable be grasped (Flavell 1963).

During adolescence, upon attaining combinatorial and proportional schemas, one first has a systematic method for isolating the various possible combinations of a set of things. Then one is capable of understanding the nature of random processes and dwelling on the chances of determining particular combinations from the total set of possibilities. In like manner, a person who has the concept of proportionality is capable of making a real quantitative comparison of probabilities. For example, only if such a proportionality concept is at hand can the adolescent be sure that a set of 2 red and 3 white tokens yields better odds for drawing a red than does a set of 1 red and 2 whites; in other words, that the proportion 2/5 is greater than the proportion 1/3. (J. H. Flavell. "Concept Development." In Mussen 1970.)

Applying Piaget's Theory With Older (12+) Children

The following discussion has to do with students who are over twelve years of age. Yet, according to Lovell (1972), there must be some differentiation of approaches depending on whether a student is classified as backward, ordinary, or able.

Backward Children. Even though some new mathematical ideas will be introduced, the class organization and active approach suggested for people who are in the concrete-operational stage will be used. Learning in mathematics for the weakest students will take place by means of algorithms that help students deal with real-life situations.

Ordinary Students. Average students will be able to handle new topics that depend on the inchoate stages of formal thought. But the structures must be introduced through concrete means. Lovell illustrates this point as follows:

> Take an envelope. Let its center be O, and suppose OX and OY are axes in the plane of the envelope, through O, and are parallel to two adjacent sides of the envelope. Suppose OZ is the axis through O perpendicular to the plane of the envelope. The twelve- or thirteen-year-old can build up a table showing the effects of rotating the envelope about the three axes—any one operation being followed by a second. He can understand the structure displayed by the table; hence, he can understand the structure of a mathematical group in this one concrete realization.

Since ordinary pupils move so slowly into formal thought, it is imperative that small group and individual work involving dialogue between teacher and pupil and between pupil and pupil be carried out.

Able Students. The abler student will generally be in the flexible formal-operational thought stage; these possibilities are offered for your consideration:

1. This type of student will be able to move away more quickly from intuitable data and work on third-level abstractions that have no concrete realizations. These structures as well as relationships between structures are now more easily attainable and, therefore, generalizable.

2. More verbal and symbol exposition in class teaching is now possible even though discussion still is necessary.

3. Students still must have the chance to devise their own questions and discuss their own answers to the questions at this stage.

TEACHING MATHEMATICAL CONCEPTS

A concept is a generalization. Even the terms *house* or *dog* are concepts because neither refers to one specific thing. Dogs have many attributes in common and to the extent that they have a set of attributes commonly ascribed to dogs they can be called dogs. If an animal had all of the attributes commonly associated with dogs and yet it meowed we might be tempted to call it a cat (or a weird dog, perhaps).

Johnson and Rising (1972) define a mathematical concept to be a mental construct or a mental abstraction of common properties of a set of experiences of phenomena. The basic kinds of mathematical concepts are illustrated by the following examples.

Set concepts. A number is the common property of equivalent sets.
Operational concepts. Addition is the common property of the union of disjoint sets.
Relational concepts. Equality is the common property of the number of elements of equivalent sets.
Structural concepts. Closure is the common property of a mathematical group.

Necessary Conditions for Learning Mathematical Concepts

Johnson and Rising (1972) use a cliche, albeit a meaningful one, to summarize the necessary conditions for learning a concept: "The learner must be *ready, willing,* and *able* to learn." Furthermore, the learner needs *guidance, resources,* and *time* for such learning. Johnson and Rising consider the following conditions to be essential in building new mathematical concepts:

1. *The learner must have the necessary information, skills,* and *experiences to learn a new concept.* For example, with only a meager understanding of rational numbers, the meaning of common denominator, the impossibility of division by zero, and the identity element for multiplication, a learner cannot consider algebraic fractions. Concepts and skills that are prerequisites to learning another concept should be listed. The students should then be pretested and the accomplishments of each student checked against the list of prerequisites in order to see where troublesome lacunae exist.

2. *The learner must have been motivated to the extent that he or she is willing to participate in learning activities.* Action-related thinking helps in this case. Rather than asking a student to learn the associative law of addition for some test, it would be better to ask the student to look for a short-cut way of solving the following:

$$26 + 39 + 61 \qquad 132 + 992 + 8 \qquad 6\ 1/2 + 4\ 2/9 + 6\ 7/9$$

3. *The learner must have the necessary capability to participate in the learning activities.* For example, if a student does not know how to compute square roots, do not ask him or her to compute cube roots. If the student is unable to solve linear equations do not ask him or her to learn to solve quadratic equations.

4. *The learner must be given some guidance so that motivation is preserved and learning is efficient.* Not only can trial-and-error learning or haphazard reflection be inefficient, it may also so discourage the potential learner that he or she never reaches the goal. If the learner is to conceptualize, ideas need to be presented so that he or she can perceive common elements. This implies giving two or more situations that contain the concept or common element that the learner is to perceive. Johnson and Rising explicate this point by

providing some examples of how learning to subtract a directed number is made possible if the learner is helped to compare the directed distances between points on the number line with the effects of adding opposites:

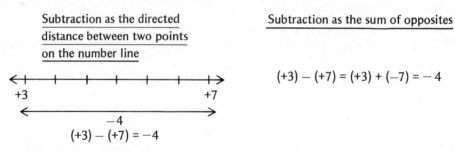

Subtraction as the directed distance between two points on the number line

Subtraction as the sum of opposites

$(+3) - (+7) = (+3) + (-7) = -4$

$(+3) - (+7) = -4$

5. *The learner must be provided with appropriate materials (e.g., a text, a model, a film, or a tape) with which to work.*

6. *The learner must be given adequate time to participate in learning activities.* If a person is to master a concept, varied experiences, applications, and uses—all time-consuming activities—must be used. Do not move on to new ideas before absorption can take place. For example, if a concept such as ratio and proportion is to be taught, take time to develop *mastery* and also use the concept in a variety of situations so that the learner will apply it as needed in chemistry class, social science class, art class, and the like.

Interrelationships for Five Related Concepts

Try the following as a demonstration with middle school students:

1. Get some students together for the purpose of developing meaning and interrelationships for five related concepts: (1) circle, (2) circumference, (3) diameter, (4) ratio, (5) pi.

2. Using hoops, circles, and the like, measure the circumference and diameter of these figures and lead the students to clarify the concepts involved and to see the interrelationships among them. Note especially that the ratio of circumference to diameter is always 3.1416; this ratio is termed pi (π).

3. Lead the students to make the appropriate generalizations. Now try to elicit from the students the generalizations involved in this situation:

    a. The diameter (D) is the distance across a circle through the middle.
    b. The distance around the circle is called circumference (C).
    c. A circumference is always about three times larger than the diameter.
    d. The ratio (or quotient) of the circumference to the diameter is 3.1416.
    e. We name this ratio pi (π).
    f. Pi is 3.1416.
    g. The formula for circumference is C = π • D
                            = 3.1416 • D

Record these generalizations and give them back as reading material. Now the students will bring meaning to the printed page.

Language Arts Analogies for Teaching Mathematical Concepts

Mathematical concepts such as commutative property and associative property have analogies in everyday experience. Capps (1970) has pointed out some of these analogies. I shall use his structure but provide my own examples, which I think are more mathematically accurate in some cases. In like manner, when teaching such concepts, you can provide such structures as an example and allow your students to extend the applications.

Concept	Mathematical Application	Language Arts Application
1. Commutative property	Addition $5 + 2 = 2 + 5$	Jellow and bananas are the same as bananas and Jello.
	Multiplication $9 \times 2 = 2 \times 9$	Nine players each scored two points. Two players each scored nine points.
2. Associative property	$(2 + 1) + 3 = 2 + (1 + 3)$	The twins and Sam joined the triplets. The twins joined Sam and the triplets.
3. Distributive property	$(5 + 2) \times 4$ or $(5 \times 4) + (2 \times 4)$	The boys and girls were nice. "Nice" applies to boys and girls. The boys were nice and the girls were nice.
4. Positional value	$234 = 432$	Lap is not equal to pal.
5. Expanded notation	$50 + 7 = 57$	School house—schoolhouse.
6. Numerals have varying meanings	$5_3 = 5_{10}$ (The context 3—base three—gives the numeral 5 a different meaning than the context 10 does.)	Please take the <u>lead</u> in the play. <u>Lead</u> is used in making batteries. The meaning of a homograph depends upon its context.
7. Numbers have many names	$12 \div 3 = 2 + 2 = 4 \times 1$	mammoth = huge Same meanings can be denoted by different symbols.
8. Exponential notation	$3.2 \times 10^{-4} = 0.00032$	Words can be abbreviated— Cash on Delivery = COD
9. Order of operations shown by parentheses	$(6 \div 2) + 7 = \underline{N}$	If you do not paint, my wife, the project will fail. If you do not paint my wife, the project will fail.
10. Sets	In mathematics numbers are classified as integers, whole, irrational, ... In geometry angles are classified as right, obtuse, acute, ...	In language sets of words are classified as noun phrases, verb phrases, adverbs, ...

DEVELOPING COMPUTATIONAL SKILLS

As a teacher and a parent, I have seen the value of computational facility. Although various kinds of electronic calculators are available, not all people can afford them, and it is still necessary to have a sense of what a set of numbers might "add up to" in order to check the reasonableness of an answer obtained with the aid of an electronic calculator.

According to Johnson and Rising (1972), psychologists and educators give the following reasons for school graduates generally lacking computational skills:

1. Inadequate understanding of numbers and operations with numbers.
2. Lack of interest in attaining computational efficiency.
3. Lack of ability to cope with the abstract ideas and symbols of computation.
4. Ineffective teaching of computational processes.

Mastery of Computation Is Necessary

Even though calculating machines have taken over computing tasks, computational skills are still essential for these purposes.

> To facilitate the learning of new mathematical concepts. If his computation is efficient, the learner can devote his mental energy to reflective thinking when facing a new problem or when exploring a new idea. If a student has mastered basic skills, he is likely to be confident in his ability to learn more mathematics.
>
> To perform many tasks in the home, on the job, and in recreational activities. Elementary arithmetic examples pervade activities such as shopping, cooking, managing a business, or playing a game.
>
> To promote productive thinking in problem solving, research, and other creative activities.
>
> To provide sources of insight into the structure of our number systems. Carrying out a computation may be a means of understanding place value, the properties of certain numbers, or the operation involved in an algorithm.
>
> *(Johnson and Rising, 1972)*

How to Practice Computational Skills

In my experience, meaningful, productive practice of computational skills is facilitated by using the following principles:

1. A student should be *motivated* to practice. Motivation is facilitated by work that the student can be successful at.

2. Motivation is also a function of *meaningfulness*. The student who understands what he or she is doing and why will be more willing to engage in the practice. Also the practice material should be related to what is currently being studied.

3. The practice should be related to *basic principles* and not just be some trick that does not fit in with the structure of mathematics.

4. Practice should be *spaced*. Brief practice periods that are spaced several hours or perhaps a day apart are better than one massed (long) practice period every day or so.

5. *Positive feedback* should be a result of practice. If the material is so difficult or meaningless that the person is not doing well, any feedback will not be positive. Also, answers should be available in some form: answer key or programmed learning feedback.

6. *Varied activities* should characterize practice. Avoid practice material that is merely an assigned page or a worksheet. Use games, programmed formats, puzzles, mental arithmetic, and the like.

Precocious mathematics students like to do mental mathematics, sans pencil and paper. In fact, one of our acquaintances managed to "get away" with mental mathematics until the eighth grade. Interestingly enough, the kind of mathematics that she learned or used prior to school age was what is now known as modern mathematics.

Austin (1970) conducted a study in the seventh- and eighth-grade classes of Margaret Lamar and found that mental mathematics taught once a week for several months resulted in the experimental group scoring statistically significantly better (.01 confidence level) than the control group. (The testing instrument was the *SRA Achievement Series,* grades 6–9.)

The method involved the assignment of problems to be brought to class on mental math day. The problems include the concepts that the class have learned and are engaged in at the time. A typical problem is: Begin with 8, add 4, multiply by 2, subtract 6, divide by 3, subtract 2, extract the square root, multiply by 3^2, multiply by 10, and subtract 5. Do you have the answer?

SUMMARY

Mathematics deals with relationships of quantities by the use of numerals and symbols. An individual's confidence in pursuing the study of a subject is increased as he or she develops facility in using the language of the subject. Mathematics is no exception.

In studying mathematics as an organized structure of knowledge, one must deal with its essential ideas and its assumptions as well as with the key laws of real numbers. These laws are, of course, taught over a period of several years.

As far as I have been able to ascertain, several leaders in mathematics education have expressed an antipathy toward the use of behavioral objectives in the area of high-cognitive processes of mathematics.

Much of Piaget's developmental theory is applicable to mathematics education, and the person (mathematics teacher and reading teacher) who would understand difficulties that a student is having in mathematics would do well to understand his or her abilities in Piagetian terms: At what stage is the learner and to what extent is the learner able to handle the basic tasks and understand the principles within a stage?

Good teachers will apply Piaget's theory with older children by differentiating among students classified as backward, ordinary, or able. Failure to differentiate instruction according to these principles will have deleterious effects on the students' mathematics achievements. Closely related to these principles is the admonition that in order to learn a mathematical concept the learner must not only be ready, willing, and able to learn but must also have guidance, resources, and time for such learning.

Concept development uses a number of strategies. A teacher should not forget to develop a collection of games for building concepts. Also, activities that use inductive principles and get students to use what they know to develop generalizations can be used to great advantage. When concepts and generalizations are developed and presented as reading material, the students will bring meaning to the page.

We know that well-devised analogies that involve everyday experiences can be especially helpful to less-capable learners. Such analogies for learning mathematical concepts are included in the chapter. On the other hand, precocious mathematics students should be provided special sessions for doing mental mathematics.

Both the importance of developing computational skills and meaningful practical guidelines for such development were presented.

ACTIVITIES AND QUESTIONS
TO PROMOTE LEARNING AND APPLICATION

1. Select at least two basic mathematical needs summarized by Johnson and Rising and expand on them in a 300-word essay.
2. Investigate the literature and find the pros and cons of using behavioral objectives in mathematics. What conclusions do you reach?
3. What does this mean: "Two equal sets of numbers are equivalent regardless of the configurations of the two sets?"
4. Take the examples of mental reversibility given in the text and explain why mental reversibility is actually important. (Here is a chance to be creative.)
5. Suppose you are writing an intelligence test. Make up some test items that require an understanding of the principle of transitivity.
6. What are some applications of the principle of reciprocity?
7. What are the implications of the difference between, "what we need in the schools are high standards" and, "one should set appropriate standards of work, expectations that are high for a given individual or group.
8. Mathematics teachers in the class may be encouraged to pursue Lovell's suggestions for classroom organization and general teaching approaches. Each student could select one suggestion to expand and illustrate in a report in class.
9. Of what value to mathematics is the ability to think in terms of the classical syllogism? Do not parrot the words in the text: make some applications to mathematics.

10. Why is hypothetical thinking useful? Fun?
11. Develop further applications of the *if-then* hypothesis to mathematics; daily living; your love life.
12. What was developed first: Archimedes' law of floating bodies or floating bodies?
13. Estimate the percentage of adults who operate in the formal-operational stage. How could you find out?
14. Make up several proportions problems and present them to the class for solution.
15. Give some examples of people not solving everyday problems by formal operations when that is what is required.
16. Develop applications of the concept of probability and share them as problems with members of the class. Be prepared to give cues to their solution.
17. Mathematics teachers may enjoy the challenge of further explicating Lovell's general applications of Piaget's work with older (15+) children who are (a) backward children, (b) ordinary students, (c) able students. This is indeed a challenge!
18. Prepare to teach a math concept to members of the class.
19. Comment on the value of language arts analogies for teaching mathematical concepts. Develop additional analogies for other mathematical concepts.
20. A seventh grader tells you that since the advent of hand calculators it is no longer important to know how to compute or calculate. What is your answer?
21. Develop a sequence of computation practice sessions related to concepts of your choice. Show how you will apply the various principles for meaningful, productive practice enumerated in the text.

SUGGESTED ADDITIONAL READINGS

CORLE, CLYDE G. "Reading in Mathematics: A Review of Recent Research." In James L. Laffey (Ed.). *Reading in the Content Areas.* Newark, Del.: International Reading Association, 1972, pp. 75–94.

GOOD, RONALD. *How Children Learn Science.* New York: Macmillan, 1977. [Excellent discussion on Piagetian theory.]

HAFNER, LAWRENCE E. (Ed.). *Improving Reading in Middle and Secondary Schools.* Second Edition. New York: Macmillan, 1974. Section 10.

SHEPHERD, DAVID L. *Comprehensive High School Reading Methods.* Columbus, Ohio: Charles E. Merrill, 1973. Chapter 11.

BIBLIOGRAPHY

AUSTIN, JOHN C. "Mental Mathematics Counts." *Arithmetic Teacher. 17* (4) (April 1970), 337–38.

BEUTEL, DONALD G., and PHYLLIS I. MEYER. "A Regular Classroom Plus a Mathematics Laboratory." *Arithmetic Teacher.* (November 1972), 527–30.

CAPPS, L. R. "Teaching Mathematical Concepts Using Language Arts Analogies." *Arithmetic Teacher. 17* (1970), 329–31.

DAVIS, FREDERICK B. "Research in Comprehension in Reading." *Reading Research Quarterly.* *3* (4) (Summer 1969), 499–545.

FLAVELL, JOHN. *The Developmental Psychology of Jean Piaget.* Princeton, N.J.: Van Nostrand, 1963.

FURTH, HANS G. *Piaget and Knowledge.* Englewood Cliffs, N.J.: Prentice-Hall, 1969.

HAFNER, LAWRENCE E. (Ed.). *Improving Reading in Middle and Secondary Schools.* Second Edition, New York: Macmillan, 1974. P. 324

——, WENDELL WEAVER, and KATHRYN POWELL. "Psychological and Perceptual Correlates of Reading Achievement Among Fourth Graders." *Journal of Reading Behavior.* *2* (4) (Winter 1970), 281–90.

HUNT, J. MC V. *Intelligence and Experience.* New York: Ronald Press, 1961.

INHELDER, BARBEL, and JEAN PIAGET. *The Growth of Logical Thinking from Childhood to Adolescence.* New York: Basic Books, 1958.

JOHNSON, DONOVAN A., and GERALD R. RISING. *Guidelines for Teaching Mathematics.* Second Edition. Belmont, California: Wadsworth, 1972.

LE FRANCOIS, GUY R. *Psychology for Teaching.* Second Edition. Belmont, California: Wadsworth, 1975.

LERCH, HAROLD. "Improving Reading in the Language of Mathematics—Grades 7–12." In Lawrence E. Hafner (Ed.). *Improving Reading in Middle and Secondary Schools.* New York: Macmillan, 1974.

LOVELL, KENNETH R. "Mathematical Concepts" In H. J. Klausmeier and C. W. Harris (eds.). *Analyses of Concept Learning.* New York: Academic Press, 1966.

——, "Intellectual Growth and Understanding Mathematics: Implications for Teaching." *Arithmetic Teacher.* (April 1972), 277–82.

MUSSEN, PAUL (Ed.). *Carmichael's Manual of Child Psychology,* Volume 1. Third Edition. New York: John Wiley & Sons, 1970.

PHILLIPS, JOHN L. *The Origin of Intellect: Piaget's Theory.* San Francisco: W. H. Freeman, 1969.

PIAGET, JEAN, and BARBEL INHELDER. *La genese de l'idee de hasard chez l'enfant.* Paris: University of Paris Press, 1951.

PIDGEON, D. *Expectation and Public Performance.* Slough, England: National Foundation of Educational Research, 1970.

RISING, GERALD. "Some Comments on a Simple Puzzle." *Mathematics Teacher.* *49* (4) (April 1956), 267–69.

CHAPTER 11

Reading Mathematics.
II. Strategies for Improving
the Reading of Mathematics

THE MATHEMATICS TEACHER AS A TEACHER OF READING

It is the job of the mathematics teacher to help students think well in mathematical situations. Reading is a thinking process, therefore the mathematics teacher should help students read mathematics material.

Lerch (1974) concurs in the above statements, pointing out that to the extent that the language of mathematics is concerned each teacher of mathematics must also be a teacher of reading. The mathematics teacher wants students to be able to read the language of mathematics, Lerch says, and to apply this reading skill as a self-learning tool. Not only must the teacher aid students in learning to read mathematical materials, he or she must also help them read in order to learn mathematical concepts.

In addition to developing in students mathematical concepts and comprehensive speaking and reading vocabularies of mathematical terms and mathematical signs, mathematics teachers will also teach students to identify familiar words and to develop speed and fluency in the reading process. Furthermore, they should help students understand the main idea or concept in sentences and paragraphs, read to note details or facts, follow a logical presentation or sequence of ideas, and develop the ability to follow written directions (Lerch, 1974).

The mathematics teacher should also help students to find and use other appropriate materials. For example, the teacher would help them use reference materials, programmed instructional materials, and other discourses related to a given topic. The teacher should also help the students develop skills in the reading of problems, maps, charts, and graphs. Finally, the teacher must help the students develop the abilities to select materials and organize what is read.

Difficulties in Reading the Language in Mathematics

It seems to me that the difficulties in reading the language of mathematics are quite obvious. These difficulties stem, in part, from the fact that mathematicians seem to write for one another instead of for students. We know, for example, that understanding can be facilitated by the right amounts and kinds of redundancy. Yet mathematicians pride themselves in writing in what they call precise language, "bare bones" stripped of what could be nourishing meat. A mathematician who wrote for students could make a fortune if he or she could convince mathematics teachers to use the books. It may well be that mathematics education has developed so greatly in order to present through the many algorithms, games, structures, and the like what some textbook writers fail to do.

Furthermore, introduction of different kinds of symbolism from one mathematics series to another can cause difficulty for students. If the mathematics series is any good, it is probably a good idea to use that series through several grade levels.

Conceptual difficulties provide a stumbling block for students. If a person is required to understand concepts and solve problems that are beyond his or her developmental level—formal operations required when person is still concrete operational—and mathematics achievement level, then the teacher is forcing failure on the student.

If the student has word-recognition difficulties with either general or technical vocabulary, then he or she is on an inappropriate level. Material on more appropriate levels should be used and corrective help in word recognition must be given.

Another stumbling block for would-be students of mathematics is the careful reading required in reading mathematics problems. Part of this is a function of the poor writing by text producers and part a function of having students placed in inappropriate materials for their level of development. Even so, the reading of mathematics requires careful, intelligent reading.

Teaching-Testing Exercises for Mathematics Symbolism and Vocabulary

Too often individuals have proferred as teaching material exercises that test. The following exercises based on Feeman (1973) are of that type. However, by suitable discussion prior to and concomitant with doing them they can be used for teaching.

Instructional Exercise: Mathematics Symbols to Printed Words

Instructions: You know what these symbols mean:

$$>, =, \cup, \#, \cap, \geqslant, \in, \nleqslant, <, \lessgtr, \leqslant.$$

Below you will find these symbols with the words standing for them written above the symbols:

greater than	is not equal to	is equal to or greater than
$7 > 5$	$3 \neq 10$	$\underline{y} \geqslant \underline{f}$

intersection   union   equals

$\underline{A} \cap \underline{B}$ $3 \cup 8 = 11$

is equal to
or less than   is not less than   is at least

$\underline{x} \leqslant \underline{y}$ $5 \nless 4$ $\underline{r} \leqslant \underline{s}$

is at most   is an element of

$1 \geqslant 5$ $\underline{z} \in \underline{R}$

Test Exercise: Matching Verbal Symbols with Correct Mathematical Symbols

Directions: At the left is a column of mathematics symbols. On the right is a column of verbal symbols. Match the appropriate symbols by placing the correct letter in the space at the left. Number 9 is done for you.

_____ 1. $\cap$ a. union

_____ 2. $\geqslant$ b. is not less than

_____ 3. $\nless$ c. is greater than

_____ 4. $>$ d. is equal to or less than

_____ 5. $\geqslant$ e. is an element of

_____ 6. $\in$ f. is not equal to

_____ 7. $\cup$ g. is equal to or greater than

_____ 8. $\leqslant$ h. is at most

_____ 9. $=$ i. equals

_____ 10. $\neq$ j. intersection

_____ 11. $\leqslant$ k. is at least

Instructional Exercise: Operations and Their Corresponding Mathematical Symbols

Instruction: Mathematical symbols can represent different sets of words that stand for the same idea. Below are symbols and various expressions that stand for the same operation or idea.

1. $-$ minus
        take away
        less
        (the difference)
        decreased by

2. $\div$ divided by
        distributed among

3. $\times$ multiplied by
        times

4. $+$ plus
        and
        increased by
        (sum of)

Test Exercise: Matching Verbal Expressions to Mathematical Symbols Denoting Operations

Directions: Below are verbal expressions. After each expression write the correct mathematical symbol for the operation denoted.

1. distributed among _____	8. divided by _____
2. plus _____	9. take away _____
3. sum of _____	10. decreased by _____
4. times _____	11. the difference _____
5. less _____	12. increased by _____
6. and _____	13. multiplied by _____
7. minus _____	

Instructional (Test) Exercise

Directions: Each set of mathematics symbols below is followed by an equivalent expression. Study them and think of alternative ways of stating each set of mathematical symbols.

1.	$1/7\ t$	one seventh of t	$1/7$ times $\underline{t}$
2.	$\underline{a} + \underline{b}$	a plus $\underline{b}$	
3.	thrice $\underline{j}$	3 times j	
4.	$6\underline{R}$	6 multiplied by $\underline{R}$	
5.	$\underline{q} - \underline{t}$	q less $\underline{t}$	
6.	$7 \cup 3$	7 union 3	
7.	$(2\underline{X})^2$	$2\underline{X}$ times itself	
8.	$10 \div 2$	10 distributed among 2	

Further Aids to Reading Mathematics Vocabulary

Vocabulary terms are the tokens or symbols that represent concepts. Attempting to teach a student a word for which he or she does not have the concept is a meaningless ritual. Therefore, the teaching of vocabulary must be rooted in concept knowledge.

Likewise, vocabulary teaching should be related to the student's general reading ability so that any sentence contexts containing new vocabulary items do not present meaning or perceptual difficulties. Some materials and activities that can be used to teach mathematics reading *vocabulary*, not the concept, are word-symbol cards, phrase-symbol cards, card readers, known to unknown matrices, and games. Place terms in sentence contexts when possible.

Word-Symbol Cards. Because we read from left to right, the conditioned stimulus is to the left of the unconditioned stimulus. If we are trying to teach the identification of the printed word by association with a known mathematical symbol, the latter should follow the printed word:

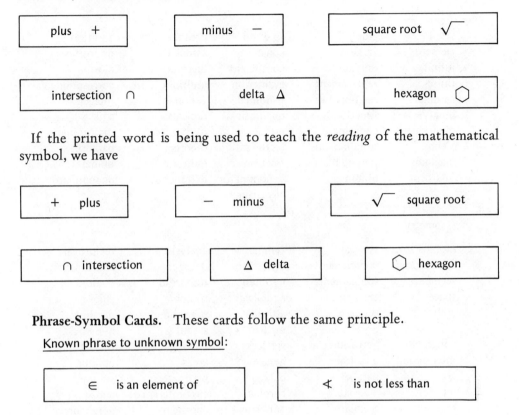

If the printed word is being used to teach the *reading* of the mathematical symbol, we have

Phrase-Symbol Cards.   These cards follow the same principle.

Known phrase to unknown symbol:

Known symbol to unknown phrase:

Card Readers.   A card reader "reads" a card by playing the audio tape affixed to the card below the corresponding visual display: the student looks at the visual display while listening to the audio display.

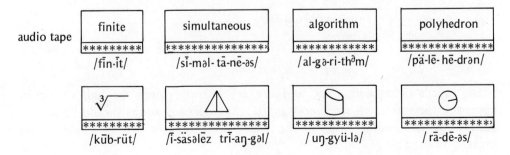

Following is a list of arithmetic, algebra, and geometry terms (in order of introduction in textbooks) especially suitable for use on card readers:

Arithmetic–Algebra

set	graph	solution	commutative	addition
elements	variable	constant	associative	opposites
infinite	domain	coefficient	distributive	closure
finite	replacement	evaluation	multiplication	correspondence
cardinal	relation	trinomial	exponent	integer
binary	function	quadratic	radicals	axis
monomial	coordinate	prime	pythagorean	discriminant
Venn	simultaneous	factorization	theorem	parabola
diagrams	polynomial	fraction	radicand	numerator
intercept	binomial	denominator	extraneous	denominator
		algorithm		

Geometry

mobius strip	vertical	symmetry	analysis	reciprocals
tetrahedron	complement	reflection	decagon	coordinates
segment	supplement	hypotenuse	trapezoid	conic
space	theorems	equidistant	rhombi	ellipse
collinear	geodesic	altitude	trigonometry	parabola
coplanar	postulate	median	secant	hyperbola
congruent	perpendicular	vertices	rectangle	trichotomy
intersection	dihedral	hexagon	areas	oblique
arc	parallel	octagon	perimeters	volume
interior	alternate	corollary	circumference	cube
exterior	auxiliary	opposite	apothem	polyhedron
obtuse	equilateral	consecutive	inscribe	cylinder
adjacent	isosceles	diagonals	circumscribe	pyramid
	equiangular	parallelogram	intercept	

Known to Unknown. A basic learning principle is to approach the unknown via the known. Some mathematical terms, because of their construction, lend themselves to comparison with other words to note common pronunciation elements. For example, aids to pronunciation of the word *coordinate* are juxtaposed with coordinate as follows:

<u>co</u> ke	known
<u>co</u> <u>ordi</u>nate	previously unknown
<u>ord</u>er	known
<u>in</u>	known
<u>ate</u>	known

The words *coke, order, in,* and *ate* are known words through which we approach the unknown word *coordinate*. Such presentations should be accompanied by discussion. Use of the overhead projector would enhance the presentation.

Following are more words from the fields of arithmetic, algebra, geometry, and trigonometry:

Known to Unknown

Arithmetic and Algebra

fact	receive	absent	ex	cart
factor	pro	abscissa	exponents	Cartesian
or	reciprocal	scissors	lone	art
	vocal			artesian
expo		slow	in	quads
exponent	grab	slope	inverse	quadrant
bent	graph	hope	verse	hydrant
	phone			
i	litter	depend	national	complete
identity	literal	dependent	rational	complex
dentist		dentist		exact
dense	equal	free		
density	equation	fraction		
city	nation	action		

Geometry and (Trigonometry)

possible	transfer	side	transport	pro
postulate	transversal	sine	transitive	protractor
late	verse	fine	it	tractor
			give	
con	verse	cold	prison	con
converse	vertex	cosine	prisms	concave
verse	tex	sine	chasms	cave
elevator	scale	chorus	tan	slow
elevation	scalene	chord	tangent	slope
nation	Gene		gentle	rope
tried	penthouse	concert	sphinx	local
triangle	pentagon	concentric	sphere	locus
dangle	gone	cent	here	us
		trick		
correct	October	pie	bike	
correspondence	octagon	pi	bisects	
respond	gone	hi	seconds	
fence	pentagon			
radio	con	sect	rec	
radius	convex	sector	rectangles	
us	vex	or	tangles	

Translating a Written Formula into its Mathematical Equivalent. Provide students with the opportunity to translate written formulas to mathematical equivalents.

Example 1:

Area equals length times width.

Math form $\underline{A} = \underline{L} \times \underline{W}$ or $\underline{a} = \underline{lw}$

Example 2:

Circumference equals pi times diameter.

Math form $\underline{C} = \pi \times \underline{D}$ or $\underline{C} = \underline{D}$

Example 3:

Final velocity equals initial velocity plus gravity times time.

Math form $\underline{v_t} = \underline{v_i} + \underline{g} \times \underline{t}$

or $\underline{v_t} = \underline{v_i} + \underline{gt}$

Now try these:

Example 4: The sine of angle $\underline{A}$ equals the opposite side divided by the hypotenuse.

Math form   _____

Example 5: Energy equals mass times the speed of light squared. (Where light = C.)

Math form   _____

Research Cues to Teaching Problem Solving

Reading and Computational Ability as Determinants of Problem Solving. Balow (1964) studied 1,400 middle school (sixth-grade) students to find relationships among reading ability, computational ability, and problem solving ability. He found that general-reading ability does have an effect on problem-solving ability. He felt that if a more normal reading situation (rather than a standardized reading test) were involved, reading skills might prove to be (even) more important. Computational ability also has a significant effect on problem-solving ability. As one might infer, for a given level of computational ability problem-solving achievement increases as reading ability increases; and for a given level of reading ability problem-solving achievement increases as computational ability increases.

Improving Problem Solving by Improving Verbal Generalizations. Irish (1964) studied fourth-grade students whose computation scores fell above the 50th percentile in computation but whose problem solving scores ranged between the 10th and 30th percentiles. For a two-year period, five minutes a day were devoted to work designed to develop the students' ability (1) to generalize the meanings of the number operations and the relationships among these operations and (2) to formulate original statements to state these generalizations as they are developed.

Members of the teacher study group analyzed the fourth-grade curriculum carefully and identified the generalizations involved in the topics covered. During the study-group sessions attention was devoted to examining and stating the associative, distributive, and commutative principles in language that children might use. When children fumbled for words, the words were *not* supplied. Needed vocabulary was carefully taught in computation instruction, but the students were not given definitions that might be memorized. The basic idea of the technique was that each student must speak for himself or herself, using his or her own words. The result of this type of instruction in the development of generalizations was that for two consecutive years the students in the experimental group made significantly greater average growth in problem solving and in computation than did the control group.

The Role of Structure in Verbal Problem Solving. Wilson (1967) compared the wanted-given structure with the action-sequence structure to determine the relative effect on the problem-solving ability of a group of fourth graders. The wanted-given structure was found to be statistically significantly superior (.01 level) to the action-sequence structure. In this program the students were trained to (1) recognize the wanted-given structure of the problem, (2) express this structure in an equation, and (3) compute by using the operation indicated by the equation. In this wanted-given program there was consistent use of expressions such as, "What are we given here, the parts to find a total, or the total and one of the parts to find the size of the other part? What does subtraction mean? Subtraction is used to find the size of one part when we know the total and size of the other part. Is the meaning in this problem?"

Teaching Problem Solving: How To?

Johnson and Rising (1972) speak of factors involved in the mental process. These relate to its being a complex mental process, requiring original and varied responses, skill in reading, and a procedure—an analysis and a sequence of steps. This process also involves a background of knowledge and structures as well as motivation and curiosity.

Johnson and Rising note that to understand all the conditions of the problem situation one must be able to *read*, that is, comprehend. For example, in his reading he applies what Wilson called the wanted-given structure: What is the particular thing the *reader* must catch in this problem?

> Suppose I have two American coins in my pocket whose total value is 60 cents. If one of them is not a dime, what coins do I have?

Are you puzzled? I was for a few seconds. One is not a dime; it is a half dollar. The *other* one *is* a dime!

Steps in Solving Written Mathematics Problems

1. Read the problem accurately.
   a. Carefully note the information; this may involve paraphrasing.
   b. Determine what you are to find.
2. Use mathematical symbols to set up the problem.
3. If possible, set up the relationships in equation form.
4. Perform the operations.
5. Fit the answer and values of unknowns back into the problem to see if the solution is satisfactory.

Sample problem: The sum of two numbers is 36. If 4 times the larger is added to 3 times the smaller, the result is 132. What are the numbers?

Steps:

1. a. Read the problem accurately; this may involve paraphrasing.*
      Add two numbers and you get 36. You do something to the numbers. Then you add the modified numbers. The sum is 132.
   b. What are we to find?
      Find the two (original) numbers.
2. Use mathematical symbols to set up the problem.
   a. Call the larger number X.
   b. Call the smaller number Y or $36 - X$.
   c. Call the sum of the larger and smaller numbers 36.
   d. 4 times the larger number, X, is represented as $4X$.
   e. 3 times the smaller number, Y, is represented as $3Y$.
3. If possible, set up the relationship in equation form.

$$4X + 3(36 - X) = 132$$

4. Perform the operations necessary to solve the equation.

$$4X + 108 - 3X = 132$$

Subtract 108
from each side

$$4X - 3X = -108 + 132$$
$$X = 24, \text{ the larger number}$$
$$36 - X = 12, \text{ or } Y, \text{ the smaller number}$$

5. Fit the answer and values of unknowns back into the problem to see if the solution is satisfactory.

$$\text{Larger number} + \text{smaller number} = 36$$
$$24 \quad + \quad 12 \quad = 36$$

Solution is satisfactory!

Study Guide Based on a Word Problem

Word Problem: In a sum of money there are three times as many dimes as nickels. If the total amount of money is $7.00, how many dimes are there?

*It is helpful to have the student read the problem enough times to be able to state the problem in his or her own words!

True or False:

1. (Literal comprehension)
   - _____ a. The problem speaks of dimes and nickels.
   - _____ b. There are three times more dimes than nickels.
   - _____ c. The nickels plus the dimes equal $7.00. (700 cents)

2. (Interpretive)
   - _____ a. The problem asks the total value of the dimes.
   - _____ b. An unknown number can be represented by $\underline{X}$.
   - _____ c. $\underline{X}$ can represent the number of nickels.
   - _____ d. The problem asks the total number of dimes.
   - _____ e. $\underline{X} \cdot 5$ could stand for the amount of money in nickels.
   - _____ f. What operations must be used to solve the problem?

Answer:

3. (Applied)
   - _____ a. What is the answer to the problem?
   - _____ b. If there are one fourth as many nickels as quarters and the total was $4.20, how many quarters are there?
   - _____ c. Make up a similar problem.

Reading Formulas and Equations

Analyzing Formulas and Equations. A useful practice to help students understand formulas and read them in both mathematical symbol and written forms is to have students translate from one form to the other. Following are samples of the kinds of mathematical formulas students will encounter in *mathematics*, *technical*, and *science* courses:

(1) $$\frac{\underline{A} \quad = \quad \underline{I} \quad \cdot \quad \underline{w}}{\text{The Area equals length times width}} \quad \text{or } \underline{A} = \underline{I}\underline{w}$$

(2) $$\frac{\underline{C} \qquad\qquad = \qquad \underline{D} \quad \cdot \quad \pi}{\text{The circumference of a circle equals its diameter times pi}} \quad \text{or } \underline{C} = \underline{D}\pi$$

(3) For any prism: $$\frac{\underline{V} \quad = \quad \underline{B} \quad \cdot \quad \underline{h}}{\text{Volume equals base area times measure of altitude}} \quad \text{or } V = Bh$$

(4) The quadratic formula. (I will start you on this. Can you finish it and then put in final form?)

$$\frac{\underline{X} \quad = \quad -\underline{b} \qquad \pm}{\underline{X} \text{ equals } -\underline{b} \text{ plus or minus (the square root of } \underline{b} \text{ squared}}$$

$$\frac{}{\text{minus four times } \underline{a} \text{ times } \underline{c}) \text{ divided by two times } \underline{a}.}$$

or $$\frac{\underline{X} = \pm \underline{b}}{}$$

(Can you finish this?)

(5) For a cylinder: $$\frac{\underline{L} =}{\text{Lateral area equals two times pi times radius times height.}}$$

(Try putting these into written form without peeking back.)

(6) $\underline{A} = \underline{l} \cdot \underline{w}$

(7) $\underline{C} = \underline{D} \cdot \pi$

(8) $\underline{X} = -\underline{b} \pm \sqrt{\underline{b}^2 - 4\underline{ac}} / 2\underline{a}$

(Translate to written form.)

(9) For any pyramid: $\underline{V} = 1/3 \ \underline{Bh}$ (where $\underline{V}$ = volume)

(10) For a sphere: $\underline{A} = 4\pi \underline{r}^2$ (where $\underline{r}$ = radius)

(11) For a sphere: $\underline{V} = 4/3\pi \underline{r}^3$ (where 3 superscript
                                                        is stated <u>cubed</u>)

(12) For power $\underline{P} = \underline{W}/\underline{T}$ (where P = power
                                                        W = work
                                                        T = time)

(13) For acceleration $\underline{a} = \underline{v} - \underline{v}_o$
                             $\overline{\qquad \underline{t} \qquad}$ or   (where $\underline{v}_o$ = initial velocity
                                                        $\underline{v}$ = the velocity
                                                           after a time, $\underline{t}$
                                                        $\underline{a}$ = acceleration
                                                        $\underline{t}$ = time)

(14) For distance in $\underline{s} = \underline{v}_o \cdot \underline{t} + \frac{1}{2} \cdot \underline{a} \cdot \underline{t}^2$
     rectilinear motion
                                        (where $\underline{s}$ = distance)

(15) For impedance
     in electricity $\underline{Z} = \sqrt{\underline{R}^2 + (\underline{X}_L - \underline{X}_c)^2}$ (where
                                                        $\underline{Z}$ = impedance
                                                        $\underline{R}$ = resistance
                                                        $\underline{X}_L$= inductive reactance
                                                        $\underline{X}_c$= capacitive reactance)

(16) For molecular
      weight of a gas $$M = \frac{wRT}{PV}$$

                                        or

                               $$M = wRT/PV$$

(where
   M = molecular weight of gas
   w = weight of a given sample
   R = the universal gas constant
   T = the temperature
   P = the pressure
   V = the molar volume)

(17) For Planck's
      constant in
      the uncertainty $$(\Delta p)\,(\Delta x) = h$$
      principle

(where
   h = Planck's constant
   Δp = the uncertainty
                in momentum
   Δx = the uncertainty
                in position)

(Now can you translate the written form into mathematical symbolism?)

(18) _____

The area of a sphere equals four times pi times radius squared.
(to <u>check</u> your answer see [10])

(19) _____

(The molecular weight of a gas equals the weight of a given sample times the

_____

temperature) divided by (the pressure times the molar volume).
(to <u>check</u> your answer see [16])

(20) _____

Impedance equals the square root of resistance squared plus the square of the

_____

difference of the inductive reactance and the capacitive reactance.
(to <u>check</u> your answer see [15])

(21) Bonus for the Brains:
      (Please finish translating this into
      mathematical symbols.)

where
   σ = standard deviation
   i = interval
   N = number
   Σ = sum of
   d = deviations

_____

The standard deviation equals the <u>quotient</u> of (the interval divided by the

_____

number in the sample) times the <u>square root</u> of the <u>difference</u> of (the number

_____

in the sample times the sum of _____ the squared deviations) and (the
square of the sum of deviations)   or $\sigma =$

Reading Statistical Representations

In the modern world people must be able to read variable quantity relationships that show status and change in status, such as growth. The distribution of height, weight, intelligence, and wealth can be depicted mathematically and graphically. The proportions of money allotted to various categories in the family, corporate, and governmental budgets can likewise be depicted. Also, variables such as the purchase of stocks, the crime rate, and the incidence of disease can be shown graphically and mathematically as a function of certain variables. Teaching people how to encode and decode such relationships is worthwhile. Following are procedures that aid in interpreting statistical representations.

Analyzing and Interpreting Frequency Distributions and Graphs. In order to obviate a tortuous path through a number of paragraphs about some mathematical phenomena a writer often resorts to methods that give a quick, clear bird's eye view—frequency distributions and graphs. Below is a table that gives a frequency distribution for the weights of 161 fourteen-year-old girls.

Frequency distribution table:

Frequency Distribution for the Weights (in Pounds) of 161 Fourteen-Year-Old Girls

Interval	f	Cumulative f	
160–169	1	161	Vocabulary and
150–159	1	160	Concepts to Clarify:
140–149	2	159	Interval
130–139	9	157	f
120–129	29	148	Cumulative f
110–119	39	119	Purpose of intervals
100–109	35	80	How to determine
90– 99	32	45	size of intervals
80– 89	9	13	
70– 79	3	4	
60– 69	1	1	

One of the best ways to help students understand frequency distributions is to develop several frequency distributions regarding phenomena of interest to the students. They can write appropriate textual materials to accompany their distributions.

Learning exercise for the frequency distribution on weights:

1. How large are the intervals?
2. What does frequency mean?
3. What is the purpose of grouping scores in large intervals?
   (Cue: think of distributing these scores if the interval were two instead of ten.)
4. Where are the fewest frequencies?
5. (Stretching your mind): If a frequency distribution were made of boys' heights,

do you think there would be many frequencies at the extremes and few in the middle? Why?

6. What is the cumulative frequency?

7. What is the relation between the word "cumulative" and the expression, "I do not see how you can <u>accumulate</u> so much junk in your closet?"

8. How many people weighed in the 130–139 pound range? In the 70–79 range? Between 60 and 149?

9. Construct two frequency distributions on topics of your choice. You may need to <u>tally</u> your data as you work. Following are lists of some of the mathematics spelling scores made in Mrs. Simmon's algebra class: 75, 90, 95, 82, 81, 76, 85, 88, 52, 77, 83, 86, 65, 97, 85, 78, 72, 66, 70, 91, 69, 62, 82, 84, 47, 77, 89.

The scores are tallied below:

(NOTE: In tallying, five is indicated by crossing the four previous tallies with a line. This provides an easier means of grouping and counting.)

Score Interval	Tally Marks	Frequency
96–100	1	1
91–95	11	2
86–90	1111	4
81–85	1111 11	7
76–80	1111	4
71–75	11	2
66–70	111	3
61–65	11	2
56–60		0
51–55	1	1
46–50	1	1

Histogram (bar graph): A histogram is a bar graph representation of a frequency distribution. It shows graphically the contrast between the middle area of the distribution and the extreme parts. Following is the histogram for frequency distribution of weights of 161 fourteen-year-old girls:

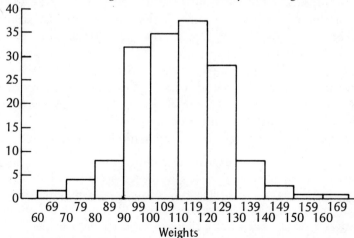

Histogram for the Weights (in Pounds) of 161 Fourteen-Year-Old Girls

Pie or circle graph: The pie graph is sometimes used to show expenditures or allotments of money, thus the expression about getting a large or small "piece of the pie." The pie or circle graph is especially popular for converting data into percentages and representing the percentages as "pieces of pie."

Below is a pie graph depicting the percentages of players on a basketball team who obtained particular averages during a season. The averages are grouped by fives.

*Distribution of the Fourteen Basketball Players on a Squad
Whose Season's Average Scores Per Game Fell in Certain Ranges*

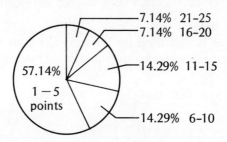

Learning Exercise:

1. How many players averaged between one and five points per game for the season?
2. What percentage of the team averaged eleven to fifteen points?
3. How many students averaged in "double figures"?
4. How many students averaged nine points or less?
5. Classify by categories how you spend your money; estimate the percentage you spend for each category; construct a pie graph to depict the results. Compare your results with those of someone who used the same categories.

THE DIRECTED READING LESSON APPLIED TO MATHEMATICS

The Directed Reading Lesson (DRL) format is a spin-off from the Herbartian method of teaching instituted early in the nineteenth century by J. F. Herbart and adopted in this country at the turn of the century by DeGarmo and by the McMurry brothers. Aspects of DeGarmo's five formal steps comprising a general method of instruction—(1) preparation, (2) presentation, (3) comparison, (4) generalization, and (5) application—appear to be related in part to directed reading lesson formats in use for decades and to Bloom's taxonomy of cognitive processes. Bloom's hierarchy is (1) knowledge, (2) comprehension, (3) application, (4) analysis, (5) synthesis, and (6) evaluation.

The steps of the DRL as adapted to reading mathematics are these:

1.0 Objectives. Listing the desired objectives of the lesson can facilitate proper planning of the lesson proper as well as the pre-test and post-test.

2.0 Pre-test. A pre-test may include two parts: (1) concepts propaedeutic to learning the concepts involved in the lesson and (2) concepts and objectives to be attained as a result of the instruction and concomitant activities. An important outcome is to determine whether given students are ready to tackle the lesson.

3.0 Preparation.*

3.1 Review of concepts propaedeutic to learning the lesson.

3.2 Set the stage for instruction by introducing needed concepts and appropriate labels (vocabulary) for the concepts. In some instances, full development can be expected only as a result of the complete tuition [instruction].

3.3 Develop purposes for reading and applying the material in terms of the objectives of the lesson. (It might be helpful for the students to indicate understanding by paraphrasing some of the developed purposes or by taking a quick quiz. (However, do not overdo such quiz taking.)

4.0 Guided silent reading in terms of purposes and challenges developed.

5.0 Discussion of what was read to determine whether purposes of reading and the appropriate concepts were attained and also to "unearth" any difficulties encountered.

5.1 It might be well to draw out the diffident members of the class to make sure that you do not proceed without clarifying troublesome areas.

5.2 Questions used in the discussion should relate to concept-vocabulary, literal understanding, and interpretation—seeing relationships and drawing conclusions.

5.3 Should difficulties in solving word problems occur, troubleshoot to find out the nature of the difficulties and (1) clarify concepts and vocabulary, if needed, and (2) work through the appropriate problem-solving steps with the student(s) involved.

5.4 Where appropriate, use relevant guided reading exercises such as those previously delineated in the present text or other appropriate exercises. (Save useful exercises for future use.)

5.5 Reread orally, where necessary, to prove a point or check a person's ability to read, that is, gather needed information to do the work.

6.0 Application and enrichment

6.1 Give students related problems to solve

6.2 Allow students to make up problems for you to solve. (That should motivate them and keep you alert.)

7.0 Post-test

7.1 Review results quickly

7.2 Each portion of the test should be keyed to materials and procedures that can provide further help.

8.0 Further help

8.1 Certain students may be helped by manipulating realia, using appropriate algorithms, viewing relevant movies, and working with models.

8.2 Programmed learning materials might be useful for some students.

8.3 If tutors or knowledgeable aides are available, use them as needed.

DIAGNOSTIC MATH CONCEPT AND READING TEST

The following inventory was devised to illustrate the formidable concepts and reading problems involved in (not a fifth- or seventh- or ninth-grade text) a *fourth*-grade text. My experience in working with students tells me that many middle school students have trouble reading material at this level of difficulty.

*Useful tips on several strategies used in reading lesson plans can be found in Marksheffel (1974) and Hafner and Jolly (1972).

This kind of inventory helps the content-area teacher and the reading teacher *face the facts* about the appropriateness of reading materials for students. This test is based on chapter 1 of *Understanding Mathematics* by Edwina Deens and others.

1.0 General vocabulary

Directions: Please read these words for me, beginning with number 1. (no prompting)

1. galaxy	2. different	3. reverse	4. suppose	5. what
6. ancient	7. separate	8. operator	9. probably	10. how

2.0 Mathematics vocabulary in isolation

Directions: Please read these words for me.

1. digits	2. open sentences	3. cardinal numbers	4. million	5. set
6. base	7. thousands	8. millions	9. period	10. equations

3.0 Reading sentences

Directions: Please read these phrases and sentences for me.

1. Does <u>many</u> have different meanings?
2. The place held by 5 in the numeral 97,650 is important.
3. This numeral is read, "Five hundred thirty-seven."
4. How many groups of 1 hundred would there be in all?
5. For each set write five different numerals that tell how many sticks there are in the set.
6. Make a list of all the names you and your classmates thought of for this number.
7. To name a number move beads from the top to the bottom on each wire.
8. Have you ever heard the name for the period just left of millions?
9. How do you think a telephone operator would read this numeral?
10. The first three digits stand for the area code.

4.0 Mathematical symbols

Directions: Write the mathematical symbols for each of the following:

1. plus	2. equals	3. minus	4. fifty seven	5. set
1.	2.	3.	4.	5.

5.0 Computations

Directions: Write the correct number in each box.

1. $3 + \square = 9$ 2. $12 - 5 = \square$ 3. $\square + \square = 4$
4. $542 = \square$ hundreds $+ \square$ tens + 12 ones.
5. $\square + \square + \square = 9$

6.0 Interpreting pictorial illustrations [To check reading <u>and</u> concepts, have student read the problem.]

abacus

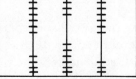

hundreds tens ones

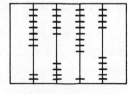

What is the simplest name for the number shown at the bottom part of the abacus?

What number is represented on this abacus?

To what number is the short hand pointing? the long hand?

7.0 Word problems [Student reads these problems.]

1. The numeral <u>10</u> stands for 1 ten. Does <u>01</u> stand for 1 ten? _____
2. Below are some equations. Tell whether each of these is true, false, or open;

   $3 + 5 = 9$ $4 - 1 = 2$ $3 + \square = 7$

3. Write the simplest name for each number.

   a.   15 hundreds + 17 ones [_____]   b.   3 tens + 8 ones [_____]

SUMMARY

There is no longer any doubt that content-area teachers must conceive of themselves as reading teachers. As a person sensitized to the problem of finding textbooks written with students in mind, the mathematics teacher will exercise great care in selecting textbooks for use in the classroom. Even when a given book is well written a student should not be placed in it if the reading challenges do not match his or her reading ability.

A teacher will want to take the appropriate steps to use the reading improvement strategies set forth in this chapter. These strategies were designed to help students read mathematics symbolism and vocabulary, relate operations to corresponding mathematical symbols, and translate written formulas into their mathematical equivalents.

One also is more successful in teaching students to read and solve word problems when one leads students carefully through the appropriate steps delineated. One should use actual problems as shown in the chapter. As an additional aid for solving word problems, one can construct study guides similar to the sample guide provided here.

A useful strategy for teaching students to understand formulas and equations and read them in mathematical symbol form is presented to help them translate the formulas from one form to another.

Reading statistical representations can be a fun thing if interesting examples are used and careful explanations given. Developing well-thought-out learning exercises contributes to understanding the various graphic representations of frequency distributions, for example.

The steps of the Directed Reading Lesson (DRL) as adapted to teaching mathematics reading can be compared to the plan given in a later chapter. Suggestions from that plan can be adapted for use in the DRL plan in this chapter.

The mathematics teacher and other content-area teachers, as well as reading specialists, must *face the facts* about the appropriateness of reading materials for students. A model diagnostic test to help a teacher do just that was provided at the end of the chapter.

ACTIVITIES AND QUESTIONS
TO PROMOTE LEARNING AND APPLICATION

1. Select a page or two from a mathematics text and rewrite it for students that you know who could profit from rewritten material. Try it out, note results, and share your project with your methods class.
2. Construct an exercise for teaching students to associate verbal symbols with their corresponding mathematical symbols.
3. Select several *arithmetic-algebra* terms and develop appropriate symbol-word or symbol–phrase cards.
4. Obtain the special cards used with card readers such as the Language Master; draw a mathematical symbol on each card and record its corresponding verbal symbol on the audio tape.
5. Select a chapter from a mathematics text and prepare various exercises and activities for teaching the concepts, the vocabulary, and the operations in the chapter.
6. Try to develop several five to ten-minute lessons (a la Irish, 1964) that will help students (1) to generalize the meanings of the number operations and the relationships among these operations and (2) to formulate original statements to state these generalizations as they are developed. (Perhaps a mathematics teacher (or major) and a reading specialist (or major) would like to team up on this project.)
7. Devise a word problem that will use a wanted-given structure for its solution.
8. Bring word problems to class. Divide the class into groups (three members per group) with a mathematics major in each group. Following the steps for solving a problem, let a member who is less adept at solving problems try to solve them. Allow the other "nonmath" person to be a "consultant." Let the math major give cues when the other two group members run into problems.
9. Let these same groups write study guides based on word problems. If possible, use these guides in middle or secondary school classrooms as well as in your methods class. Share what you have learned about problems of reading word problems and also techniques for getting solutions.
10. Find students who are taking math courses or science courses and having trouble reading formulas and equations. Offer to tutor these students, using some of the techniques outlined in the text. Report results to the class.
11. Develop a learning exercise for reading (1) a histogram and (b) a pie graph.
12. Select a section of mathematics material from a mathematics text and write a Directed Reading Lesson that can be used to teach the material.
13. Find out where a group will be in a mathematics text in two weeks. Write a *Diagnostic Math Concept and Reading Test* to fit the material they will be reading at that time. At the appropriate time administer the test to a random sample of the students. What percentage of students did not do well on the test (that is, are inappropriately placed in their text)? Draw appropriate conclusions.

SUGGESTED ADDITIONAL READINGS

AUKERMAN, ROBERT C. *Reading in the Secondary Classroom*. New York: McGraw-Hill, 1972. Chapter 10.

CATTERSON, JANE H. "Techniques for Improving Comprehension in Mathematics." In Gerald G. Duffy (Ed.). *Reading in the Middle School*. Newark, Del.: International Reading Association, 1974. Pp. 153–65.

COULTER, MYRON L. "Reading in Mathematics: Classroom Implications." In James L. Laffey (Ed.). *Reading in the Content Areas*. Newark, Del.: International Reading Association, 1972. Pp. 95–126.

HAFNER, LAWRENCE E. (Ed.). *Improving Reading in Middle and Secondary Schools*. Second Edition. New York: Macmillan, 1974. Section 10.

HERBER, HAROLD L. "Reading and Reasoning Guides: Mathematics." *Teaching Reading in Content Areas*. Englewood Cliffs, N. J.: Prentice–Hall, 1970. Pp. 265–67.

LEES, FRED. "Mathematics and Reading." *Journal of Reading*. 19 (8) (May 1976), 621–26.

MAFFEI, ANTHONY C. "Reading in Analysis Mathematics." In Lawrence E. Hafner (Ed.). *Improving Reading in Middle and Secondary Schools*. Second Edition. Macmillan, 1974. Pp. 310–24.

SHEPHERD, DAVID L. *Comprehensive High School Reading Methods*. Columbus, Ohio: Charles E. Merrill, 1973. Chapter 11.

WEBER, MARTHA GESLING. "The Demon of Arithmetic—Reading Word Problems." In A. J. Harris and E. R. Sipay. *Readings on Reading Instruction*. Second Edition. N.Y.: David McKay, 1972. Pp. 302–306.

BIBLIOGRAPHY

BALOW, IRVING H. "Reading and Computation Ability As Determinants of Problem Solving." *Arithmetic Teacher*. 11 (1964), 18–22.

FEEMAN, GEORGE. "Reading and Mathematics." *Arithmetic Teacher*. 20 (7) (November 1973), 523–29.

HAFNER, LAWRENCE E. and HAYDEN B. JOLLY. *Patterns of Teaching Reading in the Elementary School*. New York: Macmillan, 1972. Pp. 56–64.

IRISH, ELIZABETH H. "Improving Problem Solving by Improving Verbal Generalizations." *Arithmetic Teacher*. 11 (1964), 169–75.

JOHNSON, DONOVAN A., and GERALD R. RISING. *Guidelines for Teaching Mathematics*. Second Edition. Belmont, California: Wadsworth, 1972.

LERCH, HAROLD. "Improving Reading in the Language of Mathematics—Grades 7–12." In Lawrence E. Hafner (Ed.). *Improving Reading in Middle and Secondary Schools*. New York: Macmillan, 1974.

MARKSHEFFEL, NED D. "Reading Readiness at the High-School and College Levels." In Lawrence E. Hafner (Ed.). *Improving Reading in Middle and Secondary School*. New York: Macmillan, 1974. Pp. 248–52 (esp. 250 and 251).

WILSON, J. W. "The Role of Structure in Verbal Problem Solving." *Arithmetic Teacher*. 14 (1967), 486–93.

CHAPTER 12

Reading in Science and Technology:
I. Foundations

As with the other major content-area foundation chapters, this foundation chapter may be of more value to the general reader and the reading specialist than to science teachers. However, it should serve to remind the science teacher that the reading of science must be grounded in a knowledge of science and its processes as well as the language used to discuss the knowledge and processes.

THE NATURE OF SCIENCE STUDY

What Is Science?

A Body of Knowledge and a Way of Knowing. Science is an organized body of knowledge and a way of knowing. As an organized body of knowledge it is divided into (1) mathematics and logic and (2) the empirical or observational sciences. In this chapter we will be concerned mainly with the empirical sciences. As a field of inquiry, science seeks factual knowledge about natural phenomena. This knowledge is obtained through observation, classification, hypothesis making (using logic and reason) followed by experimental verification (using observational evidence) leading to the drawing of conclusions.

One kind of scientist may engage mainly in observation and classification. Another tries to develop generalizations from the particulars observed. This scientist often is the experimentalist who likes to vary experimental conditions in order to see what will result. Finally, the person of a deductive bent may ruminate about previous findings to see if he or she can develop better patterns or theories to fit these findings. Yet, the activities of these scientists are not necessarily mutually exclusive.

The scientific method is not always the best way to inquire into a subject, as first-rate scientists will be ready to admit. Note the success of the well-ordered intuitions of writers, theologians, and poets as they investigate such themes as love, loyalty, citizenship, and beauty.

Science as Inquiry

Inquiry Methods. Inquiry is basic to the scientific method, and it implies a problem-solving approach in which a person observes natural phenomena first hand. Therefore, students should be taught how to make hypotheses regarding interrelationships among natural phenomena, to gather data in a systematic fashion in order to test the validity of the hypotheses, and to draw conclusions regarding such observation and verification.

For example, one can check the validity of the claims of two companies— A and B—about the productivity of their marigold seeds by using inquiry methods. First, one hypothesizes that there will be no difference in the quality of the flowers produced by A's seeds compared with the flowers from B's seeds raised under identical conditions. Next one develops criteria for judging the quality of the flowers. Then the criterion for ascertaining whether statistically significant differences in quality between the products exists is selected. Next the seeds are planted and raised under identical conditions. Finally, at the appointed time, observations and measurements are made to assess the quality, hypotheses are tested, and conclusions regarding the quality of A's and B's seeds are drawn.

Conditions Conducive to a Spirit of Inquiry. Inquiry flourishes when people want to be and in fact are free to inquire and to disseminate the results of their inquiry. The following conditions are also conducive to inquiry:

1. Unique and/or interesting events come within a person's purview.

2. A person desires to have the events repeated or to understand aspects of the event or phenomena related to it.

3. A person has the materials to repeat the event or can be helped to acquire them or develop them.

4. A person will not be ridiculed for making a mistake, but people will understand that error as well as corrigibility are integral aspects of science.

5. One feels free to disagree and to conduct one's own investigations where one sees discrepancies in nature or in the work of others.

6. The investigator can reason both deductively and inductively.

7. A person is adept at theorizing and suggesting hypotheses.

Classes of Concepts. There are many different classes of concepts, some of which can be further subdivided. Johnson (1972) talks about the *class* or *categorical* concept. If you know the class concept *trees*, you know its place in a structure:

> •plants
>> •trees
>>> •maples
>>> •oaks
>> •flowers

Johnson also discusses *dimensional* concepts. Dimensional concepts based on salient perceptual qualities such as size, color, loudness, and fragrance are relatively easy to learn. Those based on more abstract properties are harder to learn; examples are attitude, intelligence, and rigidity.

The intelligence quotient is also a dimensional concept. Let me illustrate. The intelligence quotient—a somewhat abstract mental construct—is an index of brightness. A ratio IQ is determined by dividing mental age by chronological age and multiplying the result by 100.

Johnson also refers to *explanatory* concepts (or principles) and *singular* concepts. (A principle is of a higher order complexity than a concept because it states a relation between concepts.) Examples of explanatory principles: the angle of incidence equals the angle of reflection; cities grow near harbors. Since a principle, unlike a concept, takes the form of a proposition, it may be true or false. Principles are more important than concepts because concepts help us to refer to events, but principles help us to understand and predict events.

Singular concepts: a singular term refers to a single object or event. Johnson states that the referent of a single term may be a cluster of memories, perceptions, affects, and associations based on direct experience and on communications from others. Take, for example, the concept *moon*. One's concept of moon may be acquired by seeing the moon directly at different times, in different phases, and under different atmospheric conditions, by seeing pictures of it, and by reading about it.

Learning Science Concepts Inductively. Many science concepts are learned inductively. It is possible to learn these concepts without guidance but it can be a very slow and time-consuming process. Gagné (1966) hypothesizes that a child might learn a concept by being shown several positive instances of the concept and a negative instance or two of it. This would hold true for fairly simple concepts.

For example, in order to teach the concept *magnet*, first show the person a positive instance of magnet and say, "This is a magnet;" show that it can attract an iron-type substance. Next, show another instance of a magnet (possibly a horseshoe magnet if the first one was a straight bar) and say, "This is a magnet;" demonstrate its ability to attract metal. Then, show a negative instance of magnet, any piece of metal, and say, "This is *not* a magnet;" show that it does *not* attract an iron-type substance. Then take two bars, one a magnet and one not a magnet; as you demonstrate the metal-attracting capability of the one say, "This is a magnet." As you show the inability of the other bar to attract the same kind of metal, say, "This is *not* a magnet." Finally, test the person by saying, "Show me a magnet." (Allow the person to determine this property by testing the metal-attracting capacity.)

In actuality, this approach to learning some kinds of concepts might take many more positive instances and negative instances and need to be done over a period of time. Gagné also suggests that one might want to use a questioning form of statement rather than a declarative form.

Need for Learning Theory and Principles

Students need to learn theories if they are going to go very far in science. Those who do not may become technicians rather than individuals who can help advance the frontiers of science.

Definition of Scientific Theory. A scientific theory is a temporary proposition or set of propositions about some natural phenomena; it consists of symbolic (language, mathematical, graphic) representations of (1) the observed relationships among manipulated events and measured events, (2) the structures thought to underlie such relationships, or (3) inferred relationships and underlying mechanisms that account for data observed when direct showing of the relationships is lacking (after Melvin Marx, 1970).

Theory has a twofold function. As a *tool* it guides observation and so produces new facts and firmer facts. Theory is also a *goal* of science in that our long-range objective is to develop the most complete understanding we can of the natural world.

As a goal or objective, theory (1) summarizes or describes and (2) explains. In summarizing it provides economy of expression because it is easier, for example, to state the law of gravity as a general proposition than to state each of the myriad separate observations regarding falling bodies. The explanatory function advances us to assuming that the final objective of scientific work is understanding the order of nature. We also assume that by using theoretical constructs and hypotheses we are not just summarizing but also symbolically probing nature's structure (Marx, pp. 9, 10). Deese (1967) states the function of theory in this manner. "*Theory* serves to describe, interrelate, and explain the observations we make."

Definition of Principles. A principle or rule represents the relationships among concepts and may be called a chain of concepts (Gagné, 1970).

Some scientific principles are (1) round things roll, (2) the earth rotates, and (3) metals expand when heated. What are the constituent concepts that must be known and chained to form the latter principle? If you answer metal, heat, and expansion, you are correct.

Importance of Learning Principles of Science

1. *Principles can be applied in various situations.* The principle or rule that "metals expand when heated" was used in the development of the thermostat. This principle was used in conjunction with the principle that each metal has its own coefficient of linear expansion: copper expands more than does iron with the same change in temperature. In making the thermostat device a compound coil—made of two different kinds of metal (copper and iron)—will unwind when the temperature rises and move an attached metal pointer that makes an electrical contact and causes the furnace draft to close. A temperature drop causes the coil to wind and move the pointer in the other direction until an electrical contact that opens the furnace draft is made.

Another application of this principle is the basis for putting expansion joints in steel structures so that expansion in the summer will not cause a break in the structure.

2. *Principles allow one to deduce applications for oneself.* If a person is going to develop a mechanism that needs a part that will roll, a person can apply the principle, "round things roll" and develop a round part. On the other hand,

if one needs to place something on an inclined plane that will not roll, one will not use something that is completely round, that is, a round sphere.

3. *Principles help a person operate effectively in the environment.* Knowing that heavy objects have greater momentum at a given speed than lighter objects (principle of inertia) is a guide to inhibit a(n intelligent) person from darting out in front of a truck with a car.

Applying the principle "Black material absorbs the heat of sunlight" results in our not wearing black clothing on a hot summer day. On a cold day we might find it advantageous to wear black or dark clothing.

SCIENTIFIC METHODS

Science as usually taught means that observed facts lead to formulation of principles that can then be used to derive facts. This guideline is related to the three facets of the scientist's work: (1) The scientist develops principles. (2) The scientist makes logical conclusions from the principles in order to derive observable facts about the principles. (3) Finally, the scientist makes an experimental check of the facts (Frank, 1957). Therefore, it is accurate to say that the natural sciences are experimental. The scientist experiments because of a need for more answers to certain questions. An individual as scientist, then, is concerned with certain basic kinds of questions.

What are the fundamental questions of science?

1. *Is it so?* (Can it be experienced repeatedly? Can other observers also experience it?)

2. *To what extent is it so?* (Obtain an estimate of quantitative characteristics of the phenomenon: magnitude, amount, frequency.)

3. *Why is it so?* (Get behind the facts.)

4. *What are the conditions that bring about this phenomenon?*

In order to answer the above questions the scientist must have the attitude and methods of science, and these involve (1) observation, (2) hypothesis, (3) experimental verification leading to (4) a conclusion.

As can be seen, the natural sciences are empirical; therefore, in science matters we must resort to experience. As already implied, scientists use two basic means: *observation* and *experiment*. This section of the chapter will explore these two methods as well as the ancillary methods of demonstration and reading.

Observation

Kotarbinski on Observation. As we discuss methods of obtaining empirical data, we must first differentiate among perception, observation, and experiment. *Observation is planned perception.* Noticing something unwillingly or incidentally is only perceiving. When striving to notice it, we observe it. Experiment is a manipulation intended to bring about an effect under specified conditions so that one might observe whether under such conditions that effect is accompanied by something else (Kotarbinski, 1966, p. 299).

Uses of Observation. Observation is planned perception. It may involve a careful examination of some natural phenomenon—thing or event—to see what can be discovered. Observations may include one or more of the following modes: looking, listening, feeling, smelling, and tasting.

As a result of observations, questions may be raised by the observers. These questions may lead to more carefully planned observations in order to note structure and function of the phenomenon.

Questions may also be of the "If we did this or that, what would happen?" variety. Now we are into a kind of experimenting; observation as planned perception is also used in this instance.

Observing and questioning may lead to a higher kind of thinking in which the students predict what will happen if certain conditions are varied systematically. In any event, one important aspect of observation must not be forgotten: the recording of observations. Recording may take the form of verbal notations, charts, graphs, tables, pictures, and the like as well as combinations of these methods.

Examples of Observations. Some observations that middle school students can make about magnetism and electricity are:

1. Place a compass on the table. Note that it points in a northerly direction. Why?

2. Approaching from the right, move a magnet toward the compass. What happens?

3. Examine several discarded electrical applicances but do *not* connect them to an electric power source. Try to explain the principles of electricity involved in each appliance. (Assumes some previous knowledge.)

4. Examine a motor and an engine. On what principles does each operate?

5. Watch someone clean and repair a car battery (that has discontinued functioning but still has energy) and/or its connections. Note the results.

6. Inspect a good fuse and a blown-out fuse. How do they differ? Why does the metal strip have a low melting point? That is, what is the purpose of using a strip with a low melting point?

NOTE: The above questions can be used with secondary school students who do not have much science experience or who are "slow" students. The same basic kinds of question plus elaborations can be used with average secondary school students. Further elaborations and more theoretical explanations may be required of advanced secondary school science students. Of course, many students will develop their own questions. Also, the procedures, results, and explanations of the results can be written up to provide meaningful reading material.

Experimentation

What an Experiment Is. Broadly speaking an experiment is an inquiry in which observations are made, hypotheses are developed, variables are manipulated, results are noted, and conclusions are drawn. We daily engage in experiments but we do not control them too well so the conclusions we draw may be rather shaky. A simple experiment that *can* be controlled is to make two batches of cake batter from the same recipe, leaving the baking powder out of one of the batches and baking them under identical conditions. Note any differences in size, texture, and taste, and draw conclusions about the role of baking powder.

The discussion under inquiry methods at the beginning of the chapter overviewed the controlled experiment as a means of determining the comparable quality of company A's and company B's marigold seeds.

Experiments as Cookbook Laboratory Exercises. Apparently not many middle school and secondary school science activities are controlled experiments. Pitluga (1972) notes that today the science teacher is often torn between two philosophies of science education. The traditional point of view feels that science should be basically concerned with giving student basic facts and concepts. These facts must be mastered before the learner can do investigations. The laboratory exercises, loosely referred to as "experiments," seem to be a cookbook approach. Many of the experiments that I have come across seem to be of this type.

Open-ended Experiments. The second approach, according to Pitluga, views science as a method of investigating the world. The facts of science are viewed more as a by-product of the method of investigation. Science education should be concerned with guiding students in the process of practicing science. In this approach much emphasis is placed on "open-ended" experiments.

These kinds of activities appear to me to be real experiments involving the development of hypotheses, the testing of hypotheses, and the drawing of conclusions, although not many appear to be the classic controlled experiments. Two of the open-ended experiments offered by Pitluga follow:

> Experiment 1: What determines how long it takes a candle to burn out? Is it the kind of wax? Is it the length of the candle? Is it the size of the wick? Can you make one or more hypotheses? Can you devise a strategy for testing each one? Should we deal with just one variable at a time?
> *Materials:* Some string, waxes, cylinders, molds, and a time keeper and beam balance may be all the equipment needed.
> Experiment 2: Present students with a glass brimful of water in which an ice cube is floating. What will happen when the ice melts? Will the water overflow? or .... ?
> NOTE: This problem gives students excellent practice on a very elementary level in hypothesis making.
> Experiment 3: If you live along the sea coast and teach earth science, you, yourself, may get some surprises together with the students by posing this problem. Where is the moon in reference to our meridian when it is high tide here? (Several hypotheses suggest themselves. The strategy requires careful thought, and even after the answer has been found, you may discover that, like most true experiments, this one raises more questions than it answers.)

Reading is brought into this type of situation in several ways. Individuals may want to read about tides. After the experiment is finished, students may write it up and they will have some good science reading material. They should let various kinds of students read the material, note which kinds of students have what kinds of problems. The students can be helped with reading problems—vocabulary, comprehension, etc. by applying methods suggested in previous chapters. Also, the students who wrote the materials may get some hints on how to rewrite them for clarity. Discuss with all participants what is involved in reading science material with comprehension: the point is that after such involvement they should be able to make substantive contributions.

General Principles That Apply to Good Experimentation. The following principles of good experimentation apply particularly to the middle grades and to beginning general science students in the early secondary grades:

1. Keep the experiment simple. Whenever possible use simple, homemade equipment.

2. Provide opportunities that require children to think. If you plan to tell students the answers or let them read the answers, why bother with an experiment? Experimenting to find answers to a genuine problem raised by students is sure to be more thought-provoking than one done to "prove" something that is already known by many of them.

3. Let students do as much of the planning as they can. Then follow the plan. If it is necessary to make changes, students have some basis for making them, because they themselves helped make the plan.

4. Challenge students when they make sweeping generalizations from one experiment. "Magnets will pick up all nails." After a limited experience with a box of nails the teacher may say, "Do all of you believe that we can say this?" The discussion may well result in further experimentation.

5. Keep experiments simple and safe enough for students to do by themselves. If classes are large and sufficient material is available, students may work in groups to give many of them the opportunity to experiment. If this is not possible, the material may be left available for individual use when part of the class is engaged in other activities. The teacher should remember that it is one thing to manipulate apparatus yourself and quite another to watch while somebody else does it. The best situation exists when every person has an opportunity to experiment.

6. Provide opportunities for students to react to: "Can anyone think of something we can try or some ways of experimenting that may help us solve this problem?" Such a procedure gives a chance for real thought, careful planning, organization, predicting, and interpretation.

7. Help students to apply the information gained by experimenting to the world about them. It is this application to "real-life" situations that is often missed.

8. Urge students to keep in mind the purposes of experimenting. It is often advisable to have on the chalkboard a simple statement of purpose to guide the thinking as the experimenting goes on and as the conclusions are drawn. Of course, individual students with varying backgrounds and interests should be encouraged, as time and space allow, to follow their own paths. The examples of open endedness illustrate the point.

9. Examine the policy of requiring a complete record of all experiments performed in the (middle) school. It is not always necessary or desirable. The old idea of recording in a notebook for each experiment the object, materials used, drawing, procedure, results, and conclusions is deadly and certain to take away the natural interest in experimenting that youngsters seem to possess. Sometimes it seems

sensible to record in a sentence or two the important outcomes of an experiment, either for future reference or to be sure that the ideas are clearly understood. If the experiment is one that takes several days to complete, it may be helpful to record each day's observations by making drawings, by writing a short paragraph, or by making a graph or chart of the findings. The guiding idea may well be, "Is there any good reason for writing or communicating in some other way, anything about this experiment?"

10. Keep experiments as "scientific" as possible, stressing the importance of control of the variables. For example, if the importance of light to plants is being investigated, light should be the only variable. A number of plants should be kept in the dark, a number of similar plants in the light. But all other conditions should be the same for both groups.

11. Remember that when experiments do not follow the predicted path, real problems arise and students, in attempting to discover why, think more, plan better, and learn more than would otherwise be the case. In a truly scientific sense, every experiment "works" although it may not take the course anticipated.

12. Remember also that an experiment is an experiment in the true sense only if students do not already know the outcome. Such an experiment will provide opportunity for thoughtful observing, predicting, communicating, and interpreting (Blough, 1969).

Kitchen Experiments. Kitchen experiments are done with materials that one can find around the house or that are readily available in stores; they are so easily done that they can be performed at home. The kitchen, of course, has a sink, counters, containers, utensils, tools, and so forth, which prove useful in many experiments. There is value in doing these experiments at home because they can either be initiated there or practiced there.

1. *Making an electromagnet:* Following are some suggestions adapted from Langley (1968) for making an electromagnet:

PURPOSE: To demonstrate the principle of electromagnetism and to show how to make an electromagnet.

MATERIALS: Piece of insulated wire, 1½ volt dry cell, one large paper clip, several small clips, a large nail, two tacks, two small pieces of cork, and a thin piece of wood.

PROCEDURE: Open a large paper clip so that it looks like an "s." Wrap a piece of insulated wire around the clip about 15 turns. One end of the wire is then attached to the 1½ volt dry cell and the other end to a switch. Then complete the circuit by wiring the switch to the dry cell.

The terminals of the switch are two tacks inserted—distance apart is 1/8 of an inch more or less than the length of a regular paper clip. One tack fastens one end of the clip so that the clip can rotate in order for it to open and close the circuit at the other switch terminal (the other tack).

Close the circuit and try to pick up several paper clips and small metal objects such as toys. On opening the switch the objects will be released.

Experimental aspects are brought in as students hypothesize what will happen when the electromagnet is moved toward the clips, when the number of turns of wire is increased and decreased, when a large nail is used in the electromagnet instead of the clip. Verification follows. Discuss what has happened and why.

2. *Bernoulli's principle:*

PURPOSE: To demonstrate how to create a low pressure and what happens to objects adjacent to such a low pressure.

MATERIALS: Two round objects (such as ping pong balls) and two strings.

PROCEDURE: Suspend the two objects so they are about one inch apart. Ask the students what will happen if you blow air between the objects. (Do you know what will happen? Try it to see if your prediction is verified. Can you explain what happened?)

A principle is often more thoroughly developed if a second experiment using the same principle is performed soon after the initial experiment. Have a student or several students take a piece of paper and hold one end of it with both hands; direct the student to hold the paper about two to four inches in front of his or her mouth and blow across the top of the paper in order to hold the paper down. Can the student do it? Find out for yourself first. How do you explain what happens?

Have the students write up the experiment, using illustrations if they like. See which written versions are easier for your poor readers to read. Study the ones that are easier to read in order to determine why they are easier to read.

Contributions of Laboratory Exercises. Laboratory exercises contribute to the learning of science by young people to the extent that they:

1. Add reality to text material.
2. Develop first-hand familiarity with the tools, materials, or techniques of the profession.
3. Allow the student to demonstrate for himself something that he already knows to be true.
4. Give the student an opportunity to pit his laboratory skills "against par" in seeking an experimental answer.
5. Create opportunities wherein the student predicts events or circumstances and then designs experiments to test the accuracy of his predictions (Andrews, 1957).

Demonstration

Teaching science through demonstration can occur in two basic ways. In one way the instructor or student shows a step-by-step process such as the borax bead test for metals with a "play-by-play" description of what is taking place. Such a method may go too fast or too slow for the students, and it certainly does not involve the students in inductive inquiry and its valuable correlates such as hypothesis making and testing.

On the other hand, an inquiry method might be used in which the instructor asks the students what he or she is going to do with the materials at hand. Before doing each step, the teacher asks, "What will happen?"; after each step or several steps "Why did that happen? What happened to the such and such? Where did the this and that go?"

Students like the latter kind of demonstration because they are involved, they must constantly be thinking participants, and the constant feedback between instructor and students aids the conduct of the questioning.

Sund and Trowbridge (1967) give the following suggestions for staging a demonstration. I have abridged them.

1. Teach inductively, starting the demonstration with a question. If you are using equipment, ask the students how the equipment is going to be used.

2. Constantly ask questions that require responses telling what you are going to do, what is taking place, why they think it is taking place, and what is being proved or illustrated by the demonstration.

3. Know the purpose of the demonstration and have some questions prepared, for then you will be able and free to use the feedback from the students as a critical aid in formulating meaningful questions for the students as well as being prepared to answer some of their questions or help them answer their own questions.

4. Reinforce positively, recognizing replies with remarks such as, "Say, I think you have something there." "Good, you're thinking." "What do the rest of you think of Susie's remarks?"

5. Use the chalkboard in describing the purpose of the demonstration because pictures and diagrams attract students' attention.

At the conclusion of the demonstration you may want to have a student summarize what has happened in the demonstration and its purpose. Then evaluate your lesson orally or by means of a written summary (Sund and Trowbridge, 1967).

SUMMARY

Science is an organized body of knowledge and a way of knowing. The scientific method seems to be the best one for investigations of natural phenomena and their relationships.

Science as inquiry implies a problem-solving approach in which one observes natural phenomena, makes hypotheses about interrelationships among the phenomena, and tests the validity of the hypotheses after gathering appropriate data.

A number of conditions are conducive to a spirit of inquiry, but it flourishes particularly when people are free to inquire and to share the results of their inquiry. Much scientific inquiry is inductive but aspects of science instruction, for example, laboratory instruction in high school chemistry, lend themselves to an inductive-deductive approach. Also, many science concepts can be learned inductively; however, well-planned guidance results in more efficient learning.

Students who want to push back the frontiers of science must learn theories and principles (rules) of science. Theory guides observation and produces new facts; it also summarizes and explains. Principles can be applied in various situations, allow a person to deduce applications, and help a person operate effectively in the environment.

In science matters the scientist resorts to experience and uses the basic means of observation and experiment. Observation is planned perception that helps observers raise questions and improve subsequent observations. As a result, one can make predictions about what will happen if certain conditions are systematically varied. This step—the forming of hypotheses—is the entree into the experimental method that culminates in the testing of hypotheses and the drawing of conclusions.

An approach to science education that views science as a method of investigating the world places much emphasis on open-ended experiments. Suggestions for relating these experiments to reading were noted.

The general principles that apply to good experimentation feature keeping experiments simple and safe. Also students are urged to keep in mind the purposes of experimenting and to keep experiments as scientific as possible, stressing the importance of keeping the variables controlled.

Kitchen experiments use at-hand materials. Their values and procedures for conducting them were explained. Finally, there was a comment on the conditions under which laboratory exercises contribute to the learning of science by young people followed by several suggestions for staging a science demonstration.

ACTIVITIES AND QUESTIONS
TO PROMOTE LEARNING AND APPLICATION

1. What makes a science empirical?
2. Explain what a scientist does when observing and classifying. Give a concrete, systematic explanation that goes into some detail.
3. Design and execute an experimental study in one of the sciences.
4. Give examples of scientists thinking deductively.
5. How have you thought inductively? What, in your estimation, is the value of inductive thinking.
6. Is there any relationship between inductive thinking and the concept of corrigibility? Explain (Read in the history of science.)
7. Can you think of some explanatory principles used in science besides the ones given in the text? (Be prepared to explain their meaning to someone, please.)
8. Develop a mini lesson for teaching a scientific concept inductively. Teach it to someone in class.
9. Find what you think is a scientific theory. Subject it to Marx's three criteria. Did it pass the test?
10. State ten scientific principles that are of value to the nonscientist, that is, to the average person in everyday life. (You may need to dig around in some books and/or in your brain to come up with some.)

11. What natural phenomena would you like to examine or observe? How do you plan to go about it? (You might try some of the ones mentioned in the text.)

12. Do you subscribe to the traditional approach to teaching science or to science as a method of investigating the world? What are some examples of activities that characterize the approach that you favor? Why do you think it is superior?

13. Try some experiments with middle grade students or early secondary grades students (or classmates or room mates). Use the general principles that apply to good experimentation.

14. To what extent were you able to follow the general principles in your experimenting (in number 13)? Explain, please.

15. Obtain a book on "kitchen" experiments. School libraries usually have a number of them. Try out some experiments with friends, relatives, or students. (How did it go? Was it fun?)

16. Arrange to do a demonstration in class, following the suggestions of Sund and Trowbridge as delineated in the text. (If you are not a science teacher, do you think you might enjoy being one?)

SUGGESTED ADDITIONAL READINGS

GOOD, RONALD. *How Children Learn Science.* New York: Macmillan, 1977.

HAFNER, LAWRENCE E. (Ed.). *Improving Reading in Middle and Secondary Schools.* New York: Macmillan, 1974. Section 10.

MALLINSON, GEORGE G. "Reading in the Sciences: A Review of the Research." In James L. Laffey (Ed.). *Reading in the Content Areas.* Newark, Del.: International Reading Association, 1972. Pp. 127–52.

SHEPHERD, DAVID L. *Comprehensive High School Reading Methods.* Columbus, Ohio: Charles E. Merrill, 1973. Chapter 10.

BIBLIOGRAPHY

ANDREWS, DONALD H. *Educating a Chemist.* A report on the conference held at the Johns Hopkins University, October 16–20, 1957, sponsored by the National Science Foundation, pp. 52, 53.

BLOUGH, GLENN C., and JULIUS SCHWARTZ. *Elementary School Science and How to Teach It.* Fourth Edition. New York: Holt, Rinehart and Winston, 1969.

DEESE, JAMES. *General Psychology.* Boston: Allyn and Bacon, 1967.

FRANK, PHILIP G. *Philosophy of Science.* Englewood Cliffs, N. J.: Prentice-Hall, 1957.

GAGNÉ, ROBERT M. "Varieties of Learning and the Concept of Discovery." In Lee S. Shulman and Evan R. Keislar (Eds.). *Learning by Discovery: A Critical Appraisal.* Chicago: Rand McNally, 1966.

JOHNSON, DONALD. *Systematic Introduction to the Psychology of Thinking.* New York: Harper and Row, 1972.

KOTARBINSKI, TADEUZ. *Gnosiology: The Scientific Approach to the Theory of Knowledge.* New York: Pergamon Press, 1966.

LANGLEY, RITA. *Teaching Elementary Science.* West Nyack, New York: Parker, 1968.
MARX, MELVIN. *Learning Theories.* New York: Macmillan, 1970.
PITLUGA, GEORGE E. "Provocations to Thought: Open-Ended Experiments." In Board of
  Editors. *Best of General Science.* West Nyack, N. Y.: Parker, 1972.
SUND, ROBERT B., and LESLIE W. TROWBRIDGE. *Teaching Science by Inquiry in the
  Secondary School.* Columbus: Charles E. Merrill, 1967.

CHAPTER 13

Reading in Science and Technology.
II. Strategies for Improving Reading Skills

Abelard has said, "By doubting we are led to inquire, and by inquiry we perceive truth." Reading is a form of inquiry. You are using it now.

What role does reading play in science work? Is it necessary? To be sure, students can advance to a certain point and learn various concepts and principles without having to read, but in order to become an independent learner, one who can gather information from the written accounts of others, one must be able to read.

I have implied that although experiment, observation, and demonstration are extremely important and should be the fundamental means of developing science concepts and principles, reading has basic contributions to make. Some of the uses of reading in science are

1. To understand teachers' and students' written plans for experiments, as well as their written summaries of such activities.
2. To verify information developed in science class.
3. To expand on information previously learned.
4. To learn concepts and principles from systematic accounts.
5. To learn on one's own how to do experiments and demonstrations.
6. To aid in solving problems that cannot be solved by experimentation alone.
7. To learn the finer points of theory.
8. To enjoy the biographies and autobiographies of scientists.

It is incumbent upon the teacher to know the science literature suitable for students in the class. This means that the teacher not only knows the readability and content of available literature but also takes steps to provide materials of easy readability as well as medium and difficult readability. The teacher's responsibility also includes working with the librarian and fellow science teachers to obtain a wide variety of reading materials—textbooks, trade books, manuals, bulletins, kits, and so forth.

Who is responsible for improving the reading skills of science students? The science teacher. Why? It is very simple: because he or she as teacher is responsible for helping students think better about science concepts, principles, and the like, and science reading is a thinking process. Therefore, the teacher has the duty (and privilege) to help improve the students' thinking skills of reading science materials.

IMPROVING SCIENCE READING SKILLS

In this section we shall deal with facets of improving science reading skills such as interest-motivation, readability of materials, decoding words, vocabulary meaning and decoding, and reading science materials with comprehension. We know that by middle school years the abilities and interests of students are beginning to differentiate. There seems to be a relationship between interest and achievement.

Interest-motivation

It is a cliché in education that if some students are motivated half the battle is won. Some people talk about intrinsic motivation and extrinsic motivation; it may be that in more than a few cases intrinsic motivation has its roots in extrinsic motivation. What I mean is this: if we were to start taking away the positive feedback to individuals who are supposedly intrinsically motivated in an area of study, how long would their interest hold up?

Knowing Concepts. Most people seem to be interested in the things in which they have some degree of proficiency. The girl who runs races and wins continues to run. The boy who wins high ratings in his first piano competitions continues to practice assiduously. The girl who solves all the mathematical problems in her head until she gets to high school and does well in high school has learned many concepts and interest is maintained. Indeed, those who know concepts about a field are usually interested in the field.

Positive Feedback. Most people who are successful at learning concepts and performing in various areas do receive positive feedback. But when instruction is not modified to agree with an individual's learning rate, the individual will learn little and eventually fail. We can, however, aid people in being successful so that they can receive feedback and stay in the positive, upward, success spiral. First we get them into the spiral by pacing instruction so that mastery occurs and interest is maintained. When we get new students we not only check their ability, reading achievement, and science achievement, but we also look into their interest in science.

Science-Interest Questionnaire Starter. Anderson (1954) reports the work of Donald G. Decker who developed an interest questionnaire starter that can be used in grades 7 and 8 and adapted to lower and higher grades:

> I. Two parts: A. activities   B. subject
> II. Eighteen different activities, such as:
>   A. owning   D. hearing   G. giving reports
>   B. using   E. taking part
>   C. seeing   F. discovering

    III. Items include five major areas of science:
        A. Living Things   D. The Universe
        B. The Human Body   E. Matter Energy
        C. The Earth
    IV. Questions grouped for convenience in tabulating:
        A. Questions pertaining to <u>living things</u> are numbered 1
        B. Questions pertaining to <u>human body</u> are numbered 2 and so forth
    V. Parts of the questionnaire are shown below:
        2. What have you used?
            1. Have you used a chemical to make a plant grow better?
            2. Have you used a microscope to examine cells from a human body?
        2a. What would you like to use?
            1. Would you like to use different chemicals on plants to see what would happen to the plants?
            2. Would you like to use a machine to measure your brain waves?

I feel that this is quite a contrast to the first assignment my sixth grader brought home today, the first assignment: "Find out what you can about Eratosthenes?"

Four Kinds of Science Students. Junior high school science teachers classified science students into four groups: A: high ability, high interest; B: high ability, low interest; C: High interest, low ability; D: low ability, low interest. The teachers then delineated characteristics of the various groups. Group A was characterized by such features as does quality work, shows initiative and reflection, is prepared, formulates conclusions, and applies knowledge. Group B (high ability, low interest) showed such features as understands assignments, does little additional work, works promptly, and finishes work daily, but seldom goes beyond assignments. Group C (low ability, high interest) manifested features such as participates in class discussion at a concrete level of experience, has some ability to retain facts, completes work daily, respects knowledge, reasoning is average, improvement possible. Group D (low ability, low interest) was thought to be inattentive, careless, takes little part in discussions, is unwilling or unable to attack new work, and works only on minimum requirements (Bryan, 1959).

One, of course, wonders to what extent the curriculum and methodology were adapted to the abilities and needs of the students involved. Psychological principles intimate that when adaptations are made students profit more from their experiences and are somewhat more interested.

Readability of Materials

Commensurability a Key. To recite the litany of findings regarding the lacunae between readability of science texts and the reading ability of students for whom they were designed would be an endless and dull task; the hiatuses are great and many.

The readability of textbooks must be commensurate with the reading level of the students who are being asked to use the books. Simple logic, right? Well, I challenge you to take the *Fry Readability Graph* or another suitable readability measure and apply it to the science texts used in the nearest school and then compare the readabilities with the reading abilities of the students. Lacunae, hiatuses, and sundry kinds of gaps will abound.

In addition to the Fry and SMOG methods delineated in chapter 4, you might want to consider the Dale–Chall Readability Formula and the Flesch Readability Formula. The former is used to estimate the reading difficulty of reading materials at the fourth-grade level and above. Koenke (1971) has developed a computation ease chart to facilitate use of the Dale–Chall formula.

Project Rewrite.   A study by Williams (1969) demonstrated the value of rewriting junior-high science materials down to the fourth-grade level. In the rewritten version *simpler words* were used, technical words were more fully *explained*, and sentences were *rephrased* and *shortened* for clarity. The experimental group of students read the materials at the fourth-grade level; the control group read the original material, which was at the seventh-grade level. Both groups answered the same multiple-choice questions. The experimental group scored higher in comprehension than did the control group. A further finding was that good and average readers benefited even more from rewritten materials than the poor readers did. The implication is obvious: select a rewrite team from among a group of science teachers and replicate the study by rewriting a chapter or so of materials and conducting the same kind of experiment. An excellent article by Moore (1974) is devoted to preparing special science materials for the low-ability junior-high school student.

Vocabulary: Meaning and Decoding

If you have read the chapters on vocabulary and decoding, you know the principles of developing concepts and of decoding printed words. You are now looking for additional applications for reading science terms.

Lesson Outline for Scientific Vocabulary

1. Skill:
   Understanding special science vocabulary by means of the study of root words and the drawing of inferences.
2. Motivation:
   a. There is something in this room that moves up and down. It is not alive and it moves very slowly. What is it? Give as many clues as necessary to elicit thermometer.
   b. Show the two types of thermometers, Fahrenheit and Centigrade.
   c. Today we are going to learn to make intelligent guesses about the meanings of unfamiliar words.
3. Direct Teaching Techniques:
   a. As the word thermometer is elicited, write it on the board. Advise that when scientists invent an instrument, a thermometer, for instance, they have to give it a name. How do you suppose they decided upon the name thermometer?

b. Do you recognize any part of this word? Elicit meter. What does it mean? (Measure) The dictionary tells us that this word comes from the Greek word metron which means "measure." (Write on board) Does the other part of the word look familiar to you? Do you know a word that looks like this? Elicit thermos bottle. What does a thermos do? (Keep warm) What do you think this part of the word thermometer might mean? This also came from a Greek word, therme, meaning heat.

c. Fahrenheit (write on board) is a man's name. Can you guess why this thermometer (show Fahrenheit thermometer) should bear his name? (Inventor)

d. Show the other thermometer. Do you know the name of this thermometer? Elicit centigrade. (Write on board.) Let us see if we can discover why it is so named. Does any part of the word look familiar to you? Elicit grade and its meaning "step." This comes from a Latin word, gradus, meaning "step." Now look at the beginning of the word. What words do you know that have cent in them? Elicit century, centennial, and per cent and their meanings. This is from a Latin word centum, meaning one hundred. What is the meaning of centigrade?

e. Distribute pictures of both types of thermometers. To which of these would you give the name centigrade? Why? Write the names of the thermometers in the blank spaces provided.

f. Look at the paper. Each line is a step. What do we call these steps? Elicit degrees. (Write on board.) The dictionary tells us that centigrade and degree stem from the same Latin word, degradare, which is made from a prefix and a root word, gradus. What is the meaning of gradus? What is the meaning of de? Develop meaning of root and prefix.

g. What do we call this silvery substance? Show and elicit mercury. Did you ever hear of a Roman god named Mercury? Who was he? Elicit messenger of gods. Is this a good name? Why?

h. Now we know the meaning of several root words. Point to therm, meter, cent, and grade. If you had to guess at the meanings of the words at the bottom of your paper, could you guess intelligently? Have pupils give approximate meanings. What helped you? If you needed an exact meaning, what would you do? Elicit "Consult a dictionary."

4. Summary:
   a. What have we learned?
   b. Why should we be interested in learning the meanings of root words and their derivations?

5. Follow up:
   a. Add words to vocabulary section of science notebook.
   b. Add words to wall chart.
   c. Have pupils find other words with the same root.
      (1) Thermostat, thermometer, etc.
      (2) Gradation, gradual, etc.
      (3) Altimeter, barometer, kilometer, etc.   (Daugherty, n.d.).

Deck's Unit Teaching Plan. Teaching the Vocabulary. Deck (1974) warns against the practice of assuming that students have learned through prior experiences the needed vocabulary for topics in science. The teacher in teaching a unit in science must identify new or difficult terms in the unit and then discover and arrange learning activities to help pupils develop meanings and facility in using technical words.

1. *Preliminary planning.* Prior to introducing the unit "Our Welfare Is Tied Up with That of Other Living Things," Deck anticipated new and difficult words and came up with 138! He then segregated these words into ten categories; several are given here.

   a. Those thought to be key words of the unit, such as pollination, interdependence, and nitrification.

   b. Those terms needed to identify the key concepts of the unit: e.g., nitrate, lichen, terracing, etc.

   c. Words presenting the possibility of pronunciation difficulty, ichneumon fly, exquisite, insectivorous.

It is natural that some of the words fit into more than one group. It should help the students learn them better.

2. *Development of the unit.* An interesting account of an interdependence of living things was used to introduce the unit. Then key words relating to the first division of the unit were placed on the chalkboard and underlined with colored crayon. Another list of new words thought to be hard to understand was made. In order to make the students familiar with these words six activities were used; two are given here:

   a. Showing real flowers plus their pollen and nectar glands, and examining them with a microscope.

   b. Mounting the legs and mouth parts of bees on slides and showing on seoscope to the students.

Following are the kinds of questions suggested to stimulate purposeful reading that might help clarify and enrich the meanings of the new words: Why do fruit growers hope to have fair weather during the time their fruit trees blossom? Why are night-blooming flowers often white?

Subsequent units of the division were studied in like manner. Words or terms just learned will be remembered only if the learner has a number of opportunities to use them again and again. In order to make this possible ten different kinds of activities were carried out; three are given here:

1. Draw diagrammatic charts of the nitrogen cycle.

2. Exhibit models of practices in wildlife preservation.

3. Conduct an exhibit of pictures that illustrate the key words learned.

Deck reports that these procedures were very instrumental in yielding a number of positive specific outcomes such as making vocabulary much more interesting, making the reading of the textbook more profitable in terms of comprehension, pupils reading to learn while learning to read, and science concepts being learned as a unit of coherent and correlated facts while being built up around key words.

Illustrated Science Dictionaries. Each person may make a science dictionary but there probably will be a lot of interest in making a class dictionary of key science terminology. In a class effort, each student makes one or more pages of the dictionary. The following format may be used:

1. List word and its dictionary respelling. (pronunciation aid)

2. Give definition of word as used in the scientific context the class studied or will study.

3. Write at least two sentences using the word in the intended sense; these may come from a text source or be made up by the student. At any rate, the use should be clear and accurate.

4. Draw a clear picture or diagram illustrating the word or use an existing appropriate picture.

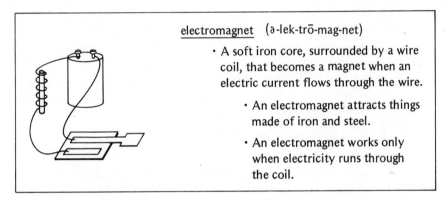

electromagnet   (ə-lek-trō-mag-net)

• A soft iron core, surrounded by a wire coil, that becomes a magnet when an electric current flows through the wire.

• An electromagnet attracts things made of iron and steel.

• An electromagnet works only when electricity runs through the coil.

Some Functional Applications of Phonics. The following strategies are not rudimentary phonics but a strategy in game form that has applications using previously learned phonics skills. They are designed to heighten the student's sensitivity to the relationships between encoding and decoding and to show how phonics can be fun.

PURPOSE: To arouse interest and competence in decoding through encoding, to illustrate graphemic options, to show utility of certain options in science terminology, and to show value of oral syllabication.

MATERIALS: Words contributed by students. Ask student to write his name on the card, too.

PROCEDURE:

1. Pick word, say it, and ask if anybody can use it in a sentence; perhaps the person who contributed the word will give a sentence.

   Example: ⟨chlorophyll⟩ ⟶ /klòrəfil/ "Chlorophyll is used in photosynthesis."

2. Ask someone to syllabicate the word orally. (Take what you get if it has all the sounds.)

   Example: /klór-ō-fil/)

3. Students may syllabicate the word together.
4. "What is the first syllable?" /klôr/
5. What sounds are in the first syllable/
6. How might we spell the first syllable? (or sound?)
   Possible responses: klor   chlor   clor
7. Why do you think it could be ⟨klor⟩ ?

   Response: _____

   Why do you think it could be ⟨chlor⟩ ?

   Response: _____

   Can you think of any other words where ⟨ch⟩ represents /k/?
   Possible response: chlorine, choir
8. How many think it is ⟨chlor⟩? ⟨klor⟩?
9. What is the second syllable?
   Possible responses: /ə/   /ō/
10. How could you represent the /ō/?
    Response: ⟨o⟩
11. Now we have ⟨chloro⟩
12. What was the last syllable?
    Response: /fil/
13. How can you spell that?
    fil   fyl   phil   phyl   phyll
14. What are some words that represent /f/ with ph?
    Possible responses: phone, graph
15. They are science words, aren't they? What have you noticed about the way /f/ is represented in many science words?
    Response: by ⟨ph⟩
16. If advanced students, or if you have studied this at all, ask which language many words come from in which /ch/ is represented by ⟨k⟩ and /f/ by ⟨ph⟩ .
    Expected response: Greek.
17. Can an /i/ be represented by ⟨y⟩?
18. Then /l/ is represented by _____ ?
    Expected responses: l ,   ll
19. Let us write out two or three ways (including the correct way) that chlorophyll can be spelled and then check in the dictionary.
20. You may want to let the students add this word to a list of ch /k/ words or ph /f/ words.

NOTE: Each word may not be that involved and require such a detailed analysis. There are advantages and disadvantages to having a heterogeneous group.

Cues to Inductive Study of Some Roots and Affixes

Regarding the study of the meanings of roots and affixes someone has said, "If the person can understand what you are talking about, he does not need it; and if he needs it, he will not understand what you are talking about." The foregoing statement is probably exaggerated. Actually, little is known about the value of such study. If, in doing this work, one points out how the understandings can be applied to other terms in the field or in general vocabulary, transfer will be increased and the value of the study will be greatly enhanced.

It probably would not be satisfactory to mimeograph lists of words with common roots and hand them to the students, if there were no provisions made for teaching and/or discussion. This is particularly true for somewhat above average students and average students. What dull students could learn by the best of methods would have to be a matter of research.

Table 13-1. Classification of Some Common Grapheme–Phoneme Relationships in Science Vocabulary

	⟨ch⟩ /k/	⟨g⟩ /j/	⟨eu⟩ /yü/	⟨ph⟩ /f/	rh /r/
Biology (human)	stomach chromosome eustachian	trigeminal gene gemmule	eugenics euglena eustachian	pharynx euryphagous oligophagous	rhesus rhebok rhea
Physics	mechanics Archimedes schematic	gigahertz gyroscope cryogenics	neutrino eudiometer	microphone photon siphon	rheostat rhythmicity
Botany	chlorophyll chromatin chlamydospore	gentian genipap ginseng	eucalyptus neurospora deutzia	phlox photosynthesis siphonophore	rhododendron rhatany reheotropism rhubarb
Chemistry	chlorine chromate technetium	germanium gel hydrogen	europium deuterium	phosphate phenol phthalin	rhenium rhodium
Geology	brachiopods ichthyosaurs chalcedony	geode fungi geanticline	eustatic eurypterid	morphology porphyry	rhodochrosite rhyolite

To do inductive teaching, at least two words containing the element in question should be known. The concepts represented by the words should be known also. Discuss with your students what the terms mean, how the roots or affixes have changed in meaning over the years, and so forth.

A second approach would be to allow pairs of students to dig out the information, re-reading the texts when necessary, and checking the glossary and dictionary for meaning and derivation [etymological] clues. Individual and class dictionaries of the type just discussed may also be consulted.

Students may keep a record of their work, may display some of it, and also explain portions of it to their classmates. I would encourage teachers and students to experiment in order to find other ways to study meanings. Where possible, use discussion in teaching because of its interest value and its value in clarifying concepts!

1. Chemistry and Physics

Word	Meaning of Root or Affix	Dictionary (optional) Definition
kinetic	moving	1. resulting from motion. 2. energetic or dynamic.
kinescope	moving to watch	1. motion picture record of a television program.
kinetic	moving	1. resulting from motion.
cinema	moving	1. movies.
kino (German)	move	1. movies.

What does kine (cine) mean? _____

Kinesiology is the study of human muscular _____ .

Kinetic art is an art style that involves the use of _____ parts, shifting lights, sounds, and so forth.

Kineto is a combining form meaning moving. What kind of words could you invent that use this form?

Word	Meaning	Definition
cent	one hundredth	1. penny; one hundredth of a dollar.
century	hundred	1. hundred years.
centigrade	hundred steps	1. hundred degrees.
centimeter	one hundredth meter	1. hundredth of a meter.

What does cent mean? _____

A centennial is the celebration of the _____ anniversary.

A centurion is the captain of a _____ soldiers.

A centipede is supposed to have a hundred _____ .

Why would you not want to have to complete report forms in centuplicate? _____ .

Would you like to have a fullback on your football team that weighed two centners? _____ Why or why not? _____

Word	Meaning	Definition
thermometer	heat measurer	1. a device for measuring heat.
barometer	pressure measurer	1. a device for measuring (air) pressure.
ammeter	current measurer	1. an instrument for measuring the strength of an electric current in terms of amperes.

What does meter mean? _____

What does odometer mean? Cue: odo is from hodos, meaning way. _____
_____ .

Why was the diet drink Metrecal so named? _____

Word	Meaning	Definition
accelerate	towards speed	1. to speed up.
decelerate	reduce speed	2. to reduce speed.

What does celer mean? _____

A person who exhibits celerity of thought would be a _____ thinker.

An accelerant increases the _____ of a process.

Word	Meaning	Definition
telephone	from afar sound	1. a communication device for talking with someone at a distance.
microphone	small sound (amplification)	1. a device that is part of a system for amplifying sound.
phonograph	sound writing (recording)	1. a device for playing back sound recorded on a disc.

What does phone mean? _____

A phoneme is a unit of _____ .

A phoney person is all _____ and no action, or his actions belie his words.

Word	Meaning	Definition
kilocycle	thousand cycles	1. radio broadcasting frequency; now called kilohertz.
kilogram	thousand grams	1. unit of weight equivalent to 2.2046 pounds.
kilometer	thousand meters	1. unit of length or distance equivalent to 3,280.8 feet.

What does kilo mean? _____

Would you lose or gain weight on a kilocalorie of food per day? _____

Has anybody ever weighed half of a kilo-kilogram? _____

What is the record weight of a person? _____

If a comedian had an audience of 10,000 people, would he be doing very well if he got a kilolaugh per joke? _____

Word	Meaning	Definition
monotone	one tone or pitch	1. a single, unchanging musical tone. 2. a person who sings in such a tone.
monochrome	one color	1. painting, drawing, or photograph in one color or shades of one color.
monograph	one writing	1. a book or paper written on one subject or topic. 2. treatise on a single genus or species.

What does mono mean? _____

Would a <u>mono</u>lingual person be a good translator? _____

Do you think you would find a <u>mono</u>stylous person to be very interesting? _____
Why or why not?

A <u>mono</u>carpic fruit bears fruit _____ and then dies.

How many replacable hydrogen atoms per molecule in a <u>mono</u>acid? _____

Word	Meaning	Definition
<u>photo</u>graph	<u>light</u> writing	1. a picture obtained by photography.
<u>photo</u>n	<u>light</u> + electron	1. a quantum of electromagnetic energy. . . : the energy of light, etc. is carried by photons.
<u>photo</u>electric	<u>light</u>, electric	1. of or having to do with the electric effects produced by light. . ., esp. as in the emission of electrons by certain substances when subjected to light. . . .

What does <u>photo</u> mean? _____

A person who has an abnormal fear of _____ is said to suffer
from <u>photo</u>phobia.

The <u>measurement</u> of the intensity of <u>light</u> is called _____y.

Word	Meaning	Definition
tele<u>scope</u>	distance, <u>seeing</u> (instrument for)	1. optical instrument for making distant objects appear nearer.
micro<u>scope</u>	small, <u>seeing</u>	1. optical instrument for making tiny things (often invisible to naked eye) visible, larger.
oto<u>scope</u>	ear, <u>seeing</u>	1. instrument for examining the tympanic membrane and external canal of the ear.
baro<u>scope</u>	(atmospheric) pressure <u>seeing</u>	1. an instrument for indicating changes in atmospheric pressure.

What does <u>scope</u> mean? _____

If you wanted to view a picture in three dimensions you could use a stereo _____ .

If the doctor wanted to "see" how your "stetho" is doing, he could use a stetho-
_____ . (Stetho refers to the chest; the stetho_____
is used to examine the heart and lungs to see what kinds of sounds they make.)

Word	Meaning	Definition
<u>hemo</u>globin	<u>blood</u>, protein component	1. the fluid that circulates in the heart, arteries, ...
<u>hem</u>ophilia	<u>blood</u>, tendency toward (bleeding)	1. tendency toward prolonged bleeding bleeding from even minor cuts and injuries.

hemocyte	blood cell (or combining form meaning cell)	1. a blood cell.

What does <u>hemo</u> mean? _____

A <u>hemo</u>toma is a local swelling or tumor filled with effused _____ .

Something that is _____ atic is filled with or colored like blood.

A <u>hemo</u>stat is a clamplike instrument used in surgery to stop _____ .

Word	Meaning	Definition
<u>proto</u>xylem	first xylem	1. Botany. the first formed xylem of a root or stem, produced by the differentiation of the procambium.
<u>proto</u>n	first	1. an elementary (first or basic) particle found in the nucleus of all atoms ... ; it carries a unit of positive charge... .
<u>proto</u>plast	first formed	1. a thing or being that is first of its kind. 2. Biology. same as energid. 3. <u>Botany</u>. a unit of protoplasm, such as makes up a single cell exclusive of the cell wall.

What does <u>proto</u> mean? _____

Adam was the _____ type of man because he was _____.

<u>Proto</u> is also used to mean basic. We see this use in the word _____ plasm which refers to a semifluid, viscous, translucent colloid that is the essential living matter of all animal and plant cells.

Word	Meaning	Definition
in<u>cis</u>ion	in, <u>cut</u>	1. the act or result of incising; cut; gash. 2. a deep notch, as in the edge of a leaf.
in<u>cis</u>ors	in, <u>cut</u>	1. a cutting tooth; any of the front teeth between the canines in either jaw.
ex<u>cis</u>e	out, <u>cutting</u>	1. to remove, as a tumor, by cutting out or away.

What does <u>cis</u> mean? _____

In<u>cis</u>ive speech _____ directly to the heart of a matter or problem.

We use a s____sors to cut cloth.

Meaning Hierarchies. Concepts seem to be easier to understand, see relationships among, and remembered if a visual structure showing some of the relationships can be developed. There are, of course, formal taxonomies available, but it makes sense to build these up as you go along by developing conceptual hierarchies. This kind of activity has its roots in the kinds of classifying done already in kindergarten and grade 1 (Hafner and Jolly, 1972).

Chapters 3 and 5 of the present work contain more complete discussions of meaning hierarchies. Following are some hierarchy *starters*:

1. *Simple Hierarchies:*

   a. Matter

states of matter	gases	liquids	solids
•gases	•hydrogen	•	•
•liquids	•oxygen	•	•
•solids	•	•	•

properties of specific gases	properties of specific liquids	properties of specific solids
•hydrogen	•	•
•		
•		
•		
•carbon dioxide	•	•
•		
•		
•		
•water vapor	•water (H_2O)	•ice
•	•	•
•	•	•
•	•	•

properties of gases in general	properties of liquids in general	properties of solids in general
•	•	•
•	•	•
•	•	•

   b. Machinery

   • Four fundamental mechanical principles on which all machinery is based
     •the lever
     •the wheel and axle
     •the screw
     •the wedge
     •(some combination)

   Lever machines
     •beam balance
     •
     •

   Wheel and axle machines
     •
     •

   Principles of levers
     •first-class lever:

   _____

   _____

     •second-class lever:

   _____

   _____

     •third-class lever:

   _____

   _____

2. Complex Hierarchies: Examples of more complex hierarchies in science are to be found in the vocabulary chapter.

"Pre-reading" Vocabulary Study Sheets. Call it readiness, warm up, or advance organizer, the name may not matter that much, but preparation for reading through pronunciation cues and meaning clues can be very helpful.

1. Study Sheet for a Section of a Biology Chapter

protozoa
(prō-tō-zō-ə)

Protozoans are tiny, single-celled animals.

parasitic
(per-ə-sit-ik)

Malaria and African sleeping sickness result from parasitic protozoa.

paramecium
(per-ə-mē-syəm)

The paramecium is a protozoa. Therefore, it is a
_____, _____ – _____ animal.
It moves around to get food, and it reproduces by dividing.

vacuole
(va-kyü-əl)

A food vacuole is the part of the paramecium that holds food from a previous meal.

cilia
(sil-yə)

Paramecia swim. How? By flapping their cilia, or tiny hair, that serve as arms and legs. How do paramecia get around? Right, by moving their cilia. _____ is their means of locomotion. Guess what the paramecium uses to get food into its gullet? Right again, c_____ .

Can you provide headings for the following:

Provide examples under the heading:
Diseases resulting from
parasitic protozoa

_____   _____

•cilia   •paramecia   • _____

•food vacuoles   •foraminifera   • _____

Words on Card Readers. For each chapter or unit of study one can prepare words for individual or small group study by placing technical terms on card-reader cards. They can be prepared in a number of ways.

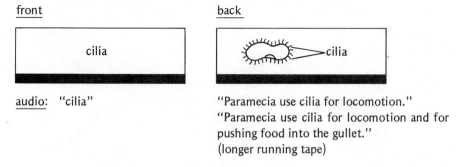

front

cilia

audio: "cilia"

back

cilia

"Paramecia use cilia for locomotion."
"Paramecia use cilia for locomotion and for pushing food into the gullet."
(longer running tape)

These cards can be filed (1) alphabetically, (2) by units, or (3) alphabetically within units.

front   back   or

| cilia | Cilla are tiny hairs. | Paramecia use cilia for locomotion. |

audio: "cilia"   "Cilia are tiny hairs."   "Paramecia use cilia
                                                          for locomotion."

Reading Science Materials with Comprehension

Many of the general comprehension skills transfer directly to reading science materials. If you have not read the comprehension strategies developed in the chapter on comprehension, you will need to. Remember that the quintessence of reading comprehension is careful, logical analysis of cognitive relationships; it is an active thinking process.

Reading Scientific Material Carefully. A technical word often represents a complex concept. Since in some textbooks we see pages crammed with technical words and little explanatory material, reading can be a very difficult task. To the extent that they have had experiences with the concepts through observation, experimentation, demonstration, and so forth, students will have fewer problems understanding the materials. If the curriculum is highly textbook oriented and a solid knowledge of concepts has *not* been developed prior to reading, serious comprehension problems can be expected.

At any rate, one must approach science material with the attitude that careful reading is required because some concepts and relationships are difficult even when the preparation has been good. An individual who cannot read carefully in order to develop relationships will not fare well in science reading.

Techniques Demanding Careful Reading. Any technique that demands that students process information should induce careful reading. Writing summaries, making notes, outlining, and study techniques such as SQ3R, NSL, and REAP require careful reading and, more importantly, understanding and organizing ideas. These techniques are explained in chapter 7.

Do not expect these techniques to work miracles. You must determine that the reading comprehension achievement of the student who is expected to read science material X is commensurate with the reading difficulty of science material X. (Remember, you might teach weight lifting techniques to a 75-pound girl but you do not ask her to clean and jerk a 500-pound weight!)

When there is a reasonable correspondence between reading ability and text difficulty, the student understands prerequisite conceptual material, and there is some motivation—some reason—for reading to comprehend, then one can expect a person to read carefully in an attempt to comprehend.

A Good Time to Use Reading in Science. A particularly good time for students to use reading in science is when they are faced with a problem they cannot solve by experiment alone. Blough and Schwartz (1969) delineate a situation in which middle grade students develop a problem, "How are sounds made?" A suggestion is made that each student bring to class something that makes a sound. The teacher reads the textbook section on sound, explores to see what other reading materials are available, locates nearby examples of things using the principles of sound, and assembles a number of things they will need that the students probably will not find.

Next day the students bring in their soundmakers. The students are to observe carefully to see (1) what makes the sound, and (2) how the sounds differ from each other. After the demonstrations, the teacher suggests that the students listen quietly to the sounds about them.

After each sound, the students state what they think may be the answers to the questions. They formulate hypotheses and discuss things that happened—throat quivering, violin strings vibrating. They agree that when a sound is made something is vibrating. Now the question remains, "What has this to do with the sound I hear in my ears, and how does the sound get there?"

This is a good time to use reading because the students now face a problem they cannot solve by experiment alone. The students read the sections on sound in the books assembled by the teacher. They read about vibrations and suggest experiments they can do with a tuning fork. They feel the vibrations in the tuning fork. They experiment with rubber bands of various sizes. Then they return to the books to "finish reading about vibrations, how they make sounds, and how sounds travel in waves from place to place."

As the study continues, the students read further, study diagrams, search for supplementary books on the subject, experiment further, and gradually come to some answers to their questions as well as to other questions that may have come up in the course of the study.

Blough and Schwartz (1969) further suggest that the effectiveness of reading can be stepped up by (1) reading for specific purposes, (2) reading from several supplementary sources that provide extra information and differing points of view, (3) reading with an open mind, deliberating and examining before drawing conclusions, going to reliable sources for evidence, (4) having teachers and students select reading materials, and (5) having students take notes on the reading.

Reading–Reasoning Guides. If you read chapter 9 you may recall the discussion on reading-reasoning guides and their use in helping students (1) process information better and (2) through their continued use become independent enough to apply such strategies without the teacher's help. Following are examples of some guides for science reading. The guides for reading the selection on "Class Angiospermae" follow it.

● FLOWERING TRACHEOPHYTES
  NONFLOWERING TRACHEOPHYTES
● NONTRACHEOPHYTES

Figure 5 · 5
Proportion of plant species
in various taxonomic groups.
Compare this graph with
Figure 4 · 20.

Phylum Tracheophyta
[trä'kē ăf'ə tə; Greek: *tracheia,*
windpipe, + *phyton,* plant]

vascular [văs'kyə lər; Latin:
vasculum, little container]

Pteropsida [tə răp'sə də;
Greek: *pteron,* feather, + *opsis,*
appearance]

Angiospermae [ăn ˌjē'ō spər'mē;
Greek: *angeion,* container, +
sperma, seed]

sepals [sē'pəlz; Greek: *skepe,*
covering]

petals [pĕt'əlz; Greek: *petalos,*
outspread]

stamens [stā'mənz; Latin:
stare, to stand]

pistils [pĭst'əlz; Latin: *pistillus,*
pestle]

pollen [päl'ən; Latin: *pollen,*
dust]

A CATALOGUE OF LIVING PLANTS: KINGDOM PLANTAE

The organisms that taxonomists commonly group in the plant kingdom lack ways to move themselves from place to place and, in general, react rather slowly to their environment. In addition, they have a chemical characteristic: they contain *cellulose,* a substance that gives their bodies more firmness.

PHYLUM TRACHEOPHYTA
vascular plants; about 211,900 species

The chances are very good that almost all the plants you can name are tracheophytes. Every tracheophyte has a continuous system of tubes (a *vascular system*) extending through its roots, stems, and leaves. By means of this conducting system, water and substances dissolved in it move rather easily from one place in the plant to another. For land plants, movement of water upward from the soil is especially important. Any land plant that stands as much as a meter high is almost certainly a tracheophyte.

SUBPHYLUM PTEROPSIDA
seed plants and ferns; about 210,700 species

The subphyla of tracheophytes are very unequal in number of species included. This subphylum contains 99 percent of the species in the phylum. It is distinguished from other tracheophyte subphyla by the fact that the position of each leaf is marked by a gap in the vascular tissue of the stem.

Class Angiospermae
flowering plants; about 200,000 species

Botanists think of a flower as a short branch bearing groups of leaves. Some of these may resemble ordinary leaves, but others are so different in structure that it is hard to think of them as leaves at all. If you examine the flower of a buttercup, for example, you see on the underside a number of green, leaflike structures—*sepals.* Before the bud opened, the sepals enclosed the other parts of the flower. The most conspicuous flower parts in a buttercup are the *petals,* which, like the sepals, are more or less leaflike in shape but of a quite different color. Attached just above the base of the petals are a number of *stamens,* each having an enlarged tip. And grouped together in the center of the flower are numerous small, rounded structures called *pistils,* each with pointed tip. Despite their shape, both stamens and pistils are believed to be modified leaves.

A flower is a reproductive structure. Stamens produce *pollen* grains; when these are transferred to the tips of the pistils, *seeds* may develop. The sepals and petals are not directly involved in seed formation, so a flower can function without them. In fact, in a few plants a flower may consist of only a single stamen or a single pistil.

Much of the diversity shown by angiosperms lies in their flowers. There is no better way to appreciate this than to examine various kinds

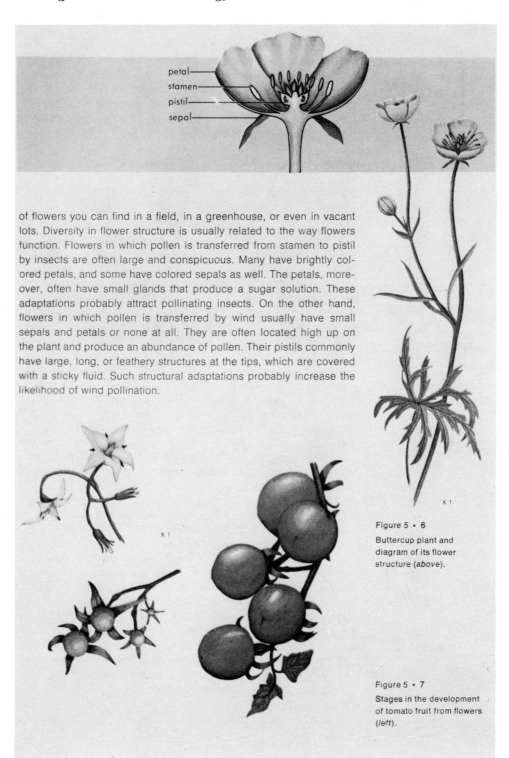

petal—
stamen—
pistil—
sepal—

of flowers you can find in a field, in a greenhouse, or even in vacant lots. Diversity in flower structure is usually related to the way flowers function. Flowers in which pollen is transferred from stamen to pistil by insects are often large and conspicuous. Many have brightly colored petals, and some have colored sepals as well. The petals, moreover, often have small glands that produce a sugar solution. These adaptations probably attract pollinating insects. On the other hand, flowers in which pollen is transferred by wind usually have small sepals and petals or none at all. They are often located high up on the plant and produce an abundance of pollen. Their pistils commonly have large, long, or feathery structures at the tips, which are covered with a sticky fluid. Such structural adaptations probably increase the likelihood of wind pollination.

x 1

x 1

Figure 5 · 6
Buttercup plant and diagram of its flower structure (*above*).

Figure 5 · 7
Stages in the development of tomato fruit from flowers (*left*).

As development proceeds, pistils are transformed into *fruits,* which contain seeds. Each seed contains a tiny new plant—an embryo. Part of an embryo consists of one or two modified leaves, called *cotyledons,* and part is a beginning of a root. Each seed also contains a supply of food that is used when the embryo starts to grow. The food may be stored in a special part of the seed called the *endosperm,* or it may be stored in the embryo itself, usually in the cotyledons.

cotyledons [kŏt′ə lē′dənz; Greek: *kotyle,* anything hollow]

endosperm [ĕn′dō spûrm′; Greek: *endon,* within, + *sperma,* seed]

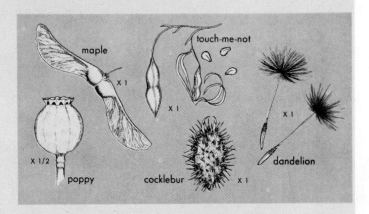

Figure 5 · 8
Diversity among fruits. How does each of the structural adaptations shown here provide for seed scattering?

Seeds and fruits show as much diversity as flowers. In many cases, part of the pistil becomes thick and fleshy, as in the fruits of peach, plum, and tomato. Other fleshy fruits, such as apples and pears, also include parts of the flower stalk. Fleshy fruits are often eaten by animals. The seeds in many such fruits have thick coats that permit them to pass through an animal's digestive tract unharmed, later to be dropped at some distance from the parent plant. Many fruits are not fleshy but have other adaptations that aid in scattering their seeds.

What kind of ecological relationship exists between plant and animal in this case?

In addition to the diversity in their flowers, there is great diversity in the size of angiosperms and in the life-span of their *shoots*—the parts that appear above ground. Many angiosperms are trees. A tree form enables a plant to bear its leaves well above the surface of the ground, where they are likely to receive more light than do those of shorter plants. Because of their size, trees can store large reserves of food in trunks and roots, allowing survival through a series of several bad years. Trees have relatively long life-spans; this increases the probability that a tree species will survive even though the entire seed crop of any one year may be destroyed. But most species of angiosperms are not trees. Some, such as roses and raspberries, are woody shrubs. Others, such as ivy, grapes, and hundreds of tropical species, are *lianas*—woody vines—which rely on rocks, walls, or other plants for support. Most, however, are neither shrubs nor vines, but nonwoody plants—*herbs.*

lianas [lī ăn′əz]. See Figure 8·20.

herbaceous [hûr bā′shəs]

Many of these herbaceous plants have roots or stems that year

after year remain alive in the soil during winter and during each growing season send up new shoots. These are *perennial* herbs, such as
goldenrod, iris, and asparagus. Others are *annuals*. These (for example, garden beans, sunflowers, and corn) produce seeds and die after
growing for only one season. Still others have life-spans intermediate
between those of perennials and annuals.

perennial [pə rĕn'ĭ əl; Latin:
per, through, + *annus*, year]

goldenrod. See Figure 2·11.
Iris. See Figure 2·2.

Subclass Monocotyledoneae
monocots; about 34,000 species

Monocotyledoneae
[mŏn'ə kŏt'ə lē'də nē; Greek:
monos, one, single, + *kotyle*]

Botanists divide angiosperms into two large groups. Figure 5·9
shows the characteristics on which these subclasses are based. In
studying the figure, keep in mind that it is a summary and does not
take all known angiosperms into consideration; for example, some
monocots have netted-veined leaves. The basic characteristic, as the
name of the group indicates, is that the embryo contains a single
cotyledon.

Many of the plants most economically important to man are monocots. All important grain-producing plants, such as wheat, rice, and
corn, are monocots; these are a major source of biological energy
for mankind. The pasture grasses that feed the cattle that are another
source of human food are also monocots. It is safe to say that without
the monocots the human population could never have reached its
present size. (Examples below.)

In addition to grains, what
other monocot plants are
important for human food?

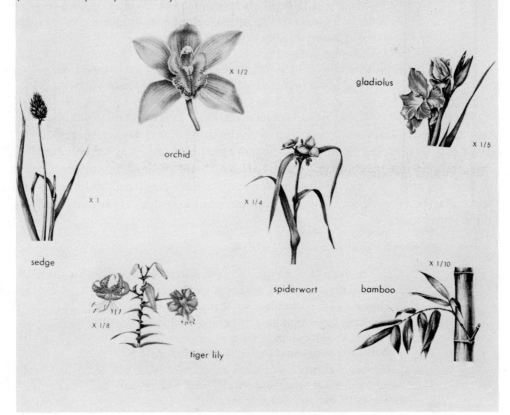

X 1/2

gladiolus

X 1/5

orchid

X 1

X 1/4

sedge

spiderwort

bamboo

X 1/10

X 1/8

tiger lily

Literal: Please follow these steps: (1) Read the statements below, (2) read the above selection on "Class Angiospermae," (3) as you read the selection, look at the statements in the guide and indicate by a check which statements the author made.

LITERAL GUIDE

_____ 1. The construction of some leaves make it difficult to think of them as leaves.

_____ 2. In the buttercup the petals are easiest to see.

_____ 3. Stamens and pistils are a form of leaves.

_____ 4. Parthenogenesis is involved in the fertilizing of class angiospermae plants.

_____ 5. The petals and sepals are particularly involved in seed formation.

_____ 6. Pollen grains fulfill a male function in fertilization.

_____ 7. Seeds may develop when pistils receive pollen grains from stamens.

_____ 8. One of the hardest ways of differentiating angiospermae is through examination of their flowers.

_____ 9. There is a relationship between transfer of pollen by insect and these factors: size and conspicuousness of petals.

_____10. Pistil transformation results in fruits which contain seeds.

_____11. The embryo of each seed contains (1) one or two modified leaves (cotyledons) and (2) the beginning of a root.

_____12. The food in each seed—used when the embryo starts to grow—may be stored in a special section of the seed called the endosperm or it may be stored in the embryo, usually in the cotyledons.

_____13. Animals play no role in dissemination of seeds.

_____14. Flowers would be affected sooner by a drought than would trees.

_____15. Perennial plants produce seeds and die after one season's growth.

Internal Interpretation: Since you have read the selection you should be ready to check each statement that you feel the author was trying to get across. Two or more pieces of information may combine to form the relationship indicated by the statement. (NOTE: In addition to internal interpretation statements some of the following statements may be literal statements and some may be false. Check only the statements obtained by combining relationships found in the text.)

INTERNAL INTERPRETATION GUIDE

_____ 1. Before the bud opens up, the sepal is more conspicuous than the pistil.

_____ 2. In the buttercup, sepals and petals are the same color.

_____ 3. The base of the petals is lower than the tips of the stamens.

_____ 4. In a sense buttercups have three kinds of leaves.

_____ 5. Flowers produce seeds.

_____ 6. Sepals and petals play a key role in seed production.

_____ 7. Flowers pollinated by insects would not likely lack sepals and petals.

_____ 8. Sticky pistils lessens the chance of wind pollination.

_____ 9. Lianas are species of angiosperms.

_____10. Asparagus roots stay alive from year to year.

External Interpretation: Your familiarity with the selection will enable you to proceed to the exercise below. If you think a statement can be supported by using the author's ideas and external related ideas on the topic, check the statement. Literal ideas, as well as internal relationships, may be combined with external sources to support a statement.

EXTERNAL INTERPRETATION GUIDE

_____ 1. Bees likely would be found in large flowers that have brightly colored sepals.

_____ 2. There are some similarities between flowers and humans.

_____ 3. "Cotyledon" would be a logical name for a helicopter.

_____ 4. Pistils are the easiest part of a flower to see.

_____ 5. Flowers must be multi-pistilled.

_____ 6. Wind pollination is not likely in a greenhouse.

_____ 7. Tomatoes develop from flowers.

_____ 8. Pistils with short structures are conducive to wind pollination.

_____ 9. The name angiospermae gives cues to at least one function of that class.

_____10. Having food in the exosperm would facilitate embryonic growth more than having the food in the endosperm.

Cause and Effect Guide. (1) Identify cause and relationships. (2) Place effects in one list and causes in another. (3) Students read the text to note relationships of details in the text and (4) relate causes and effects on the basis of the relationships; place letters in appropriate blanks. (NOTE: Watch for reversal of cause and effect.)

"Liquids"

Foundations of Chemistry, pp. 326–328
E. R. Toon and G. L. Ellis

CAUSE AND EFFECT GUIDE

Effects

a. Reduced space between molecules.

b. Diminution of spaces between molecules.

c. Ratio of volume of molecules to total volume of gas increases.

d. Volume of liquid (if temperature does not change) keeps same volume even though pressure is exerted upon the liquid.

e. Difficult to pour.

f. Molecules move more rapidly.

Causes

_____1. Compression of gas.

_____2. High viscosity of molasses.

_____3. Liquefying gases.

_____4. Temperature increase.

_____5. High pressure.

_____6. Molecules of liquid greatly attracted to one another.

Comparison Guide. A valuable method for sorting things, for noticing like-nesses and differences among theories, methods, etc., is the use of comparison. In developing this exercise one must read materials to find things that can be compared. One looks, for example, for ways of doing things, lists them hori-zontally, and then lists vertically the headings on which the comparisons will be made. Then the students are asked to read, make the comparisons, and *fill in the spaces* with appropriate information.

"Methods of Measuring Time"
Verwiebe, et al. Physics, pp. 485–86

COMPARISON GUIDE

	egg timer	sundial	common watch	grand-father clock	electric clock	ammonia clock	cesium clock
Source of power			spring				
Means of Regulation			oscillation of balance wheel				
Time Indi-cated by			hands pointing to numerals				
Accuracy			?				

Comparison. Read pages 218–220 and note the different procedures used by the various scientists in their attempts to measure light. Then reread in order to note the points of comparison and fill in the boxes with appropriate information.

Teaching a Directed Reading Lesson. There is a very important assumption that I must reiterate. Before preparing a fancy lesson plan, make sure that the recipients of and participants in your lesson (1) are being asked to read materials at their reading achievement level and (2) have prerequisite concepts that are the foundation for the material in question. Then your job is to decide whether any experiments or demonstrations occur prior to, during, or after the reading.

There are several steps in a Directed Reading Lesson (DRL): One, *Preparation,* we have treated to some extent. The other steps are *Guided Reading, Follow-up, Clarifying Activities,* and *Evaluation.* Following is an outline plan for a brief chapter on minerals written for middle school students. (Not all details of the plan will be filled in.)

1.0 *Delineating objectives and giving pre-test*
1.1 *Objectives*
1.2 *Pre-test*
2.0 *Preparation*

2.1   *Developing interest*

2.1.1 (option) Review concepts of previous lesson: (1) differentiating minerals from rocks; (2) recalling difference between element and mineral; (3) noting characteristics of mineral; (4) subjecting several substances to test of characteristics to see if they are minerals; (5) recalling the two different kinds of clues to the properties of minerals; (6) recalling the mineral detective's tools.

2.1.2 (option) Using actual mineral samples (those shown in text) or just a list of names of the minerals, ask students to arrange them in order of hardness.

2.2   *Reading and discussing the vocabulary study sheet*

2.2.1 [Construction of vocabulary study sheets (VSS) was discussed earlier in the chapter.]

2.2.2 The reading and discussing should be done a day or two before the reading of the chapter.

2.3   *Reviewing study sheet and clarifying any remaining problems*

2.3.1 Immediately prior to reading the chapter let students ask any questions they still have.

2.3.2 Spot check understanding.

2.4   *Previewing the chapter and noting questions*

2.4.1. Read target question.

2.4.2 Read section or paragraph headings, reminding students that these questions are related to the *keys* or clues from the previous chapter: hardness key, luster key, color key, and so forth.

3.0   *Guided reading*

3.1   Purposes, guides, etc.

3.1.1 (option) The questions that constitute the headings may be the guiding questions. Responses may be oral or written, free response or multiple choice.

3.1.2 (option) Reading-reasoning guide. (See previous discussion. The reader of the present text is encouraged to write a suitable guide for the chapter on minerals.)

3.1.3 Responses should be discussed and evaluated.

4.0   *Follow–up, clarifying activities*

4.1   (option) Students and teacher write a practice post-test.

4.2   (option) Play a quiz game using items contributed by students.

4.3   Doing the section "Understanding What You Have Read" individually and then discussing the answers.

4.4   (option) Bring in other minerals to classify and rate on hardness scale.

4.5   (option) Add items to individual and/or class *Illustrated Science Dictionary*.

5.0   *Evaluation*

5.1   Post–test.

5.2   Discuss results of post-test and determine whether objectives were met.

9

TARGET
How are minerals used for work? What minerals are used for jewelry?

Minerals for Work and Minerals for Beauty

1. RUB IT . . . SMOOTH IT . . . CUT IT . . .

Run your finger across the top of your school desk or the top of a wooden dresser at home. How smooth the surface is! The same is true of the body of your car and the surface of your coffeepot. Industry has great need for smoothing surfaces of wood and metal.

2. ABRASIVES ARE FOR SMOOTHING

Minerals used in rubbing and smoothing are called ABRASIVES (uh-BRAY-sivz). The *scouring powder* you have used in your Home Economics class contains abrasives. Most scouring powders contain mixtures of sand (quartz) and aluminum oxide. They feel rough to the fingers. As you rub the powder against a pot, dirt comes off and the surface of the pot becomes clean and shiny.

Fig. 46–1
These girls are using the abrasives in the scouring powder to polish the surfaces of the pots.

In the woodshop, rough wood surfaces may become smoother than your skin when you rub them with sandpaper or *emery* paper. Sandpaper is made by coating a paper surface with glue or plastic. Thousands of little quartz chips are then thinly spread into the glue. Emery paper contains the mineral CORUNDUM (kuh-RUN-dum). Look back to the chart on page 36 and you will see that corundum is very high on the "hardness key." Only diamonds are hard enough to scratch corundum. Women are quite familiar with the small emery "boards" they use to file down their fingernails. For heavy grinding and cutting in industry, grinding wheels made of corundum are used.

Fig. 47–2

The U.S. submarine "Nautilus" uses atomic energy to run her engines.

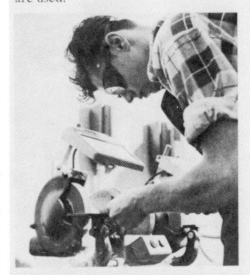

Fig. 47–1

This boy is using an abrasive wheel in his school shop to grind metal.

YOU NOW KNOW

▶ Minerals used for cutting, grinding and polishing are called "abrasives."

▶ Abrasives use the minerals quartz, corundum and diamond.

3. HEAT AND ENERGY FROM THE EARTH

When we think of heat and energy we usually think of coal and gaso-line, for these materials burn to give off heat. This heat energy can be used to run steam engines or gasoline engines. In a later chapter, we shall talk about coal and gasoline—two "treasures" from our earth.

We are beginning to hear more and more of nuclear energy—the energy that comes from splitting atoms. We sometimes think of nuclear energy in the form of destructive bombs in time

Fig. 47–3

Atomic plants are beginning to make cheap, safe energy.

of war. Most of us, however, would like to see nuclear energy used to drive car engines, to dig tunnels and to heat homes.

Earlier we mentioned the ore pitchblende. This ore, found in nature, can be purified to make uranium-235. From uranium-235 we can then make other materials. The atoms of these materials can easily be split to make nuclear energy. Pitchblende has a black luster. It can be found in Katanga in Africa. Closer to home, there are large deposits of pitchblende in Canada and in Colorado. Once again, we see how the earth is a treasure-house for man.

YOU NOW KNOW

▶ Coal and gasoline come from the earth and are used for energy.
▶ Pitchblende and uranium come from the earth and can be used for energy.
▶ The earth is a "storehouse" of energy.

4. GOLD OR FOOL'S GOLD?

The precious metals, gold, silver and platinum, can be hammered, bent and shaped into beautiful jewelry, such as rings, necklaces, cufflinks and tie clasps. Gold and silver have been known for a long time. Platinum was discovered in 1735 in South America. It was first mistaken for silver and called by the Spanish name for silver—*plata*.

There are simple but sure tests for the precious metals, mostly based on specific gravity. It is very hard to pass off other metals as the "real thing." Many gold prospectors learned quickly that what they thought was a rich "find" in gold, was really a brassy-yellow mineral, IRON PYRITE (PY-rite)—quickly named "fool's gold."

5. STONES OF BEAUTY

"What a gem!" is an expression we use often to describe anything of great beauty or great price. "He's a gem of a pitcher!" "It's a gem of a story!"

A GEM (JEM) is a mineral stone which is beautiful because of its color or the way it reflects light. As you would expect, these are quite scarce and so the price of gems is very high. There are, however, some gems that are more plentiful. These are called *semiprecious* (half-precious) and cost much less money than the rarer gems.

Gem Stones	
Diamond (DY-uh-mond)	clear, white, pale blue
Amethyst (AM-uh-thist)	purple
Topaz (TOW-paz)	yellow
Emerald (EM-uh-ruld)	green
Sapphire (SAF-fire)	blue
Ruby (ROO-bee)	red
Jade	green
Lapis Lazuli (LAP-is LAZ-you-lee)	blue
Opal (O-pal)	white (many colors)

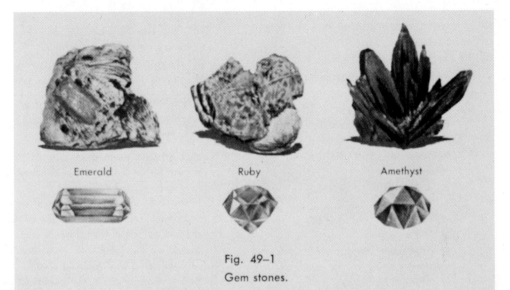

Fig. 49–1
Gem stones.

When gem stones are found they are not in the shape you usually see them and they are not smoothly polished. Skilled jewelry workers cut the stones into various sizes and shape and then polish them with abrasives to bring out their luster. Gem-stone polishers are highly skilled and well paid. Perhaps this is a job for which you would like to train.

6. JOB OPPORTUNITIES

Diamond cutting and polishing is a skill that takes training and practice. But once learned, it offers good jobs with good pay. Would you like to be a diamond cutter?

YOU NOW KNOW

▶ Some materials from the earth, such as coal and uranium, can give heat and energy.
▶ Precious metals and gem stones are used for jewelry and decoration.

UNDERSTANDING WHAT YOU HAVE READ

1. What are the two main ideas of Chapter 9?
   1. Some minerals that look like gold are really not gold.
   2. Some minerals are used in industry.
   3. Uranium is the future source of power.
   4. Gems are minerals which have beautiful colors or shine brightly.

II. In which paragraph do you find the answer?

1. Are there tests for precious metals?
2. What do scouring powders contain?
3. What is corundum?
4. What is the difference between precious and semiprecious stones?

III. Knowing What and Why

1. Pitchblende can yield uranium through
   a. metallurgy.
   b. oxidation.
   c. abrasives.
   d. mining.
2. The surface of sandpaper is usually covered with
   a. black diamonds.
   b. quartz chips.
   c. aluminum powder.
   d. coal dust.
3. Which two of these gem stones are green?
   a. jade and ruby
   b. opal and emerald
   c. jade and emerald
   d. topaz and ruby
4. Gem stones are valuable because
   a. there are so few and they are so beautiful.
   b. they can be made into jewelry.
   c. it costs much to polish them.
   d. they are found in faraway places.

IV. For the Home Laboratory

Would you like to make sandpaper? Here's how:

1. Get a heavy paper bag. Cut it into sheets about 3 inches by 3 inches.
2. Get some clean beach sand.
3. Wrap a small piece of glass in an old rag. Crush it with a hammer. *Be careful* to wrap the glass so that pieces do not jump into your face.
4. Mix the sand and glass in a jar.
5. Brush some glue on the sheets of paper.
6. Sprinkle the sand-glass mixture as evenly as you can on the wet glue.
7. Allow the glue to dry overnight.
8. You now have sandpaper! Try smoothing a block of wood with it.

V. Brain-Teaser

Can you explain the difference in the methods used to make coarse (rough) sandpaper and fine (smooth) sandpaper?

SUMMARY

Reading is a form of inquiry stimulated by doubt and the desire to discover truth. At a certain stage of development the person who wants to become an independent learner of advanced science concepts and principles will have to know how to read well.

Interest-motivation is an important facet of science reading. Readers must be gotten into a positive, upward, success spiral by pacing instruction so that mastery occurs and interest is developed and maintained. Use of a science inventory can provide important cues for hooking into what interests students.

Several projects have shown the value of rewriting science materials to make the readability commensurate with the reading ability of students. Increased comprehension results when students are able to read appropriate science materials.

The teaching of science vocabulary should not be a catch-as-catch-can procedure. One should use specific strategies designed to teach vocabulary systematically, thoroughly, and interestingly. This is also true for teaching functional applications of phonics. Inductive teaching of vocabulary, phonetic analysis, and structural analysis may take longer, but the process may be more interesting and the results more satisfactory.

As with other content areas, I recommend the use of some kind of readiness material. Since vocabulary is such a problem for so many students, one should use such techniques as "pre-reading" vocabulary study sheets, words on card readers, and the like.

Scientific material should be read carefully because many concepts and relationships are difficult to process even when the preparation has been good. Suggestions were given on how reading can be used in science.

The energetic, conscientious, bright science teacher will probably develop reading-reasoning guides to use in helping students process information better and through continued use become able to apply such strategies on their own. Furthermore, the teacher will find it very useful to teach the reading of science materials by a Directed Reading Lesson Plan when the occasion requires it. It pays off in increased understanding and it is rather an interesting way to teach!

ACTIVITIES AND QUESTIONS
TO PROMOTE LEARNING AND APPLICATION

1. What role *does* reading play in science work? Give some concrete examples, please.
2. How would you arrange to give positive feedback to science students?
3. Develop a science interest questionnaire and administer it to a number of students. (What did you find out about certain students that you did not know before?)

4. Characterize several science students as A: high ability, high interest; B: high ability, low interest; and so forth. Perhaps you could use the science interest questionnaire. How would you ascertain ability in science? What about latent ability.

5. Check the reading ability of students and compare that ability with the readability of the science texts they are using. Report lacunae. How do the hiatuses affect achievement? interest in science?

6. Rewrite some science materials so they will be readable by some of the poorer readers in a class. Try the material with these readers and report their reaction.

7. Write a lesson on teaching science vocabulary and teach it to some students who do not know the vocabulary items. (Did they enjoy it? Did it seem to be a worthwhile activity?

8. Get together with a science teacher or a pre-service science teacher and develop a plan for teaching the concepts and vocabulary in a unit of science, using Deck's Unit Teaching Plan. (For more details, see Deck's article in Hafner, 1974.)

9. Help a student make a science dictionary.

10. Try several of the many suggestions for the inductive study of roots and affixes with several kinds of students. Which kinds of students responded best? Why?

11. Find some students who are having some vocabulary difficulty in a science text. Develop a study sheet (and duplicate copies) for a section of the chapter that will soon be studied. Help the students go over the study sheets to nail down the pronunciation and work through the explanations before allowing them to take the sheets home for further study. Review and use Language Master Cards or techniques such as word-picture cards or part-whole comparison to nail down the words. (Report your success to members of your methods class.)

12. Help a student to learn and apply a technique such as summary writing, SQ3R, or note making. See Chapter 7 in order to brush up on techniques.

13. Do the reading-reasoning guides provided toward the end of the chapter. (Wherein lies their value?)

14. Select science reading material and write appropriate guides as follows: (1) literal, (2) internal interpretation, and (3) external interpretation. Try it out with appropriate students. Report results and reactions to colleagues or members of your methods class.

15. Using the same material or different material, write a cause and effect guide and try it out with appropriate students. Report results and reactions to class.

16. Write a comparison guide for suitable material. Try it out, etc.

17. Consult with a science teacher and write a Directed Reading Lesson (DRL) for a piece of science reading material. Teach the DRL to an appropriate group of students. Report results to your class and have a discussion on what you liked about the experience and how you would modify the present lesson or a future lesson which you would plan.

SUGGESTED ADDITIONAL READINGS

AUKERMAN, ROBERT C. *Reading in the Secondary Classroom.* New York: McGraw-Hill, 1972. Chapter 9.

HAFNER, LAWRENCE E. (Ed.). *Improving Reading in Middle and Secondary Schools.* New York: Macmillan, 1974. Section 10.

KNIGHT, DAVID W. and PAUL BETHUNE. "Science Words Students Know." In Lawrence E. Hafner (Ed.). *Improving Reading in Middle and Secondary Schools.* New York: Macmillan, 1974. Pp. 304–307.

MALLINSON, GEORGE G. "Reading in the Sciences: A Review of the Research." In James Laffey (Ed.). *Reading in the Content Areas.* Newark, Del.: International Reading Association, 1972. Pp. 127–52.

MOORE, ARNOLD J. "Science Instruction Materials for the Low-Ability Junior High-School Student." In Lawrence E. Hafner (Ed.). *Improving Reading in Middle and Secondary Schools.* New York: Macmillan, 1974. Pp. 312–20.

SHEPHERD, DAVID L. *Comprehensive High School Reading Methods.* Columbus, Ohio: Charles E. Merrill, 1973. Chapter 10.

SMITH, CARL B. "Reading in the Sciences." In James L. Laffey (Ed.). *Reading in the Content Areas.* Newark, Del.: International Reading Association, 1972. Pp. 153–76.

BIBLIOGRAPHY

ANDERSON, HAROLD S. "Science Interests of Junior High School Students." *Science Teacher.* (October, 1954), 15–18.

BYRAN, J. NED. *Science in the Junior High School.* Washington, D. C.: National Science Teachers Association, 1959.

DAUGHERTY, AILEEN, (Ed.). *Guide to the Teaching of Reading.* La Grange, Illinois: Lyons Township School Board, (n.d.).

DECK, RAY F. "Vocabulary Development to Improve Reading and Achievement in Science." In Lawrence E. Hafner (Ed.). *Improving Reading in Middle and Secondary Schools.* New York: Macmillan, 1974.

HAFNER, LAWRENCE E., and HAYDEN B. JOLLY. *Patterns of Teaching Reading in the Elementary School.* New York: Macmillan, 1972.

KOENKE, KARL. "Another Practical Note on Readability Formulas." *Journal of Reading.* 15 (December 1971), 206.

KOLB, HAVEN, R. D. IVEY, E. J. KORMONDY, V. LARSEN, E. M. PALMER, and B. WALLACE, plus N. L. HAYNES (Ed.). *Biological Science: An Ecological Approach.* (BSCS Green Version), Third Edition, Chicago: Rand McNally, 1973.

MOORE, ARNOLD J. "Science Instructional Materials for the Low-Ability Junior High School Student." In Lawrence E. Hafner (Ed.). *Improving Reading in Middle and Secondary Schools.* Second Edition. New York: Macmillan, 1974.

OXENHORN, JOSEPH, and MICHAEL N. IDELSON. *The Earth We Live On.* New York: Glove, 1968. Pp. 46–50.

WILLIAMS, DAVID. "Rewritten Science Materials and Reading Comprehension." *Journal of Educational Research. 61* (January 1968), 204–206.

CHAPTER 14

Teaching the Reading of English. I. Foundations and Strategies for Improving the Reading of Biography, Folk Literature, and Poetry

An English teacher is generally a well-educated person who is devoting his or her life to acquainting students with the content and form of literature, helping them improve their communication skills, and contributing to their liberal education. For years teachers have worked to develop the transmissive language arts—speaking and writing—but have neglected the receptive arts of listening and reading.

Judy Rich Lee, an English teacher and reading specialist, related to me several of the unhelpful attitudes and misconceptions of a miniscule minority of English teachers in years gone by. I will state them by questioning them:

1. Should all children learn at the same rate?
2. Do all children need what a given child needs?
3. Should the secondary English teacher be a "little" professor, spitting back to the youngsters what he or she got from a favorite professor?
4. Should English be boring?
5. Is not grammar the "all and end all" of English?
6. Should you not spend many hours trying to change the speech patterns of all students to NBC standard English or the Queen's English?
7. Can an intelligent English teacher state with a clear conscience that he or she is not responsible for improving students' ability to read?

Today hardly any English teacher would answer "yes" to any of these questions. Those answering "yes" and practicing accordingly would make it miserable and unprofitable for many students. How could anyone deny that a teacher to no small extent guides the thinking processes of students? Since reading is a thinking process, it seems clear that a good English teacher would take a very active role in helping students improve their reading skills. Further discussion of this matter is found in Hafner (1974, vii, viii, 275, 276).

VALUES OF LITERATURE

What Does Literature Include?

The reading and interpretation of literature is one of the more important facets of teaching English. Briefly stated, literature includes belles-lettres (fiction, poetry, drama, etc.) and journalistic writing having at least current social value: Hartig (1972) has given us an excellent discussion of literature as belles-lettres. I have taken the liberty of paraphrasing some of his main points:

1. A literary work is produced by the author for its own sake, and the artistic motive is primary.

2. Literary works tend to be complex in meaning, thereby providing the readers with an intellectual challenge.

3. Literature often contains universal values that go beyond interests of time and place.

4. Literature tends to deal with serious subjects.

The Role of Literature in Personal Development

Leary (1948) noted that literature plays a vital role in the lives of students if it helps them solve the problems encountered in day-to-day living. She further stated that since the student rather than the literature itself is the center of the literature program, the content of literature takes precedence over literary form.

Literature does open up to young people value systems, ideas, and practices at variance with their own. Reading also permits students to discover the world of the past and the present and to see that the world is a human one and therefore not all good nor all evil. Forays into literature allow people to view themselves and their problems a bit more objectively, too (Donelson and Haley, 1972).

Literature as a Help in Meeting Developmental Tasks. Havighurst (1946) offers direct help in explaining the relationship between developmental tasks and literature. In relating literature to life, Havighurst points out how literature can help the adolescent achieve the insight necessary for recognizing and solving the developmental task of becoming emotionally independent of one's parents. To solve this task one must attain enough self-sufficiency so that deep affection can be felt for one's parents without being entirely dependent on them in making decisions related to adult life. This task appears in some of the great pieces of literature: *King Lear*, Turgenev's *Fathers and Sons*, Galsworthy's *Forsyte Saga*, and Mann's *Buddenbrooks*. It can also be seen in books such as *Cheaper by the Dozen* and in the biographies of such people as Helen Keller, Jim Thorpe, and Glen Cunningham.

Havighurst further explains how literature helps solve this developmental task (1) by showing that all adolescents have the problem, (2) by portraying the problem sympathetically toward parents, so that the adolescent gets a well-balanced view of it, and (3) by depicting the stories of people who have made the break with their families and of those who have submitted and then showing the results of the different problem solutions.

Various types of literature can be used as aids in solving personal problems. We think of fiction, *Tom Sawyer* and *Moby Dick*, for example; drama, *Romeo and Juliet* and *West Side Story*, which could be taught together (for advanced students Ibsen and Chekhov can be explored): poetry, Frost's "The

Road Not Taken," Langston Hughes, "Life Aint No Golden Stair" and "I, Too, Sing America," and "Auto Wreck" by Karl Shapiro; biography, the lives of Ann Frank, Amelia Earhart, Madame Curie, Nathaniel Bowditch, and Helen Keller.

These kinds of literature objectively present problems and experiences that students have. Being more detached from this presentation, yet identifying with the problems, compared to one's own real problem allows the student to analyze and solve his or her problem, according to Dora Smith (1948). And there is no limit in country or time. The piece of literature that best conveys human and social values to a given reader or group of readers may come from any period or any country (Leary, 1948). Furthermore, literature has a role in fostering international relations. This topic has been ably discussed by Crowder (1971).

Bibliotherapy

We have in a sense been talking about a process called bibliotherapy, or using books for psychotherapy. Russell[1] (1970) and Russell and Shrodes in an earlier work synthesized a number of studies on bibliotherapy. The following discussion is based largely on their work.

The mentally healthy person can be characterized in three important ways: (1) he or she is adjusted to the group, (2) he or she understands and accepts himself or herself and others, and (3) he or she is prepared for living in the modern world, that is, ready for changes, aware of different sides, and able to attack and solve problems. The latter idea implies that the mentally healthy person is aware of problems and is tense enough (rather than complacent) to work on rectifying disturbing situations. Russell further states that one use of literature is to help the individual understand himself or herself and his or her associates and to wrestle with problems. Thus, reading may at times be a form of psychotherapy.

Identification is a mechanism of adjustment and is usually thought of as a basic part of bibliotherapy. When a person identifies with another person, he or she wants to be like that person.

Bibliotherapy Explained in Terms of Identification, Catharsis, and Insight. Identification: In *identification* one becomes someone in a story, poem, or drama or imagines that one is such a character or group. In this way feelings are released and one comes to a greater understanding of what impels one's behavior and what rationalizations one makes for behavior. If the character in the story is admired, the reader's self-esteem may be increased; or as a result of reducing the sense of difference from other people one's feelings of belonging may be augmented. Identification may also help one to understand better a parent or friend, have a more realistic understanding of limitations and strengths, and ameliorate guilt feelings from earlier difficulties with the parent or friend.

---

[1] Edited by Robert Ruddell.

Catharsis: Identification usually involves emotional catharsis. Therefore, one can express one's emotions vicariously because one feels one *is* the character read about. In putting oneself in the place of others one gradually understands the needs and aspirations not only of the people being read about— but also of oneself. Reading, then, may provide a tension release by allowing socially unacceptable urges to be gratified symbolically or through substituting motives approved by society. At another stage, seeing oneself in the behavior of the character and becoming aware of one's own motivations and needs represents a higher level of identification (Russell, 1970).

Value of Bibliotherapy. Careful analysis of a number of discussions of the values of bibliotherapy yields the following synthesis:

1. It may help a person to know himself or herself.

2. It may help a person to see that others have faced problems he or she is facing.

3. It may help a person to release tension through symbolic gratification.

4. It may help a person understand the humanness in himself or herself, and others.

5. It may help a person express feeling vicariously.

6. It may help a person plan, develop, and carry out a constructive solution to problems.

7. It may help a person understand different social groups and cultures.

8. It may allow a person to experience vicariously aspects of life in a non-threatening manner.

9. It may stimulate a person's imagination, broaden interests, and provide experiences upon which to draw in developing alternative solutions to problems.

10. It may help a person meet and do the developmental tasks necessary for attaining psychological and social maturity.

Research reported by Russell (1970) shows that bibliotherapy and other kinds of therapy such as art therapy, language therapy, and psychodrama, have positive effects on reading achievement and also on personal adjustment. Research analyzed by Lindeman and Kling (1968) reports more specifically the positive value of bibliotherapy for children in the elementary grades and middle grades and for adolescents. They also note its value for the gifted, the retarded reader, and the handicapped child. Therefore, I have developed the extensive annotated bibliography that follows.

SELECTIVE ANNOTATED BIBLIOGRAPHY OF BOOKS HAVING BIBLIOTHERAPEUTIC VALUE

Preadolescence

ARMSTRONG, WILLIAM H. *Sounder.* Harper, 1969. Illus. Trials and tribulations are mixed with good times in this bittersweet story of a black sharecropper who is not making it economically. Eventually he steals food to put on the family table but is put in jail. *Basic values/results of prejudice; empathy for people in distress.*

BLUME, JUDY. *Are You There, God? It's Me, Margaret.* Bradbury, 1970. A young girl discovers inchoate signs of puberty and takes her concerns to God in a series of conversations. *Problems of growing up.*

CHANDLER, EDNA W. *Almost Brothers.* Albert Whitman, 1971. Accurate depiction of rural Southwestern life today: the unemployment, government aid, polluting plant that provides jobs, and the diverse cultural backgrounds of the people. *Courage in the face of adversity.*

CHANDLER, EDNA W. *Charley Brave.* Albert Whitman, 1962. Shows how Charley and Jean, city children, win acceptance for themselves when their doctor father moves to the reservation to work in the hospital there. *Intergroup relations.*

DE ANGELI, MARGUERITE. *The Door in the Wall.* Doubleday, 1949. Illus. The bubonic plague strikes and cripples a ten-year-old child in medieval England. Triumph is the end of a long, courageous struggle. *Courage in the face of adversity.*

FENTON, HAROLD W. *Nat Love, Negro Cowboy.* Dodd, Mead, 1969. The exciting story of a real, black cowboy who earned his own way and broke broncos, roped and branded steers, and went on buffalo-hunting forays in the Wild West of the 1800s. *Dispelling stereotypes.*

FRIIS-BAASTAD, BABBIS. *Don't Take Teddy.* Charles Scribner. 1967. Little Mikkel has a big responsibility for his mentally retarded brother. The problems involved are finally resolved. *Responsibility and cooperation.*

HARNDEN, RUTH. *Runaway Raft.* Houghton Mifflin, 1968. Bart and Alec have not always been on best of terms, but learn to appreciate each other in a crisis fraught with danger. *Responsibility and cooperation.*

HASKINS, JAMES. *From Lew Alcindor to Kareem Abdul Jabbar.* Lothrop. 1972. The unusual story of the great basketball star from his early days as a lonely boy through his high school and college years to professional basketball Of his childhood Abdul said, "I was the large, economy-size child." He relates some of the problems he has encountered in being so tall—7 feet 2 inches—and black. *Conflict resolution in establishing identity.*

JENKINS, EMYL. *Greg Walker, News Photographer.* Albert Whitman, 1970. This illustrated story is by a person who has experience in teaching reading to boys whose conceptual achievements surpass their reading achievements. *Courage in the face of adversity.*

LAMPMAN, EVELYN SIBLEY. *The Year of the Small Shadow.* Harcourt, 1971. What is your heritage? Has anyone tried to deprive you of your identity? An Indian boy lives in a white community for a year and the people try to make him over. He resists these efforts. *Retaining one's identity.*

LATHAM, JEAN LEE. *Carry on, Mr. Bowditch.* Houghton, 1955. Nathaniel Bowditch is a preteen apprentice seaman. By dint of natural ability and hard study of mathematics, astronomy, and navigation, he rises to captain his own ship at age twenty. *Utilization of one's gifts.*

LESKOV, NIKOLAI. *The Wild Beast.* Funk and Wagnalls, 1968. Illus. Real meaning is given to Christmas by a conversion in Czarist Russia. *Basic values/meaning of Christianity.*

MILES, BETTY. *Save the Earth.* Knopf, 1974. Illus. What happens when greed and ignorance combine to rape land, air, and water? *Basic values/the results of greed and ignorance.*

NEIGOFF, MIKE. *Dive In.* Albert Whitman, 1965. This book is about competition swimming and should be of interest to the average child who cannot be a football or a baseball star. *How to get into the swim of things.*

NEIGOFF, MIKE. *Ski Run.* Albert Whitman, 1972. Rick gets to go on a ski vacation, but he discovers that temper control is the key to good skiing and successful friendships. *Use of patience in resolving emotional conflicts.*

NORRIS, GUNILLA B. *Lillan.* Antheneum, 1968. Illus. The eleven-year-old daughter of divorced parents eventually emerges from the turmoil to a new maturity. *Resolving emotional conflicts.*

PETRY, ANN. *Harriet Tubman: Conductor of the Underground Railroad.* Crowell, 1955. Harriet was a slave but she escaped with the help of a group of people and methods, collectively known as the Underground Railroad. She was instrumental in bringing 300 people out of slavery to freedom in the North. *Courage in the fight for freedom.*

TALBOT, CHARLENE JOY. *Thomas Takes Charge.* Lothrop, 1966. Two Puerto Rican youngsters are forced by the exigencies of life—desertion by father—to survive in the New York slums. They do it on their own. *Courage and ingenuity in the face of adversity.*

UCHIDA, YOSHIKO. *In-between Miya.* Scribner, 1967. Illus. Miya, daughter of the village priest, longs for things her father cannot give her. After a visit to Tokyo, she learns some of the real values of life; for example, that wealth does not mean happiness. *Basic values/ putting money into perspective.*

WHITE, E. B. *Charlotte's Web.* Dell, 1967. Wilbur the pig was destined to grace people's dinner tables—an eventuality low on his priority list—until Charlotte the spider spun life-saving messages to those who wanted to "ham" up the situation. *Compassion for the unfortunate.*

WHITE, E. B. *The Trumpet of the Swan.* Harper, 1970. Illus. Louis is a trumpeter swan that was born mute. After receiving a trumpet, Louis develops a way to communicate through music and makes friends with people. *Utilization of one's gifts.*

Early Adolescence

ALCOTT, LOUISA MAY. *Little Women.* World, 1969. Illus. A story of sisters, Amy, Jo, Meg, and Beth, drawn from the life of the author and her sisters. It relates the day-to-day interrelationships of family life, the search of each sister for fulfilment, and the joys and sorrows of growing up. *Basic values/search for identity and fulfillment.*

BEATTY, PATRICIA. *O the Red Rose Tree.* Morrow, 1972. Illus. Our thirteen-year-old heroine is the lively narrator of her adventures in the Northwest at the end of the last century. Her adventures are varied—a flood in Portland, a taste of Portland's "upper crust," and getting to know an Italian opera singer. *Courage in the face of diversity.*

BURCH, ROBERT. *Queenie Peavy.* Viking, 1966. Illus. Set in depression days. Queenie, a young teenage Georgia girl, is harrassed by people because her father is in prison. Queenie courageously fights back and develops an understanding of herself. *Overcoming poverty and showing courage in the face of perversity.*

CARPELAN, BO. *Bow Island: The Story of a Summer That Was Different.* Delacorte, 1971. Johan protects a retarded boy from the taunts of other children and thus learns how to cope with cruelty. *Family relationships/coping with cruelty.*

EAGLE, D. CHIEF. *Winter Count.* Golden Bell, 1968. Authentic sources provide a gripping tale about the Teton Sioux and their troubles with the uninvited, encroaching white people in the 1870s. *Basic values/adjusting to the effects of greed and larceny.*

FAST, HOWARD. *The Hessian.* Bantam. (n.d.) This American Revolution story tells how Puritans and Quakers wrestled with the grim realities of war. A young Hessian soldier, fighting for the British, is the object of a manhunt; goal: hanging. Throughout this novel run themes of religious freedom, justice, love, and the nonproductiveness of war. *Basic values/taking a stand for what one believes is right.*

FENTON, EDWARD. *A Matter of Miracles.* Holt, 1967. This story is related to the ancient art of puppeteering. Gino is an industrious thirteen-year-old boy who finds Sicily—a land of poverty and little work—to be somewhat frustrating. Sicily has its good points, though, for it is a place where miracles happen. *Vicarious escape.*

FRANK, ANNE. *The Diary of Anne Frank.* Washington Square Press, 1952. Relates the deep feelings and fears of a young Jewish teenager and her family as they hide from the Nazi terrorists during World War II. *Courage and love in the face of extreme, diabolical adversity.*

GAINES, ERNEST J. *The Autobiography of Miss Jane Pittman.* Dial, 1971. This fictional work tells of a black woman who experiences the Civil War and then lives a hundred years more to witness another emancipation of her people. Courage in the face of overwhelming adversity—man's inhumanity to man—characterizes this story. *Basic values/seeing your own troubles in perspective.*

HARRISON, DELORIS. *Journey All Alone.* Dial, 1971. A young girl growing up in Harlem discovers that it takes more than daydreams to change reality. *Problems in growing up black.*

HUNT, IRENE. *Across Five Aprils.* Follett, 1964. Divided loyalties are the theme of this Civil War story. Jethro and his brother live on an Illinois farm; Jethro is loyal to the Union, but his brother is a Rebel. In spite of this, Jethro loves his brother and also sympathizes with a deserter friend. *Resolving emotional conflicts.*

L'ENGLE, MADELEINE. *A Wrinkle in Time.* Ariel, 1962. A science fiction story of several teen agers who try to rescue a friend who has gotten himself into another world. *Far-out loyalty.*

LONDON, JACK. *White Fang.* Airmont, 1964. An animal—part dog, part wolf—battles the vicissitudes of its environment, including hostile people who make it vicious by cruel abuse. But in the last analysis it is transformed through the patience and affection of one person and is loyal to him. *Perseverance and loyalty.*

MCKAY, ROBERT. *Canary Red.* Meredith, 1968. A Teen-age "orphan" is thrown into conflict and turmoil when the father she did not know returns to her. She faces great obstacles as she tries to adjust to this situation and give him affection and trust. *Resolving emotional conflicts.*

MCSWIGAN, MARIE. *Snow Treasure.* Scholastic Book Services, 1942. Tells how Norwegian children sled nine million in gold past the Nazis and onto a waiting Norwegian freighter. A true story. *Responsibility and cooperation.*

NORRIS, FRANK. *The Octopus.* Bantam. (n.d.) The railroads encroach on nineteenth-century California wheat farmers and the latter struggle against them. *Facing inevitable change.*

SAROYAN, WILLIAM. *The Human Comedy.* Dell, 1966. Shows how a young boy is matured by his role as a telegraph messenger who is touched by the responses of people to various kinds of news in the telegrams he delivers. At the end he bears bad news to his parents about his brother's demise in battle. *Basic value/seeing human qualities in others.*

SCHECTER, BETTY. *The Peaceable Revolution.* Houghton, 1963. How have the great people coped with injustice? Through a type of revolution. But the only productive revolution is the nonviolent revolution we see in the lives of such people as Thoreau, Gandhi, and Martin Luther King, Jr. *Basic values/the soft answer.*

STEINBECK, JOHN. *The Red Pony.* Viking, 1965. A young boy, growing up on a California ranch, experiences the blatantly harsh realities of life in this story of the boy's love for a pony. *Basic values/courage in the face of adversity.*

VERNE, JULES. *Twenty Thousand Leagues Under the Sea.* Scribner, 1925. Verne looked into the future and imagined the submarine long before it was a reality. He fantasizes new underwater worlds that bring exciting adventure to the reader. *Vicarious escape.*

WEST, JESSAMYN. *The Friendly Persuasion.* Harcourt, 1956. This story of a Quaker family living in Indiana in the mid-1800s poignantly describes their views about peace and brotherhood and relates how they lived brotherhood in a moving crisis situation. *Basic values/brotherhood of man.*

Middle Adolescence

BARNWELL, ROBINSON. *Shadow on the Water.* McKay, 1967. Thirteen-year-old Cummie is overwhelmed by self-pity germinated by her parents who are on the brink of divorce. *Basic values/results of selfishness.*

BYARS, BETSY. *The Summer of the Swans.* Viking, 1970. Illus. Sara is a diffident, sensitive eighth grader whose life is complicated when she has to care for and protect her little retarded brother. Poignant, tender, and at times humorous. *Basic values/compassion and nurturance.*

CAUDILL, REBECCA. *The Far-off Land.* Viking, 1964. Young Ketty is on a boat headed for Tennessee. On her long trip she learns to accept hardship and fear but because of her Christian training she is opposed to the wide-spread hatred for the American native—the Indian. *Basic values/brotherhood of man in the matrix of love.*

CLEAVER, VERA, and BILL CLEAVER. *Where the Lilies Bloom.* Lippincott, 1969. The fourteen-year-old daughter in this poor Appalachian family that has lost its father takes the lead in courageous efforts to hold the family together. The efforts—including hiding their father's death to avert separation of the family—pays off and the family comes through all right. *Responsibility and cooperation.*

EYERLY, JEANNETTE. *Escape from Nowhere.* Lippincott, 1969. An oft told story of the child neglected by the money-grubbing father, who is seldom home, and the alcoholic mother. Result—the boy takes up smoking marijuana. The reader will become engrossed in this realistic account. *Basic values/results of serving Mammon.*

FAST, HOWARD. *Freedom Road.* Bantam. Story of an ex-slave's rise from illiteracy to Congress. This novel about race relations is honest and moving. *Race relations and struggle against adversity.*

FORMAN, JAMES. *The Traitors.* Farrar, 1968. A Bavarian pastor and his sons come to grips with the Nazi regime. *Basic values/faith in time of peril.*

HEMINGWAY, ERNEST. *The Old Man and the Sea.* Scribner, 1960. This story can be read on two levels—a great fishing story or the story of man's struggle against the forces of life. At the first level it is simple reading; at the second level, deep meanings must be probed as one introspects his soul. *Basic values/courage in the face of adversity; for what shall man struggle?*

HINTON, S. E. *The Outsiders,* 1968. Teenage gangs in New York battle each other and also society at large. The message is that self-understanding is the key to understanding and coping with the larger society. *Value of knowing oneself.*

KIDDELL, JOHN. *Euloowiree Walkabout.* Chilton, 1968. To what length will some teen-agers go to understand adults? Three Australian boys hike 900 miles to get a better understanding of grownups. *Developing empathy through outreach and caring.*

KRUMGOLD, JOSEPH. *Henry 3.* Atheneum, 1967. Henry is being intelligent and having trouble getting along in the world until he meets someone hated even more than he is. *Perspective into one's situation through comparison with another's.*

LEE, MILDRED. *The Skating Rink.* Seabury, 1969. This is a fine story of a fifteen-year-old boy who retreats within himself because of a self-concept of inadequacy. The perceptive owner of a skating rink has insight into his difficulties and helps him escape the circular failure pattern in which he was engulfed. *Problems of growing up.*

MADDOCK, REGINALD. *Thin Ice.* Little, Brown, 1971. A boy struggling to grow up gets in with a gang of boys when he moves to a new school. He gradually develops his own individuality, seeing himself in relation to (and yet apart from) his family, and learns how to stand up for his rights in the gang. *Problems of growing up; developing one's own identity.*

MCKAY, ROBERT. *Canary Red.* Meredith, 1968. How does a daughter adapt to a father who has been a convict who raised canaries while in prison and became known for new breeds of canaries? *Basic values/loving the outcast.*

ORWELL, GEORGE. *Animal Farm.* Harcourt, 1946. Can humanity cope with the demands of history? This brilliant satire depicts an allegory in which gluttonous, avaricious, domesticated farm animals try to set up a Utopian society after chasing the owner off the farm. The result is a totalitarian state. The story illuminates the range of human experience. *Basic values/avarice as a cause of confusion and destruction.*

PEYTON, K. M. *Pennington's LAST TERM.* Crowell, 1971. Pennington is sixteen and in his last term at school. His teachers are happy about that because he is not turned on by school and is a constant troublemaker—long-haired and lazy. *Responsibility.*

ROBINSON, VERONICA. *David in Silence.* Lippincott. 1965. David spends most of his life among the deaf. When he moves to a new neighborhood among hearing people, he has to convince the boys he can be part of their world. *Adapting to the exigencies of life.*

SHIRER, WILLIAM L. *The Rise and Fall of Adolf Hitler.* Simon and Schuster, 1960. An account of the conditions in Germany that allowed Hitler to take over Germany and institute his diabolical plans. It relates the heyday of Nazism as Hitler executes his plans. And finally we see the great fall of Hitler, his minions, and his legions. *Basic values/ results of hubris and its ensuing totalitarianism.*

STEINBECK, JOHN. *Of Mice and Men.* Viking, 1963. This is the story of every man's desire for his own land. Two rootless men till the soil that belongs to others. The harvest they reap does not belong to them. Although an earthy book, it tries to show that man is responsible for his fellow man since all men are brothers. *Responsibility and cooperation as aspects of brotherhood.*

STOLZ, MARY. *Who Wants Music on Monday?* Harper, 1963. An individualist who clearly knows her values is in conflict with a conservative family of conformists, her own family. One of the problems she has to cope with is her capricious younger sister who is wild about boys. The meanness of the "mean"; adapting to the average.

TWAIN, MARK. *The Adventures of Huckleberry Finn.* Bantam, 1971. A depiction of life in the Mississippi Valley, which judges many lasting weaknesses of human nature including the resulting social injustices. It is a novel of escape for Huck from his genteel censors and from his drunken father; for Jim from slavery; and for the reader from whatever. *Basic values/coping with injustices resulting from human weaknesses.*

VIPONT, ELFRIDA. *The Lark on the Wing.* Holt, Rinehart, and Winston, 1970. Carnegie Medal winner. Life takes on meaning for motherless and unhappy Kit as she visits her aunts and eventually discovers that music will be her joy and "salvation." *Meaning through love and music.*

Late Adolescence

ALDRICH, BESS STREETER. *A Lantern in Her Hand.* Appleton, 1928. After a rugged wagon train trip to Nebraska, young Abby Deal and her husband build a home. Abby is courageous and strong, and through troubled times she holds her family together. *Courage in the face of adversity.*

BAINTON, ROLAND H. *Here I Stand: A Life of Martin Luther.* Mentor, 1955. Martin Luther, a priest in the Catholic Church and a Bible scholar, rediscovers justification by faith. Accused of heresy and threatened with excommunication, Luther stands by his position against abuses in the medieval Catholic Church and his great theological discovery of sola fide (by faith alone). This is an excellent portrayal of Luther and his role in history. *Basic values/central, final meaning of life.*

BONHOEFFER, DIETRICH. *I Loved This People.* John Knox Press, 1965. Bonhoeffer was a German Lutheran pastor who spent many years in Nazi prisons. Only a few days before the Americans liberated the prison, he was executed. In the main part of the book we find a collection of brief mature essays on such topics as "Who Stands Firm?" "Concerning Stupidity," "Contempt of Man," "Some Beliefs About God's Activity in History," and "Present and Future." It is almost trite to say these essays are "thought provoking"; "earthshaking" might be more appropriate. Perhaps this work could be read in conjunction with *A Prisoner and Yet . . .* by Corrie Ten Boom. *Basic values/perfect love casts out fear.*

COX, WILLIAM. *Chicano Cruz.* Bantam. A young Mexican-American boy works his way into major league baseball in this lively action story and develops much pride in and understanding of his heritage: "I am proud I am a Chicano." *Identifying with one's culture.*

CRICHTON, ROBERT. *Secret of Santa Vittoria.* Simon and Schuster, 1966. Dell paperback. Sheer madness erupts in an Italian town when the townspeople try to hide what is dear to them—millions of bottles of wine—from the encroaching Nazi troops. Many hilarious scenes as characters such as Scheer, von Prum, and Traub try to match wits with the likes of Bombolini, Fabio, and Tufa. *Vicarious escape.*

DOSTOEVSKY, FYODOR. *The Brothers Karamazov.* Bantam. This penetrating novel explores good and evil. The story centers around Fyodor Karamazov, a sensual Falstaff kind of person. Dostoevsky delineates the effect of the murder of Karamazov on his four sons, who are kinds of lost souls who seek to redeem themselves. In the fate of these brothers every person sees the fate of humanity In this novel we also see Dostoevsky's belief that humanity enters salvation only after much suffering and through the merits of Christ. The "working out" of salvation comes through love, not through force of intellect. *Basic values/central, final meaning of life.*

FAIRBAIRN, ANN. *Five Smooth Stones.* Bantam. This story of a man in quest of dignity and love moves rapidly from a ghetto in New Orleans where a young black struggles for a better life. He later returns to the South to help in the fight for human rights. *Intergroup relations; human rights.*

FUKEI, ARLENE. *East to Freedom.* Westminster, 1964. It is 1948 and the Communists are on the move in their takeover of China. How do a schoolgirl and her fiancé react to the crises brought about by the political and social upheaval? *Courage in the face of adversity.*

GREENE, GRAHAM. *The Power and the Glory.* Bantam. A reconstituted Mexican government in the 1930s is persecuting religious leaders. All the leaders except one have either been wiped out or have chosen to recant their beliefs. The one remaining priest escapes and lives the secular life until he realizes he must return as a spiritual leader; this decision results in his death *Courage in the face of adversity.*

HOLLAND, ISABELLE. *Cecily.* Lippincott, 1967. Cecily is rotund and ugly, a square peg in the round hole known as a British boarding school. But she helps her headmistress's love affair with a Rhodes scholar. *Problems of growing up.*

KOSINSKI, JERZY. *The Painted Bird.* Bantam. A small boy is separated from his parents during World War II and spends his time wandering from village to village and witnessing many horrors. This book portrays the Nazi mentality so that one should be able to see it in other places at other times. *Basic values/results of the drift and separation from God.*

LESSING, DORIS. *The Summer Before the Dark.* Bantam, 1974. This story recounts three months in the life of a middle-aged woman who separates from her husband and children to "go it on her own." She goes to work for an international organization, but a number of physical and mental crises leave her scarred. She emerges, however, with a new outlook that enables her to come to grips both with her family and with middle age. *Facing inevitable change.*

LIPSYTE, ROBERT. *The Contender.* Bantam. Sensitively portrays the struggle of a Harlem boy to attain manhood. *Problems of growing up black.*

MCCULLERS, CARSON. *The Heart Is a Lonely Hunter.* Houghton-Mifflin, 1940. The setting of this novel by a young Georgia woman is a small southern town. John Singer, the chief character, loses his only friend, another mute, who is committed to a mental hospital. Singer then becomes the "confidante" for an odd array of some of the town's loneliest citizens. *Pathos of loneliness.*

PLATH, SYLVIA. *The Bell Jar.* Bantam. Esther Greenwood is a nineteen-year-old guest editor for a New York fashion magazine. At first she dreams of a happy life but her sense of reality is severly shaken by the tense relationships with her mother and with the men she meets. The reader is drawn into the thoughts and feelings of a sympathetic heroine. *Resolving emotional conflicts.*

SCHWARZ-BART, ANDRE. *A Woman Named Solitude.* Bantam. A child named Solitude is born on a slave ship bound for the New World. In spite of her ensuing slave life with its degredation she retains her dignity. *Retaining sanity in an aura of stupidity and avarice.*

SHULMAN, ALIX KATES. *Memoirs of an Ex-Prom Queen.* Knopf, 1972. We see Sasha Davis's reaction to the message to middle-class whites: be beautiful, marry young, and produce beautiful children. But then Sasha rethinks middle-class values, especially the dream of Mr. Right and the validity of Dr. Spock's dicta. *Basic values/intelligence versus unchallenged custom.*

TEN BOOM, CORRIE. *A Prisoner and Yet . . .* Pyramid, 1971. Corrie Ten Boom, her father, and her sister risk death at the hands of Nazis by providing a shelter for refugees. Corrie, her sister, and father are placed in a concentration camp. The father soon dies. Corrie and Betsie suffer terribly; however, they continue to minister to one another and to others of their trust in Christ. Betsie follows her father home and Corrie survives to carry on her ministry for many years. (A true story.) *Basic values/the central, final meaning of life.*

TRUMBO, DALTON. *Johnny Got His Gun.* Bantam. This is a timely novel that strongly protests against war. It is about a 19-year-old World War I veteran whose only "limb" is his head. He bangs out messages with his head, pleading to be taken out of his hospital room so that people can see the stupidity of Every War. *Vanity of avarice and hate.*

VILLASEÑOR, EDMUND. *Macho.* Bantam. Roberto, the son of a poverty-stricken Mexican family, gets a job in the states as a migrant worker. We see the exploitation of the Chicano field workers as well as Chavez's attempts to improve their plight. As a result of the years of grueling labor Roberto matures; upon his return to his homeland, he sees everything there from a different point of view. *Problems of growing up Chicano.*

Late Adolescence and Adult

BALDWIN, JAMES. *Go Tell It on the Mountain.* Dial, 1963. Harlem is the setting for a family's striving to lead a pure life even though encompassed by sin. Adolescent John hated his father, Gabriel, a lecherous man who pretended to be pious. John struggled with sin and fought his family's attempt to convert him, even as he vainly attempted to be accepted by his father. Confusion, subjugation, and despair marked the lives of these black people from slavery days to the present ghetto existence. *Basic values/struggle against spiritual, psychological, physical, and economic bondage and degredation.*

BALDWIN, JAMES. *If Beale Street Could Talk.* Dial, 1974. Relates the story of two young people, Tish and Fonny. The latter is a young sculptor who is the father of Tish's unborn child. Fonny is imprisoned for a crime he did not commit, yet Tish endures because of her hope and her loyalty to Fonny. *Loyalty and hope in the face of adversity.*

BENNETT, JACK. *Mister Fisherman.* Little, Brown, 1965. When do people of different races have to come to grips with their identity and their racial prejudices? When they are drifting alone in the ocean in one place. A rich boy and his black fishing guide find themselves in that situation. *Coming to grips with the results of racial prejudice.*

BRADFORD, RICHARD. *Red Sky at Morning.* Lippincott, 1968. Josh's Yankee father sends him and his Southern belle mother to New Mexico during World War II. Josh has to get used to a new town and also care for his alcoholic mother. The result is a reassessment of who he is and what life is about. *Problems of growing up and coping with adversity.*

COSTAIN, THOMAS B. *The Silver Chalice.* Doubleday, 1954. Legends that came into being after the death of Jesus Christ focus on Basil the artist who made the chalice used during the Lord's Supper. Much of the story is devoted to Basil's upbringing by a nobleman, his subsequent ouster upon the death of his father, his development as an artist, and his travels that eventually take him to the Holy Land. *Courage in the face of adversity and utilization of one's gifts.*

DODSON, KENNETH. *Away All Boats.* Little, Brown, 1954. Based on actual naval operations in the Pacific theatre during World War II, this fictional story gives the reader a realistic idea of the herculean task performed by the U.S. Navy during that global war. *Dedication to a cause.*

DOSTOEVSKY, FYODOR. *Crime and Punishment.* Bantam. This is a psychological novel that delves into the multiple, confused motivations of humanity and reflects the author's view that all of us are sinners who need redemption. Raskolnikov, the main character, feels that he, as a superior person, is above the ordinary laws and moral standards and therefore tries to justify his murder of an inferior person. After a psychological cat-and-mouse game with a first-rate detective, Roskolnikov finds himself disgusted with his life of lying and fear. Sonia, a prostitute who leads an evil life trying to help others, makes him see how false his pretensions are. In the novel we see the difference between morality and respectability. One is reminded of Proverbs 16:18: "Pride goeth before destruction and an haughty spirit before a fall." *Basic values/value of humility and the nature of morality.*

DOSTOEVSKY, FYODOR. *The Idiot.* Bantam. In this novel the author contrasts (and shows the conflict between) an ideal Christian and a society out of tune with Christian values. *Basic values/the nature of Christianity.*

DU MAURIER, DAPHNE. *Rebecca.* Doubleday, 1948: Rebecca was a selfish, lovely woman overcome by pride. In the story she is dead. In a mysterious way she continues to exert a weird influence over the Manderley estate, only narrowly failing to ruin her husband's second marriage. Her real character gradually unfolds as the story progresses. *Danger of hubris.*

DUTTON, MARY. *Thorpe.* World, 1967. Miss Thorpe is a Southern girl to whom the prejudice against the black is illogical and not understandable. *Paradox of prejudice in a world that claims to know what it is doing.* (Therapeutic if the reader makes the correct choices.)

ERDMAN, LOULA GRACE. *Another Spring.* Dodd, 1966. Divided loyalties among rich Missouri farm families during the War Between the States is the focus of this story. *Insight into the roots of and results of prejudice.*

FLAUBERT, GUSTAVE. Madame Bovary. Bantam, 1959. Emma Roualt is a talented woman who marries Charles Bovary, a pedestrian physician. Life with Charles bores her because it does not bring the excitement and fulfillment she desires. Emma immerses herself in the study of music, art, and languages, but does not find them fulfilling. Two liaisons with lovers bring her reprieve from a (to her) banal existence. When her creditor forecloses and she is threatened with the loss of her lover and the ruin of her dull, faithful husband Charles, she steals poison and puts an end to her life. *Degradation and denouement of a dallying dame.*

GAINHAM, SARAH. *Night Falls on the City.* Holt, 1967. The engrossing tale of Viennese life during the second global conflict as the citizens waited for the Germans to move in, and also during the occupation. *Courage in the face of adversity.*

GREEN, HANNAH. *I Never Promised You a Rosegarden.* Holt, 1964. A mentally ill girl is committed to a mental hospital and develops a perception of beauty and a feeling for others. *Growth of beauty and empathy when nurtured.*

GREENBERG, JOANNE. *In This Sign.* Holt, 1970. Deaf people have a difficult time getting along in the hearing world. Their isolation and frustration can be seen in this poignant novel. *Understanding the plight of others leading to empathy for them.*

HALEY, ALEX (ed.). *The Autobiography of Malcolm X.* Grove Press, 1966. This work should be read by everyone—particulary self-righteous and bigoted people—in order to help them understand the roots—terror, injustice and poverty—of Malcolm X's quest for social justice, humanity to humankind, and harmony among peoples. *Empathy for the downtrodden.*

HALLIBURTON, WARREN J., and ERNEST KAISER. *Harlem: A History of Broken Dreams.* Doubleday/Zenith, 1974. Illus. This book is a history of Harlem from the 1700s onward. It covers such movements as the Harlem Renaissance, the Garvey Movement, and the leadership of Malcolm X and Adam Clayton Powell. *Genesis of the broken dream.*

HANSBERRY, LORRAINE. *A Raisin in the Sun.* New American Library, 1961. This is the emotionally laden drama of Walter Lee Younger, a young black husband in the Chicago ghetto, who is bitter about his lack of power and position His mother makes a substantial down payment on a house with part of the $10,000 insurance check she receives. Walter squanders the remaining $6,500 in a deal that goes awry. Black pride is put to a severe test as Walter is tempted to sell out to the Man for a large sum of money *Intergroup relations and the quest for identity and acceptance as human beings.*

HARRISON, EDDIE, and ALFRED PRATHER. *No Time for Dying.* Prentice-Hall, 1973. Eddie Harrison is imprisoned for murder, but is rehabilitated and pardoned. Although unemployed and a high-school drop out, he finally finds an unusual route to respectability. Eddie eschews a life of crime; it is this act coupled with his abiding belief in the judicial system that is his "salvation." (A true story.) *Regeneration and renewed faith in long-awaited justice for all as keys to renewal.*

HEINLEIN, ROBERT A. *Orphans of the Sky.* New American Library, 1963. Hugh Hoyland is a fledgling scientist aboard a five-mile-long space capsule, which to the inhabitants is the universe. They have been aboard it for several generations and are slowly spinning through interstellar space, but they do not think that there is space outside the ship. Hugh's curiosity takes him up hundreds of stories to the weightless regions, the forbidden land of the muties (mutants), and eventually he and two muties find and enter the forbidden sanctuary marked Control Room, and find long-lost scientific journals and the first captain's log. Hugh studies these papers and tries to complete the voyage begun hundreds of years before. *Value of knowing where you have come from, what you are doing here, and where you are going.*

HESSE, HERMANN. *Beneath the Wheel.* Bantam. This a spiritual autobiography that attacks an educational system that nourishes intellect and ambition while neglecting emotion, soul, and instinct. *Basic values/value of nourishing feelings and spiritual aspects of man.*

HESSE, HERMAN. *Narcissus and Goldmund.* Bantam. Called by some his greatest novel. Hesse deals with themes such as freedom and order, nature and humanity. These dualities in existence are characterized in the sculptor Goldmund who finds after he leaves a medieval cloister and his teacher Narcissus that humans must not just survive but come to experience and develop a full meaningful life through expanding their capacities. *Developing one's gifts.*

HUGO, VICTOR. *Les Miserables.* Premier World Classics. Jean Valjean received a long prison sentence for stealing a loaf of bread. He escaped and began to rehabilitate himself by serving humankind. A detective, Javert, gets on his trail and tracks him relentlessly. With Javert's change of feelings and suicide Jean is a free man, and the people learn of his kindness and elevated character in spite of his early foible. *Courage and kindness in the face of social inequity.*

KELLEY, WILLIAM N. *Dem.* Macmillan, 1969. Dem refers to white Americans controlled and deluded by fantasies. How they react to encounters with blacks and the resultant suffering amounts to a "put on" of white people and their ways. In this book the blacks are nice and reasonable and do nothing wrong unless provoked. *Intergroup relations.*

KEYES, DANIEL. *Flowers for Algernon.* Harcourt, 1966. Bantam. A fascinating, poignant story of Charley's meteoric rise from the world of mental retardation to genius and love and then back to his former state. *Seeing human qualities in others.*

KOESTLER, ARTHUR. *Darkness at Noon.* Bantam. The Moscow Trials of the 1930s are the source of this novel, which shows the effects of a totalitarian philosophy. Rubashov, a member of the government, is arrested for crimes of which he is innocent. He and his captors explore the meaning of justice and the possibility of its existence in a totalitarian state. "The Party denied the free will of the individual—and at the same time it exacted his willing sacrifice." There was a "mistake in the system; perhaps it lay in the precept . . . that the end justifies the means." A horrible, but fairly predictable ending. *Results of totalitarianism, with a concomitant appreciation for freedom.*

LEWITON, MINA. *Young Girl Going Out the Door.* Delacorte, 1969. The heroine of this story has much going for her. Does she choose marriage over independence and a career? *Basic decisions at the crossroads of life.*

MICHAILOVSKAY, KIRA A. *My Name Is Asya.* McGraw-Hill, 1966. Asya's personality emerges as she carries out her job as an Intourist guide. She sees and is involved in the problems of getting along with coworkers and of making the best of seemingly inevitable strife among office workers scrambling for status. *Insights into results of hubris versus humility.*

MITCHELL, GEORGE. *I'm Somebody Important: Young Black Voices from Rural Georgia.* University of Illinois Press, 1973. This compilation allows the reader to "get to know in human terms some of the victims of America's great social ills of racism and poverty." *Struggle to grasp a chimerical freedom.*

PASCAL, BLAISE. *Pensees.* Panthon, 1965. An explanation of the Christian religion directed to the free thinkers of the seventeenth century—and still applicable today—who believed they possessed the truth. Argues that humanity left to its ratiocination is weak and that the doctrine of Vicarious Atonement is the only thing that brings meaning to human life. *Basic values/central, final meaning of life.*

ROSTAND, EDMOND. *Cyrano de Bergerac.* Bantam. Cyrano was a real person who lived in seventeenth century France. As recreated in Rostand's play, he is the "most"—in swordsmanship, wit, and length of proboscis. Those who make fun of the latter appendage succumb to a torrent of clever invective and sword play. In love with Roxane, his cousin, he fears courting her because of his nose. Cyrano supplies Christian—a good-looking, obtuse fellow Guardsman—with the poetic lines needed to court Roxane. He also writes love letters to Roxane, signing Christian's name. He has the opportunity to note Roxane's reactions; therefore, Cyrano knows she loves *his* mind and soul. Christian is killed in battle. In their old age Roxane accidentally discovers that her real lover all along was Cyrano. *Virtue, vocabulary, and valor over vacuity.*

SMITH, LILLIAN. *Killers of the Dream, Revised.* Anchor Books, 1963. This book is an autobiography of an intelligent, compassionate Southern woman and her perceptive analysis of the squelching of human rights and dignity through greed, ignorance, and a horrible misinterpretation of the Bible and Christianity. Finally it portrays the awakening and cleansing of the repressed, contaminated conscience of a few people and the dawning of a new day of rationality and love. *A new dawn for the repressed.*

SOLZHENITSYN, ALEXSANDR. *One Day in the Life of Ivan Denisovich.* Praeger, 1963. This Nobel Prize winner describes a day in the life of a prisoner in a Siberian prison camp—and almost unbelievable human made hell. This story actually portrays a day in the life of Solzhenitsyn who once was such a prisoner. This is a scathing indictment of the Communist totalitarianism and tryanny endemic in the Soviet world. Look about you. *Basic values/results of totalitarianism.*

SPEARE, ELIZABETH GEORGE. *The Bronze Bow.* Houghton, 1961. Daniel and his sister Leah are overcome by the weaknesses of hatred and fear, respectively. An encounter with Jesus opens up saner vistas. *Value of love and courage and ways of obtaining them.*

TOLSTOY, LEO. *Anna Karenina.* Bantam. Anna Karenina's world is a segment of nineteenth-century Russia. Anna and Vronsky are overwhelmed by love, but have no moral principles to guide them. She fails to reconcile the demands of society and her personal desire to achieve happiness. The result is tragic. *Passion is no substitute for rectitude; also humble, practical examples of social reform.*

TURGENEV, IVAN. *Fathers and Sons.* Bantam. The age-old story of differing points of view between parents and children and the conflicts that result. The novel is more about personal relationships than social issues. Turgenev is sympathetic to both generations. *Developing independence from parents.*

URIS, LEON. *Mila 18.* Bantam. The Warsaw Jews in World War II organized a resistance movement against the Nazis. Its command post was known as Mila 18. This story relates the work of a small group of Jews who, knowing they will die, battle the entire German Army with fists and homemade weapons. *Courage in the face of perversity.*

WERSBA, BARBARA. *Run Softly, Go Fast.* Antheneum, 1970. A reading of the diary of nineteen-year-old Dave Marks shows a frustrated young man who is trying to resolve his cyclic love-hate relationships with his father. *Resolving emotional conflicts.*

WILDER, THORNTON. *The Bridge of San Luis Rey.* Washington Square Press, 1927. Pursues the meaning and intention of a catastrophe that happened to five travelers who were gathered on the finest bridge in all Peru. Should be read in conjunction with the reading of "Ecclesiastes" in the Bible. *Basic values/the meaning of life.*

READING LITERATURE

Some people say that teaching literature and teaching reading should be two different tasks. I cannot wholly agree with that. One does not teach reading in just nonliterary selections and then hope for some kind of automatic transfer or application to literary selections. When there are generalizations or identical elements that can be transferred, transfer may take place if someone has taught for transfer.

I believe that after a certain point the person who teaches reading skills and the literature teacher are one and the same person. If not, we may have clashes among groups and a failure to teach for comprehension and appreciation of literature.

In teaching literature one deals with four major relationships that run through literature: humans and deity, humans and other humans, humans and the natural world, and humanity and itself (Burton, 1969). For this reason the foregoing annotated bibliography of books of therapeutic value is at once a bibliography of excellent literature and vice versa.

What Literary Writing Is Like

Shepherd (1973) points out that literary writing is "discursive and imaginative and tends to be descriptive and narrative." Factual data are not given or explained as is done in technical writing. In fact, literature contains little technical vocabulary—although we find some in such areas as science fiction and in some works about artists such as *Autobiography of Benvenuto Cellini* and Costain's fictional Basil in *The Silver Chalice.*

Importance of Reading Skills and of Teaching Them Directly

Axelrod (1946) states that reading skills, both the literal and the analytic, interpretive, evaluative skills, are necessary in all areas of life, are hard to teach and to learn, and will not be learned if only taught incidentally. He further notes that if the student is to learn to do the higher level reading he or she must be taught it intensively and directly and as an end in itself.

The Specialized Skills in Reading Literature

I generally shun long lists of anything. However, I would like to list literature reading skills by skills more or less specific to types of literature or reading material. Many of the general reading skills discussed in an earlier chapter apply to literature reading.

Novels and Short Stories

1. Reading to note the plot.
2. Reading to note characterization and devices used to attain it.
3. Summarizing the main idea in a situation or the gist of the author's thought.
4. Reading for evidence of change in basic character of a person and/or transient changes.
5. Noting development and function of scenes.
6. Noting development and function of settings.
7. Understanding the significance of the work.
8. Feeling, noting, and applying therapeutic insights where desirable and/or possible.

Biographies and autobiographies

1. Checking authenticity of information.
2. Noting the historical elements in a biography and differentiating it from anecdotal information.
3. Noting difference between information in a biography, an autobiography, and posthumously discovered letters and diaries.

Poetry

1. Noting purposes of particular poems.
2. Noting style of a poem.
3. Recognizing and overcoming barriers to enjoyment of poetry such as difficult structure, unfamiliar figurative expressions, and lack of informational background.
4. Using such strategies as the following to overcome the barriers: noting subject and verb; shuffling parts of inverted sentences; discussing figures of speech; developing information background through study of mythology, history, author's life, and the like; improving word-recognition skills, directing study of meaning and affective relationships.

Drama

1. Developing the setting of the plot.
2. Recognizing implied descriptions and actions.

Newspapers

1. Discovering the types of content in newspapers.
2. Learning the problems in reporter's developing accurate accounts: time factors, lack of expertise, capsule writing, and the like.
3. Learning how to be selective in reading: which section(s)? which article(s)?; read headlines and first paragraph; reading the best features and columns.
4. Testing the truth in newspapers. Doublecheck statements against authoritative sources; note assumptions of writer and general bias of the newspaper; look for logical fallacies of reasoning. (Strategies for developing these skills are developed in the chapter on comprehension and the one on social studies, but should be emphasized by the English teacher also.)

Magazines

1. (See the points regarding newspapers.)

2. Noting bias of magazines: NOW in some women's magazines; male chauvinism in some men's magazines; sensationalism.

3. (See the points regarding reading of short stories.)

Essays

1. Noting education and background of the writer in order to help determine biases.

2. Noting the purpose of the writer: to inform, entertain, or persuade the reader.

3. Testing the truth in essays. (See 4 under Newspapers.)

4. Skimming or overviewing to get the gist or broad outline.

5. Determining the pattern of exposition: definition, cause-effect, analysis, compare and contrast, analogy, chronology, dialogue.

6. Reading carefully and rereading where necessary to develop cognitive relationships and thus full meaning.

READING BIOGRAPHIES AND AUTOBIOGRAPHIES

A biography is a narrative about the life of a person. An autobiography is one that a person writes about himself or herself (*autos*). The most famous person in history had four chief biographers. Such people as Cellini, Franklin, Henry Adams, Gosse, and Wiener have written well-known autobiographies. Cellini's autobiography is fascinating because he doubtessly has embellished some facts. The other people mentioned wrote interesting and informative works.

Because of our concern with reading and teaching reading skills, we note with interest autobiographical notes that endorse reading as a pleasurable and profitable pastime. R. G. Collingwood, the eminent British philosopher, tells of his mixed feelings of excitement and discouragement upon first encountering (at age eight) Kant's *Theory of Ethics*. Another emotion was that the contents of the book "were somehow some of my business: a matter personal to myself, or rather to some future self of my own." This kind of experience is probably fairly common among people who become well educated and make reading a lifetime habit.

Some First-rate Autobiographies

Benvenuto Cellini, whose life spanned the first seven decades of the sixteenth century, was a multitalented artist-engineer-soldier who was apprenticed to a Florentine goldsmith at age fifteen. He was a spirited man, ready to fight at less than a moment's notice. He had to flee to Rome because of a duel. He received commissions from Clement VII and from King Francis I of France for a number of works. The adolescent boy will be intrigued especially by the skill with which Cellini commanded a battery of artillery in the defense of a hilltop castle. He was imprisoned for a long time and underwent some mystical experiences. Cellini was a rather self-centered person, albeit a fascinating, talented sort of rogue. In addition to being a superb goldsmith, Cellini was an excellent sculptor and even wrote a treatise on the *cire perdue* (lost wax) method of sculpting.

The Autobiography of Benjamin Franklin relates the life of one of our finest minds—a person who combined practicality with book learning. (This should not come as a surprise, for book learning is eminently practical when applied rather than shunned or scoffed at. Would that more teachers, technicians, and artisans had more and better book learning.) At a tender age Franklin would buy books such as *Pilgrim's Progress*, Defoe's *An Essay on Projects*, and Cotton Mather's *Essays to Do Good*. His father noted his bookish inclinations and decided to make a printer out of him. He soon became an author and publisher, developing the *Pennsylvania Gazette* into one of the best papers of colonial times. Franklin also became a civic leader, scientist, inventor, and statesman. His work in science and inventing was not the result of a tinkerer who shunned books; it was the result of a prepared mind! As a boy and young man, he had taught himself the basic principles of algebra, geometry, navigation, the natural sciences, and the physical sciences. He was not a Babbitt.

To arouse interest in biographies and autobiographies we can make them available, prepare some vignettes such as the two you just read on Cellini and Franklin, present skits based on such works, schedule movies based on the lives of famous people, develop pageants in which these individuals have prominent parts or are the focus of the theme, develop bookfairs in which certain individuals are featured, allow reports to be made, publish in a class or school newspaper reports, vignettes, and the like of autobiographies and biographies, and make them part of resource and teaching units on historical themes.

Autobiographical Notes

In addition to full-blown biographies and autobiographies there exist autobiographical excerpts. David Russell (1970) includes a number of these excerpts in the second chapter of his book. In these notes we learn about such matters as the dynamics of reading, the influence of people who read to authors when the authors were children, the influence of books read and of travel, reading as imaginative response, and the like.

Robert Louis Stevenson credited Kate Greenaway's book on childhood verses as the inspiration for his writing about his own childhood in *A Child's Garden of Verses*. Robert Heinlein, science fiction writer, attributes his interest in science fiction to the stories of Jules Verne and H. G. Wells and stated that when he grew up he tried to emulate them.

Carl Van Doren credits reading with general utilitarian values. In *Three Worlds* he lauds reading by saying he could not remember when he did not read and that he read hours a day. His life on the farm did not prove to be a hardship when he moved to the city because of the vicarious experiences he acquired through reading. "Books," he said, "had enlarged the village."

Russell also speaks of the whole world being changed through literature. One comes across an idea that has been vaguely formed in one's mind, but now one comes across it in a clearly limned and integrated form. This idea may then become a life-long influence. The idea is so tremendous, Russell says, that one must continue to explore and analyze it for a long time. He draws on the writings of Christopher Morley, William Cobbett, C. S. Lewis, H. L. Mencken, and Carl Van Doren to illustrate his point.

Illustrative Lesson for the Teaching of Biography

Perhaps secondary teachers are well acquainted with teaching biography. At any rate, the following is a lesson designed for use in middle school, which could be adapted for use at other levels:

Biography: "Boy of Hannibal," Scott-Foresman

Introduction
(The following sample lesson for teaching biography is written for use in middle school, grades 5 and 6. However, it is felt that it is easily adaptable at any grade level by omitting or adding any item or items necessary.)
Time: One class period, the length of which is determined by the needs of the group and the grade level.
Objectives
Thinking:
   To receive insight into patterns of human behavior.
   To recognize cause and effect relationships.
   To recognize time and place relationships.
Interest:
   To make history come alive.
   To note contributions made by the subject.
Procedure
(Word-attack skills omitted in this sample)
1. Have student read title.
2. Inquire as to those who have stopped, passed through, or know of Hannibal, Missouri.
3. Locate the town on map. Relate it to our locality.
4. Develop the idea of the time of the story.
5. Find clues to the story by discussing illustrations.
6. Have students read the story silently to find how the "great, muddy Mississippi River" affected the life of the boy, Sam Clemens.
7. List the following on the board:

licensed pilot	writer of stories and books
typesetter	cub pilot
newspaperman	

Comment that Sam Clemens became each of these at one time in his life. Have students tell you how to number the items to show the correct sequence.

Evaluation
Do the students receive insight into patterns of human behavior? _____ _____

Have the students cite words that describe Sam Clemens' character such as:

impulsive	observant	adventuresome
curious	persistent	quick-witted
enthusiastic		

As the list is being written on the board, ask for examples from the story that show that each was a part of Sam's character. Discuss how these character traits could have helped him in his work as a writer.

Do they recognize cause and effect relationships?

Discuss such questions as:

What does "mark twain" mean?

Why do you think Sam Clemens chose this name when he began to write?

Do they recognize time and place relationships?

Ask: Are we familiar with any other famous person who lived at the same time as Sam Clemens? (Lincoln, Lee, Grant)

How was Sam's childhood different from yours? Compare:

methods of transportation	recreation
education	clothing

Do they note contributions made by the biographical subject?

This will depend upon the biographical subject and what that subject offers for extending interest. In the case of Mark Twain, you might enjoy a famous scene from one of his best-loved books such as:

"The Glorious Whitewasher" from The Adventures of Tom Sawyer, Huckleberry Finn, or a scene from River Boy.

If available, listen to Jerome Kern's Mark Twain or Ferde Grofe's Mississippi Suite.

Does the book make history come alive for the students?

Allow the children to dramatize scenes from the book or an entire story, whichever they prefer. You might encourage students to illustrate a particular scene or paragraph which they enjoyed (Daugherty n.d.).

READING FOLK LITERATURE

Definitions. Folk literature in a broad sense includes all forms of prose and poetry narratives such as myths, fables, legends, and fairy tales that relate customs, beliefs, and traditions that have been handed down over the years in oral and (in later years) written forms. Folklore is more inclusive and includes stories, music, arts and crafts, and dances.

The inventors of some folk tales are known. Cervantes invented Don Quixote and his adventures. Rudolf Raspe invented Baron Munchausen who had so many unbelievable adventures. One of his stories related how the snow was once so deep in a German city that when the snow melted a team of horses and a sled were left hanging from the spire of a cathedral, which had been mistaken for a hitching post. The Munchausen stories are quite funny and preposterous.

Kinds of Folk Literature

The Myth. Myths are tales about a special kind of world that existed prior to today's order. They tell of superhuman beings and demigods, the origin of things, life and death, and the powerful forces of nature. They are related to religion. One person's truth is another person's myth; that is, what one culture or religion considers to be true another will consider to be untrue. Myths, then, embodied the mystic forces of the universe into animal and human form. The forces were generally in human form and were given superior attributes; they were good looking, highly intelligent, and immortal—somewhat immoral, too. Vengeance for slights by other gods and humans was carried out on a large scale—thunderbolts, banishment, turning people into animals, imprisonment, and the like. The gods seem to have found human pride especially repugnant. Bellerophon presumed to rise into Zeus' abode on the winged horse Pegasus and was forthwith struck blind. Niobe, a human who was extremely proud of her divine lineage and attendant supernatural powers as well as her fourteen progeny, placed herself on a par with the goddess Leto. Thereupon Leto's twin children dispatched Niobe's total brood. Niobe is petrified with grief, turning into a stone fountain and weeping for her children eternally.

Greek myths were brought together and organized by the poet Hesiod who supposedly lived during the eighth century B.C. He disliked women as much as he loved nature. His *Works and Days* contain a kind of farmer's almanac, ethical lessons on working hard, some stinging criticisms of women, and the first Greek fable—"The Hawk and the Nightingale." Furthermore, the book contained a dramatic version of Pandora and her box as well as "The Five Ages of the World" (Arbuthnot, 1947).

Which accounts can be read by students in middle school and secondary school? Time-tested versions of Greek and Roman myths include Charles John Kingsley's *The Heroes,* Macmillan, 1936; Thomas Bulfinch's *Mythology.* A simplified version of Bulfinch's work is Sally Benson's *Stories of the Gods and Heroes,* Dial, 1940. Olivia Coolidges' *Greek Myths,* Houghton Mifflin, 1949, is also written in a readable style. A version of the Greek myths that is explicit in its detailing of the gods' activities but it not too difficult to read is Geon Garfield and Edward Blishen's *The God Beneath the Sea,* Pantheon, 1971.

READING POETRY

Perhaps the biggest block to reading poetry is the inability to understand the meanings intended. I have found that to be the case. Simmons (1966) points out that teenage boys do not reject poetry because it is "fairy stuff," they do so because it is hard to read. Experience shows that people like poetry that they understand.

Problems in Reading Poetry

A composite picture—Strang, et al. (1955), Simmons (1966), and my own observations—of the several aspects of reading poetry that trouble a student follows:[2]

[2] The illustrations are mine.

1. *Compared to prose, poetry contains visual "anomalies."* Each line is capitalized, punctuation is irregular, and interrupting thoughts are interspersed here and there.

2. *The reader attends too much to the rhythm of the work instead of assiduously pursuing meaning.*

3. *Words are turned about in an unnatural manner:* "To pass there was such scanty room, the Gate descending scraped his plume" (and there is hardly anything more disconcerting than getting your plume scraped.)

4. *Sentences in poetry are often unduly long.* (At the extreme, sentences contain 150 plus words.)

5. *Unusual words in dialects.* Especially ballads written in Scottish dialect. Note these words and expressions from a poem by Burns entitled "The Cotter's Saturday Night": "frae the pleugh;" "tentie rin;" "sair-won penny-fee;" "kye;" "hawkie;" "weel-hained kebbuck, fell." The Australian poem-song "Waltzing Matilda" by Andrew Barton Paterson (music by Marie Cowan) contains such slang words as swagman, coolibah tree, billy, and Waltzing Matilda.

6. *Rare and elegant language.* For example, Keats, "Ode to a Nightingale" is full of rare and elegant language. Lines 41–50 serve as a sample:

> I cannot see what flowers are at my feet,
>   Nor what soft incense hangs upon the boughs,
> But, in embalmed darkness, guess each sweet
>   Wherewith the seasonable month endows
> The grass, the thicket, and the fruit tree wild;
>   White hawthorn, and the pastoral eglantine;
>   Fast fading violets covered up in leaves?
>   And mid-May's eldest child,
> The coming muskrose, full of dewy wine,
>   The murmourous haunt of flies on summer eves.

Another lyric poet who uses rare and elegant language, including figurative language, that adds freshness, beauty, and vividness of meaning to his poems is Shelley, "To a Skylark" and "The Cloud." Note Keats again in "Ode on a Grecian Urn."

7. *Mythological and historical illusions.* In "How Sweet I Roamed," Blake exclaims, "With sweet May dews my wings were wet, and Phoebus fired my vocal rage." Phoebus is Apollo, the Greek god of the sun; also the god of music and poetry. Wordsworth in "The World Is Too Much With Us" says, "Have sight of Proteus rising from the sea; Or hear old Triton blow his wreathed horn." Proteus and Triton are sea gods in Greek mythology.

Historical reference are found in many poems. Three poems that refer to the Civil War, the Crimean War, and the Napoleonic Wars, respectively, are "Barbara Frietchie" by Whittier, "The Charge of the Light Brigade," by Tennyson, and "Incident of the French Camp," by Browning. With the poems are specific historical references.

8. *The large number of unusual figurative language expressions.* Examples of figurative language in poetry abound. Here are several:

<u>Simile</u>

(1) Silence will fall like dews
(2) And my heart is like a rhyme
(3) Helen, thy beauty is to me
    Like those Nicaean barks of yore

<u>Metaphor</u>

(1) For each age is a dream that is dying
(2) My mind to me a kingdom is
(3) The maple wears a gayer scarf

<u>Personification</u>

(1) With the yellow and the purple and the crimson keeping time
(2) No time to turn at
    Beauty's glance,
    And watch her feet, how they dance

9. *Words and groups of words that create a feeling response.*

(1) And all I ask is a windy day with the white clouds flying,
    And the flung spray and the blown spume, and the sea gulls crying.

(The first line with its words beginning with the /w/ sound suggest movement and freedom. The second line with its /sp/ suggests a spitting or a *spritz* and a kind of action and adversity.)

(2) It shivered the window, pane and sash;
    It rent the banner with seam and gash.
    Quick as it fell, from the broken staff
    Dame Barbara snatched the silken scarf

(The /s/ and /sh/ sounds induce an uneasy-conflict-action feeling that needs to be placated or solved.)

10. *Thought is compacted into a shorter space than is typical of prose.* Compacted thought is very evident in Edwin Markam's four-line poem, "Duty," Donald Mattam's four-line poem, "In a Town Garden" and A. E. Housman's "When I Was One and Twenty." Or think of the deep meaning of this pithy verse:

    To love with no return
      Is a sad thing to befall;
    But a sadder, to come to die
      Before having loved at all.   *—Spanish Folk Song*

Helping Students Understand and Enjoy Poetry

In *Practical Criticism: A Study of Literary Judgment*, I. A. Richards notes that even Cambridge University students were unable to handle poems as a series of sentences. Therefore, they did not understand the meaning of the poems. Richards also found that the students needed guided practice in visualizing images. (I am reminded of the imagery-making exercises my father had us students engage in—I was his student for four years in my middle school years. He would have us imagine things, people, animals, and situations. We thought it great fun to have giraffes stand on their heads, wiggle their ears, wink, and the like.) Similar techniques, Hasselriis (1972) points out, are used by Sam Smiley, a drama professor at the University of Missouri. This technique can be modified for use in the teaching of poetry "because it tends to make students more sensitive to imagery and other devices used to evoke sensory impressions." Furthermore, when students are helped to imagine persons, places, and events similar to those in poems to be discussed in the near future, they will become aware of the many elements involved not only in reading poetry, but also in writing it, according to Hasselriis.

Finally, Richards found that students could not generally separate their insights about poems from experiences and thoughts not related to the poem that impinged themselves into the readers' consciousness. An aid in separating the prereading ideas from the poem's ideas might be to have the students read a poem on a given theme and then have them list all their thoughts on the theme prior to their reading the poem and then carefully compare these preconceptions with the thoughts given in the poem (Hasselriis, 1972).

I think that if one reads poetry with understanding there is a good chance that one will like it. Students of mine who did not understand poetry well changed their attitude from dislike or indifference to one varying from putting up with it to really liking it. This change took place as I taught them to read it, to listen to it, and to understand it. After all, "to be young without poetry is like being indoors in spring."

The would-be teacher of poetry should be an avid reader of poetry. Generally you should know the meaning of a poem before going into class. However, some of your better sessions might result when you go into class without knowing "all the answers." If there are things you do not know, you will be more likely to call upon the expertise of the class. Discussion is encouraged when students feel they have a real contribution to make!

Techniques to Improve Comprehension of Poetry. You help students understand poetry by using such techniques as the following:

1. *Begin with poems that your students can understand and that appeal to them.* The particular poem or limerick that you begin with depends upon the reading ability and general maturity of your reader. You might try this limerick some time:

"A decrepit old gasman, named Peter,
While hunting around for the meter,
  Touched a leak with his light;
  He rose out of sight —
And, as everyone who knows anything about poetry can tell you,
    he also ruined the meter.   *—Anonymous*

It might be fun to let people change parts of limericks. How about this:

A worn-out old gasman, named Jeter,
While hunting around for the meter,
  Touched a leak with his match
  And before they could catch
Him he was well on his way to Saint Peter.

2. *Try to imagine the first word in a line of poetry as starting with a lower case letter rather than a capital,* unless the previous word ended a sentence.

This injunction is in keeping with the idea of trying to develop sentence sense, that is, reading for meaning. A related practice in reading for meaning is to read through the lines rather than stopping at the end of the line.

3. *Take time out for emotions; react to the meanings, the freshly-minted expressions and imagery, in terms of feeling.* Poetry often touches us at the point of our basic drives and aspirations, and when it does so in a new way that cries out to move us, we should feel and enjoy it. Young people and adults alike react to lines such as these (Hafner and Jolly, 1972).

The chattering leaves
Twist and turn in the loud wind,
Autumn is here now.   *—Joey Felipe*

Rushing with the wind,
Whispering in the dark sky,
The leaves fall shyly.   *—Vickie Mitchell*

The snow is clear white
The sun blazes pale orange
To bring new morning.   *—Susan L. Mercer*

These poems were written by students of Marilyn R. Mazer. A detailed explanation of her method is found in Chapter 11 of the reading methods text by Hafner and Jolly (1972).
And to these:

It Isn't the Cough

It isn't the cough
That carries you off;
It's the coffin
They carry you off in.*—Anonymous*

King Tut

King Tut
Crossed over the Nile
On stepping stones of crocodile.
<u>King Tut!</u>
His mother said,
<u>Come here this minute!</u>
<u>You'll get wet feet.</u>
And now King Tut
Tight as a nut
Keeps his big fat Mummy
shut.
King Tut,
tut, tut.   —*X. J. Kennedy*

Or to the Psalms

Psalm 23. Cominus regit me

The Lord is my Shepherd: I shall not want.
He maketh me to lie down in green pastures:
He leadeth me beside the still waters.
He restoreth my soul: He leadeth me in the
paths of righteousness for His name's sake.
Yea, though I walk through the valley of the
shadow of death, I will fear no evil: for
Thou art with me; Thy rod and Thy staff, they
comfort me.
Thou preparest a table before me in the
presence of mine enemies: Thou anointest my
head with oil; my cup runneth over.
Surely goodness and mercy shall follow me
all the days of my life: and I will dwell in
the house of the Lord forever.

4. *Shuffle the parts of sentences mentally when you suspect they have been turned about in an "unnatural" manner.*

"At length did cross an Albatross." → At length an Albatross crossed.
The sun now rose upon the right:
Out of the sea came he," → He came out of the sea.

(Excerpts from "Rime of the Ancient Mariner" by Coleridge)

5. *Disregard temporarily some of the modifying phrases and clauses as you try to get at the key parts of a sentence to get its basic meaning.* It is quite possible for the unsophisticated reader to welter in detail to the extent that meaning is lost. One should transcribe involved sections of poetry onto

transparency paper and project them on a screen. Then, with the class, find the subject and predicate of the sentences and circle them on the transparency. When the very basic meaning is obtained, one can add the most important modifying element and underline it with one color and discuss the meaning. Marking and discussion can be continued as necessary. Follow-up work can be done by individuals and committees on worksheets and transparencies. Some students might want to develop a set of overlapping transparencies that can be presented a step at a time with discussion.

"Their eldest hope, (their Jenny,) woman grown,	1. (Who?)
In youthfu' bloom, love sparkling in her e'e,	3. Detail modifying Jenny
(Comes hame;) perhaps, to show a braw new gown	2. (What does she do?)
Or deposit her sair-won penny-fee,	4. Detail telling how she came home.
To help her parents dear, if they in hardship be."	5a. Why she might have come home.
	5b. Another reason for coming home.
	5b(1) Purpose of depositing her hard-won wages.
	5b(2) Conditions calling for help.

(From "The Cotter's Saturday Night"
by Robert Burns)

The amount of analysis done, the types of markings, and the extent of discussion, and the like, will vary with the nature of the poem, the sophistication of the students, and the purpose of reading the poem. One thing is certain: this kind of analysis along with readiness for reading the poem by working on some of the vocabulary ahead of time is very helpful to students trying to understand and appreciate poetry. However, when working with a dialect do not try to do too much at one time.

The first example showed the necessity of getting at key meaning parts. The next example is a little easier to handle:

"Ah, love, let us be true
To one another! for (the world,) which seems
To lie before us like a land of dreams,
So various, so beautiful, so new,
(Hath really neither job, nor love, nor light, . . . ")

(From "Dover Beach" by Matthew Arnold)

6. *Pinpoint figures of speech and allusions and develop their meanings.* It may be necessary to look up the allusions. Have a dictionary of mythology or some reference work such as a one-volume encyclopedia readily available to the students. Of course, mythological allusions are much more meaningful to students if they have been learned as part of a thorough study of mythology. Sources for the study of mythology are given in a previous section.

One way of studying figures of speech is to note analogous parts in figures of speech in order to clarify meanings:

"The road was a ribbon of moonlight."

The qualities that a road and a ribbon might have in common are smoothness, slenderness, length, and gentle curve. The qualities of the road and the moonlight are silver cast and glow (Strang, McCullough, and Traxler, 1968).

"He was as nervous as a cat in a roomful of rocking chairs."

If a person sees no relationship between a cat's tail which is often on the floor (when the cat is resting) and the rocking of the rockers, and if he or she cannot picture a whole room full of rocking chairs that are rocking—even after a picture is drawn, say—he or she may be doomed to living a very prosaic life.

7. *Make available, at times, an explanation of the poem or an outline of it for the student to read before he or she reads the poem.*
Such advance organizers as an explanation of a poem or an outline of it may help students to work out some of the relationships in the poem and develop a better interpretation of it.

8. *Allow students to read well-selected commentaries and notes.* Use poetry commentaries and notes in conjunction with reading poems, but not as a substitute for reading them.

Dangers in Overanalyzing a Poem

If you did not like your high school teachers or your college professors to engage in overanalyses, your students will probably reject it also. T. S. Eliot has called the overanalysis of poems "the lemon-squeezer school of criticism."

Developing Comprehension of Poetry Through Intensive Reading Exercises

I have used successfully a procedure for reading poetry that entailed vocabulary pretest and study, intensive reading, and discussion. Among other poems, I have used "Ode on the Death of a Favorite Cat" with high school students and college students; the procedure is adaptable for use in the middle school grades, also.

Step 1: Pretest and Vocabulary Study. Words and expressions that might cause the students problems can be determined by giving the students a pretest of vocabulary items from the poem to be studied. This test can be based on items that you think are difficult or the items that students in the past have found to be difficult; a multiple-choice format is acceptable. These items are for the poem, "Ode on the Death of a Favorite Cat."

Sample items sans directions:

1. lofty	A. sky	B. barn	C. high	D. nice
2. gayest	A. weirdest	B. brightest	C. saddest	D. poorest
3. azure	A. blue	B. tall	C. fragrant	D. green
4. demure	A. sneaky	B. in debt	C. old	D. modest
5. pensive	A. deep thought	B. hanging	C. in a pen	D. tired
6. jet	A. dam	B. color	C. boat	D. game
7. Genii	A. lamp	B. smart	C. spirits	D. heredity
8. Tyrian	A. Austria	B. rich purple	C. mean	D. sweet sound
9. hapless	A. footless	B. unlucky	C. sad	D. decapitated
10. Nymph	A. water maiden	B. sex	C. gland	D. genie

Vocabulary study can be approached in a variety of ways (cf. vocabulary chapter.) A simple way is to use a study sheet that contains two illustrative sentences for each word that will be studied. In a reading and discussion session, students will try to determine inductively the meaning of each word on the basis of the word used in sentence contexts. It would be well to have students give additional sentences in which the words are used correctly.

The pretest and vocabulary study can be done several days before the poem is to be read, if you like. Such a procedure will give the teacher and students a chance to use the words in their conversations and discussions. Just prior to the reading you may want to give another version of the test, either in multiple-choice form or in fill-in-the-blank form.

Step 2: Intensive Reading: I have found the following format to be very useful in guiding intensive reading. The poem may be read through silently and at a normal rate in order to get an overall idea of it. Then the student reads in order to respond to the items in column two of the exercise below. The answers may be discussed in order to find out misprocessings and then to clarify concepts so that the full meaning of the poem is obtained.

"Ode on the Death of a Favorite Cat"

DIRECTIONS: Please read the poem through one time in order to get the general sense of the poem. It may be helpful to know that the "lake" referred to in line six is the water of a fishbowl. When you have finished the first reading, please read the questions in the right-hand column and circle the appropriate letter indicating where the answer can be found. Upon completing the items, another reading of the poem should prove interesting.

'Twas on a lifty vase's side,

1

1. What line tells us that the art object was high?   1   2   3   4

Where China's gayest art had dyed

2

The azure flowers, that blow;

3

2. How do we know an art process was involved in making the vase?   1   2   3   4

Demurest of the tabby kind,

4

The pensive Selima reclined,
5
Gazed on the lake below.
6

Her conscious tail her joy declared;
7

The fair round face, the snowy beard,
8   9
The velvet of her paws,
10
Her coat, that with the tortoise vies,
11
Her ears of jet, and emerald eyes,
12   13
She saw; and purred applause.
14   15
Still had she gazed; but 'midst the tide
16   17
Two angel forms were seen to glide,
18
The Genii of the stream:
19
Their scaly armor's Tyrian hue
20
Though richest purple to the view
21
Betrayed a golden gleam.
22
The hapless Nymph with wonder saw
23
A whisker first and then a claw,
24   25
With many an ardent wish,
26
She stretched in vain to reach the prize.
27
What female heart can gold despise?
28
What Cat's averse to fish?
29
Presumptous Maid! with looks intent
30   31
Again she stretched, again she bent,
32   33
Nor knew the gulf between.
34
(Malignant Fate sat by, and smiled)
35
The slipp'ry verge her feet beguiled,
36
She tumbled headlong in.
37

3. How do we know the vase was at least partly blue in color? 2 3 4 5

4. Which line hints that she was looking into a fishbowl? 3 4 5 6

5. How do we know that her mood was a satisfied one? 5 6 7 8

6. Which line tells us that the cat was partly black? 11 12 13 14

7. How do you know the cat was partly yellow? 11 12 13 14

8. Which line tells you the cat may not have been very modest? 12 13 14 15

9. What line makes us aware that she saw several objects? 17 18 19 20

10. Where do we have an indication of the identity of the objects the cat saw? 17 18 19 20

11. Is the intended prey considered to be fortunate? 21 22 23 24

12. In which line does the poet take a jab at the intentions of the fair sex in general? 27 28 29 30

13. Do you think the cat usurped some rights? 27 28 29 30

14. Which line refers to a treacherous precipice? 36 37 38 39

15. Where is an allusion to the proverbial "nine lives" of a cat? 35 36 37 38

Eight times emerging from the flood
38
She mewed to ev'ry wat'ry god,
39
Some speedy aid to send.
40
No Dolphin came, no Nereid stirred,
41   42
Nor cruel Tom, nor Susan heard.
43
A Fav'rite has no friend!
44
From hence, ye Beauties, undeceived,
45
Know, one false step is ne'er retrieved,
46
And be with caution bold.
47
Not all that tempts your wand'ring eyes
48
And heedless hearts, is lawful prize;
49   50
Nor all, that glisters, gold.
51

16. Where do we learn
of the sea nymph?   41 42 43 44

17. Which is the first
subtle warning to
take care?   46 47 48 49

18. Which line speaks of
legitimate bounty?   48 49 50 51

19. Where does the author
refer to reckless
emotions?   48 49 50 51

20. Is all scintillating or
sparkly material of
value?   48 49 50 51

Step 3: Discussion. Discussion can be done by having people summarize the story, discuss nuances of meaning, and share favorite portions that may be read aloud. It is also very interesting to take issue with some of the author's assumptions about women and his use of various aphorisms.

HELPFUL ACTIVITIES FOR TEACHING POETRY AND ITS APPRECIATION

1. Allow students to give their interpretations of figures of speech used in poems. This might be done in a game situation where contestants ask panel members for their interpretations and then either agree or disagree with them as on "Hollywood Squares," the television game show.

2. Have students bring to class pictures illustrating several figures of speech in a poem and see if the students can identify the poems. This guessing may be done on a competitive basis if you like.

3. Allow students to describe one another in a given number of similes and/or metaphors.

4. Bring to class examples of colloquial and slang language and relate the intended meanings of the expressions to the words in which the meanings are couched. In other words, let the students discuss/explain the aptness of each expression.

Enjoying Poetry

1. Tape-record poetry written by students. Play it for the class.
2. Have professional speech people at school or in the community read both

student poetry and published poetry and have the students discuss how and what they like the poetry. The authors of the poems should not be revealed until students discuss how and why they like the poetry. Let the authors have the prerogative of not having their names revealed, especially if the "reviews" are not very favorable.

3. Let students pantomine certain poems or portions of poems as someone reads them.

4. Let certain poems be pantomined and allow the audience to identify the poems.

Noting Effect of Choosing the Right Words

1. Try to obtain copies of drafts of poems by famous poets, unknown published poets, or students. Note changes in the drafts and why the changes were for the better or, perhaps, not an improvement. If the authors are present, ask them why they made particular changes in their manuscripts.

2. Ask students to bring first drafts of their poems. Place the first draft on transparencies, making sure there is plenty of space between the lines. Allow the poet to write second draft emendations on the transparencies and explain improvements, especially in terms of using bright and fresh words and phrases.

Doing Poetry

1. Bring limerick starters to class and allow students to complete them. Allow a committee to choose the best completions in terms of several categories such as originality, humor, smoothness, and appropriateness.

2. Write incomplete poems on the chalkboard. Let the students complete the last line of each incomplete verse. Ask the students to write their own verses on the topics of the poems. A variation is to let them write poems on the topic of their choice using the same rhythm or meter as the given poem.

3. Allow students to compare verses on certain topics, using specific meters. Have students discuss why they prefer certain meters. Ask why particular meters may not be appropriate for certain topics.

4. Provide sets of rhyming words along with several topics for each set of words. (A set would be four, six, or eight words.) Have students write verses. Note differences among poems resulting from use of different topics.

5. Ask students who like to write music to provide music for poems that students write.

6. Perform in class or in assemblies songs developed by your lyricists and composers.

SUMMARY

Today more English teachers are doing what is logical—they are teaching the receptive language arts of listening and reading as well as the transmissive language arts. Furthermore, they are doing it because they understand that reading is a thinking process and that they have a responsibility in helping improve their students' thinking skills.

Literature plays a role in personal development when it helps people solve problems encountered in living. Literature opens up to people value systems and practices that may be at variance with their own Using book content for psychotherapy is bibliotherapy. The mechanism of adjustment central to bibliotherapy is identification. Included in this chapter is a selective annotated bibliography of books with potential therapeutic value.

Many people enjoy reading biographies and autobiographies. An illustrative reading lesson for teaching biography is discussed in the present chapter.

The reading of literature should not be neglected. In addition to enjoying folk literature for itself, the student will learn many mythological illusions that are useful in understanding poetry and other forms of literature.

A block to poetry reading for some people is their inability to understand the meanings intended by the poet. Systematic lessons on poetry comprehension result in increased comprehension of poetry and interest in it. Many specific strategies for improving poetry comprehension are included in the chapter. Furthermore, the would-be teacher of poetry should be an avid reader of poetry.

ACTIVITES AND QUESTIONS
TO PROMOTE LEARNING AND APPLICATION

1. Construct a questionnaire that will help you determine some important (1) teaching practices and (2) attitudes about teaching (especially reading) that middle school and secondary school teachers have. After refining your questionnaire with the help of your instructor, get his or her help in arranging the administration of the test to a sample of English teachers. Draw appropriate conclusions.
2. Select ten pieces of reading matter at random. Determine which selections are literature. On what did you base your judgment?
3. List books that *you* have read that seem to have bibliotherapeutic value. Wherein does the value of each book lie?
4. Explain the concept of *identification.*
5. Explain the concept of *catharsis.*
6. Select several of the values of bibliotherapy and expand on each.
7. From your observations of students and/or talking with their teachers, determine the psychological needs or problems of two or three students. State them. Select several books that may have therapeutic value. *Explain* why you think this is so.
8. Think of several people in the public eye (or who are historical figures). Try to determine problems they may have and select appropriate books that might have therepeutic values for them.
9. Someone has said that there is more psychological value in reading literature than in reading psychology books. Would you agree or disagree? Explain.

10. Do you agree or disagree with Axelrod's comments on reading skills. Defend your answer.

11. Collect several book reviews of a recent biography. What are the areas of *agreement* among the reviewers? Of *disagreement*? How do you account for the areas of agreement? Of disagreement? Read the biography and emend your analysis.

12. Read a first-rate autobiography. Select a given student and explain why the autobiography would be suitable for him or her to read.

13. Read a book that has been the center of controversy in a school system. Analyze the arguments of the book's detractors and state their arguments that have been logical, illogical; based on good theology, on poor theology; abide by the Bill of Rights, run counter to the Bill of Rights. In each instance be analytical.

14. Develop a lesson for the teaching of biography, teach it, and report the results to the class. What was successful? Why? What was unsuccessful? Why?

15. List some "myths" about myths.

16. Select a poem typical of the ones "assigned" for reading in a high school or middle school classroom. Have students read the poem and note pronunciation and comprehension problems. Try to discern which problems match the ten problems listed in the present text. Make notes and report in class.

17. Do a research paper on the use of imagery in reading poetry and prose.

18. Have students change parts of existing limericks. Let them write original limericks on a given theme; on a theme of their choice.

19. Teach students to write Haiku. (For useful teaching techniques see Hafner and Jolly, 1972.)

20. Read the song, "The Lord's My Shepherd. . ." in a hymnal; see, for example, Lutheran Hymnal, Methodist Hymnal, Episcopal Hymnal. Compare it with Psalm 23, King James Version. Which version do you like better, the Bible version or a hymn version? Why?

21. Construct an exercise or a lesson that uses several strategies for helping students to better understand a poem.

22. *Do* some poetry in class. See suggestions in the very last part of the chapter.

SUGGESTED ADDITIONAL READINGS

BAZEMORE, JUDY. "An English Department Builds a Meaningful Reading Program." In Lawrence E. Hafner (Ed.). *Improving Reading in Middle and Secondary Schools.* New York. Macmillan, 1974. Pp. 346–50.

BURTON, DWIGHT L. *Literature Study in the High Schools.* Third Edition. New York: Holt, Rinehart and Winston, 1970.

GALLO, DONALD R. "Reading in Literature: The Importance of Student Involvement." In James L. Laffey (Ed.). *Reading in the Content Areas.* Newark, Del.: International Reading Association, 1972. Pp. 1–29.

FINDER, MORRIS. "Teaching to Comprehend Literary Texts—Poetry." In Lawrence E. Hafner (Ed.). *Improving Reading in Middle and Secondary Schools.* New York: Macmillan, 1974. Pp. 355–66.

HASSELRIIS, PETER. "Reading in Literature: Student Involvement Is Just the Beginning." In James L. Laffey (Ed.). *Reading in the Content Areas.* Newark, Del.: International Reading Association, 1972. Pp. 31–74.

JENKINSON, EDWARD B., and JANE STOUDER HAWLEY. *On Teaching Literature: Essays for Secondary School Teachers.* Bloomington: Indiana University Press, 1967.

LICKTEIG, MARY J. *An Introduction to Children's Literature.* Columbus, Ohio: Charles E. Merrill, 1975.

OLSON, ARTHUR V., and WILBUR S. AMES. *Teaching Reading Skills in Secondary Schools.* Scranton: Intext Educational Publishers, 1972. Chapter 10.

PIERCEY, DOROTHY. *Reading Activities in Content Areas.* Boston: Allyn & Bacon, 1976. Chapter 5.

SHEPHERD, DAVID L. *Comprehensive High School Reading Methods.* Columbus, Ohio: Charles E. Merrill, 1973. Chapter 8.

SIMMONS, JOHN S. "Teaching Levels of Literary Understanding." In Lawrence E. Hafner (Ed.). *Improving Reading in Middle and Secondary Schools.* New York: Macmillan, 1974. Pp. 350–54.

BIBLIOGRAPHY

ARBUTHNOT, MAY HILL. *Children and Books.* Chicago: Scott, Foresman, 1947.

AXELROD, JOSEPH. "Steps in Understanding and Interpreting Different Kinds of Writing." *Improving Reading in the Content Fields.* Chicago: University of Chicago Press, 1946.

BURTON, DWIGHT. "Literature in No-Man's Land: Some Suggestions for the Middle School." In Stephen Dunning (Ed.) *English for Junior High Years.* Champaign: National Council of Teachers of English, 1969.

DONELSON, KENNETH, and BEVERLY A. HALEY. "Why Should Students Read?" *Reading Improvement. 9* (3) (Winter 1972), 67–69.

HAFNER, LAWRENCE E. (Ed.). *Improving Reading in Middle and Secondary Schools.* Second Edition. New York: Macmillan, 1974.

HARTIG, HUGO. "Literature and Popular Culture." *Reading Improvement. 9* (2) (Fall 1972), 39–44.

HASSELRIIS, PETER. "Reading in Literature: Student Involvement Is Just the Beginning." In James L. Laffey (Ed.). *Reading in the Content Areas.* Newark, Del.: International Reading Association, 1972. Pp. 31–74.

HAVIGHURST, ROBERT J. "Facts About Pupils and Their Development That Influence Efforts to Improve Reading in Content Fields." *Improving Reading in the Content Fields.* Chicago: University of Chicago Press, 1946. Pp. 153–56.

LEARY, BERNICE. "Meeting Specific Reading Problems in the Content Fields." In *Reading in the High School and College,* Forty-seventh Yearbook of the NSSE, part II, pp. 136–79. Chicago: University of Chicago Press, 1948.

LINDEMAN, BARBARA, and MARTIN KLING. "Bibliotherapy: Definitions, Uses and Studies." *Journal of School Psychology.* 7 (2) (1968–69), 36–41.

RUSSELL, DAVID. *The Dynamics of Reading.* Waltham, Mass.: Ginn, 1970.

SIMMONS, JOHN S. "The Reading of Literature: Poetry As an Example." In J. A. Figurel (Ed.). *Vistas in Reading.* Newark, Del.: International Reading Association, 1966. Pp. 93–100.

SMITH, DORA V. "Guiding Individual Reading." In *Reading in the High School and College,* Forty-seventh Yearbook of the NSSE, part II, pp. 180–205. Chicago: University of Chicago Press, 1948.

STRANG, RUTH, CONSTANCE MC CULLOUGH, and ARTHUR TRAXLER. *Problems in the Improvement of Reading.* Second Edition. New York: McGraw-Hill, 1955. (Third Edition, 1967.)

CHAPTER 15

Teaching the Reading of English. II. Strategies for Improving the Reading of Fiction, Drama, and Essays

READING FICTION

The Art of Short Fiction. Works of art imitate what humans have observed and reacted to, and they are designed to give aesthetic pleasure. Some individuals feel humans can achieve immortality through creating art. If by immortality they mean the artists will be remembered and appreciated over the centuries, they can achieve it.

Pannwitt (1964) tells us that good works of art have the qualities of universality and individuality, the former to satisfy one's need to recognize the familiar, the latter to satisfy one's need to uncover the new. Universality, according to Pannwitt, can be illustrated in the characters of the parable, "The Prodigal Son." Individuality is attained in the to-the-point manner in which the author has depicted the unqualified love of a father for his son.

Fiction deals with *content, material,* and *form*. The character in action produces the theme or content, for example, love. The material is the language fashioned to give individuality to the universal theme, characters, and action. Thus, in the "Prodigal Son," we find not only love, but a father's love for a son who, according to human standards, did not deserve it. Rather, the son who stayed home "deserved" the love; but the errant son received it. The form is (1) the way the author unites content and material and (2) the result of the union, the story.

W. S. Campbell (1948) notes that the adaptive human is the civilized human. Nature and society are humanity's judges. Nature (according to its "survival of the fittest" dictum) gives humans a pat on the back for killing their enemy; society screams "Guilty!" People read fiction because it reconciles happiness (doing what you want to) with goodness (conforming to social standards). Such ideal reconciliation rarely occurs in life.

Humans look for trouble, but the search is dangerous. A safer way to experience trouble is vicariously, through fiction. Therefore, "fiction is made up of struggle, strife and conflict"; when these are removed the story ends. A good story is an impossible yarn that the writer makes plausible.

Understanding the Short Story and the Novel

In working with students you will want to develop an understanding of the role of the elements of fiction. These elements are characterization, the scene, the theme, the plot, and the setting. Some of the following discussion may not reduce much cognitive uncertainty for experienced English teachers, but may prove informative to the reading specialist and the general readers. Most of it is presented from a writer's point of view, since it draws heavily on the excellent work of W. S. Campbell, a writer and teacher of writing.

The basic idea of a story is the *theme* or main thought. The theme is developed by means of the *plot*, a connected series of dramatic action-dialogue units called *scenes*. In each dramatic scene *characters* meet for a particular purpose. Some kind of encounter ensues, and then there is the final action from which a winner emerges. The final element in the scene shows the winner claiming the fruits of the endeavor—the "reward." So, as characters move into action we see the theme developed as the plot unfolds. A scene is basically an encounter and its resolution. Several scenes take place in one physical *setting* or the setting may change for each scene.

Understanding Characterization. Every character has to have traits that set him or her apart from other characters. Traits are classified as human, typical, social or moral, and individual.

Human traits are the basic ordinary appetites, feelings, and natural affections. A trait may be positive and indicate strength or negative, indicating weakness. Rip Van Winkle and the prodigal son were weak characters; the latter's father was a strong character.

Typical traits are those of a profession or a group classified by race, social class, and the like. Typical traits are used for minor and stereotyped characters.

In creating a *flat* character an author will use one of the following kinds of tags: expression, gesture or mannerism, appearance, habit of thought. The stories in which the hero is a super detective seem to stereotype police as bumbling idiots (tag of habit of thought). Hoods are swarthy and wear black shirts and long white ties (tags of appearance) and mumble (tag of expression). Unfortunately the police are characterized as not being able to spot clues or keep an open mind (tag of habit of thought). Super detective will be a *round* character who has or will find all the answers, something like an updated Sherlock Holmes. A variety of traits is assigned to round characters.

Mimics or people who do imitations use all the tags. Can you supply the names of the celebrities and historical characters who have the following tags?

1. Clenched teeth, glasses, mustache; "Bully!" _____

2. No navel, green thumb; "<u>She</u> made me do it." _____

3. White hat, tall; "This here cowpoke bothering _____

   you, Miss Kitty?"

4. Grin, well-dressed; "That's a real biggie!" _____

Social or moral traits are the ones that society approves or disapproves. They can be stated as opposing traits—pride versus humility, for example—or traits in which the Golden Mean is represented:

1. cowardice—courage—recklessness
2. quarrelsomeness—friendliness—flattery

A *flat* character would be given one of these traits, perhaps cowardice, whereas a more *rounded* character might be cowardly at one time and recklessly brave at another.

Individual traits are the distinguishing traits that make a character interesting. It may be a particular habit of thought or mind that uses a "visible" sign such as a speech tag. The individual trait is useful in creating characters in *relief* and *rounded* characters.

The author of fiction uses various traits to develop characterizations: The *flat* character will be painted, according to Campbell, by centering the attention of the reader upon a typical or social trait. The character in *relief* is painted with a dominant social or typical trait and modified with a quick dip into a "color" to develop a human or individual trait. The *round* character has bold splashes of human and individual traits, which are related to each other and to carefully selected social and typical traits. The reader will find that in serious fiction people are complex creatures not entirely comprehensible, neither all good nor all bad, not entirely rational, but very real and interesting. "A character may reveal itself by *action*; by *speech*; by *effect* upon other characters; by the *character's own reaction* to persons, things and circumstance about it" (Campbell, 1948). Actions of course, speak louder than words, but the reader has to be prepared for the action if it is going to seem plausible; therefore, the motive must be presented before the action.

Campbell also tells us that there are other methods by which the author may delineate his characters directly. The reader will want to look for these methods:

1. Explain the traits and motives of the hero.
2. Describe the hero.
3. Analyze the psychological processes of the hero.
4. Quote what other characters say about the hero.

Making Applications: Noting Characterization in Fiction. Before you have your students engage in the kinds of analysis just noted, guide them in working the exercises below, which are the kinds of exercises suggested by Campbell.

1. Prepare five columns on a sheet of paper. In column one will be the names of ten persons now in the public eye. Columns two through five will be headed tags of appearance, tags of expression, tags of gesture or mannerism, and tags of habit of thought, respectively. For each person selected fill in appropriate information. For example:

	Appearance	Expression	Gesture or Mannerism	Habit of Thought
Richard Nixon	bushy eyebrows upturned nose	"Let me be perfectly clear about that!"	pointing right index finger upward	guarded expression

You can also make such a table for fictional characters and for individuals personally known to you.

2. Familiarize yourself with the names of opposite virtues and vices and with opposites plus the Golden Mean. This can be done as an in-class exercise.

3. Determine the dominant human, typical, social, and individual traits of the people on your previous lists.

4. Buy copies of fiction magazines. Assign a particular color to each type of tag, that is, develop a color code. Go through several short stories and underline with appropriate colors the instances of each type of tag.

5. Make up a list of the characters in the stories that you have just read and note the tags used for each characters. How many <u>kinds</u> of tags did each have?

6. Assign different colors (from the ones used in 4) to human, typical, social, and individual traits. Go through a second copy of the same issue of the magazine and underscore with appropriate colors the various types of traits.

7. Try to determine the flat characters, name them; those in relief, name them; those that are round, name them.

Campbell suggests other analyses that I will not go into here. After such analyses and discussion, you could create characters of your own, giving them appropriate tags, traits, functions, and the like and then write a two-hundred word sketch of each.

NOTE: You may get your students and yourself interested not only in reading fiction more expertly but perhaps in *writing* fiction!

Understanding the Scene.   You have heard the expression, "Don't make such a scene." The expression is appropos of the meaning of scene in fiction because encounter and conflict are the very essence of scene. The *scene* is a unit of plot made up of dramatic action and dialogue.

Let me provide an illustration that includes the elements of scene. We can imagine a group of teachers trying to get a raise in pay from the school board: The champion (the school board) and the challenger (the teachers) *meet*. Each has a *purpose or intention*—to defeat the other. They engage in an *encounter* lasting two hours. During this encounter, champion and challenger land (verbal) blows. In the *final action* the challenger knocks out the champion with a left jab (finally convincing the board that education is worthwhile), a right upper cut (convincing the board that the present teachers are excellent and actually irreplaceable except at considerable expense of time and money) and a roundhouse from the left (a declaration of a city-wide intent to strike). In the *sequel* we see a teachers' picnic in which the teachers are barbecuing ribs instead of boiling oatmeal-laden wieners, their spouses are wearing their first nice clothes in five years, and the children are learning to play ball because they can now afford balls and bats.

Making applications: analyzing scenes:

1. You, as teacher, should analyze some short stories from current fiction magazines into the component scenes, indicating each meeting, purpose, encounter, final action, and sequel. Each part can be described in five to fifteen words, except the encounter, which may take up to 40 or 50 words.

2. After you have written the scenarios for a number of stories, including some of the fiction your students have read, show and explain what scenes are in terms of fiction they know.

3. Let the students try analyzing scenes. For material that they can mark, let the students underline the parts that indicate meeting, purpose, and the like in different colors. Let students who have analyzed the same works discuss what they have done.

4. Encourage the students to write one or more scenes.

Understanding the Theme and Plot. Great literary themes cause us to ponder, to feel, to experience vicariously. The theme of Cinderella—the uplifing of the humble—has its roots in both the "Magnificat" and the "Sermon on the Mount." Readers of such literature—the former piece a fairy tale—are buoyed up with hope. The plot of Cinderella is worked out to a finite happy ending. The plots of the Magnificat and the Sermon on the Mount work out in people's lives each generation to two-world solutions.

A practiced short-story reader wants to see how a theme is developed through plot. We already know how scenes are developed. Plotting deals with a connected sequence of events.

Campbell tells us that there are two basic plots and that they arise from two basic patterns of humanity: the story of the Doer and the story of the Sufferer. These plots are usually combined. The story of the doer is the basic plot of all stories of adventure, of brave men and daring enterprise—the story of Man. The second is the foundation plot of stories of endurance and is the story of Woman. Man is centrifugal; he wanders. Woman is centripetal; she stays and bears the suffering.

To me both patterns are found in all those who take a stand and who suffer even though victorious in the end, although they may be discomfited temporarily by loss of temporal life.

A plot has five essential parts: the *situation* or problem that forces the hero to get moving to solve the problem; a *complication* (or two) to make the hero's problem unsolvable; a *crisis* calling for an agonizing decision, thus action; and a *climax* in which the problem is solved in an interesting and imaginable way (Campbell, 1948).

Some applications:

1. Discuss with your students recently read short stories and have them write a sentence or two explanation of the situation.

2. Then ask them to tell you what complication was developed to make the hero's problem insoluble. What was the climax?

3. Next ask your students if they could see the solutions coming. A good writer will put the hero in a very tough spot, but cue the reader into what will happen, because one of the more important aspects of plotting is maintaining plausibility. Writers get readers ready for events that follow by informing the reader in advance of the existence of things, people, conditions, facts, attitudes, motives, and the like that will appear later in the story.

4. Taking the same stories, have your students list certain events in a story and the earlier planting of cues for each event.

Another preparation cue is *pointing*. The author points to future events in the story with a word or phrase that lets the reader know that some event might or could occur later in the story. These preparation cues aid interest because a reader's "interest will depend largely upon his feeling that something is coming," according to Campbell.

Application: Have your students go through a selection and number a set of cues and then state the event for which the cues were a preparation.

The hero does not need these clues, but the reader must know them. (Now you know why you are always smarter than the hero!) Anticipation is also aided by *transitions,* which allow everything to flow along in smooth continuity.

Discovery and reversal is a device in which the elements of interest and plausibility appear together. Discovery, according to Campbell, means a story character finding out something that causes him or her to change his or her mind or intention. The *reversal* is the change effected.

Aristotle noted four types of discovery–reversal:

1. The character makes a discovery and then changes his or her mind, that is reverses his or her intention. For example, when Cleopatra discovers that Antony is about to jilt her, she changes her intention of flattering and humoring him to a new strategy in order to retain his love. (Remember it was Cleopatra who invented the dunking seat used in the Salem Witchcraft Trials!)

2. The character does something wrong in ignorance and only later makes the discovery. For example, a sheriff shoots a man he thought was a criminal only to discover later it was his deputy.

3. The character makes a discovery but goes ahead with his or her original intention. For example, a man is about to uncork a custard pie at a target when he discovers that his tryannical boss is moving into the line of fire. Delighted, he unloads his pie on the boss.

4. The character makes a discovery, but does not carry out his or her original scheme. Thus, the coach at State plans to run up the score on his intrastate football rival, the big land grant university, that had defeated him seven years in a row, but decides to hold it at 58–7 in the third quarter.

Making applications: analyzing plots:

1. Take the stories whose scenes you analyzed in the last section. State the plot of each story in a few sentences. To give force and clarity, use mainly nouns and verbs.

2. Take each plot synopsis and underscore impossibilities in blue and gross improbabilities in yellow.

3. Bracket the sentences in each story that indicate the following parts: a. the *situation* or *problem* that sets the hero into action, b. a *complication,* c. a *crisis*, and d. a *climax* yielding a solution. In the margin adjacent to your bracketed passages identify each part by writing the corresponding plot part—complication and so forth.

4. Briefly write the main complications for each story. Discuss in class.

5. Note plants for an event. Write P1-1a, P1-1b, P1-1c by the plants and Ev1 by the event. Do this for several events; the second one would run P1-2a . . . and Ev2.

6. Do the same for *pointers* and *repetitions*. Discuss in class.

7. Note several *discoveries* and *reversals* for each story.

NOTE: Some students will get bored by doing too much of this. You have to learn to be selective.

Understanding the Setting. Setting is a useful element in fiction. It refers to the time, place and atmosphere in which the story occurs. One kind of setting is *solid*, which is the catalogue or specifications of a place. This type of setting is often used in detective stories and at times in historical fiction. The second is the *liquid* setting, which is laid out in terms of description or sensory impressions as they affect a person. Third is the *gaseous* setting, in which the atmosphere is obtained by "presenting things in terms of emotions, in terms of the reaction of the character or characters, so that the setting becomes a part of the hero instead of something extraneous to him" (Campbell, 1948).

Since so many readers have traveled widely, lengthy descriptions of setting are no longer considered necessary. Setting variety today is depicted in terms of the emotions of characters.

Settings vary with the psychological choices of the characters. If a high-school football player decides to strive for All-American status in college football, he will likely enroll at a large university that emphasizes football rather than a small college. The setting will become a part of our would-be hero.

Imagine the setting differences and the long-term effects of a given choice in these situations: woman marrying a State Department career officer or an insurance salesman; man marrying a successful opera singer or a key punch operator; a person finding successful rehabilitation or lapsing again into a life of crime. The reader sees better the reality of the choice when the author develops the setting appropriately.

The appropriate setting may be effected by the gaseous method when the author develops the setting through the reactions of the characters. In depicting the inner city, for example, the author will eschew lengthy description. Instead, there may be a neon sign here, a waif there, or a screaming ambulance over there. The author makes the setting part of the hero by noting the sensations and emotions of the hero while reacting to the physical accoutrements. We recall how so many people "like the book better than the movie." What the movie may do is to destroy the dream the writer and reader had developed.

Making applications: learning more about settings:

1. Buy a copy of a magazine and underline passages that indicate these settings:

> Solid (matter of fact), black
> Liquid (sensory impression), lavender
> Gaseous (emotional), light blue

Calculate the actual number of inches of print devoted to each type of setting. Note whether you think the balance is correct for that type of story.

2. Select several short stories you have read. Rate them. Assign a 1 to the story you liked best, a 2 to the next best, and so forth. Then determine the main type of setting used in each. Is there any relationship between your preferences and the type of setting used?

NOTE: In these down-to-earth analyses with students you may use magazine fiction. If such fiction is too difficult, use appropriate selections from student anthologies. How you handle the colored marking problem I will leave to your ingenuity. Also, I have used only a portion of Campbell's excellent book in this presentation. I recommend it highly to anyone who wants to learn more about the topics we have discussed. The Panwitt article is also excellent.

Students will read well-written fiction that they can understand and that gets through to them. In the past teachers may have tried to get students to analyze fiction by asking them questions that were too abstract, that required more familiarity with what authors do to get certain effects than the students had. The preceding information about the structure and content of fiction plus a digging into real, current fiction as suggested in the exercises constitute a concrete approach that students can enjoy. If there are any fledgling writers and critics in your classes, they will profit more from the types of work program analyses suggested here than from abstract discussions.

Illustrative Lesson for the Teaching of Short Stories. Some teachers would want to precede this type of lesson plan with the down-to-earth analyses suggested earlier. Others would reverse the procedure. I think that a plan in which you gradually familiarize your students with the elements is best. At any rate, here is one type of lesson, which I hope you would adapt to your situation if you decide to use it.

Illustrative Lesson for the Teaching of Short Stories
Junior High Level
Story: "The Legend of Sleepy Hollow" by Washington Irving.

Introduction

The aim of the teacher is to develop the power of appreciation. Many previously taught reading skills are combined for appreciation of a story. The reinforcement and culmination of these skills is the child's true enjoyment. As an example, when reading "The Legend of Sleepy Hollow" the student will be able to use many skills in discovering new meanings in literature.

Time: Two weeks.

Objectives

1. To read for enjoyment.
2. To read to gain knowledge of the early settlement of New York State.
3. To appreciate Washington Irving's humor.
4. To appreciate Washington Irving's wide choice and mastery of words.
5. To develop imagination.

6. To identify and appreciate exaggeration (caricature) in character portrayal.
7. To detect foreshadowing.
8. To identify clues.
9. To follow sequence of events.
10. To note the emphasis on atmosphere and character as predominant elements in the story.
11. To appreciate the universality of the thoughts, experiences, and feelings of the characters.

Procedures

1. Ask the questions about the title, illustrations, author, and locale of the story to arouse interest.
2. Have the students read silently the entire story.
3. Divide the story into parts for purposes of instruction in these skills:

To be aware of time and place, ask:
  When did the story take place?
  Where did the story take place?
  Why is the Van Tassel farm so vividly described?

To follow sequence of events:
  Ask the students to show sequence of events by having them dramatize the story.
  Ask the students to re-tell the story.

To read for details: Ask these and comparable questions:
  What is the name of the town where the story takes place?
  Name the various vocations that Ichabod Crane had.
  How old was Katrina Van Tassel?
  What was the name of Ichabod's horse?
  What was the name of the farmer who owned the horse?
  Who was Major Andre?

To increase vocabulary: Use the context method primarily.
  If necessary use the dictionary. Use the words in original sentences.

wight	pedagogue	caricature	specter
tarried	psalmody	credulity	ludicrous
insinuating	domiciliated	sumptuous	adjacent
mettle	affrighted	phantom	apparition
cudgeled	(Add other words.)		

To understand figures of speech, sound images, sight images:
  Have the students find examples of alliteration, simile, hyperbole, onomatopoeia.
  Ask why they are effective. Examples:

  "His arms dangled a mile out of his sleeve."
  "the brook that whimpered"
  "moan of the whippoor-will"
  "stately squadron of snowy geese"
  "long snipe nose that looked like a weathercock"
  "might have mistaken him for some scarecrow eloped from a cornfield"

To detect clues:

Ask the students to find clues for <u>character</u>.
"more <u>mischief</u> than knavery in his composition" (Brom Bones)
"peerless daughter" (Katrina)
"viciousness" (Gunpowder)
"kind and thankful creature" (Ichabod)

Ask the students to find clues for <u>thread of story</u>.
"formidable rival" (Brom Bones)
"coquette" (Katrina Van Tassel)
"whimsical persecution" (Ichabod)

To detect foreshadowing:
Ask the students how the following incidents prepare for coming events:

"The lady of his heart was his partner in the dance, while Brom Bones sat brooding by himself in one corner."

Brom Bones' account of racing with the Headless Horseman—"This tale and the others ran deep in the mind of Ichabod."

To visualize, ask:
What do you see when you read the description of the Van Tassel farm?
Of what are you reminded when you visualize the bountiful amount of food on the table for the party?
Can you find a picture in a magazine like the scene with Major Andre's tree, the bridge, or the church?

To find historical facts in a story:
Ask the students to read orally that particular section of the story.
Examples:
Major Andre's tree
The legend itself
Dutch settlements in New York State

To detect humor:
Ask the students where they can detect humor. Examples:
Gunpowder, Brom Bones, Ichabod, Hans Von Ripper, the appearance of Ichabod, Ichabod leading the choir, and the race with the Headless Horseman.

To draw inferences: Ask these and comparable questions:
Why was Brom Bones famed for his skill in horsemanship?
Why was Brom Bones' horse black?
Why did Ichabod have a "fearful pleasure" in hearing "tales of ghosts and goblins, and haunted fields, and haunted bridges, and haunted houses, and particularly of the Headless Horseman"?
Why do you think Brom Bones laughed so heartily every time the pumpkin was mentioned?

To predict outcome: Ask the students to list events that condition Ichabod's frame as he leaves the party. Examples:
Brom Bones resents Ichabod's dancing with Katrina.
The men tell ghost stories.

Brom Bones dominates the conversation with tales of the Headless Horseman.
Katrina turns Ichabod down.
It's midnight.
Ichabod is the <u>last</u> to leave.

Evaluation

Did the students develop their imagination?

Ask the students to write a dialogue that they imagine might have taken place between Ichabod and the old farmer who had been to New York.

Ask each member of the class to write about an incident in "The Legend of Sleepy Hollow," but writing it from a different viewpoint than that found in the story. Example: Katrina Van Tassel telling how she felt about Ichabod Crane and Brom Bones trying to win her favor.

Ask the students to pretend that they were students in the school where Ichabod Crane taught. Write a letter to a relative or friend telling him the disappearance of their school master.

A student might choose three experiences from the life of Ichabod Crane, pretend that he is Ichabod, and write a diary about these events.

Were the students able to appreciate the universality of the thoughts, feelings, and experiences of the character?

Ask the students to write a character sketch of Brom Bones, Ichabod Crane, and Katrina.

Did the students detect foreshadowing?

Why did Ichabod read Cotton Mather's History of New England Witchcraft?

Did the students appreciate Washington Irving's description?

Ask the students to draw pictures, or make murals of scenes found in the story.

Could the students follow the sequence of events, identify clues, and react to the mood of the story?

Following the reading of "The Legend of Sleepy Hollow," ask each member of the class to write a four-page newspaper (theme paper size) chronicling events in the story of contemporary to it. The headline story could be an item mentioning the events leading up to the disappearance of Ichabod Crane. Other items could be sports events that were popular at the time, church news, parties, newcomers to the community, and sale of horses. Include cartoons. The students may give their newspaper a title such as The Tarrytown Tribune, The Sleepy Hollow Echo, The Sleepy Hollow Sentinel, or The Dutch Post. (Daugherty, n.d.)

READING DRAMA

Various Meanings of the Term Drama

Brossell (1976) writes of dramatic pedagogy or educational drama, theater drama, and the reading of dramatic literature. Process-centered teaching, he says, can be described as dramatic pedagogy, "since its aim is to promote learning through natural action." This educational drama, then, is quite different from both theater and the reading of dramatic literature. Theater uses the creation of stylized illusion in its attempt to communicate, and "it requires people of special sophistication and talent to convey meaning through the creation of stylized illusion." Reading dramatic literature is a "passive" process —a purely verbal process that does not involve the extensive physical movement required in drama. "Theater means performing, reading means reading and drama means doing" (Brossell, 1976). The present discussion will center on reading drama.

Reading drama requires cognitive-imaginative skills. In turn, cognitive-imaginative skills should be sharpened through the reading of drama. I shall not dictate what drama students should read. However, I would like to mention some reading skills a teacher might emphasize. Some of them relate to performing but they involve reading. These reading skills are drawn from Brossell (1976), Haselriis (1971), and Daugherty (n.d.). Discussion is by the present author. The specific source for each will not be noted since there is some overlap:

1. *To read to understand dramatic structure: act and scene development; plot development.* Obviously if fiction has been taught as suggested in the previous section, there will be transfer from it to reading drama, but transfer elements should be pointed out and discussed.

Since fiction is about 30 to 40 per cent dialogue and the rest narrative, one should study how lack of narrative or author's commentary is handled in drama in which so much dialogue is used. Of course, some of the descriptions of settings in fiction are handled by visual settings in *performed* drama. Reading drama calls for much imagination.

2. *To read carefully to note how characterization is handled.* Much interpretation and imagination are called for to be able to see what kind of person a character is. One must note the various cues used in writing fiction, dig into one's own experiential background, and possibly even research the settings, the psychological and sociological processes, and the historical period involved in order to develop an adequate interpretation of the characterization intended. Cues to characterization can sometimes be found even in the discussion of settings such as in the opening of *Raisin in the Sun,* which tells how Mama selected the furnishings of the room with care and love and even hope and arranged them with taste and pride. We get cues about Ruth from the next page of the same play, for example, when it tells how she moves, what her reaction to early morning is, and then hints at how she has reacted to life. The characterization is developed throughout the play through dialogue, responses, and the author's brief narrations.

3. *To read to visualize stage sets, lighting, costumes, and the movement of characters.* Once again, one may draw on one's experiential background for this visualization. One's background may be real or vicarious. One may have seen similar plays or movies, visited or read about the type of locale or actual locale, done research on the settings and costumes. Showing films to the class, attending movies, bringing in pictures, books, pamphlets, and reference works, and making sketches of sets and costumes would certainly enhance accurate

visualization. One need not go so far as to require all class members to make sketches. That will deaden the interest of many of your students.

4. *To read to interpret stage directions.* It certainly is a source of amazement to see the difficulties people can have with stage directions. It can be fun to read through a play and work on entrances, places where people stand, move, and the like. It brings interest and hilarity to the project.

5. *To read to note the scenario and plot development, including physical and psychological conflicts and their resolutions.* As in short stories and novels, plot development and its execution in each scene centers on meeting, purpose, encounter, final action, and sequel. If one scene of a play is not as popular with students as another, analyze the elements of each scene to see if weakness in a given element accounts for lack of interest.

When psychological conflicts are portrayed, as in *A Raisin In the Sun,* the author still uses evidences of physical tension as well as dialogue to delineate the conflict.

> Walter: (frowning impatiently): . . . (straightening up from her and looking off); . . . (passionately now); . . . (In utter anguish as he brings his fists down on his thighs).

6. *To detect the motivating forces triggering the character's behavior.* We look again to *A Raisin in the Sun* to see the poverty, the lack of a good job, or prospects for short- or long-term improvement of economic or social status and resultant deflation of pride and hope to see the impelling force behind Walter's behavior.

7. *To acquire understanding needed for reading a Shakespearean play.* Shakespeare should not be inflicted on the *average* reader in high school. If you want the student to get the lessons of Shakespeare's plays, you have several choices. One, rewrite the material so that it is readable; two, select other readable literature that makes some of the same points. If you want the student to enjoy reading, you will have to present something that he or she can decode and understand. The Elizabethan vocabulary, the figures of speech, the historical, geographical, and mythological allusions, and the long, complex sentences create such a vast gulf between the reader and the distant star "Meaning" that the average high-school reader cannot traverse it.

As most of his works are ordinarily presented, Shakespeare is for the top 10 or 15 per cent of high school students. Even with these students, steps may be taken to aid meaning development:

1. Provide an overview of the plot; you will not want to divulge the ending.
2. Discuss the historical setting and the kinds of roles that characters—kings, princes, ladies, generals—might play as well as some of the related problems of the age.
3. Discuss some of the difficult general vocabulary found in the work. (This can be done over a period of time before reading the play.)
4. Provide pictures and captions of some words and expressions such as graymalkin, kerns and gallowglasses, chops, rump-fed ronyon, Posters, Hautboys, and penthouse lid (Macbeth). Use the expressions in class.

5. Use some of Shakespeare's expressions in talking with your students, although this practice might result in the expressions being adopted as a kind of "slang." (Do not complain. At least it would have meaning for them.)

. Hie thee hither   (Come here)
. has the speed of   (outstripped)
. golden round   (crown)
. cleave to my consent   (adhere to my plan)
(Macbeth)

6. Amplify some of the footnotes. For example, editions of Macbeth vary in the detail of the footnotes.

word	Edition 1	Edition 2
graymalkin	gray cat	gray cat. Witches were supposed to be accompanied by spirits in the form of animals.
rump-fed ronyon	a mangy creature fed on refuse	well-fed creature
penthouse lid	eyelid sloped like the roof of a penthouse	eyelid
gentle senses	refined tastes	—————

READING EXPOSITORY PROSE

What an Essay Is

The essay, is a short literary composition of an analytical or interpretive nature that usually deals with the subject from a personal point of view. This definition implies that readers, especially of serious essays, would engage in a thorough logical analysis of the cognitive relationships in the work.

Sources of Essays

The essayist writes to inform and/or convince the reader of something. Classical examples of essays are those of Montaigne and Bacon—arranged under such general topics as youth and age, marriage, truth, and riches—and those of Locke, Steele, and Addison. There was a profusion of interesting essays by nineteenth-century English writers such as Arnold, Carlyle, Huxley, Macaulay, Newman, and Ruskin.

American essayists include Franklin, Paine, Irving, Emerson, Holmes, Poe, Thoreau, Dunne, Mencken, Thurber, White, Cousins, and Trilling, to mention but a few. Most of the essays written by the individuals named would be understood and appreciated by only a few of the better readers in the secondary school. However, there is expository prose of various levels of difficulty, similar to essays, in the writing of syndicated columnists in newspapers and in such general interest magazines as *Reader's Digest, Family Circle, Ebony,* and *Woman's Home Companion.* Certain articles and features in the weekly news magazines *Time, Newsweek*, and *U.S. News and World Report* are expository prose that treats topics of current interest to the reader. *Atlantic Monthly* and *Harper's* contain excellent, but difficult, essays as do a number of religious publications.

What Is Exposition?

Exposition is detailed explanation that answers questions by setting forth facts and ideas and the relationships among them. The questions may be stated directly prior to the writing, included as part of the writing, or stated after the writing as study questions. On the other hand, they may have been stated by the writer as part of an outline and then included, not as stated questions, but as an implicit part of the writing.

Patterns of Explanation

The classical structure of oration, although useful, was too rigid and lengthy, resulting at times in boring prose on the one hand and inept exposition on the other. New patterns arose that were at once more pertinent to the author's purpose and, therefore, more parsiminious in expression.

Definition Pattern. Definition is a basic kind of explanation that uses *genus,* a brief statement showing the general class to which something belongs, and *differentia,* indicators of how something differs from the general class. Thus, an "orange" can be defined by the brief statement of its *genus,* "An orange is a citrus fruit," and a statement of the *differentia* that indicate how it differs from other members of its class, "reddish-yellow, round, with a sweet juicy pulp." (Edibility was not included because that is a characteristic of citrus fruit.)

An article or chapter can contain many definitions or be devoted to defining one term. In "Democracy," Carl Becker shuns vague terms, such as republic, justice, truth, and Americanism found in the "Pledge of Allegiance" and politicians' rhetoric, and attaches "to the word a sufficiently precise meaning to avoid the confusion which is not infrequently the chief result of" imprecise, overly abstract discussions.

The *genus*—"form of government"—and the *differentia*—"of the people, by the people, for the people"—constitute the basic definition. He then presents a "realistic" definition, which is more specific: "government of the people, by the politicians, for whatever pressure groups can get their interests taken care of." This definition if followed by a *paraphrased expansion* of what Becker considers the *key element,* "by the people:" . . . government by the people as opposed to government by a tryant, a dictator, or an absolute monarch. After three examples of an antithesis—Peisistratus, Caesar, and Napoleon—in which power was basically supported by the people but still dictatorships, he states the *essential test* of democratic government: "The source of political authority must be and remain in the people and not in the ruler," he *expands* on the key element, stating that the citizens or a representative group of them (utilizing established forms) freely act (1) "to appoint or recall the magistrates" and (2) "to enact or revoke the laws by which the government is governed."

This excellent article by Becker is a classic illustration of the process of definition by analysis. Teachers in the content areas should compile a list of articles exemplifying definition and use them in teaching students to get as much as possible from such material. Have the students note such elements as: (1) genus; (2) differentia; (3) further specification; (4) paraphrased expansion; (5) key element; (6) essential test; and (7) expansion of the key element. These concepts will not be understood by the students unless you can work through several pieces of material with them. After such direct teaching, students will understand the concepts and be able to analyze similar materials on their own.

The types of definition (some of which are included at least implicitly in the seven points above) are:

1. *Definition by synonym:* We define by synonym in explaining diffidence as shyness, conation as will, lassitude as lethargy, tortuous as winding, jocund as merry. There is wide overlap in the meaning of synonyms, but also areas of specificity We use a particular word to connote a special shade of meaning.

2. *Definition by analysis:* The use of genus and differentia characterizes analytic definition. The writer of analytic definition thinks of many aspects of concept he or she is analyzing. The reader tries to "milk" the explanation by asking more questions. If all the questions are not answered by the writer, the reader may need to consult related works or reference works.

3. *Definition by synthesis.* Definition by synthesis calls out one characteristic of the word to be defined and combines it with a class word. Stating that a "center is the member of a basketball team who is usually the tallest" is useful and interesting but not complete; herein lies the weakness of this type of definition.

4. *Definition by connotation.* When a person wants to suggest characteristics for a thing or idea, he or she notes another thing that has the characteristics; that is, he or she connotes meaning by using a sort of analogy. The thing to be defined would not necessarily have the individual traits as a member of the class to which it belongs; it is connoted that it has them by use of the comparison:

> Conscience is condensed character. (anonymous)
> God is like a skillful geometrician. (Sir Thomas Browne)
> The camel is the ship of the desert. (unknown)

5. *Definition by showing.* In face-to-face situations one can point, illustrate, and demonstrate. In writing, one uses pictorial representations to supplement the text.

6. *Definition by function.* This definition is a kind of low-level concrete one. Children often use it. "An orange is to eat." "A house is to live in." "A poem is to read." Such definitions are rather weak.

7. *Definition by example.* In definition by example one goes down the abstraction ladder: If I am going to define *prose* I give examples, "You know, essays and short stories and things like that." Use of these exemplars implies that the definer assumes knowledge of the concept but not the name of the concept, that is, the superordinate *prose.*

Analysis Pattern. Analysis is the distinguishing of component parts and showing their relation to one another and to the topic as a related whole. There are basic types: analysis by partition and analysis by classification.

How does *analysis by partition* proceed? That which is to be explained is divided into parts, how each part works and/or its function is explained, and their interrelatedness is explained. Analysis by partition is used in explaining one object, one idea, or one process. The component parts are not mutually exclusive, but may work in tandem or interrelatedly. Taking process, for example, one could explain the process of fluvial erosion as an interrelated complex of hydraulic action, abrasion, solution, and transport. "Fluvial Erosion and Deposition" from *A Textbook of Geology* by Chester Longwell et al. is an excellent example of analysis by partition. Each facet—hydraulic action, abrasion, etc.—is taken up in turn and explained, and any existing causal *relationships* are also noted.

How does *analysis by classification* proceed? Martin (1958) discusses one type of analysis by classification:

1. A proposition is stated.
2. The proposition is divided into a subject and a predicate.
3. Points related to the subject are classified into categories.
4. Each category is developed by an elaboration of its points.
5. Points related to the predicate are classified into categories.
6. Each category is developed by an elaboration of its points.

Martin gives a brief example without going into a lot of detail, starting with a proposition that serves as the core of an essay:

1. Proposition. "Washington's policy of avoiding 'foreign entanglements' is no longer possible for any civilized country."
2. a. The subject. "Washington's policy of avoiding 'foreign entanglements . . .'"
   b. The predicate. ". . . is no longer possible for any civilized country."
3. Classifying points related to subject into categories. We assume here that these points in his "Farewell Address" can be classified into categories which can be labeled "economic," "political," and "moral."
4. An elaboration of points is made by referring again to his address.
5 and 6. The predicate is developed and the contention inherent in it is proved by a marshaling of relevant points based on current conditions under the three categories—"economic," etc.

Cause and Effect Pattern. This pattern might more properly be termed causes and effects since a given effect can have a number of causes. Think of the complex of causes for cancer; the Civil War; a good marriage; a high IQ; and so forth. At any rate, cause and effect deals with dynamic relationships between and among phenomena. What are the causes of a given phenomenon? What effects might result from a given phenomenen or set of phenomena?

Writers, then, use certain devices to explain such relationships. Readers need to be familiar with such devices; these usually are the relationships in which cause and effect are close in time and in physical proximity:

Obvious, common C-E relationships using simple explanation:

Where causes are close in time and physical proximity to the effect or event and the relationship is stated in a way that makes the relationship obvious.

1. Some transitional (or indicator) words and phrases commonly used to indicate a cause–effect relationship (C = Cause; E = Effect):

for	Let us go, <u>for</u> all things are now ready. E C
because	<u>Because</u> she neither studied wisely nor sedulously she failed. C E

therefore	You did not hearken unto my voice, <u>therefore</u> the kingdom
	                                      C
	shall be taken from you.
	        E

accordingly	Your spelling average for the year is 98%; your certificate will
	                             C
	be adorned with a blue seal, <u>accordingly</u>.
	                           E

consequently	The coach did not bring reflected glory to the sophomoric
	                             C
	middle-aged alumni, <u>consequently</u> his contract was summarily and furtively bought up with funds provided by "boosters,"
	        E
	without consulting the team, the faculty, the students or the great majority of the alumni.

2. Transitional words that can show cause-effect or merely show relationship in time are *then, since,* and *as*.

then	The English fired a volley into the enemy, and <u>then</u> the enemy fell.
since	<u>Since</u> the other team did not show up, the game was cancelled.
as	The man was crippled <u>as</u> the result of a car accident that he had.

Complex cause–effect relationships are exemplified in the Civil War phenomenon in which a complicated, interrelated network of phenomena and associated events culminated in the Civil War (the War Between the States).

In this kind of reading, one studies history texts or the literature dealing with the Civil War and carefully traces ideas, ideals, movements, and events and sees a concatenation of interrelated phenomena that lead to a precipitating event or cause that gave the big effect, in this case the War. My notes indicate some of the relationships I encountered. I distilled them into several complexes; the points are chronological, with many cause–effect relationships.

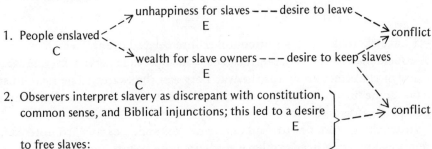

2. Observers interpret slavery as discrepant with constitution, common sense, and Biblical injunctions; this led to a desire

   E

   to free slaves:
   a. Quaker abolition movement began in the eighteenth century.
   b. Charles Finney encouraged spiritual-social reform in the form of good works.
   c. The transcendentalists were on a quest for right and justice.
   d. Women worked for reform in many areas, including slavery.

   (I will not try to label all the succeeding C-E relationships; they are obvious.)

3. Northern and southern business men had their ups and downs and blamed each other for their ills. Yet at the same time they taunted one another with their own real and assumed economic advantages, especially if war were to break out.

4. The preceding phenomena and cause–effect relationships and conflict led to bitter exchange of invective and rhetoric.

5. A comparative lull in the storm came with the Great Debate between Lincoln and Douglas.
   a. Lincoln stated, "The sentiment that contemplates the institution of slavery in this country as a wrong is the sentiment of the Republican party . . . They look upon it as being a moral, social, and political wrong."
   b. Douglas agreed that, "We ought to extend to the negro race . . . all the rights, all the privileges, and all the immunities which they can exercise with the safety of society." (Conditional for blacks, but was it for whites?) But he went on to say that each State should "mind its own business, attend to its own affairs, take care of its own negroes, and not meddle with its neighbors, then there will be peace . . ." (but still slavery).

6. Then the South lost power in Congress, and the southern leaders demanded that the Fugitive Slave Law be applied. A meeting in Vicksburg, Mississippi in 1859—a Southern Business convention—asked for a reopening of the Atlantic slave trade.

7. Violence erupted in Harper's Ferry, Virginia, when a firebrand by the name of John Brown captured white hostages. He was captured, and in court he gave a speech in which he told the country that he would be rewarded rather than punished if the benefactors of his actions had been the "rich, the powerful, the so-called great." He said prophetically just before he was executed that "the crimes of this guilty land will never be purged away but with Blood."

8. Threats and denunciations were exchanged between North and South.

9. Lincoln was elected.

10. The South seceded and . . . .

11. The secession was backed by Southern editors.

12. Rebels raised troops.
13. Ft. Sumter was fired upon by the rebels. It is ironic that the firing on Ft. Sumter which precipitated the war was due to a disobedience of orders <u>not</u> to fire on it.

I have sketched a series of complex interrelated events, which are in actuality a concatenation of cause–effect relationships that served in aggregate as the cause of the effect known as the War Between the States. The facts I used might have come from an essay, but they did not. The point is that they illustrate complex cause and effect.

In teaching students to read essays or "extended essays" to note cause–effect relationships, one needs to have students note points and see what they lead to, also looking for transitional words that indicate C–E relationships. The important "events" and ideas should be reduced to capsule form. Arrows can be drawn from one point (C) to another (E). Points can be grouped to show a movement, a force, as I did with the Quaker abolition movement, Charles Finney's reform, the transcendendalists, and the women's reform movement. This grouping is a form of the analysis discussed in the previous section. The points and categories can be revised and arranged with appropriate markings to bring out the flow of C–E relationships and their culmination in the big effect.

However, before engaging in such complex activities, you should have your students analyze sentences, paragraphs, and brief simple essays that use C–E relationships or whichever relationship you are teaching. After a while, let them analyze essays for whatever relationships they may contain.

Before going on to a very brief discussion of the remaining patterns, let me show you the kind of paragraph students can analyse for C–E (and other kinds of) relationships:

Children of the poor:

> The widest and most varied opportunities for play have surrounded the child for centuries in the country life. . . . The growth of large cities has deprived the child of these opportunities . . . . The street is all that is left to the playing child, and the street gang is his organization for purposes of play. . . . They have no purpose except to play, and this means . . . to "steal, to destroy, even to stab or shoot" . . . The collapse of home life . . . and the necessity which compels both mother and father . . . to work early and late, bereave the child of every good influence . . . Our gardens are given a place apart; flowers and plants are tended . . . by wise hands . . . but the childhood of our city is without its place, without its tending, and without its guidance.
>
> —*From Robert Hunter, Poverty, 1904.*

Comparison and Contrast Pattern. This pattern is a nonpareil method for differentiating ideas that have a number of similarities but some important, and possibly confusing, difference. Sometimes one does not know what something is until one knows what it is not. Contrast in particular helps to differentiate things that are similar in some respects but not in others.

Such methods as the following could be the end result of the analysis of someone's prose or a beginning sketch preparatory to writing a comparison and contrast piece.

Feature List Comparison–Contrast: A simple, interesting form of comparison contrast involves a feature list. A plus indicates that this is generally true, that it is characteristic; a minus indicates that this is not characteristic.

	Uses rhyme	Much figurative language	Inverted expressions	Conveys ideas	Uses meter	Arrangement of words	Each line begins with capital letter
Poetry	+	+	+	+	+	+	+
Prose	−	−	−	+	−	+	−

Two-Column Comparison–Contrast: There is no end to what can be compared and contrasted. The following example is a fairly simple analysis of aspects of the short story and the play. It is not intended to be exhausive or sophisticated.

Short story	Play
1. Has a theme and plot.	1. Has a theme and plot.
2. Uses scenes.	2. Uses scenes.
3. Setting is carefully described.	3. Setting is more hinted at.
4. Not usually written to be performed.	4. Written to be performed.
5. More written cues to characterization.	5. Characterization has to be inferred more from dialogue.

In other patterns, such as *analogy* patterns, the writer can explain a difficult subject in terms of something familiar and concrete. Edward Bellamy wrote "The Stagecoach" in an attempt to acquaint the readers of his time with the social structure of the world in 1887. This excerpt is from his work *Looking Backward* in which he writes as though he were living in the not-too-happy days of 1887. He compares "society as it then was to a prodigious coach which the masses of humanity were harnessed to drag toilsomely along a very hilly and sandy road. The driver was hunger, and permitted no lagging . . . . the top was covered with passengers who never got down, even at the steepest ascents."

It may be that by analogy writers reach readers in a very special way. I seriously recommend Bellamy's "The Stagecoach."

SUMMARY

Works of art are designed to give pleasure. Although it is stated that such works imitate what humans have observed and reacted to, some people say that life imitates art. Good works of art have the qualities of universality and individuality. Through the former, one's need to recognize the familiar is satisfied; through the latter, one's need to uncover the new is met.

Fiction helps us reconcile happiness with goodness. Since people seem to be looking constantly for trouble, one can more safely experience it vicariously rather than directly. The fiction writer aims to concoct an impossible yarn and make it sound plausible.

I have assumed that an interesting way to teach students to read fiction with understanding is to teach them how writers set about constructing their fascinating, impossible yarns. Consequently, the craft of writing fiction is discussed at great length. An illustrative lesson for the teaching of short stories provides another valuable strategy for helping students comprehend and appreciate fiction.

The term *drama*, has various meanings, but the present discussion centers on reading drama. Seven drama reading skills and strategies for teaching them are given.

The essay is an important kind of expository prose. Some essays are humorous, but most of them are of a serious nature and for proper comprehension they require thorough logical analyses of the cognitive relationships in them.

Patterns of exposition or explanation treated in this chapter are definition, analysis, cause and effect, comparison–contrast, and analogy. Some patterns are further divided and the relationships involved are explicated and illustrated. In the complex cause and effect pattern I sketched a series of complex interrelated events, which are in actuality a concatenation of cause–effect relationships, which are in sum the cause of the effect known as the Civil War. More direct teaching of how to read expository prose must be done in the schools. Teachers will, however, have to (1) use materials of appropriate difficulty and interest, (2) work at helping students understand the relationships involved, and (3) do this teaching over a long period of time.

ACTIVITIES AND QUESTIONS
TO PROMOTE LEARNING AND APPLICATION

1. What fiction have you read in which happiness is reconciled with goodness?
2. Make a list of certain kinds of people and the stereotype trait assigned to them to create *flat* characters.
3. Characterize acquaintances as rounded characters or as characters in relief. See if your acquaintances can guess given characterizations.

4. Do the exercises under "Making applications: noting characterization in fiction" in the present chapter.
5. Of what value is the *sequel* in fiction?
6. Do the exercises under "making applications: analyzing scenes."
7. How do you interpret the author's statement, "The plots of the Magnificat and the Sermon on the Mount work out in people's lives in each generation to two-world solutions"?
8. Teacher and students will probably enjoy the applications for "plot" in the text.
9. Create other examples of the four types of discovery–reversal. Let *yourself go; it can be a lot of* fun!
10. Make applications by "analyzing plots." Execute several of the seven suggestions in the chapter such as (1) "Take the stories whose scenes you analyzed in the last section. State the plot of each story in a few sentences . . . , and the like.
11. Make the applications suggested in the text to help you learn more about settings.
12. Teach the illustrative lesson for the short story "The Legend of Sleepy Hollow."
13. Write a lesson for the short story of your choice, submit it to the criticism of your peers and your instructor.
14. After doing all the exercises, plan a special seminar with students and faculty. The seminar may be for other students and faculty, and/or interested individuals in the college community, in the schools, or in the general community.
15. Read a play and find cues to characterization. Make notes of these cues and share them in a class discussion.
16. For a given play, determine which scenes are not as interesting (to students) as others. Analyze each scene in terms of its elements to see if weakness in given elements accounts for lack of interest.
17. For a given play, try to detect the motivating forces that trigger the character's behavior.
18. Develop an overview for a Shakespearean play, using the six-point plan developed in the text. Try it out with students, peers, or teachers.
19. What in your estimation are some transfer elements between reading short stories and reading drama? (This question, beginning with "what," will hopefully disabuse anyone who still believes that "what" questions require merely literal comprehension of that idea.)
20. Read and classify expository material according to the pattern(s) of explanation used. Give evidence for each classification made.
21. Write a brief essay on a topic of interest to you, using a particular pattern of explanation or patterns. Allow others to read your essay What do they like about it. What do they dislike? Try to ascertain their reasons.

SUGGESTED ADDITIONAL READINGS

AUKERMAN, ROBERT C. *Reading in the Secondary School Classroom.* New York: Mc-Graw-Hill, 1972. Chapter 8.

BURTON, DWIGHT L. *Literature Study in High Schools.* Third Edition. New York: Holt, Rinehart and Winston, 1970.

CONNELLY, JOHN E. "Techniques for Improving Comprehension in English." In Gerald G. Duffey (Ed.). *Reading in the Middle School.* Newark, Del.: International Reading Association, 1974. Pp. 130–39.

GALLO, DONALD R. "Reading in Literature: The Importance of Student Involvement." In James L. Laffey (Ed.). *Reading in the Content Areas.* Newark, Del.: International Reading Association, 1972. Pp. 1–29.

SHEPHERD, DAVID L. *Comprehensive High School Reading Methods.* Columbus, Ohio: Charles E. Merrill, 1973. Chapter 8.

BIBLIOGRAPHY

BROSSELL, GORDON. "Developing Power and Expressiveness in the Language Learning Process." In James Squire (Ed.). *Seventy-sixth Yearbook of National Society for the Study of Education.* Chicago: University of Chicago Press, 1976.

CAMPBELL, W. S. *Writing Magazine Fiction.* Garden City, New York: Doubleday, 1948.

CROWDER, WILLIAM W. "The Role of Literature in Fostering International Relations." In Helen W. Painter (Ed.). *Reaching Children and Young People Through Literature.* Newark, Del.: International Reading Association, 1971.

DAUGHERTY, AILEEN (Ed.). *Guide to the Teaching of Reading.* LaGrange, Illinois: Lyons Township School Board, n.d.

HASELRIIS, PETER. "Student Involvement Is Just the Beginning." In James L. Laffey (Ed.). *Reading in the Content Areas.* Newark, Del.: International Reading Association, 1972.

MARTIN, HAROLD C. *The Logic and Rhetoric of Exposition.* New York: Rinehart, 1958.

PANNWITT, BARBARA. *The Art of Short Fiction.* Boston: Ginn, 1964.

CHAPTER 16

Reading in Business Education

GENERAL READING REQUIREMENTS, PROBLEMS, AND SKILLS

Vocabulary Meanings—Comprehension

The world of business is broad and complex and there are many occupations within this world such as accountant, bookkeeper, executive, insurance agent, lawyer, secretary, and shipping clerk. All these people have technical vocabulary with which they must deal. Of course, there is some overlap among these occupations.

House (1953, 1954) studied vocabulary load in bookkeeping texts and the reading ability of tenth-grade bookkeeping students. He found the technical vocabulary in bookkeeping to be extremely heavy. He also noted a wide range of reading ability in secondary schools from about fourth-grade to college levels. In fact, 62 per cent of the 357 students were below the average tenth-grade student in vocabulary knowledge and 60 per cent were below average in comprehension on a standardized reading test.

Hafner, et al. (1971) also found general reading ability to be important to achievement in reading bookkeeping materials.

Concept-Vocabulary Loads. There are several problems with learning technical terms in business fields:

1. For many students both the concepts and the vocabulary used to represent them are totally foreign.

2. Many words are abstract.

3. Quite a few words are long and difficult to decode (related also to general unfamiliarity with the concepts and labels).

4. As with many technical areas, the concept density is great due to competitive concept stuffing.

5. Students after years of holding a cavalier attitude or a laissez-faire attitude toward the world of ideas think business fields are an easy out. Of course, these students receive a shock.

Terms in Bookkeeping-Accounting:

1. Technical terms.

accounts payable	invoice	subsidiary accounts
cash discount	ledger	trial balance
inventory	purchase order	unexpended balance

2. Common terms with special meanings.

abstract	capital	journal	register	terms
allot	extend	prove	surplus	

Terms in General Business, Business Law, Office Practice:

1. Sample of technical terms.

abstract	express	plaintiff
affidavit	figure discount	postscript
alien	finance	principal
asterisk	foreclosure	proofread
bankruptcy	freight	proxy
bill of lading	girth	receipt
breach	health	refund
budget	honest	repossess
capital	income tax	retail
certificate of title	installment	secretary
chattel mortgage	journal	silent partner
civil law	lawyer	stock turnover
commercial size	letter of appreciation	subsidiary
complimentary close	lien	terminate
credit letter	market	tort
cross referencing	mortgage	usury
defendant	night letter	valid
dictation	nominal	vertical file
dividend	notify	voucher
elite type	outcharge	wholesale
empathy	ownership	witness
enterprise	parentheses	zone
excise tax		

Reading Ability

When vocabulary is a problem, comprehension is a problem. Also, lack of skill in relating concepts and principles in textual materials lowers comprehension. And reading comprehension problems in business and related fields are serious. Because of them, people can get themselves and their businesses into legal and financial problems. Civil and criminal suits may follow and loss of confidence in one's business and concomitant dwindling of profits may ensue. At the extreme, bankruptcy is a threat.

Therefore, every effort must be made by the homes and the schools to improve concept-vocabulary development—general terms are a big problem, too—and reading comprehension skills. Before determining which areas need improvement, one should get appropriate data through testing. The chapter on measurement and evaluation provides many ideas that can be used directly or adapted. Some ideas on informal testing follow.

INFORMAL TESTING

Hafner, Robinson, and Gwaltney (1971) found that a very small sample of bookkeeping teachers had quite a difficult time of predicting their students' performance on a bookkeeping content cloze test. The teachers also seemed to think that intelligence is synonymous with reading performance: teacher *perception* of intelligence and reading correlated .87. However, the correlation for measured *performance* on these two variables was .58.

Ability to comprehend bookkeeping material can be measured accurately by using the content cloze test (delete certain important nouns and verbs). Actually, Hafner, et al. found that one can get a pretty good idea of how well a person reads bookkeeping material by selecting a long passage from a bookkeeping text, deleting all punctuation marks and capital letters (at beginning of sentences), and having students supply the deleted items. There is a good possibility that this phenomenon applies to other reading materials in the business field.

Of course, the business teacher will want to develop vocabulary tests to see how students understand the terminology.[1] One should develop chapter readiness tests in order to see if the students are capable of handling the concept-vocabulary-reading tasks demanded. You will remember the mathematics reading test at the end of Chapter 11.

IMPROVING THE READING OF BUSINESS MATERIALS

Vocabulary Development

Some strategies for developing meaningful vocabulary are:

1. *Associating the term with experience.* Probe the students' memories for pertinent experiences that will provide a meaningful matrix for the term.

2. *Placing the word in meaningful context.* When developing a *Directed Reading Lesson* for a section or chapter, use previously discussed techniques such as placing each new term in a meaningful sentence context. Before this preteaching and before reading the material, test the students on the items introduced.

3 *Prepare a take-home study sheet.* A day or two prior to the reading of a section, select technical and general vocabulary terms that will probably cause

---

[1] One can extend the diagnostic value by having students read group vocabulary tests and reading tests and drawing one line under any word they cannot pronounce and two lines under any word they do not know the meaning of.

the students trouble and prepare a study sheet. Put each word in sentence context; you may also provide a pronunciation key if you wish. An example from business law—*legal process* is the topic—follows.

legal process /lēg'əl prä'ses/	1. The way in which you can start an action in a court of law is called legal process.
	2. When you go to court to try to convince the judge (or jury) that someone must pay you the money he or she owes you, you are using legal process.
summons /sə'mənz/	1. When the judge sends the person who owes you money a special "letter" to come to court, he is summoning him. The "letter" is a summons.
defendant /dē fend'ənt/	The person being charged is called the defendant in court. The person who owes you money is called the defendant and hire a lawyer to help with his defense.
plaintiff /plān'tif/	The person making the complaint is known as the plaintiff. (Notice the "plaint" in complaint and plaintiff.)
lawsuit /lô'süt/	The legal process of bringing a plaintiff to court in order to try to obtain justice is known as a lawsuit.

4. *Note the special technical meanings of certain terms.* For example, a defendant in boxing puts up his *fists* and tries to ward off blows. Not so in the court. In court a defendant uses legal means that do not involve fisticuffs. Also, the word *overhead* might refer to the sky above you or to the ceiling in everyday speech. In business *overhead* refers to the expenses of running a business—the rent you pay to use a building and land for your office or shop, for example.

5. *Where possible bring realia and/or snapshots, drawings, and the like that illustrate such phenomena as business terms, transactions, commodities, and relationships.* For example, you may bring advertisements, sketches, copies of contracts, bills of lading, income-tax forms, order forms, copies of pages from ledgers, business letters, stocks and bonds (a few that are not worth very much). Discuss the purpose of these realia and point out the meaning of certain terms in their contexts. Concept-vocabulary work, including discussion (as outlined above), pays handsome dividends in comprehension and is good for class morale and motivation to read and succeed!

Comprehension Development

Some Key Questions. Aukerman (1972) points out that since one is rather concerned with main ideas, and to get at the basic points in reading business materials one asks questions beginning with *what, how, how much, how many,* and *why.* These words, of course, have to be followed by other words in order to make a meaningful question. Let us take some business situations:

1. Reading about how to start a business and applying it to plans to start a business.
   a. What business do I want to start?

b. Why do I want to start a business?
c. What is the situation in the text about starting a business?
d. How does one start a business?
e. How does that information relate to my problem?
f. How much money is usually required to start the kind of business I am thinking about?
g. How much money will it take to get my business underway?
h. How many months, years will it be before I am paying all bills, making regular installment (mortgage, etc.) payments, and still be making a decent profit?
i. How much profit do I expect to make?

Study guides in the text may be used to advantage if the instructor shows students *how* to use them. The teacher should work through at least one set of guides *with* the students. Many people in business have to read and solve mathematical word problems. Do not forget to recheck the mathematics chapters in the present text for valuable cues on how to read and solve such problems.

2. Reading business law. These are questions students are taught to ask. They are a combination of the key words—what, how, how much, etc.
    a. What is the problem?
    b. What is a tort?
    c. How do we know that Martinelli committed a tort?
    d. How many common torts are there?
    e. Why should we know about torts?
    f. What does assault mean?
    g. What are some things that qualify the meaning of assault?
    h. In the case of Pratt and Anderson, how do you think the judge ruled? Why?

What Are Some Common Torts?

Problem: Martinelli was erecting a scaffold in preparation for painting a building when the head flew off his hammer, hitting and injuring Bott, a passerby. Did Martinelli commit a tort?

A tort may be the result of a deliberately harmful act or an act that is done unintentionally, or, as in the problem, it may result from doing a legal act in a manner that is harmful to someone else. Since a tort is any invasion of a private right, some of them are discussed later in connection with other topics. A few of the more common torts are as follows:

(1) ASSAULT

A person has the right to be free from reasonable fear that he will suffer personal injury from another person. A breach of the duty or failing to observe the right is an assault. It consists of a threat to inflict physical injury upon another causing a reasonable fear that it will be carried out. Mere words do not constitute an assault; threat of violence must also be displayed. The threat must be accompanied also by an apparent ability to carry it into execution.

Anderson, an elderly and totally blind person, thought Pratt, who was not blind, was taking advantage of him. He threatened to "beat Pratt's face to a pulp" (Fisk, 1972).

Now write some questions to guide the thinking of a person who reads the following comments on the nuisance tort. I have not included the ruling at this point. The last question could ask the reader to predict the court's ruling. Discussion of this point should bring about more careful reading.

1. _____

2. _____

3. _____

4. _____

5. _____

6. _____

(2) NUISANCE

A person has the right to the use and enjoyment of his property without unreasonable interference from others. This means that one must use his property so that it does not injure others. To use one's property in a manner that unreasonably interferes with others' use and enjoyment of their property is a nuisance.

> Channel operated an asphalt plant near the homes of Mirande and Roland who had lived there before the asphalt plant was opened. They claimed the fumes, odors, smoke, dirt, and dust caused by the plant and blown by the wind over their homes created a nuisance (Fisk, 1972).

3. Materials for the poor reader.

Wylie (1975) has developed a number of personal reading modules called Life Style 70's with such titles as "My Legal Rights," "Buyer's Rights," "Money," "Marriage," and "On Your Own." The rationale for these materials, which are written at readability levels ranging from 2.0 to 2.5 and interest levels of 10.5+, is summarized briefly as follows:

1. The need for high-interest, controlled vocabulary reading materials that are personally rewarding to young adult and adult disabled readers.

2. The need for materials with high content density that address important social, economic, and personal concerns.

3. The need for materials that use more learning modalities than just pure reading.

4. The need for materials that create an interest in and a desire for learning.

Life Style 70's, according to Wylie, provides high-interest learning and an audio approach to learning in which an audio tape teaches the main concepts in context through conversation. The key concepts, then, appear (1) in print for the student to read, (2) during tape listening, and (3) for follow-up reading and study.

Each *Life Style 70's* module contains: "15 high interest, limited reading illustrated books, an audio conversation tape that extends book content, 15 four-page skill development sheets that teach and reinforce basic skills, a Teacher's Guide that provides teaching strategies, and a sturdy box for storage or display."

I should like to present the *directions for teaching* the module titled "Money" along with *excerpts from the materials:*

1. READINESS

Introduce and teach the Key Words from the last page of each book. Encourage the students to understand the relationship of each word to the topic. Write the words on the chalkboard for student reference while reading and listening.

KEY WORDS

advantages	checks	money	promise to pay
credit card	disadvantages	money order	register
deposit			

2. LISTEN AND READ

Have the students listen to the audio tape and follow along with the book. Encourage the students to think about the tape narrative and the corresponding pictures in the book. (The book contains short, controlled vocabulary sentences of the major concepts presented on the accompanying book.)

Page 3:

One form of money that shows who owns it is a check. A check is an order written by someone who has money in the bank to someone else whose name is on the check.

At first look most checks seem the same. But when you look carefully, you will see that each one is very different. Look with me at the check on this page. In the top left corner is the name of the person paying out the money (Mr. Bob Roberts, 1652 Stone Mountain Drive, Stone Mountain, Georgia). The numbers in the upper right corner tell the check number (2050) and the number of the bank. Right after the words "Pay To The Order Of" is the name of the person to whom the money will be paid (Carol George). Then, you will find the amount of money to be paid ($50.00). This amount of money is written twice, once with numbers and once in words. This is done to help stop errors and to prevent someone from changing the numbers without the writer's knowledge.

Page 4:

A checking account is an easy way to pay bills. Money in a checking account can be taken out, or withdrawn, as it is called, just by writing a check. People with checking accounts don't need to carry a lot of cash.

Each check book has two parts. Part one, the checks, and part two, a place to write deposits and withdrawals. This part is called the register.

When writing checks it is important to write clearly. If a check is not clear, the bank will not cash it.

Page 5:

The register is where you keep track of your money When you write a check, record the number of the check written, the date, to whom the check was written, the amount of the check and finally the amount of money still in your account. For example, the last check written was number 2051, July 4, 1975, to J-D Hardware, in the amount of $27.36. After the $27.36 check there is a balance of $125.00 in the checking account.

If you enter each check as you write it, you will always know how much money you have in your account.

Each month you will receive a record from the bank of all the checks that were returned as well as the checks. By comparing this record with your register, you will know who got your checks and when they got them.

If you save your cancelled checks, you will have proof of paying your bills.

Page 6:

If a check is written and there is not enough money in the account, the check is sent back to the person who wrote it. When this happens, the check is called "a bad check" and it has bounced. When there is not enough money in an account to pay the order, the check is returned to the person who received it. If this happens, the person has two choices:

1. To take the check back to the bank in hopes that there is now enough money
or
2. Contact the person who gave you the check and ask them to pay you in cash.

If you write a bad check, the bank will probably charge you five, six, or more dollars as a penalty. This money is taken from your account. So you can see it pays to be careful.

The important thing to remember about a check is that it is not cash, it is only a promise to pay cash. Before a check becomes cash, the check must go to the writer's bank and the money taken out of the account. When the money is placed in your account, it becomes cash.

3. DISCUSSION

"Discuss the concepts presented on the tape."
"Discussion Questions:

Use questions similar to the following to stimulate discussion about money:
1. Why should you have a checking account?
2. A good credit rating is important because . . .
3. The advantages and disadvantages of paper money are . . .
4. If you owned a store (you would) (you would not) be reluctant to accept checks because . . .
5. If you could invent one more type of money, what would it be? What would it do that the types we now have do not do?

4. READ

Have the students read the book. Stop and discuss at points where appropriate. (The following excerpts will be confined to the part of the book on ordinary checks; not all the subtopics on checking are excerpted.[2])

[2] The following headings on checks, along with illustrations and explanatory sentences, are found in the book: 1. CHECKS; 2. REASONS FOR A CHECKING ACCOUNT; 3. CHECKS AND REGISTER; 4. WRITING IN THE REGISTER; 5. COMPARE THE REGISTER WITH THE STATEMENT; 6. A BAD CHECK; and 7. WHAT TO DO WITH IT. I shall excerpt several of these.

CHECKS

One form of money that shows who owns it, is a check.

Most checks look the same, but when you look carefully, you will see that each one is very different.

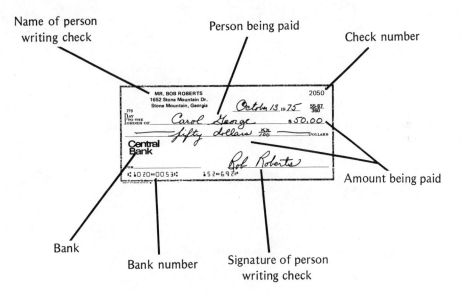

Name of person writing check

Person being paid

Check number

Amount being paid

Bank

Bank number

Signature of person writing check

REASONS FOR A CHECKING ACCOUNT

A checking account is an easy way to pay bills. The check can be sent by mail and when it is cashed, you have proof it was received.

WRITING IN THE REGISTER

Check number   Date   Person paid   Amount   Money left in account

CHECK NO.	DATE	CHECKS ISSUED TO OR DESCRIPTION OF DEPOSIT	AMOUNT OF CHECK	✓	AMOUNT OF DEPOSIT	BALANCE FORWARD
						386 55
2047	7/1	To Jean Cox (typing)	25 00			Check or Dep. 25 00
						Bal. 361 55
2048	7/1	To City Electric	23 75			Check or Dep. 23 75
						Bal. 337 80
2049	7/2	To Parkway Garage (repairs)	94 00			Check or Dep. 94 00
						Bal. 243 80
	7/3	To			20. 00	Check or Dep. 20 00
		For				Bal. 263 80
2050	7/4	To Harris Clothing (suit)	111 44			Check or Dep. 111 44
						Bal. 152 36
2051	7/4	To J-D Hardware (hinges)	27 36			Check or Dep. 27 36
						Bal. 125 00

Each time you write a check, record the information about your check in the register.

5. DO THE SKILL SHEET

Have the students complete the skill sheet.

_____

Name

_____

Date

MONEY SKILL SHEET

KEY WORDS:

Match each picture to the word or phrase that best describes the picture.

Money Order

Register

YES OR NO

Directions: Read each sentence. Write yes if you agree or no if you do not agree.

6. _____ A checkbook has two parts; checks and a register.

7. _____ A check is only a promise to pay.

8. _____ A money order and a check are the same thing.

9. _____ A charge card is like money.

10. _____ A bad check is when there is not enough money to cover a written check.

Pictures Talk

Directions: Look at each picture. Name the form of money, and how it is best used.

Name: _____

_____

Use: _____

USING ALL TYPES OF MONEY

Directions: Read each situation. Write the type of money you would use in the situation.

1. Mail money to a friend.

2. Pay bills.

3. Buy a pack of gum.

4. Buy clothing at the store

Applying Study Skills

Please review the techniques involved in SQ3R which were presented in Chapter 7. As you remember, the *Survey* works as an advance organizer for developing a cognitive framework. Developing *questions* is also part of the framework and helps motivate and guide the meaningful silent reading through which students will extricate and organize the more important ideas and relationships. As a person *reads* he or she *recites* the ideas in order to paraphrase the material and extract the key parts pertaining to the question. He or she then writes the answer and at appropriate times *reviews* the questions and answers in order to understand better the material and place it in long-term memory.

The teacher should remember that tests tend to dictate the curriculum and the way it is taught. Examinations should test for mathematical techniques and processes involved in accounting, cashiering, tax-return preparation, and the like, but also check on student ability to recall and discuss such things as *torts*—examples and implications—, finance and banking problems, government regulations, and ways of improving office practice. In other words, students should know detailed techniques as well as global processes, principles, and problem-solving approaches. Therefore, students should be taught to process ideas and to re-chunk and organize them for varying purposes and appropriate applications. Paradigms in Chapters 6 and 7 provide helpful models.

SUMMARY

One must infer from the studies on reading and bookkeeping that many students are trying to read such materials and are encountering formidable obstacles. The reading ability of such students was as low as the fourth grade at the time of the studies by House and are probably lower today.

I delineated five types of problems associated with learning technical terms in the field of business. A listing of many of these terms followed. The reader who is not conversant with the argot used in business will understand the quandary in which many fledgling business students find themselves.

Vocabulary knowledge and reasoning ability are the two most important factors in reading comprehension, so when vocabulary is a problem for the reader comprehension is a problem. Furthermore, when the reader is unskilled in manipulating ideas—that is in relating given ideas to other ideas—comprehension, perforce, suffers.

Reading-comprehension problems in business-related fields are so serious that homes and schools should team up to improve concept-vocabulary development.

Testing of the ability to read business materials can be handled by the informal methods discussed in chapter 4. Also, the ability to read such materials with understanding can be measured by using a content cloze as well as the punctuation cloze test similar to that developed by the present author and his associates. It was also pointed out that the diagnostic value of reading tests can be increased by having students draw one line under words they cannot pronounce and two lines under words they do not know the meaning of, a technique I devised a number of years ago.

Several strategies for developing meaningful vocabulary were presented in the chapter. They should be used sedulously, because they pay rich dividends in increased understanding.

Rather than re-present the numerous strategies for developing comprehension, which can be found in the present volume, I expanded on an idea of Aukerman's and applied it to the reading of material on torts.

Of special interest to the reader should be the excellent materials developed by Wylie for the poor reader. To me, these materials are exemplary.

Finally, a brief review of the SQ3R study procedure was presented. The chapter closed with a few hortatory remarks on (1) the relation of examinations to curriculum development and (2) the need to teach students detailed techniques as well as global processes, principles, and problem-solving approaches.

ACTIVITIES AND QUESTIONS
TO PROMOTE LEARNING AND APPLICATION

1. Study the reading achievement of a secondary school bookkeeping class. Correlate knowledge of technical terms, general reading achievement, math computation ability, and course grades. What interrelationships do you find?
2. How can you apply the information obtained in your study to helping students improve their reading of bookkeeping materials?
3. Devise a content cloze test to determine the ability of students enrolled in office practice or secretarial courses to read and understand segments of the material. Also, have the students draw one line under any word they cannot pronounce and two lines under any word they do not know the meaning of. Does there seem to be any relation between pronunciation problems and problems in supplying the correct words in the cloze task? between meaning problems and cloze task problems?
4. Randomly divide the poorest readers in a business class into a preparation group and a nonpreparation group. For a given segment of reading material that the students will shortly read, devise for the preparation group a take-home study sheet, discuss the pronunciation and meaning problems involved in it, and have the preparation group take it home to study overnight. Review the next day. Collect the study sheets. On the next day have the nonpreparation group and the preparation group read the material on which the study sheet was based and give them a multiple-choice test over the material. Compare mean scores and the range of scores of the two groups. (Apply test to determine if the difference in mean scores is statistically significant at the .05 level of significance. Your reading methods instructor should be able to help you with these calculations.)
5. Try point five about bringing to a business education class realia, drawings, and the like. Compare realia with the text's discussion of such items. Discuss the meanings of certain terms in the contexts supplied by these realia and note the effect of such work on interest and comprehension.

6. Devise meaningful *what, how, how much, how many,* and *why* questions for use with specific materials. Apply these questions by guiding the students in seeing the interrelationships involved in the materials. Point up cues in the text that help one see these relationships. Also check for mispronunciations of words and misunderstanding of general and technical vocabulary terms. Now you are teaching!

7. Try out in special classes materials such as the *Life Style 70s* modules and note the students' reactions to these materials. I would not be averse to receiving feedback on the value of such instructional materials, nor, in my estimation, would the authors of such materials.

8. Teach your average and above-average readers how to use the SQ3R study technique. So that they will see the "payoff" for using such techniques, utilize essay tests on chapters so studied!

SUGGESTED ADDITIONAL READINGS

AUKERMAN, ROBERT C. *Reading in the Secondary School Classroom.* New York: McGraw-Hill, 1972. Chapter 11.
HARRISON, L. J. "Teaching Accounting Students How to Read." In Lawrence E. Hafner (Ed.). *Improving Reading in Middle and Secondary Schools.* New York: Macmillan, 1974. Pp. 404–407.
MILLER, WILMA H. *Teaching Reading in the Secondary School.* Springfield, Illinois: Charles C. Thomas, 1974. Chapter 15.
MUSSELMAN, VERNON A. "The Reading Problem in Teaching Bookkeeping." In Lawrence E. Hafner (Ed.). *Improving Reading in Middle and Secondary Schools.* New York: Macmillan, 1974. Pp. 398–404.
PIERCEY, DOROTHY. *Reading Activities in Content Areas.* Boston: Allyn & Bacon, 1976. Chapter 3.
ROBINSON, H. ALAN. *Teaching Reading and Study Strategies: The Content Areas.* Boston: Allyn & Bacon, 1975. Pp. 211–16.

BIBLIOGRAPHY

AUKERMAN, ROBERT. *Reading in the Secondary Classroom.* New York: McGraw-Hill, 1972.
FISK, MCKEE, NORBERT J. MIETERS, and JAMES C. SNAPP. *Applied Business Law.* Tenth Edition. Cincinnati: Southwestern Publishing Co., 1972.
HAFNER, LAWRENCE E., WAYNE GWALTNEY, and RICHARD ROBINSON. "Reading in Bookkeeping: Predictions and Performance." *Journal of Reading.* 14 (8) (May 1971), 537–46.
HOUSE, F. WAYNE. "Factors Affecting Student Achievement in Beginning Bookkeeping in the High School." Oklahoma Agricultural and Mechanical College. Stillwater, 1953a.
_____ . "Are You Solving the Reading Problem in Bookkeeping?" *Business Education World.* 33 (February 1953), 291, 292.
WYLIE, RICHARD E. "Money." *Life Style 70's.* Indian Rocks Beach, Florida: Relevant Productions, 1975.

CHAPTER 17

Reading in Vocational-Technical Education: Construction Trades, Automotive Science, Electronics, Home Economics

One could hardly begin to list all the technical areas taught at the secondary level. I have chosen some for emphasis in this chapter. Home economics has been included, for example, because it, too, is a technical area, requiring mathematical and scientific knowhow. Also, any course can be taught at various levels of sophistication. Therefore, the vignettes presented here may seem to be too sophisticated for use in some classrooms, whereas for other classrooms they will seem too elementary.

The key strategies for testing, teaching reading acquisition, comprehension, study skills, and the like are found in previous chapters. The transfer of these strategies to the areas treated in the next three chapters is not difficult. It requires only a willingness to study the strategies treated in earlier sections in order to see their essential purposes, structures, and directions. The intelligent teacher will not encounter great difficulty in adapting them to a specific content area.

BASIC EDUCATION: READING ACQUISITION

In some vocational education curricula nonreaders are provided an opportunity to learn to read. Strategies for teaching reading acquisition are provided in Chapter 21. Additional notes of interest follow.

A Programmed Linguistic Approach

In situations in which individuals already know the letter names or can be taught to recognize and print the names of letters, a programmed linguistic method can be used to teach reading. The *Sound Reading Program,* discussed in Chapter 21, is a method that is not offensive to older students. It has been used even in secondary schools and adult reading programs. It is a systematic method that starts at rock bottom and brings a person through four decoding books and four comprehension books to the fourth-grade level in reading. Research by Morgan (1974) shows it to be quite cost effective, too.

The Language Experience Approach with Older Illiterates

The Language Experience Approach (LEA) has been widely used in elementary and middle schools. However, Becker (1970) showed that the LEA approach combined with high motivation and respect for personalities was quite successful in teaching four illiterate teenagers.

Although these four young women could comprehend seventh-grade selections *read to them*, only one of them could read as many as 8 of the 20 test words at the preprimer (early first grade) level. The subjects met five days a week as a group and discussed the ideas and objectives of the Job Corps (in which they were enrolled) and shared experiences. In this way, each person gained the feeling that "her *own* language was effective in communicating her knowledge, emotions, and ideas to others."

The first topic to be used as the basis for the LEA approach was recorded on a chalkboard using manuscript (print) writing. As the trainees pulled together the ideas that they had discussed, they formulated the following sentences:

> I am a woman. I am in the Job Corps. The Job Corps is in Charleston, West Virginia. All the girls learn a job. Some girls want to be a secretary. Some girls want to be nurses. A girl can learn to be a beautician, too. The Job Corps is my job now.

This first recorded language experience was rooted deeply in the group's experiences and interests. In the analytic language experience approach used here the progression is from whole to parts. Thus, as each sentence was written on the chalkboard, the group read the sentence aloud. The instructor pointed to each word as it was read; this procedure showed that one reads from left-to-right and from line to line. The trainees, as a result of the first session, saw that they had worthwhile ideas and that their language was acceptable for developing reading materials, that their ideas were formulated into a cohesive paragraph that one reads from left to right, and that punctuation is used in writing. Most importantly, they experienced the joy of reading successfully.

When a typewritten copy of the composition was given to each person, real joy broke out. Individuals were encouraged to try to read the selection. Of course, they could not read it perfectly, and follow-up activities were used to help master the words. (See Chapter 21 for types of activities that can be used to "nail down" words.)

The students also worked in pairs and were encouraged to keep their own individual stacks of sight word cards. Each individual's learning rate was determined by the number of words remembered the following day. Instruction was adjusted accordingly, but the learning rates "increased steadily with continuing instruction, removal of confusions, and improved study habits."

Instruction was carried on as an integrated language arts pattern; for example, for the remainder of the week attention was focused on word-recognition skills and bringing together spelling and writing with the reading. Meaning was emphasized; for example, the trainees were helped to use context clues as aids in word recognition. Phonics instruction was related to auditory-discrimination exercises and drills. Also, *Remedial Reading Drills* by Hegge, Kirk, and Kirk was used successfully as a supplemental phonics system. Spelling words came from the LEA compositions and the word lists in the Hegge materials.

Word-recognition, vocabulary, and comprehension skills were emphasized during the subsequent months. Interesting and suitable materials at the first through third reading levels, although of limited availability, did include the *SRA Reading Laboratories,* the *Reader's Digest Skillbuilders,* and *Book Series of Adult Readers* (by Education Division of Reader's Digest Services). Two volumes of easy-to-read biographical sketches of famous blacks titled *We Honor Them* were quite interesting to the group.

Each trainee developed a job-oriented book on the vocational area in which she was interested. In addition to job-oriented topics and discussions, "topics related to personal and family problems, community frictions, and controversial issues were welcomed."

After eleven months of instruction the trainees scored 2.8, 3.3, 3.8, and 5.5 (reading grade placement) on the *Diagnostic Reading Scales.* Furthermore, instructional levels at this time were determined by constructing an informal reading inventory based on the reading selections in the *Reader's Digest Skillbuilders*; two trainees were now being instructed on a third-grade level, one on a fourth level, and one on a fifth level. The findings jibed pretty well with the results obtained from the *Diagnostic Reading Scales.*

The LEA method, plus supplementary work, proved to be a very effective way of bringing these young women out of the illiterate category to the point at which they could enjoy reading and develop some pride about their reading ability.

INFORMAL TESTING

Standardized and informal tests for determining mental capacity and reading achievement have already been discussed in a previous chapter. The strategies discussed there are easy to apply to the various content areas.

Quick Survey Tests: Word Recognition and Vocabulary Knowledge

At this point I would like to list some key technical terms in a number of content areas, which are suitable for *word-recognition* and *vocabulary* tests. If a vocation is not mentioned, the reader should be able to pull samples of words in order to construct a test.

Developing and Using Word-Recognition Tests. If a teacher wants to use the lists as word-recognition tests he or she will present the student with the list and ask that the student read the words in order. On another copy, the examiner will check each word as correct or incorrect. One also has some options: (1) the words can be presented on a timed (flash) basis and/or an untimed basis; (2) partial pronunciation can be noted.

If you present the words on a *timed* or *flash* basis, use a homemade tachistoscope (See Figure 17-1). The words are typed in a column (double spaced) on stiff material that is about 2 inches wide. The column is inserted in the tachistoscope so that the words can be presented one at a time. Each word is exposed for one-half second.

Figure 17-1 shows the home-made tachistoscope. Two cards are used to make the tachistoscope. An aperture about 6/16 inch high and 1½ inches wide is cut into the front card. The tachistoscope will be slightly wider and a bit shorter than the card on which the column of words is printed.

Test the student on a flash basis first, allowing the word to be exposed for one-half second. The words that are correct can be checked in the flash column. (See the response record sheet which follows.) For the untimed presentation, give the student a copy of the test and ask him or her to read the items missed in the flashed presentation. Check the ones the student gets correct. Note partial pronunciations and also the methods used (if they can be determined) to identify a given word.

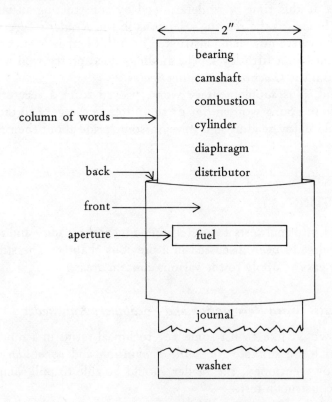

Figure 17-1. Home-made Tachistoscope for Presenting Words on a Time (Flash) Basis.

Response Record Sheet

	Word Recognition		Definition
	Name		
Engine Operation	flash	untimed	
bearing	_____	_____	_____
camshaft	_____	_____	_____
combustion	_____	_____	_____
cylinder	_____	_____	_____
diaphragm	_____	_____	_____
distributor	_____	_____	_____
engine	_____	_____	_____
exhaust	_____	_____	_____
fuel	_____	_____	_____
grooves	_____	_____	_____
ignite	_____	_____	_____
installed	_____	_____	_____
journal	_____	_____	_____
keeper	_____	_____	_____
mechanism	_____	_____	_____
oil pump	_____	_____	_____
piston	_____	_____	_____
pressure	_____	_____	_____
rotary	_____	_____	_____
sequence	_____	_____	_____
sprocket	_____	_____	_____
temperature	_____	_____	_____
vacuum	_____	_____	_____
valve	_____	_____	_____
washer	_____	_____	_____
Total	_____	_____	_____

Testing Vocabulary Knowledge.   Vocabulary can also be tested after a word-recognition test is given. Read the word (if necessary) and ask the student to define it. Since you are the expert in your field, you will need to set criteria for acceptable answers. You may want to compile a list of acceptable answers for each item. If you would like to give more credit for better quality responses, keep a list of two-point responses for each item, a list of one-point responses, and a list of no-point responses. You need to write the student's responses as they are given and check them for quality later.

I have already presented a list of words on engine operation, one facet of automotive mechanics. Below you will find samples of words from a number of technical-vocational areas. I took more samples from the construction areas in order to give you an inkling of the subareas. Also, I took many samples from the area of home economics because many students take a variety of courses in this area.

These words can be used as sources for the type of word-recognition and vocabulary test just described. They can also be used as Quick Survey Tests for the areas labeled.

Quick Survey Tests.   One can quickly get an idea of the technical words known by any given individual (either word-recognition or vocabulary) in any of the following areas by administering the appropriate 25-word tests that follow. To convert score to percentage correct, *multiply the score by four.*

Working with Wood: Wood Types and Basic Tools

beams	lumber	quarter-sawed
boards	maple	rule
dimensions	nail	running foot
drying	oak	saw
edge	paint	stacking
grain	pine	swelling
hammer	plane	timber
knots	planks	warping
log		

Carpentry

balloon framing	insulation	plaster lath
bridging	jack rafters	rafters
casings	joints	specifications
diagonal bracing	louvered vents	studs
elevation	molds	symbols
footings	mullions	valley rafters
framing	nails	ventilation
girder	outrigger scaffolds	window sash
header		

Plumbing

adjustable open-end
   wrench
bushing
centrifugal pump
cross connection
drain auger
drum trap
escutcheon
faucet

fixture
basket
hacksaw
insulation
joist
male adapter
neoprene sleeve
oakum
pipewrench

plug
reducer
septic tank
shutoff valve
T fitting
threading
valve seat
water seat

Sheet Metal: Shop Practice

angle iron
bench level shears
blowhorn stake
crimping machine
dovetail seam
elevation view
flat cold chisel
galvanize
hawkbill snips

lid stiffener
miter line
nibbler
oblique cone
plain rectangular duct
protractor
rollation
soldering

squaring shears
tacking
template
triangulation
universal stake holder
vertex
welding rod
y fitting

Air Conditioning and Heating

attic condensation
batts
British Thermal Unit
connection
duct
electrostatic
   precipitation
expansion tank
finned tube coils

furnace thimble
gable vent
germicide-treated filter
humidifier
hydronic
inside flush mounting
kilowatt
multistage thermostat
odor control

polyethylene sheeting
refractory fire pump
refrigerant tubes
steam gauge
thermostat
upflow highboy
ventilation
weatherstripping

Basic Electricity

alternating current
ampere
anode
battery
circuit breaker
condenser
direct current
dry cell
electrolysis

electromagnet
fluorescent light
grounded
inductance
insulator
left-hand generator
   rule
magneto
ohm's law

parallel circuit
rheostat
right-hand rule for motors
solenoid
thermocouple
transformer
voltmeter
watt

Electronics: Radio, Television, and Computers

assembly language
capacitance
cardioid microphone
cathode ray tube
digital computer
filament transformer
frequency modulation
grid
hertz

image orthicon
ionize
integrated-injection
   logic
microprocessors
n-type semiconductors
oscillator
pentode
photoelectric cell

photovoltaic cell
radar
scanning beam
series resonance
signal-to-noise ratio
thermionic emission
transistor
vacuum tube

Personality and Personal Care

accessories
becomingness
budget
characteristic
dental floss
ethics
fiber
grooming
hem

inverted pleat
jumper
knit
lengthwise grain
manners
nutrition
outside margin
petite

posture
religion
safety
texture
understitching
vacation
weskit
yoke

The Family: Meals, Family Relations, Family Health, and Homemaking

buffet service
caring and sharing
center of interest
dinnerware
family experiences
glaze
human relationships
informed buyer

menu
medicine
mercerized cotton
nutritious meals
operating expenses
organization
paring knife
protein

responsibility
sauté
security
spiritual guidance
sunshine
telephone etiquette
vitamins
working habits

Recipes (Cooking, Baking, Cake Decorating) and Nutrition

alternate layers
beriberi
caramelize
cardiovascular system
confection
enzymes
figure piping
groundnut protein
   isolate

hors d'oeuvres
julienne
kwashiorkor
lysine
marasmus
parboil
prenatal protein
requirement
protein synthesis

saucepan
skinfold thickness
soya milk absorption
sprig
sterilize
trace minerals
tryptophan
vegetable protein blends
waffle

Measuring Understanding

The IVCA Inventory.   You can ascertain a student's ability to comprehend a text and apply what is read by administering an informal inventory based on the text. I call this the IVCA Inventory, an acronym of *I*ndex, *V*ocabulary, Comprehension, and *A*pplication. This can be a group inventory if you require the student to write the responses. The IVCA Inventory format can be applied to any content reading material. Ten questions provide a good sample, and scores are easily converted to a percent.

IVCA Inventory
Based on Sheet Metal Shop Practice
—Leroy F. Bruce and Leo A. Meyer

Using the Index

Directions: Below you see a segment of the index of a book on sheet metal shop practice. Please read the questions and write your answers.
1. On which page(s) can you find out how to exercise care while soldering?
2. Where do we get information on the folding rule?

INDEX

R
Round taper by radial line, 211, <u>212</u>
Round taper by triangulation, 204, <u>205</u>
Rules (instruments), 7
  Common, how to read, 61, <u>62</u>
  Folding, 7, <u>7</u>
  Steel flexible circumference, 7, <u>7</u>

S
S & drive slips to join duct, project, 121, <u>121</u>
Safety
  Cornice brake, 98
  Gas furnace, soldering, 142
  General, 34, 35, 38
Sal ammonias, 147, <u>147</u>
Saw, band, 68, <u>69</u>
Soft Solder, 138
Solder, bar, 139, <u>139</u>

Vocabulary

Directions: Read the following words and tell in writing what each word means. You may make drawings as necessary. If you cannot read the word, draw a line under it.*
3. diameter
4. denominator

*These words should be defined before the student reads the textbook.

  5. circumference
  6. common rule

Comprehension: Translation

Directions: Read the following section of text material and answer the questions, please.
  7. Does the word <u>former</u> refer to 3.1416 or 3 1/7?
  8. Can a person get more accuracy with a denominator of 8 or one of 64?

FINDING CIRCUMFERENCE BY USE OF FIGURES. Occasionally the sheet metal worker desires to find the distance around a pipe without the use of a circumference rule. The method for doing this is to multiple the diameter of the pipe by 3.1416 or 3 1/7. The former is generally preferred. For example, suppose that a pipe 5″ in diameter is to be made. The first step would be to find the circumference in inches. This can be done in the following steps:

  1. Multiply 3.1416 by the diameter, 5″

     $$3.1416$$
     $$\underline{\times 5''}$$
     15.7080″   circumference of pipe

  2. Change the decimal .7080 to a fraction that can be read on the common rule. To do this, multiple the decimal .7080 by the denominator of the fraction that is to be used, such as 8, 16, or 32, depending on the accuracy required. In this problem, use 16 thus:

     $$.7080$$
     $$\underline{\times 16}$$
     11.3280 or 11/16

  3. The decimal .7080 can now be read as the fraction 11/16.
  4. This makes 15.7080″ = 15 11/16″, which can be read directly from the common rule.

Hence, we see that multiplying the decimal by the denominator of any of the fractional inch graduations on the rule will give the numerator of the desired fraction as shown by the preceding example.

Application

Directions: Please do the following problems based on the selection above:
  9. What is the circumference of a circle that has a diameter of seven inches?
  10. Convert .37 to a fraction that has 32 in the denominator.

NOTE: You may wonder why I ask the students to answer the vocabulary items *before* reading the text. This procedure will give you an idea of a student's understanding of some rather key concepts needed in the text. If a student has trouble with these concepts, you will have to do specific concept-vocabulary work. You should always be checking on this anyway!

TEACHING READING SKILLS

Teaching Students to Identify Words

Teaching sight words is easier when students know the meaning of the words you are trying to teach. When you are attempting to teach a word that is not easily depictable, or for which you have no example that can be labeled, it may be necessary to use card readers so that students may practice identifying the words.

Some Woodworking Terms. If one assumes that an individual knows the meanings of the following words taken from the areas of *plywood, hardboard,* and *wall paneling,* one can use word-picture cards for teaching students to identify the printed word:

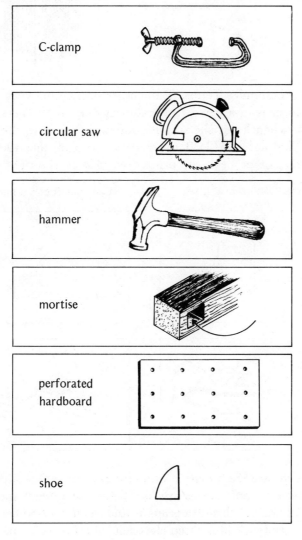

Sometimes illustrations in which several terms can be incorporated can be used:

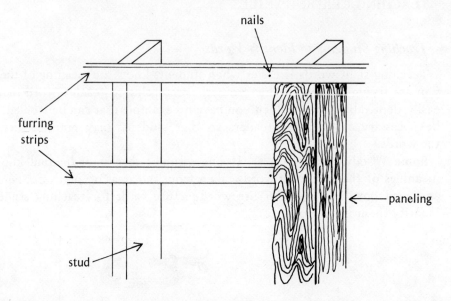

Some Home Economics Terms. Remember, in making vocabulary cards (1) if the spoken form is in a person's vocabulary (i.e., if the person can name an item or process when he or she sees it) but cannot read it, the printed word is to the *left* of the picture. (2) If the person can read, but does not know the name of the item or process, the printed word is to the right of the pictures.

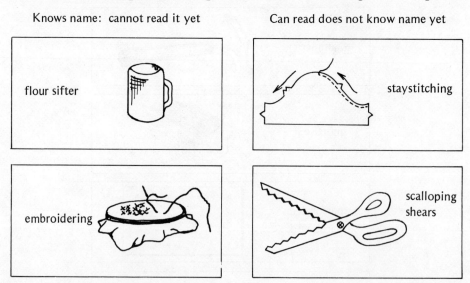

Illustrated Technical Dictionary. Sometimes a concept is somewhat involved and illustrations and applications are useful for clarifying it and helping one to remember it. Of course, this idea is *applicable to all content areas.* Figure 17-2 is a page from a student's illustrated electricity dictionary.

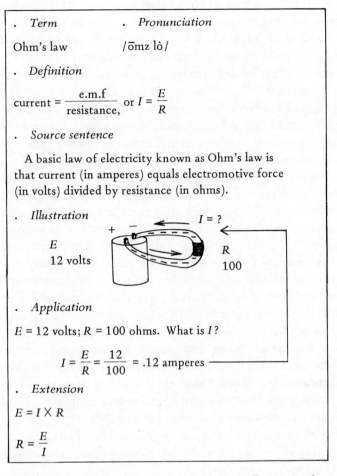

. Term   . Pronunciation

Ohm's law   /ōmz lò/

. Definition

$$current = \frac{e.m.f}{resistance,} \text{ or } I = \frac{E}{R}$$

. Source sentence

A basic law of electricity known as Ohm's law is that current (in amperes) equals electromotive force (in volts) divided by resistance (in ohms).

. Illustration

$I = ?$

E
12 volts

R
100

. Application

$E = 12$ volts; $R = 100$ ohms. What is I?

$$I = \frac{E}{R} = \frac{12}{100} = .12 \text{ amperes}$$

. Extension

$E = I \times R$

$$R = \frac{E}{I}$$

Figure 17-2. Page of Illustrated Dictionary, Illustrating the Ohm's Law Concept.

Independent Word Identification

In order to be able to identify words independently, one can use context plus a "sounding out" of the constituent parts of a word. Partial sounding out can be successful if the context is strong enough and the material is at the student's instructional reading level It is a pitiful thing to hear a teacher asking a student to "sound out" a word when the student knows only one of several elements in a word. That is like asking a student to read a long chemical formula when he or she only knows how to decode H and N or to play a Bach passacaglia in D major when all he or she can play is "Twinkle, Twinkle, Little Star" and a triad.

Some people look at phonics, *as ordinarily taught,* as a panacea for the poor reader; it is probably the least successful approach to teaching word acquisition to individuals of less than average intelligence, according to research by Mills (1956).

The Case of Ed. Newman (1965) relates the case of a ninth-grade student named Ed who on entering a remedial reading class at Vocational High School in New York tested at 2.6-grade level in both silent and oral reading. His chief problems were an inability to "sound out" words and a limited knowledge of basic sight words. What he did manage to piece together, he understood fairly well because he made intelligent use of context clues.

After five terms of remedial reading instruction Ed tested at 3.9 in reading. Even though he could "sound out" quite a few words, his oral reading showed poor phrasing, repetitions, omissions, and errors on easy words. (Not to second guess or criticize Newman, but overdependence on having to sound out very many of the words rather than having been taught more of the words directly does cause nonfluent reading and does interfere with meaning gathering!)

Newman interviewed Ed five years after remediation. Ed remarked that prior to remedial instruction he could rarely read his textbooks with understanding and often asked his father for help. Ed's ability (after instruction) to better understand his textbooks was attributed by him to his ability to "sound out" words. He was especially delighted by studying the construction of words through structural and phonic analysis. He also attributed his increased confidence in his ability to succeed in other course work to having a method of attacking new words.

A Teaching Paradigm. Some individuals in vocational-technical education classes may be of average or below-average intelligence (or have below par cognitive foundations). Phonic elements that are taught inductively would more likely stick than those taught by rules and examples. However, once a phonic element or grapheme-phoneme correspondence is learned inductively, further examples of the rule thus developed can be elicited or provided. Also, it would not hurt to use a rule and examples approach occasionally to see how it works and to provide some variety.

Do you remember the inductive paradigm? Once a *minimum* of two words containing a given grapheme-phoneme correspondence are known as sight words, that correspondence can be taught inductively:

1. <u>Select words</u>: beach and chair
2. <u>Align vertically so common elements are juxtaposed</u>:   beach
                                          chair
3. <u>Ask student, How do the words look alike?</u>   "Both contain ch"
4. <u>How do they sound alike?</u>   "Both have /ch/."
5. <u>What kind of rule can you make about pronouncing ⟨ch⟩?</u>   "If you come across ⟨ch⟩ you sound it /ch/."
6. You may underline the ⟨ch⟩ in each word.
7. <u>Can you think of other words that have ⟨ch⟩ in them?</u>

8. <u>Let us build some words</u>
   using ⟨ch⟩.
   <u>Known words:</u>   team   fill   gulf   smoke

                  tea__   __ill   gul__   __oke

9. <u>Give me some sentences, please, that use these new words that contain ⟨ch⟩.</u>
   (Write them on the chalkboard.)

   . Teach me some more phonics.
   . I get a chill when I stand on icebergs.
   . I'm all choked up about your winning the state lottery.

10. <u>Apply this new element to the list of other known elements and practice</u>
    <u>sounding out the following.</u> (Assume here the person now knows t, p, l, k, b,
    d, s; ea/ē/, ai /ā/, oa /ō/; sh /sh/, ch /ch/, ph /f/, e, /e/, and o /ä/:

    Some examples:

cheal	ched	deach	chail	pesh	bais
daish	pais	toas	shoak	poph	

Ruddell (1969) has pointed out that pronunciation combinations have high transfer value in decoding words. As I have said, however, much application and practice are necessary.

11. <u>Some simple games which can be used as follow-up activities</u> are found in books by authors such as Richard Bloomer, Selma Herr, and Evelyn Spache.

Vocabulary Development

In working on vocabulary problems the teacher needs to determine with respect to a word or group of words the following:

1. Does the student know the *concept* involved?
2. Does the student know the spoken *label* for the concept?
3. Is neither the concept nor the spoken label in the student's meaning repertoire?
4. Can the student read the *label* (vocabulary term) for the concept?

I have discussed concept development and vocabulary development at great length in other chapters. A review of *some points to consider* in developing *spoken* vocabulary follows:

1. Point to thing (hammer, nail, stud, plank) or process (hammering, sawing, measuring) and provide a spoken label. This procedure may need to be repeated.
2. Note features of thing or process. Where necessary, differentiate features of similar concepts.
3. Discuss uses of things and processes; note related vocabulary.
4. Note how the things are correctly used and processes correctly executed; note related vocabulary.
5. Encourage use of the vocabulary in appropriate situations.
6. Draw pictures of things and processes on Language Master Cards and record appropriate words, phrases, and sentences for identifying the things drawn.

Training Program for Mentally Retarded. Camacho and Smith (1975) provided a reading program for mentally retarded trainees in a meatcutting training program at an Air Force Base. The remedial reading program was not designed to improve the overall reading grade level of the trainees; it was limited only to that which was vocationally applicable. Therefore, all materials—including vocabulary lists, application forms, and the like—were designed by the teacher to meet the specific needs of the reading program.

Since many trainees had undergone formal remedial training in the public schools prior to entering the Air Force, that approach was shunned. Instead, an attempt was made to tie the vocabulary and the reading to what the trainees were doing in the meatcutting training and what they would be doing soon after they left the program. The reading segment of the program consisted of about three and one-half months of daily lessons. It was broken down into three phases:

1. a. Meatcutting vocabulary (100 words).
   b. Identification of various cuts of meat by word and illustration.
2. a. Application form vocabulary (100 words).
   b. Simulated job interviews (tape recorder used here).
   c. Working through 10 application forms of increasing complexity.
3. a. Driver's license vocabulary (300 words).
   b. Road symbols and signs.

The trainees were handled individually or in groups of two or three. Some very slow trainees did not make it through category one. Others completed all three categories and were given supplementary training related to a work situation. Overall, the training program was considered to be successful. Most trainees were placed in competitive employment.

More complete strategies for vocabulary development are found in Chapter 5 and in other content-area chapters.

Readability of Certain Technical Materials Used in the Army

How does a person determine the readability of certain reading materials which are designed for technical training? Sticht (1975) reports on the research he and his associates have been conducting in literacy training for the army. Their research on readability yielded these results:

1. One can use readability formula based only on the number of one-syllable words in a 150-word sample of material.

2. This formula called FORCAST (FORd, CAylor, STicht), produced a more accurate estimate of the reading difficulty of Army job reading materials than did the Flesch and Dale-Chall formulas.

3. Data also revealed that over half the reading materials in each of seven jobs exceeded the eleventh-grade difficulty level as measured by the FORCAST formula.

According to Caylor, in Sticht (1975), the formula is

$$\text{FORCAST readability in RGL} = 20 - \frac{\text{number of one-syllable words}}{10}$$

One obvious limitation to using the FORCAST index is its restricted range. Even if all the words in a 150-word passage were monosyllabic, Caylor notes, the passage's readability would be indexed as 5.0 RGL. No army job material of such "low" readability has been encountered, however. The average readabilities of materials designed for training certain kinds of specialists and the reading ability of high and low aptitude candidates in those fields are given in Table 17.1.

Table 17.1. Average Readabilities of Materials Designed for Training Certain Specialists and the Reading Ability of High- and Low-Aptitude Candidates in Those Fields

Specialist category	Readability of Materials	Reading Ability	
		High Aptitude	Low Aptitude
supply specialist	16+	10.5	7.7
repairman	14.5	9.5	7.4
cook	8.8	9.5	7.4
ground control radio repairman	11.2 (estimate)	——	——

One can see the parallels with the vocational-technical subareas discussed in this chapter: supply specialist (business), repairman and ground control radio repairman (technical), cook (subarea of home economics). I would suggest that the reader determine the readability of materials in the vocational area of his or her choice and compare the findings with the results in the corresponding areas above.

Comprehension Development

Assumptions. The following assumptions should be studied and taken into consideration:

1. The majority of reading materials in vocational-technical (V-T) areas are tenth-grade level and above.

2. The reading ability of many individuals who take courses in V-T areas is far less than tenth-grade level.

3. Few V-T materials are being written at a readability level that corresponds to the reading ability of the individuals who must read them.

4. Individuals who are expected to somehow tackle these materials *must* be taught to read each section in a chapter by a particular strategy.

5. Some of the reading comprehension strategies that can be used singly and in combination are the Directed Reading Lesson (DRL); the Paraphrase-Cloze

Lesson (P-CL): The Reading-Reasoning Guide (R-RG); Re-Quest Procedure (R-QP); the Hypothesis Testing Procedure (HTP); and the *Basic Idea*-Main *Idea*-'N' (and) *Inferences* (drawing conclusions) (BIMINI) discussed in this text.

6. Many more people will be able to succeed in the V-T areas as they are taught reading material as reading lessons.

7. Specialized procedures can be used to teach students to read and follow directions.

8. Comprehension improves as word knowledge develops and as students are *taught again and again* to make thorough logical analyses of cognitive relationships encoded in reading material.

9. The reading achievement of people who are systematically taught to read these materials over a long period of time will improve.

A Directed Reading Lesson Plan.   Following is a complete Directed Reading Lesson (DRL) Plan, modeled after the one presented in the chapter on basic procedures. It is thorough because what myriad numbers of students in vocational-technical programs need is a solid, comprehensive procedure for teaching them to read analytically with comprehension.

Directed Reading Lesson Plan for Teaching a Technical Selection

I. Readiness
   A. Background
      1. One prerequisite for reading this selection is knowledge of how magnetism is used to make electricity: magnets, magnetic properties, inductance, and principles of generator operation.
      2. In a discussion or introduction, bring out the fact that a car, for example, has both motors and generators. Point out that an engine is an engine and that a motor is something else. Also note that when mechanical power—say from the engine—is connected to the generator, electricity is generated as wires are moved through a magnetic field. In the operation of a motor, the process is reversed: electricity is fed into a motor mechanism and mechanical power results. In this lesson the students will learn what makes motors run. (Some of the above points may be brought out through "Socratic" dialogue in order to involve the students and keep their attention.)
   B. Pretest: magnetism used to make electricity (the generator)
      Directions: Please read the items below and answer them. Indicate true with a + and false with a 0. In the completion subtest complete the sentences by filling in the appropriate word for each blank.

      True–False

      ___1. A piece of iron can be magnetized.

      ___2. A motor is run by mechanical power.

      ___3. Like (magnetic) poles repel.

      ___4. A galvanometer can be used to detect current.

Completion

5. To magnetize a piece of iron, wind_____around it many times

and send a_____ through the wire.

6. Label correctly and complete the arrows to show current induction,

magnetic flux, and _____ in order to show understanding of
generator principles.

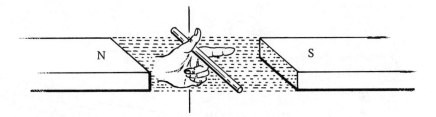

C. Review known words and teach new words
   1. Pronunciation (and meaning)
      (Technique choices, singly or in combination: diacritical marking, word-
   picture cards, card readers, discussion, using words in context)

motor	current	magnet
magnetize	polarity	magnetic field
repel	iron filings	cross section
horshoe magnet	lines of force	generator
right-hand rule	drum	

   2. Meanings: words in context (reading + discussion)

   Chart A

   . A <u>motor</u> is run by electricity.
   . Electric pumps and vacuum cleaners are run by electric <u>motors</u>.
   . The mass of electrons that move through a wire is called <u>current</u>.
   . Each of the two ends of a <u>magnet</u> is called a pole.
   . To <u>magnetize</u> a piece of iron wrap many turns of wire around it and
     send a current through the wire.
   . If one end or pole of a magnet has positive <u>polarity</u>, the other pole has
     negative polarity.
   . A <u>magnetic field</u> flows from the north pole of a horseshoe magnet
     across space to the south pole.
   . Bring two like poles (S, S or N, N) toward each other and they will
     <u>repel</u> one another.
   . Little chips of iron that result from filing are called <u>iron filings</u>.
   . The mechanism that uses mechanical power such as that provided by
     an engine (in a car) or a waterfall and converts it into electricity is
     a <u>generator</u>.
   . Current is <u>induced</u> in a wire by moving the (coiled) wire up and down
     through a magnetic field; this <u>generates</u> electricity.

3. <u>Picture dictionary</u> (Discuss each term briefly and point out that the students can refer to the chart as needed while reading. The <u>full</u> meaning of the new concepts involved will be brought out in the reading selection.)

Chart B

Picture Dictionary

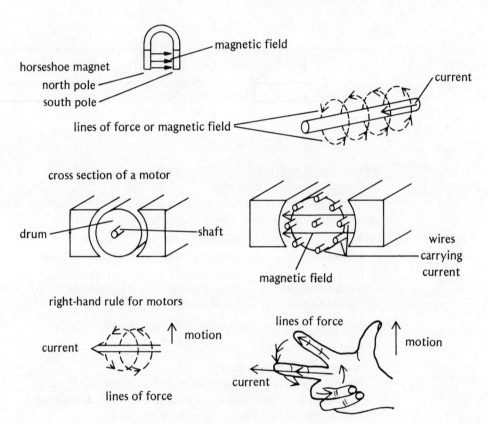

4. <u>Words in context plus questions</u>

Chart C   <u>Words in Context</u>

a.   The power that makes a <u>generator</u> work is mechanical power.

Q.   Explain briefly <u>how</u> a <u>generator</u> is powered.

b.   A magnet will attract an iron nail, not <u>repel</u> it.

Q.   Why does a <u>magnet</u> attract an iron nail?

Q.   Under what <u>conditions</u> would a <u>magnet</u> repel an iron nail?

c.   <u>Lines of force</u> is another expression for magnetic field.

Q.   Explain <u>lines of force</u> around a wire in relation to current in the wire.

5. Review*
   a. Chart A: Find the sentence that tells about machines run by motors, and read it, please.
   b. Chart A: Find the sentence that tells about lines of force moving through an open area. Read it.
   c. Chart A: Find the word that means the body of electrons that are "transported" through wire.
   d. Chart B: Explain the right-hand rule.
   e. Chart B: Complete this sketch to illustrate d.
              (place sketch on chalkboard)

   f. Chart C: Find the word that represents the thing that produces electricity; frame it and read it.
   g. Chart C: Find the word that means a mass of electrons moving through a wire; frame it and read it, please.

D. Setting a Purpose
   1. Show the picture of a cutaway model of a generator and review very quickly the principles involved.
   2. Motors utilize the same basic principles used in generators, except one goes from electrical energy to mechanical energy. Let us read to find out how this is done. Be prepared to explain the process, please.

II. Guided Reading (Leave the charts on the wall for reference.)
   A. Reading to Answer the Motivating Question
      Directions: Read silently the selection "What Makes Motors Run?" to see how electrical energy is converted to mechanical energy.
      1. Walk around the class. Note the words that are underlined and give help if desired.
      2. Quickly clarify pronunciation and meaning problems.
      3. When most of the students have finished, ask for the answer to the motivating question.
   B. Guided Rereading
      1. How can one show the effect of a magnetic field?
      2. Explain the right-hand rule for current flow and magnetic field.
      3. What happens when a current-bearing wire is introduced at right angles into a magnetic field?
      4. Explain and illustrate the left-hand rule for motors.
      5. Explain how a motor works. Make sketches as necessary.

III. Teaching Reading-Thinking Skills
   A. Vocabulary
      1. E-A-S exercise
      Directions: Write an explanation or an antonym or a synonym for each word listed below; label E, A, or S.

magnet	current	magnetic field	galvanometer
motion	cross section	repel	
magnetic field			

---

*I owe a debt of gratitude to Professor Faye Kirtland for the structural ideas of the charts and the review.

2. Contextual application
   Directions: I will give several of you a word. Either act it out or use it a sentence to show you really understand it, please.

| repel | galvanometer | magnetic field | current |

B. Comprehension: paraphrase-cloze (Delete every seventh word beginning with the second sentence.)
   Directions: Please read the selection below and fill in the missing words. Sometimes a hyphenated word will be the correct one.

A magnetic field is set up around a wire through which current flows. Iron filings placed in such _____ magnetic field will be rearranged to _____ the influence of the field. The _____ rule regarding this effect states that _____ one grasps a wire so that _____ thumb points in the direction of _____ flow, the fingers will point the _____ of the magnetic field flow.

   When _____ current-carrying wire is introduced into a _____ field in such a way that _____ two fields are "parallel" at the _____ point, the wire will be repeled _____ a direction away from the side _____ which the lines join the magnetic _____ of the magnet. This phenomenon is _____ basis for the operation of the _____ .

NOTE: The deleted words may be placed below the selection in alphabetical order depending on the sophistication of the group, your expectations, and your purposes!

"What Makes Motors Run"

One can better explain why motors run by explaining the principles underlying their operation. Let us begin. Obtain a piece of cardboard, pass a segment of copper wire through it, and spread some iron filings on the cardboard. (Figure 17-3). Then connect the wire to a 12-volt battery. As current flows through the wire, a magnetic field is set up around the wire. The filings will be arranged in a pattern showing the influence of the magnetic field. The direction of the current determines the direction of the magnetic field. Grasp an unconnected wire with your right hand. The thumb will indicate the direction of the current when connected, and the fingers will indicate the directional flow of the magnetic field.

Figure 17-3.

Figure 17-4 shows only lines of force between the opposite poles of a magnet; there is a smooth flow from north to south. In Figure 17-5 we see how the lines of force flow as expected following the right-hand (grasping) rule—thumb indicates direction of current and fingers indicate lines of force around the wire. In Figure 17-6 we see what would happen to a wire if it were introduced to the magnetic field of the magnet. The field around the wire and the field on the magnet "combine" so that there are more lines of force in the magnet above the wire and the magnet's field repels the wire's field and the wire. This effect is known as the primary motor rule: A wire having a magnetic field tends to move away from the side on which its lines are added to those of another field. Since the lines are added on the topside of the wire, the wire is pushed downward in the directions of the arrow. Figure 17-7 is the cross section of a "motor." Because the current in the N-pole side of the motor is going in the direction it is, the right-hand rule for motors is applied (Figure 17-8) On the right side of the motor (N pole) the wires, and consequently the motor drum, go up. Since on the S-pole side the current goes in the "opposite" direction, we apply the left-hand rule (modified). (Figure 17-9) The wires and motor drum go down on the S-pole side. The resultant mechanical power is conveyed by the rotating shaft in the center of the drum Thus, a motor is a device for converting electrical power to mechanical power.

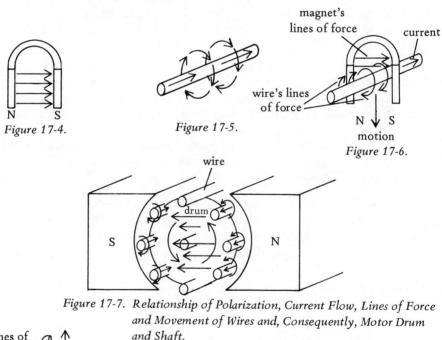

Figure 17-4.

Figure 17-5.

magnet's lines of force

current

wire's lines of force

N S
motion
Figure 17-6.

wire

drum

S   N

Figure 17-7. Relationship of Polarization, Current Flow, Lines of Force and Movement of Wires and, Consequently, Motor Drum and Shaft.

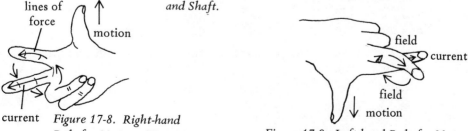

lines of force

motion

current   Figure 17-8. Right-hand Rule for Motors. (You See the Palm of Hand.)

field
current
field
motion

Figure 17-9. Left-hand Rule for Motors. (You See Back of Hand.)

Reading to Follow Directions. With some changes the following procedure for teaching students to read a recipe can be adapted to reading to follow directions in other technical areas. The products may be more durable but not as delicious.

Preparation: Teaching Concepts and Vocabulary:

1. Write the name of the recipe on the board and have it read ("Rich Christmas Stollen").

2. Ask the students to name the ingredients they think will be in the recipe. Write their offerings on the board.

3. Categorize the ingredients under headings.

4. Project the recipe on a screen, using overhead projector.

5. Place a check by each "correct" item on the chalkboard.

Rich Christmas Stollen

1 cup scalded milk	3 egg yolks
2 packages yeast	½ tsp. salt
1 tsp. sugar	½ tsp. nutmeg
1 cup margarine or butter	1 tsp. lemon extract
4 cups flour	1 cup candied fruit or orange slices
½ cup sugar	½ cup nuts

Cool scalded milk until lukewarm. Dissolve yeast and 1 tsp. sugar in ¼ cup of the scalded milk. Combine all ingredients, mix well, and knead until smooth with extra ½ cup flour. Put in large greased bowl, cover, and let rise until double in bulk (approximately 1½ to 2 hours). Punch down and divide into three equal parts. Spread with desired candied fruits and nuts. Knead again and form into loaves or rings. Put in pans. Let rise again approximately 1½ hours. Bake at 350 degrees, 30 to 35 minutes. When cool, ice with thin powdered sugar icing and decorate with extra candied fruit.

6. Write the name of each ingredient on the card and place the card by the ingredient. Spot check on students' ability to read the ingredients.

7. Also write *scalded, optional, approximately, bulk, dissolve,* and *desired* on the board and ask what they mean. Have the words used in a sentence. Be specific on the meaning of *scald.*

Checking Functions and Processes:

8. Ask what the *function* of each of the following is:

    scalded milk
    yeast
    margarine

9. Write the names of the *processes* on the board and call on individuals to pantomime the processes:

    mix well
    knead until smooth
    punch down
    divide in three parts
    spread with fruit and nuts

Reading the Recipe:

10. Distribute duplicated copies of the recipe.

11. Have the students read the recipe carefully to note the ingredients and to get the sequence of processes or procedures.

Comprehension Check (Project recipe on screen again):

12. Ask students the following questions:

    a. How does one scald milk?

    b. Is very hot milk put into the mixture?

    c. How is the ¼ cup of scalded milk used?

    d. What causes the dough to rise?

    e. Why does the dough rise after it is punched down?

    f. When are the loaves put into pans?

Sequence Check:

13. Number in the correct order the following procedures:

    Decorate with extra candied fruits.

    Combine all ingredients.

    Scald milk. (This is <u>inferred</u> from list of ingredients.)

    Knead until smooth with extra ½ cup flour.

    Punch down and divide into three equal parts.

    Put in pans.

    Mix well.

    Dissolve yeast and 1 tsp. sugar in ¼ cup of the scalded milk.

    Knead again and form into loaves or rings.

    Let rise again approximately 1½ hours.

    When cool, ice with thin powdered-sugar icing.

    Let rise until double in bulk.

    Put in large greased bowl, cover.

    Spread with desired candied fruit and nuts.

    Bake at 350 degrees, 30 to 35 minutes.

Execute and Check Product*:

14. Follow recipe and bake the stollen.

15. Serve stollen with milk and coffee.

SUMMARY

Since nonreaders enrolled in some vocational-technical (V-T) education courses are in "do or die" situations, schools have been providing a second chance for them.

Older students have learned to read by various approaches. Good results have come from both a programmed linguistics approach (SRP) and the language experience *approach*. Becker's study showed the success of the latter approach with several illiterate teenagers.

---

* I wish to thank my mother for the recipe and my mother and my wife for the times that I have been privileged to run product quality checks.

Quick survey tests for word recognitions and vocabulary were presented in the chapter as were vocabulary samples from a number of V-T areas. The reader also noted a complete example of my IVCA inventory for measuring understanding.

Independent word-identification skills are somewhat difficult to teach to the very low ability students. The utility of these skills for some students is over-rated. Such students can be taught to identify words when the words are taught by the "naildown" methods described in the chapter on reading acquisition and treated in part in the present chapter.

Clarification of concepts and the words and phrases used to represent them can be aided by developing illustrated technical dictionaries. Of course, these dictionaries—in addition to being good memory joggers—are a considerable source of pride to the contributors.

A thorough teaching paradigm for inductively teaching grapheme-phoneme associations was also presented. It was also pointed out by Ruddell that certain kinds of syllables or pronunciation combinations have high transfer value.

A teacher should ask four basic questions about a specific problem word or group of words encountered in reading materials. One should also remember that spoken vocabulary may be neglected. Six points to consider in developing spoken vocabulary were given in the chapter.

Mentally retarded people can be trained to read better. A program designed to improve the vocationally applicable reading skills of meatcutting trainees was delineated. The program was considered to be generally successful, and most of the trainees were placed in competitive employment.

Since there is some similarity between V-T training done in civilian and army schools, a formula used to ascertain the readability of V-T materials was discussed. No Army training material was found to be as easy as the lower limit of the formula, grade five.

When considering comprehension development, certain assumptions should be taken into consideration; nine such assumptions were provided. Of special interest to the reader is a complete Directed Reading Lesson (DRL) Plan for teaching a technical selection. The plan, of course, can be adapted for use in the various V-T areas, as well as in other subject-matter fields. Finally, a plan designed to teach students to read carefully and follow directions was presented.

ACTIVITIES AND QUESTIONS TO PROMOTE LEARNING AND APPLICATION

1. Select several nonreaders or poor readers and get them started at the appropriate level in programmed linguistic materials. Guide them through at least four levels. What change do you note in their reading ability? their self confidence?

2. How do you account for the success of the total reading instruction approach used with the four illiterate young women enrolled in the job corps?

3. Try out the *Quick Survey Tests: Word Recognition and Word Knowledge* in classes of your choice. Compare your rating of the ability of ten of the students to read related material to their instructor's rating of their ability to read the material. How do you account for any differences in the ratings.

4. Write an *IVCA Inventory* for a segment of material that will be read soon in a V-T class. Administer the inventory and share the results with the instructor of the class. Prepare a DRL for teaching students to read the material and teach them the lesson.

5. How would you teach V-T students to identify words?

6. Show several students how to develop entries for an illustrated technical dictionary. (This might be a group or an individual project.)

7. How are word-identification techniques sometimes misused?

8. What changes in instructional procedures would you make in approaching a case like that of Ed?

9. After determining several grapheme-phoneme associations that a few students do not know, ascertain some words (containing a given element) that they do know. Using the inductive teaching paradigm presented in the chapter, teach the students the grapheme-phoneme association. Do not forget to build words and to use them in context.

10. What are the four things a teacher needs to determine when working on a specific vocabulary problem?

11. Please take into consideration the points on developing spoken vocabulary. Try these out for several months and see what happens.

12. For a sample of retarded trainees who are being trained in a vocation, help develop and start a specific job-oriented reading program on the order of Camacho's and Smith's. Introduce techniques explained in the present text.

13. What seems to be the value of the work done by Sticht and his associates?

14. Study the assumptions stated about comprehension development. Discuss them in your methods class or reading workshop. What are you planning to do about them or with them?

15. Find a suitable group of people, if you can, and teach the DRL for the selection, "What Makes Motors Run?"

16. Write a similar plan for a technical selection of your choice and teach it.

17. Teach the lesson on reading to follow the directions for making a "Rich Christmas Stollen." Do not shortcut the lesson because you are hungry. This lesson is to help students learn to read carefully. Execute product quality check!

SUGGESTED ADDITIONAL READINGS

AUKERMAN, ROBERT C. *Reading in the Secondary Classroom.* New York: McGraw-Hill, 1972. Chapters 11 and 12.

HAFNER, LAWRENCE E. (Ed.). *Improving Reading in Middle and Secondary Schools.* Second Edition, New York: Macmillan, 1974. Section 10.

MEHRER, RON. "Improving Readability of Vocational Agricultural Students." *The Agricultural Education Magazine. 32* (October 1959), 5–7.

MILLER, WILMA H. *Teaching Reading in the Secondary School.* Springfield, Ill.: Charles C. Thomas, 1974. Chapter 16.

PIERCEY, DOROTHY. *Reading Activities in Content Areas.* Boston: Allyn & Bacon, 1976. Chapters 9 and 10.

SHEPHERD, DAVID L. *Comprehensive High School Reading Methods.* Columbus, Ohio: Charles E. Merrill, 1973. Chapter 12.

SYMKOWICZ, DOROTHY. "Home Economics and Reading." *Fusing Reading Skills and Content.* Newark, Del.: International Reading Association, 1969. Pp. 62–66.

BIBLIOGRAPHY

BECKER, JOHN T. "Language Experience Approach in a Job Corps Reading Lab." *Journal of Reading. 13* (1970), 281–84, 319–21.

CAMACHO, E. OLIVER, and FRANK SMITH. "Vocabulary Training." *Journal of Rehabilitation. 18* (1975), 541–43.

CAYLOR, JOHN S., THOMAS G. STICHT, LYN C. FOX, and J. PATRICK FORD. "Readability of Job Materials." In Thomas G. Sticht (Ed.). *Reading for Working.* Chapter 2. Washington, D.C.: Human Resources Research Organization, 1975.

MILLS, ROBERT E. "An Evaluation of Techniques for Teaching Word Recognition." *Elementary School Journal. 56* (1956), 221–25.

MORGAN, VIRGINIA R. "A Cost Study Analysis of Measured Gains in a Reading Program Utilizing Individualization of Instruction." Unpublished doctoral dissertation. Florida State University, 1974.

NEWMAN, HAROLD. "Dropout Case No. 22." *Clearinghouse. 37* (1965), 544–46.

RODGERS, T. S. "Linguistics Considerations in the Design of the Stanford Computer Based Curriculum in Initial Reading." Institute for Mathematical Studies in the Social Sciences, Technical Report No. 111, USOE Grant Number OE5-10-050, 1967.

RUDDELL, ROBERT B. "Psycholinguistic Implications for a Systems of Communication Model." In Kenneth S. Goodman and James T. Fleming (Eds.). *Psycholinguistics and the Teaching of Reading.* Newark, Del.: International Reading Association, 1969. Pp. 61–78.

SMITH, EDWIN H., C. GLENNON ROWELL, and LAWRENCE E. HAFNER. *The Sound Reading Program.* Waco, Texas: Education Achievement Corporation, 1972.

STICHT, THOMAS G. (Ed.). *Reading for Working.* Washington, D.C.: Human Resources Research Organization, 1975.

CHAPTER 18

Teaching the Reading of Foreign Languages

TEACHING THE SKILLS SUPPORTING READING: LISTENING, SPEAKING, AND WRITING—SOME RESEARCH AND PRACTICE

Listening Comprehension

Instruction designed to improve listening comprehension is necessary. Anyone who has studied a foreign language is familiar with the phenomenon of being able to construct oral and written sentences but being completely overwhelmed by normal conversational speech. Belasco (1971) found this to be true among American teachers of French in an overseas institute; they understood next to nothing when overhearing a conversation on a streetcar or in a shop.

Asher (1972) points out that "listening comprehension maps the blueprint for the future acquisition of speaking." Using students ranging from CA 17 to 60, he showed that real physical involvement in listening resulted in their attaining significantly better listening comprehension and reading scores than a control group.

People who have had some contact with a foreign language as children will likely remember some of the commands; for example, Komm mal her! Setz' dich hin! Lass' uns beten! or Mire! Vasmos! Calma! Kalivoda, et al (1971) used a strategy based on a series of spoken commands that involve the interplay of visual, auditory, and motor skills to improve listening comprehension.

Kalivoda (1972) reports on the development and use of an oral course that has been used successfully with secondary school students. Highly speeded, colloquially spiced, everyday language is used in language lessons. Radio plays, teacher's original material, recording, textual material, and the like comprise the listening lessons.

Stern and Weinrib (1971) describe language modules that use recorded radio broadcasts in French. The tapes are transcribed so that the printed text is also available. Also accessible are a glossary of words and expressions, a student-teacher guide, and a workbook.

Moral (1972) plays a game called "lotería de palabras." Similar to bingo, it uses pictures of various scenes pasted onto 8½ X 11 inch cards. A statement is made by the teacher and the students identify the corresponding picture on the bingo board.

Speaking Ability

Kalivoda (1972) notes that the new trend is a plea for reality, requiring that language be used in meaningful situations that occur spontaneously in the classroom. Reality, then, also calls for application to the personal lives of the learners (Gaarder, 1967).

Today, emphasis is placed on what the learner needs rather than on *the* "right technique" for all students. Therefore, the teacher is free to "introduce grammar into the lesson at the time and in the way he feels it would be most beneficial" (Kalivoda and Elkins, 1972). Hammerly (1972) would retain drills for the automatic use of language, but the drills must emphasize understanding and meaningfulness.

Drills can be made more meaningful. Sinnema (1971) has developed a "rotation drill," which consists of "a sequence of questions with a variety of answers to each question indicated." To encourage "flexibility, ingenuity, imagination, and creativeness" in foreign language conversation classes, Sinnema recommends the rotation drill. Material for questions or stimulation statements that could elicit fitting responses from the vocabulary range of students can be obtained from the textbook being used. A question and four logical answers seems to be adequate for each concept.

Buenos dias! ¿Como está usted?	Good morning! How are you?
1. Bien, gracias. ¿Como está usted?	1. I'm fine, thanks. How are you?
2. Muy bien, gracias. ¿Y usted?	2. I'm very fine, thank you. And you?
3. Yo tengo dolor de cabeza.	3. I have a headache
4. Yo estoy cansado.	4. I am tired.

An 8½" X 11" sheet containing both foreign language and English columns will usually hold about five or six question-answer sets. About 15 minutes of class time is used each session. Classes are divided into small conversational groups. For a given set, each person gets a chance to be leader and ask the question. Students also "rotate" to a different answer each round. In the next segment, the paper is folded so that only the English appears and the students must question-answer in the foreign language. Smith (1970) notes that personalization can be effected in drills by using a variety of *free response* and *free completion* drills.

Writing Ability

Writing graphemes and words can be thought of as perceptual reinforcement. In either tracing or copying the graphic stimulus, one is forced into visual inspection. The German *s* and *f* are similar in appearance. Having to write these graphemes and words containing the graphemes should provide experience in making fine visual discriminations. Two words can have different meanings depending on a minimal contrast. Similar-appearing words can be placed in sentence context, and differences in meanings can be noted. Some of the meaning differences can be hilarious.

Even though writing is not the same as written speech, at certain stages, before refinement, it might be similar to speech. I could visualize writing as being an intermediary between a certain level of speech facility and advanced facility. Because one has more time to formulate thoughts into language when writing, some writing might be useful in certain cases in bridging the gap between two stages of speech. This statement should not be interpreted to mean that dialogue in the second language would cease during this particular writing period.

Levels of Writing and Kinds of Writing Exercises. Chastain (1976) points out that before being introduced to writing, the students should be able to hear the phonemes of the language and be able to decode the graphemes in which the phonemes have been encoded. Students must also have a body of vocabulary and understand the grammatical structures they will use in writing.

Chastain suggests that *competence in writing words* be achieved by exercises in copying letters and in learning the graphemic options for sounds and in writing elements dictated by the teacher.

Competence in writing language forms is developed through such exercises as writing the verb form that goes with a particular subject and writing the correct verb form of the verb *to be* in blanks inserted in dialogues. Another language form exercise involves simulation: Students take the key words of "dehydrated" sentences and expand the key words into complete sentences.

Exercises designed to improve productive performance use such formats as sentence completion, answering questions, and originating questions. Finally, *sustained writing* is achieved through such activities as summary writing and semicontrolled writing.

Sentence Combining. T. Grant Brown (1975) discusses (1) a selected linguistic universal that needs to be taught to students and (2) practical classroom techniques that help assure that "students' foreign language performance is consistent with that universal."

Human languages are recursive systems. That is, we are not confined to a finite number of possible sentences. Rather, the "fluent speaker of a language controls a finite system of rules which he uses to produce and comprehend an infinite variety of possible sentences." Even in speech, Brown notes, fluent speakers utter complex sentences that are actually combinations of a number of simple propositions.

Combining simple propositions into complex sentences is called "embedding." Research shows that as students mature in their use of a foreign language the amount and quality of embedding increases—but not automatically.

To improve embedding Brown suggests using sentence-combining techniques developed by O'Hare (1971). These techniques were found to be highly successful in improving the compositional skills of junior-high students. Students instructed in these techniques for a year were writing at the level of high-school seniors.

A very practical technique for combining basic ideas into complex sentences is to elicit a series of simple responses to questions and then combine these responses into fewer, longer sentences.

Brown (1975) recommends, for example, clipping a large photograph of a person from a magazine and asking a series of questions about the photograph. A student may record the responses on the chalkboard. Questions and answers about a young woman might run like this:

Teacher	Students
1. What do you see?	I see a woman.
2. What is her name?	Her name is Mary.
3. What color is her hair?	Her hair is blond.
4. How tall is she?	She is very tall.
5. How old is she?	She is twenty years old.
6. What does she do?	She is a student.
7. What does she study?	She studies mathematics.
8. What is she doing?	She is waiting for a friend.

(One may begin with three or four sentences rather than eight if one would prefer.)

After pointing out the redundancies and possibly underlining them, one can ask the students to recombine them, the eventual product being something like the following:

Mary, a tall, blond, twenty-year-old mathematics student, is waiting for a friend.

After written material is removed or erased, individuals may be called on to describe the picture orally. For more advanced classes, creativity may be stimulated by clustering questions relating to physical descriptions of the character, to the physical environment, to motives, and the like, so that entire compositions can be developed and refined in style.

Brown explains another type of rewriting that uses *reading* passages. Complex sentences as well as whole paragraphs may be broken down into simpler sentences on worksheets. Then the students can practice combining them. If students have carefully familiarized themselves with the style and content of the original passage, the recombining proceeds more smoothly.

Meaningful Textbook Exercises.   Jarvis, et al. (1976) show their preference for a meaningful approach to language study by including after the reading selections activities that "do not force every student to do the same things or to 'come up with' single right answers." The students have to make some decisions themselves.

The first selection in their text is "J'adore, je déteste." The "activités" following the selection are:

A. QUESTIONS

Yes-or-No questions on the text:

1. Est-ce que ce jeune homme déteste les voyages?
5. Est-ce qu'il déteste porter une cravate?

Either-Or questions on the text:

4. Est-ce qu'il adore ou déteste les personnes?

Yes-or-No personal questions:

3. Est-ce que vous détestez aller chez le dentiste?

Either-Or personal questions: (If you wish, you may give your reasons.)

6. Est-ce que vous adorez ou détestez les dimanches en famille?

Personal questions: (If you wish, you may give your reasons.)

5. Qu'est-ce que vous préférez, le jazz ou la musique classique?

B. MATCHING

Make original sentences expressing your own likes and dislikes by combining items from each column or by creating your own. (Because of space considerations, I shall include only every other phrase from the right-hand column.)

J'adore . . .	voyager
J'aime . . .	parler français
J'aime bien . . .	les voitures de sport
J'aime assez . . .	travailler
Je n'aime pas . . .	les examens
Je déteste . . .	aller au cinéma
	manger au restaurant
	le camping
	jouer au tennis
	les beaux garçons
	conduire une voiture
	?

C. COMPLETION

Complete each of the following statements. Select one of the choices, a combination of them, or create an answer of your own.

4. Je suis enthousiaste quand . . .
   a. je regarde un match de basketball
   b. j'ai la possibilité de voyager
   c. j'ai une bonne idée
   d. ?
10. Je suis intimidé (e) quand . . .
    a. je parle français en classe
    b. je suis à une surprise-partie où je ne connais personne
    c. je parle à une personne d'importante
    d. ?

D. VOTRE LISTE

Imitez ce jeune chanteur et faîtes la liste des choses que vous adorez et des choses que vous détestez.

E. RELATED WORDS

(In this exercise a list of verbs is provided in the first column of a table. Related words in verb, noun, and adjective forms are provided.

	Noun	Noun	
Verb	Performer of action	Action performed	Adjective
travailler	le travailleur	le travail	travailleur
	le travailleuse		travailleuse
chanter	le chanteur	la chanson	———
	la chanteuse	le chant	———

Supply the proper word in the following sentences. Consult the preceding table if necessary.

1. Jacques Brel est un chanteur. «Ne me quittes pas» est une de ses _____ .

F. RÉACTIONS

How do you react in the following situations? Complete these sentences.

1. Quand je suis seul(e) à la maison, je . . .
9. Quand mes parents me donnent de l'argent, je . . .

G. AUTRES POINTS DE VUE

2. Imaginez que vous êtes une vieille dame ou un vieux monsieur de 75 ans. Qu'est-ce que vous aimez et qu'est-ce que vous détestez?

The types of exercises in lesson one do not exhaust the types included in the Jarvis text. There are other interesting and useful kinds of exercises in that text.

STRATEGIES FOR IMPROVING THE READING OF A FOREIGN LANGUAGE

In using the above heading I am implying that generally in the schools both the transmissive (speaking, writing) and the receptive aspects (listening, reading) are the focus of foreign language instruction, and for me to discuss reading pedagogy I must bring in the other receptive and transmissive features. Although these features are interrelated, I shall, for purpose of discussion, divide them into the topics of vocabulary reading acquisition, independent word identification, and comprehension.

Vocabulary-Reading Acquisition Strategies

A basic principle for vocabulary development is to see, hear, and practice words in a variety of contexts. Following this principle allows the student to remember the words better and use them more fluently and with greater precision. As in mathematics, new vocabulary is explained in terms of "old" or known vocabulary. Even in the first lessons—in addition to hearing, speaking, and reading basic conversational expressions such as the following—a given word should be used in several contexts.

Italian	German	Spanish	French	Chinese	Russian
Buòngiorno.	Guten Morgen.	Buenos dias.	Bonjour.	Dzău	Дóброе ýтро
Come va?	Wie gehtes Ihnen?	Como está usted?	Comment allez-vous?	Nǐ hǎu ma?	Как Вы пожцвáете?
Bene, grazie, e Lei?	Gut, danke, und Ihnen?	Bien, gracias, ¿ y usted?	Bien, merci, et vous-même?	Hǎu. Nǐ hǎu ma?	бпагодарю вас, отдично.
Arrivederci.	Auf Wieder-sehen.	Hasta la vista.	Au revoir.	Dzàijyàn.	до новой встречи.
Bono.	Gut.	Bueno.	Bon.	Hǎu.	хорошии.
Come va?	Was gibt's sanst?	¿ Que pasa?	Comment ca va?	Nǐ hǎu ma?	Как ле ла?
Per favore.	Bitte.	Por favor.	S'il vous plaît.	Chǐng.	Даите
Grazie.	Danke schön.	Gracias.	Merci.	Syèsye.	благодарю вас.
Prègo.	Bitte schön.	De nada.	Il n'y pas de quoi.	Bùshèi.	не стоит.
Parli adagio, per favore.	Bitte, sprechen sie langsamer.	Hable despacio, por favor.	Parlez plus lentement, s'il vous plaît.	chǐng nǐ sǐang màin i dǐen.	могли-бы вы говорить медле ннее?
Non capisco.	Ich verstene (nicht).	Yo (no) comprendo.	Je (ne) comprends (pas).	wǒ (bù) dǔng.	я не понимаю.
Con piacere.	Gern.	Con mucho gusto.	Volontiers.	Gāu shiňg;	
Che cosa desidera?	Was möchten sie?	¿ Que quiere usted?	Que voulez-vous?	Nǐ yàu shémma?	

I also like methods that shun translation, teach grammar by an inductive-deductive method, and totally involve the student from the outset.

Language work does not have to begin with conversational or everyday expressions but they lend face validity, are interesting to students, can be practiced readily, and provide for a degree of sociability in the class. It makes sense that *if* we want students to speak we should have them speaking. The psychologist Guthrie has said that we do in a situation what we did the last time we were in that situation; therefore, we should begin (and carefully maintain) the habit of active use of the language in our class sessions.

As prosaic as some people might consider the practice, it makes sense in reading acquisition to use terms that we use in the classroom, that are readily referred to, and that often have English cognates. Vocabulary growth is aided by using our meaning hierarchies, introducing words that are related in some way. We can pose a question each time we point to one of several related items, as in the following:

"Ou'est-ce que c'est?"	"Que es esto?"
"c'est un livre"	"es un libro"
"c'est un crayon"	"es una lapiz"
"c'est un banc"	"es un banco"
"c'est une chaise"	"es una silla"
"c'est une table"	"es una mesa"
"c'est un professeur"	"es un maestro"

As indicated above, it is absolutely vital that the ellisions be made as in natural speech. This might be indicated on vocabulary cards.

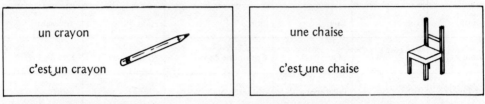

Pronunciation and ellision may be helped by phonetic respelling in the text and on vocabulary cards.

or

(voice recorded on tape) ↗

Multiple contexts and opportunities for practicing the words in these contexts (by the simple expedient of referring to the tense) should be provided:

Is this . . . .?
Here is . . . .
Where is . . . .?

Correct pronunciation is also reinforced as meanings are developed and tested by recording the appropriate words and phrases on illustrated cards for use in card readers and having the students use them appropriately.

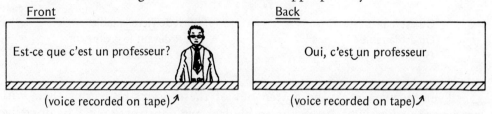

Front   Back

Est-ce que c'est un professeur?   Oui, c'est un professeur

(voice recorded on tape)↗   (voice recorded on tape)↗

NOTE: To emphasize *listening* carefully because printed word cues are not given, use recorded voice plus picture, but omit the writing.

Now to <u>another</u> context: "<u>Here</u> is . . ."

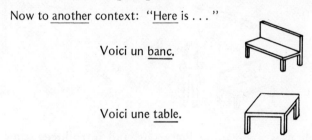

Voici un <u>banc</u>.

Voici une <u>table</u>.

And *still another* context, the position references that ask the question, "*Where* is . . .?" The instructor can introduce these constructions by demonstration, using a number of objects and calling on students to repeat the word after him or her as well as to make up their own sentences. The written construction can be on chalkboard, in a chart, in the text, and the like.

Le professeur est <u>sur</u> la table.

Le crayon est <u>sous</u> la table.

Le crayon est <u>dans</u> le livre.

Use a "programmed" learning review format by writing questions in the left-hand column and the answers in the right-hand column. While the learner is reviewing, the answer is hidden until the learner makes a response:

Ou est le professeur?   Il est <u>derriere</u> la table.
Ou est la table?   Il est <u>devant</u> le professeur.
Ou est le crayon?   Il est <u>sur</u> la table.

Still more mileage can be gotten out of these nouns by pairing them with appropriate adjectives. Again the vocabulary and construction can be done live in the class by the instructor and/or class members prior to reading.

Le crayon est <u>vert</u>.

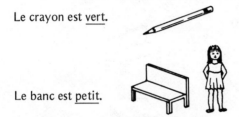

Le banc est <u>petit</u>.

The above approach uses a meaning hierarchy and introduces some useful, stable structures. At times, some class members can meet with the instructor to learn patterns or constructions and then teach them to the rest of the class.

Concomitant with this instruction is the spending of much time listening to the language being spoken so that it can be understood at normal speaking rates. If this is not done, the student will be demoralized the first time he or she is in a situation where the real thing is going on.

Interrelating the Facets of Language

Asher (1972) believes that "listening comprehension maps the blueprint for the future acquisition of speaking." Asher's strategy for physical involvement in the listening, reading, and speaking facets resulted in his experimental group achieving significantly more than the control group in listening, although the latter was in class a third more often than the former. The instructor of the course, Mrs. Silvia de Langen, is a native speaker of German. Instruction proceeded as follows:

Initial Training. The procedure involved manipulating students with commands in the German language. A student sat on each side of Mrs. de Langen. As she uttered the commands, she herself followed them and the two students also executed them. The first commands (in German, however) were Walk! Stop! Turn! Walk! Sit! Within 30 minutes the commands included utterances such as:

Point to the table.
Go to the wall.
Pick up the money under the picture.

The vocabulary items included objects on the person of the students, including that great source of "what have you?," the women's purses. At the second meeting, body parts were incorporated into the commands; several follow:

> Touch your eyes.
> Point to your toes.
> Pick up the newspaper.
> Point to the corner and touch your left hip.

In addition to body parts, "vocabulary included magazine, newspaper, floor, ceiling, light, large, small, bend, hear, see, partner, right, left, and both." The students had trouble discriminating phonemically similar words, for example, Zeitung and Zeitschrift or Zehen and Zähne.

Vocabulary Learning. Most vocabulary items were printed in German on one side of a card and in English on the other. If the German command was "Put the egg on top of the plate," the egg card was placed on the plate card. The commands got involved, including "if-then" situations. This technique worked well, too, for learning abstractions. After 32 hours of training, the students had assimilated about 500 German vocabulary items.

Syntactic Learning. During the latter part of the training, the instructor would read a story in German and then speak 10 statements about the story. The student would respond with A (true), B (false), or C (I do not comprehend).

Speaking. After 16 hours of listening training, the students asked the instructor to let them speak. They were given a list of commands such as the following and were asked to manipulate the instructor's behavior:

> "Stehen Sie auf!   Gehen sie an die Tür!
> Setzen Sie sich!   Gehen Sie an die Ecke!
> Zeigen Sie!   Zeigen Sie uns die Tür!
> Berühren Sie den Tisch!   Zeigen Sie uns die Stuhl!"
> Berühren Sie die Wand!

At the next meeting they manipulated *die Lehrerin* with abandon. Succeeding classes provided some time for students to speak.

Making a Foreign Language Dictionary

Preston (1974) suggests that students keep a foreign language notebook dictionary. Using his categories, let me illustrate his strategy:

Word	Phrase in Which It Occurred	Translation	Other Meanings	ST
siento	. . . mucho lo siento . . .	regret		
soltar	. . . soltar una carcada . . .	burst into	utter; let go	
sonreia	. . . sonreia porque . . . nadie estaba convencido	smiled		
tarjeta	. . . recibir una tarjeta postal.	card		
telón	. . . el telón construido de mosaico . . .	curtain		

Independent Word Identification

In an earlier chapter on learning theory applied to reading I explained how to use the concept of transfer of training to teach grapheme-phoneme relationships. For example, some French grapheme-phoneme relationships can be taught by using French words that have been adopted into the English language and that have retained the French pronunciation in the element concerned. The time at which this strategy is introduced is up to the discretion of the teacher; however, it does make a good "ice breaker."

Phonics Through Cognates. It is surprising how many grapheme-phoneme relationships can be taught in one class session. Even the less-well-known English words have at least been heard by many of the students. The teacher should list at least two words containing a given element (noting the element in question) and then call for words from the students in order to involve the students and create more interest. Briefly the procedure is:

1. List two words containing a given element (or give cues to elicit specific words you have in mind.)

2. Pronounce the words with the students.

3. Ask how the words *look* alike. (Underline the element.)

4. Ask how the words sound alike.

5. Ask for the generalization or rule that governs these like elements.

6. Call for more examples. (If the students have trouble, give cues. This can be much fun!)

> Example:
>
> T: "Which automobile in commercials is (was) associated with baseball and apple pie?" (Or use whatever the current associations are.)
> S: "Chevrolet." (Teacher writes it on the chalkboard.)
> T: "What would a paratrooper not be without as he prepared to enter battle?"
> S: "Parachute." (Place under Chevrolet.)
>
> > Chevrolet
> > parachute
>
> T: "Let's pronounce these two words."
> T and S: "Chevrolet, parachute."
> T: "How do they <u>sound</u> alike?"
> S: "They both have the sound /sh/."
> T: "How do they look alike?"
> S: "They both have ⟨ch⟩."
> T: "Let us underline the ⟨ch⟩ in each word."
>
> > Chevrolet
> > para<u>ch</u>ute
>
> T: "What kind of rule can we make about the ⟨ch⟩ in words that come from the French language?"
> S: "⟨Ch⟩ stands for /sh/."
> T: "What are some other words that follow this rule?" (Responses depend upon degree of sophistication of the particular class. Underline the grapheme and write it at the top of the column.)

ch → /sh/
Chevrolet
para<u>ch</u>ute
<u>ch</u>erie
<u>ch</u>emise
<u>ch</u>ateau

Other elements that may be taught and particulars containing the element follow:

(t)ique → /(t)ēk/	oir → /wär/	age → /äzh/
bout<u>ique</u>	reserv<u>oir</u>	gar<u>age</u>
ant<u>ique</u>	au rev<u>oir</u>	mont<u>age</u>
	boud<u>oir</u>	

ai → /e/	ou → /ü/	au → /ō/	é → /ā/	ie → /ē/
l<u>ai</u>ssez faire	b<u>ou</u>quet	<u>au</u> revoir	souffl<u>é</u>	sort<u>ie</u>
f<u>ai</u>re	b<u>ou</u>tique	g<u>au</u>che	consomm<u>é</u>	cher<u>ie</u>
	m<u>ou</u>sse	<u>au</u> lait		

er → /ā/	eau → /ō/	et → /ā/	en → /ȯn/
Bouvi<u>er</u>	chat<u>eau</u>	Chevrol<u>et</u>	<u>en</u>trée
parl<u>er</u> (vous)	nouv<u>eau</u>	bouqu<u>et</u>	<u>en</u>semble
	b<u>eau</u>		<u>en</u>core

ge → /zh/	ez → /ā/	ir → /ēr/
rou<u>ge</u>	rendez<u>vous</u>	souven<u>ir</u>
monta<u>ge</u>	laiss<u>ez</u> faire	

T: "Here are some French words that contain elements that we have been study-ing. Let us try to pronounce these words."

mouchoir	fromage	soirée	vouloir
Chandelle	boucher	classique	couvrir
aussi	dynamique	courage	enflé
boulanger	couteau	pique-nique	fou
voulez-vous	potage	coucher	embrasser
	lentement	vrai	
	oiseau	aider	
	cassoulet	chou	
	avoir soif		

Allow the students to discuss the meanings of the words. Some may see the relationship of *chandelle* to *chandelier,* of *potage* to *pottage,* of *pique-nique* to *picnic,* of *lentement* to *lentemente* (Spanish for slow) or to *lento* (music term—Italian—for slow), etc.

Highlighting an Element in Color. Students learning a language often have difficulty in differentiating and remembering the many grapheme-phoneme relationships of a language. For example, in German the following elements, among others, are often confused and misused: ch—ck; s—z; w—v

ch → /k̲/, not /k/	s → /z/	w → /v/
ck → /k/	z → /ts/	v → /f/

All these associations, except ck → /k/, are foreign to English. One exception is ch → /k/; *loch* as pronounced in Scottish dialect is an example.

Step 1: Noting similarities for given element *ch*. Elicit words in which ch → /k/; include the article for common nouns because students need all the practice they can get in associating each noun with its correct article. Develop the rule inductively if it has not been developed.

Step 2: Highlight the *ch* by writing it in green, for example.

Ba*ch*
das Bu*ch*
rau*ch*en
der Na*ch*bar

Step 3: Noting similarities for c̲k̲:
Step 4: Highlight the element, say, in red.

der Sto*ck*
die E*ck*e
der Rü*ck*en

Step 5: Pronounce words containing the elements. It might be better to pronounce some unfamiliar words for which they do not know the spelling so that they will have to listen carefully.

Step 6: Then write the word, leaving out the grapheme in question. Have a student write the grapheme, using the "appropriate" color:

Pronounce	Write
"das Schicksaal	das Schi_ _saal
"das Angesicht"	das Angesi_ _t
"der Koch"	der Ko_ _
"stecken"	ste_ _en
"der Briefwechsel"	der Briefwe_ _sel (tricky one)
"stechen"	ste_ _en
"die Drucksache"	die Dru_ _sa_ _e
"der Nachteil"	der Na_ _teil
"glücklich"	glü_ _li_ _

Step 7: Have the entire class pronounce the words on the list. Then select individuals to pronounce certain words.

Sh! That's Silent! or Flip the Strip! Select words in a language in which certain letters do *not* represent a sound. Write the words in a column on a (overhead) transparency; *omit* the letters in question, however. Develop an overlap of transparency strips. Although bound on the left side to keep them together, each strip should be free to be moved singly. Flip the strips down over the words and write in the missing letters.

When using this device, present the words by using the transparencies and an overhead projector. Project the whole word on the screen. Ask the student(s) to pronounce the first word. If pronounced correctly, ask which letters do not represent a sound. Then *flip the strip* to reveal core part of the word and to show which letters are pronounced and which are not pronounced!

Some words to use (here I will underline the core parts):

French

office	electrique
bain	peux
croissant	le Havre
gris	front
toits	

Variations on the theme can be worked out by the teacher.

Rapid Differentiation Drill. Write on transparencies. Cover the list and answer one syllable or word at a time.

German

Spanish

ie - ei	v - w	s - z	s - sp - st	h - j	l-ll
bei	va	si	se	he	la
bie	wa	zi	spe	je	lla
tie	wa	zi	se	je	la
sei	vi	zi	sto	hu	lle
sie	wi	sa	spo	ju	le
sie	vi	za	so	ja	lle
sei	wi	sa	spo	ja	le
nei	wo	su	spu	he	llo
nie	wo	zu	spu	je	lo
nei	vo	zu	stu	he	llo
nieder	was?	ziemlich	spotten	hay	leyendas
beide	Vater	Zahn	spielen	justo	ventanilla
lieben	womit	sauber	stolz	hermano	linda
einmal	weder	Sahne	suppe	dijo	calle
Eigentum	verstehen	sein	sehen	hasta	leche
Familie	versuchen	selten	speise	helado	loza
leise	Wiese	Zunge	selbst	hoy	lluvia
Kreide	wirklich	segnen	singen	naranja	llegar
wieder	Wolkswagen	Salz	stattlich	zanahoria	mantequilla
Weihnachten	Winter	lesen	Morgenstern	jardín	violeta

French

ure-eur

heur	geur	indicateur	meilleur
teur	ture	pointure	confiture
ture	heur	brulure	temperature
lure	leur	largeur	douleur
leur	devanture	voiture	valeur

Developing Reading Comprehension[1]

When we comprehend, we grasp ideas and the relationships among them. Teaching reading comprehension involves teaching students to analyze thoroughly the cognitive relationships represented in the printed text.

Relationship of Listening Comprehension to Reading Comprehension. Research shows the strong relationship between listening comprehension and reading comprehension. Pimsleur (1965) demonstrated that listening comprehension is one of the main factors differentiating success in a foreign language, particulary in conversational courses or any course that stresses spoken language skills both as a goal and as a medium of language instruction. Also, Asher (1972) noted the positive transfer from listening comprehension to reading comprehension in the inchoate stages of foreign language learning, although no specific training in reading was involved. Lee (1972) offers several pedagogical reasons for teaching listening comprehension along with reading comprehension:

1. It allows for greater varieties of activities in the classroom, and provides an additional kind of exposure to the foreign language.
2. Listening is more closely related to reading than any other language skill, since it would seem that the same basic processes are involved in both aural and visual comprehension of language.
3. Listening to a model read a sentence aloud provides additional exposure to the foreign language sound system, and the organization imposed upon the language along with the correct intonation and stress may help the student in becoming familiar with the structural cues to phrasing and isolating key elements in the sentence.
4. It is possible that some slower readers may be encouraged to increase their speed while reading silently by trying to keep up with a model reading aloud.

Paraphrase-Cloze Strategy. I should like to present one of my strategies for teaching comprehension that is part of a complete lesson. I call this type of lesson the "Paraphrase-Cloze Reading Lesson." It can be used with any level material and with any kind of subject matter. One of the reasons for using it in this chapter is to show its flexibility. The lesson outline is presented first. Next is part of the lesson that shows *some* of the essential elements I have developed for a lesson in French.

PARAPHRASE-CLOZE READING LESSON OUTLINE

1.0   Objectives.[2]
2.0   Materials.[3]

---

[1] The numerous strategies in the chapter on comprehension and in other chapters can be adapted for use in foreign language teaching. I shall present one rather comprehensive, new strategy.

[2] State what you are trying to accomplish.

[3] List the materials you are going to use. Be specific. At times you may want to write your own reading selection. Control readability by checking your writing against a readability formula. State the readability of the selection.

3.0   *Preparation.*[4]
3.1   *Pre-test* of Concepts and/or Words.
3.2   *Teach Unknown Words* to Mastery Criterion.
4.0   *Read Selection.*
4.1   *Options.*[5]
4.1.1   Teacher reads story to student(s).
4.1.2   Story is on cassette tape (may need to use "beeps" to show where sentences end).
4.1.3   Children read silently, then aloud.
4.1.4   Students read in response to guided questions.
4.1.5   Etc.
5.0   *Selection Paraphrased and in Cloze*[6] *Form. (Delete* every seventh word of the paraphrased version.)
6.0   *Deleted Words Placed in Alphabetical Order.* (They are placed here for reference, such as help in spelling.)
7.0   *Experience Story* (related topic)

Paraphrase-Cloze Comprehension

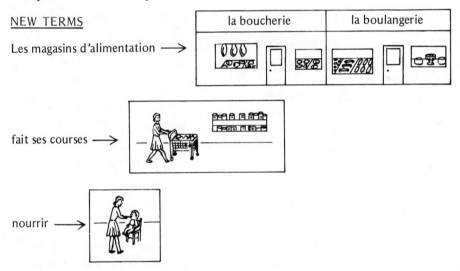

SELECTION
Les Magasins d'alimentation
(Vous et Moi, R. Cadoux)

La femme française fait ses courses tous les jours pour nourrir sa famille! Il y a maintenant dans les maisons de France un assez grand nombre de réfrigérateurs,

---

[4] Anticipate problem words. Pre-test. Teach unknown words by using "nailing down" methods suggested in the present text, Chapter 21. If the student knows enough word identification skills for the particular word(s) involved, he may be guided in sounding out the word(s).

[5] For sake of variety, try different options. Various conditions learner, learning situation, time, etc.— will also determin apprach here.

[6] The cloze procedure provides a measure of understanding.

mais tout le monde n'en pas encore un! Par conséquent, la femme française moyenne ne peut pas mettre la nourriture dans un congélateur, comme la femme américaine.

Maman va à toutes les boutiques: à la boucherie, à la boulangerie, à l'épicerie, à la crémerie et aussi chez le marchand de légumes. Souvent elle s'arrête aussi chez un fleuriste pour un petit bouquet. A présent il y a quelques supermarchés dans les grandes villes, mais, en général, les supermarchés sont plutôt rares.

SELECTION PARAPHRASED AND IN CLOZED FORM
(DELETE EVERY SEVENTH WORD)

La tâche de la mère de _____ famille est de trouver à manger.

_____ la venue des réfrigérateurs en France _____ en observe

leur absence dans plousieurs _____ français. Alors, la femme française ne

_____ pas mettre la nourriture dans un _____ comme une

femme américaine.

Maman va _____ boutiques qui s'appellent la boucherie, _____

boulangerie, la crèmerie, et l'épicerie. _____ , on achète des fleurs chez

le _____ de légumes. Il y a quelques supermarchés _____ les

grandes villes, mais ils sont _____ rares.

DELETED WORDS PLUS FOILS

a	congélateur	electricien	malgré	peut
aussi	dans	foyers	marchand	plutôt
aux	de	la	on	professeur

SUMMARY

Listening comprehension should be taught assiduously and well. Not only is it a good base for further instruction, but when it is well taught it is a valuable skill in its own right—allowing a person to understand even native speakers. Research shows that it can be significantly improved through special instruction.

If people are to become competent *speakers* of a second language, that language must be used in meaningful situations that occur in the classroom and outside the classroom. Of course, it does not hurt to practice outside the classroom situation. Any instructional strategies designed to develop speaking ability should encourage "flexibility, ingenuity, imagination, and creativeness."

Writing is at once a goal of instruction and a means of reinforcing the other three modes of language. In addition to noting a systematic hierarchy of writing techniques, a thorough discussion of the use of sentence-combining techniques for improving the composition skills of students was presented.

Practical strategies for improving the reading of a foreign language focused on the areas of vocabulary-reading acquisition, independent word identification, and reading comprehension.

Vocabulary-reading acquistion strategies involved use of listening drills in words that were related in some way, use of word-picture cards and card readers with these same words, presentation of pictorial-verbal contexts for learning function words and brief sentence contexts in which nouns were paired with appropriate adjectives.

Of special interest was the experimental instruction in a beginning German course that used commands—words, then sentences to manipulate student behavior. Reading was used when instructions were printed on cards.

The discussion on *independent word identification* began with the introduction of an "ice breaker" exercise—phonics through cognates. The familiar inductive learning paradigm was used in this fun technique. Certain similar-appearing graphemes can cause a beginning reader trouble. One strategy for dealing with this problem involved the highlighting of similar graphemes with different colors. The next strategy was called flip-the-strip and the last one was a rapid differentiation drill.

One new strategy was presented in this chapter, but it is a useful one that is part of a complete lesson plan. It is called the paraphrase-cloze strategy, and an example of its use in a French lesson was given.

ACTIVITIES AND QUESTIONS
TO PROMOTE LEARNING AND APPLICATION

1. Try to analyze the instruction you have received in foreign language. Which strategies of instruction seemed to be most effective?
2. Talk with a second language student who seems to be quite proficient in the language and one who has studied the same number of years, but who seems less proficient. Ask what instructional procedures were used in each case and how diligently the two students applied themselves. Try to account for the differences in proficiency.
3. If you were to set up listening experiences for students, what features would you include? Give the rationale for each item that you include.
4. What would you do to improve the speaking ability of second language students?
5. In your estimation, how should dialogues be used?
6. As far as you can determine, what are the essential differences between Chastain's competence exercises and his productive performance exercises?
7. What is embedding?
8. Speculate on the reasons students do not automatically transfer their command of syntactic processes to a second language.
9. Develop and execute a sentence-combining strategy (which uses a series of questions) for a foreign language student. Report results to your class.

10. Develop and execute a sentence-combining strategy in which you take reading passages, break them into simpler sentences, and then have students practice combining them into complex sentences.
11. Take a small group of "students"—middle school, secondary school, roommates, or whatever—and introduce them to a foreign language using procedures reported by Asher and taught by de Langen. Report your experiences in writing, on audio tape, on video tape, or any combination of the three. Perhaps you could talk your crew into coming to your methods class for a demonstration lesson.

SUGGESTED ADDITIONAL READINGS

CHASTAIN, KENNETH. *Developing Second Language Skills: Theory to Practice.* Second Edition. Chicago: Rand McNally, 1976.

FRECHETTE, ERNEST A. "Testing Reading Comprehension in Foreign Languages." Unpublished Study, Florida State University, 1976.

HAFNER, LAWRENCE E. (Ed.) *Improving Reading in Middle and Secondary Schools.* New York: Macmillan, 1974. Section 10.

PIERCEY, DOROTHY. *Reading Activities in Content Areas.* Boston: Allyn & Bacon, 1976. Chapter 7.

STEINER, PETER. "Using Language to Learn Language." *Foreign Language Annals.* 9 (1) (February 1976), 40–45.

VAN ESSEN, A. J., and J. P. MENTING. (Eds.). *The Context of Foreign-Language Learning.* Assen, the Netherlands: Korinklijke Van Gorcum and Company B.V., 1975.

BIBLIOGRAPHY

ASHER, JAMES J. "Children's First Language As a Model for Second Language Learning." *Modern Language Journal.* 56 (1972), 133–39.

BELASCO, SIMON. "C'est la guerre? or Can Cognitive and Verbal Behavior Co-exist in Second Language Learning?" In Robert C. Lugton and Charles H. Heinle (Eds.). *Toward a Cognitive Approach to Second Language Acquisition.* Philadelphia: Center for Curriculum Development, 1971.

BROWN, T. GRANT. "How to Apply Linguistics to Language Learning Without Scotch Tape." Unpublished Study, Florida State University, 1975.

CHASTAIN, KENNETH. *Developing Second Language Skills: Theory to Practice.* Second Edition. Chicago: Rand McNally, 1976.

GAARDER, A. BRUCE. "Beyond Grammar and Beyond Drills." *Foreign Language Annals.* 1 (1967), 109–18.

HAMMERLY, HECTOR. "Recent Methods and Trends in Second Language Learning." *Modern Language Journal.* 55 (1971), 499–505.

JARVIS, GILBERT A., THERESE M. BONIN, DONALD E. CORBIN, and DIANE W. BIRCKBICHLER. *Connaître et se Connaître: A Basic Reader.* New York: Holt, Rinehart and Winston, 1976.

KALIVODA, THEODORE B. "An Individual Study Course for Facilitating Advanced Oral Skills." *Modern Language Journal.* 56 (1972), 492–95.

_____ , and ROBERT J. ELKINS. "Teaching as Facilitation and Management of Learning." In Dale Lange and Charles James (Eds.). *Foreign Language Education: A Review.* Skokie, Ill.: National Textbook, 1972.

_____ , GENELLE MORAIN, and ROBERT J. ELKINS. "The Audio-Motor Unit: A Listening Comprehension Strategy That Works." *Foreign Language Annals.* 4 (1971), 392–400.

LEE, JEAN COX. "An Assessment of Reading in a Foreign Language with Special Reference to German." Unpublished Doctoral Dissertation, University of Washington, 1972.

MORAL, AURORA E. "Dateline: Pennsylvania." *American Foreign Language Teacher.* 2 (3) (1972), 38.

O'HARE, FRANK. "The Effect of Sentence-Combining Practice Not Dependent on Formal Knowledge of a Grammar on the Writing of Seventh Graders." Unpublished Doctoral Dissertation, Florida State University, 1971.

PIMSLEUR, PAUL, et al. "Under-achievement in Foreign Language Learning." *International Review of Applied Linguistics.* 2 (2) (1964), 113–39.

PRESTON, RALPH. "Give the Student Tips on How to Get the Most From Foreign Language Books." in Lawrence E. Hafner (Ed.). *Improving Reading in Middle and Secondary Schools.* Second Edition. New York: Macmillan, 1974. Pp 420–22.

SINNEMA, JOHN R. "Rotation Drills in Teaching Conversation." *Modern Language Journal.* 55 (1971), 269–71.

SMITH, ALFRED N. "Strategies of Instruction for Speaking and Reading." In Dale L. Lange (Ed.). *Britannica Review of Foreign Language Education, Volume 2.* Chicago: Encyclopedia Britannica, 1970.

STERN, H. H., and ALICE WEINRIB. "French-Language Teaching Modules: A New Approach to Language Teaching Materials." *Canadian Modern Language Review.* 27 (3) (1971), 25–31.

CHAPTER 19

Teaching Reading in Art, Music, Health, and Physical Education

READING IN ART

What Is Art?

We are surrounded by art. We create it, view it, use it, but when asked to define it we are often at a loss to do so. Art is concerned with the arrangement of color and space and therefore with lines. It also has to do with our reactions to such arrangements. The first example of a very simple arrangement of color and space that I can think of is the Japanese flag—a large, red dot, if you will, on a white, rectangular background. I think it is an harmonious arrangement, skilfully done; and most art will be found to have that feature. When we go beyond such a simple, harmonious arrangement of space and color as the Japanese flag we get into permutations and combinations of space and color, degrees of harmony, and varieties of taste and satisfaction.

What Place Does Art Have in the Curriculum?

I think it would be safe to say that art does not occupy the place in the curriculum that many people would like, but it holds a better place in many communities than it ever did. Art is important to people who see life as beautiful for itself and something to be shared.

Fortunately, people are imbued with the potential to create art and to appreciate the artistry of their surroundings. This ability to create and appreciate must be nurtured, however. To some art is an extra frill rather than an integral part of their lives. To others it fills voids and brings an extra dimension of beauty into their lives. To them it is a "fill," not a frill!

Living in a charming city, being blessed with beautiful children, and being married to a lovely woman who is an accomplished artist I am literally, but pleasantly, overwhelmed by art.

Is art education surviving in our town? So far it is. But at times it seems the fillers are in danger of gradually being overwhelmed by the frillers.

451

What Are the Objectives of Art Education?

Mary Hafner[1] has listed the following practical objectives of art education:

1. To make art vital to the student in and out of the classroom, thereby affecting his or her whole way of life.
2. To stimulate awareness to unlimited resources of beauty in the student's environment and help him or her to see that art is a force in our everyday life.
3. To foster the growth and development of the creative, spiritual, appreciative, and aesthetic qualities, abilities, and potentialities of students.
4. To develop the student's ability to select and competently use the appropriate materials and techniques to create art.
5. To help the student experience satisfaction in his or her own creations, to gain confidence in his or her ability and to rely on it.
6. To give the student practice in describing works of art and explaining art techniques.
7. To help the student grow in the ability to enjoy the art expression of peers, contemporaries, and that of other cultures and historical periods.
8. To enable the student to become aware of design qualities in everything and to become increasingly able to relate design to articles of practical use.
9. To help the student to express ideas and attitudes toward art in a clear and comprehensible fashion.
10. To help the student become aware that factors other than realism may be used in judging the value of an art project and to recognize some of the art elements and principles of design.
11. To help the student gain in an appreciation of the art of other nations and races leading to universal respect and tolerance.

Measuring and Evaluating Reading in Art

There are several basic ways to approach measurement and evaluation in reading art. *One* is to give standardized reading tests and relate a student's general ability to the readability of textual materials in art. The *second* is to develop a series of informal reading inventories on the specific reading materials that will be used in the art curriculum. A *third* way is to develop the special IVCA inventories on selections of your choice. A *quick* way to measure and evaluate is to develop multiple-choice cloze tests on general reading material as well as on textual materials in art. *Another* method, which I have not suggested before, is to have teams of students go through textual materials and have them list terms and expressions (1) that they have difficulty in pronouncing and (2) that they do not understand. These terms should be carefully catalogued by *selection* and/or possibly by readability level of the textual material. This information can be used to develop aids in reading. A *final* method is probing a student's ability to read specific materials.

Probing the Ability of Students to Read How-to Books. If specialized how-to books are used in middle and secondary school art classes, the teacher

---

[1] Mary Hafner—personal communication.

should know the readability of these materials. The teacher also needs to know something about the dynamics of the reading ability of the students in addition to their reading grade placement. To accomplish this, the teacher should have students of various reading achievement levels read portions of books and then probe to see what they can and cannot do without cues and with cues. This procedure will get at the dynamics of the students' reading, and the teacher will know how particular students function in reading. Problem areas in materials[2] will also come to light this way.

I selected several segments from the first few pages of Lammer's book, *Print Your Own Fabric.* The segments I selected at the 9.7 readability level are reprinted below, followed by an unstructured interview with Katie, a girl at a 5.9-grade placement who reads at a 7.0-grade level and Linda, a girl at a 7.9-grade placement who reads at the 9.5-grade level. It is predictable that Katie will not do well, but she was asked to try it anyway to see whether it could be used by students in her grade.

1. Introduction: (paragraph one of a three-paragraph introduction.)

The process is a simple one: a printing block made of one or other of the materials listed below is covered with dye and pressed on to the fabric. This method of decorating textiles differs essentially from batik, where the fabric is immersed in a dye bath, often successively in different colors, and from fabric painting, in which work is done with a brush. It therefore produces quite different results.

2. Potato blocks (three paragraphs after paragraph one)

Potato blocks are extremely easy to make, but they do not last long. By the end of the day they will have shrunk, and the outlines will have altered so much that they can no longer be used. A further disadvantage of the potato block is that only relatively small motifs can be printed from it. Its chief use is for composing varied patterns by a rhythmical repetition of formal elements alongside, above and below one another. Even a single block in the form of a triangle or square can produce very decorative results.

Moreover, printing with potato blocks is a technique which even children can employ successfully, under proper supervision and guidance.

3. Cutting a block

Having cut a large, well-shaped potato in half, you can carve a simple shape on one of the cut surfaces with either a penknife or a kitchen knife. Work free-hand, without pencilling the outline; the little irregularities are part of the charm of this kind of printing. It is best to start with a square or round form, which can be enriched by notching the edges or varying it in some other way. Thin lines should be avoided because they are liable to break down under the pressure of printing. No curlicues or complicated shapes can be cut in this medium, as you will soon discover for yourself.

---

[2] Those who have overloaded our middle and secondary school teachers with such large numbers of classes and students are ignorant of the fact that our children would get a much, much better education if the teachers had time to plan, to diagnose students' abilities, and really get to know them and interact with them.

After cutting out the pattern, stand the potato for a few minutes on a dry cloth, which will absorb most of the moisture in it. The print will be much clearer if made from a dry block.

First, Katie. Introductory Paragraph: Katie had trouble with the pronunciation and meaning of *essentially, batik,* and *successively.* She could not paraphrase, "This method of decorating textiles differs from batik." When questioned as to what "this method" referred to she was unable to refer back to the chapter heading, *Fabric Printing.* We continue:

I   (Interviewer): "In what technique is fabric immersed in a dye bath?"
S   (Student): "D.K." (did not relate this to <u>batik</u>.)
S: (mispronounced "successively" as "successfully")
I: "What does this method refer to? Name the method."
S: "Fabric printing."
I: "In which method is the fabric immersed in a dye bath?"
S: "D.K."
I: "You are going to have to read these three lines."
S: _____
I: "They are saying fabric printing differs from something else. What is the something else?"
S: "Batik."
I: "Often when you have a word followed by a comma, the expression after the comma refers to that word."
I: "What does immersed mean?"
S: "The fabric is put into the dye."
I: "How much of it?"
S: "All of it."

Potato blocks

I: "What is the advantage of potato blocks?"
S: "They are easier to make."
I: "What is the disadvantage?"
S: "They do not last long."
I: "What happens?"
S: "They shrink."
I: "What does alter mean?"
S: "They get out of shape. Don't have their hardness left."
I: "Does it say they lose their hardness or did you infer it?"
S: "I inferred it."
I: "What does motif mean?"
S: "Shapes—Squares."
I: "Can you think of another name for motif?"
S: "Pattern."
I: "When you set a visual pattern out in a certain way, what do you call it?"
S: "Design."
I: "What does the next sentence mean?"
S: "You could design your own pattern."
I: "What does varied pattern mean?"
S: "They might not all be the same."

Cutting a block

I: "Please read this section and then tell me how you would cut a block?" (There were six illustrations on the facing page.)

S: (Was able to do this.)

Next, Linda. Linda did not read the introductory paragraph.

Potato blocks

I: "What is the advantage of the potato block?"
S: "They are easier to make."
I: "What is the disadvantage?"
S: "That they won't last long and will shrink by the end of the day."
I: "What does shrunk mean?"
S: "Made smaller."
I: "What does "altered" mean?"
S: _____
I: "Ladies use that term all the time in sewing."
S: _____ (Read "relatively" as "relat' ively")
          (Read "motif" /mōtēf/ as /motif/)
I: "What does "motif" mean?"
S: "Picture or design."
I: "How could you say that sentence in your own words?"
S: "Another disadvantage of the block is that only small designs can be printed from it."
I: "What does 'it' mean?"
S: "Potato block"
I: "What does the next sentence mean?" ("Its chief . . . . one another.")
S: "That you can use it over."
I: "Oh? What does varied patterns mean?"
S: "Different patterns."
I: "You have one block. How do you get the different patterns?"
S: "Make like a diamond out of them or different shapes besides the rectangle like that."

Cutting a block

I: "Please read this section and then tell me how you would cut a block?" (I covered the six illustrations on the facing page.)

S: (Was able to do this.)

Obviously a student will have to read at the ninth-grade level or better to feel comfortable with this book. Even so, special reading guides and lessons should be devised to help certain students read this book with better comprehension. Such work by each content teacher contributes to the students' on-going development of vocabulary and reading skills. Had Katie and Linda been receiving such instruction in recent years, they would have read much better than they do!

Improving the Reading of Textual Materials in Art

Developing Vocabulary. If students were to see the large amount of diverse technical vocabulary terms in art that I have encountered recently within a short period of time, they would be overwhelmed by it. Fortunately they will be introduced to the terms gradually in relation to their interests and the projects on which they are working.

This might be a good place to reiterate the principles of vocabulary development posited in the vocabulary chapter.

1. *Create a good climate for learning words:* More vocabulary has died-a-bornin' because teachers and parents have not shown their love of words, have not interjected unusual words into their speech, nor followed up on the general and technical vocabulary found in the text material. The art teacher will use and provide students with many opportunities to use these terms.

2. *Root vocabulary development in concept development:* As long as art classes are closely tied to doing, rather than merely reading about, there is little chance of verbalism.

3. *Develop vocabulary in oral and written language contexts:* Meanings should always be illustrated. If you are going to talk about *refractory* material or know that the word occurs in some reading, have some of this material available. The definition, "Material that stands up to and resists fusibility at high temperatures" is not sufficient for me; I want more. The student who takes a pottery course or two will have no problem in learning *kaolin, engobe,* and *slurry,* but the student who is taking a survey course should perhaps see and handle slurry at least once, although i am positive he or she will not become a collector of it. My nomination for the five most undecipherable words in a series is: "*engobe:* a coating of slip." Because of a definition I read, I now have a general idea of what these words mean, but I cannot wait to get to a potter's studio to see and feel engobe. (I hope these few sentences also illustrate the idea that we should make words interesting.)

> She wanted her dinnerware to be made from <u>kaolin</u>.
> I've seen many <u>kaolin</u> pits in central Missouri.
> <u>Kaolin</u> is white clay.
> They use <u>kaolin</u> to make porcelain.

Do you remember Jenkin's basic strategy for developing vocabulary? It was individual word study using dictionary and index cards (containing word, pronunciation, meanings, plus the word in sentence contexts). Do you remember what kinds of contexts and why? That is important. On the front side of the card, among other things, was the word in the sentence context that she student found. On the back, the student wrote a meaningful sentence containing the word used with precision. If the student can use the word accurately, it shows he or she understands it. A student will be more likely to study and make the word his or her own if he or she invests time and energy. Discussion is used to clarify the meaning and provide opportunities to use the word meaningfully.

4. *Discuss experiences:* We discuss real experiences. I suggest that teachers see some of the events and places the students do so they will all have something in common to discuss. Art museums, art galleries, showings, studios, and the

like can be visited. Much excellent vicarious experience is possible. Work with other art teachers, curriculum consultants, and librarians (media specialists) in order to plan carefully an excellent program of vicarious experiences in art.

I have already mentioned some strategies. In addition to using the vocabulary cards strategy, the teacher can help students make illustrated or nonillustrated dictionaries. I still like the idea of the teacher and/or students skimming a chapter for the purpose of pulling out words that provide pronunciation and meaning difficulties and then making up study sheets comprised of the words in one column and the sentences illustrating the words in another column. Details for making and using these sheets are in the vocabulary chapter.

Catalogues and magazines provide many current examples of art and related art text. These publications can be used as sources for bulletin boards, study sheets, illustrated dictionaries, word-picture cards, and the like. Do make use of these invaluable sources and techniques.

A solid way of developing vocabulary is to connect words with aspects of things, such as color. Cataldo (1969) suggests that older students can be asked to find examples or make examples of these hues:

vermillion	lapis lazuli	magenta
cerise	indigo	burgundy
cerulean	amethyst	sloe
jet	cinnamon	ecru
puce	ocher	ivory
cinnabar	sepia	pearl

Three activities to use in conjunction with these colors:

(1) Begin a discussion about what these colors might feel like.

(2) Find examples of these colors in literature.

(3) Discuss the effect of these words on meaning.

Reading to Follow Directions. You may want to reread the lesson on reading to follow directions for making stollen in the vocational-technical chapter. You will note the following parts:

1. Preparation: Teaching Concepts and Vocabulary
2. Checking Functions and Processes
3. Reading the Recipe
4. Checking Comprehension
5. Checking Sequence
6. Executing and Checking Product

The following lesson will assume that the pottery student has already made a clay base and several clay coils. The lesson is designed to help readers who would have trouble with aspects of the vocabulary and the phraseology in the directions.

Preparation: Teaching Concepts and Vocabulary

1. Write the name of the directions on the board and have it read. ("Fixing the First Coil to the Base")

2. Ask the students to name some important terms that will be in the directions. Write their offerings on the chalkboard.

3. Categorize the terms under headings.

4. Project the directions on a screen, using an overhead projector.

5. Place a check by each "correct" item on the chalkboard, reading aloud each item checked.

"Fixing the First Coil to the Base"*

1. Place the middle of the coil on the base at 12 o'clock and gently bend each end towards 6 o'clock. Miter the right end by cutting it with a needle and place the left hand end to overlap. Mark this end a little shorter, lift it from the base and miter it.

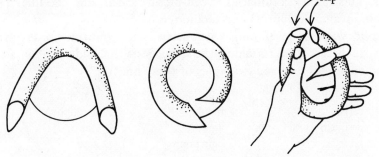

Bending coil; cutting it to size; holding it for joining with slip

2. Remove the coil from the base and hold it between the outstretched thumb and three fingers of the left hand while the forefinger passes through the loop to support the inside of the two ends. Apply slip to each end and, fully overlapping them, press firmly together to expel any surplus slip and carefully model the join.

3. Position the coil on the base by pressing the four finger tips of each hand against the edge of the base at 12 o'clock and, rotating anticlockwise at each pressure, move the coil with the thumbs towards the fingers.

4. Continuing this process, move the thumb tips to a more horizontal position and to the top of the coil and so 'beat' the inside edge of the coil towards the base. At the second revolution, the clay should just make contact with the base so that the third revolution can produce a sliding action towards the center of the base and the inside will then be smoothly finished.

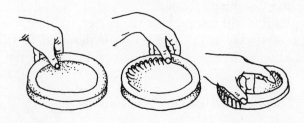

Positioning and 'beating' coil (two hands); modelling the outside of base coil

* Thorpe, Harold E. *Basic Pottery for the Student.* New York: St. Martin's Press, 1973. Pp. 20, 21.

5. Now, holding the fingers inside and the thumbs outside, both vertically at 6 o'clock, press the thumbs inwards and downwards 1/8 of an inch to model the outside of the coil to the base. The coil should now be accurately fixed to the base and all air excluded from the join. A beginner need never fear finding the base separated from the body, after firing, if this method is carefully followed.

6. Write the name of each important word and phrase on the chalk board, ask what they mean, and illustrate where possible. For example:

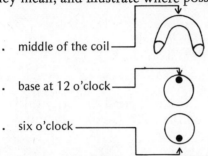

- middle of the coil
- base at 12 o'clock
- six o'clock
- miter = to fit together two bevelled pieces
- needle = a needle which has been firmly inserted into a handle
- forefinger = index finger
- slip = an even creamy mixture of clay and water
- position = place

- rotating anticlockwise   turning

- thumb tips to a more horizontal position

- revolution = turn
- beat inside edge of coil towards the base (in order to make a smooth connection between coil and base)

- vertically = |

- firing = baking

Checking Functions and Processes

7. Ask what the *function* of each of the following is

- needle
- thumbs
- slip
- base

8. Write the names of the *processes* on the chalkboard and call on students to pantomime the processes.

- miter
- applying slip
- modeling the join
- rotating anticlockwise
- moving thumb tips to a horizontal position
- modeling the inside of the coil to the base
- modeling the outside of the coil to the base

Reading the Directions.

9. Distribute duplicated copies of the directions.

10. Have the students silently read the directions carefully to notice what *things* are involved and to get the sequence of procedures.

Checking Comprehension (Project directions on the screen again.)

11. Ask the students the following questions:
    a. Where is the middle of the unjoined coil?
    b. Where is 12 o'clock on the base? six o'clock?
    c. What does "mitering" mean?
    d. Why is "slip" used?
    e. What does direction 3 mean? (You may need to clarify this!)
    f. What makes the indentations on the coil? (Look at pictures.)

Checking Sequence

12. If the students have not had much practice at this, develop a very simple sequence check. For example: Number in correct order the following procedures:

    . Rotate the coil clockwise at each pressure.
    . Miter the right end.
    . Apply slip to each end of the coil.
    . Place the middle of the coil on the base at two o'clock.
    . Model the outside of the coil to the base.

Executing and Checking the Product

13. Using preprepared coils and bases, follow the directions, and fix the coils to the bases.

14. Allow the students to comment on one another's work.

NOTE: It might be easier to demonstrate rather than to teach the reading lesson, but students will not progress in reading textual materials in art and will not advance to becoming independent readers of art materials if you do not give them lessons on reading textual materials in art.

Building Art Background Through Library Reading

Reading Topical Books. Following is a small annotated list of topical books in art. I would suggest that you add to this list from time to time.

BENENSON, LAWRENCE A. *How a House is Built.* New York: Criterion Books, 1964. Pp. 128 (Middle and Secondary) This nontechnical book "describes how houses are built and why the parts go together they way they do." (Readability = 9.2)

CHASE, ALICE ELIZABETH. *Famous Paintings.* New York: Platt and Munk, 1962. 184 plates, including 54 in full color. Pp. 120. (Middle and Secondary) The paintings in this book are arranged under 52 topics. Each topic is illustrated by one full-page color plate of a major work and several small plates. For each topic there is an interesting, informative discussion of several paragraphs. This is a very fascinating book. (Readability = 10.5)

DOWNER, MARION. *Discovering Design.* New York: Lothrop, Lee and Shepard, 1947. Illustrated with photographs and drawings. Pp. 104. (Secondary) This book on design is designed to "give new eyes to many people who have been looking at, but not seeing the beauty in the everyday world." It is of interest to the art student and to the general reader. The designs, most of which are found in nature, are classified and named. On each left-hand page is an explanatory paragraph. On the facing page are the designs exemplifying the type of design. (Readability = 11.2)

GASSER, HENRY. *Guide to Painting.* New York: Golden Press, 1964. Pp. 160, including a three-page glossary of terms. Illustrated in color. (Secondary) This book is one of the most colorful and useful books on painting. Under the section headings of oil painting, water color, and casein, we find 57 topics with titles such as material and equipment, lay-in of the subject, transferring a sketch, scumbling; watercolor quickies, the figure in watercolor, several technical devises; and casein vignettes. (Readability = 8.9)

GLUBOK, SHIRLEY. *The Art of Ancient Greece.* New York: Atheneum, 1965. Pp. 48. Illus. (Middle and Secondary) This well-illustrated book is on the "Golden Age of Greek Art," the years from about 450 B.C. until about 400 B.C. The photographs of the art works are from museums all over the world; there is also a picture of the Parthenon. (Readability = 6.4)

HAMM, JACK. *Drawing the Head and Figure.* New York: Grosset and Dunlap, 1963. Pp. 120. Illus. (Secondary) This is a very complete, well-organized, and illustrated treatise on figure drawing. The author states that "if you can draw people well, you become a wanted individual in both commercial and fine art." His approach will indeed give the student something to understand and remember.

HORVATH, JOAN. *Filmmaking for Beginners.* Nashville: Thomas Nelson, 1974. Pp. 162. Illus. (Secondary) Evidently this book has grown out of work done at the Collegiate School for Boys, New York City. It contains the information you would need to get started in filmmaking. It answers such questions as "How do you plan a film, write a script? How do you choose a camera? What is a cutaway shot, a pan, a tilt, a dolly? How do you edit a film or add sound? What are the tricks for animation or for special effects . . . . ?" (Readability = 7.8)

ISENBERG, ANITA and SEYMOUR ISENBERG. *How to Work in Stained Glass.* Philadelphia: Chilton, 1972. Pp. 237. Illus. (Upper Middle and Secondary) The first sentence in the introduction is, "Surely one of the most beautiful sights in the world is a medieval stained glass window." This is a very thorough book—I would say a real labor of love— that is a must for the secondary school library and for the library of anyone interested in the many uses of stained glass. (Readability = 8.0)

LAMMER, JUTTA. *Print Your Own Fabrics.* New York: Watson-Guptill, 1965. Pp. 59. Illus. (Secondary) The chapter headings for this delightful book are Fabric Painting, Stencilling, Painting on Fabric, and Batik. (Readability = 9.1)

MEILACH, DONA Z. and LEE ERLIN SNOW. *Creative Stitchery.* Chicago: Henry Regnery. 1970. Pp. 118. Illus., 135+ black-and-white and 16 color photographs. (Upper Middle and Secondary) The balance between informational commentary, how-to text, and illustrations is good. Materials, stitches, and the canvas stitch are explained. Following this there are chapters on ideas, colors, and designs for stitcheries; multiple fabrics; mixed media with stitchery; and sculptural stitchery. (Readability = 10.2)

MILLER, NATALIE. *The Story of the Statue of Liberty.* Chicago: Children's Press, 1965. Pp. 30. Illus. (Middle and Secondary) This is the story of the Statue of Liberty from the inception of the idea of a monument at a dinner attended by Auguste Bartholdi and other notable Frenchmen at the home of Edouard de Laboulage, the visit to America by Bartholdi and the first sketch he made as he entered New York harbor, through the statue's construction in segments in France, and its erection on Bedloe's Island in New York harbor. A brief, but engaging story. (Readability = 7.7)

PARISH, PEGGY. *Costumes to Make.* New York: Macmillan, 1970. Illustrated by Lynn Sweat. Pp. 111. (Lower Middle Grades) The costumes fall under three main divisions: Other Days, Other People; Holidays; and Storybook Characters. (Readability = 4.0)

RAINEY, SARITA R. *Weaving Without a Loom.* Worcester, Massachusetts: Davis Publications, Inc., 1966. Pp. 132. (Secondary) Any book that "talks" about "Weaving Into

Scrim," "Weaving With Straws," "God's Eyes," "Ghiordez Knot", and "Provocative Variations" has to have something going for it. It does. At the back of the book are guides for materials and techniques and materials and supplies, and a glossary. (Readability = 7.5)

SEITZ, MARIANNE. *Creating Silver Jewelry With Beads.* New York: Sterling Publishing Co., 1972. Pp. 48. (Middle School) This book is one in a series of 32 books in the Little Craft Book Series. In this book one is taught by text and illustrations how to create such things as a looped-nine and bead necklace, a wire neckloop and jeweled silver pendant, silver-and-bead-decorated velvet chokers, and a wire-and-bead decorated belt. The directions are straightforward and easy to follow. (Readability = 6.4)

TAUBES, FREDERIC. *Penn and Ink Drawing.* New York: Pitman Publishing Co., 1962. Pp. 53. 47 illus. (Secondary) In a brief introduction the author discusses the nature of drawing. In the *materials* section the author discusses pens, ink, brushes, and kinds of paper and the basic effects that can be obtained with them. In the *drawing techniques* part such techniques as the single contour definition, the staccato, single line sketch, cross-hatching, and diagonal shading are delineated. The author includes illustrations by Dürer, Raphael, Rembrandt, and himself. Wash drawings by Rembrandt and Guardi exemplify in-interesting pictorial effects. The author also explains how to work on wet paper with india ink. In the section on methods of expression Taubes discusses texture in drawing, using his own sketches in addition to one each by Van Gogh, Michelangelo, and Leonardo. (Readability = 10.8)

THORPE, HAROLD E. *Basic Pottery for the Student.* New York: St. Martin's Press, 1973. Pp. 102+ Illus. (Secondary) This is a fine book that gets rather technical so it is not always easy to read. The book "attempts to provide outlines on methods of making pottery, on design and decoration, and on technical background." (Readability = 11.7)

WEISS, HARVEY. *Paper, Ink and Roller: Print-Making for Beginners.* New York: Young Scott Books, 1958. Pp. 63. Illus. (Secondary) Although this book is generally as difficult to read as the Lammer book on the same topic, the directions on potato printing are better written and illustrated. (Readability = 9.0)

_____. *Pencil, Pen and Brush: Drawing for Beginners.* New York: Young Scott Books, 1961. Pp. 64. (Middle and Secondary) This book explains with words and illustrations how to draw animals, the figure, heads, landscapes, scenes. There are also chapters titled "Experimenting with Pencil, Pen, and Brush" and "Information About the Illustrations." (Readability = 6.9)

ZARCHY, HARRY. *Ceramics.* New York: Alfred A. Knopf, 1954. Illus. Pp. 171. Glossary. (Middle and Secondary) In ten chapters the author explains such things as hand-built pottery, using the potter's wheel, bisque firing, decorating pottery, glazing, and making ceramic jewelry. The book contains approximately 200 illustrations. The directions seem farily explicit. (Readability = 7.6)

Reading Reference Works. Reference works in almost any discipline are generally rather difficult and are useful, as far as textual material is concerned, only to the excellent reader in the secondary schools.

ASHTON, DORE. *New York.* New York: Holt, Rinehart and Winston, 1972. Pp. 288. 150 illus. (color and black and white) "The main text provides a survey of the city's cultural history from its founding by the Dutch as Nieuw Amsterdam and then as the English New York in 1664 to the present time. It is illustrated with paintings, sculpture, buildings and general views." (From the Foreword) Special photography is by Mario Carrieri.

GLOAG, JOHN. *Guide to Western Architecture.* New York: Hamlyn Publishing Group, 1969. Pp. 407. 400+ illustrations.

HUYGHE, RENE (General Editor). *Larousse Encyclopedia of Renaissance and Baroque Art.* New York: Prometheus Press, 1964. Pp. 444.

JANSON, H. W. *History of Art.* New York: Harry N. Abrams, Inc., 1969. Pp. 616. The introduction, "The Artist and His Public," is informative and interesting. This work is made up of four parts: 1 The Ancient World, pp. 18–184; 2. The Middle Ages, pp. 185–283; 3. The Renaissance, pp. 284–452, and 4. The Modern World, 453–568. Also a Postscript; Synoptic Table; and Books for Further Reading.

MURRAY, PETER and LINDA MURRAY. *A Dictionary of Art and Artists.* Baltimore: Penguin Books, 1972. Pp. 468. "The purpose of this Dictionary is to act as a companion to the inquiring gallery visitor, and, we hope, to serve as a useful quick reference work." Articles on technical terms are combined with biographies of many artists.

OSBORNE, HAROLD (Ed.) *The Oxford Companion to Art.* London: Oxford University Press, 1970. Pp. 1229 plus a 2,969 item bibliography.

READ, HERBERT. The *Thames and Hudson Encyclopedia of the Arts.* London: Thames and Hudson, 1966. Pp. 966. Many illustrations plus 79 color plates. This encyclopedia contains (1) entries for individual artists and for particular works of art (books, films, plays, operas, paintings, etc.) as well as more general articles on historical movement in the arts and (2) groups of articles. It also contains articles on techniques and materials.

READING IN MUSIC

The chief goal of reading musical compositions is performance marked by accuracy and good interpretation—dynamics, feeling, and the like. The result for the performer and listener should be satisfaction, pleasure, and edification. Music is an auditory gem. But there are many facets to music, as with other jewels. We must let the full light of excellent instruction fall upon the gem we call music if we are going to behold it in all its effulgent, many-faceted glory.

I shall leave curriculum and vocal and instrumental teaching methods to the music specialist. In this section of the chapter I shall discuss a few ideas that I hope will be useful and stimulating to the teacher in trying to help students perceive and interpret verbal and figural symbols.

Measurement Procedures

Testing Reading Vocabulary. Since there is a great amount of foreign language vocabulary in music reading, this vocabulary in particular should be learned in a natural way in oral and written contexts. The music dictionary should be a secondary but important source of vocabulary. I prefer a very small one that the student can easily carry. *The Students' Dictionary of Musical Terms* (Charles Hansen Music and Books) is such a dictionary. It gives (1) the chief signs and symbols used in music, (2) the flat and sharp key signatures, and (3) the dictionary proper, with a clear definition and an indication of the language source.

Following is a subjective vocabulary list, taken from the above dictionary, that includes common terms and some terms to challenge music majors or buffs.

bagatelles	gloria	Marseillaise	quadrille	virginal
brio	hochzeits-lied	nocturne	quire	vox
cadenza	introit	obligato	rubato	zither
celeste	Italian sixth	offertory	senza	zwischenspiel
diapason	jodeln	organ point	solfeggio	
doxology	lagrimoso	passacaglia	tenuto	
fugue	litany	pressando	tutti	

The above list can be used to check the ability of gifted music students to pronounce and define important musical terms. For the middle school and average secondary school music student, the list can be modified somewhat. The test can be used as a meaning test in group situations by having the students (1) write the definitions or (2) select the correct choice in a multiple-choice situation. Following is a 25-point test suitable for use with middle school music students. (To add to the diagnostic value, have the students draw one line under words they cannot pronounce and two lines under words they do not know the meaning of.)

1. arpeggio: A. "broken" chords   B. lively   C. a musical subject
   D. type of trumpet

2. cadenza: A. furniture   B. hesitating   C. ornamental solo passage
   D. the subject of a fugue

3. crescendo: A. melody or theme   B. increasing volume   C. modulating   D. quickly, without haste

4. embellishment: A. music store   B. with feeling   C. trills, turns, etc.
   D. make louder

5. fermata: A. a brass instrument   B. pause or hold   C. a quick release   D. tone coloring

6. fugue: A. polyphonic composition   B. gloomy, sad
   C. French march   D. fanfare

7. in tempo: A. vibration   B. urgently   C. in strict time
   D. in an undecided manner

8. legato: A. rapidly   B. in connected manner   C. undecided
   D. in a bold manner

9. maestoso: A. quiet staccato   B. hurrying the time   C. extremely loud   D. majestic; with dignity

10. mute: A. contrivance to dampen the sound   B. to open up
    C. to sustain the sound   D. to end abruptly

11. noel: A. Christmas eve song   B. a set of bells   C. a violin made in Cremona   D. a Lenten hymn

12. opus: A. pompous   B. work   C. open   D. fluently

13. piano: A. an organ   B. softly   C. bold   D. at first sight

14. presto: A. a sacred song   B. smoothly   C. melodic
    D. rapidly

15. ritenuto: A. passionately   B. a slow dance   C. holding back
    D. delicately

16. root: A. grace note   B. an old dance in triple time   C. change
    D. fundamental note of a chord

17. <u>signature</u>:   A. composer's writing   B. legend   C. slow dance
    D. signs that indicate the key
18. <u>staccato</u>:   A. crisp, quick attack   B. medley   C. lilting
    D. more motion
19. <u>syncopation</u>:   A. many voiced   B. shifting accent   C. jubilant
    D. run or arpeggio
20. <u>tenuto</u>:   A. held, sustained   B. rural, rustic   C. martial
    D. trumpet-like
21. <u>tranquillo</u>:   A. with expression   B. serious   C. calmly
    D. pompously
22. <u>troubadors</u>:   A. type of trombone   B. vocal duet   C. wandering
    singers   D. cathedral organists
23. <u>vivace</u>:   A. with love   B. sprightly   C. articulated
    D. mysterious
24. <u>woodwind</u>:   A. bellows   B. kettledrum   C. tubas and trumpets
    D. flutes, clarinets, etc.
25. <u>xylophone</u>:   A. instrument played with mallets   B. monotone   C. a
    kind of French horn   D. a kazoo

Creating Informal Reading Inventories. The music teacher and the reading specialist—working singly or in tandem—might well consider developing one or more kinds of reading inventories: (1) the ordinary informal reading inventory as discussed in the chapter on measurement and evaluation, (2) the IVCA (index, vocabulary, comprehension, and application) inventory explained and illustrated in the chapter on vocational-technical reading, and (3) the multiple-choice cloze test.

Teaching the Reading of Music Materials

In addition to using the following suggestions for teaching vocabulary and the reading of specialized materials one should consult other chapters in the present text. Instruction should always be meaningful, in context, and provide for meaningful repetition and use.

Reading the Words in Music Class. Earle and Perney (1972) point out that students who are generally poor readers in academic subjects also have trouble in reading the songs in their music books. Three factors, they say, contribute to the problem: (1) The words hold little or no meaning for some students; that is, the students cannot recognize and comprehend certain words. (2) The word syllabication (done to fit the rhythmic pattern of the songs) hinders word recognition. (3) The problem is intensified by the words being interspersed among music staves and symbols.

For accurate recognition and interpretation of lyrics one must know the background of a song and be able to identify words accurately so that, for example, one does not read foeman's chain in "The Minstrel Boy" as foreman's chain. Several unidentified or misidentified words may result in meaning being lost entirely or in a misinterpretation. Furthermore, proper musical treatment hinges on correct interpretation of lyrics. (The first thing that comes to mind is the song "Lullaby" by Brahms. How would you like to have that screamed in your ear as you prepared for a gentle repose!)

Second, the sounds must be related to symbols that are spread out by syllabication, and the sounds must be synthesized to give the word. When learning a fast-tempoed song, this process must be executed rapidly, and the result can be stumbling and confusion.

Third, seeing a song with music staves, notes, dynamic markings, and sundry kinds of signs around and near the words can be discombobulating enough to discourage a slow reader at once.

What can be done about this problem? Present words of a song in poem format prior to using them in connection with music notation:

1. Present the words of the song in poem form on a sheet.
2. Underscore words.
3. Develop their meaning.
4. Work out the pronunciation of troublesome words.
5. Discuss the overall meaning of lyrics.
6. Go to the music books and teach the musical aspects of the song.
7. Hand out the same type of song sheet as in 1.
8. Sing from the sheet.
9. Have the students mark the song sheets where they think the words should be divided.
10. Sing the song again.
11. Give the students song sheets on which the words are divided into syllables.
12. Sing the song a third time.
13. Ask the students to compare the syllabicated and nonsyllabicated song sheets and ask them which form is easier to follow.
14. Use the music books that contain the syllabicated words along with the music notes and other symbols.

This type of teaching, Earle and Perney tell us, is very helpful in dealing with the reading difficulties related to music. One would not prepare such materials for every song, nor would every music class contain students who need extra help in reading lyrics.

I can see how the reading specialist could adapt this procedure, using familiar lyrics, to teach some kinds of students to improve minimal reading skills.

Reading Technical Directions for Playing. Directions for playing musical instruments use general language, technical language, and figurative language in combination. Below are three examples of technical directions found in piano literature:

Example one

Practice first in four-four time.
Later in alle breve.
Apply the swells and diminuendos as indicated.*

* #9, "Smooth Passage Playing." Le Couppey. John Thompson. Third Grade Velocity Studies. Cincinnati: Willis Music Co., 1938.

A teacher generally should know whether students can decode the words and understand the directions A teacher will often give the directions orally in paraphrase, perhaps not paying attention to the exact words. But the teacher really should check the student's ability to decode the words, understanding of terms, and comprehension of the directions as a whole. The teacher and the student can look up the term *alle breve*, for example, in the dictionary. If the dictionary has pronunciation helps, the pronunciation can be rewritten into the student's book or into a music notebook the student is developing under the guidance of the teacher:

> alla breve
>
> Definition: 4/4 time at a higher rate of speed and counted as 2-2.
> Technical sentence: "Practice first in four-four time.
> Later in alla breve."
> Fun sentence: I walk to school in four-four time. I come home in alla breve.

Also, crescendo and diminuendo are usually found together. "Swell" is substituted for crescendo and is related to ◁ just as diminuendo is related to ▷ . The term *indicated* can be related by the teacher to the word *index* finger, or pointing finger so that *indicated* means *pointed out*.

> Example two
>
> These arpeggio figures should be tossed from one hand to the other and sound as smoothly as though played with one hand.*
>
> * #14 "By the Seaside," Streaborg. (Ibid.)

A piano student in this level book will know what an arpeggio figure is. However, even apparently simple arpeggios can be difficult to execute smoothly so the author used the figure of speech "tossed from one hand to another" to connote the idea of continuity. Again, the teacher should check the student's understanding of meaning.

In the following example, one cannot assume that good students who have studied piano several years know the meaning of all the underlined terms. As with other content areas, the teacher must continually check on the student's understanding of general and technical vocabulary. Of the terms in question, *staccato* is probably the most familiar term.

> Example three
>
> The diatonic groups should be tossed from one hand to the other. Use a slight rolling motion in combination with finger legato to give sparkle.
> Play the intervening chords with sharp forearm staccato.*
>
> * #30 "L'avalanche," Heller (Ibid.)

The term *diatonic* could have been introduced at one time and promptly forgotten and so must be retaught. "Should be tossed from one hand to another" is an expression used previously. As indicated previously, arpeggio type figures are difficult to execute so the suggestion to use a "slight rolling motion in combination . . . ." is important. If the term *legato* has not been used recently in a piece, the meaning should be doublechecked and possibly written out by the term. Responsibility for this can be given to the student.

The term *intervening* will not be nailed down unless used in several written contexts and in speech from time to time. A deductive pattern can be used at times:

> Intervene means to come between. (Vene is Latin for come as in Venite adoremus—Come, let us adore Him. Inter means between.)
> 1. The father intervened in the fight between two of his children.
>   Q.: What did the father do?
>   Expected answer: He came between them.
> 2. Pochantas intervened and stopped the execution of John Smith.
>   (Predicated on knowing this story.)
>   Q.: What did Pochantas do?
> Application: (1) "Point out the intervening chords."
>   (2) Between what do they come?

A student may have been executing *forearm staccatos* without knowing what a forearm is. One needs to point this out and make the connection between the concept and the label.

Reading Music Reviews. The only middle schoolers who regularly read music reviews in large metropolitan newspapers are a few sophisticated students who are excellent readers and who are deeply interested in music. More middle and secondary school students will read if they (1) are familiar with the particular production being reviewed and/or (2) are taught to read reviews. Some portions of any review are easier to understand than others, for example, the opening section that identifies the work, the composer, the musical group, the place of performance, and the like.

In such a review of the Mikado, Raymond Ericson in the *opening* paragraph of his review in the *The New York Times* newspaper gives some of the basic identifying information and then finishes the paragraph by commenting that the performance "induced 'modified rapture.' " (This expression is explicable but should be related to experience.)

The *second* paragraph gives some general comment about the troupe and the producers and provides few reading problems. Succeeding paragraphs and some of the expressions that could be difficult for the unsophisticated reader are:

> Third: The performers "never seem to capture the Victorian gentility with which the music should be played and sung." (Requires discussion and allusion to history and to performance by a British company that does play and sing with Victorian gentility.)
> Fourth: none
> Fifth: "even when the voices were less than sumptuous"

<u>Sixth</u>:   a. "light-voiced English tenor, phrasing with an elegant legato line" (The meaning of this could be illustrated by a teacher or student or, better yet, by a recording of the actual performance.)

           b. "Little flights into fioriture" (<u>Fioriture</u> are trills, appogiaturas, or other ornamentation added to the melody As a class name, it can be the superordinate for such terms.)

<u>Seventh</u>: "rolls out his lines and lyrics with the proper relish of Gilbert's wit." (Explainable partly through discussion, but discussion coupled with an opportunity to hear and see such performance yields better understanding and appreciation.)

<u>Eighth</u>: "he sings the 'Tit Willow' song with a proper seductiveness that is both shy and sad." (Again, seeing the performance and discussing it in connection with basic meanings of seductiveness would be fruitful. The concept might be illustrated by the music teacher or selected students.)

<u>Ninth and Tenth</u>: None.

I am not an expert on what constitutes a good review, but I must say that, in the main, Ericson's writing is quite readable and does the job. Such writing becomes more readable for middle and secondary students as they and their teachers discuss reviews and relate them to actual performances and to recordings of performances!

Music: Visiting 'Mikado'

By RAYMOND ERICSON

The D'oyly Carte Opera Company, the London ensemble that keeps alive the performing tradition of the Gilbert and Sullivan operettas, returned here last night after an absence of seven seasons. It opened a three-week engagement at the Uris Theater with "The Mikado." To use Nanki-Poo's phrase in that work, it induced "modified rapture."

To the faithful, and Savoyard operetta on hand is a cause for rejoicing, doubly so when produced by so honorable a company. But the troupe is playing it safe, or rather its local producers are, and it has brought only the three most popular works in the repertory—"The Pirates of Penzance" and "H.M.S. Pinafore" besides "The Mikado"—which are almost always with us. There were signs, at least in the Tuesday preview seen by this writer, that overfamiliarity had infected some of the company, who treated the performance as a ritual rather than a spontaneous experience.

The strength of the present company is musical. American groups that stage Gilbert and Sullivan have picked up most of the D'Oyly Carte stage business and handle it well; if without quite the same precision, but they never seem to capture the Victorian gentility with which the music should be played and sung.

It was a special pleasure to hear Royston Nash conduct the overture as if time did not matter, pacing the well-loved tunes in a leisurely manner. Yet Mr. Nash's rhythms were so steady that when tempos were slow they did not drag and when they were fast they did not rush. Sullivan's score could not have sounded more poised.

The singing was always stylish even when the voices were less than sumptuous. As Nanki-Poo, Geoffrey Shovelton was a model of the light-voiced English tenor, phrasing with an elegant legato line. Lyndsie Holland's contralto had an unusual smoothness for the grim role of Katisha. Julia Goss, a round, cuddly Yum-Yum, headed a trio of sisters, with Jane Metcalfe as Pitti-Sing and Patricia Leonard as Peep-Bo, who chirped charmingly, and Michael Raner's little flights into fioriture as Pish-Tush were neatly handled.

It was the company's veterans, however, who gave this "Mikado" its special quality. Kenneth Sandford, who is credited with almost 2,000 performances as Pooh-Bah, still rolls out his lines and lyrics with the proper relish of Gilbert's wit.

Then there was John Reed, making his sixth tour of North America in 20 years, he pranced through the part of Ko-Ko as if he hadn't aged a year. His comic spirit remains fresh, and he sings the "Tit Willow" song with a proper seductiveness that is both sly and sad.

Physically, the production is the same as for the company's previous visit, and handsome enough. The chorus sang stirringly and snapped its fans smartly, but also behaved as routinely as a Broadway musical's chorus finishing a three-year run. On balance, the D'Oyly Carte people give the Gilbert words and the Sullivan melodies their due, and perhaps one shouldn't ask for anything more.

Reading Forewords to Selections and Collections. Myriad numbers of selections and collections have forewords. One written by a distinguished composer-teacher is Percy Grainger's foreword to Grieg's Opus 16, Piano Concerto in A Minor I shall discuss it first and then Huneker's foreword to Chopin's nocturnes.

Just as Grieg's music is "clear and clean" compared to some of Chopin's work, so is Grainger's foreword to Grieg's music compared to Huneker's foreword to Chopin's Nocturne. Grainger includes two excerpts from Henry T. Finck's "authoritative and inspiring book," *Grieg and His Music*. The first excerpt discusses the quality of the concertos.

> . . . The first movement is replete with beautiful, haunting melody, and nothing could be more lovely than the orchestral introduction to the slow movement—one of the saddest preludes ever written—a prelude illustrating Grieg's gift of creating an emotional atmosphere with the simplest means . . . .

If you have any idea of the difficulty of this work you would appreciate Greig's account in the second excerpt from Frinck's book He tells of his meeting with Liszt and Liszt's agreeing to sight read the piece! Liszt first asked Grieg to play his own work. Grieg demurred because he had not practiced it:

> Then Liszt took the manuscript, went to the piano and said to the guests, with his characteristic smile: "Very well, then, I will show you that I also cannot." With that he began. I admit that he took the first part of the concerto too fast, and the beginning consequently sounded helter-skelter; but later on, when I had a chance to indicate the tempo, he played as only he can play. It is significant that he played the cadenza, the most difficult part, best of all. His demeanor is worth any price to see. Not content with playing, he at the same time converses and makes comments . . . .

Grainger was Grieg's guest during the summer of 1907 in Grieg's country home, Troldhaugen. He and Grieg spent much of their time, Grainger writes, "rehearsing the concerto for a number of performances of the work to take place the following winter in the various capitols of Europe, himself conducting and myself playing the piano part."

We get insight from Grainger's remarks on the psychology of Grieg as an artist and a man: "In performing Grieg's music . . . we should constantly remember the heroic undercurrent of the composer's personality (so dramatically evinced by his brave behavior in Paris in connection with the Dreyfus affair) and the intensity of his emotionality. Sir Charles Villiers Stanford has called Grieg 'a miniature viking,' and there is much truth in this remark; for a certain fresh or tragic primitiveness, mixed with a somewhat eerie and ethereal spirituality, marks off Grieg's muse . . . ."

Grainger makes many other comments about Grieg the man and about how Grieg played his own music. I like Grainger's one pithy remark: "Grieg eschewed all 'muddiness' or turgid obscurity of tonal effect in writing for the piano or other instruments, and the performer of Grieg's music should try to realize the composer's predilection for bright and clear and clean sonorities."

Another foreword is that written by James Huneker for the *Nocturnes for the Piano* by Chopin. These comments are historical and analytical, and I would assume that this type of prose is read as much by the fledgling music critic in order to build vocabulary, prose style, and expertise as it is by the music teacher and piano student. Although you would need some knowledge of music and familiarity with the nocturnes to truly appreciate Huneker's writing, a few excerpts—and these relate to several nocturnes—might "tickle" your ear and mind:

> Chopin loved the night and its starry mysteries; his nocturnes are true night-pieces, some wearing an agitated, remorseful countenance; others seen in profile only; while many are like whisperings at dusk—Verlaine moods.

Speaking of Opus 27, No. 1 in C# Minor, a small excerpt of prose:

> The wide-meshed figure of the left hand supports a morbid, persistent melody that grates on the nerves. From the <u>piu mosso</u> the agitation increases . . . There is a surprising climax followed by <u>sunshine</u> in the D flat part; then after mounting dissonances, a bold succession of octaves leads to the feverish plaint of the opening.

The poor reader would find this prose to be gibberish; the average reader would consider it rather unintelligible. Only the excellent reader with considerable background in music who could thoroughly check the comments against the written and performed music would understand.

Building Music Background Through Library Reading

Reading Topical Books. Much music enrichment is done by the student. If the student is made aware of readable music books that match his or her interest or in some way are intellectually and/or artistically appealing, he or she will read them. This is not a curriculum text, but I would like to share some brief notes on a few books in the field of music. Also included is the readability of each book in terms of reading grade placement as determined according to Fry's Readability Graph:

BULLA, CLYDE ROBERT. *Stories of Favorite Operas.* New York: Thomas Y. Crowell, 1964. Pp. 277. (Middle School and Lower Secondary) Abridged versions of the story line of the great operas. These stories are complete, well written, and designed to hold the interest of the reader. (Readability = 5.8)

DAVIS, LIONEL and EDITH DAVIS. *Keyboard Instruments: The Story of the Piano.* Minneapolis: Lerner Publications Co., 1963. Pp. 40. (Middle School and Secondary) A fine work that musicians, especially piano students, will enjoy. A review for the good student and an introduction to piano for the interested nonpiano student who is a good reader. (Readability = 7.2)

GILMORE, LEE. *Folk Instruments.* Minneapolis, Minnesota: Lerner Publications Co., 1962. Pp. 41. (Middle and Secondary) This is a how-to-do-it book that also includes some history of the instruments and fundamental concepts of harmony. (Readability = 7.6)

HOFFMAN, E. T. A. *The Nutcracker.* Illus. by Fumiko Hori. Tokyo: Gakken Co., Ltd., 1971. (In U.S. Distributed by Silver Burdett.) Pp. 28. (Lower Middle School) The illustrations would be enjoyed by people of all ages. Middle grade students especially would like the text as would the young-at-heart regardless of chronological age. Very early in the story we see what little Marie saw late on Christmas eve as she came down the stairs and saw an army of mice attacking her dolls: "The Nutcracker was leading the toy soldiers into battle. The drummer boys drummed, and the buglers blew their bugles. . . . The soldiers fought bravely, but more and more mice came to join the battle. All the mice seemed to be trying to reach the nutcracker doll." And you know the ending—though unbelievable—has to be true! (Readability = 3.5)

KETTELKAMP, LARRY. *Flutes, Whistles, and Reeds.* New York: William Morrow, 1962. Pp. 48. Illus. (Middle and Secondary) The woodwinds include flutes and piccolos, double bassoons and saxophones, clarinets and bagpipes, as well as the great classical organs. The author explains why woodwinds perform as they do, shows how to make simple versions of them, and gives their historical background. (Readability = 7.3)

LYONS, JOHN HENRY. *Stories of Our American Patriotic Songs.* New York: Vanguard Press, Inc., 1942. Pp. 72. (Middle and Secondary) This book contains the music and lyrics for the following songs, in addition to a page or two on the history of each: The Star Spangled Banner; Yankee Doodle; Hail, Columbia; America; Columbia, the Gem of the Ocean; Dixie; Maryland, My Maryland; The Battle Cry of Freedom, The Battle Hymn of the Republic; and America, the Beautiful. The tenor of the book is summarized in its last paragraph: "The noble words of 'America, The Beautiful' lift the hearts and minds of Americans as few songs have power to do. The plea for brotherhood and a richer, freer national life breathes through its every line and inspires us to work for that great and ennobling cause." (Readability = 9.2)

MYRUS, DONALD. *Ballads, Blues, and the Big Beat.* New York: Macmillan, 1966. Illus. Pp. 136. (Secondary) This fascinating book tells about "the power and pleasure of folk songs and how they got to be so compelling." Everyone from precocious teenagers to open-minded octogenarians who can read and have a curiosity about songs and their singers will enjoy this work. (Readability = 12.0)

POSELL, ELSA Z. *This Is an Orchestra.* Boston: Houghton Mifflin, 1950. Illus. with over 30 photos. Pp. 95. (Middle and Secondary) Informative but not very exciting. It is interesting when it talks about the history of the instrument. The section "On Choosing an Instrument" is very worthwhile. I like the suggestion that older pupils practice at least an hour a day. The record suggestions for a beginner's library are excellent. (Readability = 9.5)

SELIGMAN, JEAN and JULIET DANZIGER. *The Meaning of Music: The Young Listener's Guide.* Cleveland: World, 1966. Glossary. Pp. 128. (Upper Middle and Secondary) The language of music and its traditional forms are explained in an engaging manner. The basics—tempo, harmony, melody, and rhythm—are defined and the various kinds of instruments are introduced. Should be read by the person who has a real interest in music, preferably by one who is a performer who knows quite a bit about music already. (Readability = 10.8)

SURPLUS, ROBERT W. *The Story of Musical Organizations.* Minneapolis: Lerner Publication Co., 1963. Pp. 41. (Middle and Secondary) The seven chapters are 1. Do You Know the Organizations in a Music Department? 2. Choral Music. 3. The Orchestra. 4. The Band. 5. Small Ensembles. 6. The Dance Band. 7. People Need Music. (Readability = 7.5)

TETZLAFF, DANIEL B. *Shining Brass.* Minneapolis: Lerner Publications Co., 1963. Illus. Pp. 39. (Middle and Secondary) For such a brief book, this work does about as good a job of discussing the brass instruments as one could want. The general reader as well as the musician will find this book to be informative. (Readability = 6.5)

Reading Reference Works. The general skills for reading reference works apply to reading reference works in music. Over a lifetime one develops the ability to read such works intelligently and with great understanding. It is a developmental process that must begin somewhere. Why not in school! Reference works are one area in which people can read in a desultory manner in order to build gradually a fund of vicarious experience and connect it where possible with real experience.

Before me is an article on Enrico Caruso in Ewen's *The New Encyclopedia of the Opera.* Being a tenor myself who has had the opportunity to sing excerpts from operas while a student at the University of Wisconsin, Milwaukee, and who has heard recordings of Caruso's voice, I can appreciate this vignette of Caruso's life. Because of real and vicarious experiences I have had I can reconstruct more of the facts that lie behind the symbols than I could when I was 23 and many more than I could when I was 17.

EWEN, DAVID. *The New Encyclopedia of the Opera.* New York: Hill and Wang, 1971. Pp. 759.

PAULAKIS, CHRISTOPHER. *The American Music Handbook.* New York: The Free Press, 1974. Pp. 836.

ROXON, LILLIAN. *Rock Encyclopedia.* New York: Grosset and Dunlap, 1969. Pp. 611.

SCHOLES, PERCY A. *The Oxford Companion to Music—Ninth Edition.* New York: Oxford University Press, 1955. Pp. 1195.

STAMBLER, IRWIN and GRELUM LANDON. *Encyclopedia of Folk, Country and Western Music.* New York: St. Martin's Press, 1969. Pp. 396.

READING IN HEALTH AND PHYSICAL EDUCATION

Since the topic being discussed is health and physical education, not sports, I have included those forms of physical activity most likely to contribute to physical fitness and health. By physical fitness I do not necessarily mean certain kinds of bulky muscular development, which result from weight lifting, or particular skills such as those used in golfing and bowling. In fact, these three activities—as well as an activity such as archery—have not been included in the discussion of physical (fitness) education because they have not been shown to contribute to the cardiovascular-pulmonary (c-p) fitness associated with aerobic activities. This does not mean I can vouch for wrestling or any activity as being a contributor to c-p fitness; this fitness depends, as I will point out later, on how the activity is done by any individual.

Aerobics, according to Cooper (1970), "refers to a variety of exercises that stimulate heart and lung activity for a time period sufficiently long to produce beneficial changes in the body. Running, swimming, cycling, and jogging—these are typical aerobic exercises. There are many others." I shall list key vocabulary items for a number of physical activities, some of which are classified as sports and most of which are aerobic. I do not include certain sports because leading physical conditioning people decry the popular assumption that these activities —such as golf and bowling—contribute anything to cardiovascular-pulmonary fitness.

Golf, according to Herman Hellerstein of Case Western Reserve University, "can be a fine way to spoil a walk." The total expenditure of energy for 18 holes of golf takes 20 minutes. To derive any benefit from the 5,000 to 6,000 yards covered, the golfer would have to walk at 3 to 4 miles per hour, which golfers do *not* do.

Certainly bowlers, archers, and golfers may engage in such aerobic activities as running, cycling, and swimming, and, if they meet Cooper's criteria, they may attain certain training effects characteristic of c-p fitness.

The criteria for attaining c-p fitness are set forth by Cooper (1970). If the programs developed by him are rigidly adhered to, the objectives of an aerobic exercise program will be met and the training effects will be obtained. Cooper states that the main objective of an aerobic exercise program is to "increase the maximum amount of oxygen that the body can process within a given time." This is called your aerobic capacity." The best index of overall physical fitness is the aerobic capacity.

The training effect produced by aerobic exercise increases in several ways the capacity to use oxygen:

1. By strengthening the muscles of respiration the rapid flow of air in and out of the lungs is ultimately facilitated.

2. By improving the strength and pumping efficiency of the heart, more blood can be pumped with each stroke. Therefore, the ability to rapidly transport life-sustaining oxygen to the heart and to all parts of the body is facilitated.

3. By toning up muscles in all parts of the body general circulation will be improved and at times blood pressure will be lowered and work on the heart will be reduced.

4. By increasing the total amount of blood (and thereby hemoglobin) circulating through the body, the blood becomes a more efficient carrier of oxygen (Cooper, 1970).

In listing the following vocabulary I am not claiming that all the activities are necessarily aerobic. For a given person to obtain aerobic benefits, the activities would have to meet the criteria set forth by Cooper. For example, if a boy or girl is "out for" baseball, but the associated activities do not include enough running or walking and the person does not get enough practice and game time to meet Cooper's requirements, the aerobic capacity will not be improved. Bonalewicz (1976) states that aerobic exercises should be a vital part of a baseball pitcher's training program because according to his research, pitchers are subjected to cardiovascular stress while pitching.

The 100 items in this list can be used in several ways: (1) as a general test of knowledge of physical (fitness) education terms, (2) as a very brief test for any category, and as a starter list for any category, to which other items may be added. Two of the categories—physical fitness and running—feature aerobic concepts. These concepts apply to other areas, also.

Physical fitness	Basketball	Field Hockey
aerobic capacity	back court	bully
conditioning	fast break	dribble
heat-stress index	individual foul	goal
medical examination	jump shot	long corner
overexertion	pivot	reverse sticks
training effect	screen	striking circle
vitality	zone defense	
warm up		

Football	Gymnastics	Handball
down	bridge	ace
forward pass	dismount	double fault
interception	flex	hand-out
punt	mount	long ball
scrimmage	pommels	punch ball
touchdown	saddle	service
	uneven bars	

Ice Hockey	Lacrosse	Rhythm and Dance
clearing the puck	cradling	allemande left
goal judge	crosse	docey doe
killing penalities	free position	honor your partner
misconduct	midfielders	mazurka
pale check	penalty box	promenade
save	slashing	step hop

Running—Walking—Cycling	Baseball	Soccer
cardiovascular-pulmonary fitness	double play	dribbling
fitness categories	fielder	heading
oxygen utilization	home run	kick-off
recovery heart rate	knuckle ball	penalty kick
stamina	shoestring catch	trapping
thirty points per week	Texas leaguer	
twelve-minute test		

Speedball	Swimming	Track
aerial ball	Australian crawl	anchor man
fly ball	breast stroke	dead heat
kick-up	free style	exchange
place kick	medley relay	lap
touchdown	short course	sprint
	turn	starting block

Volleyball

deuce
game point
match
rotation
setup
spike
volley

In addition to Cooper's book *Aerobics,* the interested reader might like to read the good general overview provided by Snider (1974) in his article "The Fitness Craze" in the *World Book Yearbook.* Here are what I consider to be some of the important points in his report:

1. Evidence tends to support the belief that (aerobic) activity prevents, or at least postpones, many heart attacks.

2. Industrial studies show that sedentary workers have a slightly higher rate of heart disease than active workers. For example, professional people in one Canadian study had 5.7 times as many coronary deaths as farmers, miners, and laborers.

3. Persons who want to start an active exercise program should first have a thorough physical examination.

4. "Exercise that produces heart and lung fitness is more beneficial for most sedentary Americans than that which produces big muscles and eliminates swim-suit bulge."

5. The size and the shape of the biceps are not of importance to daily living; the conditions of the circulatory and respiratory systems are.

6. Running, swimming, cycling, walking, running in place, and either handball, basketball, or squash (in that order) are said to be the best exercises for cardiovascular-respiratory fitness, according to Cooper. Brisk walking is high on Cooper's list.

7. Golf, bowling, and isometrics, among other forms of "exercise," have *no* cardiovascular-respiratory conditioning value.

Improving Vocabulary and Reading Comprehension

One of the most important ways of developing vocabulary (in addition to the methods already given in the book) is for physical education and health instructors to develop a large collection of graded reading selections on health physical education topics. I would consult with a librarian on the best way of cataloging, housing, and making available these documents.

Sources would be *Reader's Digest*, newspapers, family magazines, *Sports Illustrated, Today's Health,* and the like plus pertinent articles, which could be located through use of the *Reader's Guide to Periodical Literature.* The teachers should enlist the help of reading and writing specialists for tips on taking selections and rewriting them to make them more readable. Besides the rewriting work done by the teachers, students can help with this work. The original sources can be catalogued and appropriate persons should check the rewritten material for accuracy.

(I like to go through *Sports Illustrated* with my middle school and high school children and let them underline problem words. I write in the margins the meanings of the words and discuss them with the children right on the spot. Teachers should do more of this. But too much dictionary work kills interest in vocabulary learning.)

The following kinds of reading aids can be developed in conjunction with the excerpted articles.

1. Key words and meanings.
2. Guided reading questions.
3. Post-reading multiple-choice quiz.
4. References to other articles on the topic that the student might like to read.

These four activities, including all the associated details could be typed on fairly stiff manila material and then laminated. Of course, each set of aids must be properly labeled and filed so that retreival is easy.

Any text material will have to be of suitable difficulty for the students expected to read it. I recommend teaching much of the material as guided reading lessons, especially when there is much of a discrepancy between the readability of the text and the reading ability of the students. You will remember, too, the pre-reading worksheets, Language Master cards, and nail-down methods that can be used for vocabulary meaning and word recognition—worksheets and Language Master cards for vocabulary meaning, and LM cards and other nail-down methods for word recognition.

Reading Topical Books.   Following is a very brief annotated list of books in physical education. I have, in keeping with my philosophical bias, included only two books of the nonaerobic sports.

ARCHIBALD, JOE   *Baseball Talk for Beginners.* New York: Julian Messner, 1974. Pp. 90. Illus. (Middle) This is a dictionary of baseball terms written in an interesting style. (Readability = 6.0)

BAKER, EUGENE. *I Want to Be a Swimmer.* Chicago: Children's Press, 1973. Pp. 31. Illus. (Middle and Secondary) Simple well-illustrated explanation of the following swimming strokes: American crawl, back stroke, breast stroke, side stroke, and butterfly. Readability = 3.3)

HENKEL, STEPHEN C. *Bikes.* Riverside, Conn.: The Chatam Press, 1972. Pp. 96. Illus. (Secondary) Cycling can contribute to cardiovascular-pulmonary fitness as well as develop many muscles. It is therefore a very important activity for real physical fitness. This book, however, is on the care and repair of bicycles. (Readability = secondary)

KNOSHER, HARLEY. *Basic Basketball Strategy.* Garden City, N.Y.: Doubleday, 1972. Pp. 102. Illus. (Upper Middle and Secondary) This carefully detailed book written by a college coach answers key questions about basketball and explains basic basketball strategy. The illustrations by Leonard Kessler are excellent. Each chapter ends with five or six brief tips. (Readability = 8.9)

LISS, HOWARD. *Bobby Orr: Lightning on Ice.* Champaign, Ill.: Garrard, 1975. Pp. 96. Illus. (Middle and Secondary) This biography will appeal to hockey players and fans.

MONROE, EARL and WES UNSELD. *The Basketball Skill Book.* New York: Atheneum, 1975. Pp. 114. Illus. (Upper Middle and Secondary) The reader is taken through the basic fundamentals of basketball by sequence-action photography and accompanying text. The material is presented from two perspectives. *Monroe* illustrates the principles of backcourt play and his special style of shooting. Unseld, although "only" 6'7", is a top defensive center. He illustrates the front court that has made him an all-pro player and the nemesis of opposing teams. (Readability = 8.5)

VAN RIPER, GUERNSEY. *Behind the Plate: Three Great Catchers.* Champaign, Ill.: Garrard Press, 1973. Pp. 95. (Middle) Biographies of Mickey Cochrane, Bill Dickey, and Roy Campanella. (Readability = 6.6)

WOODEN, JOHN. *They Call Me Coach.* Waco, Texas: Word Books, 1973. Pp. 195. Illus. (Upper Middle and Secondary) This book is a first-person story of the brilliant, God-fearing basketball coach, John Wooden of UCLA. It shows what happens when a person lets himself be guided and empowered by his Maker. David Condon of the Chicago Tribune calls it "the finest inside story of a championship sports personality since the one on Vince Lombardi." (Readability = 9.0)

SUMMARY

Art, which is concerned with the (harmonious) arrangement of color and space, is ubiquitous in nature. People come into the world with the potential to create art and to appreciate it but this capacity must be nourished When art brings beauty into people's lives it is a *fill*, not a frill.

One especially productive way of measuring and evaluating people's ability to read how-to books is to probe the individual's ability as he or she actually reads segments of it. Although a slow process, it gets at the dynamics of the student's reading and gives a realistic idea of how the student functions in these situations.

As a guide to teaching vocabulary, the principles of vocabulary development were reiterated and applications were made. Meanings, of course, are rooted in appropriate real and vicarious experiences. Provisions for developing concepts and for connecting concepts with labels in dynamic, meaningful ways must be made and carried out. When a student invests time and energy in a word, the word becomes a meaningful, integral part of him or her.

If you expect a student to be able to read to follow directions, teach him or her to do so And such teaching is not a one-shot affair. How can the idea of reading directions well be generalized if it is not developed in a matrix of numbers of lessons over a period of time. Even then, vocabulary may be a problem. Furthermore, students will not learn to read art materials well and become independent readers if not given opportunities to learn aspects of techniques by reading. Some teachers may like to have their students dependent solely on them but that is not good for the students' long-term development, nor the teacher's for that matter.

Music, like art, is another area in which harmonious imagery is both a means and an end. In art the imagery is visual; in music, auditory The goal of musical performance is performance marked by accuracy and good interpretation. The result is pleasure and edification.

Reading vocabulary can be tested by any of several methods. Certainly if vocabulary, musical symbols, and signs are worth teaching, it is sensible to test to see how much is retained and what needs to be retaught or restudied.

Besides the ordinary vocabulary reading problems faced in general reading and in other content areas, people reading the lyrics of songs in music format face the problems of literary allusions, of syllabicated words, and of the lyrics being embedded in a matrix of music staves and symbols. These problems and their solutions were delineated in this chapter.

Technical directions for playing musical instruments use several kinds of language in combination. Examples of such directions and how they might be treated in a less prosaic manner were set forth.

An example of a music review and some of the problems in understanding such a valuable piece of writing were delineated. The various strategies for teaching vocabulary apply and were therefore not reiterated. The idea of discussing reviews and relating them to performances and recordings of performances was recommended.

After a discussion of the affective and cognitive aspects of reading forewords the reader found an annotated list of topical music books. Finally, a few basic reference works were provided.

The author chose to adopt a particular philosophical bias with respect to health and physical education. It is a point of view ground in a theory of aerobics and verified by scientific evidence. Aerobic sports are fun and many of them can be engaged in by the individual as well as by groups of people. Certainly the secondary school student who is educated and trained to participate in a life-saving activity is fortunate.

After listing important points about aerobic theory and some human interest aspects of the practice, there was a discussion of a unique way of developing vocabulary and comprehension of physical education materials. Of course, this approach can also be used in other content areas.

The last part of the chapter contained a quite brief annotated list of topical books in physical education.

ACTIVITIES AND QUESTIONS
TO PROMOTE LEARNING AND APPLICATION

1. How would you define art? What might be the advantages and disadvantages of having just one definition of art? Is it really necessary to *define* art? Why or why not?

2. Is art alive and well in your town? Explain some of the positive things going on; some of the negative.

3. Prepare a 5-minute presentation on one of the objectives of art education and be ready to present it in class.

4. Prepare an IVCA inventory for reading a segment of textual material in art. (Note the example given in the chapter on vocational-technical reading.)

5. Select some textual materials in art that are commensurate in readability with a particular student's reading ability. Explain the purpose of your "experiment" and then gently probe the student's ability to read the material. You might record the interview and transcribe it later. How would the information help you to plan a reading lesson on that material for such readers as the one you interviewed?

6. Plan a lesson on reading art textual materials. Note examples of lessons in the Basic Procedures chapter and other chapters. Incorporate in the preparation and skills sections of your plan some of the vocabulary teaching principles and strategies found in the chapter. Also note how you plan to follow up on the vocabulary strategies. That is, what have you done that might transfer to the students using some of these strategies on their own?

7. Write a lesson plan designed to help students read to follow directions. Teach it to a class or even to a small group of students for whom it is appropriate. Report your results to the rest of the class (or to your peers in the school where you teach.)

8. Read five art books that are not on the list in the chapter and annotate them; also do the readability on each book. Now, with the book's list and your list, you may be in a better position to recommend some art books to people.

9. How did you do on the music vocabulary tests? Administer the 25-item vocabulary test to a music class in the middle grades and to one in the secondary grades. How do you account for any differences you might note? How would you explain a *lack* of difference?

10. Select a song and prepare to teach the lyrics to a group of readers in a music class who have had some problems in reading lyrics Use the strategy set forth in this chapter. Report to your methods class on the outcome.

11. Get a "nitty-gritty" reading on the ability of two or three students to read technical directions for playing a musical instrument. Plan to improve their reading of such directions. How do you feel about what you did?

12. Make plans for some students to attend with you a concert that will be reviewed in a newspaper. Make a recording of the concert if possible. Obtain copies of the review. Try to relate the reviewer's comments to the music as recorded (and/or your memory of the concert) in order to understand what the reviewer meant by the expressions used. To what extent do you agree with the reviewer? Disagree?

13. If you have not read the forewords to musical selections you have performed, do so. What did the reading do to your understanding of the work? Your appreciation of it? Your appreciation of the composer?

14. Distribute to members of your methods class copies of forewords to musical selections that you can perform. Try to shed light on the foreword by verbal explanation and by playing related parts of the selection. If you feel uncomfortable playing, record the musical segments in question on a cassette tape and use that. Allow the people to whom you are making the presentation to make comments at appropriate times.

15. Write annotations of several topical books on music. Bring your annotations and copies of the books to class. See if your comments induce any of your classmates to read the books.

16. What is your understanding of aerobics?

17. If you have attained cardiovascular-pulmonary fitness, share the history of your endeavor with the rest of the class.

18. What should teachers of nonaerobic sports do in order to develop credibility for their sports in terms of aerobic concepts?

19. In cooperation with a local physician and/or physical education expert who are *known to be aerobics experts,* plan an aerobics information display and demonstration. After trying it out, announce it to the public through the various communications media. In your display make sure terms are explained and illustrated. If you are a teacher, you may want to set up such an informational display at your school for the benefit of students and parents.

20. A mini display and explanation of the ideas mentioned in activity 19 might be set up in your reading methods class. Students knowledgeable in nutrition might be enlisted to explain dietary concepts that might be used by those engaged in aerobics training.

21. Determine how much students know about the various physical education terms. How do you account for differences in scores?

22. Find up-to-date articles and books on aerobics, annotate them, and share the annotations with appropriate people.

23. Develop for the content area of your choice a collection of *graded* reading selections plus reading aids—key words and meanings, guided reading questions, post-reading multiple-choice quiz, and references to other articles on the topic that the student might like to read. Laminate the materials. Properly label and file the materials for easy retrieval. Use them with students and report to your class.

24. Annotate five topical books on physical education or on topics of your choice. Share them with appropriate individuals.

SUGGESTED ADDITIONAL READINGS

Art

SHEPHERD, DAVID L. *Comprehensive High School Reading Methods.* Columbus, Ohio: Charles E. Merrill, 1973. Pp. 288–89.

THOMAS, ELLEN L. and H. ALAN ROBINSON. *Improving Reading in Every Class: A Sourcebook for Teachers.* Boston: Allyn and Bacon, 1972.

Music

OLSON, ARTHUR V. and WILBUR S. AMES, (Eds.). *Teaching Reading Skills in Secondary Schools: Readings.* Scranton: Intext, 1970. Pp. 114–115.

PIERCEY, DOROTHY. *Reading Activities in Content Areas.* Boston: Allyn & Bacon, 1976. Chapter 7.

STRANG, RUTH, CONSTANCE M., and ARTHUR E. TRAXLER. *The Improvement of Reading.* Fourth Edition. New York: McGraw-Hill, 1967. Pp. 375–77.

THOMAS, ELLEN L. and H. ALAN ROBINSON. *Improving Reading in Every Class: A Sourcebook for Teachers.* Boston: Allyn and Bacon, 1972. Pp. 437–46.

Health/Physical Education

KARLIN, ROBERT. *Teaching Reading in High School.* Second Edition. Indianapolis: Bobbs-Merrill, 1972. Pp. 305–07.

PIERCEY, DOROTHY. *Reading Activities in Content Areas.* Boston: Allyn & Bacon, 1976. Chapter 8.

SHEPHERD, DAVID L. *Comprehensive High School Reading Methods.* Columbus: Charles E. Merrill, 1973. Pp. 290–91.

THOMAS, ELLEN L. and H. ALAN ROBINSON. *Improving Reading in Every Class: A Sourcebook for Teachers.* Boston: Allyn and Bacon, 1972. Pp. 465–71.

BIBLIOGRAPHY

BONALEWICZ, RICHARD M. "Cardiovascular Training for Pitchers." *Athletic Journal.* 56 (5) (January, 1976), 25.

CATALDO, JOHN W. *Words and Calligraphy for Children.* New York: Reinhold Book Corp., 1969.

COOPER, KENNETH H. *The New Aerobics.* New York: Bantam Books, 1970.

EARLE, RICHARD and LINDA S. PERNEY. "Reading the Words in Music Class." *Music Educator's Journal.* 59 (4) (December, 1972), 55–56.

ELSON, LOUIS C. *Elson's Pocket Music Dictionary.* Philadelphia: Oliver Ditson Company —Theodore Presser Company, 1909.

ERICSON, RAYMOND. "Music: Visiting 'Mikado'." *The New York Times,* Thursday, May 6, 1976.

GRAINGER, PERCY. "Foreward to Grieg's Opus 16, Piano Concerto in A Minor." New York: G. Schirmer, 1920.

HUNEKER, JAMES. "Foreward to Chopin's Nocturnes for the Piano." New York: G. Schirmer, 1915.

LAMMER, JUTTA. *Print Your Own Fabrics.* New York: Watson-Guptill, 1965.

SNIDER, ARTHUR J. "The Fitness Craze." In the 1974 *World Book Yearbook.* Chicago: Field Enterprises Educational Corporation, 1974. Pp. 106–119.

Students' Dictionary of Musical Terms. Charles Hansen Music and Books, 1954.

THORPE, HAROLD E. *Basic Pottery for the Student.* New York: St. Martin's Press. 1973.

THOMPSON, JOHN. *Third Grade Velocity Studies.* Cincinnati: Willis Music Co., 1938.

Section Four

Basic Procedures – Teaching Comprehensive Content Area Reading Lessons and Teaching Reading Acquisition Skills

CHAPTER 20

Some More Basic Procedures for Teaching Reading Lessons in the Content Areas

A number of basic procedures for teaching reading lessons have been introduced in previous chapters. In this chapter I discuss in some detail important procedures for teaching word identification skills, a comprehensive Directed Reading Lesson plan, and key ideas to consider when working with motivational problems of reluctant readers.

BASIC PROCEDURES IN TEACHING INDEPENDENT WORD IDENTIFICATION

Interspersed throughout the book are discussions of ways of teaching word-identification skills. In this first section of the chapter, I want to consolidate some ideas, introduce more concepts and principles of word identification, and further explain some important relationships.

Reading requires that a person be able to identify the pronunciation and meanings of words. Identifying the pronunciation means to convert print to speech. Even if I would not be able to decode ⧧⊞ to an oriental language, my "translating" it to English speech or some silent internal representation is still decoding.

A reader has the task of decoding printed words in sentences rapidly enough so that the "speech" chain is fluent and intelligible. In other words, it has to be fast enough so that on reaching the end of a sentence a person remembers what the other parts were about. Placing students in reading situations where the decoding process, by virtue of the number of problem words encountered, is labored and nonfluent results in a breakdown of intelligibility for the reader. This breakdown is one of the chief causes of reading problems. The way to make a second-grade (or level) piano student a remedial piano student is to put a Chopin nocturne or a Liszt rhapsody before him or her.

Basic Word-Identification Tools

The following tools are used in various combinations to independently decode or identify word segments and words: (1) structural analysis, (2) phonemic options analysis, (3) context clues, and (4) the dictionary.

Structural Analysis. A person analyzing a word structurally looks carefully at words that are not in *his* or *her* stock of sight words in order to differentiate constituent parts of the word: syllables (com-bine), root words (help-er), prefixes (dis-avow), suffixes (reader-ship), variant endings (reads, baked, playing, happily, and so on), and graphemes (d ough, f r eigh t, ch e rr y). Structural analysis is used in conjunction with phonemic options analysis and context to decode unfamiliar words.

Phonemic Options Analysis. In phonemic options analysis a reader draws on his or her knowledge of grapheme-phoneme(s) relationships in order to decode words. A grapheme is a unit of writing used to represent one or more basic sounds or phonemes[1]; for example, ⟨eigh⟩, a grapheme, can represent the /ā/ sound or phoneme in *eight* or the /ī/ phoneme in *height*. The /ā/ and /ī/ are phonemic options for ⟨eigh⟩. Let us say that a person knows the following relationships: ⟨s⟩→/s/ or /z/, ⟨oi⟩→/òi/, ⟨o-e⟩→/ō/, ⟨r⟩→/r/, ⟨l⟩→/l/, ⟨i⟩→/ī/. Theoretically, this person could unlock the following words even if he or she did not know them as at-sight words: *oil, toil, roil, soil, role, rile, rose, rise* and the like. Of course, the person would need a context to help ascertain that the *s* in *rose* and *rise* calls for the phonemic option /z/ rather than /s/.

Context Clues. As just implied, meaning clues from the context can provide clues to the pronunciation of a word. In fact, we can use zero graphic clues for a word if the context is strong: "He hit a home _____ over the left field fence." Office workers might say, "I feel drowsy and it is ten o'clock—time for a coffee _____ !" Strong cues for supplying the word *break* are given by *drowsy, ten o'clock, time for a coffee.* Of course, context clues are also used in conjunction with partial pronunciation to decode some words.

Repetition of previous warning: It is ludicrous to ask a person to "sound out" a word if he or she knows only one of five graphemes in a word. The context would have to be very strong for the student to succeed under those conditions. Now, "strong" can be considered objectively and subjectively. Objectively the context is strong if it contains good clues. Subjectively the context is strong if the reader can decode and understand the clues it provides. The writing may be terrific, but the student must be able to understand it if it is going to provide useful clues to use along with partial pronunciation!

The Dictionary. A dictionary is usually consulted for the following information about a word: (1) meaning, (2) pronunciation, and (3) spelling. The ability to use the dictionary is predicated upon fairly sophisticated phonemic options analysis skills, structural analysis skills, and the ability to select the appropriate meaning from among several alternative meanings; that is, a person needs to

[1] Strictly speaking, a phoneme is a sound. Virgules, / /, are used to indicate the idea of phoneme in technical discussions.

check a given dictionary meaning for a word against the context in which the word was found to see if the selected meaning is correct. Also, in order to use a dictionary a person must have some spelling competence so that he or she can come close to where the word is in the dictionary and then spend a minimum of time locating the word.

A BRIEF COMPENDIUM OF
WORD–IDENTIFICATION CONCEPTS AND PRINCIPLES

At-sight words	Words that a person can read instantly at sight.
Function words	Words such as of, in, for, and, as, the, a, here, because, however, although, and the like. Also called function words, they are the "glue" that holds words together in sentences.
Phoneme	The smallest sound unit. Phonemes are grouped to form spoken words. The word /dough/ has two phonemes: /d/ and /ō/.
Grapheme	A unit of writing used to represent a phoneme. The word ⟨dough⟩ has two graphemes, ⟨d⟩ and ⟨ough⟩, which represent /d/ and /ō/, respectively. Therefore, a grapheme may be composed of one or more letters.
Vowel	One of a class of speech sounds in the articulation of which the oral part of the breath channel is not blocked and is not constricted enough to cause audible friction; a grapheme representing a vowel.
Consonant	One of a class of speech sounds (as /p/, /g/, /n/, /l/, /s/, /r/ characterized by constriction or closure at one or more points in the breath channel; a grapheme [letter] representing a consonant. However, note these graphemes that represent "consonant" phonemes: ⟨ti⟩→ /sh/ and ⟨ci⟩→/sh/.
Schwa -/ˈshwä/	1. An unstressed vowel that is the usual sound of the first vowel in the word *about* or the first and last syllables of the word *America*. 2. the symbol ∂ is used to represent the schwa. (It is also used to represent the stressed vowel in such words as hut, cup: /hət/, /kəp/.) Note its use in the stressed vowel and unstressed vowel in the word *butter*: /ˈbət-ər/. Note these examples of the schwa symbol:

Unstressed Vowels	Stressed Vowels
m**a**chine → /mə-ˈshēn/	r**u**n → /ˈrən/
happ**e**n → /ˈhap-ən/	c**o**ver → /ˈkəv-ər/
lem**o**n → /ˈlem-ən/	

Graphemic options	The various ways that a given phoneme may be encoded.

Examples:

Phoneme*	Some Graphemic Options
/ā/	⟨a⟩ in r<u>a</u>dio
	⟨a–e⟩ in c<u>ake</u>
	⟨ai⟩ in p<u>ai</u>d
	⟨ai-e⟩ in pr<u>aise</u>
	⟨ay⟩ in m<u>ay</u>
	⟨eigh⟩ in w<u>eigh</u>
	⟨ey⟩ in gr<u>ey</u>
/f/	⟨f⟩ in i<u>f</u>

*Strictly speaking, a phoneme is a sound. You should make the sound when you see the phoneme representation that uses the slant lines.

Phonemic Options The various ways that a given grapheme may be decoded. (A more complete list will appear later.)

Examples:

Grapheme	Some Phonemic Options
⟨s⟩	/s/ in <u>so</u>
	/z/ in ro<u>se</u>
	/sh/ in <u>sugar</u>
	/zh/ in plea<u>sure</u>
⟨ough⟩	/ō/ in d<u>ough</u>
	/ò/ in <u>ought</u>
	/aủ/ in b<u>ough</u>
	/ü/ in thr<u>ough</u>
⟨gh⟩	/g/ in <u>gh</u>ost
	/f/ in cou<u>gh</u>

Phonemic options analysis Drawing on one's knowledge of grapheme–phoneme relationships, selecting the correct phonemic options for the given grapheme through contextual analysis, and applying the information to decode words.

Structural analysis Analyzing a word for familiar parts; syllabicating a word in preparation for sounding (decoding) familiar graphemes, syllables, root words, prefixes, suffixes, and variant endings.

Syllable Basic pronunciation unit; each spoken syllable has one vowel *sound*.

Root word Basic meaning unit. Examples of root words are *happy, self, glad, capable,* and *fix.*

Prefix Meaning unit attached to beginning of word in order to change the meaning: *un*happy, *in*capable, *pre*fix.

Suffix Meaning unit attached to end of word to change its meaning: self*ish,* fix*er,* discord*ant.*

Variant endings Word endings such as *s, ed, ing, ly, er,* and *est.* In adding these endings to a word, changes of tense, mood, or comparative form are indicated.

Auditory discrimination The ability to hear likenesses and differences in speech sounds.

Auditory blending The ability to blend the speech sounds of a word when the same speech sounds are presented in sequence. (In test situations they are often presented at the rate of one per second. In reading situations a person develops patterns while "sounding out" words; the possible number of patterns, therefore, is infinite.)

Inductive teaching Drawing out or developing a generalization about particular phenomena that share a common element. In teaching grapheme-phoneme associations, two or more known sight words containing common graphemes that yield the same phoneme are placed in vertical juxtaposition,

<u>ph</u>one

epita<u>ph</u>

their visual likeness is noted, their sound likeness is noted, and a generalization regarding pronunciation of the grapheme is drawn.

Deductive teaching A rule about some phenomenon is stated and examples are given. The following is a syllabication rule:

Rule: If there are two nontwin "consonant letters" between "vowel letters," divide the word between the consonants. (Exceptions: So-called consonant clusters—*bl*, *gr*, *ch*, *ph*, and the like—are left intact.)

Examples: Il/ya, har/bor; ex-<u>tra</u>, re-<u>pr</u>ise

NOTE: It is better to *do* many examples than to try to memorize the rule. Also, inductive teaching generally yields better results in teaching independent word-identification skills than does deductive teaching.

Syllabication rules It is somewhat useful to know how to divide words into syllables. Some rules follow:

Rule 1. If there are twin "consonant letters" (pp, gg, etc.) between "vowel letters," divide the word *after* the twin consonant letters.

Examples: dinn-er, butt-er, happ-y, coff-ee

(*Rationale:* you do not *say* the consonants twice; the *nn* and *tt* are the graphemes)

Rule 2. If there are two nontwin "consonant letters" between "vowel letters," divide the word between the consonants. (Exceptions: So-called consonant clusters—*bl*, *fr*, *gl*, *pr*, *ch*, *th*, *ph*, *ck*, and the like—are left intact.)

Examples: Ar-min, <u>st</u>an-dard, ex-<u>tra</u>, ni<u>ck</u>-el

Rule 3. If there is only one consonant between two vowels, the consonant ordinarily goes with the second syllable.

Examples: so-lo   mo-tor   ti-ger

Rule 4. If the syllable ends in *le*, the consonant that precedes the *le* goes with the *le* to form a separate syllable.

Examples: lit-tle   ma-ple

Vowel rules   Rather than giving a number of vowel rules, which have so many exceptions and which can be a source of confusion, I suggest teaching the phonemic options for given graphemes. This procedure cuts down on the excess nomenclature associated with word identification. In a very real sense, word-identification principles should be functional: you should *do* them, not "talk about" them.

Some Phonemic Options for Key Graphemes
Vowels

Grapheme	Phonemic Options	Grapheme	Phonemic Options
a	/ā/ as in lady	ay	/ā/ as in way
	/a/ as in ask	e	/ē/ as in me
	/ə/ as in about		/e/ as in bell
ai*	/ā/ as in paid		/ə/ as in eaten
au	/ȯ/ as in auto	ea	/ē/ as in bleat
	/a/ as in laugh		/e/ as in head
augh	/ȯ/ as in daughter	ee	/ē/ as in see
aw	/ȯ/ as in law	ei-e	/ē/ as in receive
eigh	/ā/ as in sleigh	ou	/au̇/ as in out
	/ī/ as in height		/ü/ as in uncouth
eu	/yü/ as in eucalyptus		/ə/ as in double
ew	/ü/ as in new	ough	/ō/ as in though
	/yü/ as in few		/ȯ/ as in brought
ey	/ā/ as in hey		/ü/ as in through
i	/ī/ as in hi		/au̇/ as in bough
	/ĭ/ as in did	ow	/ō/ as in low
	/ə/ as in pencil		
i-e	/ī/ as in time		/au̇/ as in how
ie	/ī/ as in pie	u	/yü/ as in music
	/ē/ as in chief		/ə/ as in under
igh	/ī/ as in sight	ue	/yü/ as in cue
o	/ō/ as in told		/ü/ as in blue
	/ä/ as in cot	ui	/i/ as in build
	/ə/ as in lemon		/ü/ as in suit
	/ȯ/ as in cloth	y	/ī/ as in my
oa	/ō/ as in oak		/i/ as in gypsy
oe	/ō/ as in toe		/ē/ as in tipsy
oi	/ȯi/ as in oil		
oo	/ü/ as in spoon		
	/u̇/ as in book		

*The grapheme in ⟨aisle⟩ that cues the /ī/ pronunciation is probably ⟨ai-e⟩; note ⟨aye⟩→/ī/.

Vowels and Consonants

("Special" Combinations)

Grapheme	Phonemic Options	Grapheme	Phonemic Options
ar	/ar/ as in bar	or	/or/ as in for
er	/ə/ as in her	ur	/ər/ as in blur
ir	/ər/ as in sir		

Consonants. Because the 22 consonants in English are familiar, I shall not indicate the basic sounds they represent. Also, the same letter would be used to indicate the sound meant; for example: *b* /b/, *d* /d/, *f* /f/, and so forth. A few of the phonemic options will be given. Furthermore, if one knows the basic phonemes that graphemes such as *b, g, f, p, l, s,* and *t* represent, one may not need to be taught "blends" such as *bl, br, fl, pr, st,* and the like. These consonant blends, however, may be taught, for if each combination is learned as a unit it *might* make decoding a little more efficient.

Graphemes	Phonemic Options	Graphemes	Phonemic Options
c	/s/ as in cent*	s	/s/ as in saved
	/k/ as in cub		/sh/ as in sure
ch	/ch/ as in chill		/z/ as in rose
	/k/ as in choir		/zh/ as in closure
	/k/ as in loch	sh	/sh/ as in shrimp
	/sh/ as in chanteuse	t	/t/ as in time
		ti	/sh/ as in nation
ck	/k/ as in nickel	th	/th/ as in those
d	/d/ as in don't		/th/ as in think
(dy)	/j/ as in did you	wh	/w/ as in what
	as in /dijəlikit/? †		/hw/ as in what
dge	/j/ as in fudge	wr	/r/ as in wright
g	/j/ as in gentle‡	x	/ks/ as in tax
	/g/ as in gat, got, gut‡		/gz/ as in exam
gn	/n/ as in gnu, gnat		/kz/ as in taxi
ng	/ŋ/ as in ring		/z/ as in xenophobia
ph	/f/ as in phone	y	/y/ as in yolk
pn	/n/ as in pneumatic		/ē/ as in city
ps	/s/ as in psychology		(serves as vowel)

---

*One helpful generalization (which, of course, has exceptions), known as the "c" controller principle, is: c followed by e or i is often sounded /s/; examples: cent, celery; city, cilia. c followed by a, o, or u is often sounded /k/; examples: captain, calorie; coptic, come; Cuthbert; curry.

†This is to let the linguist know we are aware of these phenomena but cannot treat them here. They will be treated at length in a forthcoming book by T. Grant Brown and the present author.

‡This is analogous to the so-called "c" controller rule.

Example

Step 1: Determine unknown grapheme-phoneme associations. (Use a test such as the *Hafner Quick Phonics Test*.)

Step 2: Select an association to teach: for example, ⟨ch⟩→/k/.

Step 3: Determine known sight words that contain the element ⟨ch⟩ in which the *ch* represents /k/.

Go below present reading level, for example, 7.5, and pull sample of words containing the element.

Example: If the person is reading at the 7.5 level, you select words from books below that level. Let us say that out of the sample, the student knows *Christmas*, *choir*, and *chlorine*.

Step 4: Align vertically two or more known words containing the element ⟨ch⟩.

Example:

> Christmas
> choir
> chlorine

Step 5: Ask how the words *look* alike. ⟨ch⟩. Then underline the *ch* in each word.

Step 6: Have the words *pronounced*.

Step 7: Ask how the words *sound* alike. /k/

Step 8: Help the student to develop a rule about this.

Examples:

> "Sometimes ⟨ch⟩ stands for /k/."
> "If /ch/ does not sound right, try /k/."

Step 9: Help the student unlock another word (or words) that contains the element ⟨ch⟩.

    a. If the student knows several elements, such as the basic consonants in addition to *o-e*, he or she may be able to sound out a previously unknown word that contains *ch*.

    b. *Example.* If the student knows the /ō/ sound for *o-e* and knows r→/r/ and m→/m/, he or she can combine this knowledge with the new-found knowledge of *ch* and unlock:

> chrome

Step 10: Use the word in a sentence. Charlie shined the *chrome* on our car.

Step 11: *Application.* Build new words similar to known words.

> known: ford   Korea   pi
> new: _ord   _orea   _i

Step 12: *Contextual Application.*

    1. He played a chord on the piano.
    2. The dog had the nervous disorder called chorea.
    3. The Greek letter χ is called Chi.

DIRECTED READING LESSON PLAN[2]

I. Readiness
  A. *Background*
    1. Ask what you would do if you wanted to keep someone off your property.
    2. Ask what you would do to keep someone out of your country. Lead discussion to the Great Wall of China.
    3. Show a picture of the Great Wall of China. (*World Book Encyclopedia*, vol. C–Ci, p. 377.)
  B. *New concepts:* incursions, rapine, Barbarians
    1. Do you know what the *Barbarians* were? (Barbarians were the Germans who lived from the time of Julius Caesar until the fifth or sixth century A.D. The Romans considered them uncultured. *Barbarian*, then, is a term applied to crude or uncultured people.)
    2. The Barbarians invaded or made *incursions* into Roman territory.
    3. Alaric, a Barbarian chieftain, captured Rome in 410 A.D. His *rapine* followers plundered and looted the city, carrying off women and children.
  C. *New words:*

    1. *Check meaning and pronunciation.*

timorous (nations) (people)	incursions (of Barbarians)
rapine	industry (industriousness)
celerity	efficacious
preys	incessantly
vanity	surmount
solace	tediousness
reposited	satiety

    2. *Pair new words with known words* (pronunciation).

known:	amorous	hilarity	sole
new:	timorous	celerity	solace

    3. *Put words into couplets or poems:*

Jim was amorous.	The celerity
Jane was timorous.	of hilarity
Jane was glamorous.	increased
Jim was simmerous.	geometrically.

---

[2] This is a plan for teaching the reading of a selection from *Rasselas*, by Samuel Johnson. This particular selection can be taught to gifted eleventh- or twelfth-grade students who are good readers. The plan structure can be used in middle school, secondary school—and college, for that matter—if it is adapted.

4. *Words in context.*

Discuss each sentence to bring out meaning of the underlined word. (The four charts should be placed on large sheets of paper and taped to the chalkboard.)

Words in Context   (A)

1. Jim was bold, but Jane was timorous.
2. Florida suffered from FSU incursions into Florida territory.
3. The rapine enemy made off with women and children.
4. I was amazed by her industry; she worked like a horse.
5. Celerity is an attribute held in common by the hummingbird, the jet plane, and the student going home for the weekend.
6. His plans were efficacious; he was granted a scholarship.
7. A good friend is a solace in time of trouble.

---

5. *Picture Dictionary*

Point out that one refers to the picture dictionary for the meaning of certain words if one has trouble while reading.

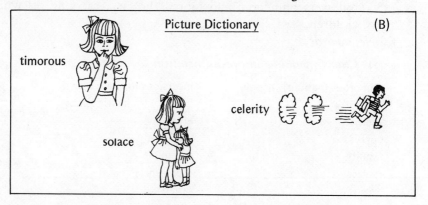

---

6. *Words in context*

Read and discuss the sentences. After each sentence, give student meaning as it will be in the story, or ask student to give it.

Words in Context   (C)

1. The owl preys upon the mouse,
   And the tornado preys upon the house.
Q. What would it mean for one country to prey upon another?
2. The Barbarians were rapine.
Q. Use rapine in a sentence.
3. His celerity showed as he ran across campus in one minute.
Q. How can you show your celerity?
4. The six doughnuts induced satiety.
Q. What induces satiety in you?

---

7. *Other words*
Ask students (1) what these words mean and (2) to use them in illustrative sentences.

	Other Words	(D)
vanity		reposited
	surmount	
incessantly		compliance

8. *Review*
   a. Chart (A). Find the sentence that tells that a scheme worked.
   b. Chart (A). Find the sentence that tells how a person finds comfort.
   c. Chart (A). Find the word that means plundering; frame it; read it.
   d. Chart (C). Find the word that means speed; frame it; read it.
   e. Chart (C). Find the word that means filled up.
   f. Chart (D). Use the word *surmount* in a sentence.

D. *Purpose:*
   1. Show picture of Great Wall of China. Ask students whether they think it took a lot of work to build it.
   2. Ask: "Why do you think the Chinese built it?" "Do you think it was worth all the effort it took?" Let us read to see what Samuel Johnson thought about the endeavor.

II. *Guided Reading*
   A. *Reading to answer the motivating question* (The reading selection is in the last part of the lesson.)
   B. *Guided Rereading*
      1. What were the motives for building the wall?
      2. State the first part of sentence two in your own words.
      3. What does the next part of the sentence mean?
      4. Paraphrase the first half of the last sentence of paragraph 1.
      5. In that same sentence, to what does the word *it* refer?
      6. Why does Johnson feel it was a ridiculous idea to build the pyramids? (List the reasons it was ridiculous.)

III. *Teaching Skills*
   A. *Vocabulary*
      1. Antonyms exercise
      Directions: Write an antonym for each word listed below. (Place on chalkboard.)

      bold _____   never _____

      slow _____   exciting _____

      excursion _____   hungry _____

      laziness _____   helps _____

2. Contextual application
   Charades.
   Directions: "I will give each of you a word. I want you to act
   it out when I call on you."

timorous	rapine

celerity	incessantly

B. *Phonic Element*
   Example 1: gn
   Ask how two known words look alike, how they sound alike.
   Develop the rule for pronouncing *gn* words.
   1. Highlighting the common element; developing the generalization.

   <u>gn</u>ash
   <u>gn</u>u

   2. Word building:

   bar   home
   _ar   _ome

   3. Contextual application:

   a. Did you hear the dog <u>gnar</u> at the intruder?
   b. He was grumpy and <u>gnarly</u> today.
   c. The king hired two <u>gnomes</u> to guard his underground treasure.
   d. The mayor hired 50 <u>gnomes</u> as subway guards.

   Example 2: ai
   Ask how two words look alike, how they sound alike. Develop the
   rule for pronouncing *ai* words.
   1. Highlighting the common element; developing the generalization.

   <u>ai</u>m
   tr<u>ai</u>n

   2. Word building: boil   seal   boat
                         b_l   s_l   b_t

   3. Contextual application:*

   p_l   a. He had to make b_l
   _ai   To get out of j_l.
   __l   b. We set <u>sail</u> to catch the seal.
                c. You get the boat and I'll get the <u>bait</u>.

   ---

   *Although the words and sentences in this exercise are uncharacteristic of this level of reading
   [college], they show the present readers a different kind of contextual application.

The Reading Selection

Of the wall (of China) it is very easy to assign the motives. It secured a wealthy and timorous nation from the incursions of Barbarians, whose unskillfulness in the arts made it easier for them to supply their wants by rapine than by industry, and who from time to time poured in upon the habitations of peaceful commerce, as vultures descend upon domestic fowl. Their celerity and fierceness made the wall necessary, and their ignorance made it efficacious.

But for the pyramids no reason has ever been given adequate to the cost and labor of the work. The narrowness of the chambers proves that it could afford no retreat from enemies, and treasures might have been reposited at far less expense with equal security. It seems to have been erected only in compliance with that hunger of imagination which preys incessantly upon life, and must be always appeased by some employment. Those who have already all that they can enjoy, must enlarge their desires. He that has built for use, till use is supplied must begin to build for vanity, and extend his plan to the utmost power of human performance, that he may not be soon reduced to form another wish.

I consider this mighty structure as a monument of the insufficiency of human enjoyments. A king, whose power is unlimited, and whose treasures surmount all real and imaginary wants, is compelled to solace, by the erection of a pyramid, the satiety of dominion and tastelessness of pleasures, and to amuse the tediousness of declining life, by seeing thousands laboring without end, and one stone, for no purpose, laid upon another. Whoever thou art, that, not content with a moderate condition, imaginest happiness in royal magnificence, and dreamest that command or riches can feed the appetite of novelty with perpetual gratifications, survey the pyramids, and confess thy folly!

—Samuel Johnson, Rasselas

MOTIVATIONAL PROBLEMS IN READING

The Reluctant Reader

The reluctant reader has been described by Alm (1972) as neither skillful nor disabled. He or she is not an efficient reader, because he or she reads very little.

In the following characterization of reluctant readers at various levels of mental ability, there will be a range of reading achievement at each level. The purpose of my sketch is to delineate some possibilities why people have the attitudes they have as well as what some of those attitudes are. Debate them if you will, and some are debatable, but think of them as stimulators to thinking that might result in insights that could be used in helping some reluctant readers.

Below-Average Mental Ability

1. Was rushed into reading at a time when concept-language development was his or her chief developmental task.

2. Developing meaning for reading material is too laborious a task; not enough mental ability for what the person is required to do.

3. Is expected to "sound out" words when this approach as ordinarily taught has been shown to be rather ineffective with low IQ people compared to, say, our "nail-down" methods.

4. Probably has poor auditory discrimination and poor auditory memory, which form part of a constellation of factors interfering with ability to succeed in phonics.

5. Not many people in peer group or family read.

6. Has been written off by individuals who do not know needs or how to help student attain some success in meeting them.

7. Needs personal help (1) to improve concept-language development, (2) to improve reading skills, and (3) to make readily available materials that he or she can read and that are of interest.

Average Mental Ability

1. Extraverts need big doses of experience to "turn them on."

2. Vicarious experience through reading may not give this extravert type enough of a "jolt." Impact is made through direct experience.

3. The need for ever-increasing amounts or differing kinds of direct experience may lead to wilder and weirder experiences.

4. Has poorly developed "Weltanschauung" (world view).

5. If overly "conservative" politically, older high average readers who have authoritarian personalities might fail to read widely for fear that the material may challenge their rigid structures and consequently pose a threat.[3]

6. Not able to or willing to process ambiguous information. In this sense, too, the person would not be creative about processing verbal ideas that required problem-solving techniques.

7. Some reluctant readers will have lower verbal abilities than nonverbal.

8. May not be self-starters; might get involved in reading if it is associated with colorful accoutrements. This done in excess can lead to the placid, passive reader who will never be a self-starter: "Here I am, 'teach.' Motivate me. Entertain me."

9. Reading for this reader has to provide something unobtainable from real experience or an extension of real experience that he or she likes.

10. Needs personal attention, then, (1) to improve reading skills and (2) to make readily available materials that are of interest and that he or she can read.

Above-Average Mental Ability

1. May have higher spatial and arithmetic reasoning abilities than vocabulary and general information ability (or achievement).

2. Does not have a self-concept of being one who knows much and who should keep well informed.

---

[3] However, the *true* conservative of high-average and above-average ability who is probably what people call a liberal would be interested in knowing the past in greater depth and breadth and be an avid reader who is really seeking to penetrate layers of certain kinds of myths in order to get at the truth. We do live by our myths; we just need to develop myths that are closer to reality and more beneficial to mankind.

3. May think that he or she knows more than he or she does.

4. May feel that reading intrudes on introspective life.

5. Does not have a vocational goal that requires reading. Or may not realize that it requires much reading.

6. Books and other interesting material may not be readily accessible; again, they may be.

7. May not like aspects of problems of disciplines that do not have a precise answer. This might be more likely if math-spatial abilities are quite high and vocabulary abilities, though above average, are not nearly so high as the former abilities. Therefore, might not prefer to read very much in areas such as social studies where solutions are sometimes equivocal.

8. May have a need, then, for neat, well-ordered structures where little ambiguity is present. Likes to run off the familiar patterns.

9. May like the spatial-mathematical aspects of geography: maps, tables, formulas; also music reading because of its spatial mathematical and tonal aspects.

10. May be proficient in music if a student in this area.

11. Might read if a Book Club member.

12. As an adolescent might read certain things. For example, girls may read certain sections of the newspaper, popular magazines, and the like; boys may read certain sections of the newspaper, parts of *Popular Mechanics, Mechanix Illustrated* or "car magazines," and may nose around in the encyclopedia reading articles that relate to specific interests. *National Geographic* and *Sports Illustrated* might be skimmed, but seldom read thoroughly.

13. Girls and boys might on occasion read *Reader's Digest, Time,* and *Newsweek,* very short books, and a brief biography or autobiography about someone they admire or are interested in.

Teachers need to be well acquainted with a variety of interesting materials, general materials as well as special materials related to their field. George Spache's *Good Books for Poor Readers* should be consulted as well as *Reading Ladders for Human Relations* by Virginia Reid (1972).

Bibliotherapy is a possible means of showing the value of books to some of the fairly good readers who may have personal problems. If they are interested in the problems and solutions in these books, and especially if a therapeutic effect is wrought, a greater interest in reading may be kindled.

Open-stack libraries that make available a wide variety of books can be useful in stimulating reading. High interest–low vocabulary books are often of interest to the reluctant readers of below-average mental ability or average mental ability who are poor readers.

Newberry and Caldecott books, because of their literary quality and interesting stories, might interest some readers. Young people might also like to read books on humor and vertical file collections on humor. Plays geared to the interests of particular young people could be appealing. Vertical files carry interesting bulletins and clippings on a host of topics. Students should be introduced to the possibilities of this marvelous phenomenon.

Finally, teachers themselves should be avid readers. The physical education teacher, mathematics teacher, shop teacher, and art teacher, for example, who reads a variety of paperback books is a good model for fledgling students. Think about it. Do it!

SUMMARY

One of the chief causes of reading problems is giving students reading tasks that are so difficult that the reading is labored and nonfluent and a breakdown in meaning development results. A person reads in order to identify the meaning and pronunciation of printed words.

The basic tools used singly or in combination to decode words independently are structural analysis, phonemic options analysis, context clues, and the dictionary. Although independent word-identification skills can be taught in a number of ways, the inductive approach is favored for teaching structural analysis and phonemic options analysis skills.

Through structural analysis, words are scrutinized to locate constituent parts so that known parts may be pronounced.

A basic plan for teaching a directed reading lesson was presented. The particular selection was difficult in order to show the value of direct teaching of vocabulary and comprehension skills. The author maintains that college students would be much better readers and better informed people had such lessons been taught them all through middle and secondary schools.

Motivational problems in reading were discussed. There is a real place for some suppositional and propositional thinking with respect to the reluctant reader. It is hoped that the suppositions and propositions set forth will be treated as idea starters. I think, too, that they might provide seminal hypotheses for research, the end result of which is some insights that could be used in helping reluctant readers.

ACTIVITIES AND QUESTIONS
TO PROMOTE LEARNING AND APPLICATION

1. What is one of the chief causes of reading problems?
2. How, then, are such problems obviated?
3. How is structural analysis used?
4. What is meant by phonemic options analysis?
5. Why is it important to think of the "strength" of contexts in objective and subjective terms?
6. Why is some spelling competence important to the use of the dictionary?
7. Which symbol is used to indicate the vowel sound in numbers of unstressed syllables? Give name and special symbol used.
8. Differentiate graphemic options from phonemic options.

9. Differentiate inductive and deductive teaching. (By the way, people induce and deduce in these situations, *not* induct and deduct.)

10. Practice writing sentences using the special symbols included in the chapter. This is fun for encoding dialects. This only works if the symbols are related to a standard Midwest "accent." For example /ī/ is said the way a native Minnesotan would say it. To get the "ah" of the Southerner, use the symbol /ä/, the so-called short "o." For example, "I'm doing fine, buddy," can be transcribed as /äm dü-in fän, bə-di/ (one type of Southern dialect) or /īm dü-in fīn, bədē/ (a type of Northern dialect). How about /īm jəst az plēzd az pənch/!

11. Try pronouncing these and see if you can pinpoint the part of the country:

    a. hā, ha⁽ē⁾ yü? äm fän, ha⁽ē⁾ yü?
    b. wē tůk thə bä-ə⁽ᴵ⁾z bak tə thə shäp- in sen- tə.
    c. ä läk kan-dē bȯrz n sō-dē.
    d. hwə-ch⁽ē⁾yü m⁽ā⁾-ēn⁽ē⁾yü dōnt läk gri-⁽ʸ⁾əts!
    e. it's däůn* bī mich-əl wer thə strēt kär bendz thə kórner räůnd.

12. What other kinds of reading skills besides grapheme-phoneme associations do you think could be taught inductively?

13. How would you follow up on grapheme-phoneme associations so that they would be retained?

14. Prepare to teach the DRL on the story about the "Great Wall and the Pyramids" to a group of high school or college students. Teach it and then share the experience with your methods class.

15. There is a complete DRL plan using this same model in the chapter on vocational-technical education. Note similarities and differences in the plans.

16. Problems of reluctant readers are complex. From your experience and observations, which of the points apply to a particular reluctant reader that you know? What characteristics not mentioned in the chapter does he or she have? How might you help him or her to become a less reluctant reader?

17. Add to the list of suggestions for helping reluctant readers.

SUGGESTED ADDITIONAL READINGS

BURMEISTER, LOU E. *Reading Strategies for Secondary School Teachers*. Reading, Mass.: Addison-Wesley, 1974. Chapter 4.

CHEEK, MARTHA. "Objective-Based Teaching of Word-Analysis Skills in Middle and Secondary Schools." In Lawrence E. Hafner (1974. Pp. 62–76).

CULLITON, THOMAS E. "Techniques for Developing Reading Interests and Attitudes." In Gerald G. Duffy (Ed.). *Reading in the Middle School*. Newark, Del.: International Reading Association, 1974. Chapter 19.

FORGAN, HARRY W., and MANGRUM, CHARLES T. *Teaching Content Area Reading Skills*. Columbus, Ohio: Charles E. Merrill, 1976. Pp. 294–28.

* Actually it takes äů to yield the "north midwest" sound and aů to yield the "southern sound", except for native speakers in Virginia who might say /ü/ as in ə-bůt (about).

HAFNER, LAWRENCE E. *Improving Reading in Middle and Secondary Schools.* Second Edition. New York: Macmillan, 1974.

MILLER, WILMA H. *Teaching Reading in the Secondary School.* Springfield, Ill.: Charles C. Thomas, 1974. Chapter 8.

MORETZ, SARA and BETH DAVEY. "Process and Strategies in Teaching Decoding Skills to Students in Middle and Secondary Schools." In Lawrence E. Hafner (1974. Pp. 76–101.)

OLSON, ARTHUR V., and WILBUR S. AMES. *Teaching Reading Skills in Secondary Schools.* Scranton: Intext Educational Publishers, 1972. Chapter 10.

SHEPHERD, DAVID L. *Comprehensive High School Reading Methods.* Columbus, Ohio: Charles E. Merrill, 1973. Chapter 6.

BIBLIOGRAPHY

ALM, RICHARD S. "The Reluctant Reader." In H. Alan Robinson (Ed.). *The Underachiever in Reading.* Supplementary Educational Monograph 92. Chicago: University of Chicago Press, 1962.

REID, VIRGINIA M. (Ed.). *Reading Ladders for Human Relations.* Fifth Edition. Urbana, Ill.: National Council of Teachers of English, 1972.

SPACHE, GEORGE D. *Good Reading for Poor Readers.* Revised Edition. Champaign: Garrard Press, 1974.

CHAPTER 21

Teaching Reading Acquisition Skills to the Nonreader and the Reader Who Has Attained Minimal Reading Skills

Do you have any students in your school who cannot read? Many schools have such nonreaders. I am not talking about first graders or even ninth graders; I mean high school seniors. That sad fact will affect these people in two basic ways: *learning* ability and *earning* ability. Let us look at earning ability first.

Figures from the U.S. Census bureau tell us that

1. The average high school drop-out will earn $192,000 in a lifetime.

2. The average college graduate will earn $388,000 in a lifetime—twice as much!

I am not equating earning ability with human worth. But let us get on to learning ability. I am talking about the aspects of learning that require reading. It is obvious that you know about reading and academic tasks. But let me remind you of its importance.

What do people say when you tell them that you teach students to read? They say—besides, "Do you teach that speed reading?"—"Oh, reading is so important. It is basic. If you can read, you can learn." Right!

How is it with the nonreader? He or she might like to (1) read a letter or a newspaper, (2) find out what Beetle Bailey is actually saying, (3) fill out a job application, (4) read the delightful prose on cereal boxes, or (5) read some poems or novels. . . , but he or she *cannot*. We have been talking about reading. What is the nature of this process?

THE READING PROCESS

In several places in this book I have talked about the reading process. Betts gives us a fairly unsophisticated, but somewhat useful, definition of reading, related, no doubt, to the work of Count Korzybski, the semanticist: Reading is the reconstruction of the facts that lie behind the symbols. Others say it is decoding print to speech; this is a partial misrepresentation of what reading is.

Visual configuration *does* yield a kind of meaning. Visual configuration mediates meaning so that when one sees ⟨symbol⟩ one does not think of a percussion instrument in the band. You can think of reading as a process that reduces informational uncertainty—uncertainty, not anxiety.

Look at this sentence:

I like to play with <u>simbəlz</u>.

Alternative interpretations can be given to this word: ⟨cymbals⟩ or ⟨symbols⟩. One alternative could be eliminated by knowing the topic of the discourse:

"Great Moments in the Life of a Percussionist"

Now there is a greater probability that ⟨cymbals⟩ is meant: I like to play with cymbals. At this point, then, the graphic cues reduce the alternatives to one: ⟨cymbals⟩. But it still does not yield the correct meaning for the reader who does not know the referent for cymbals.

What does Anisfield mean to you? Is it a place where *anise* is raised? The context of our discourse might lead some of my readers to know that I was referring to the individual whose theory of reading I have been illustrating.

Anisfield (1964) states that reading, among other things, is a process of using various kinds of interpretation to decide among alternative interpretations of a word. The alternative interpretations that might be given a word are eliminated by (1) a knowledge of the topic of the discourse, (2) a preliminary syntactic analysis of the sentence, and (3) the use by the reader of graphic clues to reduce the alternatives to one.

Ryan and Semmel (1969) claim that one does not need to look at every graphic or semantic or syntactic detail. One just samples cues. One samples just enough of the visual, meaning, and sentence construction cues to help develop the meaning. As one goes along one is developing and checking hypotheses. (You just did it.)

I should like to coin an expression for using graphic cues within a word and meaning cues within a sentence to determine the pronunciation and meaning of a word; I call this intra- and interword(s) cues decoding (IIWC-decoding). For example, within the word one has cues to differentiate a word from a similar word ⟨though⟩: ⟨ough⟩ preceded by ⟨th⟩ yields /thō/; When an ⟨r⟩ is interspersed between ⟨th⟩ and ⟨ough⟩ the word is ⟨through⟩, /thrü/. Those are intraword cues to aid decoding. "We learn through examples" is a sentence that yields interword cues to help give us meaning for ⟨through⟩. So when I use the word *decoding* in IIWC decoding I mean it in a generic sense that includes pronunciation and meaning.

Now let us check out some of Betts', Anisfield's, Ryan and Semmel's, and Hafner's ideas. Look at this:

(1) [Fun in]   (2) [New XXXXXXX]
(3) [I went for a]   (4) [xxxx]   (5) [on the]   (6) [street]   (7) [_____],
(8) [visited]   (9) [Xx.]   (10) [Louis]   (11) [Cxxxxxxxl,]   (12) [toured
the French]   (13) [xxxxxxx],   (14) [and had dinner at one of the very fine
(15) [rxxxxxxxxxx].

A quick perusal of the sentence shows a semantic network:

> (1) fun, (2) New_____, (9) Louis C., French, dinner. These point to New Orleans. Now (2) reads New Orleans.

Some solutions:

> •interwords cues: 1 + 2 + 3 + 5 + 6 yields (4) <u>ride</u> and (7) <u>car</u>.
> •intra- and interword(s) cues: 8 + 9 (intraword cue: capital letter + . = abbreviation) 10 + 11 (intrawords cues) yields (9) St. and (11) Cathedral.
> •interword cues: theme + 1 through 12, specifically French in 12 yields (13) Quarter.
> •interword cues of 1–14 + intraword cues in 15 yield (15) restaurant.

All this is predicated on some knowledge of New Orleans. But we know that word knowledge, general information, and reasoning are *sine qua non* cognitive requisites for reading achievement. Thus, we see the interaction of graphic, semantic, and syntactic cues in reconstructing, reducing, and sampling in reading; we are using those IIWC decoding strategies.

BARRIERS TO READING ACQUISITION

Psychological Barriers

Verbal Deficit. Bell, et al. (1972) investigated various factors associated with reading retardation. Among several factors associated with reading deficit on the vocabulary and reading subtests of the *Iowa Tests of Basic Skills* was verbal deficit.

Low Mental Age. At the first-grade level low mental age is one barrier to reading acquisition that can be inferred from McNinch's (1971) finding that the mental age derived from the *Lorge Thorndike Intelligence Test* made the largest contribution to predicting reading achievement.

Lack of Perceptual Skills. The ability to see likenesses and difference among visual forms is termed visual discrimination. Kerfoot (1964) found that visual discrimination of letters predicted beginning reading achievement better than auditory discrimination or intelligence did.[1] *Poor visual discrimination* was found to be a barrier to reading acquisition.

The ability to hear likenesses and differences in speech sounds is auditory discrimination. It is a necessary skill for learning grapheme-phoneme (letter-sound) associations and applying knowledge of these associations in identifying words. Kerfoot (1964) found auditory discrimination to be the third best predictor of reading achievement in grade one. *Deficient auditory discrimination*, then, is a barrier to reading acquisition, because it prevents one from learning a skill that allows one to identify the pronunciation of words independently.

---

[1] To reconcile McNinch's finding with Kerfoot's it must be pointed out that the Lorge Thorndike Intelligence used by McNinch has a non-verbal section that contains many visual perception items.

Since, as Jenkins, et al. (1972) have shown, knowledge of letter-sound relationships transfers to learning to recognize words, it can be inferred that a *deficiency in the knowledge* of letter-sound relationships serves as an obstacle to reading acquisition.

Education Barriers

Lack of a Child-Development Point of View. At all levels of education, a serious barrier to reading acquisition is the failure to adequately assess a person's psychological and educational abilities, achievements, and needs.

The lack of a child-development point of view is evident when teachers and administrators fail to gear the school program to an individual's needs and abilities. This can be seen in such practices as (1) trying to teach reading to a low-risk child (particularly in grades one and two) who may have other greater developmental needs such as the need for greater experiential background, the need for further language development, or the need to find out who he or she is, that is, to find himself or herself; (2) using mindless busywork materials that fail to aid development; (3) working at trying to teach a person letter-name or letter-sound relationships when he or she has inadequate mental age and poor auditory discrimination; and (4) using methods and materials that are not geared to either a person's needs or abilities.

Results of Lacking a Child-Development Point of View. What results when a child-development point of view is missing? (1) No accurate, up-to-date knowledge of a student's key needs, abilities (strengths), or weaknesses; (2) no real feeling of concern or responsibility by the public (look how people vote, for example), the school board, the superintendent (doesn't get the real experts to advise him), the principals, or teachers for knowing a child's key developmental needs; (3) no genuine responsibility for trying to meet a child's needs, for example, to rectify language (conceptual-vocabulary, not dialect) differences, development deficiencies, and reading-skill deficiencies, (4) use of inappropriate, ineffective methods and materials due to (a) poor teacher judgment, (b) the lack of funds, or (c) the people responsible for selecting and purchasing materials receiving and acting upon poor advice, brochures, "in" phrases, and so forth, instead of looking at the research, the theory, and the results or getting an informed advisor who will look.

As a result of the above failures, teachers often assign tasks to children that are difficult or impossible to achieve.

Failure to Pace Introduction of Material. When the teacher fails to pace the introduction of material to the student's ability and learning rate so that he or she cannot master material at each step of the way, the student falls behind, learns precious little (for example, does not learn to read), becomes frustrated, and develops a poor self-concept. (If things really go awry, the student may harm you or someone else in order to "earn" a living, and you will pay more in taxes to keep him or her in jail than it would have cost to educate the student properly.)

Coercion. Individuals who are coerced into reading instruction or who are improperly taught will probably not learn to read or to enjoy reading. They often become anxious. Do you know what happens if too much anxiety is produced? One concretizes, that is, one has trouble in dealing with abstractions and relations among abstractions and cannot think fluently and in an organized manner. Such a state of concretization is deleterious to the achievement of reading skills.

Social Barriers

Threat of Extinction by Cultural Assimilation. Walker (no date) commented on the effect of the threat of the dominant social group to the minority social group. In the 1830s the Cherokee Indians had a 90 per cent literacy rate in their native language. Since the white population took over in 1898, the Indians have viewed the schools as white institutions, which they must attend but have no control over. Also, the Cherokee parents view the white schools as alienating factors that break up families because the children who do become educated tend to leave the community, either socially or geographically.

Also, the Cherokees are viewed by whites as people who need to be assimilated socially. If the Cherokee community is to become literate again it must be convinced that learning to read will not mean the death of its society.

Walker feels that such attitudes toward education no doubt can be found in Appalachia, in urban slums, in Afro-Asia, and in "all societies where the recruitment of individuals into the dominant society threatens the extinction of a functioning social group."

PRINCIPLES OF TEACHING READING
ACQUISITION TO OLDER STUDENTS

Show That You Feel Confident That They Can Learn

Since the great majority of students in middle and secondary schools have adequate mental age for learning to read and will respond if you provide for success and positive feedback, you can be confident in showing your confidence in the student because he or she *can* be taught to read.

Use Words Significant to the Person

Anyone who has taught a language experience approach (LEA) or read *The Spinster* or the research on LEA knows the value of using reading words significant to the person you are teaching. Older (1973) found that for ten third-grade subjects from low-income families and of Puerto Rican extraction there is a significantly greater retention of the "emotionally charged" words than the neutral words. Therefore, the "content of reading materials and the methods for teaching them must be revised so that reading deals with events, ideas, and feelings which are emotionally significant to the child."

Use Language Familiar to the Person

Once again, experience with LEA shows the value of using the person's own language production for story form and content. Also Ruddell (1965) examined the effect on reading comprehension at the fourth-grade level of written patterns of language structure that occur with low and high frequency in the oral language of students. He controlled the vocabulary difficulty, sentence length, and subject content in a series of reading passages and then studied the relationship between reading comprehension and pattern complexity. He discovered that reading comprehension scores on passages written with high-frequency patterns of language structure were significantly higher than comprehension scores on passages written with the low-frequency language structure patterns.

Use Context to Improve Perception

Expectation Based on the Situational Context. Neisser (1967) found that the knowledge of language does affect print perception. For example, expectation based on the situational context in the selection or the sentence context leads to implicit hypotheses about what the reader will probably see.

Context Helps the Subjects to Read More Accurately. Goodman (1965) showed how context helps subjects to read more accurately than they can read words in a list. The percentage of words that they could read correctly in context of the ones they missed in a list are (by grade);

Grade one:	66 2/3%
Grade two:	75%
Grade three:	80 + %

Context Provides Syntactic and Semantic Constraints. Meaningful context facilitates word identification because the semantic and syntactic constraints placed upon a word lessen the amount of visual information required for identifying the word (Tulving and Gold, 1963).

Increase the Length of Congruous Text. Tulving and Patkau (1962) found that increasing the length of congrous context facilitates the identification of words. Further information on using context to determine meanings can be found in an article by Hafner (1967).

Teach the Use of Graphical Information

Letter-sound relationships transfer. Jenkins, et al. (1972) recommended the learning of letter-sound relationships because they transfer to learning to recognize words better than letter-name relationships do. (P = .001) For example, i, a, n, t, → → in, it, an, at, and the like.

Teach Graphemic Options

Most phonemes in the English language can be represented by more than one grapheme. For example, the phoneme /e/ can be represented by such graphemes as ⟨e⟩ and ⟨ea⟩. It can be said that ⟨e⟩ and ⟨ea⟩ are graphemic options for the phoneme /e/. Other examples of graphemic options are ⟨ay⟩, ⟨eigh⟩, and ⟨ai⟩, which are graphemic options for representing the phoneme /ā/.

Moretz (1971–72) used the "Graphemic Options Test" (GOT) and the *Comprehensive Test of Basic Skills* (CTB) in order to determine among third and fifth graders the relationship between knowledge of graphemic options and (1) spelling achievement and (2) reading achievement. At the third-grade and fifth-grade levels the correlations of GOT with reading achievement were .77 and .75, respectively. For GOT and spelling, the correlations were .74 and .76.

The findings suggest the need for careful investigation of teaching methods that present basic decoding and encoding skills in a mutually reinforcing manner and facilitate students' acquisition of an awareness of the ways sounds are represented in the written language.

Teach Syllabic Graphemic Options. Savin (1972) has suggested a method of teaching reading that involves teaching the spelling of each *syllable*, without analyzing the spoken syllables into phonemes. For example, one would teach that the letter sequences *doe, dow, dough*, all are (sometimes) pronounced as /dō/. A very large number of such correspondence would have to be learned, but learning several thousand syllables is much less difficult than learning several tens of thousands words, according to Savin.

Teach Construction of the Word in Order to Aid Word Identification and Word Recognition

Knowing Construction Aids Redintegration.[2] As I shall point out later, many word-recognition errors are due to the reader not using enough visual cues in reading.

Knowing the construction of the word—the beginning, middle, and ending graphic cues—helps accuracy and speed of recognition because redintegration based on a proper sampling of cues is aided. Therefore, if redintegration is to work, the word must be "nailed down" (and one must read for meaning).

Results of Failure to Use Constituent Parts of a Word. When a student does not know the constituent parts of a word, does not see how it is constructed, he or she may respond as the students in one of Diack's (1960) studies did.

Diack pointed out that the student who reads *foot* for *forest* does so "because he saw that the word he was trying to read began with *fo* and ended with *t* and the word more familiar to him which had these characteristics was *foot*. The conclusions we reached after our study of the numerous errors made by these children were that the most frequent cause of error was part-seeing of the print in front of them and whole-saying of a word they had part-seen elsewhere." The children usually gave the greatest attention to the first letter or two; the *middle* letters were given *less* attention than any other part of the word.

[2] Recalling whole on the basis of parts.

Results of Using the Constituent Parts of the Word. Briggs (1972–73) taught disadvantaged second graders to read by using a programmed linguistic program —*The Sound Reading Program* by Smith, et al. (1972)— which featured the learning of graphemic options and studying the construction of each word formally introduced by noting carefully the beginning, middle and ending graphic cues.[3] Not only was the treatment effect significantly superior, but in the experimental groups the blacks did as well as the whites and the boys as well as the girls. The material is high interest level; it is used in elementary, middle, and secondary schools as well as in adult reading programs.

Emphasize the Continuous Progress Formula

Hafner and Jolly (1972) suggest eleven principles that the teacher will apply in order to do the best job of teaching reading. These principles are encapsulated in this minimum formula: "continued progress in learning to read = correct pacing + practice of correct responses + mastery at each step + continued language and concept development."

METHODS THAT WORK

I will not be so crass as to say the methods that I will briefly delineate are the only ones that can be used to teach nonreaders to read. Other methods, particularly if they use the principles of teaching reading set forth here, can be successful too. Because of space limitation, I shall be briefer than I originally intended.

The Language Experience Approach: Analytic

In the language experience approach to teaching the nonreader to read the students read sentences or stories about an experience they have had or about something in which they are interested. Since the students cannot read or spell, they dictate the story to the teacher (or aide or peer or tape recorder) who writes it on the chalkboard or on a piece of paper.

The next step is for the student to hear the selection often enough so that he or she commits it to memory. Then the teacher has the student "read" the story sentence by sentence, pointing to each word while saying it. In one of my books (Hafner 1974), I recommend this procedure for teaching LEA analytically:

1. Establish rapport.
2. Student tells story and teacher records it (in writing).
3. Rehearse story so student can memorize it in sequence (may use a cassette tape).

---

[3] How? By systematically teaching the students to work through all parts of the word:

judge
bed
head

4. Point to words as student "reads" them.
5. Make two charts of the story.
6. Cut one of the charts into sentences.
7. Scramble the order of the sentences and have student match sentences to story on the intact chart. Student reads each sentence of the chart.
8. Continue to scramble and rearrange sentences; read them.
9. Cut sentences into phrases; match phrases to intact phrases and read them. Reassemble phrases into sentences. Read the assembled sentences.
10. Continue to scramble and rearrange phrases.
11. Cut phrases into word cards; reassemble and read as necessary.
12. Read chart and segments of the chart and note problem words.
13. Make a card for each word taught; scramble order of cards and test words in isolation. Note problem words.
14. Teach problem words by procedures explained [in the last section of this chapter].

The LEA is effective but quite time consuming.

The Language Experience Approach: Synthetic

Instead of going from the whole story to the parts and taking advantage of the semantic and syntactic constraints afforded by the sentences in the LEA: analytic, the LEA: synthetic goes from individual words and builds to sentences. The words can be taught as sight words by any of the techniques described in the last section of this chapter. In order to provide stylistic variety and to see the elements of the procedures used in teaching the synthetic language experience approach, I shall present it in outline form. It is expected that a teacher will want to adapt these procedures. Accomplishing what is set forth here would take a number of class periods and in-between practice.

1.0   Objectives
1.1   Learn to recognize several words; Kay, rock, pet, has, a, the, Herbert, smart, etc.
1.2   Learn to read sentences that use these words.
1.3   Be able to *identify* the words in isolation and in context.
1.4   Substitute words in appropriate slots in given syntactical patterns.
1.5   Use some different syntactical patterns (1.4 and 1.5 are the second phase of the procedure and are instituted when deemed appropriate.)

2.0   Materials
2.1   Paper and pen or pencil.
2.2   Crayons or colored pens.
2.3   Chalkboard and chalk.
2.4   File folder or notebook for keeping stories.

3.0   Basic Idea
3.1   Teach words by "nail-down" techniques.
3.2   Select words that are meaningful to the student(s) involved and that can be put into sentences.
3.3   The sentences bring meaning to the words and to the learning situation.
3.4   This is one approach to teaching a child to read.

4.0   Procedure

4.1   Teach words that are meaningful to the child and that the child can and will "nail down."

4.1.1 Teach some nouns, verbs, function words (at, in, for, of and the like), and direct objects.

4.1.2 Hafner-Jolly nail-down procedures (see the last section of this chapter for details of the procedures noted below):

· Word-picture cards.

· Card reader such as Language Master.

· Visual scrutiny by comparing parts of two words just introduced.

· Using magnetic letters or felt letters to construct words and note parts, etc.

· Tracing a word while saying it.

· Illustrated rhyme phrases.

· Knowing what a word is and what it is not.

· Programmed learning and review book.

· Teaching function words by mediating procedures (see last section of chapter).

4.2   On chalkboard or piece of paper write in a vertical column (upper right-hand corner) the words as they are learned.

4.3   Illustrate nouns, verbs, and other parts as necessary and feasible.

4.4   Combine the words into brief, appropriate sentences; place at bottom of paper.

5.0   Examples of Cumulative Sequences

7

Herbert can roll over.

8

Herbert can play dead.

9

Herbert can "play possum."

10

Kay puts Herbert to bed.

11

Kay sings to Herbert and "rocks" him to sleep.

12

Herbert sleeps well and dreams of . . .

6.0   Theme and Variations

N   V   O

Theme: John runs home.

6.1   Substitute words in slots.

Sue runs <u>home</u>.
Sue <u>eats</u> <u>oranges</u>.
Sue eats <u>apples</u>.
Sue <u>drinks</u> <u>cokes</u>.

6.2   Add syntactic segments.

Sue drinks cokes <u>in</u> <u>class</u>.

6.3   Rearrange and use different syntactical patterns.

John and Sue eat oranges.
Because I enjoy eating oranges, I eat them everywhere, even in class.

6.4   Use known words in sentence building and then have students engage in random selection to read "crazy" sentences. (Example in dotted lines)

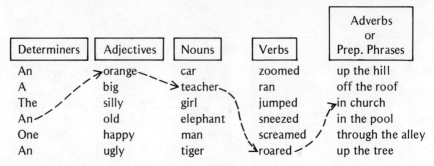

Determiners	Adjectives	Nouns	Verbs	Adverbs or Prep. Phrases
An	orange	car	zoomed	up the hill
A	big	teacher	ran	off the roof
The	silly	girl	jumped	in church
An	old	elephant	sneezed	in the pool
One	happy	man	screamed	through the alley
An	ugly	tiger	roared	up the tree

Programmed Linguistic Reading Methods

In "programmed materials, small amounts of information are given, a problem is posed, a response is elicited, and the response is then corrected or reinforced at once" (Hafner and Jolly, 1972).

Sullivan Associates Program. *Programmed Reading for Adults* is a linear program developed by Sullivan Associates, (1966). It is comprised of the following books:

1. Letters of the Alphabet
2. The Sounds of the Letters
3. From Words to Sentences
4. Sentence Reading
5. Paragraph Reading

There are other books but they would not be considered beginning reading. Although the material works and it has some strengths, one disadvantage is that the program espouses a letter-sound constancy philosophy; that is, there is only one graphemic option for a phoneme for page after page in the introductory book. This tends to make the material somewhat dull. Also transfer value is low under these conditions. Furthermore, I have not seen any research studies that support this program. Otherwise, the material seems effective.

The Sound Reading Program (SRP). *The Sound Reading Program* developed by Smith, Rowell, and Hafner (1972) is a programmed linguistic reading series that teaches decoding and comprehension skills from the very beginning levels to a level 4 equivalent. Emphasis is placed on the learning of graphemic options, career awareness, and character development while teaching comprehension skills inductively.

Books 1, 3, 5, and 7 teach decoding options through the use of picture cues and written context.[4] The first word taught is ⟨bed⟩. Page 1 shows the picture of a bed with the word *bed* written under it; this allows the student to make the association between ⟨bed⟩ and /bed/. In order to learn the constituent parts of the word and the grapheme option ⟨e⟩ for /e/, the student fills in graphemes that have been systematically deleted from the word. For example, in the word

---

[4] A set of read-along cassette tapes is available for use with the series of books.

box to the right of the box in which the picture of the bed and the word *bed* were presented there is the visual array ⟨_ed⟩. The student has the task of filling in the blank with the correct letter. On turning the page the student sees the correct answer, *bed*. Next the student fills in the middle part of the word—the part Diack (1960) reported as being neglected—and then in the third frame the letter *d*.

Through this approach the student learns how the word is constructed, to look at all of the constituent parts for visual cues, and the pronunciation of the word as well as the graphemic option.

The next word taught is ⟨head⟩. Here the student learns the graphemic option ⟨ea⟩ for the same phoneme /e/. Such an approach teaches the flexibility conducive to transfer.

Books 2, 4, 6, and 8 are the comprehension books. They use a series of related stories. In each selection a number of words are deleted; the first letter of the deleted word remains. In order to determine the word that has been deleted the student must take into consideration semantic and syntactic constraints; in short, the student must think. Spelling the word will not be a problem because the intact word will be nearby in the context. A set of questions follows each comprehension selection. At first the questions are literal comprehension only; soon one finds interpretation questions, also. Research by Briggs (1971–72) has shown SRP to be an effective program. Morgan (1974) used the *Sound Reading Program* as the core reading program to teach reading acquisition and reading improvement skills to disadvantaged youth in a federally financed program in Albany, Georgia. The program is very cost effective: it yielded good results and did so more economically than had been obtained previously with those students. This exemplary program[5] is still in operation.

TECHINQUES FOR "NAILING DOWN" WORDS

Regardless of the method used to teach reading acquisition, situations arise in which solid techniques are needed to teach students to identify printed words. Some excellent techniques used to develop associations between the printed word and the spoken word are given by Hafner and Jolly (1972):

Association of the Printed Word with a Picture

Print on the left-hand side of a card the word you want to teach; on the right-hand side draw a picture of the thing or process. For the words *apple* and *run* your cards might look like this:

---
[5] So designated by the U. S. Department of Health, Education and Welfare.

After a number of paired presentations of ⟨apple⟩ and 🍎 , just ⟨apple⟩ should elicit / apple /. This side, word and picture, is the teaching side. The other side of the card is the testing side; the word alone appears there.

A good way of teaching words is to teach several "at one time." Not only does one need to add many words to one's reading vocabulary but one really needs to differentiate a given word from other words. Therefore, after you present the first word, present the second word to be learned. Then shuffle the two words so the student will not know the one you are going to present. Next present the test side of one of the words, say *apple*. Shuffle again so that the student has to look at the visual configuration (graphic stimulus) of the word; it may be the first word, *apple*, or it may be the second word, say *run*. Add as many words in the teach-test cycle as you think the student can handle. The student can then be given the words to practice and to self-test. This will give the student a lot of response time in which he or she is differentiating given words from other words. In this manner the student will learn.

Card Reader

Card readers such as the *Language Master* can be used by a teacher, an aide, or the student to teach words and even phrases and sentences. The word to be learned is written or printed on the card and its name is recorded on the recording (audio) tape on the bottom of the card.

As the student is learning, he or she will look at the word, then run the card through the machine in order to hear the word. Again, the student will want to work with several cards at the same learning session in order to differentiate words. Of course, some known words can be in the stack of words, just as they can for the printed word-picture technique. Several students with similar needs can work in a small group situation, too. Since teachers are so busy, this method is ideal for *self-instruction* by students.

Part-Whole Comprehension

Previously we have referred to this as visual scrutiny. However, all methods require careful visual scrutiny. This technique teaches a student to inspect very carefully the component parts of a word so that he or she can identify given words and differentiate them from other words.

> T: [Print word on the chalkboard or magnetic board.]
>
> cool
>
> "Here is the beginning of the word [pointing to c], here is the middle part of the word [pointing to the oo], and here is the ending part [pointing to l]."
>
> T: "Now, watch again as I write cool on the chalkboard. It begins like this [write c], then you write this [oo], and at the end you write this [l]."
>
> T: "Look carefully at the word cool. —Now close your eyes. Can you see the word cool? —If you can't, take a quick peek."

T: [If you are using the magnetic board, you can allow children to manipulate the letters, going from a slightly jumbled form of the word to the correct form. You may want to use a model at first. After a while you can check to see if they can rearrange the letters from memory.]

T: [Put another word, such as <u>can</u>, on the board. Go through the same procedure.]

T: [Leave the two words, <u>cool</u> and <u>can</u>, on the board and then write parts of each word on the board, one word at a time, and ask which word it is a part of. This procedure sets the stage for examining these components of the words: <u>ool</u>, <u>an</u>, <u>coo</u>, <u>ca</u>, <u>co</u>. The first two segments require a grosser discrimination to be made than do the last two—<u>ca</u>, <u>co</u>.]

The advantage of using magnetic letters is that they can be moved up to the model words for comparison as necessary.

Tracing a Word While Saying It

Sometimes we find a student who will not focus visually on the word and consequently cannot learn to make the **association**. Forced visual inspection results when you have the student trace over the word while saying it. The word may be printed or written. The word should be written large enough so that the student can trace over it (with a finger or a writing instrument). In instances where students are having a particularly difficult time remembering a given word, have them trace the word while saying it until they feel they can write it without looking at the model. If a student falters, he or she should go back to tracing it until he or she can write it from memory without error. The words so learned can be filed for the student in an appropriate kind of informal file (box).

Illustrated Phrases

Rhyme Phrases. Phrases that rhyme have an attraction for students and are useful for teaching concrete and abstract words. Actually the students can produce the phrases as well as the illustrations, and the whole procedure is fun as well as useful. Some phrases that students produce are:

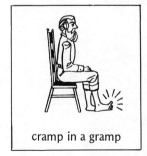

cramp in a gramp

pup in a cup

nose in a rose

star on a car	pie on a tie	crumb on a thumb
goat in a boat	fish in a dish	duck in a truck
ace in a race	lass in the grass	dirt on a shirt

Abstract Words Through Phrases.   One can readily teach those elusive, hard-to-pin-down abstract, function words such as *a, and, are, have, here, how, (I), in, is, it, of, the, this, that, to what, when,* and *where* by placing them in phrases that provide associations.   Hafner and Jolly (1972) devised a strategy for teaching these words:

1. Present a large illustrated card that contains a phrase. . . .
2. Help the students memorize the phrase (associate it with the picture), and be able to point to each word corresponding to the one they are saying.
3. Present on a duplicated sheet the picture and phrase that were on the card, along with other pictures and matching phrases. Do not present more items than the students can master in a session.
4. Help the students read the phrases and make the association of phrase and illustration. The students must say the phrase correctly.
5. "Below the pictures have dotted outlines of the word in question so that the children may trace over it as they say it." Examples from Hafner and Jolly (1972) follow:

and

chair and table

here

Look here

of

2 of hearts

when

say when

The large illustrated phrase cards that mediate the function word *may* be placed on the wall of the room so that students have them for reference in case they have a memory lapse. They may also be kept in a special book in the room library or in the student's notbeook; but *they must be taught first.* Do not leave things to chance; that is how the students got to be nonreaders and poor readers in the first place!

SUMMARY

Reading disability affects learning ability and earning ability negatively. Conversely, ability to read opens up a host of vocational opportunities as well as intellectual delights.

Reading can be defined in various ways. (1) Reading is the reconstruction of the facts that lie behind the symbols. (2) Reading is decoding print for the purpose of reducing informational uncertainty. (3) Reading is making thorough logical anlayses of cognitive relationships which have been symbolized in print. All these definitions of the reading process are useful.

In this text I have coined an expression for using graphic cues within a word and meaning cues within a sentence to determine the pronunciation and meaning of a word; I call this IIWC, intra- and interword(s) decoding. Included in this chapter was an analysis of how one could read a partially mutilated selection through developing the interaction of graphic, semantic, and syntactic cues in reconstructing, reducing, and sampling in reading.

There are many barriers to reading acquisition. The psychological, educational, and social barriers were thoroughly discussed and their effects on the would-be reader were delineated.

There are a number of principles of teaching reading acquisition to an older student. The chief ones are: show that you feel confident that the person can learn; use words significant to the person; use language familiar to him or her; take advatnage of the fact that knowledge of language affects the actual perception of print; teach the use of graphical information; teach the construction of the word in order to aid word identification and word recognition; and emphasize the continuous progress formula.

Certain teaching approaches are useful in teaching reading acquisition. The analytic Language Experience Approach is one such approach. In this approach a meaningful story of the student is written by the teacher and gradually analyzed into increasingly smaller units until the entire work and the consittuent parts are mastered. In the synthetic LEA, the student learns to read words by "nail-down" methods and after awhile constructs stories with these words. Both approaches are interesting to students. Finally, a programmed linguistic method has been known to work well.

Techniques for "nailing-down" words include association of the printed word with a picture, use of card readers, part-whole comparison, tracing a word while saying it, illustrated rhyme phrases, and learning abstract words through concrete mediating phrases.

ACTIVITIES AND QUESTIONS
TO PROMOTE LEARNING AND APPLICATION

1. Obtain some recent data on illiteracy in this country. What were the criteria used for determining whether a person is illiterate or literate?

2. In discussions of literacy it is often claimed that newspapers are written on the sixth-grade level. To either confirm that type of statement or negate it and provide more trustworthy figures, sample several papers and sections of the papers and apply your Fry Readability Graph system or the SMOG readability formula. Disseminate your information along with educational and news writing implications where it needs disseminating.

3. I once told a reporter for a Montgomery, Alabama, newspaper that more people would read his newspaper if some of the news were reported at a much lower grade level (not a page devoted to it, but articles interspersed in each edition). Of course, I told him this would be a service to people as well as a potential method for increasing circulation. He apprised me that the writers on his newspapers would not deign to do *any* of their writing in a more readable style. Please discuss.

4. Try to convince a local editor that it would be mutually beneficial to the newspapers and the new potential readership of the paper to make portions of the paper much easier to read, for example, third-grade level. Show the editor how this could be done.

5. Explain how visual information yields a kind of meaning. Give *several* examples.

6. What is meant by the term IIWC decoding?

7. I believe it was Kolers who said that reading is only partly visual. What did he mean by that statement?

8. How would you go about removing the psychological barriers to reading acquisition?

9. How would you obviate the education barriers to reading acquistion?

10. Delineate plans for removing social barriers to reading acquisition. (Did you get the most help from "super patriots" or from another group?)

11. Compare and contrast the helping group with the nonhelping group. You now have taken a great stride in acquiring a liberal education.

11. Under what kinds of conditions can you show older students that you feel confident they can learn to read?

12. Why should a person learn letter-sound relationships prior to (or at least concurrently with) learning to read?

13. Make a list of graphemes and some phonemic options for the graphemes, for example:

$$\langle \text{ea} \rangle \nearrow\!\!\!\searrow \begin{array}{l} /\bar{\text{e}}/ \text{ meat} \\ /\text{e}/ \text{ bread} \end{array} \qquad \langle \text{eigh} \rangle \nearrow\!\!\!\searrow \begin{array}{l} /\bar{\text{i}}/ \text{ height} \\ /\bar{\text{a}}/ \text{ weight} \end{array}$$

14. What is the relationship between the GOT and reading at the fifth-grade level? What does that mean?
15. How did E. H. Smith, et al. provide a means that facilitated using the constituent parts of a word in reading?
16. How do you account for Barbara Briggs, now Palmer, finding that in the experimental group of disadvantaged children using the *Sound Reading Program* the boys did as well as the girls and the blacks did as well as the whites?
17. Expand on the continued progress formula. (See Hafner and Jolly, 1972.)
18. Obtain a middle school student who cannot read and teach him or her reading acquisition through the Langauge Experience Approach or a programmed linguistic approach such as the *Sound Reading Program.*
19. Obtain a middle or secondary school student who reads below the fourth-grade level or who does not have a functional grasp of using grapheme-phoneme associations (options) for identifying words. Select a method designed to teach reading acquisitions and grapheme-phoneme associations (options) and also allow for self-instruction with feedback. (That narrows the field considerably, but the above needs and conditions for learning are real.) Carry out your plan.
20. In your reading instruction use "nail-down" methods as needed!

SUGGESTED ADDITIONAL READINGS

BLAU, HAROLD and HARRIET BLAU. "A Theory of Learning to Read." In Eldon E. Ekwall (Ed.). *Psychological Factors in the Teaching of Reading.* Columbus, Ohio: Charles E. Merrill, 1973. Pp. 379–83.

CARILLO, LAWRENCE W. *Teaching Reading: A Handbook.* New York: St. Martin's Press, 1976. Chapters 2 and 4.

EKWALL, ELDON E. (Ed.). "Linguistic-Psycholinguistic Implications for Reading." *Psychological Factors in the Teaching of Reading.* Columbus, Ohio: Charles E. Merrill, 1973. Chapter 10.

HAFNER, LAWRENCE E. (Ed.). *Improving Reading in Middle and Secondary Schools.* Second Edition. New York: Macmillan, 1974. Section 12.

LA PRAY, MARGARET. *Teaching Children to Become Independent Readers.* New York: The Center for Applied Research in Education, 1972. Chapters 10, 11, and 12.

MILLIGAN, JOSEPH P. "Using Language Experience with Potential High School Dropouts." *Journal of Reading.* 18 (3) (December 1974), 206–211.

BIBLIOGRAPHY

ANISFIELD, M. "The Child's Knowledge of English Pluralization Rules." *Project Literacy Reports.* 7 (1966), 45–51.

BELL, D. B., F. D. LEWIS, and R. F. ANDERSON. "Some Personality and Motivational Factors in Reading Retardation." *Journal of Educational Research, 65.* (January 1972), 229–33.

BETTS, E. A. *Foundations of Reading Instruction.* New York: American Book Company, 1957.

BRIGGS, B. C. "An Investigation of the Effectiveness of a Programmed Graphemic-Option Approach to Teaching Reading to Disadvantaged Students." *Journal of Reading Behavior.* 5 (Winter 1972–73), 35–46.

DIACK, H. *Reading and the Psychology of Perception.* New York: Philosophical Library, 1960.

GOODMAN, K. S. "A Linguistic Study of Cues and Miscues in Reading." *Elementary English. 42* (October 1965), 639–43.

HAFNER, L. E. "Using Context to Determine Meanings in High School and College." *Journal of Reading. 10* (7) (April 1967), 491–98.

———, and HAYDEN B. JOLLY. *Patterns of Teaching Reading in the Elementary School.* New York: Macmillan, 1972.

———, (Ed.). *Improving Reading in Middle and Secondary Schools.* Second Edition. New York: Macmillan, 1974.

JENKINS, J. R., R. B. BAUSELL, and L. M. JENKINS. "Comparisons of Letter Name and Letter Sound Training as Transfer Variables." *American Educational Research Journal. 9* (1) (Winter 1972), 75–86.

KERFOOT, J. F. "The Relationship of Selected Auditory and Visual Reading Readiness Measures to First Grade Reading Achievement and Second Grade Reading and Spelling Achievement." Unpublished doctoral dissertation, University of Minnesota, 1964.

MC NINCH, GEORGE, "Auditory Perceptual Factors and Measured First-Grade Reading Achievement." *Reading Research Quarterly. 6* (Summer 1971), 471–92.

MORETZ, S. A. "Relationships of Reading, Spelling and Knowledge of Graphemic Options." *Journal of Reading Behavior. 4* (3) (Summer 1971–72), 9–16.

NEISSER, U. *Cognitive Psychology.* New York: Appleton-Century-Crofts, 1967.

OLDER, E. "Recall and Printed-Word Recognition of Recently Taught Emotionally Charged Words as Compared to Recently Taught Neutral Words." *The Slow Learning Child. 20* (2) (July 1973), 92–101.

RUDDELL, R. B. "Effect on the Similarity of Oral and Written Patterns of Language Structure on Reading Comprehension." *Elementary English. 42.* (April 1965), 403-10.

RYAN, E. B., and M. I. SEMMEL. "Reading as a Constructive Language Process." *Reading Research Quarterly. 5* (1) (Fall 1969), 59–83.

SAVIN, H. B. "What the Child Knows About Speech When He Starts to Learn to Read." *Language by Ear and By Eye.* Edited by J. F. Kavanaugh and I. G. Mattingly. Cambridge, Mass.: MIT Press, 1972.

SMITH, EDWIN H., C. GLENNON ROWELL, and LAWRENCE E. HAFNER. *The Sound Reading Program.* Waco, Texas: Education Achievement Corporation, 1972.

TULVING, E., and J. E. PATKAU. "Concurrent Effects of Contextual Constraint and Word Frequency on Immediate Recall and Learning of Verbal Material." *Canadian Journal of Psychology. 16* (2), 1962, 83–95.

———, and C. GOLD. "Stimulus Information and Contextual Information as Determinants of Tachistoscopic Recognition of Words." *Journal of Experimental Psychology. 66,* (1963), 319–27.

WALKER, W. "An Experiment in Programmed Cross-Cultural Education: the Import of the Cherokee Primer for the Behavioral Sciences." Mimeo, no date.

Appendixes

The Hafner Comprehensive Group Reading Inventory

MANUAL OF DIRECTIONS FOR THE READINESS SECTION OF THE HAFNER COMPREHENSIVE GROUP READING INVENTORY

A. *Visual Discrimination*

Procedure: To the examinee: "We are going to take a test. I want you to show me that you can read the letters of the alphabet." (Distribute the test papers. If a given examinee cannot write his or her name, write it on the paper for him or her.)

"Now find capital A." (Illustrate this on the chalk board or have lines A, B, and 1 prepared on a piece of poster board and printed large enough for the students to see. Check to see that they have the right place. The examinees may use markers to help them keep their place.)

"See the five letters to the right of the capital A. (Pause) I will say the name of one of those letters and you draw a line under the letter on your page." "Draw a line under the letter 1." (Illustrate and then check to see that everyone understands.)

(Now have the examinees move to line B and repeat the procedure.) (The letter name is b.)

The letters for the remaining 10 items are

1. k	6. u
2. c	7. e
3. o	8. q
4. n	9. g
5. x	10. f

Evaluation of scores. If a student scores less than nine correct, you may want to retest him or her with an individual test of all letters to see which letters he or she can and cannot name. The following test from *Patterns of Teaching Reading in the Elementary School* by Hafner and Jolly may be used:

Letter-Knowledge Test

<u>Directions</u>: Here are some letters. Read the letters to me.

b	d	v	z	o
h	s	x	f	q
l	a	c	w	u
p	j	e	g	y
t	n	i	k	m
r				

B. *Auditory Discrimination   RS: Rhyming Sounds*

Procedure: To the examinees: "We are going to take another test. I want you to show that you know rhyming words. On the right side of the page you see rows of pictures. Find the top row, Row A, the one with pictures of the sun, wagon, tree, building, and hammer. I will say a word that rhymes with one of those, and you draw a line under the picture. Ready?"

A. "fun"

(Check to see that everybody understands.) "Now move to row B." (Pause) "Find the word that rhymes with *star.*"

B. "star"

(Check to see that everyone understands. You need to differentiate between those who do not understand the directions and those who cannot discriminate rhyming sounds. If it is the latter, you cannot do anything about it at this time. There is a propensity for teachers to stop and teach the test. I know that you will not succumb to that urge and thereby invalidate the test.)

Now continue in the same manner with items 1–10. The stimulus words are

1. fox	6. up
2. rake	7. see
3. moon	8. blue
4. floor	9. fight
5. man	10. lap

Evaluation of Scores.

10 = Fine.	6 = Not so good.	Needs help in auditory
9 = Right good.		discrimination.
8 = Not too bad.	4 and 5 = Good grief!	Needs much help . . .
7 = Barely passing	1–3 = "Emergency:"	Check pulse. Arrange for auditory acuity (audiometer) test.

Name _____

Grade _____

Visual Discrimination Score _____

Auditory Discrimination Score _____

The Hafner Comprehensive Group Reading Inventory
Lawrence E. Hafner
Florida State University

I. READINESS

A. Visual Discrimination	B. Auditory Discrimination
LN: Letter Name Test	RS: Rhyming Sounds Test

A.	c	t	l	r	x	A.
B.	f	o	n	b	j	B.
1.	q	k	g	a	p	1.
2.	m	s	h	f	c	2.
3.	r	t	o	w	v	3.
4.	v	f	w	n	k	4.
5.	j	l	g	x	i	5.
6.	u	r	m	k	h	6.
7.	a	m	o	s	e	7.
8.	q	r	p	f	n	8.
9.	t	o	h	a	g	9.
10.	c	s	d	f	q	10.

MANUAL OF DIRECTIONS FOR THE SILENT SECTION OF THE HAFNER COMPREHENSIVE GROUP READING INVENTORY

WR: Word Recognition (levels 1.1 to 3.0)

Directions: "I would like to see how many words you can read. I am going to give you a piece of paper with words on it." (Distribute test papers). "Please print (or write) your name in the upper right hand corner. (indicate by pointing to appropriate place on test paper, check to see that names are written.)

"Now find the picture of circle (or ball). Next to it is a capital A; point to it. To the right of that are five words. (You may allow the students to use markers if necessary). I am going to say one of the words, then a sentence using the word. You draw a line under the word. O.K.? Now listen:

    A. "jump   I like to run and jump."

(Check to see that the correct response was made.) "Now find the box. Find the capital B next to it. Now listen:

    B. "ride   I can ride a horse."

(Check to see that students understand they are to make the word you call. You cannot stop and teach the words. You should *not* teach tests anyway.) The remaining words and sentences are

1.	blue	The chair was painted blue.
2.	can	She bought a can of soup.
3.	big	Giants are big men.
4.	bed	I sleep in my bed.
5.	what	I know what time it is.
6.	grass	Grass grows in yards.
7.	talk	Little babies can't talk.
8.	guess	Some people like to guess your name.
9.	night	At night it is dark.
10.	ground	The men dug a hole in the ground.
11.	coat	Do you wear a coat when it's cold?
12.	trouble	You're not supposed to get in trouble.
13.	always	We always try to be polite.
14.	laugh	I laugh when I hear something funny.
15.	together	The neighbor children play together.
16.	fence	The boy climbed over the fence.
17.	minute	We'll be finished in a minute.
18.	forest	There are many trees in a forest.
19.	puddle	The lady fell into a mud puddle.
20.	question	The teacher asked the students a question.

Scoring and Evaluation. Since the purpose of this test is to determine if students can recognize words at the first two grade levels, grade level equivalents do not go beyond 3.0. One point is given for each correct item.

$$\text{Reading Grade Placement (RGP)} = \frac{\text{Total Points}}{10} + 1$$

Example for student who scores thirteen.

$$\text{RGP} = \frac{13}{10} + 1 = 1.3 + 1 = 2.3$$

Name _____

Total Points _____

Reading Grade Placement _____
(Maximum is 3.0)

The Hafner Comprehensive Group Reading Inventory

Lawrence E. Hafner, Florida State University

II. Silent Reading

WR: <u>Word Recognition</u> Test (levels 1.1 to 3.0)

Sample Items (Do A and B as examples.)

○	A.	jump	see	ride	come	mother
☐	B.	is	will	run	work	ride
	1.	run	little	blue	father	boy
	2.	can	is	fish	come	he
	3.	she	big	like	fish	stop
	4.	boy	blue	red	far	bed
	5.	that	funny	what	basket	where
	6.	green	car	blue	now	grass
	7.	frog	hat	paint	talk	wall
	8.	people	guess	some	dress	get
	9.	nine	friend	that	some	night
	10.	under	ground	light	round	change
	11.	coat	floor	oak	caught	paper
	12.	because	clown	tail	trouble	out
	13.	left	together	always	ought	along
	14.	loud	piece	laugh	leg	breakfast
	15.	together	gate	tomorrow	gather	through
	16.	when	fell	cream	fence	suddenly
	17.	hit	mine	mighty	minute	friendly
	18.	foot	forest	hornet	born	feather
	19.	pilot	puddle	mud	puppet	silver
	20.	question	quickly	quarrel	heavy	guess

Name_____

Grade_____

Reading Grade Placement _____

The Hafner Comprehensive Group Reading Inventory

Lawrence E. Hafner, Florida State University

II: Silent Reading

COMP: <u>Comprehension</u>

Directions: (To beginning readers): "Find the *star* on the page. Do you see it? Next to the star is the sentence. The sentence is 'My name is Jim'. Do you see it? The next sentence is I am a _____? A word is missing. What word do you think should be in the blank? (Pause for responses). Move your pencil to the right and find the capital A. Do you see the four words? Find the word *boy* and draw a line under the word boy. (Check the responses.) Now read the next sentence. What word comes after blue. See the capital B under the blank? That means you go to the capital B on the right to find the correct answer. What word comes after blue? (Pause) Yes, it is house. Draw a line under it. The next blank has a 1 under it. Find the answer and mark it. (Pause) Now do as many as you can."

Level 1

★ My name is Jim. I am a _____.
  A

I live in a blue _____. My blue
  B

house is _____ big. It is little. _____
  1   2

have a big brother _____ a cat. We
  3

like _____ play in our yard. _____
  4   5

we run so hard _____ fall on the
  6

ground.

Level 2

_____ day we got in _____.
  7   8

Mother cleaned the floor _____ we
  9

walked on it _____ it got dry.
  10

Level 3

Jack _____ , "Wait a minute,
  11

Mother. _____ you want to be
  12

A. girl	B. house
boy	sky
wagon	frog
hat	tree

1. so	2. We	3. and
very	I	for
not	Can	frog
red	Mother	now

4. our	5. Something	6. we
the	Sometimes	he
an	Besides	they
to	Look	head

7. The	8. time	9. because
Some	trouble	and
One	better	yet
Last	asleep	until

10. before	11. Sprat	12. After
after	Jones	As
until	said	If
lazily	jumped	Hey

_____ that we don't walk _____
  13   14

your wet floor, you _____ put up
                15

a sign. _____ we wouldn't make the
        16

13. sad   14. up   15. carefully
    old   on   won't
    grumpy   around   needn't
    certain   behind   should

Level 4

_____ journey across the wet
  17

_____ ."
  18

16. Often   17. bus   18. flour
    Then   happy   wall
    How   stilted   surface
    There   stupid   lake

Mother's Side of the Story

"This was quite a _____ for a
                  19

mother to _____ . After a bit of
          20

19. decision 20. have
    sign   come
    discovery   make
    journey   do

Level 5

_____ I took command and
  21

_____ as they had asked."
  22

21. preparation 22. did
    relief   went
    mystery   hoped
    encouragement   came

Mr. Brown's Occupation

Mr. Brown, Jim's father, _____
                       23

to have a very _____ job. He is the
            24

_____ of a police helicopter.
  25

23. is   24. low   25. mechanic
    and   suspicious   owner
    in   interesting   player
    appears   dumb   pilot

Level 6

_____ has an immense amount
  26

_____ work, in my humble
  27

_____ . He helps other policemen
  28

_____ traffic on crowded roads,
  29

26. Police   27. of   28. home
    He   in   estimation
    Jim   hard   language
    It   from   situation

29. over
    guide
    supplant
    help

Level 7

_____ at times he pursues _____
  30   31

bank robbers and other _____ of
                   32

criminals.

Although he _____ to do many
             33

routine _____ in his job of
        34

30. then   31. past   32. kinds
    if   fleeing   old
    when   funny   parts
    and   with   mean

33. how   34. habits   35. stifling
    will   tasks   helping
    has   vital   avoiding
    comes   happenings   abetting

Level 8

_____ crime and enforcing laws,
  35

_____has always served with
36

_____ . Part of his success
37

_____due to the intensive_____
38   39

which he received, and _____
40

Level 9

is due to his _____ mind and his
41

cool _____.
42

Grandma Brown

Grandma Brown is a _____ reading
43

teacher. Suffice it _____ say, she
44

enjoys teaching _____ people how to
45

Level 10

read. _____ factors account for her
46

_____ success in teaching. One
47

_____ real mutual trust existing
48

_____ her and her students.
49

Level 11

_____ second is the excellent
50

_____ she received at the _____ .
51   52

Another factor is her _____
53

intuition. Then the final _____
54

in her great success _____ a
55

Level 12

mentor are the _____ skill with
56

which she _____ the sometimes
57

nebulous problems _____ the
58

prodigious and also _____ manner
59

in which she _____ these problems.
60

36. it
    he
    man
    then

37. treachery
    hesitation
    distinction
    camouflage

38. happens
    is
    were
    by

39. training
    rewards
    heat
    courtesy

40. all
    what
    that
    some

41. stealthy
    melancholy
    lamentable
    ingenious

42. dedication
    badge
    expansion
    jurisdiction

43. remedial
    dejected
    festive
    grouchy

44. for
    can
    we
    to

45. feudal
    delinquent
    illiterate
    brazen

46. Numberless
    Five
    Confounding
    Which

47. poor
    gratifying
    mediocre
    piteous

48. are
    has
    sees
    is

49. by
    for
    between
    happily

50. One
    That
    My
    The

51. oratory
    symposium
    quandary
    curriculum

52. university
    high school
    book store
    library

53. fastidious
    unerring
    statistical
    impending

54. things
    factors
    scores
    deficits

55. as
    with
    story
    in

56. obsequious
    gauche
    chimerical
    consummate

57. creates
    identifies
    redresses
    vindicates

58. freeing
    and
    or
    in

59. sagacious
    voracious
    vicarious
    ostentatious

60. adjures
    sublimates
    inveigles
    rectifies

Level 13

How the _____ of life
                61
seem to _____ exemplified in these
              62
brief _____ ! Please do not take
          63
_____ at our manner of _____
    64   65
aspects of our characters' lives.

61. vicissitudes
    sycophants
    panegyrics
    judicatures

62. have
    me
    be
    come

63. cupidities
    vignettes
    satraps
    irascibilities

64. lien
    fruition
    virago
    umbrage

65. vindicating
    desiccating
    exacerbating
    delineating

Table 5. Answer Key for the Reading Comprehension Section of the Hafner Comprehensive Group Reading Inventory

1. not	2. I	3. and
4. to	5. sometimes	6. we
7. one	8. trouble	9. and
10. before	11. said	12. if
13. certain	14. on	15. should
16. then	17. stupid	18. surface
19. decision	20. make	21. encouragement
22. did	23. appears	24. interesting
25. pilot	26. he	27. of
28. estimation	29. guide	30. and
31. fleeing	32. kinds	33. has
34. tasks	35. stifling	36. he
37. distinction	38. is	39. training
40. some	41. ingenious	42. dedication
43. remedial	44. to	45. illiterate
46. five	47. gratifying	48. is
49. between	50. the	51. curriculum
52. university	53. unerring	54. factors
55. as	56. consummate	57. identifies
58. and	59. sagacious	60. rectifies
61. vicissitudes	62. be	63. vignettes
64. umbrage	65. delineating	

(See table 6 on page 536.)

MANUAL OF DIRECTIONS OF THE WORD IDENTIFICATION SKILLS TEST (TWIST) OF THE HAFNER COMPREHENSIVE GROUP READING INVENTORY[1]

Lawrence E. Hafner
Florida State University

Since time is not an important factor in this test of word-identification skills, directions will be minimal.

LN Letter Name Directions. Pass out copies of the response sheets. Have students find the star. Point out that there are five letters in that row and that you will say one of the letters and that they should draw a line under the letter. Then check to see that the students understand what they are to do. Do the "box" row in the same manner.

Sample items stimuli

a

g

[1] The test can be found after the manual of directions.

Table 6. Conversion Table for the Reading Comprehension Section of the Hafner Comprehensive Group Reading Inventory

Raw Score	Grade 16 % tile	Grade Placement	Raw Score	Grade Placement
65	93+	——	34	5.8
64	91	——	33	5.7
63	89	——	32	5.6
62	85	——	31	5.4
61	80	——	30	5.3
60	74	——	29	5.2
59	68	——	28	5.0
58	62	16.5	27	4.8
57	54	16.1	26	4.7
56	45	15.3	25	4.6
55	37	14.4	24	4.4
54	28	13.8	23	4.3
53	21	13.5	22	4.2
52	15	13.1	21	4.0
51	10	12.8	20	3.8
50	6	12.4	19	3.7
49	4	11.9	18	3.6
48	3	11.0	17	3.4
47	2	10.2	16	3.3
46	1	9.4	15	3.2
45	——	8.8	14	3.0
44	——	8.1	13	2.8
43	——	7.5	12	2.7
42	——	7.0	11	2.6
41	——	6.6	10	2.4
40	——	6.5	9	2.3
39	——	6.4	8	2.2
38	——	6.3	7	2.0
37	——	6.2	6	1.8
36	——	6.1	5	1.7
35	——	6.0	4	1.6
			3	1.5
			2	1.4
			1	1.2

Test stimuli

1. g	6. x	11. z	16. f	21. y	26. r
2. s	7. d	12. w	17. e	22. h	
3. v	8. j	13. l	18. m	23. i	
4. n	9. d	14. o	19. u	24. k	
5. b	10. q	15. t	20. c	25. p	

CB Consonant Blends Directions. Use the same general directions as in the previous subtest. However, the sample items are referred to by A and B. Have the students find row A, give the sample combination /fl/ and a nonsense word that uses the blend. Do sample B in the same manner, using the stimulus /gr/.

Sample items stimuli

A. /fl/ flim
B. /gr/ grax

Test stimuli

1.	/tr/	trib	11.	/pr/	prode
2.	/sm/	smiv	12.	/sw/	swawj
3.	/fr/	frobble	13.	/fl/	flar
4.	/gl/	glidge	14.	/dr/	dreeg
5.	/st/	steek	15.	/bl/	bloy
6.	/cr/	croyg	16.	/gr/	grile
7.	/sp/	speev	17.	/sn/	snilk
8.	/pl/	ploon	18.	/cl/	clob
9.	/br/	brate	19.	/sl/	sleen
10.	/sk/	skile	20.	/sc/	scap

CD Consonant Digraphs Directions. Use the same general directions as in the previous subtest.

Sample items stimuli

A. /ch/* chor
B. /k/ kaz

Test stimuli

1.	/n/	nod	6.	/zh/	zheeg
2.	/th/	thīm	7.	/ŋ/ [†]	ming
3.	/w/	wub	8.	/k/	kor
4.	/r/	rif	9.	/ŋk/ [†]	zank
5.	/sh/	shanz	10.	/f/	fole

* Say the <u>sounds</u> throughout this test, not the letter names.

† Point out that the sound in question is at the <u>end</u> of the nonsense word.

VC Vowel Clusters Directions. Use the same general directions as in the previous subtest, except that a nonsense word will not be given since vowel phonemes are easier to hear and discriminate.

Sample items stimuli

A. /ü/

B. /ī/

Test stimuli

1. /ē/	6. /ȯi/	11. /ō/	16. /au̇/	21. /ō/
2. /au̇/	7. /yü/	12. /ā/	17. /ē/	22. /ē/
3. /ā/	8. /ō/	13. /yü/	18. /ȯ/	23. /ü/
4. /e/	9. /ī/	14. /ā/	19. /ü/	24. /e/
5. /ü/	10. /ē/	15. /ȯ/	20. /ȯi/	25. /ē/

OC Other Combinations Directions. Make sure each student has a response sheet. State that you will make a spoken sound and that the students are to draw a line under the letter or letter combinations (graphemes) that represent the sound. Begin with number 1.

Test stimuli

1. /shən/	5. /ər/	9. /ər/
2. /r/	6. /əns/	10. /är/
3. /ȯr/	7. /ər/	11. /ōm/
4. /ər/	8. /ak/	12. /sh/

Name_____

Total Score_____

The Hafner Comprehensive Group Reading Inventory

Lawrence E. Hafner
Florida State University

III. Independent Word Identification

THE INDEPENDENT WORD IDENTIFICATION SKILLS TEST (TWIST)

LN: Letter Name

★ m   a   t   j   r
☐ u   m   o   x   g

1.	h	g	q	j	v	14.	a	e	d	o	v
2.	s	o	c	f	x	15.	m	t	q	e	b
3.	j	w	v	b	y	16.	f	h	v	t	g
4.	e	m	h	k	n	17.	i	a	e	b	h
5.	d	a	m	b	g	18.	n	o	a	x	m
6.	y	k	s	r	x	19.	y	n	u	f	o
7.	l	o	a	b	e	20.	e	d	s	k	c
8.	j	g	i	z	m	21.	w	y	p	u	v
9.	v	d	u	b	h	22.	h	a	n	b	i
10.	b	z	q	k	g	23.	o	i	a	j	l
11.	z	s	o	j	v	24.	c	q	h	k	a
12.	d	v	m	y	w	25.	p	m	b	q	e
13.	e	i	h	l	r	26.	q	n	o	r	m

CB: Consonant Blends (Digraph/Consonant Diphone)

A.	fr	kl	fl	gr	ph						
B.	gr	pl	pr	fr	gl						
1.	tr	dr	tn	wh	gn	11.	sm	pr	fl	wh	br
2.	sn	cl	gn	cr	sm	12.	vr	tw	sw	ch	fr
3.	vr	fl	pr	fr	sp	13.	fl	sl	fr	sp	sk
4.	dl	gl	cl	st	gr	14.	br	sc	pl	ph	dr
5.	sp	wh	st	cr	ng	15.	cl	br	sk	bl	gn
6.	cr	sh	gl	sn	cl	16.	zh	gt	kl	gr	pl
7.	ch	fr	zn	gr	sp	17.	sn	gl	fr	sm	sk
8.	sw	pr	sc	pl	dr	18.	pr	cl	fr	st	cr
9.	sc	kl	br	wh	pr	19.	fl	sw	zh	fr	sl
10.	sk	sg	zt	ch	fr	20.	sh	cr	sc	sm	wr

CD: Consonant Digraphs (Digraph/Consonant Uniphone)

A. gn   ch   ph   sh   zt
B. ck   sh   gn   wr   nk
1. ng   pr   nm   ch   kn
2. tw   sh   th   ng   wh
3. ch   sw   gn   wh   wr
4. wr   wh   br   tw   kn
5. cn   ch   zh   gn   sc

6. sh   sn   wr   ch   zh
7. -nk   sg   ph   -kn   -ng
8. th   ch   br   pl   kn
9. sn   -ng   zt   -nk   -zh
10. fr   sc   ph   sh   pn

VC: Vowel Clusters

Group one

A. ay   ee   uo   ie   ew
B. ie   aw   ue   ow   au
1. oy   oo   ai   ew   ea
2. ai   aw   ie   ow   oe
3. ue   ao   ai   ie   ew
4. ea   au   ee   oy   ey
5. eu   oo   oi   aw   oa

Group two

6. oy   ea   aw   ue   oo
7. aw   ue   ay   oe   eigh
8. oe   augh oi   ew   oo
9. oo   ow   ui   au   ie
10. ae   ee   ue   oy   aw

Group three

11. eigh ew   oo   ai   ough
12. ew   ay   eigh ow   ee
13. oa   eigh ew   ea   ay
14. ue   ow   ei   ay   au
15. ough eigh oo   ue   ai

Group four

16. ou   ie   oo   ea   ue
17. eu   ai   ee   oy   ay
18. ae   ue   au   oo   oa
19. augh ie   ai   uy   ew
20. ay   oi   ie   oe   ay

Group five

21. ey   oo   au   oa   ei
22. ie   ew   eigh aw   ue
23. ay   ee   ough eu   ae
24. aigh ue   ey   ie   oo
25. ew   oy   ai   ow   ei

OC: Other Combinations

1. zhom   tion   shem   sol   ton
2. wr   ar   oor   ay   eer
3. ar   ur   or   wr   oi
4. ink   im   ang   enk   ing
5. ier   or   in   ur   ay
6. osh   ious   tion   uz   ance

7. er   ahr   en   ru   eer
8. ip   et   ic   ack   uc
9. eh   eer   im   or   ir
10. ohr   an   ur   ar   oo
11. ine   ome   in   ing   im
12. e   o   ti   ea   ay

Applying Test Results. Grapheme-phoneme relationships that a student misses should be taught utilizing procedures suggested in this textbook and relevant materials listed in the materials appendix.

Name _____

Score _____

Reading Grade _____

Placement Score _____

The Hafner Quick Reading Test (Expanded Version)

Lawrence E. Hafner
Florida State University

To the Teacher: 1. Have the student read horizontally across the page. 2. Mark the items missed. Stop after five consecutive words are missed.

						Score
1.	bed	ride	funny	old	ground	_____
	catch	name	in	she	could	_____
2.	floor	together	river	minute	question	_____
	thank	enough	anyone	happen	lady	_____
3.	empty	which	stupid	glance	island	_____
	rather	weight	easily	alive	certain	_____
4.	saucer	command	future	majesty	encourage	_____
	orchard	quiver	improve	range	trumpet	_____
5.	flexible	emperor	operator	enclose	niece	_____
	warmth	mosquito	ravine	neglect	ceiling	_____
6.	mortal	physician	essential	geranium	document	_____
	possess	scroll	monstrous	forfeit	orphanage	_____
7.	complexion	conceit	reluctant	siege	monotonous	_____
	geology	chivalry	plague	unique	asylum	_____
8.	nourish	exquisite	camouflage	intrigue	hereditary	_____
	occupant	mythology	calamity	juror	reinforce	_____
9.	accomplice	regime	grimace	ecstacy	belligerent	_____
	idolize	encore	judicial	stealthy	physique	_____
10.	cynical	annihilate	uncouth	marital	deteriorate	_____
	reimburse	linear	anonymous	suave	feign	_____
11.	awry	guise	slovenly	emaciated	typify	_____
	indict	boudoir	glower	cuisine	meander	_____
12.	gauche	prosaic	visage	bourgeois	inveigle	_____
	quiescent	liaison	pedagogy	iridescent	myriad	_____
13.	inchoate	chimerical	miscegenation	sinecure	schism	_____
	satiate	avarice	matrix	cynosure	hyperbole	_____
14.	zeitgeist	persiflage	ratiocination	haricot	apotheosis	_____
	euphemism	suigeneris	caesura	klieg	syzygy	_____
					Total Score	_____

NOTE: Please do *not* try to administer this *Hafner Quick Reading Test* until you have looked up all the pronunciations! You may have been mispronouncing some of these words without being aware of it. Be careful in administering the test; if a pronunciation is wrong, it is wrong. Just mark it. Do not give any kind of indication that it is incorrect. Of course, if you did that, the student could finally "stumble" on to the correct pronunciation. Your test results would be inordinately high and invalid.

Determining the Reading Grade Placement. Count the number of correctly pronounced words and enter the raw score in the appropriate blank.

$$\text{Reading Grade Placement} = \frac{\text{Raw Score}}{10} + 1$$

An Informal Reading Inventory
(Comprehension, Pronunciation, and Vocabulary)

Readability level = 7.7

Plane Airways*

Skyways, or airways, are routes through the air followed by airplanes in flight. Most airways extend thousands of feet above the ground. Jet routes are above 25,000 feet altitude.

Each airway is ten miles wide. This results in each airplane being surrounded by a large block of airspace ten miles wide, twenty-five to fifty miles long, and two thousand feet high.

In the United States there are more than 65,000 miles of airways. These are operated by the Federal Aviation Agency. This agency's regulation is called air-route traffic control. The control centers receive flight plans and reports from pilots. The centers keep in contact with the pilots by means of radio.

Planes are separated in flight levels according to their destinations. They fly west and south at even-numbered thousands of feet altitude. Airplanes flying east or north must fly at odd-numbered thousands of feet altitude. When above towns or cities, at least 1,000 feet altitude must be maintained.

Today pilots are aided in their flights by radio, light beacons, and radar. In the early days of airplane flights, the airways were simply routes over which pilots flew as they looked for such landmarks as towns, lakes, mountains, and rivers.

# of errors_____

% correct_____ (Divide # of errors by 2 and subtract from 100 to get % correct)

Do silent reading and answering of questions first. Then have the subject read orally. Mark pronunciation errors on duplicate copy of the selection. Finally, have the student define the vocabulary items in the last part of the tests.

Plane Airways

Literal Comprehension (15 points each)

_____ 1. What can you tell me about an airway? (Any detail.)

_____ 2. Who operates the more than 65,000 miles of airways in the United States? (Federal Aviation Agency)

_____ 3. Where do pilots send their flight plans and reports? (To air-route traffic control or traffic control or control center)

_____ 4. Give me an example of a landmark. (Any of the following: town, lake, mountain, river - or any correct example of a landmark)

Interpretation (10 points each)

_____ 5. What might happen in flying if there were no airways? (There would be many crashes)

* Used by permission of Harper and Row Publishers.

_____ 6. How does a radio help a pilot in his work? (Any reasonable answer relating to communication useful in his job, e.g., communicate with control centers)

_____ 7. Why would a plane flying west probably not crash into a plane flying north? (They fly at different altitudes.)

_____ 8. How did pilots use landmarks? (navigation guides, or they helped the pilots tell where they were going)

_____ TOTAL

Criteria Met

Silent Reading _____ points or % comprehension   YES   NO

Oral Reading: _____% accuracy   YES   NO

Vocabulary: (Read the items to the student and ask him or her to define them.)

1. skyways	4. regulation	7. agency	10. communicate
2. altitude	5. destination	8. landmark	
3. radar	6. navigation	9. ascent	

Library Reference Skills Tests

Reference Skills Library Diagnostic Test
Ada Louise Anderson

1. To determine whether the library has a particular book, one would consult
   the _____ .

2. Suppose you read an article in a magazine a month ago but you do not
   remember in which magazine it appeared. How would you go about finding
   the magazine and the article?
   _____

3. The three different kinds of catalog cards are: _____ ,
   _____ and _____ .

4. What does the call number of a book show? _____

5. Are the markings on the spine of a book the same as those on the author,
   subject and title cards for the same book? _____

6. Are works of fiction arranged in alphabetical order according to the last name
   of the author? _____

7. What is the name of the system used for classifying most nonfiction books?
   _____

8. Define the following:

   almanac   circulation desk
   atlas   gazetteer
   yearbook   encyclopedia
   call number   periodical

9. What are vertical files and what types of material do you find in them?
   _____

10. What would the following in the <u>Readers Guide</u> mean? Identify each part.

②
① → Acrobats in space, c. Blinsky. New Repub ← ③

④→ 152; 14-15 Ap3'65
⑤   ⑥

1.   4.
2.   5.
3.   6.

11. Identify each numbered part. Place answers in spaces provided below the card.
    ①   ②
    T577s   Tolkien, J.R.R.
                                        ④
                ③— Smith of Wootton Major. Boston,

        ⑤ -   Houghton Mifflin, 1967 - ⑥

            ⑦ - 62p.   illus. - ⑧

    1.   5.
    2.   6.
    3.   7.
    4.   8.

12. Below is an entry from the index of an encyclopedia. Correctly identify the
    parts. Put your answers in the spaces provided

            ①   ② ③ ④   ⑤   ⑥
    Caesar: 3 — 424 b: 6 - 478 d

    1.   4.
    2.   5.
    3.   6.

Comprehensive Library Reference Skills Test
Ada Louise Anderson

PLEASE PUT ALL YOUR ANSWERS ON THE ANSWER SHEET PROVIDED! ! ! !

1. How are FICTION books classified and arranged on the shelves?
2. How are NONFICTION books classified and arranged on the shelves?
3. In the MHS library, what is the number that appears in the upper left hand corner of cards in the card catalog and on the spine of the book. Name the complete group that appears in the diagram at the right of this question.   (837.9 F34)

4, 5 What are the three types of cards in the card catalog?
6. for EVERY book in the library?
7. If you know the subject, title, author, or first line of a poem, you can find the NAME of a book containing that poem by looking in what reference book?
8. A book written about the life of a person is called a

_____ .

9. A list of reference sources used (books, magazine articles, etc.) to prepare an article on paper on a subject is called a _____.
10. What is a book of maps called?
11. A dictionary of synonyms is a _____.
12. A dictionary of geographical names is a _____.
13. The index to all the books in the library is the _____.
14. A reference source in our library containing magazine articles, newspaper clippings, pictures and other loose reference material is the _____

_____ .

15. A book containing famous sayings and phrases traced back to their sources is called a book of _____.

16. A _____ is a book that is published annually to bring an encyclopedia up to date.

17. The index to the periodicals in the library is the_____.

18. A book that lists words in alphabetical order and gives their meanings, pronunciations, derivations, etc. is a _____.

19. We studied two types of cross references. The (19)_____

_____ reference indicates where related or additional

20. material on a subject can be found; the (20) _____ reference indicates the actual subject heading under which the information can be found.

21. What is the type of reference book that is published annually and gives facts and figures about a variety of subjects such as population, sports, awards, famous person, etc.?

22. A card in the card catalog that has page numbers at the top and refers you to information that is only PART of a book is a _____.

23. A book or set of books that has general information on many subjects is an

_____ .

24. The B on the spine of a book above the rest of the call number, indicates that the book is a _____ .

25. An R on the spine of a book above the rest of the call number indicates that the book is a _____ .

26. Is the book shown in the diagram at the right a fiction or a nonfiction book?

           26 → | 837.5 |
                 | R52 |

27. Is the book shown in the diagram at the right a fiction or a nonfiction book?

           27 → | J37 |

28. What kind of catalog card is the one in the diagram below?

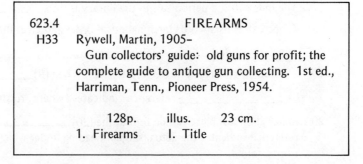

```
623.4
R33     Rywell, Martin, 1905–
            Gun collectors' guide: old guns for profit; the
        complete guide to antique gun collecting. 1st ed.,
        Harriman, Tenn., Pioneer Press, 1954.

                128 p.       illus.       23 cm.

        1. Firearms      I. Title
```

29. What kind of card is the one below?

```
623.4                           FIREARMS
H33     Rywell, Martin, 1905–
            Gun collectors' guide: old guns for profit; the
        complete guide to antique gun collecting. 1st ed.,
        Harriman, Tenn., Pioneer Press, 1954.

                128p.       illus.       23 cm.
        1. Firearms      I. Title
```

30. What kind of card is the one below?

623.4 Gun collectors' guide: old guns for profit; the
R33 complete guide to antique gun collecting. 1st ed.,
   Harriman, Tenn.,

     128 p.   illus.   23 cm.

    1. Firearms I. Title

---

31. What kind of card is the one below?

834.7 Merchant of Venice   pp. 34–58
M54   Shakespeare, William

   Merrick, Henry
    Ten Elizabethan plays: a book of selected sixteenth
   century English plays. 3rd ed., Random House, N.Y.,
   1964.

     347 p.   illus.

   1. Drama

32, 33, 34, 35, 36, 37. Identify each numbered area of the card below.

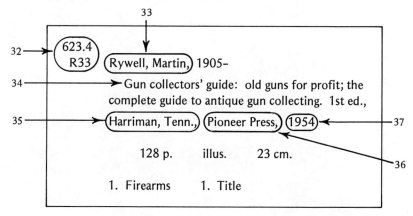

38. Is the entry from the Readers' Guide below a subject entry or an author entry?

KING, Larry L.
    Washington's money birds. Harper 231:45–54
    Ag '65

39, 40, 41, 42, 43, 44. Identify each circled and numbered area of the Readers'
Guide entry below.

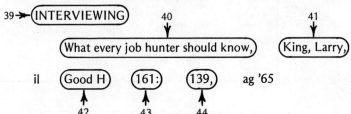

45. Name the area circled in the diagram at the right.

    45 → | 795.2 |
           | R65 |

46. Name the area circled in the diagram at the right.

    46 → | 795.2 |
           | R64 |

47. What is a book that tells about the lives of famous living Americans?
     (Give the title!)
48. What is a book that tells about the lives of persons who have been in the
     news headlines? (Give the title).
49. What is a book that tells about the lives of Americans who are no longer
     living? (Give a title).
50. What is a book that contains a BRIEF summary of the lives of people from
     all periods of history and from all over the world? (Give the title).

Answers to Comprehensive Library Skills Reference Test

1. Alphabetically by author
2. Dewey Decimal System
3. Call Number
4. Title
5. Author
6. Subject
7. Granger's Index to Poetry
8. Biography
9. Bibliography
10. Atlas
11. Thesaurus
12. Gazetteers
13. Card Catalog
14. Vertical File
15. Famous Quotations
16. Yearbook
17. Readers' Guide
18. Dictionary
19. See also
20. See
21. Almanac
22. Analytical Card
23. Encyclopedia
24. Biography
25. Reference
26. Nonfiction
27. Fiction
28. Author
29. Subject
30. Title
31. Analytical
32. Call Number
33. Author
34. Title
35. Place of Publication
36. Publisher
37. Copyright
38. Author
39. Subject
40. Title
41. Author
42. Magazine
43. Volume
44. Page
45. Dewey Decimal Number
46. Author Letter
47. Who's Who in America
48. Current Biography
49. Who Was Who in America
50. Webster's Biographical Dictionary

Annotated Bibliography of Materials
For Reading Instructions – Eva Berg

BEGINNING READING

Kits and Audiovisual Aids

Action Kit I and II. Kit designed to develop decoding and comprehension. Contains 3 unit books, two readers, Take 12/Action Plays, posters, LP record and teacher's manual. For high school students reading on second grade level. Reading level 2.0–2.9. Scholastic.

Auditory Discrimination in Depth Kit. Kit designed to develop discrimination of sounds, perception of order of sounds and correspondences of sound-symbols, by first giving in depth experience of the phonological structure of spoken words and then moving to the symbol system. Contains letter symbol tiles, colored wooden blocks, colored felt tiles, sound-symbol card deck. For preschoolers through adult. Teaching Resources.

Breaking the Code Program. An intensive code-breaking approach to reading for 4–9th graders reading on a primary level, and for students in high school needing additional reading development. Open Court.

Clues to Reading Progress. High-interest low readability program designed for grades 5+ who have not mastered basic reading skills. Employed magazine-style workbooks with black and white pop art, and accompanying audio tapes. Story content relevant to student. Components include 3 student response booklets, 36 audio tapes in 3 separate trays, 3 test booklets, a teacher's guide and a Dialect and Language Interference Tape. Educational Progress.

Keys to Reading. A multilevel core reading program designed to develop decoding and comprehension skills. Structural analysis skills and study skills are emphasized at intermediate levels. Supportive material includes activity books, duplicating masters, symbol, word, and phrase cards, story charts, and a competency skills test. High interest contemporary material contained in the three books. Grades 6–8 Economy.

Point 31 Reading Center. Designed for students who need practice in the most basic phonics skills. Builds vocabulary and comprehension. Contains readers, activity books and correlated audio lessons of high interest to teenagers. Interest level 7–12. Reading level 0–4.9. Reader's Digest.

Programmed Reading for Adults. A programmed linguistic approach designed to bring the non-reader to a 6th grade reading level. Eight books beginning with the letters of the alphabet and ending with functional reading. Grades 7–12. Webster.

Spelling Word Power Laboratory IIa. Designed to develop spelling rules and various graphemic options and sounds. Contains 55 different learning wheels, 22 different check test and key cards, student record booklet, handbook. Check tests to measure improvement. Grades 4–9. SRA.

Webster Word Wheels Kit. Kit contains 63 word wheels for sound blending practice of consonants and prefixes-suffixes. McGraw Hill.

Workbooks

Decoding for Reading Program. Highly structured decoding program containing two record albums and two readalong books designed for intermediate students. Macmillan.

Ginn Word Enrichment Program. Seven workbooks that include skill progress from visual and auditory discrimination through word origins. A diagnostic test begins each skill unit and a diagnostic mastery test follows each skill unit. Ginn.

Hip Reader. A workbook designed for minority children that presents sound-spelling patterns in brief stories emphasizing sound blending. Interest level 5–12. Book-Lab.

Mott Basic Language Skills Program Books 1300–1310. Ten semiprogrammed workbooks designed to develop decoding for middle and secondary students. Allied Education Council.

Sound Reading Program. Eight programmed workbooks stressing various graphemic options for phonemes, context clues and context processing. Pretests for placement. Manual. Interest level primary-adult. Education Achievement.

Word Attack Manual. Workbook designed to develop decoding common grapheme–phoneme correspondences, syllabication, structural analysis and dictionary use for junior high students. Educators.

Games

Get Set Series. Eight separate games to supplement and reinforce phonics concepts and reading instruction. Houghton.

Group Sounding Game. Bingo-type listening game to develop the habit of listening to sounds and the letter-sound combinations. Grades 3–8. Garrard.

Phonics We Use Learning Game Kit. Ten separate games designed to supplement and reinfoce phonics concepts and reading instruction. Lyons.

Sullivan Reading Games Kit. Ten separate games designed to supplement and reinforce phonics concepts and reading isntruction. Behavorial.

Time for Phonics Flash Cards. Three sets of 32 large illustrated cards-Touch and Learn Cards; Consonant Blend Cards; The Vowel Sounds Cards. Grades 2–7. Webster.

BASIC SIGHT VOCABULARY AND WORD IDENTIFICATION

Kits and Audiovisual Aids

Aural Reading Lab. The program develops comprehension, word attack skills, and builds vocabulary through tape-directed reading exercises. Includes 40 tapes, 6 story cards for each tape, 30 student response books, teacher's manual and a placement test kit. For grades 7–9. Reading level 4.0–8.5. Imperial.

Be Informed Series. 10 units primarily designed for adults with high interest selections. Skills developed include context processing, word processing and some decoding. New Readers Press.

Clues to Reading Progress. High-interest, low readability program designed for grades 5+ who have not mastered basic reading skills. Employs magazine-style workbooks with black and white pop art, and accompanying audio tapes. Story content relevant to student. Components include 3 student response booklets, 36 audio tapes in 3 separate trays, 3 test booklets, a teacher's guide and a Dialect and Language Interference Tape. Educational Progress.

Keys to Reading. A multilevel core reading program designed to develop decoding and comprehension skills. Structural analysis skills and study skills are emphasized at intermediate levels. Supportive material includes activity books, duplicating masters, symbol, word, and phrase cards, story charts, and a competency skills test. High interest contemporary material contained in the three books. Grades 6–8. Economy.

Macmillan Spectrum of Skills—Vocabulary Development Kit. Six color-coded linear programmed workbooks to develop word/context processing skills. Includes teacher's guide and pupil record book. Intermediate and upper grades. Macmillan.

Picto-Cabulary Series Sets 111, 222. Two sets each containing 6 different workbooks that develop meaning of adjectives. Pre-post tests available Grades 5–9. Barnell-Loft.

Plus-10 Vocabulary Booster. Levels D & E. A systematic and comprehensive vocabulary expansion program Includes exposure to Greek and Roman mythology, Hebrew history, etc.; a complete dictionary training program; audio instruction of vocabulary. Grades 7–8. Webster.

Point 31 Reading Center. Designed for students who need practice in the most basic phonics skills. Builds vocabulary and comprehension. Contains readers, activity books and correlated audio lessons of high interest to teenagers Interest level 7–12. Reading level 0–4.9. Reader's Digest.

Power Reading System III. A diagnostic/prescriptive approach to reading which focuses on specific behavioral objectives. Contains 3 units (Word Recognition, Comprehension, Study Skills) in a manageable file drawer. Grades 7–12. Winston.

The Radio Reading Series ARL-2. This program contains 10 copies each of 30 high interest, easy readability stories to develop word attack skills, comprehension and vocabulary study. Includes 15 tape cassettes, student booklet, manual. Grades 6–8. Psychotechnics, Inc.

Reach Program. An individualized self-paced program about show business. High-interest material in which student participates in the shows while learning audio and/or reading selection, audio comprehension and evaluative testing Grades 4–9. Economy.

Reading Improvement: Word Recognition Skills (film). Useful tips in developing quick and accurate recognition of words by form, context, and sound. Grades 7–12. Coronet Films, Inc.

Reading Incentive Language Program. Low vocabulary, high interest reading program designed to provide sequential skill development. Includes 10 books, a sound filmstrip, and a long playing record or cassette. Sample titles: Drag Racing, Mini Bikes, Surfing. Bowmar.

Reading Skills Library. 134 Skill builders and 72 audio lessons of high interest reading/ listening for grades 1–12. Reading level 1–9. Reader's Digest.

Scope/Word Skills Visuals. Visual masters and transparencies for vocabulary building and to develop word identification skills for middle and secondary students. Reading level 4–6. Scholastic.

SRA Reading Laboratories. Series of boxed kits or laboratories containing graded materials for development of basic reading skills of word identification, vocabulary, comprehension and rate. Manual. Placement tests. Grades 1–14. SRA.

Turning Point I. A comprehensive, individualized program designed to develop basic word attack skills. Junior High interest level. Educational Products.

Vocabulab III. Designed to develop ability to use derivational clues. Each lesson includes a reading selection followed by questions that call for context clues, structural analysis and meaning relationships. Pre-post tests available. Grades 4–9. SRA.

Vocabulary Development Programs. Each unit in a volume presents 10 words on a record first in a sentence, than in another sentence with a synonym. Contains 3 volumes. High School+. Scott Foresman.

Wordcraft 1, 2, 3 Vocabulary Programs. Multimedia approach using filmstrips, tapes and workbook to develop word processing skills. Developmental 4–8; Remedial 7–13. The Reading Laboratory.

Wordpacers Kit. Designed to develop 10 word processing skills. Includes 10 definition cards, practice cards, progress plotter, skill spotter test, thesarurus cards and teacher's manual. Pretest for placement. Grades 4–6. Random.

Books and Workbooks

Basic Vocabulary Skills. Branching, programmed text designed to develop word processing skills with exercises for application in subject areas of physical, life and biological sciences and humanities. Grades 9–12+. McGraw-Hill.

Be A Better Reader Series. Variety of word identification, vocabulary, comprehension, and reference skills taught in a setting of the content areas of social studies, new math, literature, and biological sciences. Grades 4–12. Prentice.

Conquests in Reading. An aid in teaching such word-identification skills as phoneme-grapheme relationships, compound words, prefixes, suffixes, and sylalbication. Dolch sight words also taught. Grades 6–9. Webster.

Designs for Reading. Two texts containing several color-coded levels designed to develop word/context processing skills. Self-teaching and self-scoring Skills include compounds, affixes, Latin roots, synonyms and antonyms, heteronyms, idioms, and cliches. Grades 4–9. SRA.

Discoveries. 21 colorful, high interest paperback readers containing fables, myths, factual articles, contemporary stories and novellas. Skill development accompanies the six stages of the series. Interest level 7–12. Reading level 4–6. Houghton Mifflin.

Easy-To-Read Biographies. Series of four biographies designed to appeal to slow or reluctant readers and reinforce basic skills in vocabulary, retention of information, and comprehension. Interest level 7+. Houghton Mifflin.

Know Your World. Weekly newspaper designed for ages 10–16 to build comprehension and interpretation skills. Each high-interest selection brings a variety of skill builders: Getting the Message, Using Clues, Using Sounds, Building Words, etc. Reading level 2.5–3.5. Xerox.

New Practice Readers. Each of seven books in the series contains brief reading selections and related exercises designed to improve vocabulary and comprehension, to teach pupils to note details, identify antecedents of words, identify words similar in meaning, detect opinions, and select true statements. Books A–G. Grades 2–8. Webster.

Power and Speed in Reading. Text designed to make good readers superior in perception, comprehension and interpretation through articles, exercises and tests. Includes inventories and guides for self-diagnosis. Grades 7–12. Prentice.

Reader's Digest Reading Skillbuilders. Interesting stories plus exercises for developing word identification, vocabulary and comprehension skills. Audio lessons available. Grades 1–10. Reader's Digest.

Really Reading! Workbook containing one-page exercises with self-evaluations designed for a developmental reading skills program. Sample skills: critical reading, context clues, synonymys, etc. Grades 10–12. Vocabulary level 8. Bell.

Scope/Word Skills Book. Three separate workbooks designed to develop word identification skills through high-interest puzzles, stories, exercises and articles. Interest level 7–12. Reading level 4–6. Scholastic.

Games

Baffle. Anagram-type game for developing a pupil's ability to construct patterns and words. Lyons.

Basic Sight Vocabulary Cards. Dolch's 220 words that make up 50 to 75 per cent of all reading material. Directions for playing games with the cards. Garrard.

Cagey. Anagram-type game stimulates the pupil's vocabulary potential through the use of three-, four-, and five-letter patterns. Lyons.

CrossCountry. Board game that encourages pupil recognition of phoneme-grapheme relationships through diacritical marks and phonetic spellins. Lyons.

Goldcup Games. Games designed to reinforce reading skills giving practice in building vocabulary and word recognition and comprehension. Interest level 3–12. Reading level 3.5–4.0. Bowmar.

No Nonsense. Card game designed to give experience in building words through reinforcing morphemic principles. Lyons.

Phonetic Quizmo. Designed to aid reading and spelling competence, this game is played like Lotto to teach sounds of letters and groups of letters. Milton Bradley.

Spill and Spell. A fine classroom game to brush up on spelling. Parker Brothers, Inc.

VOCABULARY AND CONCEPTS: GENERAL AND CONTENT AREA

Kits and Audiovisual Aids

Audio Reading Progress Laboratory: Developmental reading program that makes extensive use of an audio approach. The program supplements and is correlated with basic reading programs.

Aural Reading Lab. The program develops comprehension, word attack skills and builds vocabulary through tape-directed reading exercises. Includes 40 tapes, 6 story cards for each tape, 30 student response books, teacher's manual and a placement test kit. For grades 7–9. Reading level 4.0–8.5. Imperial.

Bergen Evans Vocabulary Program. Designed for the college bound student. 500 core words and their derivatives in 50 separate lessons and presented on 10 filmstrips and 5 cassettes. Grades 8–13. Reading Laboratory.

Building Reading Skills in the Content Areas. A 120 lesson cassette tape program to develop phonic analysis, structural analysis and contextual analysis in the content subject areas of geography, history, science, and mathematics at 5 graded reading difficulty levels (2–6). Junior-Senior High Interest. Educational Activities, Inc.

Building Verbal Power I, II. Each kit contains 5 LP records each designed to develop an aspect of word recognition Includes exercises on signal words, multi-usage words, sentence completion, etc. Includes teacher's guide. Grades 3–adult. Miller-Brody.

College Reading Program I and II. An aid to help college-bound students improve their reading skills, learn to recognize unfamilar words, and build comprehension High interest material. Components: Each box contains Booster Readings, answer sheets, answer keys, timed readings, teacher's guide and a student book Grades 9–14. SRA.

Discover Your World Programs. Series DW-11, China; DW-12, Pakistan; DW-13, India. A transparency series designed to help teach concepts in the following areas about each country: geography, history, anthropology, sociology, economics and political science. Teacher's guide. Elementary and high school. AEVAC, Inc.

Double Action. Multimedia program for secondary students whose skills and vocabulary levels are between 2.0–5.0. Contains: 2 LP records, 2 unit books, anthology of 20 short stories, collection of plays, 6 motivational posters, teacher's guide. Scholastic.

How to Develop a Good Vocabulary (filmstrip). EP.

Plus-10 Vocabulary Booster Levels D & E. A systematic and comprehensive vocabulary expansion program. Includes exposure to Greek and Roman mythology, Hebrew history, etc; a complete dictionary training program; audio instruction of vocabulary. Grades 7–8. Webster.

Reading Improvement: Vocabulary Skills (film). Suggests specific vocabulary building skills and exercises. Grades 7–12. Coronet Films, Inc.

Reading Improvement: Vocabulary Skills (film). Suggests specific vocabulary building skills and exercises. Grades 7–12. Coronet Films, Inc.

The Reading Line. A multi disciplinary reading and study skills improvement program. The 6 student books each contain 10 reading selections in all content areas, each written at 4 levels of difficulty. Teaches students to read with purpose, collect data and evidence, think critically, take notes, etc. Grades 7–12. Polaski Company, Inc.

Reading Tutors Levels 7–9. Self-pacing lessons for individual pupils to zero in on specific listening and reading skills. Develops vocabulary and comprehension skills. Each level contains 10 books and 6 audio cassettes. Includes Teacher's Guide and answer keys. Grades 7–9. Reader's Digest.

Science Adventures. Forty full-color captioned filmstrips in ten sets: atoms and their energy; magnetism and electricity; weather; nature of light; four metallic elements; the cell: basic unit of life; astronomy; electronics; automation; important chemical elements. Grades 5–9. Filmstrip.

Scope/Word Skills Visuals. Visual masters and transparencies for vocabulary building and to develop word identification skills for middle and secondary students. Reading level 4–6. Scholastic.

Solar Science Projects. Low-cost solar energy projects to construct and use; diagrams included. Scholastic.

Student Project Planetarium. Table-top planetarium designed to help pupils explore relationships of the sun and planets. Instructions. Ages 9–17. Creative Playthings, Inc.

Vocabulary For the College Bound. Five records of cassettes containing 600 words that appear most often on college admission examination. Words are defined, used in sentences and their derivative, synonyms and antonyms are included in the practice manual. Increases speaking and reading vocabulary. Miller-Brody.

The Vocabulary of Biology. Series of filmstrips that present the basic vocabulary of biology, precisely defining each word with self-explanatory illustrations. Junior-Senior High. Educational Activities, Inc.

Wordcraft, 1, 2, 3, Vocabulary Programs Multi-media approach using filmstrips, tapes and workbook to develop word processing skills. Developmental 4–8. Remedial 7–13. The Reading Laboratory.

Books and Workbooks

Breaking the Word Barrier. Text designed to extend vocabulary by building word interest in a variety of approaches and exercises. Provides a list of general and occupational words. Grades 7–12. Prentice.

Building Reading Power. Series of fifteen booklets in programmed learning format designed to improve vocabulary and comprehension. Grade 5+. C. E. Merrill.

Dictionary of Basic Words. This dictionary contains over 21,000 entries and features full-color illustrations on nearly every page. Age 9–adult. Childrens Press.

Grow in Word Power. Exercises from the high school edition of Reader's Digest. Grade 7+. Reader's Digest.

How to Improve Your Reading. Text emphasizing vocabulary and word building and to help student adjust reading rate to purpose and nature of the material. Grades 7–14. SRA.

Lessons for Self-Instruction in Basic Skills: Vocabulary. Programmed booklets designed to teach vocabulary. Grades 3–9. California.

Macmillan Reading Spectrum. Consists of eighteen booklets providing systematic instruction in word identification, vocabulary development and reading interpretation. Grades 4+. Macmillan.

New Practice Readers. Each of seven books in the series contains brief reading selections and related exercises designed to improve vocabulary and comprehension, to teach pupils to note details, identify antecedents of word, identify words similar in meaning, detect opinions, and select true statements. Books A–G, grades 2–8. Webster.

Reader's Digest Reading Skillbuilders. Interesting stories plus exercises for developing word identification, vocabulary, and comprehension skills. Audio lessons available. Grades 1–10. Reader's Digest.

Rochester Occupational Reading Series. Text providing reading instruction and information about the working world for nonacademic students. Printed at three reading levels (2–5). Mature content and relevant subject matter that interests students. Book title: *The Job Ahead.* Interest level 9–Adult. SRA.

Science Tutor Books. Individualized science help for problem readers to make difficult concepts clear. Simulated news stories, comic strips and cartoons build motivation. Four separate books: *Learn About Atoms, Molecules, Machines,* and *Energy Conversions.* Self-instructional. Interest level 5+ Reading level 4. Xerox.

Short World Biographies. Stories about over 30 outstanding men and women including Winston Churchill, Pablo Picasso and Ralph Nader. Exercises stress comprehension and vocabulary development. Grades 7–12. Reading level 5–6. Globe.

Stanford/McGraw Hill Vocabulary. Six-book vocabulary improvement series designed to teach words for immediate use in everyday speaking, listening, reading and writing. Built-in systematic review. Short lesson format. Grades 7–12. Webster.

Stranger than Fiction. Short interesting magazine and newspaper stories written on 2–3 level for middle and secondary students. Comprehension and vocabulary skills are stressed. Globe.

Unesco Science Book. Incorporates more than 700 easily done and clearly explained demonstrations and experiments that require everyday items found around the house. Prepared under the aegis of UNESCO. Ages 8–15. Creative Playthings, Inc.

Vocabulary Improvement: A Program for Self-Instruction. Book designed to expand the vocabulary for advanced students in high school. Grades 10–12. Webster.

Words are Important. Series of books designed to teach more unusual words in the *Teacher's Word Book* by Thorndike and Lorge. Reviews to help "nail down" words. Grades 7+. C. S. Hammond & Co.

You and Your World. Weekly newspaper for students 14 and older who read at 3.5–5.0 grade level. Highly motivating selections including skill builders: Word Power, Map, Graph, Cartoon, etc. Xerox.

Games

Glory Road, Black History Games. Learning games about such great black Americans as Crispus Attucks, Harriet Tubman, and Matt Henson. Creative.

Gold Cup Games. Games designed to reinforce reading skills giving practice in building vocabulary skills and word recognition and comprehension. Interest level 3–12. Reading level 3.5–4.0. Bowmar.

Know Your States. Players build the names of the states from syllables found on 170 cards. Grades 4–12. Garrard.

Remcraft Space Science Kits. Chemical compound forming, weather forecasting, jet propulsion, mechanical physics Expecially good for older boys who are interested in science. REMCO.

Tufabet. Tufabet cubes to construct interlocking words similar to those found in crossword puzzles. Builds vocabulary. Creative Visuals.

Undersea World of Jacques Cousteau. Good game for learning some oceanography concepts. Parker Brothers.

Wff 'n Proof. Game of logic that is a series of 21 progressively more difficult games. The games use symbols for words. Logical, orderly thinking is rewarded. Includes 36 logic cubes, timer, 224-page game manual. Ages 6–Adult. Creative Playthings.

COMPREHENSION AND STUDY-REFERENCE

Kits and Audiovisual Aids

Action Kit I and II. Kit designed to develop decoding and comprehension. Contains 3 unit books, two readers, Take 12/ Action Plays, poster, LP record and teacher's manual. For high school students reading on second-grade level. Reading level 2.0–2.9. Scholastic.

Advanced Reading Skills Library. 61 different reading selections and 30 different Audio Lessons to appeal to students in grades 7–12. Useful as a center for students who want an extra challenge or who need work on a specific comprehension skill. Quizzes and exercises follow each selection. Reading levels 7–9. Reader's Digest.

Aural Reading Lab. The program develops comprehension, word attack skills, and vocabulary through tape-directed reading exercises. Includes 40 tapes, 6 story cards for each tape, 30 student response books, teacher's manual and a placement test kit. For grades 7–9. Reading level 4.0–8.5. Imperial.

Basic Skills Series. Kit designed to develop reading and interpretive skills necessary for understanding maps, charts, and other visual data. Grades 4–8. SRA.

Be Informed Series. 10 units primarily designed for adults with high interest selections. Skills developed include context processing, word processing and some decoding. New Readers Press.

Building an Outline (film). Step-by-step procedures for developing an outline. 7+. Coronet Films, Inc.

Clues to Reading Progress. High-interest low readability program designed for grades 5+ who have not mastered basic reading skills. Employs magazine-style work books with black and white pop art, and accompanying audio tapes. Story 36 audio tapes in 3 separate trays. 3 test booklets, a teacher's guide and a Dialect and Language Interference Tape. Educational Progress.

College Reading Program I and II. An aid to help college-bound students improve their reading skills, learn to recognize unfamilar words, and build comprehension. High interest material. Components: Each box contains Booster Readings, answer sheets, answer keys, timed readings, teacher's guide and a student book. Grades 9–14. SRA.

Critical Reading and Listening Skill Development. Multimedia approach providing an extensive comprehension and study skill development program. Fiction and non-fiction high interest selection can be used in any one of three instructional approaches or the Tri-Level Approach—Book Reading, Listening (cassettes), Guided Reading (filmstrips). Grades 1–12. Taylor Associates.

Crossroads. A nongraded reading program designed to develop reading, composition, oral language, critical thinking and writing skills for grades 7–12. Contains 4 student anthologies, activity books, LP record for each volume and whole library of appealing paperbacks. Reading levels 4–9. Noble.

Dictionary Skills Series. 15 auto-instructional lessons to develop dictionary skills. Each lesson presented by a sight-sound filmstrip, and students respond in the Dictionary Skills Lesson Book. Levels 4–8. EDL.

Dimensions in Reading—Manpower and Natural Resources. Designed for adults or adolescents to develop interest in reading through high interest topics. 10 questions follow each selection to develop comprehension skills. 8 reading levels are represented. Levels 4–11+. SRA.

Doing an Assignment (filmstrip). Clues on what to do and what not to do when working on an assignment. Grade 7+. EP.

Doing Homework (filmstrip). Ways of getting to the task of doing homework profitably. Grade 7+. EP.

Double Action. Multimedia program for secondary students whose skills and vocabulary levels are between 3.0–5.0. Contains 2 LP records, 2 unit books, anthology of 20 short stories, collection of plays, 6 motivational posters, teacher's guide. Scholastic.

Finding Information (filmstrip). How to save time in finding the information needed. 7+. EP.

Graph and Picture Study Skills Kit. Designed to help students read and interpret illustrative Materials—photographs, charts, diagrams, etc. Grade level 4–8. SRA.

How to Improve Reading Skill. One LP record or cassette with printed text describing the elements necessary for improving reading skill and comprehension. Grades 7–12. Miller-Brody.

How to Read Essays (film). Tips to help make essay reading more enjoyable and profitable. 7+. Coronet Films, Inc.

How to Read Novels (film). Helps unveil the mysteries of reading the novel. 7+. Coronet Films, Inc.

How to Read Poetry (film). How to get more out of poetry and increase one's liking for it. Grade 7+. Coronet Films, Inc.

How to Read Plays (film) Helps the student learn to read plays with more finesse 7+. Coronet Films, Inc.

How to Remember (film). Specific procedures for tackling study tasks. Grades 7–9. Coronet Films, Inc.

How to Study (filmstrip) Provides a number of useful tips that help improve the results from time spent in study EP.

Importance of Making Notes (film). Explains why it is a good idea to make good notes. Grades 7–9. Coronet Films, Inc.

Jamestown Classics. High interest, low level classic stories—Jack London, Edgar Allen Poe, O. Henry, etc.—to develop interest and comprehension. Includes 4 tape cassettes and 100 student booklets. Reading level 5.0. Jamestown.

Keys to Reading. A multilevel core reading program designed to develop decoding and comprehension skills. Structural analysis skills and study skills are emphasized at intermediate levels. Supportive material includes activity books, duplicating masters, symbol, word and phrase cards, story charts, and a competency skills test. High interest contemporary material contained in the three books. Grades 6–8. Economy.

Know Your Library (film) Provides useful tips on using the library Grades 7–12. Coronet Films, Inc.

Learning to Use Maps (filmstrip). Series of 6 filmstrips providing a unique approach to understanding and using maps. Grade level 6–9. Encyclopedia Britannica.

Library Skills. These skills are taught by Minisystem—a self-contained instructional package composed of a tape reel or cassette program, 30 pupil activity sheets correlated with the taped instruction sequence, and a teacher's guide. Electronic Futures, Inc.

Listening Progress Laboratory: Series 789. Designed to develop concepts that will provide general background and also an information base for various reading endeavors. The following basic listening skills are developed: tracking, focusing, discriminating, recalling, attending, following directions, and following actions. Cognitive listening skills developed are topics, main ideas, details; note-taking and summarizing; fact and opinion; tone and mood; creative anticipation; cause and effect; inference; critical analysis. The laboratory contains content material in literature, music, science, social studies, speech, and culture. Grades 7–9. EPC.

Macmillan Spectrum of Skills—Vocabulary Development Kit. 6 color-coded linear programmed workbooks to develop word/context processing skills. Includes teacher's guide and pupil record book. Intermediate and upper grades. Macmillan.

Making an Outline (filmstrip). How to organize ideas for presentation 7+. EP.

Maps and Globe Skills Kit. Designed to help develop skills that are essential to the effective use of maps and globes. Grades 4–8. SRA.

Pal Paperback Kits. Color keyed, high-interest paperbacks that include topics like mystery, supernatural, science fiction and teenage problems. Designed to create interest in reading and to develop vocabulary and comprehension skills. Kit includes 3 copies of 18 titles in a sturdy bookcase. Teacher's guide included. Interest level 7–12. Reading level 1.5–5.5. Xerox.

Plus-4 Reading Booster. An intensive program that provides flexible, individualized instruction in word perception and comprehension skills. Self-instructional. Components include 20 copies of the basic instructional text—*Code Book*, 12 teaching cassettes, 20 copies of *Dr. Spello*—a companion remedial spelling text, Sight Word Cards, Sight Word Test Wheels, Word Ending Wheels, Word Blending Wheels, Prefix and Suffix Wheels, Reading Cards, Answer Pads, Answer Key templates and Oral Tests. Also included is an *Every Reader Library* of 20 classic stories for additional reading practice. Grades 4+. Webster.

Power Reading System III. A diagnostic/prescriptive approach to reading which focuses on specific behavioral objectives. Contains 3 units (Word Recognition, Comprehension, Study Skills) in a manageable file drawer. Grades 7–12. Winston.

The Radio Reading Series. ARL-2. This program contains 10 copies each of 30 high interest easy readability stories to develop word attack skills, comprehension, and vocabulary study. Includes 15 tape cassettes, student booklet, manual. Grades 6–8. Psychotechnics, Inc.

Reach Program. An individualized, self-paced program about show business. High-interest material in which student participates in the shows while learning audio and/or reading selection, audio comprehension, and evaluative testing. Grade level 4–9. Economy.

Reading Development Kits. Three kits (A,B,C) to develop comprehension skills—fact recall, inference and critical reading. Self-pacing and self-correcting. High interest content for below grade level readers. Level 1–10+. Addison.

Reading Dexterity Kit. Kit comprised of two parts. Part I is designed to develop flexibility in reading for different purposes and Part II geared to increase reading speed while maintaining high level of comprehension. Grades 6–8. Economy.

Reading for Understanding, Jr. and Sr. Each boxed laboratory contains 40 lessons cards containing 4,000 brief exercises designed to teach comprehension, meaning and interpretation skills. Grades 3–12. SRA.

Reading Improvement: Comprehension Skills (film). Useful tips to aid in reaching better comprehension in reading. Grades 7–12. Coronet Films, Inc.

Reading Improvement Skill File. Comprehension and vocabulary development are emphasized in this program. There are 180 graded, illustrated, color-keyed exercises in this multilevel program. Selections are on a wide variety of topics. Grades 6–13. The Reading Laboratory, Inc.

Reading Incentive Language Program. Low vocabulary, high interest reading program designed to provide sequential skill development. Includes 10 books, a sound filmstrip, and a long playing record or cassette. Sample titles: Drag Racing, Mini Bikes, Surfing. Bowmar.

The Reading Line. A multidisciplinary reading and study skills improvement program. The 6 student books each contain 10 reading selections in all content areas, each written at 4 levels of difficulty. Teaches students to read with purpose, collect data and evidence, think critically, take notes, etc. Grades 7–12. Polaski Company, Inc.

Reading Skills Library. 134 skill builders and 72 audio lessons of high interest reading/listening for grades 1–12. Reading level 1–9. Reader's Digest.

Reading Tutors Levels 7–9. Self-pacing lessons for individual pupils to zero in on specific listening and reading skills. Develops vocabulary and comprehension skills. Each level contains 10 books and 6 audio cassettes. Includes Teacher's Guide and Answer Keys. Grades 7–9. Reader's Digest.

Scope/Activity Kits. High-motivational readings and activities to develop reading, reasoning, and language skills contained in each of nine kits. Titles such as: Television, Sports, Frauds and Hoaxes, Mystery, etc. Included in each kit; 30 copies of student illustrated booklet, 6 ditto masters of related games and exercises for reinforcement of skills. Interest level 8–12. Reading level 4–6. Scholastic.

Scope/Reference Skills Visuals. Visual masters and transparencies to develop reference skills (Where to Look, How to Use). Grades 7–12. Reading Level 4–6. Scholastic.

Scope/Reference Skills Visuals. Visual masters and transparencies to develop reference skills (Where to Look, How to Use). Grades 7–12. Reading Level 4–6. Scholastic.

SRA Reading Laboratories. Series of boxed kits or laboratories containing graded materials for development of basic reading skills, of word identification, vocabulary, comprehension and rate. Manual. Placement tests. Grade level 1–14. SRA.

Study Skills. Eight filmstrips with records or cassettes designed to help students study more effectively. Sample titles: Outlining, Summarizing, Note-Taking, Writing a Paper. Grades 7–12. Miller-Brody.

Thinking Box. A teaching tool developed specifically to improve critical thinking skills. Utilizes 240 skill development cards that present activities requiring thought processes such as classifying, hypothesizing, and criticizing. Student also works out answers to questions that help him determine how he came to solutions while engaged in the previous thought processes. Also self-help thinking-skill cards, student reference books, student activity record sheets, and teacher's guide. Six curriculum and interest-content sections. Twelve thinking operations. 6+. Benefic.

Turning Point II. A comprehensive, individualized program designed to develop skills using reference materials and skill in reading comprehension. Junior High Interest Level. Educational Products, Inc.

Using a Library (filmstrip). How to take advantage of all the resources of a library. EP.

Using the Library (filmstrips). Series of 6 filmstrips demonstrating how to use a library to its fullest advantage. Grade level 7–9. Encyclopedia Britannica.

Using Maps and Globes. Uses minisystem to teach important reference skills. Electronic Futures, Inc.

The Way It Is. A high interest reading program to develop and improve reading skills of inner-city adolescents. Includes 5 LP records, learner log, reading selections and teacher's manual. Interest level 8–10. Reading level 4–7. Ginn.

We Are Black Kit. Contains high interest short selections followed by questions for comprehension and word meaning. Includes reading selections, skill cards, key booklets and teacher's handbook. Levels 2–6. SRA.

We Discover the Dictionary. (film). Shows the importance of the dictionary and how it can be used to the best advantage. Grades 4–6. Coronet Films, Inc.

Writing a Research Paper (filmstrip). How to gather, organize, and present information. 7+. Jam Handy.

Books and Workbooks

Action I and II. Four anthologies of short, high interest selections to develop skills of listening, speaking, reading, and writing using the student's own environment: billboards, newspapers, sports, television, and radio. Games to reinforce skills are included in practice books. Interest level 7–12. Reading level 4–6. Houghton-Mifflin.

Activities for Reading Improvement. Set of 3 workbooks to develop greater comprehension skills and fundamentals of skimming and speed reading. Grades 7–9. Steck.

Basic Skills System. 4 programmed texts that provide both drill and application of specific skills: main idea, details, critical reading, skimming and scanning. Each book deals with a separate skill. Grade level high school and college. McGraw Hill.

Be a Better Reader Series. Variety of word identification, vocabulary, comprehension and reference skills taught in a setting of the content areas of social studies, new math, literature, and biological and physical sciences. Grades 4–12. Prentice.

Better Reading Books. Three 90-page books designed to develop reading speed and comprehension. Each text contains 20 selections and a span of reading levels. Book 1 (5.0–6.9); Book 2 (7.0–8.9); Book 3 (9.0–10.9). Grades 4–12. SRA.

Breaking the Reading Barrier. Text requiring reader to visualize, discriminate, organize, draw inferences and conclusions in appropriate exercises to develop speek and comprehension. High interest selections. Grades 7–12. Prentice.

Developing Reading Efficiency. Designed to promote development of speed and comprehension; also contains exercises stressing word recognition. Grades 7–10. Educational Activities, Inc.

Directions: Original fiction written especially for the program as well as works by well-known contemporary authors is featured in 2 anthologies and 6 novelettes. Reading Skills Books develop comprehension skills. Special appeal to Black and Hispano-American in grades 7–12. Reading level 4. Houghton-Mifflin.

Discoveries. 21 colorful, high-interest paperback readers containing fables, myths, factual articles, contemporary stories and novellas. Skill development accompanies the 6 stages of the series. Interest level 7–12. Reading level 4–6. Houghton-Mifflin.

Ease-to-Read Biographies. Series of 4 biographies designed to appeal to slow or reluctant reader and reinforce basic skills in vocabulary, retention of information and comprehension. Interest level 7+. Houghton-Mifflin.

Gates-Peardon Reading Exercises. Designed to develop 3 basic skills: following directions, recognizing important details and main idea. Book devoted to each skill at elementary, intermediate and advanced levels. Grades 1–8. Teachers.

How to Become A Better Reader. Designed to sharpen reading skills through selections by writers such as Dickens, O. Henry, and Munro. Grades 8–14. SRA.

How to Study. A 64 page booklet on how to develop successful study habits and methods through the PQRST method of study. Middle and secondary. AGS.

Know Your World. Weekly newspaper designed for ages 10–16 to build comprehension and interpretation skills. Each high-interest selection brings a variety of skill builders: Getting the Message, Using Clues, Using Sounds, Building Words, etc. Reading level 2.5–3.5. Xerox.

Learning to Learn. Primary emphasis is application of SQ4R study method with some rate builders, lessons in how to read and content area reading to apply skills developed. Self-correcting. For High School, College. Harcourt.

The Magnificent Myths of Man. 29 myths from different lands and different ages followed by questions stressing comprehension skills. Sound filmstrips available. Middle and Secondary students. Reading level 4.3–5.5. Globe.

McCall-Crabbs Standard Test Lessons in Reading. Rate of reading and comprehension skills emphasized in these booklets. Each booklet contains 78 lessons. Book A, grades 2–4; B, 3–5; C, 4–6; D, 5–7; E, 7–12. Teachers.

Merrill Mainstream Books. Series of 5 paperback anthologies for use in suggested order, designed to develop comprehension skills. Separate teacher's manual for each anthology. Grades 7–12. Merrill.

A Mixed Bag: A Contemporary Collection For Understanding and Response. An integration of photos, paintings, poems, ads, cartoons, pop songs, etc. designed to stimulate and improve students' reading and writing. Teacher's Manual available. Grades 7–12. Prentice.

New For You, Edition A. A weekly newspaper containing content of a regular daily newspaper. Designed for adults reading on 2–3 reading level. Globe.

New Practice Readers. Each of seven books in the series contains brief reading selections designed to improve vocabulary and comprehension, to teach pupils to note details, identify words similar in meaning, detect opinions, and select true statements. Books A–G; grades 2–8. Webster.

Newspaper Workshop. Workbook designed to be used with the daily newspaper to familiarize students with all parts of the newspaper, stressing how to read it. Globe.

Power and Speed in Reading. Text designed to make good readers superior in perception, comprehension and interpretation through articles, exercises and tests. Includes inventories and guides for self-diagnosis. Grades 7–12. Prentice.

Programmed Study Techniques. A programmed study workbook designed to help students develop effective study habits. Grades 7–12. AGS.

Reader's Digest Reading Skillbuilders. Interesting stories plus exercises for developing word identification, vocabulary, and comprehension skills. Audio lessons available. Grades 1–10. Reader's Digest.

Reading Essentials Series. Ten worktexts designed to develop a variety of reading skills. Such titles as *Fun Time* and *Mastery in Reading.* Grades 1–8. Steck.

Reading for Meaning Series. Workbooks for levels 4 and 5 emphasize word meaning, detailed meanings, and central thought. Books 6–12 also include organizing and summarizing skills. Grades 4–12. Lippincott.

Reading Success Series. High-interest books for students 10 years and older to develop basic skills. Mature format and contemporary visuals. Skills progress gradually through 6 carefully planned books, using a discover method. Teacher's guide included. Reading level 2–4. Xerox.

Really Reading! Workbook containing one-page exercises with self-evaluations designed for a developmental reading skills program. Sample skills: critical reading, context clues, synonyms, etc. Grades 10–12. Vocabulary level grade 8. Bell.

The Research Paper. Supplementary handbook on research techniques that includes a step-by-step guide to using library reference tools, selecting a working bibliography, preparing an outline, writing a rought draft, using documentation and revising. Grades 9–12. Prentice.

Six-Way Paragraphs. 100 passages of mature interest level to develop six essential categories of comprehension—subject matter, main idea, supporting details, conclusions, clarifying devices, vocabulary in context. Level 6–13. Jamestown.

A Skill At A Time. 10 booklets containing detailed lessons teaching clearly and completely each of ten comprehension skills. Self-instructional. Secondary level. Jamestown.

Sound Reading Program. 8 programmed workbooks stressing various graphemic options for phonemes, context clues and context processing (comprehension). Pretests for placement. Manual. Education Achievement.

Specific Skills Spectrum. Self-teaching programmed texts to improve study skills. Standardized test available to measure pre-post gains. Levels—High School, College. McGraw Hill.

Study Skills for Information Retrieval. Series of 3 workbooks that considers study skills in depth and provides discrimination in use of materials. Grades 4+. Allyn.

Study Type of Reading Exercises: High School Level. Work-type reading material for senior high school students or advanced pupils in the upper elementary grades. Teacher.

Stranger Than Fiction. Short interesting magazine and newspaper stories written on 2–3 level for middle and secondary students. Comprehension and vocabulary skills are stressed. Globe.

Thorndike Barnhart Advanced Dictionary. Grades 7–12. Scott Foresman.

Thorndike Barnhart Intermediate Dictionary. Grades 5–8. Scott Foresman.

Venture: A Reading Incentive Program. 2 separate volumes each containing 6 books of high interest, low difficulty about sports. Corresponding skill material is presented for each reading book to develop comprehension. Filmstrips and cassettes available. Grades 7–12. Reading level 4.6–5. Follett.

Webster's Biographical Dictionary. Level 7+. ABC.

Webster's Geographical Dictionary. Level 7+. ABC.

Webster's New Practical School Dictionary. Level 4–8. ABC.

Webster's New Students Dictionary. Level 9–12. ABC.

You and Your World. Weekly newspaper for students 14 and older who read at 3.5–5.0 grade level. Highly motivating selections including skills builders: Word Power, Map, Graph, Cartoon, etc. Xerox.

You Can Read Better. Workbook that includes simple techniques for developing vocabulary, reading rate and comprehension. Grades 6–10. SRA.

INDEPENDENT READING BOOKS

Kits and Books

Action Reading Kits. High-interest, low difficulty books with coordinated filmstrips, records or cassettes and teacher's guide. Contemporary interests with titles such as *Motocross*

Racing, Karate Girl. For elementary through high school. Reading level 3-4. Scott Foresman.

Adapted Classics. High-interest classics adapted for students in grades 4-8 reading on a 4-6 reading level. Sample titles: *The Call of the Wild, Silas Marner, Tom Sawyer.* Scott Foresman.

Adventure Library. Ten LP records or cassettes containing great adventure and sea stories recreated with dramatic music and sound effects. Sample titles: *Around the World in 80 Days; Captains Courageous; Kidnapped.* Grades 7-Adult. Miller-Brody.

Adventure Poems and Stories. Six poems and novels contained on 8 color filmstrips that tell exciting stories in pictures and captions. Sample titles: *Lochinvar, Robinson Crusoe, Treasure Island.* Grades 7-12+. Miller-Brody.

The America Reads Program. Two anthologies of enduring literature for students who enjoy reading. Works by contemporary and traditional authors. Grades 7-8. Scott Foresman.

Anthology of Children's Literature for Grades 4-8. Cassette library containing 50 recorded classic books. Grades 4-8. Troll Associates.

Coping With Series. Series of 23 paperback books about the interests, values and concerns of young people. American Guidance.

Contemporary Reading Series. High-interest, low difficulty true to life stories for grades 7-12. Titles such as *Drunk, Uptight, Crisis.* Readers are helped to make personal value judgments and learn basic facts about contemporary subjects. Includes set of 6 paperback books, 12 Read-Along Cassettes, posters, and teachers guide. Reading level 4-5. Educational Activities, Inc.

Crossroads Series. Set of 10 individual books for high school students. Noble.

Easy Reading Packets. Packets of 8 page original stories to motivate reluctant reader in grades 4-8. Includes 8 biographies and 8 mystery stories. Scott Foresman.

Everyreader Series. High-interest low-difficulty level readers with titles such as *Cases of Sherlock Homes* and *The Gold Bug and Other Readers.* Reading level 4. Webster.

Falcon Classroom Library A & B. Series of specially abridged and edited "best sellers" that have been adapted to minimize reading difficulties. Contains best-selling novels, engrossing autobiographies and science fiction. Library A has 42 copies of 8 books (*Fail-Safe, Go Tell it on the Mountain*); Library B has 7 copies of each of 6 paperbacks (*West Side Story, Diary of Anne Frank*). Interest level 7-Adult; reading level 3-8. Noble.

Folklore of the World Books. Set of 14 appealing stories collected from the four corners of the world: Africa, Egypt, China, Mexico, etc. Interest level 2-8. Reading level 3. Garrard.

Impact: Short Stories for Pleasure. Text containing 33 high-interest stories featuring outstanding Black and Latino writers. Study Guide in book involves students in each story and its language through author biographies and exercises. Grades 7-12. Prentice.

Insight and Outlook. A collection of 16 short stories by well-known authors for junior and senior high students. Globe.

Mark Twain Library. Series of 5 records containing the best of Mark Twain read by Hiram Sherman. Cassettes also available. Grades 7-12+. Miller-Brody.

Pilot Books. High interest mystery and sports books. Titles such as: *Dive In!, Ski Run, Lighthouse Mystery, Surprise Island.* Interest and reading level 3-10. Xerox.

Pilot Library IIa. Independent reading books for grade levels 2-7. SRA.

Playbooks. Six books containing scripts of plays to let 6-9th graders play people like themselves. Titles such as: *Plays for Laughs, Plays about Sports, Science Fiction Plays, Mystery Plays.* Reading level 3.5-4.5. Xerox.

Play the Game. Four high-interest supplemental readers, each containing 8 stories about significant events in the lives of famous athletes such as Joe Louis, Peggy Fleming and Willie Davis. Grades 3-8. Reading level 2.5-4.0. Bowmar.

Pleasure Reading Books. Set of 13 old classics written on a fourth grade level, of interest to children in grades 3-12. Garrard.

Random House Reading Program. Program contains 10 books in 5 interest centers; Interesting People, This Could Be You, Fun and Fantasy, High Action, Marvelous But True. A

Skillpacers Unit is also available to provide correlated activities for books read. Reading level 3.8–8.0. Random.

Reluctant Reader Libraries. Low-cost, easy-to-read paperbacks of high-interest and low difficulty for grades 7–12. Adventures, sport stories, biographies, short stories and suspense tales are all included in the library. Reading level 4–8. Scholastic.

Scope/Play Series. Ten high-interest anthologies that include stage plays, teleplays, adaptations of short stories, screenplays, open-ended dramas—all on a 4–6 grade reading level for students in grades 7–12. Scholastic.

The Sea. A series of 6 filmstrips presenting 6 dramatic stories of ships and the men that saved them. Questions for review and suggestions for further activity are included. Sample titles: *Moby Dick, Billy Budd.* Grades 7–12+. Miller-Brody.

Sherlock Holmes Adventures. Series of 6 filmstrips presenting 6 Sherlock Holmes' Adventures. Sample titles: *Silver Blaze, The Final Problem.* Cassettes also available. Grades 7–12+. Miller Brody.

Sports Action Skill Kits. 36 high-interest reading modules, each containing 10 books with live-action photographs and easy text. Includes cassette tapes and a sound filmstrip for each module. Grades 4–8 ERS.

Tales of Mystery and Terror. Four records of eight cassettes presenting full-scale dramatizations of passages of some of the most exciting tales ever told. Sample titles: *Dracula, Frankenstein.* Grades 7–12+. Miller-Brody.

Target Books. 15 high-interest low-difficulty biographies about subjects relevant to students in grades 5+. Sample titles: *Men of the Wild Frontier, Black Crusaders for Freedom, Football Replay.* Reading level 3–4. Garrard.

Toward Freedom. Set of 6 books portraying the black people's struggle through centuries for freedom and equality. Interest level 5–9. Reading level 6. Garrard.

Treasury of Great Educational Records. Series of 12 records presenting a collection of some of the best known works in the English language. Sample titles: *Moby Dick, The Tell-Tale Heart, Kon-Tiki.* Grades 7–12+.

XEP Extended Reading Library. Eight 25-volume paperback libraries of high-interest contemporary fiction and nonfiction material. Sample titles: *Brian's Song, The Blue Dolphins.* Ginn.

The Young Adventure Series. Modern adventure stories with topics ranging from scuba diving to firefighting. Interest level 4–12, reading level 4–6. Bowmar.

TEACHER REFERENCES

ALLMAN, FLORENCE. "Short Fiction for High School Students," *Wilson Library Bulletin,* 18 (October 1943), 158–59.

ALM, RICHARD S. *Books for You: A Reading List for Senior High School Students,* Booklist of the National Council for Teachers of English, New York: Washington Square Press, 1964.

AMERICAN LIBRARY ASSOCIATION. Young Adult Services Division, "Easy Adult Books for Slow High School Readers," *Top of the News,* 17 (December 1960), 19–21.

BENEDICT, STEWART H. *A Teacher's Guide to Contemporary Fiction.* New York: Dell Publishing Co., Inc.

BURTON, DWIGHT L. *Literature Study in the High School.* Third Edition. New York: Holt, Rinehart and Winston, 1970.

CARLSON, G. ROBERT. *Books and the Teen-Age Readers.* New York: Harper and Row, 1971.

CARTER, SIDNEY. "Books for Backward Readers," *Forward Trends,* 7 (Winter 1962–3), 19–24. National Book League, 7 Albemarle St., London, W.I.

CHASE, JUDITH WRAGG. *Books to Build Word Friendship.* Dobbs Ferry, New York: Oceana.

EAKIN, MARY K. *Subject Index to Books for Intermediate Grades* (3rd ed.) Chicago: American Library Association, 1963, 320.

EMERY, RAYMOND C., and MARGARET B. HOUSHOWER (Compilers). *High-Interest-Easy Reading for Junior and Senior High School Reluctant Readers.* Champaign, Ill.: National Council of Teachers of English, 1965.

FADER, DANIEL N., and ELTON B. McNEIL. *Hooked on Books: Program and Proof.* New York: Berkley Medallion Books, 1968.

FADER, DANIEL. *The Naked Children.* New York: Macmillan, 1976.

HAEBICH, KATHRYN A. *Vocations in Biography and Fictions: An Annotated List of Books for Young People.* Chicago: American Library Association, 1962, 82.

NORVELL, GEORGE W. *The Reading Interests of Young People.* Boston: D.C. Heath and Co., 1950.

PILGRIM, GENIEVA HANNA. *Books, Young People and Reading Guidance.* New York: Harper and Row, 1968.

REID, VIRGINIA M. (Ed.). *Reading Ladders for Human Relations.* Fifth Edition. Washington, D.C.: American Council on Education, 1972.

ROSSOFF, MARTIN. *The School Library and Educational Change.* Littleton, Col.: Libraries Unlimited, 1971.

RUSSELL, DAVID H., and ETTA KARP. *Reading Aids Through the Grades.* New York: Bureau of Publications, Teachers College, Columbia University, 1974, 114–116.

SPACHE, GEORGE. *Good Reading for Poor Readers.* Revised Edition. Champaign, Ill.: Garrard, 1974.

STRANG, RUTH, et al. *Gateways to Readable Books.* New York: H.W. Wilson, 1966.

WALKER, ELINOR (Ed.) *Book Bait: Detailed Notes of Adult Books Popular with Young People.* Chicago: American Library Association, 1957. Pp. 96.

WALKER, ELINOR. *Doors to More Mature Readers.* Chicago: American Library Association, 1964.

WALLACE, VIOLA. *Books for Adult Beginners* (3rd ed). Chicago: American Library Association, 1963.

Directory of Publishers

Addison. Addison–Wesley Publishing Co., Sand Hill Road, Menlo Park, Calif. 94901

AEVAC, Inc. 404 Sette Drive, Paramus, N. J. 07652.

Allied Education Council. P. O. Box 78, Galien, Mich. 49113.

Allyn. Allyn & Bacon Books, Inc., Rockleigh, N. J. 07647.

ABC: American Book Company. Orders to Van Nostrand-Reinhold Books, 450 W. 33rd St., New York, N. Y., 10001.

AGS. American Guidance Service, Inc., Publishing Bldg., Circle Pines, Minn. 55014.

Barnell Loft, Ltd., 111 South Centre Ave., Rockville Centre, N. Y. 11570.

Behavioral. Behavioral Research Laboratories, P. O. Box 577, Palo Alto, Calif. 94302.

Bell. Bell and Howell Co., Audio Visual Products Division, 7100 McCormick Road, Chicago, Ill. 60645.

Benefic. Benefic Press, 10300 W. Roosevelt Rd., Westchester, Ill. 60153.

Berkely Publishing Corp. 200 Madison Ave., New York, N. Y. 10016.

Book Lab Inc., 1449 37th St., Brooklyn, N. Y. 11218.

Bowmar. 622 Rodier Dr., Glendale, Calif. 91201.

California. California Test Bureau, a Division of McGraw-Hill Book Company, Inc., Del Monte Research Park, Monterey, Calif. 93940.

Cambosco. Cambosco Scientific Co., Inc. 342 Western Ave., Boston, Mass.

Childrens. Children's Press, Inc., 1224 W. Van Buren St., Chicago, Ill. 60607.

Coronet Films, Inc., 65 E. South Water St., Chicago, Ill. 60601.

Creative. Creative Environments, Inc., 565 Fifth Ave., New York, N. Y. 10017.

Creative Playthings, Inc., Edinburg Rd., Cranbury, N. J. 08540.

Creative Visuals. P. O. Box 310, Big Spring, Tex. 97920.

Dell. Dell Publishing Company, 750 Third Ave., New York, N. Y. 10017.

Economy Co., 1901 N. Walnut, Oklahoma City, Okla. 73105.

EDL. Educational Development Laboratories, Inc. (a Division of McGraw-Hill Company, Inc.,) 284 Pulaski Road, Huntington, N. Y. 11744.

Educational. Educational and Industrial Testing Service, San Diego, Calif. 92107.

Education Achievement Corporation, P.O. Box 7310, Waco, Texas. 76710.

Educational Activities, Inc. Freeport, L. I., N. Y. 11520.

Educational Products, Inc., 1211 West 22nd St., Oak Brook, Ill. 60521.

Educational Progress. Educational Development Corporation, P. O. Box 45663, Tulsa, Oklahoma 74145.

EP. Educational Projections Corp., 527 S. Commerce St., Jackson, Miss. 39201.

ERS. Educational Reading Services, 320 Rt. 17, Mahwah, N. J. 07430.

Educators. Educators Publishing Service, Inc., 75 Moulton St., Cambridge, Mass. 02138.

Electronic Futures, Inc., 57 Dodge Ave., North Haven, Conn. 06473.
Encyclopaedia Britannica, Inc. per BIP., 425 N. Michigan Ave., Chicago, Ill. 60611.
EPC. Educational Progress Corporation, 8538 E. 41st Street, Tulsa, Okla. 74145.
Filmstrip. Filmstrip House, Inc., 432 Park Ave. South, New York, N. Y. 10016.
Follett. Follett Educational Corp., 1010 W. Washington Blvd., Chicago, Ill. 60607.
Garrard. Garrard Publishing Company, Champaign, Ill. 61820.
Ginn. Ginn and Company, Waltham, Mass. 02154.
Globe. Globe Book Company, Inc.,175 Fifth Ave., New York, N. Y. 10010.
Grolier. Grolier Educational Corp., 845 Third Ave., New York, N. Y. 10022.
C. S. Hammond & Co., Inc., 515 Valley St., Maplewood, N . J. 07040.
Harcourt. Harcourt Brace Jovanovich, Inc. 757 Third Ave., New York, N. Y. 10017.
Harper. Harper and Row Publishers, Inc., 39 E. 33rd St., New York, N.Y. 10016.
Holt. Holt, Rinehart and Winston, Inc. 383 Madison Ave., New York, N. Y. 10017.
Houghton. Houghton Mifflin Company, 2 Park St., Boston, Mass. 02107.
Imperial Productions, Inc., 247 W. Court St., Kankakee, Ill. 60901.
Jamestown Press, P. O. Box 6743, Providence, R. I. 02904.
Jam Handy. Jam Handy School Service, 278 E. Grand Blvd., Detroit, Mich. 48211.
Learning Through Seeing, Inc., 8138 Foothill Blvd., Sunland, Calif. 91040.
Lippincott. J. B. Lippincott Company, E. Washington Square, Philadelphia, Pa. 19105.
Lyons. Lyons & Carnahan, 407 E. 25th St., Chicago, Ill. 60616.
McGraw Hill. McGraw Hill Book Company, Inc., 330 W. 42nd St., New York, N. Y. 10036.
Macmillan. Macmillan Publishing Co. Inc., 866 Third Ave., New York, N. Y. 10022.
Merrill. Charles E. Merrill Books, Inc., 1300 Alum Creek Drive, Columbus, O. 43216.
Miller-Brody Productions, Inc., 342 Madison Ave., New York, N. Y. 10017.
Milton Bradley Company. East Longmeadow, Mass. 01101.
New American Library, 120 Woodbine St., Bergenfield, N. J. 07621.
New Reader's Press, Box 131, Syracuse, N. Y. 13210.
Noble. Noble & Noble, Publishers, Inc., 750 Third Ave., New York, N. Y. 10017.
Open Court. Open Court Publishing Company, Box 402, LaSalle, Ill. 61301.
Parker Brothers, Inc., 190 Bridge St., Salem, Mass. 01970.
Polaski Company, Inc., Box 7466, Philadelphia, Pa. 19101.
Prentice. Prentice-Hall, Inc., Englewood Cliff, N. J. 07632.
Psychotechnics, Inc., 7433 N. Harlem Ave., Chicago, Ill. 60648.
Random. Random House, Inc., 201 E. 50th St., New York, N. Y. 10022.
Reader's Digest Services, Inc., Educational Division, Pleasantville, N. Y. 10570.
The Reading Laboratory, Inc., 55 Day St., South Norwalk, Conn. 06854.
REMCO. Remco Industries, Inc., 200 Fifth Ave., New York, N. Y. 10010.
Rheem Califone, 5922 Bancroft St., Los Angeles, Calif. 90016.
Richards. Richards Research Associates, Inc., 353 Shangrila Circle, Painwell, Mich. 49080.
Scholastic. Book Services, Scholastic Magazines, 50 W. 44th St., New York, N. Y. 10036.
Scott Foresman and Company, Glenview, Ill. 60025.
SRA. Science Research Associates, Inc., 259 E. Erie St., Chicago, Ill. 60611.
Steck. Steck-Vaughn Co., P. O. Box 2028, Austin Tex. 78767.
Taylor Associates and Instructional/Communications Technology, Inc., Hawk Drive, Lloyd
   Harbor, N. Y. 11743.
Teachers. Teachers College Press, Columbia University, 525 W. 120th St., New York, N. Y.
   10027.
Teaching Resources, Inc., 100 Boylston St., Boston, Mass. 02116.
Troll Associates, 320 Rt. 17, Mahwah, N. J. 07430.
Webster. Webster Division of McGraw Hill Book Company, Inc., Manchester Rd., Manchester,
   Mo. 63011; 330 W. 42nd St., New York, N. Y. 10036.
Winston. See Holt, Rinehart & Winston, Inc.
Xerox Corp., Curriculum Programs, 12000 High Ridge Road, Stamford, Conn.
Young Reader's Press, Inc. A Simon & Schuster Co., 1 West 39th St., New York, N. Y. 10018.

Index

Acquisition of reading (*See* Reading acquisition)
Adams, E. K., 171, 186
Adams, S., 190–191, 222
Adler, M., 135
Allinsmith, W., 31, 38
Alm, R. S., 497, 502
Analysis of reading test items
  dynamics involved in, 130–134
  understandings as a result of, 134
Anderson, A. L., 547
Anderson, H. S., 294, 325
Anderson, R. C., 45, 56
Anderson, R. F., 521
Anderson, R. G., 62
Andrews, D. H., 288, 291
Anglin, J. M., 96–98, 100–101, 124
Anisfield, M., 504, 521
Arbuthnot, M. H., 347, 361
Art
  annotated bibliography of books, 460–463
    reference books, 462–463
    topical books, 460–462
  comprehension, strategies for teaching, 457–460
  curriculum in, 451
  definition of, 451
  following directions, strategy for teaching, 457–460
  objectives of art education, 452
  reading
    guides and lessons, need for, 455
    measurements and evaluation strategies, 452–455
      informal reading inventories, 452
      IVCA, 452
      listing difficult terms by selection, 452
      probing ability to read how-to books, 452–455
      standardized reading tests, 452
  vocabulary
    principles of teaching, 456–457
    strategies for teaching, 457–459
      dictionaries, illustrated, 457
      dictionary-context cards, 456

      discussion, 456
      real experiences, 457
      vicarious experiences, 457
    word recognition
      strategies for teaching, 457–459
Asher, J. J., 429, 438, 444, 448
At-sight words, definition of, 487
Auditory blending, definition of, 489
Auditory discrimination
  definition of, 489
  test, 526
Aukerman, R., 390, 400
Austin, J. C., 253, 255
Ausubel, D., 22–25, 32–34, 37
Automotive Science (*See* Vocational-technical education)
Axelrod, J., 341, 361

Baldwin, J., 6, 15
Balow, I. H., 264, 277
Barraclough, G., 197, 204
Basic procedures for teaching reading lessons, 485–ff. and *passim*
  independent word identification, 485–492
    basic word identification tools
      context clues, 486
      dictionary, 486–487
      phonemic options analysis, 486
      structural analysis, 486
    compendium of concepts and principles, 487–490
    necessity of fluent decoding, 485
    paradigm for teaching grapheme-phoneme associations, 492
    phonemic options for key graphemes, 490–491
  directed reading lesson plan, 493–497
    guided reading, 495
    readiness, 493–495
    teaching skills, 495–497
Bausell, R. B., 522
Becker, C., 194, 204, 377
Becker, J. T., 402, 428
Belasco, S., 429, 448

Bell, D. B., 505, 521
Bellamy, E., 383
Berg, E., 553
Betts, E. A., 503–504, 521
Bever, T. G., 98, 124
Bickley, A. C., 112, 124
Bickley, R., 112, 124
Birkbichler, D. W., 448
Blanton, W. E., 59, 91
Bloom, B., 61, 142, 272
Blough, G. C., 287, 291, 309, 325
Bonalewicz, R. M., 475, 482
Bonin, T. M., 448
Bormuth, J., 84, 91
Bousfield, W. A., 99, 124
Brekke, M. L., 160
Briggs, B. C., 142, 510, 515, 522
Brossell, G., 373–374, 386
Brown, L. T., 32, 38
Brown, R., 96, 124
Brown, T. G., 431–432, 448, 491
Brown, W. F., 77
Bruner, J., 29, 31, 37
Bryan, J. N., 295, 325
Buck, J., 209, 238
Bugelski, B. R., 21, 37
Buros, O. K., 59, 91
Burton, D., 341, 361
Business (education)
    comprehension, 388–394
        factors lowering, 388
        strategies for teaching
            audio-visual modules for the poor reader, 392–397
            key questions, 390–391
            study guides, 391–392
    processes, principles, and problem-solving approaches as basic tools, 398
    study skills, 398
    testing reading skills
        informal procedures for
            cloze procedure as test of content knowledge, 389
            punctuation and capitalization as tasks measuring comprehension, 389
    vocabulary
        importance of, 387
        problems with learning technical terms, 387–388
        strategies for teaching, 389–390, 393–394
Byrne, M. A., 84, 91

Cadoux, R., 445
Caemmerer, R., 195, 204
Caesar, J., 198
Camacho, E. O., 416, 428
Campbell, B., 202, 204
Campbell, W. S., 363–370, 386
Capps, L. R., 251, 255
Cartwright, W. H., 198, 204
Cataldo, J. W., 457, 482
Caylor, J. S., 416–417, 428
Chambers, B., 5–6, 15
Chase, S., 146, 156, 160, 224, 238
Chastain, K., 431, 448
Chomsky, N., 98

Clark, E. V., 98, 124
Clark, H. H., 98, 124
Classical conditioning
    nature of, 17
    use in word identification, 17–18
Cognitive structures
    subsuming material into, 23–25
Collingwood, R. G., 193, 199, 204
Commager, H. S., 193–194, 204
Commins, W. C., 21, 37
Comprehensibility of materials, semantic and syntactic factors affecting, 129
Comprehension
    basic factors in mature reading
        following the structure of the content, 129
        making inferences about the content, 129
        subsidiary steps to, 130
        word meanings, 129
    definition of, 127
    development of,
        literal comprehension, 10–11, 129–132
        inferential comprehension, 11, 130, 132–133
    of explicitly stated meanings, 129 ff.
    good and poor readers
        factors to consider when comparing
            approach to organization of material when reading for details, 128
            approach when reading for general impressions, 128
            establishing own purposes, 128
            proportion reading every word, 128
            reading for stated purposes, 128
            reasons for rereading, 128
            review(ing) while reading, 128
            stating purpose, 128
        good reader's basic strength, 127
        poor reader's basic weakness, 127
    problems in comprehending text, 127–128
        poor readers' approach as cause of, 127–128
        understanding paragraph structure, 128
    teaching strategies that improve, 136–145
        chaining, 141–142
        dynamic process-product, 138–139
        hierarchy of patterns, 142–145
        hypotheses testing, 136–137
        paraphrase-cloze, 444
        Re-Quest, 134–135
        six-step strategy for drawing conclusions, 140–141
        test, 531
    of words, phrases, and sentences, 9–10
    (*See also* subject-matter headings)
Comprehension of explicitly stated meanings in a specific test
    dynamics of thinking involved in, 130–132
    skills involved in, 129–130
        following the structure of the content, 129–130
        remembering word meanings, 129–130
        understanding the content stated explicitly or in paraphrase, 129–130
        weaving ideas in the content, 129–130
Comprehension of implicitly stated meanings
    dynamics of thinking involved in, 132–133
    skills involved in
        inferring word meanings from context, 130
        making inferences about the content, 130

Comprehension in relation to appreciation in a specific test
  dynamics of thinking involved in, 133–134
  skills involved in, 130
Concept(s)
  attributes and values of, 28–29
  concept-vocabulary growth as a generalization process, 98–100
  criterial features or properties of, 96–97
  definition of, 207
  development of, 27–29
  hierarchical relationships of, 96–98
    as an aid in processing and retaining information, 98
    relation to reading, 98
  studies of the generalization process, 99–102
  types of, 29
Conditioning, classical (*See* Classical conditioning)
Consonant
  definition of, 487
  phonemic options for consonant graphemes, 491
Construction trades (*See* Vocational-technical education)
Context (clues)
  definition of, 486
  values of, 486, *passim*
Cooper, K. H., 474–476, 482
Corbin, D. E., 448
Corman, B. R., 32, 37
Crawford, W. R., 28–29, 36
Critical reading
  checkpoints for teaching, 150–157
    ascertain causes of effects, 154–155
    check for evidence of over-generalization, 156–157
    determine motives of the writer, 152
    investigate information sources, 151
    question custom, 152–153
    question stereotyped opinion, 153–154
    use materials at hand, 150
  definition of, 146, 152, 155–156
  description of those who do, 147
  examples of materials that must be subjected to, 148 and *passim*
  fallacies to look for while doing, 146–157
    ad hominem, 146–147, 224
    false assumptions, 146, 222
    non sequiturs, 152, 155, 224
    overgeneralizing, 156–157, 223–224
    post hoc ergo propter hoc, 146, 224
    right because it's custom, 152–153
  guidelines for, 146–147
  historical figures who read critically, 147–148
  personality factors related to attitude change, 148
  propaganda techniques, effect of teaching, 148
  reasons for reading critically, 146
  reasons for writers treating material differently, 152
  relation of type of question asked to attitude and ability to answer questions after reading, 148
  teaching strategies that improve, 147–148
  see also checkpoints for teaching

Daniels, R. V., 204

Danzer, G. A., 193–194, 199, 204
Daugherty, A., 297, 325, 373, 386
Davies, G. F., 204
Davis, C. C., 69, 129, 160, 224
Davis, F., 103
Davis, F. B., 69, 95, 125, 129–130, 160, 224, 239, 256
DeCecco, J. P., 28–29, 38
Deck, R. F., 298, 325
Decker, D. G., 294
Decoding
  and comprehension as a unified process, 10
  definition of, 10
  see also Independent word identification; Reading acquisition
Deductive teaching, definition of, 489
Deens, E., 274
Deese, J., 98, 124, 282, 291
DeGarmo, C., 272
de Langen, S., 438
Deutsch, C. P., 91
Developmental reading skills, list of, 11–13
Dewey, J., 4, 25
Dewey, J. C., 220, 238
Diack, H., 509, 515, 522
Diagnosis (*See* Measurement and evaluation)
Diagnosis-prescription flow chart, 72–73
Dictionary, uses of, 486–487
Dinnan, J. A., 112, 124
Directed reading lesson plan, 493–497
Discovery learning
  claimed advantages of, 31
  criticism of claims for, 31–32
  definition of, 30–31
  guided, 30–32
  misconceptions about, 32–33
  versus expository teaching, 30–34
Donelson, K., 328, 361
Donimowski, R. I., 38
Donne, J., 197
Dougherty, A., 297, 325, 373, 386
Durost, W. N., 62
Durrell, D., 60, 63, 69

Eanet, M., 179, 186
Earle, R., 465–466, 482
East, W. G., 192, 205
Ebbinghaus, H., 41–42, 56
Electronics (*See* Vocational-technical education)
Elkins, R. J., 430, 448
Elson, L. C., 482
Emerson, R. W., 136
English
  bibliotherapy, 330–341
    annotated bibliography of books having bibliotherapeutic value, 330–341
    explained in terms of identification, catharsis, and insight, 329–330
    research on, 330
    value of, 330
  definition
    by analysis, 377–378
      elements to note in, 378
    as a pattern of explanation, 377
    types of
      analysis, 378

English (*cont.*)
    connotation, 378
        example, 379
        function, 378
        showing, 378
        synonym, 378
        synthesis, 378
    explanation, patterns of
    analysis, 379
    cause and effect, 379–382
    comparison and contrast, 382–383
    definition, 377–379
    exposition, definitions of, 377
    literature
        as belles-lettres, 328
        reading literature, 341–343
        role of in meeting developmental tasks, 328–329
        role of in personal development, 328
        use of in bibliotherapy, 329–330
        values of, 327–330
        what it includes, 327–328
    misconceptions of some English teachers, 327
    reading
        autobiographies and biographies
            autobiographical notes, 344–345
            definition of, 343
            specialized skills for reading, 342
            strategies for teaching, 345–346
            vignettes of, 343–344
    drama
        meanings of, 373–374
        specialized skills for reading, 342
        strategies for teaching, 374–376
    essays
        definition of, 376
        patterns of explanation in, 378–383
        skills for reading, 343
        sources of, 376–377
    folk literature
        definition of, 346
        kinds of, 346–347
    magazines
        specialized skills for reading, 343
    newspapers
        specialized skills for reading, 342
    novels and short stories
        specialized skills for reading, 342
    poetry
        activites for teaching appreciation of, 357–358
        developing interest in, 350–351
        imagery in, 350, 351, 354
        problems in reading, 347–349
        skills for reading, 342
        teaching strategies and techniques for improved comprehension of, 350–357
        visualizing images, 350
        vocabulary, 355 ff.
    short stories
        illustrative lesson for teaching, 370–373
    short story and the novel, strategies for understanding
        characterization, 364–366
        scene, 366–367
        setting, 369–370
        theme and plot, 367–369
Entwisle, D., 112, 124
Erasmus, D., 234
Ericson, R., 468–469, 482
Examinations
    pitfalls in taking, 181–182
    preparing for, 175–181
    procedures for writing essay examinations
        assumptions in, 183
        rationale for, 183
        steps in the, 183
    techniques for taking objective and new types of examinations, 182
    see also Study and notemaking skills

Fagin, B., 21, 37
Farr, R., 59, 68, 91
Farrar, C. R., 204
Feeman, G., 258, 277
Feins, D. M., 191, 204
Feldhusen, J., 84, 91
Felipe, J., 351
Figurative language, 349, 351, 353–354, 355, 371
Fisk, M., 392, 400
Flavell, J., 247, 256
Ford, J. P., 416, 428
Foreign language (education)
    comprehension (*see* listening comprehension and reading comprehension)
    dictionary making, 439
    independent word identification
        strategies for teaching
            flip the strip, 442–443
            highlighting an element, 441–442
            phonics through cognates, 440–441
            rapid differentiation drill, 443
    interrelating the facets of language
        related strategies for, 438–439
            commands, 438
            speaking, 439
            syntactic learning, 439
            vocabulary learning, 439
    listening comprehension
        basic to speaking competency, 429
        problems in, 429
        strategies for teaching
            game of "loteria de palabras," 430
            oral course, 429
            recorded radio broadcasts plus supplementary material, 429
            spoken commands, 429
    reading comprehension
        rooted in listening comprehension, 444
        strategies for teaching
            paraphrase-cloze lesson outline, 444 ff.
    reading vocabulary
        basic principles for vocabulary development, 434
        meaning hierarchy, value of, 439
        strategies for developing
            card reader, 436–437
            conversational expressions, 435
            programmed learning review, 437–438
            textbook exercises, 432–434
            word-picture, 436 ff., 445

sentence combining (embedding)
 human languages as recursive systems, 431
 success of in improving compositional skills, 432
 techniques for teaching, 432
speaking (ability)
 need to use language meaningfully, 430
 strategies for meaningful teaching
  free completion drills, 430
  free response drills, 430
  rotation drills, 430
writing (ability)
 as intermediary between levels of speech facility, 431
 prerequisites to
  body of vocabulary, 431
  understanding of grammatical structures, 431
 strategies for teaching
  answering questions, 432
  copying letters, 431
  expanding key words into complete sentences, 431
  learning graphemic options, 431
  originating questions, 431
  perceptual reinforcement through writing graphemes and words, 430–431
  sentence combining, 431–432
  sentence completion, 431
Forgetting curves, 41–42
Forlano, G., 47, 56
Fox, L. C., 428
Frank, P. G., 283, 291
Fremont, A., 241
Friedman, M., 91
Fry, E. B., 86, 91, 472
Function words, definition of, 487
Furth, H. G., 24–25, 38, 241–242, 256

Gaarder, A. B., 430, 448
Gagne, R. M., 29, 32, 38, 281, 291
Garber, H., 91, 160
Gardner, E. F., 62, 69
Gates, A. I., 47, 56
Goethe, 4
Gold, C., 508, 522
Good, C. V., 199, 204
Goodman, K. S., 508, 522
Goodwin, W., 38
Grainger, P., 470–471, 482
Grapheme-phoneme associations, paradigm for teaching, 492
Graphemes
 associating phonemes with, 9
 definition of, 8, 486, 487
 grapheme-phonemes associations, 9–10
 phonemic options of, 8
Graphemic options, definition of, 487
Gray, W. S., 131, 160
Grimes, J. W., 31, 38
Guice, B. M., 3, 15, 65, 153, 160
Guthrie, E. R., 435
Gwaltney, W., 389, 400

Haentzschel, A., 15
Hafner, L. E., 3, 15, 44, 48, 51, 56, 58, 65, 70, 74, 86–87, 91, 95, 124, 127, 143–145, 153, 160, 200, 204, 209, 238, 239, 256, 273, 277, 305, 325, 327, 351, 361, 387, 389, 428, 504, 508, 510, 514–515, 518, 522
Hafner, M. L., 452
Haley, B. A., 328, 361
Hammerly, H., 430, 448
Hanna, P., 192, 204
Harper, S., 235, 238
Harris, S., 189
Hartig, H., 328, 361
Hasselriis, P., 350, 361, 374, 386
Havighurst, R. J., 328, 361
Hayes, M. T., 63, 69
Haynes, N. L., 325
Health and physical education
 aerobics, 474 ff.
  definition of, 474
  training effect of, 474–475
  values of, 476
 annotated bibliography of topical books, 477–478
 cardiovascular-pulmonary fitness, 474–476
  criteria for attaining, 474
 comprehension
  strategies for teaching, 476–477
 physical (fitness) education
  definition, 473–474
  terms, general test of knowledge of, 475–476
 vocabulary, strategies for teaching, 476–477
Hebb, D. O., 44, 56, 65, 91
Heber, R., 66, 91, 153, 160
Hegel, G. W. F., 195
Hellerstein, H., 474
Herber, H., 228–230, 238
Hieronymus, A. N., 77
Hitler, A., 189, 199
Hobbes, T., 196
Holtzman, W. H., 77
Home economics (*see* Vocational-technical education)
House, F. W., 387, 400
Howards, M., 148, 160
Huneker, J., 470–471, 482
Hunt, J. McV., 245, 256
Hunter, R., 382

Idelson, M. N., 325
Illiterates, problems of, 3
Independent word identification
 basic procedures in teaching
  basic tools, 486–487
   context clues, 486
   dictionary, 486–487
   phonemic options analysis, 486
   structural analysis, 486
 concepts and principles, compendium of, 487 ff.
 grapheme-phoneme associations
 see also subject matter headings
Inductive teaching, definition of, 489
Inference
 basic process, 11
 questions for a given story, 372
 see also Comprehension
Informal measurement
 of capacity for reading, 66–67
 of reading skills
  cloze procedure, 84–85
  informal inventories, 77–84
 of study-reference skills, 72, 74–77

Inhelder, B., 244, 246–247, 256
Intelligence
  kinds of, 65–66
  and organization as reciprocal agents, 161
  as related to comprehension, 161
  result of cognitive therapy on, 66
  tests of
    group, 61–63
    individual, 66–67
Irish, E. H., 264, 277
Ivey, R. D., 325

James, P., 192, 204
James, W., 4
Jarvis, G. A., 432, 433, 448
Jenkins, J. R., 506, 508, 522
Jenkins, L. M., 522
Jenkins, M., 103, 107, 124, 456
Jenkinson, M. E., 84, 91
Jensen, L. C., 148, 160
Jesus Christ
  central figure in history, 195, 199
  redemption of humanity by, 195, 199
  saving unity through, 197
Johnson, A. L., 160
Johnson, D. A., 240, 249, 252, 256, 265
Johnson, D. M., 27–28, 34, 38, 280–281, 291
Johnson, S., 493, 497
Jolly, H. B., 44, 48, 51, 56, 58, 74, 91, 95, 124
      142–145, 160, 273, 277, 351, 510, 514–
      515, 518, 522

Kalivoda, T. B., 429, 430, 448
Kane, R. B., 84
Kant, I., 5
Karlsen, B., 69
Kates, S. L., 38
Kennedy, X. J., 352
Kerfoot, J. F., 505, 522
King, M. L., Jr., 147
Kirk, R., 5–6, 15
Kirtland, F., 421
Klausmeier, H. J., 38
Kling, M., 330, 361
Knecht, S., 148, 160
Koenke, K., 296, 325
Kolb, H. R., 325
Kormondy, E. J. 325
Korzybski, A., 7, 15, 503
Kotarbinski, T., 193, 204, 283–284, 291
Kulhavy, R. W., 45, 56

Lamar, M., 253
Lammer, J., 453, 482
Larsen, V., 325
Learning
  advance organizers and, 24, 34
  conditioning
    classical, 17–18
    operant, 21–22
  developmental stages related to, 25–27
  discovery, 30–33
  effects of varying degrees of guidance on, 32
  intelligence theory and, 19–21
  laws of
    effect, 19

    exercise, 18–19
    readiness, 19
  learning and earning, 503
  mediated, 45–46
  practice as an aid to, 46–51
  programmed, 48–51
  reception, 22–23
  retention (of)
    kinds of, 39
    measuring, 39–41
  subsumption and, 23–25
  theories (*See* Learning theories)
  transfer of, 51–53
  transfer theory and, 19–21
Learning theories
  explanation of and application to reading, 17–25
    classical conditioning (Pavlov), 17–18
    cognitive developmental (Piaget), 25–27
      see also Mathematics
    connectionism (Skinner), 21–22
    connectionism (Thorndike), 18–21
    meaningful verbal learning (Ausubel), 22–25
Leary, B., 328, 329, 361
Lee, J. C., 444, 448
Lee, J. R., 327
Lefrancois, G. R., 241, 256
Leinwand, G., 191, 204
Lerch, H., 239, 256, 257, 277
Levin, J. R., 45, 56
Levine, I., 103, 124
Lewis, F. D., 521
Liberal education
  consequences of not having a, 189
  value of, 189
Lincoln, A., 381
Lincoln, C. E., 5–6, 15
Lindeman, B., 330, 361
Lindquist, E. F., 77
Literature (*See* English)
Locke, J., 196
Longwell, C., 379
Lorge, I., 62
Lovell, K. R., 243, 248, 256
Luh, C., 42, 56
Luther, M., 147, 234

McCracken, R. A., 103, 124
McCullough, C., 354, 361
McDonald, A. S., 102–103, 124
McKillop, A., 148, 160
McLaughlin, H. G., 88, 91
McNinch, G., 505, 522
Mackey, W. F., 111, 124
Madden, R., 62, 69
Mandler, G., 99, 124
Manzo, A. V., 134–135, 160, 179, 186
Marksheffel, N. D., 273, 277
Martin, H. C., 379, 386
Marx, K., 195
Marx, M., 282, 292
Materials for reading instruction (*See* Teaching
    materials)
  annotated bibliography, 553–567
  teacher references, 567–568
Mathematics
  behavioral objectives in, 240

comprehension of (*See* directed reading lesson and problem solving)

computation skills, development of, 252–253
  how to practice, 252–253
  necessity of mastery, 252
  reasons for lack of, 252

concepts, mathematical (*See* mathematical concepts)

directed reading lesson applied to
  its prototypes, 272
  steps in, 272–273

formulas and equations, strategies for understanding and reading, 267–269

goals and objectives of, 239–240

language in
  difficulties of, 257–258

mathematical concepts
  interrelationships for five related concepts, 250
  language arts analogies for teaching, 251
  necessary conditions for learning, 249–250

mathematical sentences, 264

Piaget's psychology in the concrete operations stage, 240–244
  applying the theory
    applications to classroom organization and teaching, 243–244
    attitudes and expectations affecting scholastic educability, 243
  concrete logic in conservation, 241
  mental differentiation, 241–242
    comprehending the system of numbers, 242
    mental inversion, 242
    mental reciprocity, 242
    mental reversibility, 241
    seriation, 241
  principles that characterize operational thought
    associativity, 243
    closure, 243
    identity, 243
    reversibility, 243

Piaget's psychology in the formal operations stage, 244–248
  applying Piaget's theory with older children, 248
    able students, 248
    backward children, 248
    ordinary students, 248
  classical syllogism, 244–245
  combinatorial logic
    basis for scientific reasoning tasks, 247
    lattice as a mathematical model, 246–247
  operating in the area of possibilities, 245
    basis for hypothetico-deductive thinking, 245
    floating bodies problem, 245
    types of hypotheses, 245
  probability, 247
  thinking about thinking, 244–245

problem solving
  improving verbal generalization as an aid to, 264–265
  reading and computational ability as determinants of, 264
  role of structure in verbal, 265
  strategies for teaching

steps in solving written mathematics problems, 266

study guide based on a word problem, 266–267

statistical representations, strategies for reading
  frequency distribution, 270–271
  graphs, 271–272

teachers of
  duties, 257
  how they help with reading, 257

test, diagnostic math concept and reading, 273–275

vocabulary and symbols
  strategies for teaching
    card readers, 261–262
    exercises, 258–260
    known to unknown, 262–263
    phrase-symbol cards, 261

Mazer, M., 351

Measurement and evaluation
  aptitude and capacity for reading, 60–67
  basic areas for, 59–60
  reading, 60, 67–73, 77–85, 525 ff.
  reliability, 58
  steps in the process of, 58–59
  validity of, 57–58
  see also Tests

Memory
  kinds of
    long term, 44–45, 98
    short term, 44, 98
  schemes to aid memory
    chunking semantic information, 98
    coding, 44
    hierarchical organization, 98
    imagery, 44–45
    mediating instructions, 45–46
    paraphrasing, 98
    rehearsal, 44

Mental capacity tests
  standardized group tests
    academic aptitude, 61–63
    capacity for reading, 63–65, 66–67
  standardized individual tests
    capacity for reading, 66–67

Mercer, S. L., 351
Merton, P., 160
Mieters, N. J., 400
Mill, J. S., 5, 138
Miller, G. A., 42, 98–99, 124
Mills, R. E., 413, 428
Mitchell, V., 351
Moore, A. J., 296, 325
Morain, G., 448
Moral, A. E., 430, 449
Moretz, S. A., 509, 522
Morgan, V. R., 402, 428, 515
Morrill, R. L., 205

Motivational problems in reading
  basic problem, 497
  "conservatives," problems of, 498
  extraverts, problems of, 499
  lack of readiness for activities attempted, 497–498

reluctant readers

Motivational Problems (*cont.*)
  characteristics of
    above-average mental ability, 498–499
    average mental ability, 498
    below-average mental ability, 497–498
    conditions helping readers, 498–500
  self concept, problems of, 498
  spatial-reasoning/verbal discrepancies, problems
    of, 498–499
  verbal/non-verbal discrepancies, problems of, 498
Mouly, G., 23–24, 32–33, 38
Music
  annotated bibliography of books, 471–473
    reference books, 473
    topical books, 471–473
  forewords to selections and collections, 470–471
  informal reading inventories, creating, 465
  goal of performance in, 463
  measurement
    reading comprehension, 465
    reading vocabulary, 463–465
  reviews of performances, 468–470
  technical directions for playing
    strategies for teaching, 466–468
  word recognition
    strategies for teaching, 465–466
Mussen, P., 247, 256
Musson, J. W., 150, 160

Nailing down words (*See* Reading acquisition)
Nardelli, R. R., 148, 160
Neisser, U., 508, 522
Newman, H., 414, 428
Nietzsche, F., 4

Ogden, C. K., 111, 124
O'Hare, F., 432, 449
Older, E., 507, 522
Organization skills
  reading and organizing in research-study situa-
    tions, 161–186
  related to intelligence, 161
  value of, 161
Ortega y Gassett, J., 7, 15, 147, 160, 193, 205
Outlining
  keying notes to the outline, 174
  as a step in writing essays, 183
  in studying, 176–177
  in writing papers, etc., 165–166
Overgeneralization
  some types of
    I know a man who . . .
    "lovers and wheeler-dealers"
    in a nutshell
Oxenhorn, J., 325

Palmatier, R. A., 180, 186
Palmer, E. M., 325
Pannwitt, B., 363, 374, 386
Paradigmatic relationships, 100–101, 112–117
Patkau, J. E., 508, 522
Patriotism
  meanings of, 190
  in relation to attitudes towards revolution, 190–
    191
Pavlov, I., 17–18, 38

Peirce, C. S., 4
Perney, L. S., 465–466, 482
Phillips, J. L., 242, 245–246, 248, 256
Phoneme(s)
  associating with graphemes, 9–10
  definition of, 8, 487
Phonemic options
  examples, 490–491
Phonemic options analysis, definition of, 488
Physical education (*See* Health and)
Piaget, J., 25–27, 95, 210, 241, 244, 246–247
Piagetian developmental stages
  concrete-operational, 26–27
  formal operational, 27
  preoperational, 26
  sensorimotor, 26
  see also Mathematics
Pidgeon, D., 243, 256
Pierkaz, J. A., 148, 160
Pimsleur, P., 444, 449
Pitluga, G. E., 285, 292
Plato, 196
Pledge of allegiance
  conceptual problems of for middle school stu-
    dents, 209–210
Plumb, J. H., 197, 204
Popkin, R. H., 195, 205
Powell, K., 95, 124
Practice
  distributed vs. massed, 47–48
  meaningful, 47
  overlearning through, 48
  purpose of
    differentiating responses, 46–47
    fixing material in repertoire, 46–48
    recalling amterial, 46–48
    retaining material, 46–48
  uses of self-recitation in, 47–48
Pragmatism, 4–5
Prefix, definition of, 488
Preston, R., 439, 449
Programmed instruction
  advantages of in reading, 51
  examples of, 48–50
Proletarian, 5–6
Proper instruction, 48
Publishers, directory of, 569–570

Rates of reading
  helping the compulsively slow reader, 163–164
Readability
  factors that contribute to, 86
  fromulas for determining, 86–88
  guidelines for improving, 86
  increasing readability of science materials, 296
  problems in science, 295–296
  problems in the social studies, 200–201
Reading
  basic tasks of, 8–11
    comprehension, literal and inferential, 10–11
    decoding and comprehension, 10
    visual perception of printed symbols, 10
  basic uses of, 3–6
  language base for, 7–8
  misconceptions of, 6–7
  process of, 7–8, 503
  tests (*See* Measurement and evaluation)

use of alphabetic code in, 8
see also Reading acquisition
Reading acquisition, teaching skills to the nonreader
  barrier to, 505–507
    education, 506–507
      coercion, 507
      failure to pace introduction of material, 506–507
      lack of a child development point of view, 506
    psychological, 505–506
      lack of perceptual skills, 505–506
      low mental age, 505
      verbal deficit, 505
    social, 507
  methods that work
    language experience approach
      analytic, 510–511
      synthetic, 511–514
    programmed linguistic approach
      Sound Reading Program, 514–515
      Sullivan Associates Program, 514
  nailing down words
    association of the printed word with a picture, 515–516
    card reader, 516
    illustrated phrases, 517–518
      abstract words through, 518
      rhyming, 517
    part-whole comprehension, 516–517
  principles of teaching to older students, 507–510
    emphasize the continuous progress formula, 510
    instill confidence in learner, 507
    teach construction of the word, 509–510
    teach graphemic options, 509
    teach syllabic graphemic options, 509
    teach the use of graphical information, 508
    use context to improve perception, 508
    use language familiar to the person, 508
    use words significant to the person, 507–508
  reading process related to, 503–505
Reading organization skills
  card catalogue
    activities for learning to use, 170–171
    description of, 169–170
  examinations, preparing for and writing, 175–183
    (*See* study and note-making skills; examinations)
  index, using the, 171
  making notes, keying notes to outline, synthesizing notes, and writing the draft
    activities for, 174–175
    how to, 173–174
  outline of, 162–163
  reader's guide to periodical literature
    activities for learning to use, 172–173
    description of, 172
  reading newspapers and weekly news magazines, 163–164
    editorials and letters to the editor, 164
    news, 164
    political cartoons, 164
  reading nonfiction books, 165
  reference (selected) works
    art, 167–168
    general, 166–167

history, 167
literature, 168
miscellaneous, 168
music, 168
science, 167
selecting and evaluating information, questions to guide, 173
vertical file index, 172
writing a paper
  steps in
    1. Initiating the inquiry and writing the preliminary outline, 165–166
    2. getting an overview; selecting appropriate general sources, 166–169
    3. zeroing in on specific sources, 169–173
    4. recording and organizing information for retention, new synthesis, and reproduction, 173–174
    5. writing the paper, 174
  see also subject matter headings
Reading process
  definitions, 7–8, 503–504
    as cue sampling, 504
    as development and checking of hypothesis, 504
    as IIWC decoding, 504
    as reconstruction of facts, 7, 504
    as reduction of informational uncertainty, 504
    as thorough logical analysis of cognitive relationships, 126
  discussion of, 7–8, 503–505, *passim*
  see also Comprehension; Reading; Reading acquisition
Reading skills
  outline of, 11–13
  why post-elementary teachers must teach, 7
Reid, V. M., 499, 502
Relearning
  recall score, 41
  savings score, 40–41
Remembering
  meaningful organization and, 42–43
  recitation as an aid in, 43
  recitation without correction as a test of, 43–44
Research-study skills (*See* Reading organization skills)
Retention of learned material
  kinds of
    recognition, 39
    recall, 39
  measurement of, 39–42
  recitation without correction, as a test of, 43–44
Richards, I. A., 111, 124, 350
Rickover, H., 148
Rising, G. R., 240, 249, 252, 256, 265
Ritter, J. H., 181, 186
Ritter, O. P., 200, 205
Robinson, F. G., 24, 33, 37, 177, 186
Robinson, R., 389, 400
Rodgers, T. S., 428
Rogers, B., 131, 160
Root word, definition of, 488
Rowell, C. G., 142, 160, 428, 514, 522
Ruddell, R. B., 329, 415, 428, 508, 522

Rules
  definition of, 29
  learning and, 29–30
  using concepts and, 30
Russell, D., 329–330, 344–345, 361
Ryan, E. B., 504, 522

Sabaroff, R. E., 204
Sachs, H. J., 103, 124
Savin, H. B., 509, 522
Scates, D. E., 199–204
Schwartz, J., 291, 309, 325
Schwa, definition of, 487
Science
  attitudes and methods of, 283
  comprehension
    teaching strategies
      careful reading, 308
      cause and effect guide, 315
      comparison guide, 316
      directed reading lesson, 316–322
      reading-reasoning guides, 309–315
  concepts
    classes of, 280–281
      categorical, 280
      dimensional, 280–281
      explanatory, 281
      singular, 281
    knowing concepts, 294
    learning inductively, 281
    positive feedback in learning, 294
  definition of, 279
  directed reading lesson for, 316–322
  as inquiry, 280–281
    inquiry methods, 280
    spirit of inquiry, conditions conducive to, 280
  interest
    kinds of science students, 295
    questionnaire starter, 294–295
  principles
    definition of, 282
    science principles
      importance of learning, 282–283
  readability of materials in, 295–296
    formulas for determining, 296
    project rewrite, 296
  reading
    careful reading of scientific material, 308
    interest-motivation, 294–295
    techniques demanding careful reading, 308
    uses of, 293
  scientific methods
    demonstration, suggestions for staging a, 289
    experimentation
      cookbook laboratory, exercises for, 285
      definition of, 284–285
      general principles that apply to good experimentation, 286–287
      kitchen experiments, 287–288
      laboratory exercises, contributions of, 288
      open-ended experiments, 285–286
    fundamental questions asked in, 283
    observation
      definition of, 283–284
      examples of, 284
      uses of, 284

scientific theory
  definition of, 282
  functions of, 282
scientist, facets of his/her work, 283
theory and principles
  need for learning, 281–283
  principles, definition of, 282
  theory, definition of, 282
vocabulary
  illustrated science dictionary, 299
  meaning hierarchies in study of, 305–307
  teaching strategies for
    card readers in studying, 307–308
    lesson outline for teaching, 296–297
  unit teaching plan for, 298
word identification
  independent, 299–300
  roots and affixes, 300–301
    grapheme-phoneme relationships, 301
    inductive study for meanings, 301–305
Seibert, L. C., 47, 56
Semantic networks, 111–112
Semmel, M. I., 504, 522
Serra, M. C., 201, 205
Shepherd, D., 341, 361
Shrodes, C., 329
Simmons, J. S., 347, 361
Sinnema, J. R., 430, 449
Skinner, B. F., 21, 38
Smith, A. N., 430, 449
Smith, D. E. P., 136, 137, 160, 224
Smith, D. V., 329, 361
Smith, E. H., 142, 160, 428, 510, 514, 522
Smith, F., 416, 428
Smith, H. K., 7, 15, 127, 148, 160, 220, 238, 220
Snapp, J. C., 400
Snelbecker, G., 37, 38
Snider, A. J., 476, 482
Social studies
  bias of textbooks, 222–223
  central goal of educating in, 190
  comprehension and critical reading
    instructional frameworks, 228–229
    see also reading-reasoning guides
    problems in, 220–224
      poor readers in grade 12, 220
      typical difficulties, 220–221
    teaching strategies
      cause and effect, 233
      comparison-contrast, 234–235
      drawing conclusions, 227–228
      important ideas, 226–227
      main ideas, 224–227
    see also reading-reasoning guides
  comprehension, author's responsibility in increasing, 200–201
  concept-vocabulary burdens of instructional materials, 200–201
  geography as aspect of, 191–193
    cruciality of knowledge about, 192–193
    definition of, 191–192
  history as aspect of, 193–200
    definition of, 193
    philosophies of, 195–196
    processes of, 193–195
    purposes and values of, 196–198

writing of in relation to reading of, 198–200

readability problems in, 200

reading-reasoning guides

cause and effect, 233

comparison-contrast, 234–235

interpretation

external, 230–231

internal, 230–231

literal comprehension, 230–232

text adoption problems in, 190–191

vocabulary and concepts, problems in, 207–210

vocabulary and word recognition

teaching strategies

category game, 211–212

common prefixes, 218–220

simple categorizing game, 212–215

syllables, 216–217

take-home study sheets, 210–211

Socrates, 146

Spache, G. D., 499, 502

Spector, R. M., 191, 205, 223, 238

Speer, A., 189

Spitzer, H. F., 43, 56

Springman, J. H., 208, 238

Stern, H. H., 429, 449

Stevens, V., 128, 160

Sticht, T. G., 416–417, 428

Strang, R., 347, 354, 361

Stratton, R. P., 34, 38

Stroll, A., 195, 205

Strommen, M. P., 155, 160

Structural analysis

definition of, 488

used with phonemic options analysis and context, 486

Study and note-making skills (preparing for examinations), 175–181

making notes, 176

NSL: a notetaking system for learning, 180–181

outlining, 176–177

REAP: a reading-writing-study skills strategy, 179–180

SQ3R, modified, 177–179

underlining, 181

and making study sheets, 181

writing summaries, 175–176

writing the examination (*See* Examinations)

Study-reference skills, 161 ff.

informal inventories, 72, 74–77

standardized tests, 77

see also Organization skills; Study and note-making skills; Subject matter headings

Subsumption

cognitive structures and, 23–25

types of

combinatorial, 24–25

correlative, 24–25

derivative, 24–25

obliterative, 24–25

Suffix, definition of, 488

Sund, R. B., 289, 292

Sustained silent reading, 103

Swain, E., 148, 160

Syllabication rules, 489–490

Syllable, definition of, 488

Syntagmatic relationships, 100–101, 112

Teaching, expository, 33–34

Teaching materials

basic sight vocabulary and word identification

books and workbooks, 556

games, 556–557

kits and audiovisual aids, 554–556

beginning reading (acquisition)

games, 554

kits and audiovisual aids, 553–554

workbooks, 554

comprehension and study-reference

books and workbooks, 563–565

kits and audiovisual aids, 560–563

independent reading kits and books, 565–567

vocabulary

books, and workbooks, 558–559

games, 559

kits and audiovisual aids, 557

Teaching strategies, *Passim*

see also subject matter headings and skills headings

Terman, L., 153

Tests

intelligence, individual

Slosson Intelligence Tests, 66–67

Stanford-Binet Intelligence Test, 67

Wechsler Adult Intelligence Scale, 66–67

Wechsler Intelligence Scale for Children, 66–67

intelligence-aptitude, standardized group

Analysis of Learning Potential, 62–63

Durrell Listening Test, 60, 63–65

Kuhlmann-Anderson Intelligence Test, 62

Lorge-Thorndike Intelligence Tests, 62

library reference skills, 545–551

reading, group inventories

auditory discrimination, 526

cloze (comprehension), 84–85

comprehension, 531

consonant blends, 71, 537, 529

consonant digraphs, 71, 537, 540

letter names, 71, 535, 539

other combinations, 538, 540

visual discrimination, 525

vowel clusters, 538, 540

word recognition, 528

reading, individual inventories

Hafner Quick Reading Test, 70, 541

IRI: Comprehension, pronunciation and vocabulary, 77–84, 543

reading, standardized group

Davis Reading Test, 69

Durrell Reading Test, 69

Iowa Silent Reading Tests, 68

Stanford Diagnostic Reading Test, 69–70

study-reference, individual (or group) inventory, 72, 74–77

study-reference, standardized group

Iowa Tests of Basic Skills—Work-Study Skills, 77

Survey of Study Habits and Attitudes, 77

Thompson, J., 466, 482

Thorndike, E. L., 18–21, 38

Thorndike, R. L., 62

Thorpe, H. E., 458, 482

Thurstone, T. G., 144

Transfer of training, teaching for, 51–52

kinds of things that transfer

attitudes, 53

Transfer of training (*cont.*)
  principles, 51–52
  skills, 53
Traxler, A., 354, 361
Trevelyan, G. M., 200
Trowbridge, L. W., 289, 292
Tuinman, J. J., 59
Tulving, E., 99, 124, 508, 522
Turner, F. J., 193, 205

Underwager, R. C., 160
Underwood, B., 47, 56
Uses of reading
  in learning a trade or profession, 4
  in living the examined life, 4–6
  in promoting family welfare, 3, 4
Utilitarianism, 4–5

Variant endings, definition of, 488–489
Vaughn, A., 198, 205
Verbalism
  dangers of, 106
    in vicarious experience compared to real experi-
      ence, 201
  definition of, 106
Vernon, P. E., 65, 91
Visual discrimination
  definition of, 505
  importance of, 8–9, 505
  test, 525
Visual perception (*See* Visual discrimination)
Vocabulary
  clarifying meanings of, 96, 103
  consciousness and conscience, 105
  factors related to success in acquisition of, 103
  fallacies in development of, 102
  growth of word meaning, 99–100
    tasks in studying
      free association, 100
      free recall, 99, 101
      predicate generation, 102
      sorting, 99, 101
      structural relations, 99, 102
  as labels for concepts, 95–96
  relation to reading comprehension, 95
  use of paradigmatic relationships as indications
      of cognitive maturity, 112, 113
  value of, 95
  see also the subject matter headings
Vocabulary development
  principles of
    creating a good climate for learning words, 104
    developing vocabulary in language contexts,
      106–107
    discussing experiences, 107–108
    rooting vocabulary in concept development,
      106
  responsibility for, 104
  teaching procedures
    antonymns [*See* opposites (below)]
    books, 110–111
    building meaning hierarchies, 115
    catalogues, 111
    classification, 115–117
    dictionaries, 109
    discussion of real and vicarious experiences,
      103, 107–108

newspapers, 110
opposites, 113–114
roots and affixes, 103
search-insert-verify, 114–115
sentence meaning, 117–121
synonym booklet, 109–110
synonym jamboree, 115
vocabulary cards, 108–109
word relationships, 111–117
  see also subject matter headings
Vocational-technical education
  acqusition, reading
    strategies for teaching
      language experience, 402–403
      programmed linguistic, 401–402
  charts, use in teaching reading skills, 419–421
  comprehension
    assumptions regarding development, 417–418
    inventory for measuring, 409–410
    strategies for teaching
      directed reading lesson plan, 418–423
  directed reading lesson plan for teaching a tech-
      nical selection, 418–423
  following directions, reading to key strategy
      (lesson plan) for teaching, 424–425
  independent word identification, 413–415
    phonics, role of, 413–414
    pronunciation combinations, transfer value of,
      415
    teaching paradigm, 414–415
  informal testing, 403–410
    comprehension (*See* understanding)
    understanding
      IVCA inventory, 409–410
      use of tachistoscope in, 404–405
    vocabulary
      quick survey test, 406–408
    word recognition tests
      developing and using, 403–405
      quick survey tests, 406–408
  language experience approach
    basic procedures in teaching, 402
    as an integrated language arts pattern, 402–403
    learning rate, determining, 402
    measuring gain as a result of, 403
    phonics instruction, 403
    supplementary materials, 403
  mentally retarded trainees, a reading program for,
      416
  paraphrase-cloze, use in (pre-) testing, 422
  readability of technical materials, 416–417
    average readabilities of selected materials, 417
    formula for determining, 417
  reading
    acquisition, 401–403
    comprehension, 409–410, 417–423
    independent word identifications, 413–415
    informal testing, 403–411
    vocabulary, 412–413, 415–416
    word identification, 411–412
  vocabulary
    guidelines to consider when developing, 415–
      416
    questions to consider when developing, 415
    strategies for teaching
      illustrated technical dictionary, 412–413
      see also Vocabulary development

word identification
  strategies for teaching, 411
    word-picture cards, 411–412
  see also Reading acquisition
Vowel, definition of, 487
Vygotsky, L. S., 95

Walker, W., 507, 522
Wallace, B., 325
Washington, G., 191
Weaver, W., 95, 124
Weinrib, A., 429, 449
Whimby, A., 66, 91
Whimby, L. S., 66, 91

Wiener, P., 196, 205
Williams, D., 296, 325
Williams, M., 128, 160
Wilson, J. W., 265, 277
Wilson, M. C., 201, 205
Wittrock, M. C., 30–31, 38
Wooldridge, S. W., 192, 205
Word recognition (*See* Reading acquisition; Independent word identification)
Wylie, R. E., 392, 400

Youssef, M., 34, 37
Yudin, L., 38

DATE DUE

5. 21 '81	
11. 05 '81	
11. 26 '81	
5. 06 '82	
7. 15. '82	
12. 02. '82	
4. 21. '83	
5. 12. '83	
12. 15. '83	
6. 23. '83	
5. 17. '84	
8. 20. '86	
8. 26. '87	
JUL 2 8 1887	

BRODART, INC.   Cat. No. 23-221